Law and the Christian Tradition in Modern Russia

This book, authored by an international group of scholars, focuses on a vibrant central current within the history of Russian legal thought: how Christianity, and theistic belief generally, has inspired the aspiration to the rule of law in Russia, informed Russian philosophies of law, and shaped legal practices.

Following a substantial introduction to the phenomenon of Russian legal consciousness, the volume presents twelve concise, non-technical portraits of modern Russian jurists and philosophers of law whose thought was shaped significantly by Orthodox Christian faith or theistic belief. Also included are chapters on the role the Orthodox Church has played in the legal culture of Russia and on the contribution of modern Russian scholars to the critical investigation of Orthodox canon law.

The collection embraces the most creative period of Russian legal thought—the century and a half from the later Enlightenment to the Russian emigration following the Bolshevik Revolution.

This book will merit the attention of anyone interested in the connections between law and religion in modern times.

Paul Valliere is Emeritus Professor of Religion at Butler University in Indianapolis, Indiana, and a fellow of the Center for the Study of Law and Religion at Emory University in Atlanta, Georgia.

Randall A. Poole is Professor of History at the College of St. Scholastica in Duluth, Minnesota, and a fellow of the Center for the Study of Law and Religion at Emory University.

Law and Religion

The practice of religion by individuals and groups, the rise of religious diversity, and the fear of religious extremism, raise profound questions for the interaction between law and religion in society. The regulatory systems involved, the religion laws of secular government (national and international) and the religious laws of faith communities, are valuable tools for our understanding of the dynamics of mutual accommodation and the analysis and resolution of issues in such areas as: religious freedom; discrimination; the autonomy of religious organisations; doctrine, worship and religious symbols; the property and finances of religion; religion, education and public institutions; and religion, marriage and children. In this series, scholars at the forefront of law and religion contribute to the debates in this area. The books in the series are analytical with a key target audience of scholars and practitioners, including lawyers, religious leaders, and others with an interest in this rapidly developing discipline.

Series Editor
Professor Norman Doe, Director of the Centre for Law and Religion, Cardiff University, UK

Series Board
Carmen Asiaín, Professor, University of Montevideo, Uruguay
Paul Babie, Professor and Associate Dean (International), Adelaide Law School, Australia
Pieter Coertzen, Chairperson, Unit for the Study of Law and Religion, University of Stellenbosch, South Africa
Alison Mawhinney, Reader, Bangor University, UK
Michael John Perry, Senior Fellow, Center for the Study of Law and Religion, Emory University, USA

Titles in this series include:

Labour Rights and the Catholic Church
The International Labour Organisation, the Vatican and Catholic Social Justice
Paul Beckett

Law and the Christian Tradition in Modern Russia
Edited by Paul Valliere and Randall A. Poole

Christianity and the Law of Migration
Edited by Silas W. Allard, Kristin E. Heyer, and Raj Nadella

For more information about this series, please visit: www.routledge.com/Law-and-Religion/book-series/LAWRELIG

Law and the Christian Tradition in Modern Russia

Edited by Paul Valliere and Randall A. Poole

Produced by the Center for the Study of Law and Religion, Emory University

Routledge
Taylor & Francis Group
LONDON AND NEW YORK

First published 2022
by Routledge
2 Park Square, Milton Park, Abingdon, Oxon OX14 4RN

and by Routledge
605 Third Avenue, New York, NY 10158

Routledge is an imprint of the Taylor & Francis Group, an informa business

© 2022 selection and editorial matter, Paul Valliere and Randall A. Poole; individual chapters, the contributors

The right of Paul Valliere and Randall A. Poole to be identified as the authors of the editorial material, and of the authors for their individual chapters, has been asserted in accordance with sections 77 and 78 of the Copyright, Designs and Patents Act 1988.

All rights reserved. No part of this book may be reprinted or reproduced or utilised in any form or by any electronic, mechanical, or other means, now known or hereafter invented, including photocopying and recording, or in any information storage or retrieval system, without permission in writing from the publishers.

Trademark notice: Product or corporate names may be trademarks or registered trademarks, and are used only for identification and explanation without intent to infringe.

British Library Cataloguing-in-Publication Data
A catalogue record for this book is available from the British Library

Library of Congress Cataloging-in-Publication Data
Names: Valliere, Paul, editor. | Poole, Randall Allen, 1964-editor.
Title: Law and the Christian tradition in modern Russia/edited by Paul Valliere and Randall A. Poole.
Description: Milton Park, Abingdon, Oxon; New York, NY: Routledge, 2021. |
Series: Law and religion | Includes bibliographical references and index.
Identifiers: LCCN 2021007463 (print) | LCCN 2021007464 (ebook) | ISBN 9780367861315 (hardback) | ISBN 9781032054421 (paperback) | ISBN 9781003017097 (ebook)
Subjects: LCSH: Church and state–Russia (Federation) | Law–Russia (Federation)–Christian influences–History. | Christianity and law. | Christian lawyers–Russia (Federation) | Christian philosophers–Russia (Federation) | Religion and law–Russia (Federation) | Law–Russia (Federation)
Classification: LCC KLB2688 .L39 2021 (print) | LCC KLB2688 (ebook) | DDC 349.47–dc23
LC record available at https://lccn.loc.gov/2021007463
LC ebook record available at https://lccn.loc.gov/2021007464

ISBN: 978-0-367-86131-5 (hbk)
ISBN: 978-1-032-05442-1 (pbk)
ISBN: 978-1-003-01709-7 (ebk)

DOI: 10.4324/9781003017097

Typeset in Galliard
by Deanta Global Publishing Services, Chennai, India

Contents

Contributors

Paul Valliere is Emeritus Professor of Religion at Butler University in Indianapolis, Indiana, and a fellow of the Center for the Study of Law and Religion at Emory University in Atlanta, Georgia. He is the author of *Modern Russian Theology: Bukharev, Soloviev, Bulgakov: Orthodox Theology in a New Key* (T&T Clark, 2000), *Conciliarism: A History of Decision-Making in the Church* (Cambridge University Press, 2012), and many articles and book chapters on Russian Orthodoxy and Russian religious thought. He is a member of the Association for Slavic, East European, and Eurasian Studies and lectured regularly at the Kiev Summer Theological Institute from 2003 to 2016. He holds a Ph.D. in religion from Columbia University and a B.A. in English from Williams College.

Randall A. Poole is Professor of History at the College of St. Scholastica in Duluth, Minnesota, and a fellow of the Center for the Study of Law and Religion at Emory University. He is the translator and editor of *Problems of Idealism: Essays in Russian Social Philosophy* (Yale University Press, 2003); co-editor (with G. M. Hamburg) of *A History of Russian Philosophy, 1830–1930: Faith, Reason, and the Defense of Human Dignity* (Cambridge University Press, 2010, 2013); co-editor (with Paul W. Werth) of *Religious Freedom in Modern Russia* (University of Pittsburgh Press, 2018); co-editor (with Caryl Emerson and George Pattison) of *The Oxford Handbook of Russian Religious Thought* (2020); and author of many articles and book chapters on Russian intellectual history, philosophy, and religion. He holds a Ph.D. in history from the University of Notre Dame and an A.B. in government and Russian studies from Cornell University.

Konstantin M. Antonov is Professor and Head, Department of Philosophy of Religion and Religious Aspects of Culture, St. Tikhon's Orthodox University of Humanities, Moscow, Russian Federation.

Martin Beisswenger is Assistant Professor of History, National Research University Higher School of Economics, Moscow, Russian Federation.

Julia Berest is Adjunct Assistant Professor of History, University of Western Ontario, London, Canada.

Tatiana Borisova is Associate Professor of History, National Research University Higher School of Economics, St. Petersburg, Russian Federation.

William E. Butler is John Edward Fowler Distinguished Professor of Law, Dickinson School of Law, Pennsylvania State University, Carlisle, Pennsylvania, United States.

Gregory L. Freeze is Victor and Gwendolyn Beinfield Professor of History, Brandeis University, Waltham, Massachusetts, United States, and an affiliate at the Institute of World History at the Russian Academy of Sciences.

Gary M. Hamburg is Otho M. Behr Professor of History, Claremont McKenna College, Claremont, California, United States.

Vera Shevzov is Professor of Religion and Director of the Program in Russian, East European, and Eurasian Studies, Smith College, Northampton, Massachusetts, United States.

Vladimir A. Tomsinov is Professor and Head, Department of the History of State and Law, Moscow State University, Moscow, Russian Federation.

John Witte Jr. is Robert W. Woodruff Professor of Law, McDonald Distinguished Professor of Religion, and Director of the Center for the Study of Law and Religion, Emory University, Atlanta, Georgia, United States.

Foreword

Twenty years ago, Paul Valliere published a pathbreaking volume, *Modern Russian Theology: Orthodox Theology in a New Key.* There he brought to brilliant light and life three great Russian Christian minds—Aleksandr Bukharev, Vladimir Soloviev, and Sergii Bulgakov—whose profound and original theological insights deserved much greater appreciation in the Christian West. Seven years later, Valliere led a team of experts in producing another hefty title, *The Teachings of Modern Orthodox Christianity on Law, Politics, and Human Nature* (2007), with lengthy case studies and translations of the theological jurisprudence of three Russian sages—Soloviev again, now joined by Nicholas Berdyaev and Vladimir Lossky—along with other Eastern Orthodox thinkers. These two pioneering volumes helped deepen our collective understanding of the hearts and minds of the Russian people and the distinct teachings and practices of Orthodox Christianity, both in Russia and abroad. Valliere's later superb monograph, *Conciliarism: A History of Decision-Making in the Church* (2012), added further depth and nuance to our understanding of the role of church councils in Eastern and Western churches historically and today.

In the past ten years, Randall A. Poole has published three signature collections on Russian philosophy and religion. *A History of Russian Philosophy, 1830–1930: Faith, Reason, and the Defense of Human Dignity* (2010), coedited with Gary M. Hamburg, redirected attention away from the ideological precursors of Russian communism (emphasized by many older histories of Russian thought) to the Russian tradition of religious-philosophical humanism. The volume included careful analysis of a range of Russian arguments for human dignity, religious freedom, rule of law, and ordered liberty—ideas which placed Russia squarely within the broader European intellectual context. Poole's *Religious Freedom in Modern Russia* (2018), coedited with Paul W. Werth, maintained the focus on human dignity but explored it in connection with the various meanings of religious freedom, toleration, and freedom of conscience in Russian history since the early modern period. Poole's latest collection, *The Oxford Handbook of Russian Religious Thought* (2020), coedited with Caryl Emerson and George Pattison, is a landmark volume detailing the rich tapestry of religious ideas in Russian intellectual and cultural history.

In the present volume, Paul Valliere and Randall Poole have combined their talents and networks to create a brilliant new account of *Law and the Christian Tradition in Modern Russia*. The volume features fresh, crisp essays commissioned from a dozen leading experts from Russia, Europe, and North America. Two opening chapters offer a sweeping analysis of the complex interactions of church and state, theology and jurisprudence, canon law and civil law, Russian Orthodoxy and European thought over the past millennium. Thirteen exquisite case studies follow, focused on some of the most original and influential Russian jurists of the nineteenth and twentieth centuries, the period when formal jurisprudence finally came into full flower in Russia. Most of the names headlined in these chapters will be new to nonspecialist readers—Vasilii Malinovskii, Mikhail Speranskii, Aleksandr Kunitsyn, Konstantin Pobedonostsev, Boris Chicherin, Anatolii Koni, Leonid Kamarovskii, Vladimir Soloviev, Aleksei Pavlov and other Russian canonists, Pavel Novgorodtsev, Sergei Kotliarevskii, Nikolai Alekseev, and Ivan Ilyin. These are, however, the Russian equivalents of Western legal titans like Grotius, Blackstone, Beccaria, Story, Savigny, Gasparri, and Maritain, all of whose writings were known to their Russian legal contemporaries.

The authors of these chapters have made these earlier Russian jurists vividly present to us by translating their texts, terms, and ideas into accessible and authoritative forms for Anglophone readers. Most of these figures served as professors of law or philosophy, principally in Moscow. Several also worked as judges, diplomats, civil servants, church bureaucrats, legislative draftsmen, legal digesters and encyclopedists, practicing lawyers, and canonists. Some were conservative apologists for the political and ecclesiastical status quo; others were radical reformers who often suffered for their nonconformity. What this group held in common was a deep Orthodox sensibility and a profound interest in the religious dimensions of law, the legal dimensions of religion, and the interaction of legal and religious ideas, institutions, methods, and practices. Collectively, these jurists ranged widely across international laws of trade, war, and peace; Russian public, private, penal, and procedural law; Orthodox canon and ecclesiastical law; and administrative law, municipal law, and social justice reforms. Several of them offered creative natural law theories of sovereignty, constitutionalism, rule of law, human dignity, rights, equality, and liberty. Often, they developed ingenious combinations of distinct Russian theological and philosophical tropes with Western liberal theories, as well as various forms of historical, sociological, and analytical jurisprudence.

This volume is the first such comprehensive history (in English) of law and Christianity in Russian history. I have dipped into Russian literature, history, theology, and law since college days, and was privileged to learn more from my mentor and colleague, Harold J. Berman, perhaps the greatest scholar of law and religion and of Russian and Soviet legal history. But I was astonished by how much new material on law and Christianity I found efficiently and expertly presented in these pages. This book can be read in a day but savored for a career.

This title is part of a multivolume series on Great Christian Jurists in World History, presenting the interaction of law and Christianity through the intellectual histories of a thousand legal figures of the past two millennia. Commissioned by the Center for the Study of Law and Religion at Emory University—where Professors Valliere and Poole are nonresidential senior fellows—each volume in this series focuses on a specific country, region, or era and samples the life and work of a score or more of its greatest legal minds over the centuries. These figures include not only civil and canon lawyers and judges but also theologians, philosophers, and church leaders who contributed decisively to legal ideas and institutions, or who helped create landmark statutes, canons, or cases. Thus, familiar Christian jurists like Gratian, Grotius, Blackstone, Story, Kuttner, and Scalia appear in this series, but so do Augustine, Isidore, Aquinas, Calvin, Barth, Maritain, and Romero. This approach is not intended to deprecate institutional, doctrinal, social, or intellectual histories of law, nor will it devolve into a new form of hagiography. It is, instead, designed to offer a simple method and common heuristic to study the interaction of law and Christianity around the world over the past two millennia.

Columbia University Press opened this series in 2006–07 with a three-volume work on *Modern Christian Teachings on Law, Politics, and Human Nature*, featuring nearly thirty modern Catholic, Protestant, and Orthodox Christian figures. Cambridge University Press has new titles on great Christian jurists in the first millennium, as well as in English, Spanish, French, Lowlands, and American history. Routledge has taken up the Italian, Nordic, Welsh, and Latin American stories; Mohr Siebeck the German story; and Federation Press the Australian story. Forthcoming titles will cover great Christian jurists in the history of Scotland, Ireland, Austria, Switzerland, Greece, Poland, and, eventually, various countries and regions in Eastern Europe, the Middle East, Africa, and Asia.

It has been a joy for me to work with Professors Valliere and Poole and the wonderful group of scholars from Russia, Europe, and North America who contributed to this volume. I learned much from these experts and thank them for their sterling contributions. I was particularly touched to share memories with several contributors of our common mentor, Harold Berman, whose influence can be seen throughout these pages.

This volume was made possible by a generous gift from Mr. Richard L. Wyatt Jr., a distinguished Emory Law School alumnus and major litigation and labor lawyer, whose life was inspired by his college mentor, the Russian Orthodox monk Brother John Harwell. The editors join me in extending our deep gratitude for Richard's generosity as well as our deep condolences to his family and friends on Richard's premature death in 2018. I also join the editors in their kind acknowledgments and thanks to the many colleagues who contributed so generously to this project and volume.

It is a delight to publish this volume and several others in the distinguished Law and Religion series edited by one of the world's preeminent scholars of law and religion, Professor Norman Doe. Professor Doe and his many colleagues in the Cardiff Centre for Law and Religion have been vital trans-Atlantic allies with the Emory Center for the Study of Law and Religion. On behalf of the Center, I extend thanks for their leadership in this expanding global field of interdisciplinary legal study, and for their partnership with us in publishing this and parallel volumes on law and Christianity. Finally, I express warm thanks to Alison Kirk and her colleagues at Routledge in taking on this volume and applying their usual standards of excellence in their editing, production, and marketing.

John Witte Jr.
Director, Center for the Study of Law and Religion
Emory University

Acknowledgments

The editors express deep thanks to the individuals and institutions that assisted us in the preparation of this volume. We are indebted above all to the Center for the Study of Law and Religion at Emory University for the invitation to do this project and for the financial support that sustained it, including facilitation of a conference of the volume's authors in Atlanta in 2019. Collaboration with the CSLR was a rare pleasure thanks to the good counsel and extraordinary hospitality of John Witte Jr., director of the Center, and his associates: Professor Rafael Domingo, director of the great Christian jurists project; Ms. Amy Wheeler, administrative director of the law and Christianity project; Ms. Anita W. Mann, director of business and finance; and Dr. Gary S. Hauk, senior editorial consultant. We are also grateful to Ms. Paula A. Tavares, Ms. Sharon Kimbell, and their colleagues at the Emory Conference Center Hotel. We owe special thanks to Professor Witte for kindly contributing the Foreword to this volume.

We thank William G. Wagner, the Brown Professor of History, Emeritus, at Williams College, for joining our conference in Atlanta and offering us expert advice throughout the project. Philip T. Grier, the Thomas Bowman Professor of Philosophy and Religion, Emeritus, at Dickinson College, also gave us valuable advice. We are grateful, too, to Boris Jakim for assistance with the translation of chapters originally written in Russian. We thank Columbia University Press and the editors of *Dialogue and Universalism* (Warsaw, Poland) for permission to use previously published material.

The administration and staff of our home institutions were a source of encouragement and support throughout the project. At Butler University, we thank President James M. Danko, Dean Jay Howard, and the staff of Butler University Libraries, especially Ms. Barbara Howes. At the College of St. Scholastica, we thank Dean Bret Amundson, reference librarian Todd White, and Sister Mary Catherine Shambour †.

We are especially grateful to Ms. Alison Kirk and Ms. Emily Summers at Routledge and to the three anonymous readers who filed reports on our book proposal.

Finally, we thank our international cohort of contributors for bringing their expertise, good advice, hard work, and collegial spirit to *Law and the Christian Tradition in Modern Russia*.

Editors' note

Transliteration of Russian follows the Library of Congress system. In the volume narrative, the names of cities, rulers and well-known cultural figures are Anglicized. Russian dates prior to February 1918 are rendered according to the Julian calendar (Old Style). The use of italics in quoted material reflects the original source unless otherwise noted.

Introduction

A Russian conception of legal consciousness

Randall A. Poole

Harold J. Berman (1918–2007) was the intellectual architect of the modern field of law and religion.[1] In 1985, he moved to Emory University from Harvard, where he had taught for thirty-seven years. At Emory he was the Robert W. Woodruff Professor of Law and senior fellow at the Center for the Study of Law and Religion, the sponsor of this book. Berman was also one of the great scholars of Russian law. In *Justice in the U.S.S.R.*, he wrote: "Law is a monument of history, constructed over many centuries.... Law is more than rules; it is the legal profession, the law schools, the technique and tradition of judging, administering, and legislating. Law is also the sense of law, the law-consciousness, of the people."[2] Here he identified the research area in which his contributions would be most renowned: legal consciousness in its historical development. One of his sources for this concept was the Polish-Russian legal theorist Leon Petrażycki (1867–1931), who advanced a psychological theory of legal consciousness against legal positivism.[3] Berman took a broad approach to understanding law as a psychological phenomenon, "rooted in the intellectual, emotional, and spiritual life of the people of a community." He adopted Petrażycki's terminology

1 John Witte Jr., "The Integrative Christian Jurisprudence of Harold J. Berman," in *Great Christian Jurists in American History*, ed. Daniel L. Dreisbach and Mark David Hall (Cambridge: Cambridge University Press, 2019), 230–44.

2 Harold J. Berman, *Justice in the U.S.S.R.: An Interpretation of Soviet Law*, rev. ed. (Cambridge, MA: Harvard University Press, 1963), 187.

3 Berman, *Justice in the U.S.S.R.*, 279, 420n3. On Petrażycki, see Andrzej Walicki, *Legal Philosophies of Russian Liberalism* (Oxford: Oxford University Press, 1987), ch. 4. *Legal Philosophies of Russian Liberalism*, a work of profound analysis, interpretation, and insight by an eminent historian of ideas, has served as a source of great inspiration for the editors and contributors to the present volume. (Walicki died on August 20, 2020, as this book was nearing completion.) It includes chapters on three Russian philosophers who are also subjects of our book: Boris Chicherin, Vladimir Soloviev, and Pavel Novgorodtsev. In addition to Petrażycki, the two other legal thinkers whom Walicki treats at length in his book are Bogdan Kistiakovskii and Sergius Hessen. Other jurists belonging to the "golden age of Russian legal philosophy" (the period between the Judicial Reform of 1864 and the Russian Revolution), as William Pomeranz calls it, include Nikolai Korkunov, Sergei Muromtsev, and F. F. Martens. See William E. Pomeranz, *Law and the Russian State: Russia's Legal Evolution from Peter the Great to Vladimir Putin* (London: Bloomsbury Academic, 2019), 52–55.

DOI: 10.4324/9781003017097-101

of "legal emotions" (sentiments, intuitions), which are related to but distinct from moral sentiments, in order to make clear that a robust legal consciousness involves more than an intellectual commitment.[4] It involves "man's whole being" or, in short, faith.[5]

According to Berman, religion and law share four elements: ritual, tradition, authority, and universality.[6] These four elements "symbolize man's effort to reach out to a truth beyond himself."

> They thus connect the legal order of any given society to that society's beliefs in an ultimate, transcendent reality. At the same time, these four elements give sanctity to legal values and thereby reinforce people's legal emotions: the sense of rights and duties, the claim to an impartial hearing, the aversion to inconsistency in the application of rules, the desire for equality of treatment, the very feeling of fidelity to law and its correlative, the abhorrence of illegality. Such emotions, which are an indispensable foundation of every legal order, cannot obtain sufficient nourishment from a purely utilitarian ethic. They require the sustenance of a belief in their inherent and ultimate rightness.[7]

The fourth common element, universality, is "the claim to embody universally valid concepts or insights which symbolize the law's connection with an all-embracing truth."[8] This element suggests a connection with the theory of natural law, which has had very different meanings over the centuries, but which has tended toward normative identification with the very principle of justice and with the morality inherent in the idea of law. Possibly natural law might stand on its own, or rather on the grounds of morality and reason alone, without religious sanction. Berman noted that in fact this ambition to autonomy was characteristic of modern natural-law theory. But he was skeptical. More viable, he thought, was a legal consciousness in which law "as man's sense of the just" drew on religion "as man's sense of the holy."[9]

A very similar conception of legal consciousness was advanced by the Russian legal philosophers featured in the present volume. Legal consciousness was a central concept for Boris Chicherin, Vladimir Soloviev, Pavel Novgorodtsev,

4 Harold J. Berman, *Faith and Order: The Reconciliation of Law and Religion* (Grand Rapids, MI: William B. Eerdmans Publishing Company, 2000), 367–68. He cites Leon Petrażycki, *Law and Morality*, trans. Hugh W. Babb, intro. Nicholas S. Timasheff (Cambridge, MA: Harvard University Press, 1955).

5 Berman, *Faith and Order*, 9. Like Berman, Petrażycki held that law was a basic psychological phenomenon that encompassed very much of human thought and life, but unlike Berman, he was not a religious thinker.

6 See also Harold J. Berman, "Law and Logos," *DePaul Law Review* 44, no. 1 (1994): 143–65, here at 159.

7 Berman, *Faith and Order*, 5.

8 Ibid., 9.

9 Ibid., 13–14, 19.

Sergei Kotliarevskii, Nikolai Alekseev, and Ivan Ilyin. These six legal philosophers were also religious thinkers (predominantly so in Soloviev's case) who believed that Christianity could help remedy what Novgorodtsev diagnosed as the "crisis in modern legal consciousness" by reorienting that consciousness toward the supreme value of law: the sacredness of the human person. For them, the rule of law depended ultimately on a legal consciousness that was nourished by a deep moral sense and by faith. As philosophical idealists, they were committed to natural law, following their predecessor Aleksandr Kunitsyn. As Christian theists, they believed that the moral norms of natural law (human dignity and human rights) entailed, and were grounded in, a transcendent ontological reality—God.

Natural law exemplifies law in its pure form because it is upheld by consciousness (moral respect and religious reverence), not by coercion. The more closely positive law approximates natural law (which approximation is legal progress), the less it, too, will need to rely on the threat of coercion. The general tendency of Russian philosophy of law as represented in this volume was to deemphasize coercion in favor of consciousness, but there was debate among the jurists over the proper relationship between law and morality and over the justification for the use of force. Like natural law, though perhaps not as pristinely, canon law and international law also exemplify the pure form of law. A distinctive feature of our book is its attention to natural law, canon law, and international law.

The Papal Revolution, canon law, and Western legal culture

In the West, the development of the type of legal consciousness that could support the rule of law has a long history and deep religious roots. Harold Berman stressed the paramount importance of the Papal Revolution of 1075, when Pope Gregory VII (1073–85) declared the independence of the Roman Catholic Church from Emperor Henry IV and from imperial, royal, and civil rule generally.[10] Gregory and his successors established the church as an autonomous legal entity with jurisdictional claims over many areas of life in Western Christendom. They asserted that the pope was the supreme lawmaker. The result, from the twelfth to fifteenth centuries, was a marked upsurge in the promulgation of canon laws (papal decretals being the most important), together with the formation of a corps of church jurists (canonists) to administer them and the establishment of a hierarchy of church courts (culminating in the Roman curia) to enforce them. Canon law was now systematized and codified for the first time. Gratian's *Concordia discordantium canonum* (Concordance of discordant canons), known as the *Decretum Gratiani*, was completed in 1140. The compiler may have been a monk who taught in Bologna, the center of the new science of jurisprudence and the site of Europe's first university, founded in 1088. Another collection was

10 Harold J. Berman, *Law and Revolution: The Formation of the Western Legal Tradition* (Cambridge, MA: Harvard University Press, 1983). Sergei Kotliarevskii (see Chapter 12 of this volume) assessed the significance of Gregory VII's reforms in the same way as Berman.

completed by the Spanish canonist Raymond of Peñaforte in 1234. It is known as the *Decretales Gregorii IX* because Pope Gregory IX authorized it (the same year) as a standard text for the teaching of canon law at the University of Bologna. The *Corpus iuris canonici*, compiled in the twelfth and thirteenth centuries, was published in 1582 and remained the standard collection down to 1917.[11]

Berman regarded canon law, as it developed in the wake of the Papal Revolution, as the first modern Western legal system and as the foundation for the further development of law. In Europe's new universities, both Roman and canon law ("the two laws") were studied, abetting the development of the new science of jurisprudence.[12] Roman law was more important in the early history of the law curriculum—a manuscript copy of Justinian's *Corpus iuris civilis* (529–34) having been discovered about 1080 in an Italian library. Canon law was added as the new texts became available. Berman underscores the importance of Gratian's *Decretum*, calling it "the first comprehensive and systematic legal treatise in the history of the West, and perhaps in the history of mankind."[13] Especially significant (even momentous) was Gratian's invocation of natural law. According to Berman's exposition, Gratian held that 1) natural law is found both in divine revelation and in human reason and conscience; 2) the laws (*leges*) of princes and other secular authorities ought not to prevail over natural law (*ius naturale*); 3) ecclesiastical laws must not contravene natural law; 4) *ius* (right, justice) "is the genus, *lex* [law] is a species of it"; 5) as a matter of natural law, "princes are bound by and shall live according to their laws"; 6) secular laws are subordinate to ecclesiastical laws; and 7) customary law must yield to natural law.[14] Though Justinian's *Digest* (the main part of his *Corpus*) contains many references to *ius naturale* (natural law or natural right), the concept is much better developed in Gratian. With him, the principle of the subordination of positive (enacted or statutory) law to natural law became clear, and it applied to the laws of the church as well: "Enactments, whether ecclesiastical or secular, if they are proved to be contrary to natural law, must be totally excluded."[15]

Gratian's appeal to natural law is a prescient statement of the philosophical and religious basis underlying the principle of the rule of law. His ideas, together with their roots in the classical and Christian heritage (especially with the Stoics, Cicero, and church fathers such as Irenaeus, Lactantius, and Origen) and with similar formulations among other canonists, laid the groundwork for the development of natural-rights theory among later medieval and early modern thinkers,

11 Berman, *Law and Revolution: The Formation of the Western Legal Tradition*, chs. 2, 5. See also John Witte Jr., "Introduction," and R. H. Helmholz, "Western Canon Law," in *Christianity and Law: An Introduction*, ed. John Witte Jr. and Frank S. Alexander (Cambridge: Cambridge University Press, 2008), 9–15, 71–87.

12 Berman, *Law and Revolution: The Formation of the Western Legal Tradition*, ch. 3.

13 Ibid., 143.

14 Ibid., 145. The quotations are from Gratian's *Decretum*, in Berman's translation.

15 Gratian, as quoted by Berman, *Law and Revolution: The Formation of the Western Legal Tradition*, 147.

such as St. Thomas Aquinas, William of Ockham, Francisco de Vitoria, Francisco Suarez, Hugo Grotius, Samuel von Pufendorf, and John Locke.[16] But Berman thought that the Papal Revolution was the crucial threshold: "the concept of the rule of law was supported by the high level of legal consciousness and legal sophistication that came to prevail throughout the West in the twelfth and thirteenth centuries." Important steps toward the realization of the concept were taken, he notes, with the Magna Carta of 1215 and with the Hungarian Golden Bull of 1222.[17]

Legal culture in early modern Russia

In Russia, the development of a rule-of-law type of legal consciousness was a much later phenomenon, beginning with the Enlightenment in the late eighteenth century but not reaching maturity until the middle third of the nineteenth century, on the eve of the Great Reforms, and then only among a relatively small group of jurists, enlightened bureaucrats and reformist officials, professors, and other professionals.[18] Orthodox canon law was not a significant source of this development, although the study of canon law became increasingly important within the Russian Orthodox Church and its seminaries and academies in the course of the nineteenth century, with far reaching consequences for church life—and not only for it (see Chapters 1 and 10). Russian religious philosophy, drawing on Orthodox theology, became a factor in the development of Russian philosophy of law after Vladimir Soloviev brought those spheres together beginning with *A Critique of Abstract Principles* (1880) (see Chapter 9).

The delayed development of legal consciousness in Russia had very much to do with basic facts of Russian history, and very little to do with any alleged "Russian mentality." The first Russian state, Kievan Rus, did not appear until the late ninth century. Having adopted Orthodox Christianity in 988, it flourished until the Mongol conquest in 1240. Two centuries later, Muscovy emerged as a large and powerful Eurasian polity. In both Kievan Rus and Moscow, indigenous law codes were produced and enforced. A body of law was also administered by the Orthodox Church (see Chapter 1). Thus, it would be wrong to deny that nascent

16 Brian Tierney, "Natural Law and Natural Rights," in *Christianity and Law: An Introduction*, 89–103; Tierney, *The Idea of Natural Rights: Studies on Natural Rights, Natural Law and Church Law, 1250–1625* (Grand Rapids, MI: William B. Eerdmans Publishing Company, 2001).

17 Berman, *Law and Revolution: The Formation of the Western Legal Tradition*, 293.

18 The classic study is Richard S. Wortman, *The Development of a Russian Legal Consciousness* (Chicago: University of Chicago Press, 1976, 2010). Wortman's liberal, comparative perspective informs the present essay. For a different approach (with its own valuable insights) to understanding Russia's legal tradition, see Tatiana Borisova and Jane Burbank, "Russia's Legal Trajectories," *Kritika: Explorations in Russian and Eurasian History* 19, no. 3 (2018): 469–508. Their approach emphasizes "the connection between law and sovereignty in the transforming polity, the law in its everyday functions, the intermediaries of legal connection, and the technical processes of lawmaking and communication" (472).

elements of legal consciousness existed in premodern and early modern Russia. Recent scholarship on Muscovy in particular has challenged the traditional stereotype of this state as an unrelieved despotism.[19] Nevertheless, Russian legal culture fell far short of the intellectual sophistication and institutional dynamism of medieval Western law. No authority structure comparable to the Roman papacy existed in Orthodox Christianity, nor did premodern Russia possess institutions of higher learning where law—Roman law, church law, or Russian law—could be systematically investigated and expert jurists could be trained.

Following the crisis of the Muscovite state in the Time of Troubles (1598–1613), the founding of the Romanov dynasty in 1613 brought about a period of recovery in which the Russian Orthodox Church played an important role. In 1589, the metropolitanate of Moscow had been elevated to the status of a patriarchate, and in the first decades of the new dynasty, church and state enjoyed a symbiotic relationship. Patriarch Filaret (in office 1619–33) used the title "Great Sovereign" and was effectively coruler with his son, the first Romanov tsar, Mikhail (r. 1613–45). Muscovite Russia reached the pinnacle of its development at midcentury, at the time of the promulgation of Tsar Aleksei's *Ulozhenie* (Law code) of 1649 and the printing of the chief source of Russian Orthodox law, the Slavonic nomocanon, under the auspices of Patriarch Iosif and his successor Nikon (1653). The rapid decline of the Muscovite state thereafter was in large part a consequence of the Russian Church schism brought about by Patriarch Nikon's liturgical reforms (see Chapter 1).

With Peter the Great's assumption of power in 1689, Russia entered the modern period. Peter and his successors aggressively pursued the country's modernization and Westernization. Though Russia had few of Europe's societal and institutional resources (which had developed over a long period in favorable historical circumstances), the model embraced by Peter and his successors was the absolutist *Polizeistaat*, the cameralist well-ordered police state of early modern Europe.[20] Absolutist rulers of the time regarded law as an instrument of state power, not a limit on it: rule by law, not rule of law. They sought to use law to regulate and rationally organize society in order to harness its resources for the purpose of expanding its (and the state's) wealth and power, which they saw as also promoting people's welfare and well-being. The overall framework was, or came to be, the Enlightenment ideology of progress. In the West, modernizing monarchs, in pursuing their policies, not only had to contend with but also made active use of a rich and variegated social reality, replete with long-standing,

19 See Nancy Shields Kollmann, *Crime and Punishment in Early Modern Russia* (Cambridge: Cambridge University Press, 2012). To appreciate the precise meaning of Kollmann's provocative conclusion—"Russia was not a despotism" (426)—one must read this impressive study in its entirety. For a similar assessment of the premodern and early modern Russian state, see Daniel Rowland, "Did Muscovite Literary Ideology Place Limits on the Power of the Tsar (1540s–1660s)?," *Russian Review* 49, no. 2 (1990): 125–55.

20 Marc Raeff, *The Well-Ordered Police State: Social and Institutional Change through Law in the Germanies and Russia, 1600–1800* (New Haven: Yale University Press, 1983).

relatively autonomous social groups, estates, and orders; towns, guilds, professional associations, and various types of corporations; and institutions such as the French *parlements*, other courts, and the church. These "intermediary bodies" (Montesquieu), which enjoyed various freedoms and privileges, mediated the new centralizing state power and helped to distribute and moderate it. Not least important were lawyers, who tried to uphold the standards of their profession, which long antedated the absolutist, instrumental approach to law. Rulers might disdain them, judges in particular, but they could not dispense with them.[21]

In Petrine Russia, these intermediary bodies were generally absent, and society remained largely subjugated to the state, as in the Muscovite period. The nobility was not released from compulsory state service (military or bureaucratic) until 1762. The plight of the peasantry was bad to begin with and worsened under Catherine the Great (r. 1762–96); serfdom was not abolished until 1861. The church was the one institution that could potentially threaten autocratic power; Peter neutralized the threat in 1721 when he replaced the patriarchate with the Holy Synod, a collegiate board of bishops overseen by a lay official, the chief procurator. Russian social reality meant that Russian cameralism would be highly autocratic, with the sovereign's will regarded as the ultimate source of the laws that were to be directly implemented by government officials, without social mediation. Judges were expected to enforce statutory laws, not interpret them according to higher principles. The courts, including the Senate, were subject to supervision or oversight (*nadzor*) by a procurator general and the procurators under him. Written, inquisitorial procedure was designed to ensure that judicial officials correctly applied the law. This system governed the courts down to the Judicial Reform of 1864.[22] *Zakonnost'* (legality) was a narrow interpretation of the cameralist ideal of rule by law. In William Pomeranz's words, it meant strict observance of the laws "issued by the ruler as a set of instructions for state institutions and their officials."[23]

The immediate problem Peter and his successors faced in building the well-ordered police state was the absence of a corps of jurists and of institutions to train them. Peter hoped to create a *noblesse de robe*, but the nobility's sense of identity was invested in the military and in martial values.[24] They would not easily be persuaded to take up law, especially in view of its narrow, clerical conception in early modern Russia. Meanwhile Peter, advised by Leibniz and Christian Wolff, planned the Russian Academy of Sciences.[25] It opened in December 1725,

21 See Marc Raeff, "The West European Model," in Raeff, *Understanding Imperial Russia*, trans. Arthur Goldhammer (New York: Columbia University Press, 1984), 24–31.

22 Wortman, *The Development of a Russian Legal Consciousness*, 12–16. On Petrine judicial culture, see also Kollmann, *Crime and Punishment in Early Modern Russia*, ch. 8.

23 Pomeranz, *Law and the Russian State*, 19.

24 Kollmann, *Crime and Punishment in Early Modern Russia*, 190.

25 On Peter's discussions with Leibniz about the Academy of Sciences, Russian universities, and legal education, see Vladimir A. Tomsinov, *Iuridicheskoe obrazovanie i iurisprudentsiia v Rossii v XVIII stoletii*, Uchebnoe posobie, 2nd ed. (Moscow: Zertsalo-M, 2012), 69–76.

ten months after his death, combining research and teaching (in the attached university and gymnasium).[26] Initially all members of the Academy were foreign (the first Russian member was Mikhail Lomonosov in 1745). In 1738, Empress Elizabeth invited Friedrich Heinrich Strube de Piermont (1704–90), a follower of Grotius and Thomasius, to teach law at the Academy.[27] The first professor of law at Moscow University (founded in 1755) was the Austrian Philip Heinrich Dilthey (1723–81), who taught there from 1756 to 1764, and again from 1766. Karl Heinrich Langer was appointed in 1764 and retained his position even after Dilthey's return.[28] At the Academy of Sciences and Moscow University, Roman and natural law were the main jurisprudential subjects, but Dilthey taught Russian law after 1766.[29] The Corps of Cadets was established in 1731.[30] "The Cadet Corps," Wortman writes, "was where a nobleman was most likely to learn about the law in eighteenth-century Russia.... The courses taught were in natural law and sought to convey to the noblemen the importance of the law and a general understanding of its basic principles."[31] In this period, both in Germany and in Russia, natural law was generally taught according to its Wolffian interpretation, which was absolutist in its view that the ends of human society consisted in human perfectibility, and that the realization of these ends required and justified the state's absolute (and paternalistic) power. It was not until the beginning of the nineteenth century that a more liberal, Kantian interpretation of natural-law theory could be taught, usually in eclectic combination with more traditional approaches.[32]

Russian autocrats ran a considerable risk in fostering the legal education of their officials: such officials might well learn that law had a higher calling than serving as an instrument of absolutist rule. By the middle third of the nineteenth century, that risk became a reality.

Legal enlightenment in Russia

The Enlightenment in Russia spurred the development of legal consciousness. Empress Catherine II (the Great), who took seriously the image of herself as an enlightened monarch, was the preeminent sponsor of the ideas of the *philosophes*

26 Tomsinov, *Iuridicheskoe obrazovanie i iurisprudentsiia v Rossii v XVIII stoletii*, 88–96, 99–101.

27 Ibid., 96–98, 102–110; and Tomsinov, *Rossiiskie pravovedy XVIII–XX vekov: ocherki zhizni i tvorchestva*, 2nd rev. ed., 3 vols. (Moscow: Zertsalo-M, 2015), 1:99–113. See also W. E. Butler, "F. G. Strube de Piermont and the Origins of Russian Legal History," in *Russia in the Age of Enlightenment: Essays for Isabel de Madariaga*, ed. Roger Bartlett and Janet M. Hartley (New York: Palgrave Macmillan, 1990), 125–41.

28 On Dilthey and Langer, see Tomsinov, *Iuridicheskoe obrazovanie i iurisprudentsiia v Rossii v XVIII stoletii*, 142–56.

29 See also Wortman, *The Development of a Russian Legal Consciousness*, 25.

30 Tomsinov, *Iuridicheskoe obrazovanie i iurisprudentsiia v Rossii v XVIII stoletii*, 111–16.

31 Wortman, *The Development of a Russian Legal Consciousness*, 30–31.

32 See Julia Berest, *The Emergence of Russian Liberalism: Alexander Kunitsyn in Context, 1783–1840* (New York: Palgrave Macmillan, 2011), ch. 5, "The Natural Law Tradition in Russia."

in Russia. She was committed to spreading legal enlightenment in Russia, to strengthening the country's legal culture, and to improving its laws and institutions. To this end, on December 14, 1766, she issued a manifesto announcing her intent to convene an Imperial Legislative Commission, charged with preparing a draft of a new code of laws (the last having been issued in 1649).[33] Law code commissions had met earlier in the century, but this one was different. When it convened on July 30, 1767, the commission brought together 564 delegates from all over Russia. They were elected from the "free" estates of the realm (the nobility, townspeople, state peasants, and others), as well as from governmental offices. In addition to drafting a new law code for Catherine's consideration, the delegates were to inform her about the needs and problems of their communities. The Legislative Commission met in numerous sessions, first in Moscow in 1767, then in St. Petersburg in 1768. On December 18, 1768, at the 195th session, it was announced that the Russo-Turkish War made it necessary to prorogue the full assembly, though subcommittees would continue to meet. The Legislative Commission was an unprecedented event in imperial Russia.

On the opening day of the commission, Catherine's *Nakaz* (Instruction) to the assembled delegates was published. Isabel de Madariaga called it "one of the most remarkable political treatises ever compiled and published by a reigning sovereign in modern times."[34] The main part of the *Nakaz* consists of twenty chapters divided into 526 articles.[35] Much of it was taken, often verbatim, from works of Enlightenment political philosophy. The author from whom Catherine borrowed the most was Montesquieu; 294 of the 526 articles came from *The Spirit of the Laws* (1748). Another 108 articles came from Cesare Beccaria's *On Crimes and Punishments* (1764). "Although the *Instruction* was decidedly not an original work of political philosophy," Gary Hamburg writes, "its very dependence on Montesquieu and Beccaria placed it squarely in the moderate Enlightenment current of thinking about politics."[36] In the context of autocratic Russia, that was something remarkable. In the *Nakaz*, Catherine appears to have accepted the proposition that every state should be based on certain fundamental laws. According to de Madariaga's summary and analysis:

> The fundamental laws, though few in number, are permanent, exist independently of the reigning sovereign, and provide the framework within which he must operate. Power is limited, if only by the existence of laws which the

33 On the Legislative Commission and Catherine's famous *Nakaz* (Instruction) to it, see Isabel de Madariaga, *Russia in the Age of Catherine the Great* (New Haven: Yale University Press, 1981), 139–83; and G. M. Hamburg, *Russia's Path toward Enlightenment: Faith, Politics, and Reason, 1500–1801* (New Haven: Yale University Press, 2016), 381–402, 586–87. My account relies on these two works.

34 de Madariaga, *Russia in the Age of Catherine the Great*, 151.

35 *The Nakaz of Catherine the Great: Collected Texts*, ed. William E. Butler and Vladimir A. Tomsinov (Clark, NJ: The Lawbook Exchange, 2010).

36 Hamburg, *Russia's Path toward Enlightenment*, 393.

> sovereign regards as binding. The area within which the arbitrary will of the ruler can act is limited by distinguishing between the ruler and the state. This concept was not entirely new in Russia, but it had never before been clothed in the dignified language of the *philosophes* nor publicly proclaimed from the throne.[37]

Not until the 1905 revolution would the tsarist government constitutionally adopt a similar conception. It did so in the Fundamental Laws of April 1906.

Catherine's *Nakaz* was widely distributed. In 1767, instructions were issued for it to be sent to fifty-seven government offices throughout Russia, where it was to be read regularly. It was reprinted several times for circulation at home and abroad, and was translated into French, German, English, and Latin. The first seven sessions of the full Legislative Commission were devoted in large part to reading the *Nakaz*; thereafter it was to be read (or reread) regularly for the duration of the commission.[38] The other business of the commission involved reading and discussion of the country's existing laws, and discussion of the local conditions and state of affairs of the represented social groups, based on the *cahiers*, or notebooks (*nakazy*), that the deputies brought with them to the assembly. Subcommissions produced draft codes on the rights of the various estates and orders.[39] In the end, the Legislative Commission failed to produce a draft of a new law code; nevertheless, it must have awakened a sense of law among some of its delegates, and among some other readers of the *Nakaz*.[40]

Though its work remained unfinished, the Legislative Commission had important consequences. It contributed to Catherine's 1775 reform of provincial administration and to her 1785 charters to the nobility and to the cities. The provincial reform established new district (*uezd*) courts, with judges and assessors elected by the nobility (there were also new land courts, which had appointed judges but elected assessors). The Charter to the Nobility was a veritable bill of rights for nobles—though it was bought at the terrible price of giving them almost unlimited power over serfs tied to their lands (which they now held outright as private property).[41]

In Catherine's reign, Moscow University grew in stature as the center of Russian legal education. In 1761, the Russian government sent Semen Desnitskii (1740–87) and Ivan Tret'iakov (1735–76) to study law at the University of

37 de Madariaga, *Russia in the Age of Catherine the Great*, 154.

38 de Madariaga, *Russia in the Age of Catherine the Great*, 163, 166; Hamburg, *Russia's Path toward Enlightenment*, 394.

39 de Madariaga, *Russia in the Age of Catherine the Great*, 164–83.

40 True, there seems to be little evidence of this. But de Madariaga recounts the following: "P. Nakhovskoy, one of the Decembrists sentenced to death in 1826, described in a letter to Nicholas I on the eve of his execution, with what emotion he had attended meetings of peasant communes and listened in these little republics to the simple eloquence of the Russian peasant. Here, he added, 'for the first time I heard extracts from the Nakaz of the Great Catherine'" (de Madariaga, *Russia in the Age of Catherine the Great*, 163).

41 Pomeranz, *Law and the Russian State*, 23–24.

Glasgow, where they earned LLD degrees in 1767. Then they joined the law faculty at Moscow University. Tret'iakov retired in 1773, but Desnitskii served as a professor for the rest of his life. According to Gary Hamburg, "Around them they created, almost *ex nihilo*, a network of students and intellectuals interested in the history and philosophy of law and in the patient construction of a modern Russian *Rechtsstaat*."[42] Desnitskii was the more original and significant thinker. In Glasgow he studied Roman law under John Millar (1735–1801) and attended Adam Smith's lectures on moral philosophy, political theory, economics, and jurisprudence. He admired William Blackstone (1723–80) and later (in 1780) prepared an annotated translation of the first volume of Blackstone's *Commentaries on the Laws of England*, which he bought while in Glasgow. Among the things that Desnitskii valued most in Blackstone was his defense of natural rights. The English jurist wrote that society's principal aim "is to protect individuals in the enjoyment of their absolute rights, which were vested in them by the inimitable laws of nature." Statutes, he continued, "when prudently formed, are by no means subversive but rather introductive of liberty, for (as Mr. Locke has well observed), where there is no law, there is no freedom."[43]

In 1767, Desnitskii returned to Russia to assume his professorship at Moscow University. He arrived in time for Catherine's Legislative Commission and produced two writings in connection with it. The first was "A Proposal on the Establishment of Legislative, Judicial, and Executive Authority in the Russian Empire," which he submitted to the commission in March 1768. The second was "A Lecture on a Direct and Most Sensible Method of Studying Jurisprudence," which he delivered in June 1768 as a public address at Moscow University. The lecture was directed at his new law students, "but also at the political sophisticates in the Legislative Commission," and as such was intended to provide a more general juridical and philosophical framework for the proposal.[44] According to Hamburg's analysis, the proposal attempted to reconcile the Russian tradition of strong monarchy with the Western idea of separation of powers. In some respects, Desnitskii was (in Hamburg's characterization) a Russian religious traditionalist, whose aim was to construct a just Orthodox realm. He was committed to Orthodoxy as the established Russian church and clearly hoped that it would convert Old Believers and non-Christians—by moral suasion but not by coercion, which he said was "utterly contrary" to the Orthodox faith.[45]

42 Hamburg, *Russia's Path toward Enlightenment*, 566. My summary of Desnitskii relies on "Law and Enlightenment: Ivan Tret'iakov and Semen Desnitskii," Chapter 13 of Hamburg, *Russia's Path toward Enlightenment*, 566–610. On Desnitskii, see also Tomsinov, *Iuridicheskoe obrazovanie i iurisprudentsiia v Rossii v XVIII stoletii*, 156–69; Tomsinov, *Rossiiskie pravovedy XVIII–XX vekov: ocherki zhizni i tvorchestva*, 1:131–56; and Bill Bowring, *Law, Rights and Ideology in Russia: Landmarks in the Destiny of a Great Power* (Abingdon: Routledge, 2013), 21–32.

43 Blackstone, *Commentaries on the Laws of England*, vol. 1, as quoted by Hamburg, *Russia's Path toward Enlightenment*, 567–68.

44 Hamburg, *Russia's Path toward Enlightenment*, 587, 599.

45 Ibid., 593, 595–96, 609.

In "A Lecture on a Direct and Most Sensible Method of Studying Jurisprudence," Desnitskii addressed such topics as the difference (and relationship) between moral philosophy and jurisprudence; "natural jurisprudence" (in which he reprised Smith's critique of Grotius, Hobbes, and Pufendorf, and endorsed the natural-rights theory of Blackstone and Smith); Roman law, which he thought was a "complete system" that had attained a higher degree of "perfection" than any other legal code; Russian law, in which he suggested the possibility of a rights-oriented approach; and the origin of social ranks. He concluded the lecture with a "Discourse on Parental Authority," in which, as Hamburg perceptively surmises, "he imbedded an oblique but powerful critique of autocracy" and of serfdom.[46]

For good reason, Desnitskii has been called "the father of Russian jurisprudence."[47] After Dilthey's initial efforts, Desnitskii was largely responsible for introducing the scientific study of Russian law into the curriculum of the law faculty at Moscow.[48] Hamburg lists the Russian philosophers of law whom he considers to be Desnitskii's followers: Aleksandr Petrovich Kunitsyn (1783–1840), Petr Grigor'evich Redkin (1808–91), Konstantin Dmitrievich Kavelin (1818–85), Boris Nikolaevich Chicherin (1828–1904), Aleksandr Dmitrievich Gradovskii (1840–89), and Pavel Ivanovich Novgorodtsev (1866–1924).[49] Redkin, Kavelin, Chicherin, and Novgorodtsev were also professors of law at Moscow University. As Hamburg suggests, Blackstone's defense of natural rights, which so impressed Desnitskii, anticipated Kant's and Chicherin's theories of law.[50] By the 1880s, Chicherin had embraced Kant's conception of human dignity and personhood, as Hamburg shows in Chapter 6 of the present volume. This order of intellectual lineage would make Kunitsyn the immediate link between Desnitskii and Chicherin.[51] Kunitsyn is the subject of Chapter 4.

"The emergence of a legal ethos"

Kunitsyn was the first Russian thinker to advance a consistently liberal, Kantian interpretation of natural law. This, together with the other reasons that Julia

46 Ibid., 599–603.

47 A. H. Brown, "The Father of Russian Jurisprudence: The Legal Thought of S. E. Desnitskii," in *Russian Law in Historical and Political Perspectives*, ed. William E. Butler (Leyden: A. W. Sijthoff, 1977), 117–41.

48 Tomsinov, *Iuridicheskoe obrazovanie i iurisprudentsiia v Rossii v XVIII stoletii*, 168–69.

49 Hamburg, *Russia's Path toward Enlightenment*, 610.

50 Ibid., 568.

51 Aleksandr Radishchev (1749–1802) might deserve this distinction, since his theory of natural rights very likely drew on Blackstone and possibly on Kant. For the Blackstone connection, see Hamburg, *Russia's Path toward Enlightenment*, 651–52. On the Kant possibility, see Randall A. Poole, "The Defense of Human Dignity in Nineteenth-Century Russian Thought," in *Iosif Volotskii and Eastern Christianity: Essays across Seventeen Centuries*, ed. David Goldfrank, Valeria Nollan, and Jennifer Spock (Washington, DC: New Academia Publishing, 2017), 271–305, esp. 275–76.

Berest adduces in her chapter, provides good grounds for identifying Kunitsyn as the first Russian philosopher of liberalism. His magnum opus, *Natural Law* (1818–20), lays out a "liberal theory of human rights."[52] In 1811 he began teaching at the new and elite Tsarskoe Selo Lycée, where young noblemen were to be educated for high state service. His teaching marked a new stage in the development of Russian legal consciousness. "Kunitsyn inspired many of his students with a genuine devotion to the law," Wortman writes, "and several entered judicial posts directly upon completing the lycée." These included Dmitrii Zamiatnin, who became minister of justice in 1862.[53] In 1817, Kunitsyn began to teach as a law professor at the Main Pedagogical Institute, which in 1819 was upgraded to become St. Petersburg University. He also continued to teach senior courses at the lycée until 1820. As Berest recounts, in February 1821 Kunitsyn's book was officially banned because it was allegedly based on ideas "contrary to the truths of Christianity and tending toward overthrowing all family and state ties." The next month, he was dismissed from St. Petersburg University. Over the following years, the quality of teaching in natural law at Russian gymnasia and universities declined, and in 1833 such courses were discontinued altogether.

The fate of Kunitsyn's book and of the teaching of natural law was a consequence of the conservative turn in Russia that began in the second half of the reign of Alexander I (1801–25) and that sharpened with the Decembrist rebellion of 1825 which opened the reign of Nicholas I (1825–55).[54] The rebellion reinforced the emperor's conservatism and conviction in the necessity of firm autocratic rule, but he did not abandon law as an instrument of exercising his absolute will—indeed, he took measures to make the law a more effective instrument. Nicholas established a new branch of his own chancellery, the Second Section, to complete the work of preparing a new law code. He placed Mikhail Speranskii in charge. Nicholas's approach to law was broadly akin to that of the German historical school of jurisprudence, which, in Wortman's words,

> presented the laws of each nation as expressions of that nation's particular characteristics and needs. It banished the notion that law had to conform to universal natural norms, and consecrating the statutes issued by the autocrat, exempted them from outside judgment. Codification then became the ordering and compilation of the ruler's legislative acts, the precondition to the precise implementation of his will.[55]

52 Berest, *The Emergence of Russian Liberalism*, 155.

53 Wortman, *The Development of a Russian Legal Consciousness*, 41, 251.

54 The Decembrists were a group of liberal and radical military officers who attempted a *coup d'état* upon the accession of Nicholas I in December 1825. The attempt failed, the leaders were executed, and almost three hundred others were imprisoned or exiled to Siberia.

55 Wortman, *The Development of a Russian Legal Consciousness*, 43.

Speranskii resisted this approach. His jurisprudential philosophy was informed by his Christian universalism. As the distinguished historian of Russian law, Vladimir Tomsinov, states in Chapter 3 of this volume, Speranskii believed

> that the Christian religion, state power, and legal culture have a common purpose—to strengthen, support, and preserve the humanity of human beings, to preserve universal spiritual values and the social norms that correspond to the essential nature of human beings (67).

Tomsinov argues persuasively that it was Speranskii's faith, genius, and determination—more than any other factor—that brought the codification project to success, resulting in the Complete Collection of Laws of the Russian Empire and the Digest of Laws of the Russian Empire (1828–33). It was an enormous accomplishment.

Codification was one of two prerequisites which Speranskii thought essential for the further development of Russian jurisprudence. The other was legal education. Here he was involved in three significant initiatives. First, in 1828, six outstanding students were selected from the Moscow and St. Petersburg theological academies for training in law at the Second Section. Another six were assigned in 1829. Then they (among others) were sent to the University of Berlin to study with Friedrich Carl von Savigny (1779–1861), the leading legal historicist of the time. According to Robert Nichols, "The students sent to Germany justified Speranskii's confidence. Beginning in 1835, with the return of the first group from Savigny's lectures in Berlin, they began occupying the chairs of jurisprudence in Russian universities."[56] Among them were Nikita I. Krylov (1807–79), an expert in Roman law who became a professor at Moscow University in 1835, and Konstantin A. Nevolin (1806–55), who in the same year joined the law faculty of the new St. Vladimir's University in Kiev.

Second, the University Statute of 1835 revised the law curriculum to emphasize the teaching of Russian law, based on the new Digest of Laws.[57] The statute also formally ended the teaching of natural law as a separate discipline, replacing it with the study of jurisprudence as a specialized science, as an independent scholarly discipline emphasizing the history of law, including Roman law.[58] Third, a new elite (noble) institution was established in 1835: the Imperial School of Jurisprudence.[59] Its graduates numbered (according to Tomsinov's count)

56 Robert L. Nichols, "Orthodoxy and Russia's Enlightenment, 1762–1825," in *Russian Orthodoxy under the Old Regime*, ed. Robert L. Nichols and Theofanis George Stavrou (Minneapolis: University of Minnesota Press, 1978), 65–89, here at 72. See also Wortman, *The Development of a Russian Legal Consciousness*, 45; and Vladimir A. Tomsinov, *Iuridicheskoe obrazovanie i iurisprudentsiia v Rossii v pervoi treti XIX veka*, Uchebnoe posobie, 2nd ed. (Moscow: Zertsalo-M, 2010), 109–28.

57 Vladimir A. Tomsinov, *Iuridicheskoe obrazovanie i iurisprudentsiia v Rossii vo vtoroi treti XIX veka*, Uchebnoe posobie, 2nd ed. (Moscow: Zertsalo-M, 2015), 33, 47–48.

58 Ibid., 49–61.

59 Ibid., 173–93. See also Wortman, *The Development of a Russian Legal Consciousness*, 49–50.

684 by May 1866, when the Judicial Reform of 1864 came into effect. "They injected," he concludes, "a spirit of truth and justice into Russia's judicial system, thereby assuring the success of the judicial reform carried out by Speranskii's student, Alexander II."[60]

Like Peter I before him, Nicholas I intended that specialized legal education would create officials who were obedient technicians. Instead, it led to "the emergence of a legal ethos" among the young jurists educated in the reformed or new institutions.[61] The professors in the law faculty at Moscow University in the 1840s—Petr Redkin, Timofei Granovskii (1813–55) (a historian of medieval Europe), Konstantin Kavelin, and Nikita Krylov—were especially effective in creating this ethos among their students.[62] They taught that law was a science of great intellectual stature. Chicherin, who was a student in the law faculty, later wrote: "Before us arose a full sketch of Juridical Science, not as a dead enumeration of facts, but as a live organism, penetrated by high principles. We learned by heart the teachings of Roman jurists that law [*pravo*] came from justice [*pravda*]."[63] The Hegelian idealism of the period was more than an adequate substitute for the proscribed teaching of natural law. It assured the young jurists that they were instruments not of the absolutist state, but of the Absolute. They would become, in Redkin's words, organs of "the full consciousness of law."[64]

The Judicial Reform of 1864 and its fate

Beginning in the 1840s, graduates of the university law faculties and of the Imperial School of Jurisprudence (*pravovedy*) staffed the Ministry of Justice and other parts of the government. Russia's defeat in the Crimean War (1853–56) precipitated a "crisis of autocracy" that gave them the opportunity to transform the Russian court system. The Judicial Reform of 1864 was the most comprehensive and far-reaching of the Great Reforms. It provided for a system of independent civil and criminal courts, open adversarial trials, a jury system, autonomous regional bar associations, and judges with lifetime tenure. In short, the reform established an independent judiciary—which made it fundamentally incompatible with autocracy. For this reason, Jörg Baberowski has written, "The

60 See Chapter 3 of this volume (90). Speranskii had served as one of the tsarevich's teachers from October 1835 to April 1837. According to Tomsinov, he gave Alexander "a complete course of lectures on jurisprudence and statecraft" (88).

61 Wortman, *The Development of a Russian Legal Consciousness*, 197–234.

62 Ibid., 223–29. See also Tomsinov, *Iuridicheskoe obrazovanie i iurisprudentsiia v Rossii vo vtoroi treti XIX veka*, 66–102.

63 B. N. Chicherin, *Vospominaniia Borisa Nikolaevicha Chicherina: Moskva sorokovykh godov* (Moscow: Izdanie M. i S. Sabashnikovykh, 1929), 37–38, as quoted by Wortman, *The Development of a Russian Legal Consciousness*, 226.

64 P. G. Redkin, *Kakoe obshchee obrazovanie trebuetsia sovremennostiu ot russkogo pravovedtsa* (Moscow: Universitetskaia tipografiia, 1846), 10, as quoted by Wortman, *The Development of a Russian Legal Consciousness*, 225.

1864 judicial reform created Russia's first constitution." "At least *de jure*, Russia was transformed into a state under the rule of law on the European model."[65] The reform provided the institutional framework (legal institutions and court procedures) for the development of civil society and the rule of law. Previously, the courts had merely enforced statutory law; now they were empowered to interpret law, which made them a source of law. The highest civil court was the Senate's Supreme Civil Cassation Department. Through judicial review, it developed family, property, and inheritance law.[66] The Judicial Reform also contributed to the development of a viable system of private law. On this point, Pomeranz cites the testimony of Russian liberal Maksim Vinaver, who in 1905 wrote that the civil law process had become the very embodiment "of the multiple guarantees of freedom of the individual against the unlimited dominion of the administration."[67]

"The task of the judicial reform was to make universal the legal consciousness of the enlightened officials," as Baberowski aptly put it.[68] To accomplish this task, the reformers placed great hope in the jury system, which they saw as a school of citizenship. Surely it would turn "peasants into citizens." Anatolii Koni, Russia's best known jurist, lent his eloquence to these hopes. He is the subject of Chapter 7, by Tatiana Borisova. She shows how Koni's "civic hagiography" celebrated the heroes of the new courts who worked tirelessly for justice in Russia. They and Koni himself understood justice as *pravda*, with all its popular and religious inflections. Koni related it especially to Christian love, mercy, and reconciliation. He rejected the view that the new courts, which drew heavily on Western models, were too advanced for Russia. Rather, he was confident that they would provide the necessary juridical form, and *pravda* the necessary moral-religious content, for the further development and expansion of Russian legal consciousness.

The hoped-for universalization (or popularization, in a sense) of the legal consciousness of Russian jurists was not achieved. Why not, and whether it might

65 Jörg Baberowski, "Law, the Judicial System and the Legal Profession," in *The Cambridge History of Russia*, vol. 2, *Imperial Russia, 1689–1917*, ed. Dominic Lieven (Cambridge: Cambridge University Press, 2006), 344–68, here at 344. See also Baberowski, *Autokratie und Justiz: Zum Verhältnis von Rechtsstaatlichkeit und Rückständigkeit im ausgehenden Zarenreich 1864–1914* (Frankfurt am Main: Vittorio Klostermann, 1996).

66 William G. Wagner, *Marriage, Property, and Law in Late Imperial Russia* (Oxford: Oxford University Press, 1994), and Wagner, "Family Law, the Rule of Law, and Liberalism in Late Imperial Russia," *Jahrbücher für Geschichte Osteuropas*, Neue Folge, 43, no. 4 (1995): 519–35.

67 M. M. Vinaver, *Iz oblasti tsivilistiki* (St. Petersburg: Tipografiia A. G. Rozena, 1908), 335, as quoted by Pomeranz, *Law and the Russian State*, 51. For an account which emphasizes the tenacity of autocratic culture within the tsarist administration and its resistance to legal limitations on *proizvol* (arbitrary power), see E. A. Pravilova, *Zakonnost′ i prava lichnosti: Administrativnaia iustitsiia v Rossii (vtoraia polovina XIX v.–oktiabr′ 1917)* (St. Petersburg: "Obrazovanie-Kul'tura," 2000).

68 Baberowski, "Law, the Judicial System and the Legal Profession," 347.

have been, is one of the fundamental questions of Russian history. Richard Wortman maintains that

> although the development of a consciousness of the transcendent importance of the law was of great significance for its own time and subsequent decades, it encountered formidable and eventually insuperable obstacles, and its rise appears more of a glorious but tragic episode than a central trend of Russian history.[69]

The main "formidable and insuperable" obstacle was the autocracy itself, Wortman argues. Any possibility of establishing a law-based government under Alexander II all but vanished under Alexander III (r. 1881–94) and Nicholas II (r. 1894–1917), both advised by Konstantin Pobedonostsev, chief procurator of the Holy Synod from April 1880 until October 1905. In *Scenarios of Power: Myth and Ceremony in Russian Monarchy*, Wortman shows how a new myth of autocratic power was forged under Alexander III, one which presented the Russian Orthodox Church, autocratic state, and Russian people (*narod*) as one. The myth continued under Nicholas II but emphasized the tsar's personal divine authority, unencumbered by institutions of church and state. In both forms it excluded Russia's liberal development.[70] The last tsar's notion of personal monarchy was strikingly retrograde, seeking to return Russia to a putative Muscovite unity of tsar and people, without institutional or legal mediation. The autocracy's power to enforce the myth was strong, while civil society's power to resist it was weak. Thus, Wortman concludes, "the forces inimical to a law-based state remained dominant."[71] Among those forces must be counted Konstantin Pobedonostsev himself. A nuanced and balanced portrait of him (no mean task) is presented in Chapter 5, by Gregory Freeze.

The deepening of Russian legal consciousness

The tsarist autocracy may have been able to limit the expansion of Russian legal consciousness, but it could not prevent its deepening. There was a certain logic in this: faced with the external constraints of the autocracy, Russian legal consciousness developed internally. Our volume demonstrates that the deepening of Russian legal consciousness was conspicuous in three areas: international law, canon law, and the religious-idealist philosophy of law (focused on natural law). In these areas, a distinctive Russian conception of legal consciousness took shape.[72]

69 Richard Wortman, "Russian Monarchy and the Rule of Law: New Considerations of the Court Reform of 1864," in Wortman, *Russian Monarchy: Representation and Rule* (Boston: Academic Studies Press, 2013), 3–32, here at 6.

70 Richard Wortman, *Scenarios of Power: Myth and Ceremony in Russian Monarchy*, 2 vols. (Princeton, NJ: Princeton University Press, 2000), 2: parts 2 and 3.

71 Wortman, "Russian Monarchy and the Rule of Law," 30.

72 This was also the case in the area of criminal justice, in which Vladimir Soloviev was a pioneering figure, as he was in the religious-idealist philosophy of law. See Frances Nethercott,

Vasilii Malinovskii helped to lay the foundations for the development of international law in Russia. He is the subject of Chapter 2, by William E. Butler. The remarkable extent of that development is clear in Vladimir Tomsinov's portrait of Leonid Kamarovskii in Chapter 8.[73] Kamarovskii was a professor in the law faculty of Moscow University, where he served for thirty-eight years. A person of deep faith, he believed that "Christianity is the most sublime teaching of peace the world has ever known" (ch. 8, 175). His vision was of an international order transformed by that teaching. In 1909, Nicholas II appointed him as the Russian delegate to the Permanent Court of Arbitration in The Hague. Ten years earlier, F. F. Martens (1845–1909), another eminent Russian figure in international law, had drafted the Martens Clause of the 1899 Hague Convention with respect to the Laws and Customs of War on Land. In Chapter 13, Martin Beisswenger examines the further linking of Christianity and international law through Nikolai Alekseev's active involvement in the ecumenical Life and Work movement of the 1930s. Alekseev emphasized the positive role that religion and the churches could play in the search for international peace and security.

Two chapters of our volume are devoted to canon law—Chapter 1, by Paul Valliere, and Chapter 10, by Vera Shevzov. The golden age of Orthodox legal studies, as Valliere puts it, was the second half of the nineteenth century and the first two decades of the twentieth. The Russian Orthodox Church long had been subordinated to the tsarist state through the Holy Synod, in violation of its canonical order and liberty. The desire to rectify the canonical order was one of the main reasons that Russian canon-law studies experienced a remarkable upsurge in the period following the Great Reforms. The outcome of the deepening of canon-law consciousness was momentous: the All-Russian Council of Moscow of 1917–18, which Valliere characterizes as one of the great church councils in the history of Christianity.

Six chapters of our book follow the development of Russian religious-idealist philosophy of law by focusing on some of its main figures: Boris Chicherin (Gary M. Hamburg), Vladimir Soloviev (Paul Valliere), Pavel Novgorodtsev (Konstantin M. Antonov), Sergei Kotliarevskii (Randall A. Poole), Nikolai Alekseev (Martin Beisswenger), and Ivan Ilyin (Paul Valliere). For all of the differences among this extraordinary group of thinkers, they were "religious idealists" in the same basic ways.

First was their idealist conception of human nature. They understood the quintessentially human capacities to be reason and free will. Chicherin defined reason as consciousness of the absolute, not in a specifically Hegelian sense but rather in the general sense that reason is the capacity to recognize or posit absolute ideals. Through free will, human beings are capable of self-determination according to these ideals. Kant called this dual capacity "practical reason" (he

---

Russian Legal Culture Before and After Communism: Criminal Justice, Politics, and the Public Sphere (Abingdon: Routledge, 2007).

73 More generally, see V. E. Grabar, *The History of International Law in Russia, 1647–1917: A Bio-Bibliographical Study*, ed. and trans. W. E. Butler (Oxford: Clarendon Press, 1990).

also referred to it as autonomy). In their idealist conception of human nature, Chicherin and Soloviev closely followed Kant (though not only him),[74] and in this crucial respect the other four Russian philosophers followed Chicherin and Soloviev. Second, as a whole the group held that reason and free will are the grounds of human dignity and of natural rights—that they are what make us persons. All six Russian philosophers were, in this sense of the word, *personalists*.[75] Third, all thought that their idealist, personalist conception of human nature refuted naturalism and had metaphysical implications, which (fourth) they understood in terms of Christian theism. Hence, their "religious idealism."[76] In individual ways, it was both a source and confirmation of their faith.

Vladimir Soloviev, Russia's greatest religious philosopher, was the most important link in the development of Russian religious idealism and the Christian conception of law in Russia.[77] If Chicherin had elucidated the rational foundations of faith, then on them Soloviev built one of the great modern systems of religious philosophy. According to his idealist conception of human nature, human beings combine in themselves three principles: the absolute or divine principle, the material principle, and (between them) the distinctively human principle, which is rational autonomy or the capacity for self-determination.[78] Together the divine and human principles form "divine humanity" (*Bogochelovechestvo*), Soloviev's central concept.[79] It is the free human realization of the divine principle in ourselves and in the world—in patristic terminology, *theōsis* (deification). *Bogochelovechestvo* is the divine-human project of building the Kingdom of God.

Soloviev always maintained that the Kingdom of God would come through the kingdom of ends—Kant's ideal of a moral community of persons who respect each other as ends-in-themselves, whose highest end is nothing other than the

74 F. W. J. Schelling was also an important source for Soloviev. See Paul Valliere, "Solov'ëv and Schelling's Philosophy of Revelation," in *Vladimir Solov'ëv: Reconciler and Polemicist*, ed. Wil van den Bercken, Manon de Courten, and Evert van der Zweerde (Leuven: Peeters, 2000), 119–29.

75 On personalism, see Thomas D. Williams, *Who Is My Neighbor? Personalism and the Foundation of Human Rights* (Washington, DC: Catholic University of America Press, 2005); and *Rozhdenie personalizma iz dukha Novogo vremeni: Sbornik statei po genealogii bogoslovskogo personalizma v Rossii*, ed. V. N. Boldareva (Moscow: Izdatel'stvo PSTGU, 2018).

76 For further development, see Randall A. Poole, "The Liberalism of Russian Religious Idealism," in *The Oxford Handbook of Russian Religious Thought*, ed. Caryl Emerson, George Pattison, and Randall A. Poole (Oxford: Oxford University Press, 2020), 255–76.

77 For a classic account of Soloviev's philosophy of law, see Andrzej Walicki, "Vladimir Soloviev: Religious Philosophy and the Emergence of the 'New Liberalism,'" in Walicki, *Legal Philosophies of Russian Liberalism*, 165–212. See also *Politics, Law, and Morality: Essays by V. S. Soloviev*, ed. and trans. Vladimir Wozniuk (New Haven: Yale University Press, 2000).

78 See Randall A. Poole, "Vladimir Solov'ëv's Philosophical Anthropology: Autonomy, Dignity, Perfectibility," in *A History of Russian Philosophy, 1830–1930: Faith, Reason, and the Defense of Human Dignity*, ed. G. M. Hamburg and Randall A. Poole (Cambridge: Cambridge University Press, 2010), 131–49.

79 For a study of the concept in Russian religious thought, see Paul Valliere, *Modern Russian Theology: Bukharev, Soloviev, Bulgakov: Orthodox Theology in a New Key* (Edinburgh: T&T Clark, 2000).

Kingdom of God, and who are self-governed by freely and inwardly accepted laws of virtue.[80] The kingdom of ends rests on and develops out of a lower stage, the political community (or state) whose laws are external and backed by coercion. Soloviev agreed with Kant that law is the basic enabling condition of all human progress and that it makes possible the advance to the kingdom of ends, which both philosophers thought of as a spiritual community or church.[81] Soloviev called it "free theocracy." For him it seems to have signified the penultimate stage of human perfectibility, the highest development of legal consciousness and morality before the full realization of divine humanity in the eschatological Kingdom of God, when God will be all in all (1 Corinthians 15:28).[82]

Chicherin and Soloviev laid the foundations for the "Moscow school" of the Russian philosophy of law. The final four chapters of this book are devoted to the school's most outstanding jurists.[83] Pavel Novgorodtsev's theory of natural law was central to the school's religious-idealist conception of legal consciousness. In 1902, proclaiming Kant's kingdom of ends to be "the supreme good of the moral world," Novgorodtsev defined natural law as "a norm and principle of personhood." He wrote of "the absolute foundation of natural law that is revealed to us in the moral idea of personhood" and of the way that the modern conception of natural law limits state power by "the idea of the inalienable rights of the person."[84] Toward the end of his life he made it more explicit that the "moral idea of personhood" entailed, for him, Christian personalism. His colleague Sergei Kotliarevskii similarly stressed that the type of legal consciousness capable of sustaining the rule of law had to draw its strength from a religious reverence for human dignity. Novgorodtsev's students Nikolai Alekseev and Ivan Ilyin concurred. Like his teacher, Ilyin wrote a major treatise on the concept of legal consciousness, which he closely related to the idea of natural law. All four philosophers recognized that natural law rests ultimately on faith, since personhood itself, in its self-determination by and aspiration toward the absolute ideal, transcends the natural world. Their faith was centered in the sacredness of the human person—the luminous core of the Russian conception of legal consciousness.

80 See Randall A. Poole, "Kant and the Kingdom of Ends in Russian Religious Thought (Vladimir Solov'ev)," in *Thinking Orthodox in Modern Russia: Culture, History, Context*, ed. Patrick Lally Michelson and Judith Deutsch Kornblatt (Madison: University of Wisconsin Press, 2014), 215–34.

81 Immanuel Kant, *Religion within the Boundaries of Mere Reason*, in Kant, *Religion and Rational Theology*, ed. and trans. Allen W. Wood and George di Giovanni (Cambridge: Cambridge University Press, 1996), 39–215, here at 130–33, 135.

82 Both Kant and Soloviev repeatedly quote this verse.

83 Another member of the group was Evgenii Trubetskoi (1863–1920). See *Evgenii Trubetskoi: Icon and Philosophy*, ed. Teresa Obolevitch and Randall A. Poole (Eugene, OR: Pickwick/Wipf and Stock, 2021).

84 P. I. Novgorodtsev, "Ethical Idealism in the Philosophy of Law (On the Question of the Revival of Natural Law)," in *Problems of Idealism: Essays in Russian Social Philosophy*, ed., trans., and intro. Randall A. Poole (New Haven: Yale University Press, 2003), 274–324, here at 305, 303, 313.

1 Law and the Orthodox Church in the history of Russia

Paul Valliere

This chapter introduces the reader to the role the Orthodox Church has played as a source and subject of law in the history of Russia. The church was a source of law because it came to Russia with a law of its own: the classical Orthodox canon law, which was highly developed by the time the Russian lands were Christianized in the tenth and eleventh centuries. The church was a subject of law because no Russian state could afford to overlook it. For centuries, the Orthodox Church was the largest and best-organized institution in Russian society—far better organized, certainly, than the princely polities of medieval Russia. The Muscovite state of the fifteenth and sixteenth centuries was a more effective political structure than its antecedents, but it did not fundamentally alter the church's juridical tradition. In the seventeenth century, however, the Russian Church endured two crises that eventually led to significant changes in its constitution: a schism within the church itself, and the arrival of Western-style political absolutism in Russia. The result of these crises was the subordination of church to state in the imperial system created by Peter the Great (r. 1682–1725). The Petrine system, which lasted until 1917, violated the church's canonical order and liberty.

Tensions arising from the conflict between traditional canonical principles and the new imperial order, and from the pressures of existence in a society struggling to modernize itself, generated confusion but also creativity in the Russian Orthodox community. In the nineteenth century, successive generations of canonists, intellectuals, and church leaders sought to envision a new constitution for their venerable church. Their labors, frequently marked by discord, culminated in an event that could take place only because of a significant degree of concord: the All-Russian Council of Moscow of 1917–18. The All-Russian Council replaced the Petrine system with a new constitution based on an unprecedented synthesis of traditional and modern elements. This chapter ends with a word about the historical significance of the council's achievement.

Law in the Orthodox Church

Clarity about the dynamics of law in Orthodox Christianity depends on a couple of distinctions. The first is the distinction between canon law and church law. The terms overlap and are often used interchangeably, but this fluidity can lead

DOI: 10.4324/9781003017097-1

to misunderstanding. In the most restrictive sense of the term, canon law in the Orthodox Church refers to the body of positive laws of ecclesiastical provenance that attained its classical form in a Greek-language collection datable to the late ninth century (883)—the Nomocanon in Fourteen Titles, or Nomocanon of Photius, as it came to be known. Collections of canons (*kanones*, rules) appeared in the ancient Christian church as early as the fourth century and developed thereafter in both Eastern and Western venues of the still-undivided Christian community. Some of these compilations evolved into the ninth-century collection, which gained general acceptance in the Byzantine church during the ninth to twelfth centuries.[1] The ninth-century core—the "canon of canons," as we might call it—consists of laws, rules, and advice about church organization and moral issues authored by church councils and ecclesiastical writers from the fourth through the ninth centuries. The ordering of the texts constitutes a fixed pattern in its own right. The Apostolic Canons come first. These are a set of eighty-five rules traditionally regarded as actual teachings of Jesus's apostles, although they derive from a later time. Next come the canons framed by the seven ecumenical councils (325–787), followed by those of influential regional councils. A body of writings on moral and disciplinary topics by revered church fathers completes the collection. Apostles, councils, and fathers—namely, *these* apostles, councils, and fathers—constitute the classical canon law of Orthodoxy.[2]

What, then, is church law? In the first instance, the term refers to civil laws pertaining to the church. The Orthodox Church achieved its definitive shape as the established church of the Christian Roman Empire. In that status, it enjoyed considerable freedom to manage its internal affairs, but state establishment subjected it to imperial legislation in the many areas of life where it impinged on civil and political matters. In Byzantine political theory, imperial law had divine authority in its own right. The emperor received his mandate directly from God without ecclesiastical mediation, just as the church received its divine mandate in spiritual affairs without the mediation of the state.[3] Each with its own vocation,

1 For an introduction, see John A. McGuckin, *The Ascent of Christian Law: Patristic and Byzantine Formulations of a New Civilization* (Yonkers, NY: St. Vladimir's Seminary Press, 2012). The best treatment of the conceptuality of the classical Orthodox canon law is David Wagschal, *Law and Legality in the Greek East: The Byzantine Canonical Tradition, 381–883* (Oxford: Oxford University Press, 2015). See also *The History of Byzantine and Eastern Canon Law to 1500*, ed. Wilfried Hartmann and Kenneth Pennington (Washington, DC: The Catholic University of America Press, 2012). Standard Russian surveys offer an excellent introduction to the subject: A. S. Pavlov, *Kurs tserkovnogo prava* (St. Petersburg: Izdatel'stvo "Lan'," 2002), and Vladislav Tsypin, *Kurs tserkovnogo prava: Uchebnoe posobie* (Klin: Fond "Khristianskaia zhizn'," 2002).

2 There is a broad consensus on this point. Citing leading Orthodox canonists and theologians (Paulos Menevisoglu, Peter L'Huillier, John Meyendorff, Nikodim Milaš, Vladislav Tsypin), Wagschal observes: "the 883 corpus will emerge in the manuscripts as the regular and sealed 'core' of the canonical tradition—a position it retains to this day in the modern Byzantine Orthodox churches" (*Law and Legality in the Greek East*, 48).

3 The distinction is found in Justinian's sixth *Novella*. See the discussion of the Byzantine understanding of "the church in the world" in John Meyendorff, *Byzantine Theology: Historical Trends and Doctrinal Themes* (New York: Fordham University Press, 1974), 212–23.

church and state were called to collaborate in "symphony" (*symphonia*, harmony) for the welfare and salvation of the human race. However, the Byzantines did not fuse church and state, nor did they elide canon law and imperial law. The distinction between the church's rules (*kanones*) and the empire's laws (*nomoi*), between the "divine" (*theios*) order and the "civil" (*politikos*) order, was carefully observed in theory, if not always with the same degree of consistency in practice. Imperial edicts dealing specifically with the church were still considered laws, not canons. Only the church could make canons.

In the Byzantine system, bishops obviously needed to be expert (or to employ experts) not only in canon law but also in civil law pertaining to the church. Beginning in the late sixth century, to facilitate fluency in both laws, collections of imperial legislation concerning the church began to be made. These collections were transmitted in tandem with the church's canons and were eventually combined with them to form composite collections—nomocanons, as these sourcebooks came to be called in later Byzantine usage.[4] The popularity of nomocanons was based on convenience, not theory. The fact that canon law and imperial church law were transmitted together did not abolish the distinction between them. The two laws stood side by side in nomocanonical manuscripts but were still readily distinguishable. The idea of rationalizing the two sets of laws by subsuming them under an overarching scheme was completely foreign to Byzantine and Orthodox jurisprudence.

The term "church law" is ambiguous, however, because it refers to more than civil legislation alone. It also signifies the church's own lawmaking subsequent to the formation of the classical canon law. Defining the core of the canon law did not obviate the need for new law in the church. Liturgical, clerical, penitential, moral, doctrinal, and other matters continued to demand attention as the church followed its historical path. These matters were adjudicated by bishops—diocesan, metropolitan, or patriarchal; more rarely, by councils of bishops. The rulings of these instances were church law. Speaking loosely, one can even call such judgments canon law, in that they were viewed as Spirit-guided continuations of the canonical tradition in a later context. It is important to note, however, that the ninth-century core was not pried open so that later rulings could be added to it, as if the canon law were a code, periodically updated. The classical canons became as sacrosanct as the classical dogmas. Both belonged to the holy tradition of the church: the one, the sacred deposit of faith; the other, the sacred deposit of practice.

The makers of postclassical church law labored under a basic limitation: they could not claim the universal authority that belonged to the classical canon law. Councils can claim universal authority if they are "ecumenical" (worldwide), but the Orthodox Church has not convened an ecumenical council since the Second Council of Nicaea (Seventh Ecumenical Council, 787). Councils

4 The term "nomocanon" has a history of its own; see Wagschal, *Law and Legality in the Greek East*, 41–44.

that have taken place since that time are "local," which in Orthodox usage means national or regional.[5] As for hierarchical judgments, they apply to the diocese, metropolitanate, or patriarchate of the hierarch. Even the patriarch of Constantinople, called the ecumenical patriarch, is no exception to this rule, despite the fact that his title might be taken to imply universal jurisdiction. If the ecumenical patriarch exercised universal jurisdiction, Orthodoxy would have a papacy. But the Orthodox Church has consistently rejected the notion that it has a papal polity, even if individual patriarchs of Constantinople have occasionally acted as if it did.

One might wonder why limited jurisdiction should present a problem, since the scope of each judicial instance seems clear enough. A bishop governs a diocese; a metropolitan, a metropolitanate; a local council, a national or regional church. This apparent clarity masks two problems. First, what happens when one national or regional Orthodox church disagrees with another on a matter perceived by the parties to be important? Second, what happens when a conflict arises with respect to an office, practice, or institution which the classical canon law does not address, either because the *disputandum* did not exist until after the classical canon law was completed, or because it existed in such a different form that whatever the classical canons say about it does not clarify the later case?

The Russian church schism of the seventeenth century presents an example of the first problem. When it was discovered that the faithful people of the Russian Church performed their prayers differently than the faithful people of the Greek Church—not different prayers, but the same prayers performed differently—no one knew what to do.[6] In the absence of a judge or council enjoying universal authority, who was to decide which church was praying aright? In a tolerant, live-and-let-live ethos, one would say, "Let the Russians pray in the Russian manner, the Greeks in the Greek manner, and there's an end of it." But this approach, too, represents a decision. Who is to make that decision? Who is to say, "This, and not some other way, is how we will proceed?" And not just say it, but win acceptance because the decision applies a universally recognized standard?

The office of patriarch presents an example of the second problem. Most national and regional churches in the Orthodox world today are headed by patriarchs. Because patriarchs also existed in the ancient church (although the term

5 Strictly speaking, an ecumenical council requires the participation of the Roman see; so until the healing of the East/West schism, an ecumenical council is impossible. However, a Pan-Orthodox council is possible, although such a meeting did not occur during the second millennium. The need for a Pan-Orthodox council was widely recognized following the collapse of the Russian and Ottoman empires, although efforts to convene such a council in the twentieth century came to naught. A Pan-Orthodox council assembled on Crete in 2016, but its status was compromised when the Russian Orthodox Church (the world's largest Orthodox church) and three other local (national or regional) churches failed to attend.

6 A good introduction by an author who focuses on the ecclesiological issues is Paul Meyendorff, *Russia, Ritual, and Reform: The Liturgical Reforms of Nikon in the 17th Century* (Crestwood, NY: St. Vladimir's Seminary Press, 1991).

was not applied to hierarchs before late antiquity[7]), it might seem natural to assume that the evolution of the modern patriarchates must have been an organic process guided by canon law or longstanding consensus. In fact, almost the opposite is the case. The classical canon law has little to say about patriarchs and patriarchates, and what it has to say pertains to the ancient sees (Rome, Alexandria, Antioch; later, Constantinople and Jerusalem). Most of the Orthodox patriarchates that exist today arose long after the end of antiquity, and the motives and circumstances governing their appearance, as well as the functions they serve, differ substantially from those of the ancient sees. Canon law sheds little light on such questions as: Why should there be patriarchates in the first place? How should they be instituted? What are a patriarch's rights and responsibilities? What are the limits of his authority? Who or what governs the relations of patriarchs with each other?

The history of the Moscow Patriarchate illustrates the force of these questions. The patriarchate was a late arrival in Russia. The Russian Orthodox Church was six hundred years old before an enterprising Muscovite politician outfitted it with a patriarchate in 1589.[8] The history of the institution since then has not been smooth. Almost immediately, the patriarchate was swept up in the political chaos of the Time of Troubles (1598–1613). Patriarch Filaret (1619–33), another agile Muscovite politician, whose son became the first Romanov tsar in 1613, functioned more like a co-tsar than a traditional spiritual leader. Patriarch Nikon (1652–66) set a different example. Deploying an exalted notion of patriarchal power, he upset the traditional "symphony" of church and state. Simultaneously, by unleashing an ill-conceived program of ecclesiastical reforms, he provoked a vast schism in a church which had been almost entirely free of schisms before his time. Having alienated both church and state, Nikon was deposed in 1666.

In 1700, Peter the Great let the patriarchate lapse. It would not reappear until 1917, when the All-Russian Council of Moscow reinstituted it. It lapsed again in 1924, when the Bolshevik regime prevented the election of a successor to Patriarch Tikhon. The revival of the institution under state supervision in the Soviet period is not a story we can get into here, nor can we discuss the tensions surrounding the institution at the present time. To be sure, the Moscow Patriarchate has been shaped by many factors, some of them quite external to the

7 For the early history of the term "patriarch" in the canonical tradition, see Wagschal, *Law and Legality in the Greek East*, 241–42, 247–49.

8 "When Patriarch Jeremiah II of Constantinople traveled to Moscow on a fund-raising trip in 1588–1589, the Russian government did not miss its chance. With the capable and ambitious Boris Godunov already at the helm during this period of Tsar Fyodor's nominal reign (1584–1598), Moscow demanded an actual status commensurate with its rhetorical glory. Jeremiah had no desire or mandate to elevate Moscow to the status of a patriarchate. However, intimidation, confinement, harsh treatment, and economic incentive eventually broke him. The Muscovite regime simply would not let him go until he gave them a patriarchate." Isaiah Gruber, *Orthodox Russia in Crisis: Church and Nation in the Time of Troubles* (DeKalb: Northern Illinois University Press, 2012), 37.

church. But one of the causes of its instability is internal: the absence of agreement about what a patriarch is supposed to be and do. Orthodox canon law does not answer this question.

Autocephaly (the juridical independence of a national or regional church) is another example of the same problem. Autocephaly has played a huge role in the self-definition of Orthodox national churches and in inter-Orthodox relationships, especially in modern times. For this reason, one might think that it has a place in the canon law. In fact, the term does not appear in the classical canons.[9] Only through dubious analogies with ancient arrangements of a very different sort can the notion of autocephaly be inserted into classical canonical discourse. This explains why autocephaly, prevalent as it is, generates so much conflict in global Orthodoxy. The Orthodox Church has no agreed protocols that respond to questions such as why autocephaly should be instituted in the first place, how or by whom it should be instituted, or how conflicts between autocephalous churches should be adjudicated. In most cases, autocephaly exists because a national or regional church, at some point in time, seized it. Legitimation came later, often much later.[10]

There is nothing uniquely Orthodox about the problems posed by the demarcation of a classical canon, be it a canon of scripture or a canon of laws. All literate religious traditions face such problems. The commonest way of dealing with them is through a commentary tradition. The classical canon is not reopened, but reasoned discourse on the canon in relation to the challenges of later times makes it a usable resource. Lawmaking continues by means of religious jurisprudence.

In theory, this is the idea in Orthodoxy, too. "Each autocephalous Orthodox Church follows its own statute, which applies the principles found in the ancient canons to the concrete requirements of church life in specific parts of the world."[11] But such a procedure is intellectually sophisticated. It requires a continuous, written commentary tradition. What is exceptional about Orthodox law since the late

9 Neither nominally nor adjectivally is "autocephaly" indexed in Paulos Menevisoglou, *Lexikon tōn hierōn kanonōn* (Katerinē: Ekdoseis Epektasē, 2013) or in Périclès-Pierre Joannou, *Discipline générale antique*, *Fonti*, fasc. 9, Pontificia Commissione per la Redazione del Codice di Diritto Canonico Orientale, 4 vols. (Rome: Tipografia Italo-Orientale "St. Nilo," 1962–64). Nor does it appear in the index (*alfavit*) of *Kniga pravil* (1893; reprint: Izdanie Sviato-Troitskoi Sergievoi Lavry, 1992). Bishop Nikodim (Milaš) discusses "autocephalous churches"; see references in the index of *Pravila pravoslavnoi tserkvi s tolkovaniiami Nikodima episkopa Dalmatinsko-Istriiskogo*, 2 vols. (St. Petersburg, 1911–12; reprint: Izdanie Sviato-Troitskoi Sergievoi Lavry, 1996).

10 For an excellent description of the problem with a proposal for its resolution through the advancement of church law, see A. V. Shishkov, "'Respublika avtokefal'nykh tserkvei' kak model' ustroistva Pravoslavnoi Tserkvi," *Vestnik Sviato-Filaretovskogo instituta*, no. 34 (2020): 75–95.

11 John Meyendorff, "Contemporary Problems of Orthodox Canon Law," in John Meyendorff, *Living Tradition: Orthodox Witness in the Contemporary World* (Crestwood, NY: St. Vladimir's Seminary Press, 1978), 99–114, here at 102. For a statement of the same principle by one of the leading canonists of the nineteenth-century Russian Church, see Pavlov, *Kurs tserkovnogo prava*, 27 (Vvedenie, sec. 8).

Middle Ages is the relative weakness of its commentary tradition. The closest the medieval and early modern Orthodox Church came to developing robust jurisprudential commentary was in the twelfth century, when three Constantinopolitan jurists with experience in both civil and ecclesiastical government commented on the church's law. Aristenus, Zonaras, and Balsamon produced important, if not particularly speculative or expansive, commentaries.[12] After them, the commentary tradition declined. The last canonists before the destruction of the Byzantine state in 1453—Vlastaris (Blastares) and Harmenopoulos (Armenopoulos)—were encyclopedists and indexers. Not until the end of the eighteenth century did a vigorous commentary tradition reemerge in the Orthodox world.[13]

The church's law in Russia

The Russian Church was a juridical institution from the start. Its head, the metropolitan bishop of Kiev, was more than a chief priest. He was also a judge. He oversaw the canon law and asserted jurisdiction in civil and criminal matters traditionally claimed by the church. Princely statutes adapting these claims to the Russian context form Russia's earliest body of church law.[14]

The metropolitan of Kiev was also a diplomat. Until 1448, when it declared its independence, the Russian Church was juridically dependent on the patriarchate of Constantinople. Despite geographical challenges and limited means of communication, Constantinople and the Russian Church cultivated their bond with extraordinary consistency. Even in political affairs, the metropolitan of Kiev was by far the most important link between the Byzantine Empire and the Russian principalities.[15]

The reception of Byzantine civil law in medieval Russia was limited.[16] The legal norms in the judicial texts of Kievan Rus and early Muscovy reflect East Slavic and northern European customary law more than the laws of the Christian

12 See M. Krasnozhen, *Tolkovateli kanonicheskogo kodeksa vostochnoi tserkvi: Aristin, Zonara i Valsamon*, 2nd ed. (Yuriev: Tipografiia K. Mattisena, 1911).

13 McGuckin reminds us that even in the twilight of the Byzantine state, "the main ecclesiastical courts functioned confidently and their decisions were supported by extensive and well maintained archives" (268). True enough, but distinguished practice in the church of Constantinople could not take the place of an ongoing, generally available jurisprudential tradition in Orthodoxy generally.

14 Church law, specifically the competence of episcopal courts, is the concern of several monuments of early Russian law. For the texts (bilingual), see *The Laws of Rus'—Tenth to Fifteenth Centuries*, ed. and trans. Daniel H. Kaiser (Salt Lake City, UT: Charles Schlacks Jr., Publisher, 1992), 41–65. For a discussion, see Pavlov, *Kurs tserkovnogo prava*, 99–121.

15 The best treatment of the subject in English is John Meyendorff, *Byzantium and the Rise of Russia: A Study of Byzantino-Russian Relations in the Fourteenth Century* (Crestwood, NY: St. Vladimir's Seminary Press, 1989).

16 For a somewhat different assessment of the impact of Byzantine law and education on premodern Russia, see V. A. Tomsinov, *Istoriia russkoi iurisprudentsii: X–XVII veka*, 2nd rev. ed. (Moscow: Zertsalo-M, 2018).

Roman Empire.[17] Given the history and ethnography of the Russian lands, this is not surprising. The Byzantine approach to missionary activity was also a factor. The Byzantines were selective in what they transmitted to the peoples they Christianized. They exported their religious system but not most other aspects of their civilization, and the fact that they exported the religious system in translation (in the Russian lands, in Slavonic) meant that the recipients did not have direct access to the full range of Byzantine culture in any case. Before modern times, Russians did not study Roman and Byzantine civil law in its own right. The chief conduit of Byzantine law was, in fact, the church. The missionaries could not install Orthodoxy without its canon law, and, as we have noted, Orthodox canon law was transmitted in nomocanons that included a significant body of imperial legislation. In this indirect and selective way, Byzantine civil law came to be known in Russia. But it never became the driving force of Russian law. In penal law, for example, the Russians followed their own practices for centuries despite their awareness of the harsher prescriptions of Byzantine law. The most self-conscious effort to incorporate Byzantine law occurred quite late, in the middle of the seventeenth century, when elements of Byzantine penal law were woven into Tsar Aleksei's *Ulozhenie* (Law code, 1649).[18]

While the church did not bring the fullness of Roman and Byzantine law to Russia or displace Russian customary law, it still shaped Russian legal culture in important ways. First, it promoted the cultivation of written law and the evidentiary use of documents. In law, as in all other areas of culture, the higher uses of literacy came to Russia with Christianization. Second, the Orthodox Church modeled a level of complexity and sophistication in law without parallel in the indigenous tradition. The finest monument of indigenous Russian law in the medieval period is the *Russkaia Pravda* (Russian justice).[19] The *Pravda* conveys a powerful sense of legality, but it is a brief, relatively homogeneous document. The short redaction amounts to four pages of printed text; the expanded

17 For overviews of pre-Petrine Russian law, see Richard Hellie, "The Law," and Nancy Shields Kollmann, "Law and Society," in *The Cambridge History of Russia*, vol. 1, *From Early Rus' to 1689* (Cambridge: Cambridge University Press, 2006), 360–86 and 559–78, respectively; Daniel H. Kaiser, *The Growth of the Law in Medieval Russia* (Princeton, NJ: Princeton University Press, 1980); Richard Hellie, "Early Modern Russian Law: The Ulozhenie of 1649," *Russian History/Histoire Russe* 15, nos. 2–4 (1988): 155–80; Tomsinov, *Istoriia russkoi iurisprudentsii: X–XVII veka*; George G. Weickhardt, "Pre-Petrine Law and Western Law: The Influence of Roman and Canon Law," *Harvard Ukrainian Studies* 19 (1995): 756–83; and Richard Hellie's Foreword in Kaiser, *The Laws of Rus'*, xi–xl.

18 Hellie, "Early Modern Russian Law," 169–72; N. S. Kollmann, *Crime and Punishment in Early Modern Russia* (Cambridge: Cambridge University Press, 2012), 205–07, 223–30, 423–25. See also *The Muscovite Law Code (Ulozhenie) of 1649*, pt. 1: Text and Translation, ed. and trans. Richard Hellie, The Laws of Russia, ser. 1: Medieval Russia, vol. 3 (Irvine, CA: Charles Schlacks Jr., Publisher, 1988).

19 The date and provenance of *Russkaia Pravda* are matters of debate. See Tomsinov, *Istoriia russkoi iurisprudentsii: X–XVII veka*, 66–78. For an overview of the *Pravda*, see F. Feldbrugge, "The Earliest Law of Russia and Its Sources," in *The Law's Beginnings*, ed. F. J. M. Feldbrugge (Leiden: Martinus Nijhoff Publishers, 2003), 93–113.

redaction, fourteen pages. The most important Muscovite law code before the mid-seventeenth century, Ivan IV's *Sudebnik* (Law book, 1550), runs to about thirty pages.[20] Slavonic nomocanons are much more copious and complex documents. They incorporate a wide variety of judicial sources and can well exceed a thousand manuscript pages.

Third, the Orthodox Church introduced Christian ethical norms into Russian law. Even if one should be guarded about how extensively Christian morality was assimilated in practice (caution on this point is appropriate in every historical context), Christian teachings certainly reoriented Russians' moral horizon.

Finally, Orthodoxy promoted the ideal of a Christian polity, a godly society where the church and the worldly authority work together in harmony to institute God's law on earth. A compelling picture of this ideal appears already in Metropolitan Ilarion (Hilarion) of Kiev's "Sermon on Law and Grace," one of the jewels of medieval Russian literature. Writing only a few decades after the Christianization of Kiev under Prince Vladimir in 988, Ilarion likened Vladimir to Emperor Constantine at the First Ecumenical Council (325):

> O [Vladimir], [you are] like the great Constantine, equal in mind, equal in the love of Christ, equally honoring His servants [that is, bishops]. He [Constantine], with the holy fathers of the Nicaean Council established the law [*zakon*] for his people. You, in turn, meeting often with our new fathers, the bishops, deliberated in great humility on how to establish the law among [our] people, who have only recently come to know the Lord. He [Constantine] brought Hellenes and Romans, you brought Rus, to God.[21]

Slavonic nomocanons were a crucial conduit of Byzantine moral and legal culture in Russia.[22] The oldest extant manuscript is datable to the eleventh or

20 "The 1550 *Sudebnik*," in *Muscovite Judicial Texts 1488–1556*, ed. and trans. H. W. Dewey, Michigan Slavic Materials, no. 7 (Ann Arbor, MI: Department of Slavic Languages and Literatures, The University of Michigan, 1966), 45–74.

21 Ilarion, *Slovo o zakone i blagodati*, ed., trans., and intro. V. Ia. Deriagin et al. (Moscow: Stolitsa/Skriptorii, 1994), 91. The word *zakon* in Ilarion's *Slovo* has more than one meaning. In the quoted passage, it means the entire religious-political system instituted by a ruler to produce a godly society.

22 In Slavonic, a nomocanon is called *zakonopravil'nik* (a calque of "nomocanon") or *kormchaia kniga* ("pilot book" or "pilot's book"). The best introduction in English is Ivan Žužek, *Kormčaja Kniga: Studies on the Chief Code of Russian Canon Law*, Orientalia Christiana Analecta 168 (Rome: Pont. Institutum Orientalium Studiorum, 1964). Authoritative Russian monographs are Ia. N. Shchapov, *Vizantiiskoe i iuzhnoslavianskoe pravovoe nasledie na Rusi v XI–XIII vv.* (Moscow: Izdatel'stvo "Nauka," 1978) and E. V. Beliakova, L. V. Moshkova, and T. A. Oparina, *Kormchaia kniga: ot rukopisnoi traditsii k pervomu pechatnomu izdaniiu* (Moscow and St. Petersburg: Tsentr gumanitarnykh initsiativ, 2017). For a brief introduction with substantial bibliography, see E. V. Beliakova and A. A. Turilov, "Kormchaia kniga," *Pravoslavnaia entsiklopediia* (Moscow: Tserkovno-nauchnyi tsentr "Pravoslavnaia Entsiklopediia," 2000–), vol. 38: 52–58; and for a brief introduction to the manuscript history, see Kaiser, *The Growth of the Law in Medieval Russia*, 19–23.

twelfth century, although the best-documented import was received at a council of Russian bishops in Vladimir in 1273 or 1274.[23] Not long before then, Metropolitan Kirill II sent to Bulgaria for a copy of the recently minted Slavonic nomocanon attributed to Sava, the Serbian prince-monk and saint (d. 1236). The Nomocanon of Sava was accepted by the Council of Vladimir, and some copies were circulated. A new redaction was prepared a few years later, giving rise to additional transmission lines. All Slavonic nomocanons share a common core because the classical Orthodox canon law was constituted before they were produced. Nevertheless, there are significant differences between them. Some nomocanons present the canons in abbreviated form. Some provide a sampling of the twelfth-century commentators, others do not. Some append indigenous Russian legal texts. And because nomocanons were manuscripts rather than printed texts, each had its own peculiarities. As Žužek observes, "there were almost as many different *Kormčajas* [that is, nomocanons] as there were manuscripts."[24]

The manuscripts were prized possessions of the bishops, yet they did not become objects of formal study. There were no higher schools in Kievan Rus or old Muscovy. Education was by apprenticeship. A young man learned how to be a priest by interning in the household of a priest, often his father or a male relative. A young man became an adept in Russian law by working as a scribe in a government office. Here, too, family dynasties were common. Nothing comparable to the study of the two laws in the universities of the medieval West developed in Russia. Canon law and civil law were cultivated for strictly practical purposes. There was no speculative horizon, whether in political philosophy (systematic reflection on the relationship between ecclesiastical and worldly authority) or philosophy of law (definition of normative principles, concept of natural law, etc.).

In the seventeenth century, Patriarch Iosif of Moscow supervised the preparation of a printed nomocanon. The project was stimulated by the production of Russia's first printed law code, Tsar Aleksei's *Ulozhenie*. After a delay (variously explained), an edited and expanded version of Iosif's nomocanon reached the printing press in 1653 under the supervision of his successor, Patriarch Nikon. Twelve hundred copies were circulated. After this promising beginning, however, printing of the nomocanon came to a halt for over a century. The next edition, sponsored by Old Believers, came out in Warsaw in 1785. The Holy Synod of the Russian Church brought out an edition of its own in 1787.[25]

Judicial practice provided another conduit of the Orthodox Church's influence on Russian legal development. The areas of judicial competence allotted to the church in premodern Russia varied, but the general pattern was relatively stable. Church authorities were responsible for most aspects of the life of the

23 The work of the council is described by Žužek, *Kormčaja Kniga*, 145–52.

24 Žužek, *Kormčaja Kniga*, 13.

25 Tsypin, *Kurs tserkovnogo prava*, 125–28; Žužek, *Kormčaja kniga*, 52–63. An edition of Iosif's nomocanon is available: *Kormchaia (Nomokanon)*, Otpechatana s podlinnika Patriarkha Iosifa, 5th ed. (St. Petersburg: Voskresenie, 2004).

clergy. As Gregory Freeze put it, "The clergy of old Muscovy were not the tsar's subjects, but the bishop's."[26] Episcopal authority also extended to lay servitors of the church. Exceptions involved serious criminal acts on the part of church people. While the more zealous hierarchs claimed authority even over these cases, the civil authorities usually succeeded in maintaining control of felony law.

Property was a more intractable issue. The premodern Russian Church possessed vast holdings in land and was responsible for the resident population. Such a concentration of wealth and power naturally generated tension with the state, especially when the government was in the hands of an energetic ruler. Ecclesiastical wealth also evoked criticism from within the church, most famously from the "nonpossessors" of the fifteenth and early sixteenth centuries.[27] Not until the reduction of the power of the church by Peter the Great and the wholesale confiscation of church property by Catherine the Great (r. 1762–96) did conflicts over church property abate.

Marriage, family, and sexual morality formed another area of ecclesiastical jurisdiction. By the time it arrived in Russia, the Orthodox Church was on its way to acquiring a monopoly over the definition and regulation of marriage in its flock. The system involved a complex calculus of the degrees of separation, with additional rules tailored for the clerical class. The impact of church law was more palpable in the elite ranks of society than farther down the social chain.

The church's marriage law illustrates the force of tradition in Orthodox law. Consider the following passage by Vladislav Tsypin, a contemporary Russian Orthodox canonist. He is discussing the extent to which church laws of defunct political regimes (Byzantine, Muscovite, imperial Russian) have continuing validity:

> Inasmuch as some of the laws of the Byzantine emperors entered Russian law via the Nomocanon and have retained their force not because of the dependence of Rus on the political regime that promulgated them but because of the church's own needs and by virtue of ecclesiastical tradition, we should at least recognize the relative importance even of laws of Byzantine [civil] provenance included in the Nomocanon, in particular in a section such as the church's marriage law, which is comparatively little regulated by the canons. And so, in certain cases, we have to refer to Byzantine *Novellas* which have been sanctified by centuries-long ecclesiastical tradition.[28]

Given the centrality of marriage law in the judicial activity of the Russian Church, it is noteworthy that the classical canon law has little to say on the subject. Most

26 Gregory L. Freeze, *The Russian Levites: Parish Clergy in the Eighteenth Century* (Cambridge, MA: Harvard University Press, 1977), 46.

27 The "nonpossessors" were monks who believed that monastic communities should be places of asceticism and contemplation, not nodes of economic and political power. Nil Sorskii (1433–1508) was the leading figure among these "Trans-Volga Elders," as they are also called.

28 Tsypin, *Kurs tserkovnogo prava*, 159.

Orthodox marriage law derives from civil legislation. Nevertheless, as Tsypin holds, this legislation remains in force because it has been sanctified by ecclesiastical tradition. Thus, besides the three components of Orthodox law already noted—canon law, imperial church law, and postclassical ecclesiastical law—a fourth must be recognized. Tsypin calls it tradition. In another place, he calls it custom. Both terms signify the authority conferred by longstanding practice.[29]

The impact of church law in Russia sprang not only from its contents but also from the way it was applied in practice. There is much we do not know about the episcopal administration of the Russian Church before modern times, but we can be reasonably sure that it was fairly remote from the lives of most Russians. The Russian episcopate was small and did not expand much before modern times. At the end of the Kievan period (1240), the Russian Church had fifteen bishops. Three centuries later (1551), there were ten, with a few more in the western borderlands. In 1720, there were nineteen.[30] Ordinary Russians experienced episcopal oversight mainly through visitations of the bishop's tax collectors, lay servitors who also exercised a measure of judicial authority at the local level.

Church law and civil law were concurrent traditions in Russia, as they were in Byzantium, but they were not exactly parallel. Balsamon, the twelfth-century canonist, stated the difference:

> This is the difference between judges, who impose corporal punishment through their sentence, and bishops, who determine ecclesiastical punishment for penitents: that judges can neither diminish nor augment the punishment established by law without the emperor's will; bishops, who have taken upon themselves the burden of our sins through their desire to intercede with God for us, both increase and decrease punishments. For that reason, they have authority not only to shorten the period of punishment, but even to commute punishments.[31]

The fact that punishment by the church was oriented to amendment of life made it in theory a more hopeful thing than punishment by the state. In practice, the

29 For custom, see Tsypin, "Kanonicheskoe pravo," *Pravoslavnaia entsiklopediia*, vol. 30: 371–72, where the author's example is the institution of a monastic episcopate in Orthodoxy, another practice based on custom, not canons. For Orthodox marriage law, a good place to start is Vladislav Tsypin, "Brak," *Pravoslavnaia entsiklopediia*, vol. 6: 146–66. For the evolution of Russian marriage law in the period on which the present volume focuses, the most important study in English is William G. Wagner, *Marriage, Property, and Law in Late Imperial Russia* (Oxford: Clarendon Press, 1994).

30 Robert O. Crummey, *The Formation of Muscovy 1304–1613* (London: Longman, 1987), 116–17; Nancy Shields Kollmann, *The Russian Empire 1450–1801* (Oxford: Oxford University Press, 2017), 248; James Cracraft, *The Church Reform of Peter the Great* (Stanford, CA: Stanford University Press, 1971), 160.

31 This passage from Balsamon (who was commenting on St. Basil) is quoted in the "Supplement to the Spiritual Regulation" (1721). The translation is from *The Spiritual Regulation of Peter the Great*, ed. and trans. Alexander V. Muller (Seattle: University of Washington Press, 1972), 64.

distinction was less clear. Episcopal courts and monastic prisons could be harsh, while civil courts could show mercy. "Venue shopping" also occurred.[32]

Another channel of hope in the administration of church law was the exercise of *oikonomia*—"flexibility" (its opposite is *akribeia*, "exactitude").[33] *Oikonomia* is the discretion allowed to a bishop to bend the law in a particular case to avoid a merciless or intuitively unjust result. *Oikonomia* is like equity, although it was not institutionalized. In religious terms, the virtue of *oikonomia* is that it allows bishops to play a pastoral, not just a judicial role in relation to their flock. It also enables the church to respond to the needs of a changing world without constantly rewriting the church's rules. The vice of *oikonomia* is that it opens the door to favoritism and venality.

The conciliar tradition

The conciliar history of the Russian Church and of Orthodoxy generally is pertinent to an overview of law in the Orthodox Church. There is a consensus in Orthodoxy that councils are the supreme authority structure in the church, a view inherited from antiquity and reinforced in later times by antipapal polemics. In the global church, the ecumenical council is supreme; in a national or regional church, the local council. Yet Orthodoxy's self-definition as a conciliar tradition must be qualified in two ways.

First, the conciliar principle has always had to compete with the primatial principle, that is, with the authority of powerful hierarchs occupying influential sees.[34] Aside from ideological claims advanced in its favor, primatial authority has an obvious practical advantage over conciliarism. Councils are episodic; hierarchical office is continuous. Day-to-day administration of the church naturally devolves upon the hierarchs.

Second, the conciliar principle in Orthodoxy has been compromised by uneven practice. Periods of conciliar decline and drought greatly outnumber periods of conciliar activism. In the Byzantine church, conciliar practice contracted after the ninth century as ecclesiastical decision-making became centralized in the office of the patriarch of Constantinople. The patriarch did not dispense with conciliarism altogether. He governed in collaboration with a "home synod" (*synodos endēmousa*) composed of bishops who resided in, or happened to be visiting, the capital. Compared with the robust conciliar practice of antiquity, however, Constantinopolitan synodicalism represented a significant diminishment.

32 Kollmann, *Crime and Punishment in Early Modern Russia*, 36–41, 85–86, 174–76 ("venue shopping," at 40).

33 For an overview with extensive bibliography, see Dmitrii Pashkov, "Ikonomiia," *Pravoslavnaia entsiklopediia*, vol. 22: 51–58. The root meaning of *oikonomia* is "household management." In a judicial context, it means "wise" management, adapted to the needs of a particular case.

34 See *Primacy in the Church: The Office of Primate and the Authority of Councils*, ed. John Chryssavgis, 2 vols. (Yonkers, NY: St. Vladimir's Seminary Press, 2016).

It is not surprising that conciliar practice was attenuated in medieval Russia, since the Byzantine mother church did not offer a better example at the time. Councils were convened mainly for the purpose of electing new bishops. In Orthodox canon law, bishops cannot simply be appointed. They must be elected by the bishops of the province to which they are called, the province in the Russian case being the entire jurisdiction of the metropolitan of Kiev. We know, however, that Russian electoral councils were not well attended. Moreover, episcopal election constitutes the bare minimum of a conciliar program. Councils addressing broader agenda (disciplinary, liturgical, doctrinal, etc.) were rare.[35] By the early sixteenth century, however, the Russian Church's independence from Constantinople (1448), conflicts over church landholding, the appearance of dissident religious movements, and the activism of the grand princes of Moscow served to stimulate conciliar activism. This led to the most impressive conciliar gathering of the premodern Russian Church: the Council of Moscow of 1551. This council was exceptional for many reasons, not least because it produced a text: one hundred articles touching on a wide range of disciplinary, liturgical, moral, and other topics. The document subsequently lent the council its name—the Stoglav (the Hundred Chapters).[36]

The only premodern Russian church council that can be compared with the Stoglav took place a century later. The purpose of the Great Council of Moscow in 1666–67 was to address the schism that had exploded in the Russian Church in the 1650s under Patriarch Nikon. The failure of the council to settle the schism is not a story we can tell here. For our purposes, what is significant about the Great Council of Moscow is that it unceremoniously abrogated the *other* great Council of Moscow, that is to say, the Stoglav. In its articles on liturgical practice, the Stoglav affirmed a number of local Russian usages that figured in the schism a century later, such as how to make the sign of the cross, how to recite the Alleluia, and how to address the Holy Spirit in the creed. On these and other points, one party to the schism (eventually called Old Believers) insisted on the practices sanctified by the Stoglav. The Great Council of Moscow demanded conformity with seventeenth-century Greek practices. The Russian Church had no ready means to deal with the phenomenon of warring councils.[37]

35 Meyendorff, *Byzantium and the Rise of Russia*, 81–83.

36 On the Stoglav, see Jack Edward Kollmann, "The Moscow *Stoglav* ('Hundred Chapters') Church Council of 1551," PhD diss., The University of Michigan, 1978; E. B. Emchenko, *Stoglav: Issledovanie i tekst* (Moscow: Izdatel'stvo "Indrik," 2000); and *Stoglav: Tekst, Slovoukazatel'* (Moscow and St. Petersburg: Institut rossiiskoi istorii RAN and Tsentr gumanitarnykh initsiativ, 2015). Paul Bushkovitch argues that there was a shift from monastic to episcopal dominance in the Russian Church after 1500, the new conciliarism being a manifestation of the latter. See Bushkovitch, *Religion and Society in Russia: The Sixteenth and Seventeenth Centuries* (New York: Oxford University Press, 1992).

37 The settlement imposed by the Great Council of Moscow was to excommunicate and anathematize the Old Believers, a blatant abuse of conciliar authority. That the liturgical practices of the Old Belief were provincialisms is a fact; that they were a violation of Orthodoxy is nonsense.

To be sure, one should not reduce the meaning of *sobornost'*—conciliarity, fellowship, community—to formal councils. *Sobornost'* was a pervasive ethos in the Orthodox Church. As Dmitrii Khomiakov wrote of the pre-Petrine church, "One cannot deny that church government there [in premodern Russia] was not what we call *conciliar* in the strict sense, but it was thoroughly conciliar in spirit."[38] To an extent, one can see an ethos of fellowship and conciliarity at work also in the Muscovite political realm, as, for instance, in the notion of the ideal ruler as a tsar who listens to boyars and clergy rather than simply governing on his own.[39] On the village level, the shared ethos of church and society was even stronger because "the Russian [Orthodox] parish had one very striking characteristic: it was identical to the commune; the parish and community (*obshchina* or *mir*) were the same."[40]

The church's constitution in modern Russia

The upheaval in the Russian Church in the seventeenth century facilitated Peter the Great's *coup d'église* at the dawn of the eighteenth. Barring the election of a primate following the death of Patriarch Adrian in 1700, Peter imposed a novel church constitution, called the *Spiritual Regulation*, in 1721. Designed by Bishop Feofan Prokopovich, the system entrusted governance of the church to a small "college" of ecclesiastics supervised by the imperial state. The college was soon renamed the Holy Governing Synod, a title with ecclesial resonance, but the new name did not change the design. Peter was determined to integrate the church into the modernizing regime he was fastening upon Russia. Moreover, for all its novelty, the Synodal system was not unprecedented in Orthodoxy. As Alexander Schmemann pointed out, the Holy Governing Synod bore a distinct resemblance to the home synod of the patriarchate of Constantinople.[41] Despite major differences in the political context, both synods represented a centralizing, elitist form of episcopal government.

Peter's church constitution violated the tradition and canons of the Orthodox Church in at least three ways. First, it upended the ideal of symphony between ecclesiastical and worldly authority by tilting sharply to the side of the state, a power now shaped by modern political absolutism. Second, the Synodal constitution violated the primatial principle that had figured in the headship of the Russian

38 D. A. Khomiakov, *Sobor, sobornost', prikhod i pastyr'* (Moscow: Pechatnia A. I. Snegirovoi, 1917), 7. Khomiakov was writing in 1906.

39 Kollmann, *The Russian Empire 1450–1801*, 129–59, and Figure 9.1, 209. Cf. Rowland's observation that "several recent students have suggested that Muscovy's image of its political authority was more collegial than autocratic," in Daniel Rowland, "Did Muscovite Literary Ideology Place Limits on the Power of the Tsar (1540s–1660s)?," *Russian Review* 49, no. 2 (1990): 125–55, here at 126.

40 Freeze, *The Russian Levites*, 149.

41 Alexander Schmemann, "The Idea of Primacy in Orthodox Ecclesiology," in *Primacy in the Church*, ed. Chryssavgis, 1:339–66, here at 362–63.

Church from the beginning. While the patriarchate was of recent provenance, the metropolitanate was not; yet it, too, was abolished by Peter's decapitation of the church's administration. Third, the Synodal system suppressed conciliarism. While the *Spiritual Regulation* gave lip-service to the conciliar principle, the set-up amounted to little more than pseudoconciliarism.[42] Conciliar practice—that is, the work of assemblies in the government of the church—was extremely attenuated throughout the Synodal period. Before the Great Reforms of the 1860s, neither parish councils, nor clergy convocations, nor plenary episcopal councils were permitted. During and after the Great Reforms, parish trustee boards and clerical assemblies at the diocesan level were authorized in the hope that they would find means of enhancing the material support of the clergy and the church's schools. The authority of these institutions was limited, however; they did not evolve into fundamental structures of church government.[43] Only during the crisis of the Russian state in 1905–17 did fully fledged conciliar activism reemerge. In short, the Synodal constitution subverted the political, canonical, and ecclesial principles of Orthodox church government.[44] Admittedly, the church's practice of these principles in the past had left much to be desired. But a shortfall of practice is a different kind of problem than subversion of the church's constitution. After 1721, Orthodox canonical order fell outside the law of the Russian state.

The Petrine regime did endow the Russian Church with a resource that eventually empowered it to address its constitutional problems in an articulate way. That resource was education. One of the provisions of the *Spiritual Regulation* was that "each bishop have in his house, or attached to his house, a school for the children of priests, or of others, who have been assigned there as likely prospects for a priestly vocation."[45] It took some time for this mandate to be implemented, but by the end of the eighteenth century, most Russian dioceses supported such a school. These seminaries, as they were called, were not traditional institutions. The name derived from Catholic usage, Latin was the language of instruction, and the curriculum was heavily dependent on scholastic imports from the West. Nevertheless, the enterprise of formal theological education got underway. Reforms in the early nineteenth century, including the upgrading of select

42 "In the first place, truth is to be found more certainly by conciliar concurrence than through one individual" (*The Spiritual Regulation of Peter the Great*, 9 [part 1, sec. 1]).

43 On parish trustee boards (*popechitel'stva*), see Gregory L. Freeze, *The Parish Clergy in Nineteenth-Century Russia: Crisis, Reform, Counter-Reform* (Princeton, NJ: Princeton University Press, 1983), 253–59, 289–95; on diocesan assemblies, ibid., 278, 326, 362–63, 435–36, 439.

44 In a justly admired article, Gregory Freeze argued that the Synodal church was a more independent player in the Russian imperial system than most previous scholarship recognized. His argument is not contradicted by the statement that the Synodal system subverted the church's canonical order. Freeze's point pertains to the empirical church, the church as an interest group, not to the church as an entity embodying canonical ideals. See G. L. Freeze, "Handmaiden of the State? The Church in Imperial Russia Reconsidered," *Journal of Ecclesiastical History* 36, no. 1 (1985): 82–102.

45 *The Spiritual Regulation of Peter the Great*, 20.

seminaries to graduate theological academies and the introduction of Russian as the language of instruction, further enhanced the church's educational system. An educated clergy and a growing cadre of theological scholars paid significant dividends to the Russian Church over the course of the nineteenth century.

Addressing the church's constitutional challenges required the reexamination of canon law and of church law generally. Courses in canon law began to be offered in Russian seminaries at the end of the eighteenth century. From 1835, canon law was also taught in the law faculties of the universities.[46] Like the theological schools, Russia's universities were the fruit of the Petrine regime's promotion of education. A university opened in St. Petersburg in tandem with the Russian Academy of Sciences in 1725, although it operated intermittently and had disappeared by the end of the century. Moscow University, founded in 1755, was a more successful institution. A law faculty was one of its original components (with medicine and philosophy). As in St. Petersburg, the first law professors were Germans, since there were no indigenous academic jurists in Russia. The professors taught what one would have expected them to teach, given their background: Roman law and the modern natural law tradition in its Germanic iteration (Grotius, Pufendorf, Thomasius, and others). The first native-born Russian professor of jurisprudence was Semen Efimovich Desnitskii (1740–87), who had studied in Glasgow under Adam Smith and other Scottish Enlightenment thinkers. Desnitskii taught Continental jurisprudence but also instituted the study of Russian law, making Moscow University the original home of this subject in Russian academe.[47]

Russian law was a difficult subject to study, not just because of the lack of pedagogical tools but because of "the chaotic state of Russian legislation."[48] Peter the Great and his successors flooded Russia with new laws but did not succeed in codifying or even organizing their legislation, not to speak of integrating it with pre-Petrine Russian law. A further problem was the mentality of secrecy in the state bureaucracy. The first professor of jurisprudence at Moscow University, P.-H. Dilthey, lamented: "Hiding the laws as if they were some sort of secret is the usual practice of Russian chancelleries—I won't say all of them, but of some, as I myself have amply learned through experience."[49]

In the first half of the nineteenth century, progress in the organization of Russian law began to be made in both the civil and ecclesiastical spheres. Mikhail Speranskii, a veritable Russian Tribonian, accomplished the epic task of collecting

46 Tsypin, *Kurs tserkovnogo prava*, 25.

47 For the rise of academic jurisprudence in Russia in the eighteenth century, see V. A. Tomsinov, *Iuridicheskoe obrazovanie i iurisprudentsiia v Rossii v XVIII stoletii*, Uchebnoe posobie, 2nd ed. (Moscow: Zertsalo-M, 2012); also G. M. Hamburg, *Russia's Path toward Enlightenment: Faith, Politics, and Reason, 1500–1801* (New Haven: Yale University Press, 2016), 566–610.

48 Tomsinov, *Iuridicheskoe obrazovanie v Rossii v XVIII stoletii*, 123.

49 Quoted in Tomsinov, ibid., 47.

and anthologizing the laws of the Russian Empire (1828–33).[50] Speranskii's project prompted efforts at a comparable collection of the church's law. In 1839, the Holy Synod published the first new edition of Orthodox canon law since the nomocanon of 1653. The *Kniga pravil* (Book of canons) was a conservative product in that the canons were published in Slavonic, not Russian, and without commentary. On the positive side, the book presented the full text of the canons rather than abridged versions, and it eliminated the civil laws that formed part of the traditional nomocanons.[51]

Two collections of church law were ready for publication by 1836. One was the work of the retired bishop of Orenburg, Avgustin (Sakharov). It consisted of some two thousand canons and church laws of the first millennium (50–1143) followed by Russian state laws culled from Speranskii's corpus. The second collection was the work of Aleksandr Kunitsyn.[52] It consisted of acts of the Holy Synod retrieved from the Synodal archive. Unfortunately, neither Avgustin's nor Kunitsyn's work saw the light of day in its time. The Holy Synod decided that

> it would not be convenient to make public various decrees from the old days rendered in cases and events which do not serve to strengthen due respect for representatives of the church and which may also inspire views contrary to church teaching on various church ordinances which are still in effect.[53]

Such an outcome was typical of the period. Bishop Avgustin and Professor Kunitsyn fell victim to the pathological fear of public discussion.

The absence of clear, accessible written rules was a problem on all levels of church government. A good example is the diocesan consistory, the clerical board that administered a diocese under the supervision of the bishop. Instituted throughout the Synodal church in 1744, consistories exercised enormous administrative, investigative, and even police powers, yet a statute for the institution was not adopted until 1841.[54] The local parish community stands as a second example. Neither in Orthodox canon law nor in Russian church law could one find a clear, accessible definition of what a parish was or what it was supposed to do.[55]

Work on a collection of Russian church law resumed during the Great Reforms of the 1860s and 1870s. Shortly after his appointment as chief procurator of

50 See Chapter 3 of this volume.

51 *Kniga pravil sviatykh apostol, sviatykh soborov vselenskikh i pomestnykh, i sviatykh otets* (1893; reprint: Izdanie Sviato-Troitskoi Sergievoi Lavry, 1992).

52 See Chapter 4 of this volume.

53 The jurists' labors and the Synod's response are described in the unpaginated introduction to *Polnoe sobranie postanovlenii i rasporiazhenii po vedomstvu Pravoslavnogo ispovedaniia Rossiiskoi Imperii*, vol. 1, *1721* (St. Petersburg: V Sinodal'noi Tipografii, 1869).

54 *Ustav dukhovnykh konsistorii* (St. Petersburg: V Sinodal'noi Tipografii, 1843). See the discussion of consistories and diocesan justice in Freeze, *The Russian Levites*, 52–56, 65–74, and *The Parish Clergy in Nineteenth-Century Russia*, 27–42.

55 See Vera Shevzov, *Russian Orthodoxy on the Eve of Revolution* (Oxford: Oxford University Press, 2004), 22–23.

the Holy Synod in 1865, D. A. Tolstoi received Alexander II's permission to appoint a commission for the purpose of "bringing greater clarity and order" to the Synod's archive. The commission promptly launched two ambitious publication projects: a detailed description of the archive and a complete collection of the Synod's decrees and administrative rulings since its founding in 1721. The inventory began to appear in 1868.[56] The first volume of decrees came out a year later.[57] Both series advanced slowly, at the rate of two or three volumes per decade. Neither project was completed before the collapse of the Russian Empire in 1917.

The new canonists

The renewal of canon law studies was a sine qua non for the advancement of ecclesiastical jurisprudence in Orthodoxy. From the fall of Byzantium to the late eighteenth century, one cannot speak of the *study* of canon law in the Orthodox East in the systematic or scholarly sense of the word. Canon law was administered in episcopal chancelleries, but in the absence of readily available primary sources and a robust commentary tradition, the level of reflection on episcopal practice was low. Two concurrent developments connected with modernity altered this situation. One was the arrival of the critical-historical method, which became available to the Orthodox world as the Enlightenment moved eastward. The other was the rapidly changing social and political situation in the Orthodox lands resulting from the decline of the Ottoman Empire, the emergence of Orthodox nation-states, and the growing complexity of the Russian Empire. These epochal changes challenged longstanding traditional arrangements for the support of Orthodoxy, making plain the need for fresh adaptations.

The renaissance of canon law studies in Orthodoxy began with the publication of a new edition of the Greek nomocanon in 1800.[58] Prepared by the Athonite monks Agapios and Nikodemos, the *Pēdalion* (*The Rudder*) was not a critical edition in the modern sense of the term, but it was a harbinger of change. First, it provided an accessible edition of the canon law, a handbook that any cleric or literate Greek layperson could consult. Second, the authors outfitted the canons with a commentary, drawing on the twelfth-century Byzantine commentators but also offering copious observations of their own. Third, the language of their commentary was modern Greek, an innovative choice in a church where patristic Greek had iconic status. Fourth, the authors made extensive use of non-

56 *Opisanie dokumentov i del khraniashchikhsia v arkhive Sviateishogo Pravitel'stvuiushchogo Sinoda*, vol. 1 (1542–1721) (St. Petersburg: V Sinodal'noi tipografii, 1868).

57 See note 53.

58 *Pēdalion tēs noētēs nēos tēs mias hagias katholikēs kai apostolikēs tōn orthodoxōn ekklēsias, ētoi hapantes hoi ieroi kai theioi kanones.* An English translation, complete but of poor quality, is available: *The Rudder of the Metaphorical Ship of the One Holy Catholic and Apostolic Church of the Orthodox Christians, or All the Sacred and Divine Canons*, trans. D. Cummings (Chicago, IL / West Brookfield, MA: The Orthodox Christian Educational Society, 1957).

Orthodox sources. The most important of these was the *Synodikon* of William Beveridge (1637–1708), a scholar and bishop of the Church of England.

The renewal of canon law studies spread throughout the Orthodox world in the nineteenth century. In Russia, G. A. Rozenkampf (1764–1832) launched the modern source-critical study of Slavonic nomocanons. Rozenkampf was a Baltic nobleman who completed his higher education in Leipzig and served as a jurist in St. Petersburg during the reign of Alexander I. He was a reformist, but like other conservative jurists of the age, he believed that reform should be grounded in history, which in the Russian case demanded scrutiny of the nomocanons. The essential modernity of Rozenkampf's approach comes through in his preface to his study:

> The aim of these investigations has been to explain the most important sources of ancient Russian canon and civil law contained in the printed Nomocanon [*Kormchaia kniga*], but even more in the ancient manuscripts of its various contents from the thirteenth to the very end of the fifteenth century—sources which, to this day, are little known and which have not been subjected to critical analysis.[59]

Rather than assuming that Russians already knew what they needed to know about their canon and civil law, Rozenkampf set out to investigate what was actually there and how it came to be there, a mission which turned out to be extremely complicated and continued for the rest of the century. Other pioneers of canon law studies in Russia during the first half of the nineteenth century were Bishop Ioann (Sokolov), who made "the first serious attempt at a scholarly exposition, not just a compilation, of the system of [Orthodox] church law," and I. M. Skvortsov, who authored the first textbook on the subject.[60]

The second half of the nineteenth century and the first two decades of the twentieth were the golden age of Orthodox legal studies. The period began with the publication of a new edition of the classical Byzantine canon law edited by two scholars in the independent Kingdom of Greece.[61] The Athenian Syntagma, as it is usually called, went beyond the *Pēdalion* by adding full commentaries of Aristenus, Zonaras, and Balsamon, a volume of episcopal and patriarchal synodical judgments, a body of Byzantine imperial law, and the Alphabetical Syntagma of Matthaios Vlastaris. Many Orthodox scholars regard the Athenian Syntagma as the most authoritative edition of their canon law, although it cannot be considered a critical edition. A critical edition came out in the middle

59 *Obozrenie Kormchei knigi v istoricheskom vide*, soch. Barona Rozenkampfa (Moscow: V Universitetskoi Tipografii, 1829), Predislovie, v. A second edition came out posthumously in 1839.

60 Tsypin, *Kurs tserkovnogo prava*, 26.

61 *Syntagma tōn theiōn kai hierōn kanonōn*, ed. G. A. Rallēs and M. Potlēs, 6 vols. (Athens: Ek tēs typographias G. Khartophylakos and [vol. 6] Ek tou typographeiou tēs avgēs, 1852–59).

of the twentieth century, the work of Périclès Pierre Joannou, a Uniate Roman Catholic.[62] However, because Joannou larded his edition with Catholic apologetics, Orthodox scholars do not hold it in high regard, even though they consult it.

In the Balkan churches, the most important figures for our subject were Metropolitan Andrei (Şaguna) and Bishop Nikodim (Milaš). Metropolitan Andrei headed the Orthodox churches of Transylvania; Bishop Nikodim, the Serbian churches of Dalmatia and Istria. The fact that these hierarchs served in the Austrian Empire (from 1867, Austria-Hungary) is important. Unlike their counterparts in states where Orthodox Christianity was the religion of the vast but complacent majority, Metropolitan Andrei and Bishop Nikodim managed their churches' affairs in the cosmopolitan world of the Danube Monarchy, a polity where Orthodox Christianity was a minority faith. The complexity of their situation in relation to civil and constitutional law, along with their proximity to Roman Catholic and Protestant communities, made legal studies—Orthodox and Western—a matter of vital practical importance. Bishop Nikodim's contributions were a monumental study of Orthodox canon law, published in Serbian in 1890 and translated into Russian and German in 1897, and an edition of the classical canons with his own commentary.[63] Metropolitan Andrei's contribution was his vision of the church as an inclusive "organic unity," which he implemented through creative practices of church government, including extensive involvement of the laity.[64]

In Russia, the study of canon law benefited profoundly from the Great Reforms of the 1860s and 1870s, which the counterreforms of the 1880s and 1890s assailed but could not reverse. Talented canonists appeared throughout the church.[65] Most of them came from provincial clerical families and received much of their education in theological schools. In their maturity, they taught not only in theological academies but also in the universities. A. S. Pavlov (1832–98) taught in Kazan, Odessa, and Moscow. I. S. Berdnikov (1839–1909), one of Pavlov's first students, had a distinguished career in Kazan. M. I. Gorchakov

62 Joannou, *Discipline générale antique* (see note 9).

63 Nikodim, *Pravoslavnoe tserkovnoe pravo*, trans. Mil. G. Petrovich (St. Petersburg: Tipografiia V. V. Komarova, 1897); Nikodemos Milasch, *Das Kirchenrecht der morgenländischen Kirche*, trans. Alexander R. v. Pessić, 2nd ed. (Mostar: Verlag der Verlagsbuchhandlung von Pacher & Kisić, 1905); *Pravila pravoslavnoi tserkvi s tolkovaniiami Nikodima, episkopa Dalmatinsko-Istriiskogo* (see note 9).

64 See Johann Schneider, *Der Hermannstädter Metropolit Andrei von Şaguna: Reform und Erneuerung der orthodoxen Kirche in Siebenbürgen und Ungarn nach 1848* (Cologne: Böhlau Verlag, 2005). It is no accident that the most comprehensive Orthodox study of the participation of the laity in church governance was written by a Romanian scholar in the tradition of Şaguna. The work came out in 1939 but remained untranslated and ignored for decades. A German translation is now available: Liviu Stan, *Die Laien in der Kirche: Eine historisch-kirchenrechtliche Studie zur Beteiligung der Laien an der Ausübung der Kirchengewalt*, trans. Hermann Pitters, ed. Stefan Tobler, Orthodoxie, Orient und Europa, ed. Martin Tamcke, vol. 4 (Würzburg: Ergon Verlag, 2011).

65 See Chapter 10 of this volume.

(1838–1910) taught at St. Petersburg University, where he mentored N. S. Suvorov (1848–1909). Suvorov taught at the Demidov Law Lycée in Yaroslavl. N. P. Aksakov (1848–1909), from an aristocratic family that helped launch the Slavophile movement, was a philosopher, journalist, and lay theologian who wrote extensively on canonical issues toward the end of his life. N. A. Zaozerskii (1851–1919) spent his career at Moscow Theological Academy. M. E. Krasnozhen (1860–1934?), a student of Pavlov's in Moscow, taught at Yuriev University (originally Dorpat; now the University of Tartu, Estonia). A. A. Papkov (1868–1920), a lay canonist and statesman who served as governor of the province of Tavastgus (Hämeenlinna) in the Grand Duchy of Finland, contributed essential works on the Orthodox parish. V. N. Beneshevich (1874–1937), based in St. Petersburg, became an internationally prominent Byzantinist.

The scholarship of the new canonists revealed that Orthodoxy was a much more diverse and contested religious tradition than most of its adherents suspected. This discovery was challenging for a church that likes to present itself as a choral body, a locus of unanimity. The canonists were not a choir. Their debates were animated, their differences of opinion, substantial. The golden age of legal studies in the Russian Orthodox Church was an age of discordant canonists.

A new constitution: the All-Russian Council of 1917–18

Discord among the canonists should not cause us to overlook the remarkable outcome of their labors and the labors of other church intellectuals, clergy, and hierarchy in the late imperial period. The outcome was one of the great church councils in the history of Christianity, the All-Russian Council of Moscow of 1917–18. The All-Russian Council replaced the Synodal church system with a new constitution—a conciliar constitution incorporating both traditional and modern elements in a remarkable ecclesial synthesis. How was an event of this magnitude possible? How did the Russian Orthodox Church of the Synodal period find its way to the All-Russian Council of Moscow?

The outlines of a conciliar settlement for the Russian Orthodox Church emerged in the later nineteenth century through a process that would gratify a good Hegelian. The church's course from the middle of the century to 1917 was, to all appearances, a path of discord, division, and rival interests, yet out of these antagonisms emerged a council that embodied *sobornost'*—fellowship, synthesis, solidarity. While the process leading up to the council was complicated, the conceptual evolution stands out clearly. First, the word *sobornost'* was coined in 1867 by N. P. Giliarov-Platonov, a follower of the Slavophile lay theologian A. S. Khomiakov (1804–60), to indicate the ideal of spiritual unity, fellowship, integral community.[66] *Sobornost'* became the watchword of the church reform movement.

66 Giliarov-Platonov coined the term in his 1867 Russian translation of an article Khomiakov published in French in 1853. For details, see Paul Valliere, "The Conciliar Fellowship of the Church in Karl Barth and Modern Orthodox Theology," in *Correlating Sobornost: Conversa-*

But Khomiakovian *sobornost'* alone would not have generated a great council. Khomiakov and the other early Slavophiles were antilegalists. Their vision of a renewed Orthodoxy was thoroughly spiritualized. They saw no place for juridical values in the church. In the empirical church of the time, however, parties with specific, often divergent institutional agenda emerged and played a central role in discussions of reform.[67] Parish clergy generated a "clerical liberalism" designed to enhance their social standing and material well-being. Bishops appealed to canon law to justify their monopoly of church government. State bureaucrats looked for ways to reduce the church's influence in civil affairs where its role had become a nuisance—in marriage and divorce law, for example.

The breakthrough to a new constitutional formula came through the efforts of prophetic Orthodox publicists as they addressed these antagonisms. First, A. N. Murav'ev, a layman, floated the idea of modifying the Synodal regime by convening periodic episcopal councils.[68] It is noteworthy that the bishops themselves did not propose this idea, even though they were its ostensible beneficiaries. They failed to come up with the idea because of the desuetude of conciliar practice in their church. In the later nineteenth century, however, the idea of episcopal conciliarism began to channel the hierarchy's sense of its corporate identity. A. M. Ivantsov-Platonov, a Moscow priest with close ties to the Soloviev family, completed the formula.[69] In a series of articles published in 1882, Ivantsov-Platonov imagined a church council that would bring bishops, secular clergy, and laity together in an inclusive assembly.[70] In this vision, Slavophile *sobornost'* took institutional form—juridical form—while the narrow conciliarism of the bishops was flooded with the spirit of *sobornost'*. This was the formula that delivered the All-Russian Council of Moscow.

Much work remained to be done by canonists and other thinkers and activists before the formula could be put into practice. Many disagreements arose, which, because the council had not yet happened, seemed insuperable. The term *sobornost'* itself became one of the chief points of contention. Many were preaching it, but what did it mean? A council of bishops? A council of bishops, clergy, and laity? Was the latter canonical? Were the Slavophiles right to insist that *sobornost'* was a purely spiritual thing? Would the church do better to avoid adding conciliarism to its juridical burdens? What about the parish community? Where did it fit

---

tions between Karl Barth and the Russian Orthodox Tradition, ed. Ashley John Moyse, Scott A. Kirkland, and John C. McDowell (Minneapolis: Fortress Press, 2016), 3–33, at 11–14.

67 The description that follows relies on Freeze, *The Parish Clergy in Nineteenth-Century Russia*. The conclusion—that the outcome of the period was not failure but an astonishing juridical and ecclesial achievement—is mine.

68 On Murav'ev's intervention, see Freeze, *The Parish Clergy in Nineteenth-Century Russia*, 330–32.

69 Sergei Mikhailovich Soloviev (1820–79), one of Russia's greatest historians, was a professor and rector of Moscow University. His son Vladimir (1853–1900) was Russia's greatest religious philosopher. On the latter, see Chapter 9 of this volume.

70 A. M. Ivantsov-Platonov, *O russkom tserkovnom upravlenii.* Dvenadtsat' statei iz №№ 1–16 gazety "Rus'" 1882 goda (St. Petersburg: Tipografiia A. A. Porokhovshchikova, 1898).

in? The discourse of *sobornost'* was indeed "uncomfortably discordant."[71] Amid all the disagreements, however, what Irina Borshch has called "a new canonical consciousness" emerged: a strong awareness of the need to retrieve, reexamine, and reappropriate Orthodoxy's historic canons.[72] Consensus on this point kept the conciliar movement energized until it found its way to a council. And when the council took place, the Russian Church discovered something other churches have discovered on such occasions: that a great council has a charisma and an ethical reality of its own. The fact of assembly itself inspires achievements that seemed—and arguably were—impossible before it.

The All-Russian Council opened on August 15, 1917 (August 28, New Style), the Feast of the Dormition of the Mother of God, in the Cathedral of the Dormition in the Moscow Kremlin.[73] The membership numbered 564 persons, the majority of them elected from various ecclesiastical constituencies. All stations and vocations in the church were represented: bishops, secular clergy, monastics, and laity.[74] The lay contingent was the majority: 299, compared with 264 clerics. But this did not signify lay domination of the council, as is sometimes alleged. The council consisted of a plenary assembly and an episcopal assembly, the episcopal house retaining a veto over all conciliar decisions—a privilege spelled out, however, in clear rules of procedure. The council conducted much of its business in twenty-two working groups, each composed of bishops, secular clergy, and laity, and dedicated to a particular aspect of church life. In November 1917, the council restored the patriarchate while at the same time defining the church's system of governance as inclusive conciliarism: "In the Orthodox Church of Russia, the supreme power—legislative, administrative, judicial, and supervisory—belongs to the local council, which is convoked periodically, at determined times, and which is composed of bishops, clerics, and laity."[75]

The legislative productivity of the council was enormous, a testimony to the intellectual power and spiritual depth of the clerical and lay leadership of

71 Shevzov, *Russian Orthodoxy on the Eve of Revolution*, 53.

72 I. V. Borshch, *Russkaia nauka tserkovnogo prava v pervoi polovine XX veka: Poisk metodologii*, prefaces by A. Arzhakovskii [Arjakovsky] and O. A. Sedakova (Moscow: Izdatel'stvo LKI, 2008), 24–45.

73 For an introduction to the council, one should begin with John Meyendorff, "Russian Bishops and Church Reform in 1905," in *Russian Orthodoxy under the Old Regime*, ed. Robert L. Nichols and Theofanis George Stavrou (Minneapolis: University of Minnesota Press, 1978), 170–82; then proceed to James W. Cunningham, *A Vanquished Hope: The Movement for Church Renewal in Russia, 1905–1906* (Crestwood, NY: St. Vladimir's Seminary Press, 1981); Gregory L. Freeze, "The 'Long' Church Council of 1917–1918: Institutional Crisis, Intellectual Capital," *Ostkirchliche Studien* 67 (2018): 187–211; and Hyacinthe Destivelle, *The Moscow Council (1917–1918): The Creation of the Conciliar Institutions of the Russian Orthodox Church*, ed. Michael Plekon and Vitaly Permiakov, trans. Jerry Ryan (Notre Dame, IN: University of Notre Dame Press, 2015). See also Chapter 10 of this volume.

74 Women, however, were excluded.

75 Quoted in Destivelle, *The Moscow Council*, 192. See also Catherine Evtuhov, "The Church in the Russian Revolution: Arguments for and against Restoring the Patriarchate at the Church Council of 1917–1918," *Slavic Review* 50, no. 3 (1991): 497–511.

the modern Russian Church. The council left virtually no aspect of church life unaddressed. Its documents, only now being published for the first time in their entirety, will fill thirty-four weighty volumes.[76]

It is easy to overlook the magnitude of the All-Russian Council because of the tumultuous historical drama in which it was caught up: the Bolshevik *coup d'état* of October-November 1917, the Russian Civil War (1918–21), the emigration of hundreds of thousands of Russians, the founding of the USSR (1922), the Soviet regime's violent repression of the Orthodox Church, and the emergence of schisms in the church itself. These events, which altered the destiny of Russia, made it impossible to implement the new church constitution. Although the council managed to hold 170 meetings, the upheaval of the time finally overpowered it. Its last meeting took place on September 20 (September 7, Old Style), 1918.

For the rest of the twentieth century, the council's status was moot. In Soviet Russia, its legislation was a dead letter. In the Russian emigration, once the generation that had participated in the council passed away, the event seemed to belong to an irretrievable past.[77] Moreover, the council's inclusiveness, especially its accommodation of laity in the governance of the church, came to be seen by the Neopatristic thinkers who dominated twentieth-century Orthodox theology as a "democratic" subversion of proper canonical order.[78] In Western histories of twentieth-century Russia, the event slipped from view almost entirely.

At the present time, the council's legacy is being retrieved, but the reception of its work in the contexts where it ultimately belongs—the Orthodox Church and the universal church—is proceeding slowly. The post-Soviet Russian Orthodox Church, while its polity owes something to the great council, has restored episcopal centralism.[79] The wider Orthodox world, not to speak of global Christianity, has yet to take the measure of the All-Russian Council.[80] These obstacles notwith-

76 *Dokumenty Sviashchennogo Sobora Pravoslavnoi Rossiiskoi Tserkvi 1917–1918 godov*, ed. A. I. Mramornov et al. (Moscow: Izdatel'stvo Novospasskogo monastyria, 2012–).

77 On the postrevolutionary decline of the dialogue between jurists and religious thinkers in Russian Orthodoxy, see Borshch, *Russkaia nauka tserkovnogo prava v pervoi polovine XX veka*, 44–45 and throughout. Borshch is one of the few scholars who have explored this development.

78 On the issue of "democratic" conciliarism, see Paul Valliere, "L'évaluation du Concile de Moscou par les théologiens de l'"École de Paris,"" in *Comment vivre et partager la conciliarité ecclésiale? La réception du Concile de Moscou (1917–1918), Contacts: Revue française de l'Orthodoxie*, no. 263 (2018): 357–66; and Valliere, "The Idea of a Council (Σύνοδος, Собор) in Orthodox Tradition and Ecclesiology," in *The Pan-Orthodox Council of 2016—A New Era for the Orthodox Church? Interdisciplinary Perspectives*, ed. Vasilios N. Makrides and Sebastian Rimestad (forthcoming).

79 The reconstruction of the polity and law of the Russian Orthodox Church in the post-Soviet period is a subject that lies beyond the boundaries of this volume. For an introduction, see Alexander Ponomariov, *The Visible Religion: The Russian Orthodox Church and her Relations with State and Society in Post-Soviet Canon Law (1992-2015)*, Erfurter Studien zur Kulturgeschichte des Orthodoxen Christentums, vol. 14 (Frankfurt am Main: Peter Lang, 2017).

80 For the time being, the truest heirs of the ideals of the All-Russian Council are some of the Orthodox jurisdictions in the West that derive wholly or in part from the post-revolutionary

standing, a dispassionate observer can still recognize an obvious fact: that the All-Russian Council of Moscow of 1917–18 was by far the greatest church assembly in the history of Orthodox Christianity since the end of antiquity. In the breadth of its agenda, its canonical and theological acumen, and the degree of consensus and synthesis achieved, it bears comparison with the other great councils of the second millennium—Fourth Lateran, Constance, Trent, and Vatican II. Indeed, it more than holds its own among these precisely because it was an Orthodox assembly. It introduced (or reintroduced) distinctive ideas and practices of the Christian East into the conciliar life of the universal church.

The All-Russian Council of Moscow was the endpoint of the effort to reform the law of the Russian Orthodox Church in the imperial period. It is an indispensable starting point for the reform of Orthodox law globally in the twenty-first century.

Russian diaspora, such as the Orthodox Church in America. In the context of global Orthodoxy, these are small players, but they set an important example, the force of which will grow as the All-Russian Council becomes better known.

2 Vasilii Malinovskii

A Russian Christian on war and peace

William E. Butler

In his monumental treatise on the history of international law in Russia, Vladimir Emmanuilovich Grabar (1865–1956) drew attention to "diplomat-jurists," calling them Russian "legists"—individuals who served in ambassadorial or diplomatic administrative posts and, *inter alia*, drew up diplomatic instructions (*stateinye spiski*, "lists of items") for Russian diplomats abroad.[1] To this body of literature should be added the diplomatic reports sent home to Moscow or St. Petersburg by active diplomats fulfilling their instructions and the occasional substantial contribution to international legal doctrine made by Russian diplomatic personnel in books or other documents. The earliest original work in the Russian language on public international law originated from this milieu in 1717.[2] So, too, did another original work, some eight decades later, on the law of peace and war.

The work in question was initially a puzzle. The author concealed himself behind the initials "V. M." Only later did the author disclose in correspondence

1 An earlier version of this chapter appeared in a festschrift honoring Harold J. Berman (1918–2007) on the occasion of his seventieth birthday. See *The Weightier Matters of the Law: Essays on Law and Religion; A Tribute to Harold J. Berman*, ed. John Witte, Jr. and Frank S. Alexander (Atlanta, GA: Scholars Press, 1988), 163–75; and, with revisions, in W. E. Butler, *Russia and the Law of Nations in Historical Perspective: Collected Essays* (London: Wildy, Simmonds and Hill, 2009), 282–95. This chapter was "the first West European consideration of [Malinovskii's] contribution to the international debate on war and peace": see Paola Ferretti, *A Russian Advocate of Peace: Vasilii Malinovskii (1765–1814)* (Dordrecht: Kluwer Academic Publishers, 1998), 4.

V. E. Grabar, *The History of International Law in Russia, 1647–1917: A Bio-Bibliographical Study*, ed. and trans. W. E. Butler (Oxford: Clarendon Press, 1990), 6: "It would be a very rewarding task to survey the views of our diplomatic-jurists, ambassadorial secretaries—these are our 'legists'—regarding individual norms of international law and to elucidate the role of these secretaries in general and their influence in international politics and on the formation of international legal customs."

2 P. P. Shafirov, *A Discourse Concerning the Just Causes of the War Between Sweden and Russia: 1700–1721*, ed. and intro. W. E. Butler (Dobbs Ferry, NY: Oceana Publications, 1973); Butler, "P. P. Shafirov and the Law of Nations," *Sudebnik*, vol. 7 (2002): 701–56. Petr Petrovich Shafirov (1673–1739) was the vice chancellor of the Russian Empire.

DOI: 10.4324/9781003017097-2

with contemporaries that the work belonged to his pen. The author was Vasilii Malinovskii. The title of the work was *A Discourse on Peace and War*.[3]

Biographical and career data

Vasilii Fedorovich Malinovskii (1765–1814) was born in Moscow into the family of Archpriest Fedor Avksent'evich Malinovskii (1738–1811), himself the son of a clergyman of the Moscow Church of the Trinity, and Anna Nikolaevna Arsen'eva (1744–78). Vasilii was the second son of three, together with three sisters. His elder brother, Aleksei Fedorovich (1762–1840), was and remains the best known of the six children, eventually becoming director of the Moscow Archive of the Ministry of Foreign Affairs, a well-known writer, and a teacher of religion at Moscow University.

Vasilii Fedorovich graduated in 1781 from the faculty of philosophy at Moscow University. The details of his pre-university life and education are not known,[4] but the Malinovskiis were among the venerable Moscow families, tracing their lineage back to 1041. Malinovskii's father served Moscow University in his clerical capacity and was well known to old Moscow society. After completing his university studies, Vasilii entered state service as an archivist in the Moscow Archive of the College of Foreign Affairs under the direction of Gerhard Friedrich Müller (1705–83) and was close to Nikolai Mikhailovich Karamzin (1766–1826). A linguist of considerable accomplishment, Malinovskii had a command of French, German, English, Turkish, and ancient Hebrew—all sufficiently to qualify for appointment to the Russian diplomatic establishment abroad.

He received his first diplomatic assignment abroad in 1789 as translator/interpreter to the Russian mission in London (he may have visited earlier as a courier). There he spent twenty months, resident at least part of the time in nearby Richmond, where the ambassador and other members of the mission maintained a residence to avoid the "stench of London." In addition to his post duties, he devoted his spare hours to beginning his treatise on war and peace and to completing a translation of Alexander Hamilton's *Report on the Subject of Manufactures* (1791).[5] England made an enduring impression on Malinovskii. According to his anonymous biographer,

3 [V. F. Malinovskii], *Rassuzhdenie o mire i voine* (St. Petersburg: Pri gubernskom pravlenii, 1803). The title is interesting in two respects. First, Malinovskii speaks of peace and war, not war and peace, thus reversing the classical Grotian formulation. Second, he chose the term "discourse" to characterize his work, following the example of Shafirov. Reviewed in *Severnyi vestnik*, pt. 2 (1804): 311–23.

4 The records of Moscow University from this period were burned during Napoleon's sacking of Moscow.

5 The translation appeared in print after Hamilton's death. See [A. Hamilton], *Otchet general-kaznacheia Aleksandra Gamil'tona, uchinennyi Amerikanskim shtatam 1791 g. o pol'ze manufaktur i otnoshenii onykh k torgovle i zemledeliiu* (St. Petersburg: Tipografiia V. Plavilshchikov, 1807).

> A close acquaintance with this enlightened and industrial country made a profound impression on [Malinovskii]; he retained his memories of this period to the end of his days; he loved to chat about England and knew how to give the great figures and true dignitaries of that country their just due.[6]

Malinovskii returned to Russia from London in late March 1791, interested in becoming involved in the part of the world where Russian energies were concentrated: the Black Sea and Balkan region in the war against Turkey. Russia and Turkey were at war from 1787 to 1792; by late 1791, the Russian victory over the Ottoman Empire was secure, and Russia had urgent need for diplomatic personnel with a command of the Turkish language to assist with the peace arrangements. Malinovskii was attached to the Russian army to assist at the peace negotiations in Jassy. His services at the peace congress gave him occasion to petition to become an assessor of the College of Foreign Affairs, a rank equivalent to the eighth class in the Petrine Table of Ranks. His petition was unsuccessful, however, and instead he was attached to the College of Foreign Affairs in St. Petersburg without a special assignment or post, allegedly because he was unwilling to use his numerous contacts to advantage. In 1798, he was made a court councilor (*nadvornyi sovetnik*), corresponding to the seventh class in the Table of Ranks, elevated to the next rank two years later, and appointed consul general in Moldavia, where he served until May 1802.

Recalled to Moscow in connection with the reorganization of state service initiated by Emperor Alexander I, Malinovskii continued to devote himself to writing and translation. He petitioned to become a state councilor (*statskii sovetnik*) in 1805 (fifth rank) and was awarded the Order of St. Vladimir in 1806. The return to St. Petersburg brought a period of economic privation for Malinovskii. He was a founder and fervent supporter of the Imperial Philanthropic Society,[7] but in June 1810 he appealed to Count Nikolai Petrovich Rumiantsev (1754–1826) for "rent money" to augment his inadequate salary.

6 See "Vasilii Fedorovich Malinovskii," in *Pamiatnaia knizhka Imperatorskogo Aleksandrovskogo litseia na 1856–1857 god* (St. Petersburg: Tipografiia E. Veimara, 1856), 131. But Malinovskii goes unmentioned in the history of the Russian church in London, as do other translator/interpreters. See C. Birchall, *Embassy, Emigrants, and Englishmen: The Three-Hundred-Year History of a Russian Orthodox Church in London* (Jordanville, NY: Holy Trinity Publications, 2014). It is now considered highly likely that Malinovskii was the author of a series of letters between October 31, 1789, and March 31, 1791, describing his sojourn in England, published anonymously in the journal *Priiatnoe i poleznoe preprovozhdenie vremeni* in 1796 under the title "Rossiianin v Anglii: otryvki iz pisem odnogo puteshestvennika." The author remained anonymous "by his own will and modesty." The letters collectively "constitute a sort of summa of Malinovskii's philosophical conceptions." See Ferretti, *A Russian Advocate of Peace*, 33–34.

7 The Medical-Philanthropic Committee was established by the Imperial Philanthropic Society on May 18, 1802, to provide free medical assistance to the poor. In 1805, the society founded the Committee for the Relief of the Poor and remained active in various organizational forms and titles until 1917.

His repertoire of writings and translations was formidable. The Malinovskii archive in the Institute of Russian Literature in St. Petersburg contains dozens of translations from English, Turkish, ancient Hebrew and Greek, German, French, and other tongues. He favored philosophical works but included William Shakespeare along with several books of the Bible, presumably as part of his interest in the Russian Bible Society. The religious translations were unknown to the public and preserved within the family.

In connection with the Alexandrine ministerial reforms, Malinovskii drew up a Memorandum of the Emancipation of Slaves in 1802.[8] The next year he initiated a weekly journal, *Osennye vechera* (Autumn evenings), in which all the articles published were his own.[9] In the same year Malinovskii completed his reflections on transforming the state structure of Russia that he had begun writing in his diary in 1799 while at his St. Petersburg home, Belozerka.[10] He also finished an epic tale intended for his journal about a hermit who returns to a provincial Russian city after years of absence and deplores the "French morality" which he views as subverting the moral fiber of society.[11]

His most notable publication was *A Discourse on Peace and War*, begun at Richmond in 1790 (part one), completed in 1798 at Belozerka (part two), and published five years later, around the time when he completed part three, which did not appear during his lifetime. From a letter to Kochubei, written in late 1802 or early 1803, it is evident that Malinovskii left London for Jassy partly in order to witness the evils of war against Turkey in person and to gather additional data for his *Discourse*.[12] In a sense, the peace negotiations, where he served as secretary, frustrated his desire to witness the evils of war because the battles had ended.

Malinovskii left in manuscript form several political articles on Jews, land ownership, and on the history of Russia, and published an article during the wars

8 First published in V. F. Malinovskii, *Izbrannye obshchestvenno-politicheskie sochineniia*, ed. E. A. Arab-Ogly (Moscow: Izdatel'stvo Akademii Nauk SSSR, 1958), 111–14. The memorandum was drafted by Malinovskii in Jassy and sent to the minister of internal affairs, Viktor Pavlovich Kochubei (1768–1834), a friend from his London days and the peace congress at Jassy. Kochubei was one of the young liberals who participated in Alexander I's Unofficial Committee to prepare a program of social and governmental reforms.

9 Publication commenced on September 26, 1803. Malinovskii apparently intended to publish twelve weekly issues per year during the three months of autumn.

10 First published during World War I by V. Semevskii, in *Golos minuvshego*, no. 10 (1915): 247–64, and reprinted in Malinovskii, *Izbrannye obshchestvenno-politicheskie sochineniia*, 115–32, with annotations. One of the shortcomings of Russia, said Malinovskii, was that there were "not enough laws," but at least some foreign laws were being translated (115). See also Tatiana Borisova, "Russian National Legal Tradition: *Svod versus Ulozhenie* in Nineteenth-century Russia," *Review of Central and East European Law* 33, no. 3 (2008): 295–341, here at 303.

11 "Pustynnik," in Malinovskii, *Izbrannye obshchestvenno-politicheskie sochineniia*, 136–45.

12 The letter was first published in *Chteniia v Imperatorskom Obshchestve istorii i drevnostei rossiiskikh pri Moskovskom universitete*, no. 1, pt. 5 (1863): 172–75.

against Napoleon concerning a general peace.[13] As noted above, moreover, he left a third unpublished conclusion to his *Discourse on Peace and War*. The text was dated "1801–1803. Jassy, Petersburg."

Insofar as Malinovskii is known to Russian history, this is mostly due to his appointment in 1811 as the first director of Tsarskoe Selo (later Aleksandrovskii) Lycée. In that capacity he encouraged the development of international legal studies in Russia.[14] The appointment was the subject of speculation among the cognoscenti of his time. Baron Modest Andreevich Korf (1800–76) believed the directorship arose out of Malinovskii's marriage in London to Sofia Andreevna Samborskaia (1772–1812), daughter of Andrei Afanas'evich Samborskii (1732–1815), clergyman, agronomist, and author of books on English agronomy. The English connection surfaced time and again in Malinovskii's career. Samborskii had served with the Russian mission in London, served as the spiritual tutor of the future Emperor Alexander I and his brother, Grand Duke Konstantin Pavlovich (1779–1831), and was close to Alexander's law reformer, adviser, and confidant, Mikhail Mikhailovich Speranskii (1772–1839). Malinovskii's interest in the Russian Bible Society also is believed to have originated in England.[15] He was a cofounder of the society, which was authorized by the tsar in December 1812 and held its first organizing meeting in St. Petersburg in 1813.

Dmitrii Fomich Kobeko (1837–1918) attributed Malinovskii's appointment at the Tsarskoe Selo Lycée to his relationship with the Russian Bible Society. A letter dated June 16, 1811, to his brother Pavel Fedorovich Malinovskii (17??–18??) praised the efforts of Senator Mikhail Ivanovich Donaurov (1758–1817), A. K. Razumovskii (1748–1822), and Rodion Aleksandrovich Koshelev (1749–1827) on his behalf (which indicated that on this occasion Malinovskii was using his contacts).[16] All three were elected vice presidents of the Russian Bible Society in 1813. Like-minded in their attitude toward propagation of the faith, they were interested, Kobeko suggested, in placing their people in high positions and, conversely, in attracting important individuals to their ranks.[17]

13 [V. F. Malinovskii], "Obshchii mir," *Syn Otechestva* 10, no. 51 (1813): 235–44. Although the article appeared anonymously, contemporary sources confirm Malinovskii as the author. In content, it is either a conspectus or a continuation of the 1803 *Discourse*.

14 Aleksandr Kunityn, pioneer of the study of natural law in Russia, began teaching at the lycée in the same year. On Kunitsyn, see Chapter 4 of this volume.

15 I. Ia. Seleznev, *Istoricheskii ocherk Imperatorskogo byvshego tsarskosel'skogo, nyne Aleksandrovskogo litseia za pervoe ego piatidesiatiletie, s 1811 po 1861 god* (St. Petersburg: Tipografiia V. Bezobrazova, 1861), 45. Leading Western works on the Russian Bible Society make no mention of Malinovksii. See Stephen K. Batalden, *Russian Bible Wars: Modern Scriptural Translation and Cultural Authority* (Cambridge: Cambridge University Press, 2013).

16 The letter is included in Malinovskii, *Izbrannye obshchestvenno-politicheskie sochineniia*, 153–55.

17 D. F. Kobeko, "Pervyi direktor tsarskosel'skogo litseia," *Zhurnal Ministerstva Narodnogo Prosveshcheniia*, Novaia seriia, no. 58 (July 1915), Otdel po narodnomu obrazovaniiu: 28–42. On the founding of the lycée and its development during Malinovskii's directorship,

Malinovskii's tenure as director of what was to become the most distinguished Russian lycée was auspicious but all too brief. He died in 1814 at the age of forty-nine and was buried in the Bol'sheokhtenskii Cemetery.[18]

Authorship of the *Discourse*

It is now beyond doubt that Malinovskii was the author of *A Discourse on Peace and War*. At the time of publication, however, the title page did not bear the author's name. At the end of part one of the *Discourse*, the designation "Richmond 1790" appears; at the end of part two, "Belozerka near Petersburg in 1798," followed by the initials "V. M."; and at the end of the unpublished part three, "1801–1803. Jassy, Petersburg. V. M." These dates and places coincide with Malinovskii's career and places of service and residence. He later confirmed his authorship in letters to Count Aleksandr Romanovich Vorontsov (1741–1805) and to Gavriil Romanovich Derzhavin (1743–1816). He wrote to Vorontsov that he had the "honor to present my work to the public, a book on war and peace."[19] In a letter to Derzhavin dated August 1812, Malinovskii reminded him that the "book on war and peace [was] written by myself in England and the nearby vicinity; there is a continuation."[20] Grabar possessed a presentation copy (dated 1862) of the *Discourse* from Malinovskii's son to a recipient, which confirms the authorship of the volume. The book, now in the Russian State Library, bears Grabar's rubber-stamp ex libris.

The third, concluding section of the *Discourse*, prepared in Jassy and St. Petersburg, also was signed "V. M." and reposes in the Malinovskii family archive. Part three is further confirmation of his authorship.

Malinovskii's authorship has likewise been confirmed by jurists who alerted an international readership to the importance of his contribution to the literature on international law. Dmitrii Ivanovich Kachenovskii (1827–72), addressing the London Peace Society during his visit to London in 1858–59, recited extracts

---

see Dmitrii Kobeko, *Imperatorskii Tsarskosel'skii litsei: Nastavniki i pitomtsy, 1811–1843* (St. Petersburg: Tipografiia V. F. Kirshbauma, 1911), 1–66.

18 Malinovskii's contributions to international law and to scholarship generally have not received the attention they deserve. Most Russian and Soviet works on sociopolitical and historical thought overlooked him. He was rescued by literary specialists on Alexander Pushkin because of his directorship of the school where Pushkin was educated. Grabar, *The History of International Law in Russia,* drew attention to the *Discourse*, but it remains unknown to most nonjurists. On the early neglect of Malinovskii, see E. A. Arab-Ogly, "Vydaiushchiisia russkii prosvetitel'-demokrat (K 150-letiiu vykhoda v svet 'Rassuzhdeniia o mire i voine')," *Voprosy filosofii*, 1954, no. 2: 181–97.

19 *Arkhiv kniazia Vorontsova*, kn. 30 (Moscow: V Universitetskoi tipografii [M. Katkov], 1884), 394.

20 *Sochineniia Derzhavina s ob"iasnitel'nymi primechaniiami Ia. Grota*, 9 vols. (St. Petersburg: Tipografiia Imperatorskoi Akademii nauk, 1864–83), 6:239. The "nearby vicinity" refers in all probability to Belozerka; the "continuation" may refer to the unpublished continuation of Malinovskii's manuscript.

from the *Discourse* to his audience. These extracts were published in the *Herald of Peace* and reprinted in the organ of the American Peace Society in the same year.[21]

Religious views and practices

Malinovskii grew up in a family dedicated to and in the service of the Orthodox Church. His grandfather and father were clergymen, as were possibly generations before them. He himself devoted his energies to philanthropy and was, as mentioned, a key figure in the founding and development of the Russian Bible Society. What precisely led him early in life, it would seem, to address the evils and horrors of warfare remains shrouded in the past. So far as can be determined, family tragedies or experiences do not account for this. But his antiwar, anticonflict views were in evidence early on, for he was composing his *Discourse* in England, when he had not yet reached his mid-twenties, and wrote the concluding part at Jassy and upon his return to St. Petersburg after completing his diplomatic service.

Another manuscript attributed to Malinovskii, by reason of its being in his own hand, is preserved untitled at the Institute of Russian Literature in St. Petersburg under the designation "Materials on the History of German Religious Philosophy." It was at one time believed to be autobiographical, through the medium of a fictional German young man. This document would reinforce the proposition that Malinovskii grew up in a household in which broad strata of Moscow society visited to chat about religious and moral issues. The manuscript mentions nonconformist religious thinkers such as Ernst Christoph Hochmann von Hochenau (1670–1721) and Gerhard Tersteegen (1697–1769), both influential radical Pietists. Hochmann was noted for opposing war and the accumulation of excessive wealth. The manuscript indicates that Malinovskii was well acquainted with these views. But recent evidence suggests that whatever autobiographical overtones the manuscript may contain, it is in fact Malinovskii's translation of *Theobald, oder die Schwärmer* (*Theobald, or the Zealots*; Frankfurt, 1785), a novel by the physician and mystic Johann Heinrich Jung (1740–1816), better known by his assumed name, Heinrich Stilling. Malinovskii dated the manuscript January 9, 1804, a year after his *Discourse* appeared in Russia. How long he labored on the translation is unknown. If, as is likely, it was for a lengthy period, the work may have influenced the *Discourse*. It is at least evidence of Malinovskii's familiarity with some of the novel's religious intellectual origins.[22]

21 D. I. Kachenovskii, "Dissertation on War and Peace, by Basil Mahnofsky [sic]. St. Petersburgh, 1803," *Herald of Peace* (July 1, 1859), 71–72; reprinted in *Selected Works of D. I. Kachenovskii: Ukrainian International Lawyer*, ed. W. E. Butler (Clark, NJ: Talbot/The Lawbook Exchange, Ltd., 2014), 259–63. Kachenovskii delivered his remarks to the Peace Society in London on May 18, 1859.

22 See M. Shippan, "V. F. Malinovskii—perevodchik fragmenta romana 'Teobal'd, ili mechtateli' I. G. Iunga-Shtillinga," *XVIII vek: Sbornik 22* (St. Petersburg: "Nauka," 2002), 310–19. In the Russian version of the novel, *Schwärmer* is translated "dreamers."

The novel mentioned the translation of the Bible into the German language as an event leading to spiritual liberation.[23] Similar factors help account for the formation of the Russian Bible Society. Malinovskii's manuscript legacy includes his translations of books of the Bible, including Genesis, Ecclesiastes, Job, and Psalms.[24]

Malinovskii's Christian faith was central to his thinking about the causes of war and the prospects for peace, as *A Discourse on Peace and War* makes clear.[25] War, he wrote, "is a spontaneous evil and a combination of all the evils in the world," for it combines "all the savageness of beasts with the art of human reason directed toward the destruction of people." Enlightened Europe should demonstrate to the world how to eradicate the evils of war "through the restoration and confirmation of a universal and indissoluble peace" (2–3). To achieve this, Europe could draw on its two great resources: reason and faith. Malinovskii thought Christianity was a great moral force that gave Europeans an advantage over others, because "our God is a God of peace and love" (7). At the same time, he held that the institutional church, by succumbing to the temptations of wealth and power, had in important respects betrayed Christianity's moral teachings. He had particular disdain for monasticism:

> The idle crowd of monks, whose prosperity is dependent upon the ignorance of nations, have maintained themselves, and the greater part of the people have given an absurd respect to those extravagant and wealthy monks, who have converted the God of Peace into a god of war.

Among the consequences of this perversion was vicious religious persecution, according to which "those who differ in their opinions about the predominant faith are damned, deluded, and unfortunate, and are to be killed in order to please God" (8–9). Yet Malinovskii held out hope that Christianity, by returning to its core moral principles of peace and love, could inaugurate a new era in the life of nations.

23 Ibid., 316.

24 O. K[ornilovich], "Malinovskii Vasilii Fedorovich," in *Russkii biograficheskii slovar' (Maak – Miatleva)* (Moscow: Aspekt Press, 1999), 62. This is one of the new volumes of previously unpublished entries from the classic *Russkii biograficheskii slovar'* (St. Petersburg: Imperatorskoe Russkoe Istoricheskoe Obshchestvo, 1896–1918).

25 References are to the original 1803 edition: [Malinovskii], *Rassuzhdenie o mire i voine*; page references are enclosed in parentheses in the text. The work was published in full in Malinovskii, *Izbrannye obshchestvenno-politicheskie sochineniia*. Substantial excerpts appear in V. F. Malinovskii, "Rassuzhdenie o mire i voine," *Vestnik Universiteta imeni O. E. Kutafina*, no. 6 (2015): 224–49. Also see Kachenovskii, "Dissertation on War and Peace," for a concise summary. My summary of the *Discourse* is adapted from Grabar, *The History of International Law in Russia*, 202–08, and from the transcript of an unpublished codicil to the manuscript discovered by a Polish scholar: J. Skowronek, "'Rozważania o pokoju i wojnie' Wasyla F. Malinowskiego," *Teki archiwalne*, no. 4 (1978): 30–53 (the text is in Russian); reprinted in *Vestnik universiteta imeni O. E. Kutafina*, no. 4 (2019): 248–71.

Towards ensuring international peace and security

War continued to be endemic in the Europe of Malinovskii's time. Even though the domestic order of states had been strengthened, "the general administration of Europeans among themselves has remained in a barbaric state," with disputes continuing to be resolved by fire and sword (10). Far from promoting domestic prosperity, war was inimical to it, because the "prosperity of our state is inseparable from the general prosperity of Europe." The wars of Europe had (or should have) "become as unacceptable and harmful to all in general as were the internecine wars of barons in former times" (11).

As for the arguments adduced in support of war, Malinovskii examined several and refuted each. Some viewed war and pestilence as nature's corrective against overpopulation. Leave future prosperity to our descendants, he said, "for they, of course, will find enough places to live and the means to maintain themselves" (14). Against the view that Europe at peace will in the long term forget how to wage war and will fall prey to other nations, Malinovskii suggested that Europe united could be overcome by no one. Indeed, the present situation is the worse because "Asians, Americans, and Africans are entwined in our wars and, little by little learning the art of warfare, may use this against their teachers by taking advantage of their divisions and disunity" (15).

Malinovskii maintained that the power of states is not dependent on territorial possessions or increased population acquired by wars; in fact, these may lead to a state's decline. States will acquire more pride, more enemies, and thus more reasons for others to reduce their power. He supported his case by reference to the respective positions of Sweden and Denmark, which were vulnerable to Russian (and other European) pressures but not seriously considered by anyone at the time to be subject to appropriation by conquest. "Conquests are now different and virtually impossible" (23).

Malinovskii decried the prejudices of nations. The shortcomings and virtues of nations, being so diverse, should actually bind them closer together, so that they "might through their mutual virtues help one another with regard to their mutual shortcomings" (29). In his chapter on "Respect for War, Heroism, and Magnanimity of Spirit," he reserved his highest accolade for the "lawmaker" or legislator, for through the exercise of wisdom the lawmaker reaches millions of people over many races and centuries (39). This praise reflected Malinovskii's hope that law could become the educator of humanity, restraining our lower impulses and raising "the better angels of our nature," as Abraham Lincoln later put it.

The misfortunes of war are levied on society as a whole:

> War destroys the primary bases of society, the safety of life and property. Laws punish by death certain unfortunate murderers and thieves, but the keepers of those laws, the rulers of nations, in not knowing how to avert war, subject the entire state to murder and plundering.
>
> (45)

Peace, on the other hand, would bring "prosperity and justice" to Europe. The appearance of nations and lands would be altered beyond recognition (65).

Malinovskii concluded his analysis of the causes of war before he departed England and went on to the settlement of the Russo-Turkish War in Jassy. The European powers, he wrote, "habitually consider their neighbors to be implacable and natural enemies ... always ready to attack the enemy or to repulse his attack." The only rules which "European powers observe among themselves are the rules of politics" (69–70). Like the rites of the ancient Egyptians, these rules are concealed from the common people—"the priests send them away from the inner parts of the temple, and with reason" (70). The Italians

> introduced their politics into European cabinets, where they have been present to this day. The monks hurried to confirm them, rose to state office, and sowed there the principles of pretense, injustice, and secrecy which bear sufficient witness against politics [since it is] useful and decorous in the behavior of dishonorable people to endeavor to deceive one another, but not in the conduct of nations.
>
> (70–71)

The "management of politics by individuals at court could not make it . . . more accustomed to injustice and guile." Cardinal Armand-Jean du Plessis, Duke of Richelieu (1585–1642), and Cardinal Giulio Raimondo Mazarin (1602–61) are considered outstanding ministers, yet "coercion, deceit, arrogance, baseness, and perfidy marked their behavior" (71).

Malinovskii condemned political writers who "within the political composition of Europe are maggots born in the wounds of the human body" (75). They "defend the sophistry of politics, confirm its most ridiculous rules, and justify it in matters which it would itself be ashamed to admit to" (76). He divided political writers into three categories: (1) "those writers who apologize for the fact that there are those who are blinded by love for their fatherland"; (2) "those who write ex officio or in the interest of the court" ("the most dangerous of all political writers," in whose works "truth and the law of nations yield their place to injustice and lies"); and (3) "the most common political writers, the newspaper writers," who write in order to write and "are suborned to think in a particular way" (76, 77, 78).

At the family dacha in Belozerka, Malinovskii directed his attention to ways in which the international system could rid itself of the habit of war. He began with the law of nations (*obshchenarodnye zakony*), or what in 1780 Jeremy Bentham (1748–1832) began to call "international law." Malinovskii reasoned that states, just as individuals,

> need to base their behavior on absolute rules which, without prejudicing their independence, restrain them within the bounds of common advantage.... Every sovereign power administers its internal affairs according to its own discretion, and any interference, direct or indirect, is a violation of its independence.
>
> (81)

According to this logic, the establishment of laws of nations does not constitute interference in internal affairs, since such laws may be confirmed only by consent (82). Here Malinovskii may have been expressing his general understanding of the concept of Westphalian sovereignty.

Nations, he continued,

> conclude peace treaties, treaties of alliance, and defensive treaties, and these serve as the rule and law of conduct *inter se*, which are changed as frequently as the chief inducements of interest of those who are concerned in them. Those who are bound are both the judges and the judged, both the aggrieved and those who aggrieve.
>
> (83–84)

Under these conditions, "there is neither security of a court, nor justice, nor equality" (84). There must be a better way of organizing international relations, he concluded.

Malinovskii distinguished among levels or degrees of alliance. A general alliance, he suggested, might subsume all the advantages of special alliances, and then, "instead of treaties, there should be laws to confirm the independence and ownership of territory … and to establish the conduct of all nations" (86–87). Such laws would require a structure to systematize and enforce them. For the observance of such laws, a general council

> should be established, composed of plenipotentiaries of the allied nations. This council should preserve general security and ownership, prevent any disturbance of the peace, and decide disputes between nations submitted according to an established procedure, and its decisions must be unanimously implemented by all the allies (nations).
>
> (87)

If the decision of the general council is not implemented, "the recalcitrant power shall be excluded from all general privileges and intercourse, and in the event of obduracy, a common force shall be used to enforce the law" (88). The country housing the headquarters of the council shall be deemed to be "sacred and independent for the perpetual and safe sojourn of council plenipotentiaries.... Its personnel shall be inviolate in all territories" (89). All negotiations, Malinovskii proposed, would take place through mutual plenipotentiaries in the council. This new arrangement will render the custom of maintaining envoys superfluous, together with the various ways they have caused hostility among nations, such as issuing false and biased reports, interfering in a country's internal affairs, stealing secrets, and stirring passions (89–90).

In Malinovskii's vision of the new order, the first laws of nations will concern their frontiers. Other laws will aim to unite nations through trade. With still others it will be necessary, as is done in treaties of alliance, to define the *casus foederis* "even more precisely in the general alliance." This *casus* shall be an attack, the meaning of which Malinovskii thought was obvious: the incursion of a foreign army into one's own country (90–92). Except for parrying an attack, he doubted whether there could be another instance of a just or lawful war. An "insult to national honor" ought to be punished by a reprimand, since powers are obliged to respect one another. Finally, to remove any incentive for war, Malinovskii deemed it essential to deprive an aggressor

> of the expectation of acquisitions and advantages, and therefore all European powers, after having precisely demarcated their frontiers [must] acknowledge them to be mutually absolute and guarantee their integrity so that they may not be disturbed by war or conquest; equally, the advantages of trade should be absolute and might be changed only by mutual and voluntary consent. (94)

According to Malinovskii, the tribulations of warfare could be confined by limiting the spatial sphere within which European powers might engage in war. If Europeans quarrel, why should America, Africa, and Asia become embroiled? European settlements in those parts of the globe should be neutral territory, with European powers stationing only enough troops there to ensure protection against the local inhabitants. To this policy he proposed adding stipulations against European powers seeking further possessions, punishment of those responsible for committing an attack, compensation for losses sustained, and compulsory negotiations or proceedings between nations (94–95). Malinovskii did not favor disarmament per se, but noted that war is always preceded by movements of troops and arms. Such movements should be confined to imminent expectation of an attack, and the council should be notified of any such movements beforehand.

Malinovskii next contraposed the natural state of society to a state, or civil society. Legal order should exist not merely between private individuals united in a civil society but also between nations. European powers should recognize that they "constitute a single society, by reason of Christianity and of their mutual relations." In this international, law-governed, Christian society, "each power concedes its absolute right to spontaneously govern itself in its disagreements," and in return

> it receives the major advantage of mutually, with others, preserving itself from spontaneous misfortune. The Christian regions … are bound in every possible way to endeavor to settle their disputes peacefully and may not consider their rival an enemy, until he is recognized as such by all society. (111)

In the chapter titled "Unification by Consent," Malinovskii argued that the "slightest violation of universal laws is equally dangerous and harmful to all.… The rulers of a nation who have violated an oath to society subject their nation to the danger of vengeance and are guilty before it" (114–15). He makes reference to his sojourn in London: "In England representations are made by the people to the king concerning war and peace. In this fortunate land the people are allowed to judge their government in quarrels with other powers" (115–16).

The final chapter undertakes to draw the consequences of his *Discourse*. The first is that the "observance of justice between nations is as essential as it is between private individuals." Failure to observe justice between nations also "violates it for each of them separately, subjecting the innocent to destruction and death" (118–19). War, continued Malinovskii,

> cannot be lawful when there are not laws between nations. These laws of nations are duties and obligations based on their own well-being. When all governments are agreed on the unity of their intentions, they will be agreed on everything.... Politics must be the science of rights and laws among nations, just as jurisprudence is among private individuals.
>
> (123)

The turn to the law of nations

The unpublished section of Malinovskii's *Discourse* addresses the law of nations in greater detail and more directly. Malinovskii clearly used one source: the works of Emer de Vattel (1714–67).

Malinovskii emphasized the universality of the law of nations. The law belongs, he said, to Africans and Asians as much as to Europeans. He resolutely opposed slavery. All the peoples in their entirety comprise society, which has similar rules and grounds for crimes. In Europe there was never a threat of a universal monarchy, but events in France led Malinovskii to consider the possibility that a universal European republic might emerge. He supported a variant of self-determination: "every people has the right to govern itself, being subordinate externally in its relations to laws of the whole people."[26]

Self-determination, he suggested, ought to be linked to language. Equilibrium in Europe would be improved, he advised, by a new division of Europe according to the peculiarities of the languages which Europeans speak: Slavic-Russian, German, French, and Italian being the principal examples. Each individual should have his or her own land, and a legacy to pass to family members and kin. Land, he wrote, is "the Lord's, and we are newcomers and strangers to it."[27] There was enough land in any domain so that no one need be deprived of it. Preoccupation with land distribution, he said, is not a departure from the main question of peace and war, since the structuring of a new system depends on its internal components. International peace is unrealistic when there is domestic war between the rich and the poor throughout all of Europe. For Malinovskii, the Christian faith truly observed was the best means of uniting all peoples and bringing peace

26 Skowronek, "'Rozważania o pokoju i wojnie' Wasyla F. Malinowskiego," 34.
27 Ibid., 41.

among cohabitants, properly reflecting all the languages of Europe. War, he said, is contrary to all Christian teaching, citing the example of the Quakers,[28] who deny the permissibility of war, do not accept the consequences of war, and may even choose not to defend a besieged city.

Malinovskii then turned to the "science of the law of nations." He distinguished between the natural law of nations and what he called the "voluntary law of nations." By the former he meant raw force; by the latter, law proper. Under the voluntary law of nations, the European powers "preserve security and ownership of their possessions" and therefore mutual peace. Under the natural law of nations, they arbitrarily violate ownership and security and produce war. Consequently, Malinovskii said, "insofar as peace is preferable to war, it is essential to subordinate natural law to voluntary law."[29]

Security and freedom, Malinovskii said, are the natural right of each people, but no one may appropriate this benefit to himself. Following the example of Russia, which confirmed the right of free navigation of neutral peoples in Europe, the rules of general peace might also be confirmed as follows: (1) any particular violation of the boundaries of ownership of a people is a general violation of ownership; (2) any violation of the independence of one power is a violation of general security and freedom; (3) the discussion of the affairs of Europe should be common, as should its defense when the boundaries and security of a people are violated (52).

Malinovskii concluded this last portion of his treatise by addressing the declaration of war. After commenting on the practices of individual states (Sweden, England), he stated that the "right of a people to declare war is a matter for all of Europe," essential for mutual security and the hope of peace. Such a policy would make the declaration of an unjust war less likely (52).

By way of conclusion and assessment

Some would classify Malinovskii's work as part of the utopian literature proposing schemes for perpetual peace in Europe, although his actual commitment to this idea is doubtful. Whether he thought his proposals had prospects outside Christian civilization is a separate subject. Grabar would appear to be right that the *Discourse* is a "comprehensive and independently conceived work."[30]

28 The reference to Quakers is of interest because, assuming Malinovskii wrote the letters in Russian in England, he describes very favorably a visit to a Quaker meeting in Scotland. See "Vasilii Fedorovich Malinovskii," in *Pamiatnaia knizhka Imperatorskogo Aleksandrovskogo litseia na 1856-1857 god*, and accompanying text.

29 Skowronek, "'Rozważania o pokoju i wojnie' Wasyla F. Malinowskiego," 44–49.

30 Grabar, *The History of International Law in Russia*, 203. There is no evidence of, for example, the influence of Immanuel Kant on Malinovskii. Kant's work on perpetual peace came out in 1795, several years after Malinovskii had started his work. It is possible, but unproven, that Malinovskii met Jeremy Bentham while in London between 1789 and 1791. He did circulate in Benthamite circles, especially the Samborskii family. On the question of the influ-

By coincidence or serendipity, Malinovskii had completed the first two parts of his book before events in France brought Napoleon to power. The French Revolution seems to have influenced the third part. Although he is critical of diplomacy in general and of French diplomats particularly, there is no reason to believe that he pretended to foretell the pan-European conflagration in the offing, pertinent as many features of his analysis were to those events. His *Discourse* was inspired initially by a regional conflict between Russia and Turkey and completed when the clouds of war were gathering all over Europe. By then Malinovskii was beginning to apply his propositions to continental foreign policy in his journal *Osennye vechera*.

By the time of Napoleon's invasion of Russia, in 1812, the scene had changed fundamentally. Malinovksii's letter to Derzhavin[31] suggests that his journal article on a "general peace," published in 1813, was envisaged as a continuation of the *Discourse*.[32] Whatever the case, he believed the time had finally arrived for his diagnosis of events to take effect. "A general peace," he wrote, "is no longer a chimera.... Germany and virtually all of Europe desire it." Having restored

> freedom by their common efforts, all are aware that this cannot be preserved without their common consent, and already they do not rush, as before, to seek any private advantage or to conclude a separate peace.... Entire states and peoples, as one man, endeavor collectively to overcome the common enemy and are as one joyously and solemnly celebrating their mutual triumphs.[33]

Malinovskii counseled that the previous treaties of alliance against Napoleon should be transformed into one common or general new alliance that "would serve as a kind of codex [*ulozhenie*] and confirm reliable and stable rules for the security and integrity of possessions."[34] Further, he suggested that the "general spirit of heroism, love for the fatherland, and disposition of nations to defend and assert their rights, together with intolerance of force and suppressions," would lead the present generation to preserve the fruits of their common achievement for posterity. The "confluence of present circumstances," he presciently foresaw, "constitutes an epoch; we will be accountable to posterity, and will ourselves bitterly regret it if we do not take advantage of them."[35] When printing Malinovskii's last article, the editor of the journal observed that, shortly after he received the manuscript for press, the allied monarchs proclaimed their grand alliance.

---

ence of other thinkers on Malinovskii, also negative, see Ferretti, *A Russian Advocate of Peace*.

31 See note 20.

32 [Malinovskii], "Obshchii mir" (see note 13).

33 Malinovskii, *Izbrannye obshchestvenno-politicheskie sochineniia*, 94.

34 Ibid., 97.

35 Ibid., 97–98.

Malinovskii passed away in 1814 before the Congress of Vienna brought into being the framework for the structure of Europe in which he had placed such hopes. The Napoleonic wars also led to the formation in England, the United States, and other countries of the organized peace movement—in England, the London Peace Society, and in the United States, the American Peace Society. Unbeknown to the organizers of those societies, mostly if not entirely Christians of one denomination or another, a Russian Orthodox Christian had formulated a substantial and original independent contribution to proposals for structuring the international system. His untimely death deprived Russia and the international peace movement of an influential voice in post-Napoleonic Europe, but he left behind an enduring legacy to the literature of international law.

3 Mikhail Speranskii

Statesman, jurist, and Christian thinker

Vladimir A. Tomsinov

The phenomenon of Speranskii

Mikhail Mikhailovich Speranskii (1772–1839) is one of the most extraordinary figures in Russian history.[1] The son of a village priest, he achieved a brilliant career in government service. He became one of the most influential Russian statesmen of the first third of the nineteenth century and was universally acknowledged to be the leading reformer among public officials. He developed plans for reform of the state structure of the Russian Empire—the system as a whole as well as its components, including the Senate, the State Council, the ministries, judicial and executive institutions, and provincial administration. He drafted imperial decrees on new rules of government service, developed a new model for the administration of Siberia, and worked on a plan for the administration of the Grand Duchy of Finland. He drafted the founding documents of elite schools: the Tsarskoe Selo Lycée and the Imperial School of Jurisprudence. In addition, he established new rules for theological seminaries, greatly improving the education of the clergy. He authored a draft of a Civil Code of the Russian Empire in 1809–11 and led the enormous task of compiling the Complete Collection of Laws of the Russian Empire and the Digest of Laws of the Russian Empire (1828-33).

Characterizing Speranskii's government service, the historian S. M. Seredonin remarked:

> There is no doubt that Speranskii was an utterly exceptional phenomenon in the higher levels of our government in the first half of the nineteenth century. Without much exaggeration, he can be called the organizer of the bureaucracy in Russia.[2]

1 Many books have been written about Speranskii's life. The fullest treatment, relying on documentary materials, is V. A. Tomsinov, *Svetilo rossiiskoi biurokratii: Istoricheskii portret M. M. Speranskogo*, 5th rev. ed., Velikie russkie liudi (Moscow: Zertsalo-M, 2013). The most complete study in English is Marc Raeff, *Michael Speransky: Statesman of Imperial Russia*, 2nd rev. ed. (The Hague: Martinus Nijhoff, 1969).

2 S. M. Seredonin, *Graf M. M. Speranskii, 1772–1839: Ocherk gosudarstvennoi deiatel'nosti* (St. Petersburg: Tipografiia tovarishchestva "Obshchestvennaia pol'za," 1909), 179–80.

DOI: 10.4324/9781003017097-3

V. O. Kliuchevskii opined: "Since the time of [Afanasii] Ordin-Nashchokin [1605–80], no mind as powerful as his has stood beside the Russian throne. After Speranskii, I do not know if a third shall appear."[3]

Pragmatism was the distinctive feature of Speranskii's thought. As a reformer, he acquired the reputation of one whose goal was to subordinate social life to artificial schemes. In actuality, Speranskii was quite skeptical about plans to reform the governmental and social structures that had evolved in Russia over the centuries. He thought that the chief purpose of reform should be to preserve the existing state order and avert revolution. In his memorandum "Order and Its Consequences in the State," he reflected on how the state order evolves and is strengthened over the course of time and on the threats the state faces:

> Continual, prolonged order is transformed, in the end, into destiny—into physical necessity. It subdues all people, curtails the dreams of their hearts and minds. It merges with all the interests of life and molds life in its image. The consequences of this are as follows: 1) change becomes difficult; 2) minds grow calm; 3) hearts become attached to prevailing interests. But once the order is shaken, the following ensue: 1) impatience and endless change; 2) confusion and rage; 3) warring interests—revolution.[4]

For Speranskii, reforms were the only way to avert a catastrophe such as the one that occurred in the 1790s in France:

> In order to avoid such upheavals, it is necessary to take all possible measures to preserve the existing order. That is, it is necessary 1) to monitor it constantly and, harmonizing it with the spirit of the time, to fix what has become outdated; and 2) to introduce continuous and gradual reforms without radical changes. (848)

In 1809, Alexander I entrusted Speranskii with the task of creating a general plan of government reorganization. In Speranskii's opinion, it was crucial that the transition from existing institutions to new ones should be instituted

> in the simplest and most natural way, so that the new institutions would appear to arise spontaneously from the old. Furthermore, one should not take chances but should always retain the ability to put a stop to the reforms and retain the old order in all its force if insuperable obstacles to the new order were unexpectedly to arise.[5]

3 V. O. Kliuchevskii, *Kurs russkoi istorii*, pt. 5, in *Sochineniia v deviati tomakh* (Moscow: "Mysl'," 1987–90), 5:200.

4 M. M. Speranskii, "Poriadok i ego sledstviia v gosudarstve," in *V pamiat' grafa Mikhaila Mikhailovicha Speranskogo, 1772–1872*, ed. A. F. Bychkov (St. Petersburg: Izdanie Imperatorskoi publichnoi biblioteki, 1872), 847.

5 M. M. Speranskii, "Obshchee obozrenie vsekh preobrazovanii i raspredelenie ikh po vremianam," in M. M. Speranskii, *Proekty i zapiski*, ed. S. N. Valk, et al. (Moscow and Leningrad: Izdatel'stvo Akademii nauk SSSR, 1961), 231–37, here at 233.

Speranskii also criticized changes based on artificially conceived plans in his "Memorandum on the Establishment of Judicial and Government Institutions in Russia." "It should be noted," he wrote, "that any change that is unnecessary or not obviously useful is harmful, since almost all facile methods of government are unreliable.... Some changes might appear to be brilliant for a while, but over time, evil can arise from the remedies used to counteract it."[6] In a memorandum with the striking title "On Gradualism in the Improvement of Society," he remarked: "Every station of civil society possesses its vices and its virtues. In which of these stations people are happiest is an open question." Following these words, he makes a declaration that astonishes us with its tragic pragmatism: "Fate has decreed that human societies can only change their vices."[7]

Speranskii was a thinker who relied more on common sense and a realistic assessment of the conditions of state and society than on some sort of doctrine. For this reason, the scholarly debate about his political orientation—was he a liberal or a conservative?—should be regarded as meaningless. Speranskii did not adhere to any system of ideas. He was very critical of the constitutional doctrines of European thinkers, calling these doctrines unfounded and superficial. He wrote in a note to members of the commission drafting a law code:

> Notions concerning constitutions are products of modern philosophy and, in our opinion, are as useless as all other theories that are based on empty dreams and never come to fruition. From this I must conclude that you, having studied ancient philosophy and having acquired the habit of thinking in the company of Aristotle, Grotius, and Pufendorf, have penetrated into all the twists and turns of the new notables and have come to see the groundlessness of their ideas—the Montesquieus, the Blackstones, and other superficial minds of this type; that having spent your life laboring over a few pages of these thinkers, you have grasped their errors and the absurdity of their precepts, and by means of deep reflection have forged your own direct path to truth.[8]

Speranskii's dismissal of Montesquieu's ideas as "groundless" notwithstanding, John Gooding has called Speranskii a "disciple of Montesquieu."[9] *On the Spirit of the Laws* was highly influential among Russian intellectuals of Speranskii's time, as confirmed by the fact that several translations of the work were published in

6 M. M. Speranskii, "Zapiska ob ustroistve sudebnykh i pravitel'stvennykh uchrezhdenii v Rossii," in Speranskii, *Proekty i zapiski*, 86–139, here at 138.

7 M. M. Speranskii, "O postepennosti usovершeniia obshchestvennogo," in Speranskii, *Proekty i zapiski*, 75-76, here at 76.

8 M. M. Speranskii, "Otryvok o Komissii ulozheniia," in Speranskii, *Proekty i zapiski*, 17–28, here at 20.

9 John Gooding, "The Liberalism of Michael Speransky," *The Slavonic and East European Review* 64, no. 3 (1986): 401–24, here at 403.

Russia in the late eighteenth and early nineteenth century.[10] Catherine the Great used Montesquieu's ideas in her *Nakaz* (Instruction, 1767) to the commission on the establishment of a new code of laws.[11]

Speranskii agreed with Montesquieu's view that, in establishing laws, one should take into account the distinctive characteristics of the national spirit. He also agreed with Montesquieu's idea that there is an interrelationship between monarchical rule and the existence of privileged classes. But he did not accept Montesquieu's view that respect for the constitution and restrictions on the will of the ruler could be guaranteed solely by preserving class privileges. Montesquieu argued that the privileged classes (nobility and clergy) could check the extension of the ruler's ambitions "just as the sea, which seems to want to cover the whole earth, is checked by the grasses and the smallest bits of gravel on the shore."[12] Speranskii argued against this view:

> They greatly err who think that the rights granted to various classes or the privileges conferred on judicial or even legislative estates can provide a stable foundation for laws or establish a form of government.... This is a building erected on sand.... It is useless to write or publish codes of law or constitutions if one does not base them on the actual power of the state. The documents might be outstanding, but they cannot stand on their own.[13]

Speranskii's legacy retains its significance. He reflected on jurisprudential issues that contemporary jurists still regard as central. He sought solutions to problems of the organization and functioning of the state which are still unsolved. The most important of these are the formation of political elites corresponding to today's level of social development; the development of effective mechanisms for restraining the arbitrariness of ruling groups; the maintenance of a system of legality; the maintenance of constitutional stability; and the effective protection of civil rights and freedoms. The question of a constitution or fundamental laws that cannot be changed at the caprice of rulers was discussed by Russian intellectuals before Speranskii.[14] But it was Speranskii who reflected on this question from the point of view of the actual conditions of social life and state power in Russia.

10 *O razume zakonov: Sochinenie gospodina Monteskiuia*, vol. 1, trans. Vasilii Kramarenkov (St. Petersburg: v Imperatorskoi Akademii Nauk, 1775; 2nd printing, 1801); *O sushchestve zakonov: Tvorenie Montesk'e*, trans. Dmitrii Iazykov, pt. 1 (Moscow: Tipografiia S. Selivanova, 1809); pts. 2–3 (Moscow: Universitetskaia tipografiia, 1810); pt. 4 (Moscow: Tipografiia I. Ioannesova, 1814).

11 See *The Nakaz of Catherine the Great: Collected Texts*, ed. William E. Butler and Vladimir A. Tomsinov (Clark, NJ: The Lawbook Exchange, Ltd., 2010).

12 Montesquieu, *The Spirit of the Laws*, ed. and trans. Anne M. Cohler, Basia Carolyn Miller, and Harold Samuel Stone (Cambridge: Cambridge University Press, 1989), 18 (pt. 1, bk. 2, ch. 4).

13 M. M. Speranskii, "O korennykh zakonakh gosudarstva," in Speranskii, *Proekty i zapiski*, 28–55, here at 33.

14 See V. A. Tomsinov, "The Constitutional-Monarchical Tradition in Russian Political Culture," in "*The Best in the West*": *Educator, Jurist, Arbitrator. Liber Amicorum in Honour of*

Speranskii on the significance of Christian ideas in politics and law

Speranskii was educated in Orthodox seminaries where theology was the main subject of study, but through diligent reading he was able to acquire a profound and extensive knowledge of the secular sciences, especially law and philosophy. Over the entire course of his government service, he retained the Orthodox Christian worldview which he had absorbed in his childhood and youth. This worldview influenced all his work, especially in the fields of statecraft and jurisprudence.

Speranskii believed that the power of the state and the juridical life of society could be organized in harmony with the spiritual foundations of the Christian religion. "Those who assert that the spirit of the Kingdom of God is incompatible with the principles of political societies err greatly. Is not rulership a kind of priesthood?" he wrote in 1816.[15] This declaration becomes understandable if one takes into account that the Christian religion, state power, and legal culture have a common purpose—to strengthen, support, and preserve the humanity of human beings, to preserve universal spiritual values and the social norms that correspond to the essential nature of human beings. Historical experience throughout the world shows that the downfall of states, the destruction of the legal order, and the collapse of the system of common spiritual values in one country or another through natural or social catastrophes (e.g., political revolutions) inevitably lead to civil wars and the dehumanization of large numbers of people, who are transformed by such events into murderers and robbers.

Because he was a statesman, Speranskii also considered Christian spiritual values from the standpoint of their significance for solving governmental and legal problems. He assumed that political science could garner a multitude of useful truths from the holy books of Christianity. "I do not know of a single problem of statecraft that could not be solved by reference to the spirit of the Gospels," he declared. "All such things, even the pricing system [*do samogo tarifa*], can be treated in this spirit and under its guidance."[16] In his treatises on religious questions, he developed the idea that secular legislation is viable only when it is in agreement with divine law. In *On the Liturgy*, he wrote:

> Religion is a divinely ordained law, the aim of which is to separate good from evil in the spiritual world. Conforming with and subordinate to this law is another law—the law whose purpose is to separate good from evil in the physical world.[17]

Professor William Butler, ed. Natalia Iu. Erpyleva and Maryann E. Gashi-Butler (London: Wildy, Simmonds and Hill, Publishers, 2014), 103–29.

15 Pis'mo M. M. Speranskogo k F. I. Tseieru, 22 ianvaria 1816 g., *Russkii arkhiv*, 1870, vyp. 1, col. 188.

16 Pis'mo M. M. Speranskogo k F. I. Tseieru, col. 189.

17 M. M. Speranskii, "O liturgii," in I. V. Katetov, *Graf Mikhail Mikhailovich Speranskii kak religioznyi myslitel'* (Kazan: Tipografiia Imperatorskogo Universiteta, 1889), 313.

Speranskii's view that Christian spiritual values were vitally important for the statecraft and legal culture of every European country was not purely speculative. Neither was his argument that it is possible to ground the political and legal life of a society upon the teachings of Christ. After the defeat of Napoleonic France, the Russian emperor endeavored to institute such a policy. With the participation of the monarchs of Austria and Prussia, he attempted to establish an international union of Christian countries based on religious principles. On December 25, 1815, Alexander I published the proclamation "On the Creation of a Holy Alliance between Their Majesties the Emperors of Russia and Austria and the King of Prussia." The proclamation stated:

> We [Alexander I] publicly proclaim: Having learned from experience and universally catastrophic events that the course of political relations among the Powers of Europe in the past was not based on those true principles which Divine Wisdom has revealed to be the foundation of peace and prosperity among nations, We, in concert with Their Highnesses the Emperor of Austria, Franz I, and the King of Prussia, Friedrich Wilhelm, have decreed an alliance (inviting other Christian powers also to join) in which We assume the obligation, with each other and in relation to our subjects, to accept as the sole means of realizing this [alliance] the rule of life drawn from the words and teachings of Our Savior Jesus Christ, who calls people to live as brothers, not in enmity and anger, but in peace and love.[18]

Speranskii welcomed this proclamation with great enthusiasm. On January 6, 1816, he sent Alexander a letter expressing full support of his initiative. To this letter he appended a commentary that began: "The alliance announced in the Proclamation of December 25 is the greatest public act since the introduction of the Christian faith."[19] Speranskii went on to direct Alexander's attention to the sad state of international relations and to the futility of attempting to rectify the situation by political means alone:

> Continual wars, frequent internal disturbances, the widespread degradation of moral values—these things have long demonstrated the shakiness of the foundations of societies. But those responsible for statecraft have found it necessary to adhere to these foundations because they have not found better ones. They have not noticed, or have neglected, the fundamental principle to

18 *Polnoe sobranie zakonov rossiiskoi imperii*, Sobranie 1 [hereinafter 1-PSZ], vol. 33, no. 26045: 417.

19 Pis'mo M. M. Speranskogo k imperatoru Aleksandru Pavlovichu s podneseniem zapiski, v kotoroi izlozheny mysli po povodu Manifesta 25 dekabria 1815 goda, in *Sbornik istoricheskikh materialov, izvlechennykh iz arkhiva Pervogo otdeleniia Sobstvennoi ego imperatorskogo velichiia kantseliarii*, vyp. 1, otd. 2 (St. Petersburg, 1876), 36–42, here at 37. A slightly different version of the letter was published in *Russkii arkhiv*, 1867, vyp. 3, cols. 447–53.

> which all things must be subordinated in states that profess belief in *Christ*, in *Divine Power* and *Divine Wisdom*.
>
> (38)

In the Holy Alliance of Russia, Austria, and Prussia, Speranskii saw the sign of an intellectual clarity that had finally reached the rulers themselves, leading them to accept the necessity of subordinating international relations to the principles of the Christian religion. "A sudden light penetrated the heart of the powers, the souls of the rulers, prompting them to found a new [system of] political law in Europe to replace [the rule of] *decrepit* and *ignoble* passions" (38). As he explained it, the essence of the new law consisted of two truths:

> 1) The true goal of human societies lies in guiding people to union with Christ by inculcating moral values and teaching people to live together in faith and love. 2) Jesus Christ is and ought to be the head of all Christian states. The true rules of government can be obtained only from His rules and teachings.
>
> (38)

The idea of grounding relations among states on the principles of the Christian religion was utopian in nature. Yet as he developed this idea, Speranskii did not ignore the fact that the great powers base their foreign policies on their national interests and aspire to make those interests supreme and to embody them in international law. He was quite familiar with how the world order actually comes into being. Nevertheless, he clearly understood that the balance of interests among the great powers cannot be maintained for long, and that this balance will change periodically, giving rise to conflicts among nations, conflicts which inevitably lead to wars. This understanding led him to conclude that it was necessary to create an international legal order not only by harmonizing the interests of separate nations but also by implementing a system of common spiritual values that would be accepted as indubitable dogmas. For Speranskii, these values existed only in Christianity.

"I am a poor and weak mortal": family background and education

Speranskii is remembered not only because of his statesmanship but also because of his amazing destiny, the peripeteias of which resemble an absorbing novel. He came from a family in which, for two centuries, the oldest sons invariably became priests. Speranskii's father, Mikhailo Vasil'ev (or Vasil'evich) was a village priest. His mother, Praskov'ia Fedorovna, was the daughter of a village deacon. Speranskii was born on January 1, 1772, in the village of Cherkvatino, about twenty-five miles from the city of Vladimir. He spent his entire childhood in this village. The name of the place is derived from *cherkva*, a variant of *tserkva* (church). The village got its present name, Cherkutino, at the beginning of the twentieth century.

The parents of the future statesman were very pious, and they nurtured their six children in the same spirit. Mikhailo—the original form of his name—learned to read at an early age, taking up whatever books came his way, most of them religious. From the age of six, he accompanied his blind grandfather to the local church and, standing at the lectern like a deacon, read the old man the Book of Hours and the Apostle Book.

In the summer of 1781, Mikhailo's family sent him to study at the diocesan seminary in Vladimir. Seminary records show that the boy was enrolled under the surname Speranskii, although neither his father nor his grandfather, nor presumably their forebears, were known to have a surname. "Speranskii" was formed from the Latin verb *spero* (hope).

In the summer of 1788, the seminary in Vladimir merged with the seminaries in Suzdal and Pereiaslavl and moved to Suzdal. Mikhailo stayed in Suzdal only briefly. In December 1788, he departed for St. Petersburg to continue his studies at the Major Seminary, an institution established at the Alexander Nevsky Monastery to prepare instructors for other seminaries.[20] Aside from the traditional seminary disciplines (theology, metaphysics, rhetoric, and others), the program of the Alexander Nevsky Seminary included rather advanced courses in mathematics, experimental physics, mechanics, and history. Students also had to become familiar with the most recent trends in philosophy. Studious seminarians had the good fortune of having access to an excellent library. Speranskii thus had the opportunity to read the works of Voltaire, Diderot, Leibniz, Condillac, Newton, Locke, and many other Western European writers popular at the time. His spiritual world expanded through long, diligent study of the sciences. He became one of the best-educated men in Russia.

A sermon Speranskii delivered on October 8, 1791, in the Alexander Nevsky Monastery gives us an idea of the young man's worldview at the time. The sermon is highly unusual. The ideas expressed in it seem to be those of a man grown wise through experience, not an adolescent seminarian. What is most remarkable is that the sermon is permeated with the spirit of freedom, in sharp contrast to the servile obedience in which the seminarians were educated. How strange and audacious the following exhortation and warning to the monarch must have sounded, coming from the lips of a recluse within the walls of a seminary:

> If, on your throne, you fail to be a human being; if your heart fails to recognize the obligations of a human being; if mercy and peace are not dear to your heart; if you fail to descend from your throne to wipe away the tears of the least of your subjects; if your knowledge serves only to feed your love of

20 On December 18, 1797, the Major Seminary became the Alexander Nevsky Theological Academy.

> power; if you use it only to gild the chains of slavery as artfully as possible and to make those chains as imperceptible as possible, to feign love for your people while, under the veil of generosity, diverting your people's goods to sate your lusts and those of your favorites; if you use your knowledge to support universal error, to expunge the idea of freedom, to appropriate your subjects' property by secret means, making them feel your heavy hand and using fear to make them think you are more than human—you will then, with all your talents and all your brilliance, be nothing but a privileged scoundrel; your sycophants will inscribe your name in gold letters on the list of the greatest geniuses, but later, with black brushstrokes, history will add that you were a tyrant of your fatherland.[21]

The sermon combines political reflections with a Christian way of thinking.

Because of his academic excellence, Speranskii was asked to stay on as an instructor at the Alexander Nevsky Seminary after completing his studies. On May 9, 1793, he was appointed teacher of mathematics, and after three months, he was asked to teach physics and rhetoric as well. On April 7, 1795, philosophy was added to his assignment. Besides his pedagogical duties, Speranskii tried his hand at writing. He wrote essays on philosophical and religious themes as well as works of fiction. In 1795, he wrote (but did not publish) *A Brief Sketch of the Sacred History and Teaching of the Christian Faith.* His conclusion was: "God, in His love for human beings, created all people in such a way as to call them from vice to virtue. But the merciful benefits of the religion of Jesus Christ are lost to those who choose not to follow its rules."[22] Speranskii's most significant piece of writing as a teacher at the seminary was *Rules of Higher Eloquence*, distributed among seminarians in manuscript but not published until 1844.[23]

Speranskii's early writings show that his worldview was not altered by his study of Western European philosophers critical of the church. His Orthodox Christian education defined how he viewed his society, the world around him, and himself. At the time, his chief desire was to overcome his inner vices. In September 1795, he wrote in his private notebook:

> Who can say to himself: every day I am advancing towards perfection, every day I tear some vice, some weakness out of my heart?
>
> I have three enemies to combat: laziness, timidity, and vanity.... My God! what enemies! They have joined forces against me since childhood. My temperament keeps lending them new weapons; and what can I do, one

21 "Propoved', proiznesennaia Speranskim v 1791 godu," in A. I. Bychkov, ed., "K biografii gr. M. M. Speranskogo," *Russkaia starina*, 1902, vol. 109, no. 2: 283–91, here at 287.

22 M. M. Speranskii, *Kratkii ocherk sviashchennoi istorii i ucheniia Khristianskoi very* (St. Petersburg, 1861), 16.

23 Mikhail Speranskii, *Pravila vysshego krasnorechiia* (St. Petersburg: V Tipografii Vtorogo Otdela Sobstvennoi Ego Imperatorskogo Velichiia Kantseliarii, 1844).

> against three—I, a poor and weak mortal, with my vivid imagination and weak reason![24]

In January 1795, in addition to his teaching duties, Speranskii accepted the position of domestic secretary for Prince Aleksei Borisovich Kurakin, who at the time served in the Office of State Revenues (*Ekspeditsiia o gosudarstvennykh dokhodakh*). This event played a fateful role in Speranskii's life. Catherine the Great died on November 6, 1796, and was succeeded by Paul I. New men were appointed to high positions in the government. On December 4, Prince Kurakin was named procurator general. As Speranskii had shown extraordinary ability as his secretary, Prince Kurakin proposed that he leave the seminary and accept a post in government service. Speranskii agreed. On January 2, 1797, he started working as a clerk in the chancellery of the procurator general with the rank of titular councilor.

This turning point in Speranskii's destiny defined the rest of his life and gave Russia one of its most talented and most enigmatic statesmen. On April 5, 1797, Speranskii was elevated to the rank of collegiate assessor (class eight in the Table of Ranks), a rank which made him a member of the nobility. On January 1, 1798, he was elevated to the rank of court councilor, and on September 18 to the rank of collegiate councilor. On December 8, 1799, he was elevated to the rank of state councilor (class five in the Table of Ranks). In less than three years, the son of a simple country priest was transformed from a domestic secretary of a highly placed aristocrat into an important official of the Russian Empire.

In 1797, Speranskii experienced another life-changing event. At the end of the summer, he met Elizabeth Stevens, the sixteen-year-old daughter of an English pastor. Having fallen in love with her, and learning that she loved him too, he proposed. Because Elizabeth belonged to a non-Orthodox faith, namely Anglicanism, Speranskii could not marry her without the emperor's permission. He petitioned the emperor, who handed the matter over to the ecclesiastical consistory of St. Petersburg. Mikhailo and Elizabeth had to swear affidavits in which they agreed to raise their children in the Orthodox faith. Elizabeth was not required to renounce her "Reformed faith" (*Reformatskii zakon*), but she did have to promise "not to lure, coax, or in any other way incline her husband to the Reformed faith nor to abuse or reproach him for keeping the Orthodox faith."[25]

On October 29, 1798, Mikhailo Speranskii and Elizabeth Stevens received permission to marry. The wedding took place on November 3 in the Church of St. Sampson in St. Petersburg. Unfortunately, this highly promising marriage was of short duration. On the day of their betrothal, Speranskii gave Elizabeth

24 *Druzheskie pis'ma grafa M. M. Speranskogo k P. G. Masal'skomu, pisannye s 1798 po 1819 god, s istoricheskimi poiasneniiami, sostavlennymi K. Masal'skim, i nekotorye sochineniia pervoi molodosti grafa M. M. Speranskogo* (St. Petersburg: V Tipografii II-go Otdeleniia Sobstvennoi Ego Imperatorskogo Velichiia Kantseliarii, 1862), 134. Speranskii wrote this diary entry in French.

25 Otdel rukopisei Rossiiskoi natsional'noi biblioteki (OR RNB), f. 731, ed. khr. 2, l. 5.

a large gold clock. It is possible that this clock played a fateful role in her life. A few days later, Elizabeth was riding in a coach with her mother to pay a visit to Princess Ditrikhstein, who was summering at a dacha near Peterhof. For some reason, the horses bolted, and the coach overturned. The clock fell on Elizabeth's chest, causing serious injury. On September 5, 1799, Elizabeth gave birth to a daughter, but two months later, on November 6, 1799, she died of consumption. Speranskii named his daughter Elizabeth in memory of his wife.

Government service in the first decade of Alexander I's reign

Speranskii's influence on state affairs was always greater than what one would have expected of someone in the positions he held. His Orthodox Christian education and his skill at putting his thoughts down on paper singled him out among the other bureaucrats, who, for the most part, were poorly educated. From Speranskii's colleagues and his own recollections, we learn that, literally from the first year of his service in the procurator general's chancellery, Paul I employed him to compose state documents. As I. I. Dmitriev recalled,

> Proclamations, decrees, memoranda—Speranskii was the sole person empowered to compose such texts, for none of his colleagues in the chancellery was better educated or wrote as well. Ministers might change, but he remained equally indispensable to all procurators general, all of whom rewarded him for his service.[26]

On March 12, 1801, Alexander became emperor following the murder of his father, Paul I. The new emperor planned to transform the system of state power, give the country a constitution, reform the bureaucracy, and systematize legislation. This gave fresh momentum to Speranskii's career. On March 19, 1801, Speranskii was given the title of imperial state secretary and appointed to assist D. P. Troshchinskii, who "stood at the side of His Imperial Majesty." Troshchinskii's duties included reporting to the emperor and editing his drafts. Speranskii, with his adroit mind, extensive knowledge, and unparalleled skill in composing chancellery documents, became Troshchinskii's right-hand man. Troshchinskii began entrusting Speranskii with the task of composing proclamations and decrees, of which there were many during the first months of the new reign. For the capable young bureaucrat, this opened up new opportunities for advancement. On July 9, 1801, he was elevated to the rank of active state councilor, class four in the Table of Ranks.

26 I. I. Dmitriev, *Vsgliad na moiu zhizn': Zapiski deistvitel'nogo tainogo sovetnika Ivana Ivanovicha Dmitrieva v trekh chastiakh*, Izdanie M. A. Dmitrieva (Moscow: Tipografiia V. Got'e, 1866), 197.

The extraordinary competence of Troshchinskii's assistant attracted the attention of the four young friends of the emperor who made up the so-called Unofficial Committee (*Neglasnyi komitet*): Count Pavel Aleksandrovich Stroganov, Nikolai Nikolaevich Novosil'tsev, Count Viktor Pavlovich Kochubei, and Prince Adam Czartoryski. Assembled to develop plans for reform, the committee met, with hiatuses, from June 24, 1801, to the end of 1803. Its goals were formulated at the first meeting: first, to study the actual state of affairs in the country; second, to reform various branches of government; and third, to develop a constitution corresponding to the true spirit of the nation. None of the members of the committee had the ability to translate political ideas into concrete plans for reform. This is where Speranskii became indispensable, even though he was not allowed to attend the committee's meetings. Assignments were usually conveyed to him by Kochubei.

The most significant reform developed by the Unofficial Committee was the institution of ministries to replace the colleges which had functioned since the time of Peter the Great. This reform was formulated juridically in the imperial proclamation of September 8, 1802, "On the Institution of Ministries."[27] F. F. Vigel', who had access to sources describing how the emperor and his four friends worked out this reform, described the process in his memoirs:

> All five reformers were inept when it came to writing. Speranskii offered them his artful pen: after collecting their opinions, he would integrate and systematize them. It would be correct to say that he was the true author of the plan to institute ministries.[28]

On the same day as the publication of the aforementioned proclamation, an imperial decree announced that state secretary Speranskii would be transferred to the Ministry of Internal Affairs. On January 7, 1803, a chancellery for the ministry was instituted, and Speranskii was chosen to direct it. In this capacity, his principal task was to draft plans for administrative reform. Not infrequently, the emperor himself was the recipient of Speranskii's plans. In the course of 1802–04, Speranskii penned memoranda on various aspects of policy: "On Gradualism in the Improvement of Society," "On the Fundamental Laws of the State," "Reflections on the State Structure of the Empire," "On the Power of Public Opinion," "Further Thoughts on Freedom and Bondage," and many more.[29]

27 Manifest "Ob uchrezhdenii ministerstv," September 8, 1802, 1-PSZ, vol. 27, no. 20406: 243–48.

28 *Zapiski Filipa Filipovicha Vigelia*, pt. 2, Izdanie "Russkogo arkhiva" (Moscow: Universitetskaia tipografiia, 1892), 8.

29 "O postepennosti usovershenia obshchestvennogo" (see note 7); "O korennykh zakonakh gosudarstva" (see note 13); "Razmyshleniia o gosudarstvennom ustroistve imperii," "O sile obshchego mneniia," "Eshche nechto o svobode i rabstve," in Speranskii, *Proekty i zapiski*, 56–67, 77–83, 83–85.

In 1806, an event occurred that was destined to play an enormous role in Speranskii's life. Kochubei, frequently ill, began sending Speranskii to make reports to the emperor. This gave Speranskii the opportunity to demonstrate his talents to the emperor directly. Alexander saw that Speranskii was the kind of man he needed and engaged him in conversation that went far beyond the purview of the Ministry of Internal Affairs. Long conversations on various political topics soon became a regular habit. When the two men met, they would often read and discuss political and legal works by Western European thinkers.

On October 19, 1807, the emperor removed Speranskii from the Ministry of Internal Affairs while keeping him on as his own state secretary, thus bringing Speranskii even closer to himself. On November 29, 1807, Speranskii was named a member of a committee on improving theological schools and the material support of the clergy. The other members were Amvrosii, metropolitan of Novgorod and St. Petersburg; Feofilakt, bishop of Kaluga; Archpriest Ioann Derzhavin; and Prince A. N. Golitsyn, chief procurator of the Holy Synod. On June 26, 1808, the committee sent draft rules for the establishment of seminaries to the emperor for approval. This plan for the reform of theological education in Russia was written entirely by Speranskii. It was confirmed by an imperial decree, which began with the words: "The education of youth dedicated to the church based on right conduct and Christian teachings has always rightly been recognized as a most worthy object of the state's attention."[30]

On December 16, 1808, Speranskii was appointed to the post of deputy minister of justice. In the order confirming the appointment, Alexander I instructed the minister of justice to put Speranskii in charge of the commission on the drafting of laws.

Speranskii's growing importance in the hierarchy of the state was reflected in the pages of *Kamer-fur'erskii tseremonial'nyi zhurnal* (Court-manager's ceremonial journal) in reports about persons invited to dine with the emperor and the empress. According to the journal, their majesties started inviting Speranskii to dinner in 1807. That year, he was invited six times; in 1808, twenty-three times; in 1809, seventy-seven times. Commenting on these changes in his life in a letter to Alexander written years later, Speranskii recalled: "At the end of 1808, besides various particular matters, Your Majesty began occupying me more continually with matters of higher administration [and] acquainting me more closely with Your way of thinking."[31] The emperor also proposed that Speranskii prepare a general plan for the reform of the state.

With a proclamation on January 1, 1810, Alexander I instituted Speranskii's plan to establish a State Council, which was charged with discussing all aspects

30 Imennoi ukaz, dannyi Sinodu, 26 iiunia 1808 goda "O usovershenii dukhovnykh uchilishch; o nachertanii pravil dlia obrazovaniia sikh uchilishch i sostavlenii kapitala na soderzhanie dukhovenstva," 1-PSZ, vol. 30, no. 23122: 368–95, here at 368.

31 "Spisok s pis'ma tainogo sovetnika Speranskogo k Gosudariu Imperatoru. V ianvare 1813 goda iz Permi," in *Druzheskie pis'ma grafa M. M. Speranskogo k P. G. Masal'skomu*, 32–52, here at 33–34.

of government "as they relate to legislation." Speranskii was appointed to the position of state secretary of the council. He had authority over all documents passing through it, prepared the agenda for meetings, and composed the reports to the emperor. Outwardly, the function of state secretary might have seemed to be a routine chancellery function, but in practice it was exceptionally important. Speranskii's contemporaries recognized this. "The great and all-powerful Speransky, Secretary-General of the Empire and *de facto* prime minister, perhaps even the only Minister"—this was how Joseph de Maistre, Sardinian ambassador in St. Petersburg, described Speranskii.[32] His words were hardly an exaggeration. Between 1809 and 1811, Speranskii was the most influential statesman in Russia, the second most important person in the country after the emperor. His influence on governmental affairs was nearly all-encompassing, embracing administrative matters, the judicial system, finances, legislation, education, culture, and both internal and foreign affairs. Speranskii also had at least an indirect say in the appointment of officials, even to high positions. Among all these activities, however, there was one to which this unusually hard working and capable man devoted himself above all others: reforming the political system of Russia.

Speranskii as reformer

Entrusted at the end of 1808 with the task of preparing a general plan for the reform of the Russian state, Speranskii devoted almost a year to the task. He completed it at the beginning of October 1809. He gave the plan a title that promised much: "Introduction to a Code of State Laws."[33] Along with this introduction, he presented the emperor with an outline of the code itself titled "A Brief Outline of State Formation" and with "A General Survey of All Reforms and Their Distribution in Time."[34]

In the summer of the following year, a new reform of the organs of executive power was unveiled, continuing the reform of 1802. Its aim, announced in the proclamation of July 25, 1810, was "to introduce greater proportionality in the distribution of state affairs, to establish greater uniformity in their operation, to simplify and facilitate their operation, to designate precisely the limits of power and responsibility, and hence to offer executive authority greater means of rapid and precise execution."[35] The new principles were confirmed in "The General

32 Quoted by Raeff, *Michael Speransky*, 55, from Joseph de Maistre, *Oeuvres complètes—Correspondance*, vol. 4 (Paris, 1884–93), no. 304 (2/21 April 1812), 101–02.

33 "Vvedenie k Ulozheniiu gosudarstvennykh zakonov" and "Proekt Ulozheniia gosudarstvennykh zakonov Rossiiskoi imperii," in Speranskii, *Proekty i zapiski*, 143–221 and 222–25.

34 "Kratkoe nachertanie gosudarstvennogo obrazovaniia" and "Obshchee obozrenie vsekh preobrazovanii i raspredelenie ikh po vremianam," in Speranskii, *Proekty i zapiski*, 225–31 and 231–37.

35 Manifest "O razdelenii gosudarstvennykh del na osobye upravleniia," July 25, 1810, 1-PSZ, vol. 31, no 24307: 278.

Institution of Ministries," implemented by the Imperial Proclamation of June 25, 1811.[36] Speranskii also drafted a plan for reform of the Senate. The plan called for separating the judicial and administrative functions of the Senate, creating two separate bodies.[37]

Speranskii's plans for government reform were based on an understanding of society as a self-evolving organism, a view corresponding to his Christian worldview. For him, the main condition of fruitful reforms was their implementation with the cooperation of society itself and of time. In his opinion, the problem of reforming state power was reducible to the elimination of obstacles on the path of social progress and to the maintenance (and, where necessary, the restoration) of the normal conditions of social life.

Russian society was not aware of Speranskii's ideas. He developed his plans and projects in secret at the behest of the emperor. From the very beginning, therefore, his reform activity appeared in a false light. Where knowledge is absent, rumor takes its place. Speranskii appeared to be a liberal reformer trying to cast the state order of the Russian Empire into the mold of speculative schemes based on Western European ideas, to squeeze the life of Russian society into alien forms that did not correspond to Russian traditions, the spirit of the Russian people, or the special conditions of Russian society. A significant portion of Karamzin's note "On the Old and the New Russia" (1811) was prompted by this utterly fanciful notion of Speranskii's reform activity. According to Karamzin,

> the principal error of the lawgivers of this reign consists in the fact that they have too much regard for the outward forms of government; this leads to the invention of various ministries, the institution of the council, and so on.[38]

In fact, Speranskii clearly recognized that it was impossible to reform the state structure in a short period of time by means of state power alone, however strong that power might be. "If one compares the [ideal] image of monarchical rule with the form of rule existing in Russia at the present time," he declared, "there cannot be the slightest doubt that no human power can transform the latter into the former without having recourse to the passage of time and the gradual progress of all things toward perfection."[39] The techniques of state reform Speranskii devised were based on his knowledge of life and social reality and on his understanding of the true condition of the Russian state. "One of the first rules for state administrators," he declared,

36 "Obshchee uchrezhdenie ministerstv," June 25, 1811, 1-PSZ, vol. 31, no. 24686: 686–718.

37 M. M. Speranskii, *O gosudarstvennykh ustanovleniiakh*, in *Arkhiv prakticheskikh i istoricheskikh svedenii, otnosiashchikhsia do Rossii, izdavaemyi Nikolaem Kalachovym* (St. Petersburg: V Tipografii II Otdeleniia Sobstvennoi E. I. V. Kantseliarii, 1859), kn. 3: 53–54.

38 N. M. Karamzin, *Zapiska o drevnei i novoi Rossii v ee politicheskom i grazhdanskom otnosheniiakh*, ed. Iu. S. Pivovarov (Moscow: "Nauka," 1991), 98.

39 M. M. Speranskii, "Zapiska ob ustroistve sudebnykh i pravitel'stvennykh uchrezhdenii v Rossii," in Speranskii, *Proekty i zapiski*, 119.

> is to know their people and to know the age.... Theories are rarely useful in practice. They take into account only one component and do not reckon with the friction points of the system as a whole, and end with complaints about the human race.[40]

At the same time, Speranskii understood quite well that the state should not carry out reforms unsystematically and thoughtlessly, without a plan worked out in advance. "Why are all human enterprises so imperfect?" he asked:

> Among many other reasons, because they are for the most part implemented fragmentarily and without a general plan. People's natural impatience, their illusions of national happiness and rapid improvement, their hope that, by improving just one component, the whole system will work more smoothly—all these things can lead the wisest and most prudent of governments to partial solutions which, so to speak, do not allow a general plan to mature.[41]

The state reforms prepared by Speranskii were intended to solve a multitude of problems in Russia at the time. If one were to total up these problems, one could say that Speranskii was developing a plan for nothing less than *the modernization of the state structure of the Russian Empire*. By an irony of history, the principal vice of the Russian state in our own day is the same one that afflicted the state order of the Russian Empire at the beginning of the nineteenth century: the excessive *personalization of the supreme state power*, leading to the heightened influence, on both domestic and foreign policy, of the deficiencies of persons in high office. The experience of revolutions shows that such a condition can, in some circumstances, pose a threat to the very existence of a country.

The attempt to modernize the state order in Russia in the early years of Alexander's reign took place at the same time as the state reforms in France and proceeded on exactly the same principles. Like Napoleon, the Russian emperor strove first of all to modernize the bureaucracy, to establish a new organization of central and regional administration. Second, these reforms were to be crowned by a constitution. Third, like the French emperor, the Russian emperor viewed the comprehensive systematization of law to be a necessary condition of this modernization. Speranskii's labors were deployed in all three directions, but his chief task was the preparation of a constitution, or to use the Russian juridical expression common at the time, the preparation of "a code of state laws" (*ulozhenie gosudarstvennykh zakonov*).

40 M. M. Speranskii, "O postepennosti usovershenia obshchestvennogo," in Speranskii, *Proekty i zapiski*, 76.

41 M. M. Speranskii, "Zapiska ob ustroistve sudebnykh i pravitel'stvennykh uchrezhdenii v Rossii," in Speranskii, *Proekty i zapiski*, 111.

Among Western European and American intellectuals from the second half of the eighteenth century to the beginning of the nineteenth, a constitution was viewed primarily as a document of supreme judicial authority which regulated the interaction of powers in the state, guaranteed civil rights and freedoms, and protected people from the capriciousness of the powers that be. Speranskii was not an ivory-tower scholar who studied constitutions with the aim of grasping their inner essence. He was interested in constitutions not from a scientific but from a practical point of view. He saw a constitution above all as a means of reducing the personalization of the supreme state power. However, his practical standpoint led him inevitably to ask how effective a constitution would be as a means of controlling the capriciousness of rulers and limiting the influence of their vices on domestic and foreign policy. The question Speranskii asked himself was: "How can the fundamental laws of the state be made so stable and immutable that no authority could transgress them, and the ruling monarchical power would have no effect on them?"[42]

Speranskii viewed a constitution as a juridical model of a new state order, where the main role was played not by persons in authority but by institutions, principles, and juridical norms. He also regarded the legitimization of state power as one of the chief goals of a constitution. In his opinion, "every legitimate government must be based on the general will of the people."[43] For Speranskii, this meant that a constitution must emanate not from the supreme state power, but from the people. As he noted,

> In all sound monarchical systems, all fundamental laws must be created by the people, for it is a contradiction to propose that the people should entrust the same person to define the limits of power for whom the limits are intended, because the limits of power cannot be found in power itself.[44]

It is clear, however, that what Speranskii had in mind was only the people's approval of a constitution drafted in advance on the instructions of the supreme state power.

Speranskii had been working on such a draft since the end of 1808. This was a grand work of research involving the study of both the essence and the fundamental concepts of state laws. As he noted at the beginning of his "Introduction to a Code of State Laws," "In order to define a plan for a state constitution, it is first necessary to formulate a true general conception of state laws."[45] Indeed, this work was more like a learned treatise than an introduction to a constitution for the Russian Empire.

42 M. M. Speranskii, "O korennykh zakonakh gosudarstva," in Speranskii, *Proekty i zapiski*, 28.
43 Ibid., 34.
44 M. M. Speranskii, "Otryvok o Komissii ulozheniia," in Speranskii, *Proekty i zapiski*, 22.
45 M. M. Speranskii, "Vvedenie k Ulozheniiu gosudarstvennykh zakonov," in Speranskii, *Proekty i zapiski*, 144.

In "A General Survey of All Reforms and Their Distribution in Time," Speranskii listed the subjects defined in his plan:

1) the rights of the sovereign power;
2) the rights of the throne and its heirs;
3) the mode of establishing laws, their force and effect;
4) the rights of subjects; the separation of classes; definition of the political rights of each class and of the general civil rights emanating from them;
5) organic laws, that is to say, the organization of the statutes from which the law is formed and by which it is executed.[46]

While seeing the constitution as a juridical model of a new state order, Speranskii had no intention of incorporating the actual life of society and the state into this model by force. The techniques of government reform he envisaged did not contemplate the negation of the past for the sake of the future, but its preservation into the future—not a leap from the old state to the new, but a gradual migration into the new. Such a cautious approach resulted not from indecisiveness on Speranskii's part but from his recognition of a sad truth, namely, that people's knowledge of how a society actually functions and how a state organizes itself and operates is extremely limited. For this reason alone, reformers risk doing irreparable harm to their country if their reforms fail. In practice, however, most reforms are dictated not by knowledge of the real condition of a country but by the interests of the dominant groups in a society. The influence of group interests on the content of reforms often proves strong enough to overwhelm the common interest. In this case, reforms do not renew the state order but disfigure it, transforming state power, which is called to serve the common good, into an instrument of selfish interests and, at times, criminality.

Speranskii considered it useless "to write or to publish law codes or constitutions without grounding them upon the actual power of the state."[47] But how did he think this power could be induced to respect the constitution? The idea of a constitution, as it took shape in political and legal thought around the beginning of the nineteenth century, assumed that the people themselves would be the surest foundation of the constitutional order and the chief source of state power in a country. Speranskii declared that "the government can have no other power than that assigned to it by the people" (34). However, he recognized that the people on their own are incapable of ensuring respect for the constitution. In order to perform this role,

> the people must know the precise limits of power and be prepared to defend those limits at all times, and all groups must be unified in a single mass. Otherwise, given the slightest separation of the interests of the various

46 M. M. Speranskii, "Obshchee obozrenie vsekh preobrazovanii i raspredelenie ikh po vremianam," in Speranskii, *Proekty i zapiski*, 232.

47 M. M. Speranskii, "O korennykh zakonakh gosudarstva," in Speranskii, *Proekty i zapiski*, 33.

> classes, the people will exhaust themselves in internecine struggle and will not be able to stand up to the government.
>
> (36)

But the people do not and cannot possess these qualities. They are divided into various classes with different, often opposing interests, while the power entrusted by the people to the government is unified in a single mass and monopolized by state organs.

If the people as a whole cannot be the force capable of restraining the arbitrariness of the supreme state power and assuring respect for the constitution, where might such a force be found? Is it possible to create one? Speranskii thought so. To do this, however, it would be necessary to eliminate the circumstance—namely, the fragmentation of the people—which in all forms of government renders the power of the people negligible and produces autocracy.

Not trusting the people *as a whole* to defend the constitutional order against the arbitrariness of the state, Speranskii thought that this role could be played by a segment of the population:

> a special class, interposed between the throne and the people, enlightened enough to know the precise limits of power and independent enough to be fearless, whose own interests coincide with the people's interests to such an extent that this class can never profit from betraying the people.
>
> (39)

As Speranskii averred, this special class could fulfill its mission only if its interests coincided with those of the people. Otherwise, this elite could turn out to be destroyers of the state and even greater oppressors of the people than the most autocratic ruler. Yet Speranskii was optimistic about his plan. He believed it would be "very simple" to establish solidarity between the people and the political elite provided that "1) the children of this higher class, excepting the first-born, are members of the people, thus making oppression of the people tantamount to oppression of one's own children, [and provided that] 2) everything touching upon the property of this higher class is adjudicated in courts chosen by the people" (40).

Summing up what Speranskii had to say about this national political elite, we can see that, in character and social function, it corresponded most closely to the Orthodox clergy. This is what Fyodor Dostoevsky guessed when he wrote in a notebook of 1876–77 about the consequences of putting this idea into practice:

> It was easy for Speranskii to design the creation of estates in Russia following the English example, the lords, the bourgeoisie, and so on. With the elimination of the landowners, the seminarist immediately took over and did much harm with his abstract understanding and interpretation of things and events.[48]

48 F. M. Dostoevskii, *Polnoe sobranie sochinenii v tridtsati tomakh* (Leningrad: Izdatel'stvo "Nauka," 1982), 24:241. Dostoevsky refers here to seminary graduates who did not take up a church vocation but entered the secular world.

As Speranskii tried to find a social basis for a "legislative class" of fifteen hundred to two thousand persons possessing an "estimable" degree of education, property, and public trust, he concluded that it could not be formed from any one social class unless additional measures were taken. The highest degree of education, he admitted, "without any doubt belonged to the nobility," but most nobles were military officers and civil servants, who, owing to their dependence on those in authority, could not make up the special class that would guarantee observance of the laws. As for the rest of the nobility, they were

> children and old people, people habituated to urban or rural idleness, people familiar with agriculture but not at all concerned with important political questions; people whom neither theory nor experience has equipped to deal with such matters, and in any case too few in number.[49]

Nor did Speranskii think that merchants and the petty bourgeoisie could be the basis of the legislative class.

> The nature of their trade, for the most part domestic and tending to fragmentation, requiring mechanical activity and petty local knowledge rather than broad, general considerations and reflections, does not lead us to believe that we will find [the requisite] knowledge or skill in this class.
>
> (816)

Speranskii did not regard the peasantry as a serious political force owing to its lack of property. The only deficiency he saw in the priesthood—like the nobility, an educated class—was its poverty; but obviously this deficiency could be remedied. Hence, Speranskii concluded that the special class that would "guard and protect the law" would most easily be formed from the clergy. To accomplish this, however, it would be necessary to increase the income of the church. In 1808, Speranskii developed a plan to this end. Published on June 26, 1808, and presented to the Holy Synod, an imperial decree stipulated decisive measures for improving the organization and content of seminary education and at the same time augmented the material resources of the clergy.[50]

Speranskii's fall and life in exile

When he began his reforms, Speranskii clearly understood that the emperor was his sole basis of support. He recognized that any intrigue that convinced Alexander I that the reforms posed a serious threat to autocratic rule could lead to the removal of the reformer and the termination of the reforms. Intrigues

49 M. M. Speranskii, "Ob iziashchnom, osnovannom na soedinenii mnozhestva v edinstve," in *V pamiat' grafa Mikhaila Mikhailovicha Speranskogo*, 816.
50 See note 30.

always play an important role in a regime based on personal power, where general interests are dissolved into molecules of personal ambitions, passions, and motives, and where political life is subordinate to no rules except those that satisfy exclusively personal, egoistic interests. Intrigue takes the place of politics, and the most artful intriguer becomes the most artful politician. It was precisely such intrigue that Speranskii's foes in high society used to remove him from the pedestal of power and put an end to his reform plans. The intrigue turned Alexander I against Speranskii and prompted him to exile the reformer from the capital.[51]

On March 17, 1812, Speranskii was summoned to the imperial palace for a conversation with the emperor. The specific topic of their conversation has remained a secret. Only a few details were later revealed, thanks to Speranskii's own account. The rest has come down to us from people who were not present; hence, their account is not reliable. The only certainty is that the conversation lasted over two hours and was highly unusual. At the end of the meeting, Alexander declared his intention to distance himself from Speranskii in light of the seriousness of the rumors against him and because of the imminence of war with Napoleon. At home, Speranskii received the emperor's order that he depart at once into exile in Nizhnii Novgorod.[52] This event has gone down in history as "the fall of Speranskii," but we should recognize that what took place was not simply the fall of a high public official from the heights of power, which happens often in the complex game of chance called politics, but the fall of a reformer.

On September 17, 1812, Speranskii was sent to the city of Perm, in the Urals, where he spent almost two years. In January 1813, in a personal letter to Alexander, the exile beseeched the emperor to allow him to move from Perm to his personal estate, Velikopol'e, not far from Novgorod. He characterized this modest favor as a reward for his diligent labors in government service, assuring the emperor that he sought no compensation besides "freedom and oblivion." But it was only on August 31, 1814, the day of the imperial proclamation of the end of the war with Napoleon, that Speranskii was allowed to move to his estate.

In a letter to his daughter, Elizabeth, dated January 1, 1817, Speranskii declared: "I consider the period of my misfortune and the two years I devoted to you to be the most beneficial time of my life."[53] He was thinking of the years he spent with his daughter in Velikopol'e, where he devoted his time not only to her but also to religion. Although Speranskii lived on his own estate, he was still an exile. He was permitted to leave Velikopol'e only to attend the Sunday liturgy in the nearby Savvo-Visherskii Monastery. He supported this monastery

51 Speranskii's fall is described in detail in Tomsinov, *Svetilo rossiiskoi biurokratii*, 195–228.

52 "Ssylka Speranskogo v 1812 godu. (Iz bumag akademika A. F. Bychkova)," *Russkaia starina*, 1902, vol. 110, no. 4: 5–44, here at 5–12.

53 "Pis'ma grafa M. M. Speranskogo k ego docheri," *Russkii arkhiv*, 1868, vyp. 7–8, cols. 1103–1212, here at col. 1125.

as far as his means permitted. He had a new bell constructed and the iconostasis refurbished. In the monastery library, he discovered the works of the Holy Fathers, from which he copied passages that seemed most relevant to the time in which he lived.

In the quiet of the country, far from the venality and vileness of the capital, one does well to read about love of neighbor, about the sublimity and power of such love. One of the best books on this subject is the fifteenth-century devotional work by Thomas à Kempis, *On the Imitation of Christ.* The entire work is permeated with the idea of love. "Love is a great thing, a truly great good. It alone makes all burdens light and bears all inequities with equanimity. It bears its burden without feeling the weight of it and transforms bitterness itself into sweetness and pleasure."[54] Such sayings fill the entire book. The book is now largely forgotten, but in past centuries, it ranked second only to the Bible in the canon of Christian literature.

Speranskii kept *On the Imitation of Christ* by his side throughout his life, and not just by his side: he constantly extracted wisdom from it. While he was still in government service, Speranskii began translating the Latin text of *On the Imitation of Christ* into Russian, sacrificing rare hours of leisure to the project. He continued translating the treatise in Nizhnii Novgorod, Perm, and Velikopol'e. The content of the book conformed perfectly with his state of mind. And who knows? Perhaps Speranskii's search for "freedom and oblivion" in exile was sustained by this Christian thinker who had lived four centuries earlier, the thinker who said: "You will enjoy inner freedom when you desire and seek nothing except to please God and to benefit your neighbor."[55]

Return to government service

On August 30, 1816, Alexander I issued a decree that returned Speranskii to government service. The disgraced official was appointed governor of Penza Province. The emperor still did not wish to have Speranskii in his presence, so during his service in Penza the governor was not allowed to visit St. Petersburg. On March 22, 1819, Speranskii was named governor general of Siberia, a post that took him thousands of miles from the capital. Not until March 1821, exactly nine years and nine days following the beginning of his exile, did Speranskii reappear in St. Petersburg. The year before his return, he concluded his reorganization of the government of Siberia. On January 26, 1822, Alexander issued a decree on the division of Siberia into eastern and western parts. On March 22, Speranskii appointed governors general for these two entities. He had once again become an influential statesman.

54 Foma Kempiiskii, *O podrazhanii Khristu* (St. Petersburg: V Tipografii Sviateishego Sinoda, 1835), 181–82. The quotation is from *On the Imitation of Christ*, bk. 3, chap. 5: "On the Wonderful Effect of Divine Love."

55 Foma Kempiiskii, *O podrazhanii Khristu*, 119. The quotation is from *On the Imitation of Christ*, bk. 2, chap. 4: "On Purity of Mind and Simple Intention."

The death of Alexander I and the accession of his brother Nicholas did not change Speranskii's status as a statesman. Under the new emperor, he continued to work on plans for state reform.

The accession of Nicholas I was accompanied by a coup attempt carried out by revolutionary military officers. On December 14, 1825, the day on which the army was to pledge its loyalty to the new emperor, the revolutionaries led their troops to a square near the Winter Palace in St. Petersburg. The leaders' indecisiveness led to their defeat. On December 23, an investigative committee instituted by Nicholas I began the interrogation of those who would come to be called the Decembrists. In the perpetrators' testimonies, Speranskii's name came up. One of the Decembrists, Second Lieutenant A. N. Andreev, declared:

> The hope of [our conspiratorial] society rested on the assistance of the Council and the Senate, and I was told there were members of the former—Messrs. Mordvinov and Speranskii—who were prepared to take action if it came to that. Monsieur Ryleev [a Decembrist leader] assured me that these members of the government had been informed of our society and approved of our intentions.[56]

Subsequently, when confronted with testimony by Ryleev, Andreev retracted his words, but the suspicion that Speranskii was connected with the revolutionaries remained. The investigation ascertained that the Decembrists planned to offer Speranskii and Admiral N. S. Mordvinov posts in their provisional government. On January 4, 1826, Ryleev told investigators: "I must admit that I thought Speranskii would not refuse a post in the provisional government. I based my belief on his love for the fatherland."[57]

Of course, Speranskii never agreed, and could never agree, to enter the provisional government the conspirators intended to form. This was due not only to his political caution. He was a staunch opponent of violent changes of government, changes that threaten the very existence of the state. The emperor's proclamation of July 13, 1826, that passed judgment on the Decembrists expressed this conviction with great clarity:

> It is not from brazen and destructive dreams but from above that the country's laws are gradually improved, deficiencies overcome, and abuses corrected. In this gradual improvement, every modest aspiration for what is better, every thought directed toward making the force of law more secure, toward the expansion of true enlightenment and productive activity, reaching Us by a lawful path open to all, will always be received by Us with reverence, for We do not have, and cannot have, any other desire than to see Our

56 *Vosstanie dekabristov. Dokumenty*, vol. 15 (Moscow: "Nauka," 1979), 228.
57 *Vosstanie dekabristov. Dokumenty*, vol. 14 (Moscow: "Nauka," 1976), 55–56.

> Fatherland at the very apex of happiness and glory to which Providence has destined it.[58]

Speranskii wrote this document. It should not surprise us, therefore, that Nicholas I rejected the Decembrists' imputations against the reformer and let him remain at his post.

The new emperor entrusted Speranskii with the same function he had performed under Alexander I: drafting laws and instructions. The plans and drafts he produced at Nicholas's behest were wide-ranging: "Remarks on the Organization of the Judicial System in Russia" (1827), "Memorandum on the Cause of the Poor Performance of the Factories of Nerchinsk and Measures for Improving the Situation" (1827), draft of a "Regulation on the Procedure for Promotion to the Ranks" (1830), "Plan for the Establishment of District Administration" (1830), "Note on the Organization of Towns" (1831), "Plan for the Establishment of Provincial Administration" (1831), "Draft of the Rescript to the Minister of National Education Regarding the Draft of the Statute on Gymnasia and District Schools" (1837), and others.[59] But Speranskii's main work during the reign of Nicholas I was the systematization of Russian law.

Creator of the Complete Collection of Laws and the Digest of Laws

Speranskii spent five years, from 1828 to 1833, creating the Complete Collection of Laws of the Russian Empire and the Digest of Laws of the Russian Empire, an endeavor that his biographers would rightly call the chief accomplishment of his life. With the production of the Complete Collection and the Digest, Speranskii completed the work of nearly a century and a half of Russian history, crowning the numerous attempts to systematize Russian legislation dating back to Peter the Great.[60] This grand work, comparable to the famous systematization of Roman law under Emperor Justinian exactly thirteen hundred years earlier (528–34), grounded Russian jurisprudence solidly upon legislation that had evolved since the middle of the seventeenth century, that is, from the *Ulozhenie* (Law code) of 1649, which in turn summed up the earlier development of Russian legal culture.

58 *Vosstanie dekabristov. Dokumenty*, vol. 17 (Moscow: "Nauka," 1980), 253.

59 "Zametki po organizatsii sudebnoi sistemy v Rossii," "Zapiska o prichine ubytochnosti Nerchinskikh zavodov i merakh po uluchsheniiu ikh polozheniia," "Polozhenie o poriadke proizvodstva v chiny," "Proekt uchrezhdeniia uezdnogo upravleniia," "Zapiska ob ustroistve gorodov," "Proekt uchrezhdeniia dlia upravleniia gubernii," "Proekt reskripta ministru narodnogo prosveshcheniia o proekte ustava gimnazii i uezdnykh uchilishch."

60 See V. A. Tomsinov, *Iuridicheskoe obrazovanie i iurisprudentsiia v Rossii v XVIII stoletii*, Uchebnoe posobie, 2nd ed. (Moscow: Zertsalo-M, 2012), 43–58, 126–33, 211–23, and Tomsinov, "Sistematizatsiia rossiiskogo zakonodatel'stva vo vtoroi polovine 20-x—nachale 30-x godov XIX veka," *Vestnik Moskovskogo universiteta*, Seriia 11: Pravo, 2008, no. 4: 38–77.

Speranskii's work on the Complete Collection continued until March 1, 1830. The printing of its forty-five volumes began on May 21, 1828, and was concluded on April 1, 1830. The printing of the fifteen volumes of the Digest was completed at the beginning of 1833. On January 19, 1833, all volumes of the Complete Collection and the Digest were officially presented to Nicholas I. An imperial proclamation issued on the same day announced that the Digest would go into effect on January 1, 1835.

The Digest of Laws of the Russian Empire was based upon a solid historical foundation. First, it rested upon the Complete Collection of the Laws of the Russian Empire, which included all the legislative acts, judicial decisions, treaties, and normative acts issued since 1649. Second, the compilation of the Digest took into account more than a century of work by earlier codification commissions. Third, in his work on the Digest, Speranskii drew on principles formulated by Francis Bacon (1561–1626). Bacon expounded these principles in the form of aphorisms in his *Treatise on Universal Justice, or the Sources of Law* (*Exemplum Tractatus de Justitia Universali, sive de Fontibus Juris*) in the eighth book of *On the Dignity and Advancement of Learning* (*De Dignitate et Augmentis Scientiarum*). Speranskii singled out and paraphrased the following recommendations of the English jurist and philosopher:

1) exclude from the digest all laws which have fallen out of use;
2) exclude repetitions, and in place of numerous articles that say the same thing, incorporate the one that is most complete;
3) preserve the words of the law, deriving articles of the digest from the text of those words, even the smallest and most fragmentary; then bind and unite these small parts together in proper order, for in law the important thing is not so much elegance of expression as force and authority, and for authority, antiquity is precious;
4) laws that are too wordy and prolix must be shortened;
5) among contradictory laws choose the one that is best;
6) the corpus of laws compiled in this way must be confirmed by the appropriate authority, so that new laws do not creep in by appearing to be old.[61]

Speranskii was fully aware that the publication of the Digest of Laws could bring only a temporary order to existing law. New laws, appearing in ever-greater numbers, could eventually produce a new state of chaos in the legislative sphere.

61 M. M. Speranskii, *Obozrenie istoricheskikh svedenii o svode zakonov* (St. Petersburg: Tipografiia II Otdeleniia Sobstvennoi Ego Imperatorskogo Velichiia Kantseliarii, 1833), 104–10. For the Latin original of *Exemplum Tractatus*, see *The Works of Francis Bacon*, ed. James Spedding, Robert Leslie Ellis, and Douglas Denon Heath, 14 vols. (1857–74; reprint, New York: Garrett Press, 1968), 1:803–28; English trans., *Example of a Treatise on Universal Justice or the Fountains of Equity, by Aphorisms: One Title of It*, in *The Works of Francis Bacon*, 5:88–110. Speranskii's paraphrases nos. 1, 2, 4, and 5 are drawn from Bacon's Aphorism 60; no. 3, from Aphorism 62; no. 6, from Aphorism 63.

Bacon addressed this problem by following Justinian, who, in his systematization of Roman law, prescribed that the stable and permanent part of the legal heritage should be expounded in one digest (the Digest/Pandects); the variable part, composed of individual statutes adopted from time to time, in another (the Codex). As Bacon advised,

> It will be very useful in a new digest of laws to digest and arrange separately on the one side all the laws received as Common Law, the existence whereof is as it were from time immemorial; and on the other side the statutes, which have from time to time been superadded.[62]

On this point, however, Speranskii did not accept Bacon's approach:

> We do not make such a distinction, but we do have laws that apply throughout the empire and laws that are particular to some of its regions. For this reason, it has been decided to assemble the laws of the first type in the general Digest and the laws of the second type in two particular digests: one for the West Russian provinces, the other for the Baltic provinces.

Speranskii did acknowledge that "the Digests embrace only the past and do not determine anything in the future." For this reason, he prescribed an arrangement whereby laws adopted in the future would be incorporated in the appropriate sections of subsequent editions of the Digest.[63]

The creation of the Digest of Laws of the Russian Empire was Speranskii's grandest and most important work. No other work of his can compare with it in terms of its scope and benefit for the future of Russia. The creation of the Digest led to the reform of legal education in Russia, to the further development of Russian jurisprudence, and to the comprehensive reform of the Russian court system.[64]

Speranskii at the end of his life

Speranskii lived another six years after completing his work on the Digest of Laws, still developing plans for reform and drafts of imperial laws. In 1834, he was appointed one of the teachers of the tsarevich, Alexander Nikolaevich, the emperor's oldest son. From the beginning, Speranskii's task was to prepare Alexander for the throne. From October 12, 1835, to April 10, 1837, for twelve hours a week, he gave Alexander a complete course of lectures on jurisprudence and statecraft. He discussed the true state of the country with the future tsar

62 *The Works of Francis Bacon*, 5:100 (Aphorism 61).

63 M. M. Speranskii, *Obozrenie istoricheskikh svedenii o svode zakonov*, 111–13.

64 On legal education, see V. A. Tomsinov, *Iuridicheskoe obrazovanie i iurisprudentsiia v Rossii vo vtoroi treti XIX veka*, Uchebnoe posobie (Moscow: Zertsalo-M, 2015).

with great candor, planting the idea of the need for sweeping reforms. Speranskii called these exhortations "conversations." As his biographer Baron Korf wrote:

> They were in fact conversations in the full sense, but they were not conversations conducted by a scholastic professor with a student whose only goal was to do well on examinations. They were conversations that a statesman with profound practical knowledge of the life and needs of Russia conducted with a future monarch, a student eager to learn the science of monarchical government. With his eloquence and intellectual clarity, Speranskii did not find it difficult to capture the attention of his inquiring student. The teacher devoted his whole soul, his noblest aspirations, to this task.[65]

On January 24, 1835, Speranskii presented Nicholas I with a memorandum on the need for an educational institution to prepare legal specialists. He addressed this need with specific reference to the Russian judiciary of his day:

> Judges everywhere need capable and well-educated assistants, but in Russia the need for such people is greater than elsewhere, because we do not have, and for a long time will not have, either learned judges or learned lawyers. In the lower and middle ranks, our judges are chosen from the nobility, the military nobility for the most part; in the higher ranks, they are appointed from the ranks of officials, military and civil. And there is no reason to change this practice, even if it were possible to change it. If he is capably assisted, a judge chosen because of the trust his class has invested in him, a man of common sense and clear conscience, albeit without technical knowledge, is generally better than a judge who is merely learned. If he is poorly assisted, however, the same trustworthy judge will be able to conceal his bias or ignorance only from himself. Our universities cannot produce good specialists for our judicial system, first, because university students study but do not get a real education; second, because the graduates enter the military or other [general] types of employment, since they were not required to pursue a definite goal. The same may be said about our lycées. Their graduates, who in any case are not numerous, enter government service but rarely work in the judicial system. Hence, it is clear that the establishment of a special school where students would receive theoretical and practical training for service in the judicial system would be an indisputable benefit.[66]

On May 29, 1835, Nicholas I announced the establishment of the Imperial School of Jurisprudence and approved the first version of its charter. A solemn

65 M. A. Korf, *Zhizn' grafa Speranskogo*, 2 vols. (St. Petersburg: Izdanie Imperatorskoi Publichnoi biblioteki, 1861), 2:344–45.

66 M. M. Speranskii, "O spetsial'nykh uchilishchakh," *Russkaia starina*, 1885, vol. 48, no. 12: ii–iii. For more discussion of this institution, see Tomsinov, *Iuridicheskoe obrazovanie i iurisprudentsiia v Rossii vo vtoroi treti XIX veka*, 173–93.

ceremony inaugurating this unusual school was held on December 5. The School of Jurisprudence was not just a place where a student could receive a good general education and the specialized legal knowledge necessary for work in the courts. It was a school for molding jurists of a new type—educated, honest, incorruptible individuals who saw service to the law and to the fatherland as their calling. The first graduating class, in 1840, numbered fourteen. Every year thereafter saw the graduation of some twenty-five jurists on average. By May 1866, when the Judicial Reform of 1864 came into effect, 684 graduates specially trained for judicial work had emerged from the school. They injected a spirit of truth and justice into Russia's judicial system, thereby assuring the success of the judicial reform carried out by Speranskii's student, Alexander II.

Many of Speranskii's ideas for the reform of the Russian state were implemented only after his death. His heart ceased to beat on February 11, 1839. The following day, Korf wrote in his diary: "The shining light of the Russian administration has gone out."[67]

News of Speranskii's death spread rapidly throughout Russia and also had an impact in Europe. Nearly every important foreign periodical reported it. On March 12, *Allgemeine Zeitung* (Augsburg) published the following report from St. Petersburg:

> Our government has lost one of its most outstanding and honored statesmen. Last Saturday, Count Mikhail Speranskii, actual privy councilor and chairman of the department of law in the State Council, died here at the age of 68, after years of suffering, which, however, did not prevent him, indefatigable in his activities until his death, from holding various high imperial positions. He has left a lasting memory in the history of our internal state administration.... The burial of the earthly remains of this statesman, whose loss the monarch and the empire will feel for a long time, will take place today in the St. Alexander Nevsky Monastery, the final resting place of all our high imperial dignitaries of the Greek confession.[68]

K. P. Masal'skii, who was close to Speranskii during the last years of his life, noted Speranskii's surprisingly calm attitude toward his own death—the quality of a truly religious person: "His last days, like all of his life, were full of activity, bright serenity, and tenderest concern for others; with a smile he awaited his end, in which he saw only an easy transition to the most perfect state of being."[69]

67 "Iz dnevnika barona (vposledstvii grafa) M. A. Korfa," *Russkaia starina*, 1904, vol. 117, no. 2: 275–302, here at 285.

68 *Allgemeine Zeitung*, March 12, 1839 (no. 71): 567–68. The report from St. Petersburg was dated February 15 (February 27, New Style). The report was reprinted in *Bayreuther Zeitung*, March 14, 1839 (no. 63): 250–51.

69 K. P. Masal'skii, "Vospominaniia o grafe Speranskom," *Syn Otechestva*, 1844, no. 1: 20–24, here at 22. Konstantin Petrovich Masal'skii was the son of Speranskii's most devoted friend, Petr Grigor'evich Masal'skii. Konstantin Petrovich knew Speranskii from childhood and

Masal'skii was present at the burial of Speranskii and left a heartfelt description of this sad and solemn event:

> Everyone was deeply moved by the death of this man when, a few days later, the solemn funeral procession approached the Alexander Nevsky Monastery, the first shelter of his youth in the capital—when his body was brought into the church under a gilded baldachin through the very same gates he passed through a half-century ago when he arrived as a poor, unknown, defenseless youth with nothing but his exceptional gifts and noble self-assurance![70]

Political power is difficult to combine with morality, science, and religion, and it is very rare for a statesman to be wise, conscientious, and religious. Speranskii was an exception in the cruel world of politics. He was a Christian in his outlook and in his soul. He managed to unite what might seem impossible to unite—the qualities of a brilliant scholar, an outstanding statesman, and a true human being.

---

enjoyed his confidence. It was to him that Speranskii presented the cherished notebook of his youth containing his early works. Masal'skii prepared the notebook along with Speranskii's letters to his father for publication (see note 24).

70 Masal'skii, "Vospominaniia o grafe Speranskom," 22–23.

4 Aleksandr Kunitsyn

Pioneer of natural law in Russia

Julia Berest

Aleksandr Petrovich Kunitsyn (1783–1840) had an unusual intellectual life and career which reflected the major shift from liberal to conservative policies in Russia under Alexander I. The son of a sacristan from a small village, Kunitsyn rose to become a professor at the newly established Tsarskoe Selo Lycée and later at St. Petersburg University. Taking advantage of the relaxation of censorship, Kunitsyn published *Natural Law* (1818–20), a pioneering contribution to Russian legal studies. Alas, it appeared at a time when the tide of conservative reaction was about to sweep away many of the academic freedoms granted in 1803–04. The book and Kunitsyn's teaching career fell victim to the conservative attack on the faculties of law and philosophy, but Kunitsyn soon reemerged as a government official working on the legal codification project and moving steadily up the Table of Ranks. The vicissitudes of Kunitsyn's life were symptomatic of the imperial government's oscillation between the need to modernize Russia and the desire to guard the educational system against ideas that might threaten Russian autocracy.[1]

Kunitsyn's place in Russian intellectual history has long been underappreciated, in part because his book, meticulously removed from public libraries on official order, reached only a limited audience in prerevolutionary Russia. Most commonly, Kunitsyn is known as a favorite teacher of Russia's great poet Alexander Pushkin, who studied at the lycée and was influenced by Kunitsyn's views on the rule of law. Kunitsyn is also frequently mentioned in connection with the Decembrists, some of whom attended his public lectures and attested to his intellectual influence. However, Kunitsyn's legal thought has been overlooked in studies of Russian legal philosophy.[2]

As a person who was once accused of promoting ideas contrary to Christian faith and morality, Kunitsyn might appear an odd figure in the company of

1 This chapter draws on my book *The Emergence of Russian Liberalism: Alexander Kunitsyn in Context, 1783–1840* (New York: Palgrave Macmillan, 2011).

2 See, for instance, M. V. Antonov, *Istoriia pravovoi mysli Rossii* (St. Petersburg: NIU, 2011); *Russian Legal Realism*, ed. Bartosz Brozek, Julia Stanec, and Jerzy Stelmac (Cham, Switz.: Springer, 2018); Andrzej Walicki, *Legal Philosophies of Russian Liberalism* (Oxford: Clarendon Press, 1987).

DOI: 10.4324/9781003017097-4

Christian legal thinkers. However, the story of Kunitsyn's academic purge highlights an important chapter in the history of law and religion in Russia. His book inadvertently triggered a controversy over the question of the relationship between natural law and religion—a question that in Russia was decided in a typical autocratic fashion by removing the subject of natural law from the curricula of Russian universities and gymnasia. It was abolished as abruptly as it had been introduced. More than five decades passed before natural law ideas reemerged in the works of Russian Neo-Kantians, only to be banished again soon thereafter by the Bolshevik regime.[3] Kunitsyn's life illuminates the development of the natural law tradition in tsarist Russia. Taking a closer look at his view of religion in *Natural Law* also provides an opportunity to examine whether the charges leveled against him in 1821 had any merit. Kunitsyn himself never had a proper chance to defend his position.

Early years: the beneficiary of educational reforms

Kunitsyn was born in 1783 in the village of Koi, Tver Province.[4] Kunitsyn's early education was apparently meant to prepare him for a church career, as was typical for sons of the clergy.[5] After completing his studies in the district church school, he enrolled in Tver Theological Seminary, which offered a six-year program culminating with courses in philosophy and theology.[6]

Kunitsyn's graduation from the seminary coincided with the beginning of Alexander I's liberal reforms and the expansion of secular education in Russia. In 1803, Kunitsyn found himself among the students selected to study (at government expense) in the Teachers' Gymnasium, which was upgraded to the status of the St. Petersburg Pedagogical Institute a year later.[7] In 1808, along with eleven other students, he qualified for a three-year period of study abroad sponsored by the government.[8] Kunitsyn spent most of his time at the University of Göttingen, then popular among Russian nobility who sought education in prestigious institutions abroad. One of the students, Nikolai Turgenev, later known for his association with the Decembrists, became Kunitsyn's roommate and long-term friend.

3 On Russian Neo-Kantians, see Walicki, *Legal Philosophies of Russian Liberalism*, 291–341. On natural law and Soviet scholarship, see F. N. Smirnov, *Obshchestvenno-politicheskie i pravovye vzgliady A.P. Kunitsyna* (kand. diss., Moskovskii gosudarstvennyi universitet, 1966), 14.

4 *Russkie pisateli 1800–1917. Biograficheskii slovar'*, ed. P. A. Nikolaev, vol. 3 (Moscow: Bol'shaia rossiiskaia entsiklopediia, 1994), 229.

5 See S. A. Ershov, "Koiskaia rodoslovnaia Kunitsynykh XVII–XIX vekov," in *"Dlia blaga obshchego": Aleksandr Petrovich Kunitsyn (1783–1840)—prosvetitel', pravoved, gosudarstvennyi deiatel': sbornik materialov*, ed. S. A. Ershov, A. V. Bolshakova, and T. N. Zhukovskaia (St. Petersburg: "Dmitrii Bulanin," 2018), 26–38, here at 33.

6 M. A. Liubavin, *Litseiskie uchitelia Pushkina i ikh knigi* (St. Petersburg: Izdatel'stvo "Sudarynia," 1997), 26.

7 Tsentral'nyi gosudarstvennyi istoricheskii arkhiv Sankt-Peterburga (TsGIA SPb), f. 11, op. 1, d. 3727, l. 2.

8 TsGIA SPb, f. 13, op. 1, d. 231, l. 4.

Turgenev's diary and letters provide insights into Kunitsyn's life and personality during this period and for several years after their return to Russia, compensating for the lack of Kunitsyn's own epistolary output.[9]

The Göttingen period had a significant impact on Kunitsyn's intellectual development. In the early nineteenth century, the university boasted talented and popular professors in political economy, history, and law. All of them were political moderates, leaning toward conservatism under the influence of the Napoleonic Wars. However, their discursive style of lectures, as Turgenev noted, was conducive to effective learning and critical thinking—something that was often missing in the more tightly controlled Russian institutions. Turgenev recalled that the lectures of Georg Sartorius, a popularizer of Adam Smith, were particularly stimulating.[10] Kunitsyn's intellectual maturation was also boosted by his extensive reading of Western thinkers, now unobstructed by any supervision. The rich Göttingen library as well as the lack of diversions in a small university town aided students' zeal for study.[11] Turgenev wrote that Kunitsyn returned to Russia in 1811 with his head full of ideas and excitement, eager to share the fruits of his education.[12]

A decade of teaching

Upon returning to St. Petersburg, Kunitsyn passed examinations qualifying him for the position of adjunct professor of philosophical and political sciences and was appointed to teach at the Tsarskoe Selo Lycée, scheduled to open in October 1811.[13] It was a prestigious and lucrative appointment. The lycée was created as an elite institution for the purpose of educating "youth meant for higher civil positions."[14] Its charges were drawn from the nobility, but in keeping with the meritocratic approach (strongly defended by Mikhail Speranskii, who composed the initial plan), the students had to pass entrance examinations, and those who failed were not admitted regardless of their title or connections.[15] The teachers, too, were expected to meet high professional and moral requirements.[16]

The opening ceremony, attended by the tsar and high-ranking officials, provided the first occasion for Kunitsyn to make his name known. He delivered a

9 *Dekabrist N. I. Turgenev. Pis'ma k bratu S. I. Turgenevu*, ed. N. G. Svirin (Moscow: Izdatel'stvo AN SSSR, 1936); *Arkhiv brat'ev Turgenevykh,* ed. E. Tarasov, 6 vols. (St. Petersburg: Imperatorskaia akademiia nauk, 1911–21).

10 *Arkhiv brat'ev Turgenevykh* 1:361–62, 379, 396; *Dekabrist N.I. Turgenev,* 238–43.

11 *Arkhiv brat'ev Turgenevykh* 1:327.

12 Ibid., 1:296.

13 TsGIA SPb, f. 13, op. 1, d. 934, ll. 1–3.

14 *Sbornik postanovlenii po Ministerstvu narodnogo prosveshcheniia,* 17 vols. (St. Petersburg: Ministerstvo narodnogo prosveshcheniia, 1864–1904), 1:558.

15 B. Meilakh, *Pushkin i ego epokha* (Moscow: Goslitizdat, 1958), 46.

16 *Sbornik postanovlenii po Ministerstvu narodnogo prosveshcheniia* 1:558; Allen A. Sinel, "The Socialization of the Russian Elite, 1811–1917: Life at the Tsarskoe Selo Lyceum and the School of Jurisprudence," *Russian History* 3, no. 1 (1976): 1–31.

speech which made a lasting impression on his students and was noted by the tsar himself, who awarded Kunitsyn a medal of St. Vladimir of the Fourth Degree.[17] The speech gave an early indication of the themes Kunitsyn would later develop in his writings—the rule of law, meritocratic principles of social mobility, and the importance of civic and moral virtues in public servants, including the *prostoserdechie* (simpleheartedness, sincerity) traditionally prized in Russian Orthodox ethics.[18]

At the lycée, Kunitsyn gained a reputation as a talented and popular teacher who "had a vivid imagination," as one of his students remembered.[19] Alexander Pushkin, a gifted but not very disciplined student, was enrolled in the first class, from 1811 to 1817. According to the recollections of Pushkin's classmate, Ivan Pushchin, Kunitsyn was Pushkin's favorite teacher: "Most willingly Pushkin studied in Kunitsyn's classes but in his own way; [he never] reviewed his lessons and wrote down little."[20]

In September 1816, Kunitsyn petitioned to publish his lecture notes on natural law and political science, citing the inconvenience to his students of having to copy out his handwritten notes. The petition was supported by the lycée and quickly approved by the minister of education, Aleksandr Golitsyn.[21] This was a very productive and successful period in Kunitsyn's life. In 1817, on the graduation of the lycée's first class, Kunitsyn received a monetary award and a medal of St. Anne. He continued to teach at the lycée but moved to the capital to take up a position as law professor in the Pedagogical Institute, upgraded in 1819 to the status of St. Petersburg University.[22] Along with pedagogical training, the institute now offered public courses for nondegree students.[23] One such course on political economy was entrusted to Kunitsyn, in addition to his regular classes on natural law. Most of the students enrolled in these courses were public officials preparing for the examinations now required for obtaining the ranks of collegiate assessor (*kollezhskii asessor*) and state councilor (*statskii sovetnik*).[24] The new learning opportunities also attracted progressive nobility and military officers, some of whom were future Decembrists.[25]

17 TsGIA SPb, f. 3727, d.11, op.1, l. 3.

18 *Antologiia pedagogicheskoi mysli Rossii pervoi poloviny XIX v.*, ed. M. I. Kondakov (Moscow: Pedagogika, 1987), 141–42.

19 Ia. Grot, *Pushkin, ego litseiskie tovarishchi i nastavniki* (St. Petersburg: Tipografiia Ministerstva Putei Soobshcheniia, 1899), 228.

20 I. I. Pushchin, *Zapiski o Pushkine* (Moscow: Izdatel'stvo "Sovetskaia Rossiia," 1979), 52.

21 Liubavin, *Litseiskie uchitelia Pushkina i ikh knigi*, 34–35.

22 TsGIA SPb, f. 11, op.1, d. 3727, ll. 6–7; on the Institute's reorganization, see *Sbornik postanovlenii po Ministerstvu narodnogo prosveshcheniia* 1:829–74; James T. Flynn, *The University Reform of Alexander I* (Washington, DC: Catholic University of America Press, 1988), 122.

23 *Sbornik postanovlenii po Ministerstvu narodnogo prosveshcheniia* 1:829–74.

24 Ibid., 1:510–17.

25 *Vosstanie dekabristov: Materialy po istorii vosstaniia dekabristov. Dela Verkhovnogo ugolovnogo suda i sledstvennoi komissii*, vol. 18, ed. M. V. Nechkina (Moscow: Izdatel'stvo "Nauka," 1984), 164.

In St. Petersburg, Kunitsyn's name was becoming known in progressive circles. He reconnected with Nikolai Turgenev and frequented the gatherings at the Turgenev brothers' apartment, which attracted intellectuals and bureaucrats with aspirations for reforms.[26] Aleksandr Turgenev recalled that in 1818 Kunitsyn "caused a sensation" with his article on foreign peasants published in *Syn Otechestva* (Son of the Fatherland).[27] The article exalted the freedoms of foreign peasants, including the right to conclude contracts and engage in free economic activity.[28] Kunitsyn wrote the article in response to an anonymous essay published in *Dukh Zhurnalov* (Spirit of the Journals), which argued that Russian serfs were in a better position because they enjoyed the economic protection of their masters, while foreign peasants suffered from the uncertainties of the market economy. Kunitsyn's sharp and sarcastic rebuttal was a bold move. Although he did not explicitly discuss Russian serfdom, everybody understood his Aesopian device inviting comparisons between the freedom of foreign peasants and the slave-like position of Russian serfs. According to Aleksandr Turgenev, the government responded to Kunitsyn's article by issuing a ban on "writing pro and contra" about the position of Russian and foreign peasants.[29] Nevertheless, the journal which published Kunitsyn's article did not suffer any penalty. In the next two years, before his expulsion from the university, Kunitsyn published four more articles in *Syn Otechestva*, all of them written in a liberal spirit.[30]

Natural law in Russian universities

The publication of Kunitsyn's *Natural Law* in 1818–20 was part of a larger trend toward the expansion of academic publishing during the first two decades of the nineteenth century. It was occasioned by the relaxation of censorship as well as the growth of universities, which created a demand for teaching manuals. The subject of natural law was no exception to this growth in publishing. More textbooks on natural law appeared during the first two decades of the nineteenth century than in the entire eighteenth century. Most of the publications were undertaken by visiting German professors, some by their Russian colleagues, drawing primarily on the German natural law tradition, with adaptations suitable for the Russian audience.[31]

It was no coincidence that virtually all textbooks on natural law published in Russia during this period originated from German legal thought. Natural law as a

26 See Berest, *The Emergence of Russian Liberalism*, 61, 85, 91–92.

27 Quoted from V. N. Speranskii, "Sotsialno-politicheskie vzgliady A. P. Kunitsyna," *Uchenye zapiski Gor'kovskogo Gosudarstvennogo Universiteta* 72 (1964): 830. See also *Dekabrist N. I. Turgenev*, 261.

28 N. N. "O sostoianii inostrannykh krest'ian," *Syn Otechestva* 45, no. 17 (1818): 162–86. See also Berest, *The Emergence of Russian Liberalism*, 76–81.

29 P. A. Viazemskii, *Ostaf'evskii arkhiv kniazei Viazemskikh,* ed. V. I. Saitova, 4 vols., Izdanie S. D. Sheremet'eva (St. Petersburg: Tipografiia M. M. Stasiulevicha, 1899–1913), 1:137.

30 Berest, *The Emergence of Russian Liberalism*, 68–72, 89–90, 188–89.

31 Ibid., 105–42.

philosophical discipline was not native to Russia. It played only a small role in the Russian and Greek Orthodox tradition compared to the Christian West, where natural law went back to the early church fathers who adopted the idea from the Stoics.[32] In Russia, natural law was an imported science. It was introduced by the autocratic state for the purpose of bringing Russian legal education and the training of officials closer in line with European standards. It first appeared in the curriculum of the Academy of Sciences, established by Peter the Great in 1724. In the absence of native teaching cadres at that time, the Academy relied on visiting professors selected by the government.[33] From the beginning, preference was given to German scholars because their interpretation of natural law, based primarily on Christian Wolff and, to a lesser extent, on Samuel Pufendorf, appeared more congruent with the Russian political order than did the French or English variants, which developed in the direction of liberal rights theory.[34] At the core of German natural law theory was the idea of a divinely established rational order and its corollary, human perfectibility. Secular power was viewed as instrumental in facilitating the pursuit of perfection and moral order. In this form, Wolffian duty-oriented natural law proved helpful in justifying the concept of the well-ordered, paternalistic state which Peter the Great sought to establish in Russia.[35]

By the late eighteenth century, Kantian philosophy of right made its way into German academic teaching, and by the first decade of the nineteenth century it began to appear in Russian universities via the courses of German visiting professors.[36] Kant rejected the idea of the paternalistic state which "treats citizens as children" and sees itself as responsible for the perfectibility of its subjects. Instead,

32 See Paul Babie, "Natural Law in the Orthodox Tradition," in *Christianity and Natural Law: An Introduction*, ed. Norman Doe (Cambridge: Cambridge University Press, 2017), 36–57, here at 37. On natural law in early Western thought, see J. M. Kelly, *A Short History of Western Legal Theory* (Oxford: Clarendon Press, 1992), 102–10; H. A. Rommen, *The Natural Law: A Study in Legal and Social History and Philosophy* (New York: Herder Book Co., 1959), 34–69.

33 V. F. Pustarnakov, *Universitetskaia filosofiia v Rossii: Idei, Personalii, Osnovnye tsentry* (St. Petersburg: Izdatel'stvo Russkogo Khristianskogo Gumanitarnogo Instituta, 2003), 71–72; S. Shevyrev, *Istoriia Imperatorskogo Moskovskogo Universiteta k 100-letnemu iubileiu 1755–1855* (Moscow: Universitetskaia Tipografiia, 1855), 31–33, 187, 228. See also V. E. Grabar, *The History of International Law in Russia, 1647–1917: A Bio-Bibliographical Study*, ed. and trans. W. E. Butler (Oxford: Clarendon Press, 1990).

34 On Wolff, see Knud Haakonssen, "German Natural Law," in *The Cambridge History of Eighteenth-Century Political Thought*, ed. Mark Goldie and Robert Wokler (Cambridge: Cambridge University Press, 2006), 249–90, here at 268–78.

35 See Marc Raeff, "The Well-Ordered Police State and the Development of Modernity in Seventeenth- and Eighteenth-Century Europe: An Attempt at a Comparative Approach," *The American Historical Review* 80, no. 5 (1975): 1221–43; Marc Raeff, "Les Slaves, les Allemands et les 'Lumières,'" *Canadian Slavic Studies* 1, no. 4 (1967): 521–51.

36 Thomas Nemeth, "Kant In Russia: The Initial Phase," *Studies in Soviet Thought* 36, no. 1 (1988): 79–110; Franklin A. Walker, "'Renegade' Monks and Cultural Conflict in Early Nineteenth-Century Russia: The Russia of I. A. Fessler and J. B. Shad," *Religion, State and Society* 28, no. 4 (2000): 347–58; Z. A. Kamenskii, "I. Kant v russkoi filosofii nachala 19 veka," *Vestnik istorii mirovoi kul'tury* 19, no. 1 (1960): 49–66.

Kant proclaimed that "there is only one innate right"—"freedom ... insofar as it can coexist with the freedom of every other in accordance with a universal law."[37] Kant also undermined the legitimacy of the paternalistic state by making a distinction between duties of right and duties of virtue. Duties of right are regulated by positive laws in keeping with the principle of the universal law of freedom, while duties of virtue "cannot be subject to external lawgiving," for they belong to the sphere where rational beings are autonomous. "No external lawgiving can bring about someone's setting an end for himself because this is an internal act of the mind."[38] Underlying this claim was a conception of the human being as autonomous and capable of following the self-prescribed laws of reason, the most important of which is the categorical imperative—an injunction to "treat humanity ... never merely as a means to an end, but always ... as an end."[39]

Not all of Kant's ideas made their way into the works of his German followers, despite their self-professed Kantianism. Most commonly, they accepted Kant's idea of moral self-legislation and his categorical imperative, but preserved the Wolffian absolutist tradition of natural law and social contract, which undermined Kant's emphasis on individual freedom as an innate right. In this diluted form, and through German textbooks rather than Kant's original writings, Kantian philosophy was transmitted to Russia and considered safe enough to be taught in Russian universities—until the authorities came across Kunitsyn's book.[40]

Kunitsyn on natural law

What set Kunitsyn's book apart from other works on natural law published in Russia during this period was his strong emphasis on individual rights, freedoms, and legal equality. "Natural law," he wrote in the opening section, "is a science about rights [*nauka prav*] or the conditions under which the external freedom of individuals can exist."[41] Kunitsyn took pains to explain that in contrast to the older tradition of natural law, where ethics, law, and politics were linked together, Kantian "critical philosophy has now shown a clear distinction between these sciences" (210). "Moral science" (*nravouchenie*) is concerned with "man's internal freedom" and "virtue," while "law ... has as its subject ... external freedom" and

37 Immanuel Kant, *Metaphysics of Morals*, ed. and trans. Mary Gregor, intro. Roger J. Sullivan (Cambridge: Cambridge University Press, 1996), 30, 94.

38 Ibid., 31.

39 Immanuel Kant, *Groundwork of the Metaphysics of Morals*, ed. and trans. Mary Gregor, intro. Christine M. Korsgaard (Cambridge: Cambridge University Press, 1998), 38. See also Haakonssen, "German Natural Law," 279–90.

40 See Berest, *The Emergence of Russian Liberalism*, 115–30.

41 A. Kunitsyn, *Pravo estestvennoe*, in *Russkie prosvetiteli ot Radishcheva do dekabristov: Sobranie proizvedenii v dvukh tomakh*, ed. I. Ia. Shchipanov, 2 vols. (Moscow: Izdatel'stvo sotsial'no-ekonomicheskoi literatury "Mysl'," 1966), 2:204–351, at 210–11. Page references to *Natural Law* in this chapter are to this edition. First edition: Aleksandr Kunitsyn, *Pravo estestvennoe*, 2 pts. (St. Petersburg: v Tipografii Ios. Ioannesova, 1818–20).

"justice." Law sets the standard of justice and "limits the means used in politics, admitting only those that are lawful [*zakonnye*]" (211).

It is clear that Kunitsyn's central contentions—that each individual is entitled to freedom by virtue of being human, and that the system of law ought to ensure the freedom of everyone—were inspired by the Kantian philosophy of right. Kunitsyn drew heavily on Kant's notions of personal autonomy and human dignity, as well as on the categorical imperative as the main standard of right and wrong. However, he was not merely a popularizer of Kantian ideas. He gave Kant's principle of moral autonomy a more empirical and individualistic interpretation, which resembled the concept of individual liberty developed later in the nineteenth century by John Stuart Mill. Moreover, Kunitsyn made creative use of Kant's ideas on rational religion, which were virtually unknown in Russia at that time.[42] Kant's *Religion within the Boundaries of Mere Reason* was not yet available in Russian translation, while other Kantians in Russia preferred to bypass this sensitive topic, for which Kant himself had gotten into trouble with censorship in Germany.[43]

Kunitsyn's view of the foundation of law, which concerns the relationship between law and religion, was the most provocative segment of his work. It occurs in chapter two, where he provides a review of various legal philosophies followed by his own formulation of what constitutes the source of law. Like Kant, he argued that "rights and duties ... should have a single foundation [*odno obshchee nachalo*], or criterion," by which we can judge the validity of law (218). Positivist legal thinking, according to Kunitsyn, is invalid because it does not meet the criterion of universality of obligation. If we accept that law derives from historical customs and government institutions peculiar to each nation, there will be no notion of right whatsoever: "Not only each nation but also each person will have a different notion of what is right, and one and the same action will appear as just and unjust" (219). Kunitsyn also dismissed utilitarian legal theory, arguing that utility (or pleasure) is a "misleading" criterion because the notion of pleasure varies greatly from person to person (220). "Finally," he wrote, "some have viewed God's will as a foundation of law: what does not go against God's will is allowed to humanity." "This view is correct," Kunitsyn continued,

> but it cannot serve as a foundation of law, for it requires another criterion by which one would be able to tell what is in accordance with God's will and what goes against it. Since God is a moral being [*nravstvennoe sushchestvo*], God's will is ... expressed through moral laws, but in order to define God as a moral being, one already has to have moral notions.
>
> (221)

42 In 1792, when Göttingen-educated I. V. L. Mel'man (J. W. L. Mellmann) attempted to introduce his Moscow students to Kant's view of religion, he was quickly removed from the university for spreading the seeds of irreligion. See Kamenskii, "I. Kant," 52.

43 On Kant's problems with censorship, see James J. DiCenso, *Kant's Religion within the Boundaries of Mere Reason: A Commentary* (Cambridge: Cambridge University Press, 2012), 3–9.

Kunitsyn's implication in this passage is that human moral consciousness is innate and prior to religion; otherwise, men and women would not be able to recognize God's moral essence. "It follows from this," Kunitsyn concluded, that "the foundation of law can only be deduced from reason" (221).

Kunitsyn then argued that reason, if used "impartially," leads each person to a recognition that the freedom of everyone is the most fundamental "principle of right" and thus the standard of justice. Since freedom is a condition which implies both rights and duties on the part of each individual, "the main principle of right" can be expressed in two forms. In the first formulation, the emphasis is on the individual's freedom, limited only by the corresponding freedom of everyone else: "*A person has a right to all actions that are compatible with the freedom of all people according to the universal law of reason*" (222).[44] In the second formulation, drawn from Kant's categorical imperative, the same principle implies a prohibition binding on all individuals: "*do not use other people as a means to your ends*" (222).

It is easy to understand why this section of Kunitsyn's book would raise the authorities' suspicion. In Russia, where the natural law tradition had a short and limited history, Kunitsyn's rationalistic stance must have sounded provocative, especially for those educated on the textbooks by the Wolffian popularizer Christian Baumeister, which had been in use in Russia since the 1760s.[45] Kunitsyn's view of the foundations of law was inspired by Kant's a priori approach to law and religion. Kant's concept of rational religion was a significant departure from traditional Christian theology. For Kant, God is a "thought-entity,"[46] a postulate of practical reason for the needs of morality. Reason, according to Kant, can posit the existence of God as an embodiment of the highest good, but it cannot prove God's existence, because humans have no knowledge of the divine in this world. Breaking away from a centuries-old tradition, Kant denied that religious revelation is required for our determination to act in accordance with moral laws. Nor did he believe in the possibility of proving revelation as a fact.[47] Even if proven empirically, the law revealed to some particular individuals

44 It is the Kantian principle of right in a slightly modified form. Cf. Kant, *Metaphysics of Morals*, 24.

45 A. F. Abramov, "Khristian Vol'f v russkoi dukhovno-akademicheskoi filosofii," in *Khristian Vol'f i filosofiia v Rossii*, ed. V. A. Zhuchkov (St. Petersburg: Izdatel'stvo Russkogo Khristianskogo Gumanitarnogo Instituta, 2001), 189–209, here at 190, 198. Baumeister traditionally maintained that "natural law is . . . rooted in human nature itself," but "God is the creator of natural law." Khristian Baumeister, *Nravouchitel'naia filosofiia, soderzhashchaia estestvennoe pravo, etiku, politiku, ekonomiu i drugie veshchi, dlia znaniia nuzhnye i poleznye*, trans. D. Sin'kovskii (Moscow: Kompaniia Tipograficheskaia, 1788), 55, 103. This view remained unchallenged. In the textbook by Moscow professor L. Tsvetaev, for instance, the question of the source of natural law is omitted altogether. He simply begins with a Kantian categorical imperative: "The first foundation of natural law is the following: never treat humanity in other people as a means." Lev Tsvetaev, *Pervye nachala prava estestvennogo* (Moscow: Universitetskaia tipografiia, 1816), 10.

46 Kant, *Metaphysics of Morals*, 33.

47 See Denis Savage, "Kant's Rejection of Divine Revelation and his Theory of Radical Evil," in *Kant's Philosophy of Religion Reconsidered*, ed. Philip J. Rossi and Michael Wreen (Bloomington: Indiana University Press, 1991), 54–76, here at 62.

or peoples, such as Jews or Christians, would not, in Kant's view, meet the criterion of universality.[48]

Kunitsyn shared Kant's view of the limited human capacity to know God, and, like Kant, he was concerned with the universality of moral principles. In *Natural Law*, his implication is that religion, with its diverse creeds, cannot yield a universal system of morals. Later in the book, he returns to this point when discussing the justification for religious toleration: "If people are often mistaken and contradict each other even in things that concern practical experience, how is it possible for them to agree on what concerns abstract notions of reason?" (237). Kunitsyn's rationalistic position, however, was more extreme than Kant's. In Kant, reason is ultimately God's voice in humanity, much as it was understood in traditional Christian thought.[49] In Kunitsyn, there is no mention of that, nor does he say (as does Kant) that morality necessarily leads to religion. One gets the impression that, for Kunitsyn, reason is an entirely autonomous agent which generates moral maxims from itself, with no connection to the divine mind. In Kunitsyn, Kant's idea of rationality as the ability to act from duty alone is brought to its extreme logical conclusion, implying that rational human beings need no other motive, not even a religious one.

Nevertheless, Kunitsyn's position did not amount to irreligion. When discussing the concept of punishment for criminal offenses, Kunitsyn brings up the image of God as the ultimate moral judge. He notes that "punishment should not be considered moral retribution [*nravstvennoe vozmezdie*]," for no one can look so deep into the human conscience as to be able to determine the degree of moral guilt. "Only the all-knowing being [*vsevedushchee sushchestvo*] can define the measure of good and evil in human will" (231).

Interestingly, Kunitsyn's insistence on the need to distinguish between punishment and moral retribution stood in contrast to the Kantian retributive concept of punishment, which some commentators today view as a serious flaw in Kant's philosophy because "it openly contradicts some fundamental tenets of his ethics."[50] According to Kant, "punishment ... is the physical evil visited upon a person for moral evil.... Such punishments ... are moral in character" and ought to be proportional to the criminal's "inner wickedness."[51] By contrast, for Kunitsyn, moral punishment lies beyond the purview of law: "In order to define

48 Ibid., 58. See also Leslie A. Mulholland, "Freedom and Providence in Kant's Account of Religion: The Problem of Expiation," in Rossi and Wreen, *Kant's Philosophy of Religion Reconsidered*, 77–102, here at 81–82.

49 Kant, *Metaphysics of Morals*, 229. On the pre-Kantian tradition, see Kelly, *A Short History of Western Legal Theory*, 103, 144, 226,

50 Allen Wood, "Punishment, Retribution and the Coercive Enforcement of Right," in *Kant's Metaphysics of Morals: A Critical Guide*, ed. Lara Denis (Cambridge: Cambridge University Press, 2010), 111–29, here at 112, 126–27. See also Arthur Shuster, "Kant on the Role of the Retributive Outlook in Moral and Political Life," *The Review of Politics* 73, no. 3 (2011): 425–48, here at 433.

51 Quoted from Wood, "Punishment, Retribution and the Coercive Enforcement of Right," 113, 115.

the measure of moral retribution one would have to know … how far a person *deviated* from the laws of conscience, which a human court [*sud chelovecheskii*] is not able to determine" (230). Kunitsyn concluded that the measure of moral as opposed to legal guilt can be judged only by God.[52]

Kunitsyn devoted considerable attention in his book to the discussion of the individual's "innate rights." Having established in the opening chapter the concept of universal freedom as the foundational legal principle, Kunitsyn sought to explain the idea of freedom in more concrete terms. With Kant, he argued that freedom is an innate right due to everyone by virtue of their humanity. The equality of formal rights sets the limits to the freedom of each: "Since the right to freedom is shared by all people, each [individual] can do only what agrees with the freedom of everyone else. Freedom within these limits is called lawful" (234). Kunitsyn also adopted Kant's notion of freedom as an expression of the individual's moral autonomy, which presupposes the right "to set one's ends [and] choose the means for achieving them" (232). However, he went beyond Kant in expanding the concept of autonomy and setting more firmly the boundary between the individual and society in a way that prefigured the ideas of J. S. Mill in *On Liberty* (1859). The catalogue of rights Kunitsyn attributed to the individual was intended to secure not just individual freedom per se but the conditions in which the individual would achieve security, material well-being, and personal happiness. Revealingly, in arguing for the "right to achieve well-being,"[53] Kunitsyn insisted, like Mill, that "only a person himself can determine what is conducive to his well-being.… Even though he might err in choosing the means for … the enjoyment of life, nobody can direct his actions." "Every person," he added, "has a right to choose the way of life and occupation suitable to his well-being" (238).[54] It was a bold statement in Russia, where serfdom, limited social mobility, and limitations on property ownership strongly affected the way people could conduct their lives.

Kunitsyn's concept of freedom included a wide range of specific rights—from the innate "right to one's person," which implies the unimpeded use of one's "moral and physical powers" (231), to acquired rights originating in civil society, such as the right to own property (243). It is remarkable that Kunitsyn insisted on extending innate rights to "children, the feebleminded, the insane, and the like." Rights, he argued, might remain inactive if a person is not able to use them, but "the lack of intellectual or physical abilities does not justify depriving a person of his innate rights," because, "first of all, this may not be a permanent

52 A similar idea was later expressed by Vladimir Spasovich, law professor at St. Petersburg University. See N. S. Tagantsev, *Russkoe ugolovnoe pravo*, 2 vols. (Tula: Avtograf, 2001), 2:47.

53 Here he used the word "well-being" (*blagopoluchie*) in the sense of "happiness."

54 Cf. J. S. Mill, *The Basic Writings of John Stuart Mill*, ed. J. B. Schneewind (New York: The Modern Library, 2002), 14. In this emphasis on happiness as a right (rather unusual for Russia at that time), Kunitsyn must have been influenced by Jeremy Bentham, whose works he read while studying abroad. In a chapter on "well-being" he wrote: "man by his sensual nature seeks what is pleasant and avoids what is unpleasant" (*Pravo estestvennoe*, 238).

condition … [and], second, a person does not become merely a thing by virtue of inability [to exercise rights]" (240–41). Moreover, Kunitsyn noted that those who possess superior

> bodily and mental qualities have no right to humiliate those who do not have such virtues, because this right … would not be in accord with the law of reason.… The lack of natural abilities does not change one's humanity, thus there is no justification for [treating such individuals] with contempt. (240)

The significance of Kunitsyn's claim can be better appreciated if we recall how little respect was accorded to disability in the political and moral theories of the time.[55] Kant, in particular, has recently come under intense criticism for failing to include persons with disability into his conception of justice and personhood.[56] Interestingly, Kunitsyn's work shows that Kantian moral philosophy could also inspire a different interpretation of disability, one that takes as its starting point the imperative to treat all persons as ends in themselves by virtue of their humanity. What Kunitsyn added to this was the affirmation that a person's humanity is essentially the same in both able and disabled individuals. Thus, everyone should be treated with dignity and have the same innate rights.

Equally unusual for its time was Kunitsyn's assertion that "the claims [*pritiazaniia*] of some European peoples to the freedom and property of nomadic tribes in different parts of the world are entirely contrary" to the principle of inalienability of innate rights (241). By putting this statement in the same segment in which he discussed the rights of people with disabilities, Kunitsyn implied that the perceived backwardness of nomadic people does not justify their treatment as merely a means by more civilized nations. Like people with disability, they are entitled to be treated with dignity, as autonomous agents rather than the objects of someone's will.

Regarding the right to property, Kunitsyn recognized that exercising this right requires proper material means, so some people are not able to make use of it.

55 See Barbara Arneil and Nancy J. Hirschmann, "Disability and Political Theory: An Introduction," in *Disability and Political Theory*, ed. Barbara Arneil and Nancy J. Hirschmann (Cambridge: Cambridge University Press, 2016), 1–19, here at 3–4.

56 Lucas G. Pinheiro, "The Ableist Contract: Intellectual Disability and the Limits of Justice in Kant's Political Thought," in *Disability and Political Theory*, ed. Arneil and Hirschmann, 43–78, here at 50. See also Barbara Arneil, "Disability, Self-Image, and Modern Political Theory," *Political Theory* 37, no. 2 (2009): 218–42, here at 224–25. In Russia, the attitude toward mental disability was more accepting than in the West during the same period. See Julie V. Brown, "Societal Responses to Mental Disorders in Prerevolutionary Russia," in *The Disabled in the Soviet Union: Past and Present, Theory and Practice*, ed. W. O. McCagg and Lewis Siegelbaum (Pittsburgh: University of Pittsburgh Press, 1989), 13–37, here at 34. Anne Finger notes that the tradition of holy fools in Russia might have played a role in shaping Russian perceptions of insanity. See Anne Finger, "The Left Hand of Stalin: Eugenics in the Soviet Union," in *Disability Politics in a Global Economy: Essays in Honour of Marta Russell*, ed. Ravi Malhotra (London: Routledge, 2017), 199–219, here at 203.

But he insisted that as a "formal right," it belongs to everyone without exception (232). In the Russian context, this argument implied a critical stance against serfdom and, more broadly, against the tradition of restricting ownership rights based on an individual's social status. Kunitsyn also rejected the idea of birthright privileges, arguing that "special honor is not an innate right but an acquired one. No one by nature has a right to demand an exclusive honor, [or] to make others praise him and humiliate themselves before him" (239).

Kunitsyn on religious toleration

In his conception of freedom, Kunitsyn put special emphasis on the right to religious toleration and social tolerance in general. In Russia, the issue of toleration was a particularly thorny one, especially when it came to the needs of Russia's Muslim subjects. Non-Orthodox (more commonly referred to as "foreign") confessions were tolerated out of political expediency, but the Orthodox Church retained its dominant position and served as a symbol of Russian national identity.[57] Few Russian thinkers, even on the liberal and radical side, engaged the topic of toleration, and those who did tended to concentrate "not on the abstract, theoretical justifications for toleration but on its practical advantages," as Gary Hamburg has pointed out.[58] Kunitsyn's approach was different. He drew mainly on Kant's ideas about rational faith, autonomy, and freedom of expression in civil society, which he brought together into a coherent and bold argument, expanding Kantian premises in a way that closely resembled John Stuart Mill's defense of toleration four decades later.[59]

Kunitsyn's starting point was the claim that one's existence as a moral being capable of setting one's own ends requires the ability to think freely and search for truth in one's own way.

> To embrace [something as] the truth [*uverit'sia v istine*], a person has to explore the proof for it through his own reasoning. The conviction that [something] is true depends not on a person's will but on the strength of the arguments directed toward reason. Therefore, a person cannot be forced to accept something as true against his own conviction.
>
> (235)

57 See Paul W. Werth, *The Tsar's Foreign Faiths: Toleration and the Fate of Religious Freedom in Imperial Russia* (Oxford: Oxford University Press, 2014), 56.

58 G. M. Hamburg, "Religious Toleration in Russian Thought, 1520–1825," *Kritika: Explorations in Russian and Eurasian History* 13, no. 3 (2012): 515–59, here at 555. See also Werth, *The Tsar's Foreign Faiths,* 107.

59 Kant did not produce a specific work on toleration, but the idea of tolerance is implicit in his concept of freedom. See Joaquin Abellan, "Immanuel Kant: Tolerance Seen as Respect," in *Paradoxes of Religious Toleration in Early Modern Political Thought*, ed. John Christian Laursen and María José Villaverde (Lanham, MD: Lexington Books, 2012), 207–20, here at 215–19.

This formulation resembled Mill's argument in *On Liberty* that a person should be free to subject any accepted truth or opinion to intellectual scrutiny.[60] Like Mill, Kunitsyn asserted that "erring against the common opinion is not a crime." Punishment for errors of this sort is "unfair and self-defeating.... An assumption that a person might mislead others should not pose an obstacle to the free expression of opinion, for ... the individual's right to express his thoughts is indisputable" (235).[61]

Applied to religion, the innate right to freedom, according to Kunitsyn, presupposes religious toleration in the broadest sense, limited only by the principle of mutual freedom. He emphasized that freedom of conscience ensures the sincerity of faith by enabling the individual to explore and practice religion in his own way. "The right to freedom of religion," Kunitsyn wrote, "is based on the right to the freedom of thought and action," so long as the freedom of other individuals is preserved. "The virtue and holiness of religion consists in its ability to encourage and sustain morality. Only a person himself can judge the degree to which [religion] plays a role" in his moral development. Faith, he argued, is not a matter of accepting beliefs through an act of will; it comes from autonomous reasoning about religious teaching which allows the individual to internalize his religious beliefs. This process inevitably leads to differences in interpretation, which should be protected, according to Kunitsyn, under the freedom of expression. In the absence of absolute certainty about religious dogmas (or any other beliefs), who "can assume total infallibility and the exclusive right to present their beliefs as the law for everyone else?" "Any persecution on behalf of religion," Kunitsyn concluded, "is an unlawful act of violence." "Persecution only encourages and strengthens the most superstitious sects. Tolerance is the best weapon for fighting against schisms, for it gives people time to reflect upon their religious dogmas" (237). Kunitsyn added that "inner religious worship," expressed in the form of "devotion, love, and gratitude" to "divinity," belongs to "internal" acts and "by its nature cannot violate other people's rights.... External worship, too, is not subject to any limitations, if it allows the lawful freedom of other people to be preserved" (238).[62]

While Kunitsyn was not the first Russian thinker to ground religious toleration in innate human rights, it is fair to say that his position was the most robust and inclusive ever presented in Russia. The argument from human fallibility, which Kunitsyn invoked so forcefully to buttress his defense of toleration, was rare even in European thought during this period.[63] It was only in Mill's *On Liberty* that the notion of fallibility would acquire proper recognition.[64]

60 See Mill, *The Basic Writings*, 19–21.

61 See ibid., 18.

62 See ibid., 14–15. Mill also distinguished between internal and external spheres of liberty and set the principle of harm as the only limit to toleration.

63 See Vicky A. Spencer, "Human Fallibility and Locke's Doctrine of Toleration," in *Toleration in Comparative Perspective*, ed. Vicky A. Spencer (Lanham, MD: Lexington Books, 2018), 41–59.

64 Mill, *The Basic Writings*, 25, 58.

Natural Law and the censorship regime

Kunitsyn's trouble with censorship began when he decided to present his book to the emperor. In such cases, the rules required an approval from the Academic Committee of the Main School Administration, which functioned as the highest censorship organ at that time.[65] The fact that Kunitsyn deemed his book worthy of the tsar's attention underscores how little he anticipated any trouble for his ideas. However, by 1820, when he made the submission, the signs of upcoming conservative changes in Russia were already visible. Rooted in the post-Napoleonic reaction against Enlightenment ideas of rationalism and universally applicable principles of justice, the return to conservative policies in education was launched by the minister of education, Aleksandr Golitsyn, who came to believe that "the past century spread the harmful idea about the irreconcilable enmity between religion and knowledge.... For this," he argued, "Europe paid with rivers of blood and tears."[66]

Golitsyn's vision of how to reconcile faith and enlightenment was spelled out in more concrete terms by A. S. Sturdza, the tsar's analyst of foreign affairs, who shared Golitsyn's concern about the erosion of religious foundations in the Russian system of education. According to the "Instruction" which he wrote in 1818, the goal of "establishing in Russia ... harmony between Christian piety, intellectual enlightenment, and the duties of citizenship" was to be achieved through the revision of the academic curriculum and closer censorship of textbooks.[67] The first calls to restrict the teaching of natural law were voiced in 1819 after the review of Kazan University, which was found deficient according to the criteria supplied by the "Instruction."[68] That same year, courses on natural law and philosophy were removed from the curriculum of Russian gymnasia, and the discussion about censorship reform began.[69]

In June 1820, when Kunitsyn's *Natural Law* came under review, the censor Dmitrii Runich judged the book entirely contrary to the guidelines provided by Sturdza. It is "not only dangerous," he argued, "but also destructive with respect to the foundations of faith"—an apparent reference to Kunitsyn's argument concerning the right to explore religious truths through a process of reflection and reasoning.[70] Runich was appalled that Kunitsyn proclaimed reason as "the only

65 *Sbornik postanovlenii po Ministerstvu narodnogo prosveshcheniia*, 1:896.

66 Quoted from F. A. Petrov, *Rossiiskie universitety v pervoi polovine XIX veka: Formirovanie sistemy universitetskogo obrazovaniia*, 4 vols. (Moscow: Gosudarstvennyi istoricheskii muzei, 1996–2003), 2, pt. 3: 70.

67 *Sbornik rasporiazhenii po Ministerstvu narodnogo prosveshcheniia,* 17 vols. (St. Petersburg: Ministerstvo narodnogo prosveshcheniia, 1866–1905), 1:321–33.

68 See Flynn, *The University Reform*, 84–103; Berest, *The Emergence of Russian Liberalism*, 163–64.

69 Institut russkoi literatury (IRLI [Pushkinskii dom]), f. 263, op. 3, d. 6, 1.62; S. V. Rozhdestvenskii, *Istoricheskii obzor deiatel'nosti ministerstva narodnogo prosveshcheniia 1802–1902* (St. Petersburg: Ministerstvo narodnogo prosveshcheniia, 1902), 118.

70 IRLI, f. 263, op. 3, d. 12, l. 24.

source of motivation in a human being" and that he imputed "a code of rights to some natural man." It was "the notorious Rousseau" who, according to Runich, introduced all these "pernicious and false ideas," while "Marat was nothing but a sincere and practical follower of this science."[71] In February 1821, Kunitsyn's book was officially banned as "contrary to the truths of Christianity and tending toward overthrowing all family and state ties." Some of the committee members were more moderate than Runich, but none raised their voice in Kunitsyn's defense.[72]

Within the next few months, Runich proceeded to review textbooks on natural law written by both Russian and German scholars, hoping to convince the tsar that natural law should be removed from the university curriculum altogether. However, Alexander I hesitated. He asked Count Laval to inquire about the methods of teaching philosophy in France. The report indicated that France exercised a "cautious and wise" policy of supervision rather than banning philosophy courses altogether. Laval's personal opinion was that philosophy could still be useful if presented "in a monarchical spirit" and with due attention to religious truths.[73] During this period of uncertainty, the textbooks by Kant's followers were replaced with the time-tested manual by Baumeister as well as some newer Russian works hurriedly written in the spirit of Sturdza's "Instruction."[74] The final resolution came under the more conservative Nicholas I, when the decision was made, in 1833, to terminate the teaching of natural law in Russian universities.[75]

Kunitsyn after his expulsion

Kunitsyn was dismissed from St. Petersburg University shortly after the announcement of the Academic Committee's verdict. His abrupt dismissal at the height of his career became widely known in the capital.[76] Pushkin responded to it with a sarcastic "Message to the Censor," ridiculing the censors' effort to present Kunitsyn as a "Marat."[77] Nikolai Turgenev's brother, Aleksandr, hoped that the curator of the St. Petersburg Educational District, Sergei Uvarov, would interfere to save "not only … Kunitsyn but scholarship itself from the attacks" of such reactionaries as Runich.[78] Uvarov indeed attempted to intercede for Kunitsyn, but to no avail. Emboldened, Runich proceeded to investigate St. Petersburg

71 IRLI, f. 263, op. 3, d. 12, l. 27 ob.

72 Liubavin, *Litseiskie uchitelia Pushkina*, 44–45.

73 IRLI, f. 263, op. 3, d. 6, l. 38.

74 Berest, *The Emergence of Russian Liberalism*, 176–78; Pustarnakov, *Universitetskaia filosofiia v Rossii*, 131–37, 527, 634.

75 *Zhurnal Ministerstva narodnogo prosveshcheniia*, 1834, no. 1: v–vi.

76 See A. I. Turgenev, *Khronika russkogo. Dnevniki (1825–1826 gg.)* (Moscow and Leningrad: Izdatel'stvo "Nauka," 1964), 435.

77 Meilakh, *Pushkin i ego epokha*, 70.

78 *Dekabrist N. I. Turgenev*, 65.

University. As a result, in 1821, four more professors were dismissed for spreading "pernicious" ideas.[79]

Kunitsyn's reaction to the condemnation of his *Natural Law* was one of indignant astonishment. When the ministry began removing his book from public libraries, Golitsyn realized that many copies were missing. In a report requested by Golitsyn, Kunitsyn wrote unapologetically: "having published [my] book according to the established laws and with a pure conscience, I did not restrain myself in giving it away."[80] It turned out that many students at the lycée were allowed to take the book with them when they graduated, for which Golitsyn strictly reprimanded the director. In the end, the ministry stopped short of confiscating the book from private libraries. Copies sold in bookstores were also impossible to retrieve.[81]

Kunitsyn's dismissal did not bring his career to an end, although it did put an end to his philosophical writing. In July 1821, with the help of Nikolai Turgenev, he obtained a position in the chancellery of the Ministry of Finance. In 1826, Kunitsyn's name came up during the investigation of the Decembrist uprising, when some of the accused testified that they had taken Kunitsyn's public courses on natural law and political economy in 1819–20.[82] The convicted Decembrists included two of Kunitsyn's former students from the lycée, who ended up in Siberia for twenty years.[83] However, the investigation had no impact on Kunitsyn's career. The authorities must have understood that the education of the future Decembrists was not much different than that of many loyal government officials, whose qualifying examinations had included the disciplines of natural law and political economy in those years.

The codification project

In 1826 Kunitsyn was appointed to work on the legal codification project which was taken over from the Codification Committee by the newly established Second Section of His Imperial Majesty's Own Chancellery.[84] The project had a long but intermittent history. Throughout the eighteenth century, there had been several attempts to collect and order Russian laws issued since the Law Code of 1649, but none of the efforts came to fruition. In 1801, Alexander I reorganized the committee created by Paul I in 1796 and entrusted it with the task of codify-

79 See Cynthia H. Whittaker, *The Origins of Modern Russian Education: An Intellectual Biography of Count Sergei Uvarov, 1786–1855* (DeKalb: Northern Illinois University Press, 1984), 82–83; Flynn, *The University Reform*, 110.

80 Quoted from Liubavin, *Litseiskie uchitelia Pushkina*, 53.

81 TsGIA SPb, f. 11, op. 1, d. 148, l. 10. See also Liubavin, *Litseiskie uchitelia Pushkina*, 56.

82 *Vosstanie dekabristov: Materialy po istorii vosstaniia dekabristov. Dela Verkhovnogo ugolovnogo suda i sledstvennoi komissii*, vol. 1, ed. M. N. Pokrovskii (Moscow and Leningrad: Gosudarstvennoe izdatel'stvo, 1925), 226; vol. 18, ed. Nechkina, 164.

83 M. Rudenskaia and S. Rudenskaia, *Oni uchilis s Pushkinym* (Leningrad: Lenizdat, 1976), 67.

84 TsGIA SPb, f. 11, op. 1, d. 3727, l. 10.

ing Russian laws.[85] Considering that many laws were issued in manuscript form, codification was a mammoth task that required extensive archival research. More importantly, in Russia, where laws were issued not only by the autocrat but also by various government agencies, codification was greatly complicated by uncertainty regarding the selection criteria and by the absence of "fundamental laws" (*korennye zakony*) defining the scope of monarchical power.[86]

Kunitsyn was aware of these challenges long before his appointment. In 1819, he published a series of articles in *Syn Otechestva*, criticizing the committee's approach to compiling its Systematic Digest of Active Laws of the Russian Empire with the Foundations of Law Derived from Them (*Sistematicheskii svod sushchestvuiushchikh zakonov Rossiiskoi Imperii s osnovaniiami prava iz onykh izvlechennymi*), which began to be issued in 1815 as the first stage of the project. Each volume was meant to be accompanied by the Foundations of Russian Law (*Osnovaniia Rossiiskogo prava*) published separately.[87] Kunitsyn focused on the first volume of the Foundations, arguing that some of the foundational laws were missing, including, most importantly, the Charter on the Election of Tsar Mikhail Fedorovich issued in 1613,[88] and Peter the Great's decree of 1722 specifying the duty of the Senate to "report to the Emperor" regarding cases that require "new laws" and laws that are "vague."[89] He also pointed out, once again referring to Peter the Great's legislation, that the Foundations omitted "many decrees that made it clear that *laws must be implemented according to their exact formulation and meaning, impartially and without regard to social standing* [*ne smotria na litsa sil'nykh*]."[90]

A response to Kunitsyn's daring criticism came the same year from Baron Gustav Rozenkampf, who was in charge of the committee at that time. He sternly reminded Kunitsyn that the committee had "a sacred duty to stick to the letter of the law and does not allow itself ... to enter into abstract reasoning [*otvlechennye umozreniia*] and subtleties ... which are not only useless but also pernicious."[91] It was clear that Rozenkampf found such public discussion of the committee's

85 See William Benton Whisenhunt, *In Search of Legality: Mikhail M. Speranskii and the Codification of Russian Law* (New York: Columbia University Press, 2001), 49–52; I. V. Ruzhitskaia, *Zakonodatel'naia deiatel'nost' v tsarstvovanie Imperatora Nikolaia I* (Moscow: Institut Rossiiskoi Istorii RAN, 2005), 152–54.

86 Raeff, *Michael Speransky*, 321–22; Whisenhunt, *In Search of Legality*, 70–73; S. V. Kodan, "Popytki sozdaniia Osnovnykh zakonov Rossiiskoi imperii v politike, ideologii i iuridicheskoi praktike Rossiiskogo gosudarstva (XVIII-nachalo XIX vv.)," *Pravo i politika*, 2012, no. 3: 560–69, here at 563.

87 Kodan, "Popytki sozdaniia Osnovnykh zakonov," 565.

88 A. Kunitsyn, "Zamechaniia na knigu: Osnovaniia rossiiskogo prava, izdannuiu Komissiei sostavleniia zakonov," *Syn Otechestva* 51, no. 6 (1819): 241–52, here at 244–45.

89 A. Kunitsyn, "Pribavlenie pervoe k zamechaniiam na Osnovaniia rossiskogo prava (okonchanie)," *Syn Otechestva* 55, no. 34 (1819): 3–18, here at 15–17.

90 Ibid., 12.

91 Baron G. Rozenkampf, "Otvet na zamechaniia na knigu: Osnovaniia rossiiskogo prava," *Syn Otechestva* 52, no. 12 (1819): 241–72, here at 246.

work entirely inappropriate, even though the author had "good intentions," as he conceded. If someone wished to make comments on the project, Rozenkampf noted, they should "refer their comments directly" to the committee for further consideration (241).

With the arrival of Nicholas I, the committee was transformed into the Second Section and its work was significantly expedited. After the Decembrist uprising of 1825, the new tsar was eager to strengthen the monarchy's prestige and legitimacy, and one way to do that was by bringing order to Russian laws and the judicial system.[92] In need of educated cadres, the tsar did not hesitate to enlist Kunitsyn and two other purged professors from St. Petersburg University to work on the project.[93] Unfortunately, Kunitsyn's service career is the least documented period of his life, with most of the information coming from his brief official file preserved in the archives. From what we know, his diligence and expertise as a member of the project were amply rewarded. In 1830, Kunitsyn was promoted to the rank of actual state councilor (*deistvitel'nyi statskii sovetnik*), followed by a reward of hereditary land ownership nine years later.[94] However, it appears that in the atmosphere of reinforced censorship and under the watchful eye of the tsar, Kunitsyn was no longer in a position to voice his independent opinion on the project's proceedings.

As part of his work for the project, Kunitsyn was commissioned in 1835 to compile ecclesiastical laws issued by the Holy Synod since its formation in 1721. Kunitsyn completed the work by 1836 and was rewarded with a lavish personal gift from Nicholas I.[95] But the tsar postponed publication of the collection because of the Synod's objections. The church authorities reasoned that

> it would not be convenient to make public various decrees from the old days rendered in cases and events which do not serve to strengthen due respect for representatives of the church, and which may also inspire views contrary to church teaching on various church ordinances which are still in effect.[96]

It was not until 1865, during the Great Reforms of Alexander II, that the task of compiling ecclesiastical laws was taken up again at the behest of D. A. Tolstoi, the new chief procurator of the Holy Synod. Kunitsyn's work, discovered in the Synod's archive, served as one of the sources for the new project.[97]

92 See Tatiana Borisova, "The Digest of Laws of the Russian Empire: The Phenomenon of Autocratic Empire," *Law and History Review* 30, no. 3 (2012): 901–25, here at 906–07.

93 See Ruzhitskaia, *Zakonodatel'naia deiatel'nost v tsarstvovanie Imperatora Nikolaia I*, 211. After returning from exile, Speranskii became "the main driving wheel" of the committee, but the official chairman was Mikhail Balug'ianskii, Kunitsyn's former teacher and colleague. See Raeff, *Michael Speransky*, 320.

94 TsGIA SPb, f. 11, op. 1, d. 3727, ll. 11, 13.

95 TsGIA SPb, f. 11, op. 1, d. 3727, l. 14.

96 Quoted from P. M. Maikov, *O svode zakonov Rossiiskoi imperii*, ed. V. A. Tomsinov (Moscow: Izdatel'stvo "Zertsalo," 2006), 68.

97 Kunitsyn is credited in the introduction (unpaginated) of the first volume of the project, *Polnoe sobranie postanovlenii i rasporiazhenii po vedomstvu Pravoslavnogo ispovedaniia Rossiiskoi*

In 1840, Kunitsyn was appointed director of the Department of Foreign Confessions, but he died unexpectedly a few months later.[98] He was survived by his wife, whose name and origin remain unknown.

Conclusion

Looking at Kunitsyn's life before and after his academic trial, one is struck by the twists of fate he experienced. In a curious way, Kunitsyn's dismissal from the university allowed him to escape the humiliating fate of professors who survived the purges but had to adjust their views and lectures to the new atmosphere of suspicion and control. Students could not help noticing the gaps in their professors' lectures and the demoralizing effect the new prohibitions had on once-enthusiastic teachers. Yet for all Kunitsyn's newfound success as a government official, the choice of a career path—an important individual freedom according to his philosophy—was not entirely his any longer. In retrospect, even more unfortunate was the fact that the confiscation of Kunitsyn's book consigned his ideas to oblivion for many years, interrupting the discourse on natural law and individual rights in Russian thought.

Kunitsyn's Kantian-inspired defense of human dignity, individual rights, and religious toleration places him firmly in the tradition of Russian philosophical humanism. As Gary Hamburg and Randall Poole have argued,

> Russian philosophers in the long nineteenth century concerned themselves almost obsessively with the importance of human dignity, conceived either as an intrinsic property of the individual or as a project to be realized as the final goal of social development.[99]

The beginning of this tradition has been located in the 1830s and 1840s, the time of the Slavophile-Westernizer controversy. However, it is fair to say that Kunitsyn was an important harbinger of the humanist tradition in Russia, even though his ideas, muted by conservative reaction, did not reach a wide audience. Moreover, as a thinker who strongly believed in the rule of law, he exemplified the liberal strand of Russian humanism, which, for a variety of historical and philosophical reasons, remained underdeveloped in Russia.[100] Despite his forced

---

Imperii, vol. 1: *1721* (St. Petersburg: V Sinodal'noi tipografii, 1869). See also Chapter 1 of the present volume.

98 TsGIA SPb, f. 11, op. 1, d. 3727, l. 14.

99 G. M. Hamburg and Randall A. Poole, "Introduction: The Humanist Tradition in Russian Philosophy," in *A History of Russian Philosophy 1830–1930: Faith, Reason, and the Defense of Human Dignity*, ed. G. M. Hamburg and Randall A. Poole (Cambridge: Cambridge University Press, 2010), 1–23, here at 4. See also Derek Offord, "Alexander Herzen," in *A History of Russian Philosophy 1830–1930*, ed. Hamburg and Poole, 52–68, at 66.

100 On the distinction between liberal and illiberal currents within Russian humanism, see Hamburg and Poole, "Introduction: The Humanist Tradition in Russian Philosophy," 12–13.

retirement from philosophical writing, Kunitsyn's name remained in the public memory, in part due to Pushkin's famous quatrain to his teacher:

> To Kunitsyn—the tribute of heart and vine!
> He created us, he sparked our fire,
> He laid the foundations,
> He lit the light.[101]

101 A. S. Pushkin, *Sobranie sochinenii v desiati tomakh* (Moscow: "Khudozhestvennaia literatura," 1974–78), 2:553 (trans. Julia Berest).

5 Konstantin Pobedonostsev

Law, religion, and Russian conservatism

Gregory L. Freeze

Biography

Konstantin Petrovich Pobedonostsev (1827–1907) was a highly prominent—and highly controversial—political figure in late imperial Russia.[1] Home-schooled by his father (a priest's son who opted out of a clerical career and became a literature professor at Moscow University), Konstantin matriculated in the newly established Imperial School of Jurisprudence for the elite and well-connected. After graduating in 1846, he received an appointment to serve in the Moscow branch of the Senate, the supreme judicial organ. For the next fifteen years he not only oversaw several central provinces but also conducted research on the history of Russian law.

In 1859, amid plans to emancipate the serfs and embark on the other Great Reforms under Alexander II (r. 1855–81), Pobedonostsev published a study about the manifold shortcomings in Russian civil procedure.[2] Moscow University accepted that work as a master's thesis and appointed him to teach civil procedure, which in turn led to a lithograph of his lectures.[3] His publications and apparent interest in reform elicited an invitation to serve on the commission that eventually produced the very liberal and very Western-oriented Judicial Reform of 1864, featuring such provisions as juries, publicity, and the irremovability of judges.[4] The

1 This chapter is part of a project supported by the Russian Science Foundation (No. 19–18–00482: "Entangled Histories: Russia and the Holy See, 1917–1958").

The historiography on Pobedonostsev is stupendous. For a review, emphasizing Western and émigré literature, see Tom E. Dykstra, "Evil Genius and Guardian Angel: The Image of Constantine Pobedonostsev in Russian Historiography," *Symposion: A Journal of Russian Thought* 7–12 (2002–7): 81–105. For the ever-expanding post-Soviet scholarship, see A. Iu. Polunov, *K. P. Pobedonostsev v obshchestvenno-politicheskoi i dukhovnoi zhizni Rossii* (Moscow: ROSSPEN, 2010), 3–24.

2 K. P. Pobedonostsev, "O reformakh v grazhdanskom sudoproizvodstve," published in *Russkii vestnik* in 1859 and reprinted in Pobedonostsev, *Iuridicheskie proizvedeniia*, ed. V. A. Tomsinov (Moscow: Izdatel'stvo "Zertsalo," 2012), 219–313.

3 K. P. Pobedonostsev, *Grazhdanskoe sudoproizvodstvo. Lektsii*, lithograph (Moscow, 1863).

4 For detailed accounts, see M. G. Korotich, *Samoderzhavie i sudebnaia reforma 1864 goda v Rossii* (Voronezh: Izdatel'stvo Voronezhkogo universiteta, 1989); Richard S. Wortman, *The Development of a Russian Legal Consciousness* (Chicago: The University of Chicago Press,

DOI: 10.4324/9781003017097-5

official records do not fully document Pobedonostsev's role,[5] but his diary and correspondence indicate growing discord with the Western, liberal direction that prevailed in the commission. In 1861 Pobedonostsev also began serving as a tutor for the tsar's successor, Nikolai Aleksandrovich (1843–65), whom he accompanied on a tour through the Russian interior that gave both of them a firsthand exposure to the "real Russia" outside the two capitals.[6] After Nikolai's tragic and premature death, Pobedonostsev became the tutor for the new successors—first the future Alexander III (r. 1881–94) and then Alexander's son Nicholas II (r. 1894–1917).[7]

A dyed-in-the-wool Muscovite, Pobedonostsev nonetheless moved to St. Petersburg in 1865 to perform his tutorial duties and to serve in the central government, first in the Senate (1868) and then the State Council (1872). He also became a voice of Russian conservativism, not only inside state offices but also in public discourse, publishing some forty—anonymous—articles in the conservative press, texts that he later recycled in his famous and widely translated *Moskovskii Sbornik* (Moscow compilation) of 1896.

The 1870s were indeed turbulent, violent times, witnessing not only the rise of revolutionary terrorism but also growing opposition among the privileged and propertied classes. All of that impelled the state to rethink the Great Reforms and even contemplate convoking a public advisory body. In the midst of this "crisis of autocracy,"[8] Alexander II appointed Pobedonostsev to be the chief procurator (*ober-prokuror*) of the Holy Synod (April 24, 1880), a post that he would occupy for a quarter century. In late 1880, he joined the Committee of Ministers, where he became a leading critic of the Great Reforms and of political concessions that he castigated as a "constitution." On March 1, 1881, the very day that Alexander II approved the plan for a consultative body, terrorists made good on their vow to assassinate the tsar. Pobedonostsev famously persuaded Alexander III to reject his father's last measure and helped draft the manifesto of April 29, 1881, reaf-

---

1976, 2010); Friedhelm Berthold Kaiser, *Die russische Justizreform von 1864* (Leiden: Brill, 1972).

5 A. E. Nol'de offered the classic analysis in his *K. P. Pobedonostsev i sudebnaia reforma* (Petrograd: Obshchestvennaia pol'za, 1915). Traditional scholarship portrayed the young Pobedonostsev as liberal, with the rightward turn coming later, e.g., Robert F. Byrnes, *Pobedonostsev: His Life and Thought* (Bloomington: Indiana University Press, 1968), 69–71. Recent scholarship, however, discerns a conservative orientation even in the early phase, enhanced by his experience on the reform commission, e.g., A. S. Kharitonov, "K. P. Pobedonostsev: konservativnaia kritika 'Sudebnykh Ustavov' 1864 g.," *Probely v rossiiskom zakonodatel'stve*, 2012, no. 4: 160–63.

6 Pobedonostsev and fellow tutor I. K. Babst described the trip in a joint publication: *Pis'ma o puteshestvii Gosudaria naslednika Tsesarevicha po Rossii ot Peterburga do Kryma* (Moscow: v tipografii Gracheva i komp., 1864).

7 F. I. Melent'ev, "Formirovanie predstavlenii naslednikov prestola o Rossii v epokhu velikikh reform" (kand. diss., Moskovskii gosudarstvennyi universitet, 2018).

8 Peter A. Zaionchkovskii, *Russian Autocracy in Crisis, 1878–1882*, ed. and trans. Gary M. Hamburg (Gulf Breeze, FL.: Academic International Press, 1979).

firming unlimited autocracy. The liberal ministers resigned forthwith, inaugurating a new era of counterreforms.

Pobedonostsev was highly prominent in the early 1880s and earned a reputation as the leading spokesman of unrelenting conservatism. His rhetoric and court connections encouraged contemporaries to exaggerate his influence, which in fact largely vanished after the mid-1880s, save a short interlude when Nicholas II came to the throne in 1894.[9] But Pobedonostsev had an uncanny knack for making enemies, not only among liberals but even among conservatives, including most of the bishops with whom he worked as chief procurator of the Holy Synod.[10] By the turn of the century, liberation and revolutionary movements were again besieging the state and, in the 1905 Revolution, forced Nicholas II to issue the October Manifesto (October 17), granting civil liberties and creating a parliament. Forced to resign two days later, Pobedonostsev withdrew from public life, had little social or political contact, and died quietly on March 10, 1907.

Throughout his long and tempestuous career, Pobedonostsev had the unbending support of his wife, Ekaterina Aleksandrovna (1848–1932). In contrast to her husband's modest origins, she descended from an illustrious family (Engel'gardt), which had kinship ties to the Catherinean favorite Grigorii Potemkin and substantial holdings in land and serfs (some two thousand serfs in her father's case). Pobedonostsev, twenty-two years her senior, met her during a provincial trip at a time when she was only seven years old. He initially provided some informal guidance on reading, a relationship that eventually turned romantic and led to their marriage in 1866.[11] The pair never had children of their own, but in 1897 did adopt a foundling (Marfa), to whom Pobedonostsev was attached. The couple were also generous philanthropists, devoting not only funds but much time and energy to a teachers' school for girls at a St. Petersburg monastery. Indeed, Pobedonostsev chose an adjacent cemetery as his last resting place, and his wife joined him there when she died in 1932.[12]

Institutional context

Pobedonostsev thus pursued a double career—serving both in the state (initially at the provincial level, later in central organs in St. Petersburg) and as the chief lay

9 I. V. Lukoianov, "Imperator Nikolai II i K. P. Pobedonostsev: trudnosti otnoshenii uchenika i uchitelia," in *Konstantin Petrovich Pobedonostsev: myslitel', uchenyi, chelovek,* ed. V. V. Vedernikov (St. Petersburg: Izdatel'stvo Politekhnicheskogo universiteta, 2007), 52–59.

10 General A. A. Kireev welcomed Pobedonostsev's appointment as chief procurator but quickly became disillusioned. See M. V. Medovarov, "K. P. Pobedonostsev glazami A. A. Kireeva," *Klio,* 2012, no. 9: 113–17.

11 Pobedonostsev's personal archival collection includes abundant materials on his marital life. These include his letters to Ekaterina in 1860–65 (Rossiiskii gosudarstvennyi istoricheskii arkhiv [RGIA], f. 1574, op. 1, d. 53), a poem dedicated to her in 1857 (d. 23), her letters to him in 1865–92 (d. 103), and her memoirs (d. 29).

12 For a brief overview, see A. Iu. Polunov, *Pobedonostsev, Russkii Torkvemada* (Moscow: Molodaia gvardiia, 2017), 40–46.

official in the Russian Orthodox Church (1880–1905). In his years overseeing the Moscow office of the Senate, he developed a hands-on and unflattering picture of everyday tsarist administration and law. Convinced that jurists must not only know theory but also have practical experience, he took a keen interest in legal history and included a praxis dimension in his teaching at Moscow University. His many years as tutor of the tsar's successors were important: he cemented strong ties at court (especially helpful for someone with a modest genealogy) and helped instill conservative views in the last two tsars. The court connection also enabled a brilliant career, culminating in his appointment to the Committee of Ministers (October 1880) that provided an important venue to address sundry secular issues—from poll tax reform to university statutes, from local governance to foreign policy. By challenging bureaucratic elites in the Committee of Ministers, he earned the eternal enmity of many. As a public symbol of reaction, he ranked high among the targets for terrorists—who repeatedly tried, but failed, to assassinate him.[13]

As chief procurator of the Holy Synod, Pobedonostsev was responsible for overseeing the church, its administration, and its relationship with the state. He had a well-earned reputation for personal piety and had even been offered this position in 1865, which, for family reasons, he declined. When it was again tendered in 1880, he eagerly accepted, convinced that he could repair the problems arising in the church from the Great Reforms of the 1860s. From Pobedonostsev's perspective, there were three main problems: (a) the new statutes for seminaries and academies in 1867–69 entailing changes in curriculum and management; (b) the parish reform of 1869 that merged small parishes and reduced clerical staffs to make them economically viable; and (c) the decline of parish schools in favor of state and zemstvo schools. In all three areas, Pobedonostsev enjoyed considerable success: by 1885 he had persuaded the Holy Synod to rewrite the reform statutes and the state to help fund the initiatives.

Because of his sheer longevity in office, far longer than any other chief procurator—indeed, longer than *any* other minister—contemporaries and historians long assumed that Pobedonostsev exercised extraordinary power over the church. However, he was not the "head of the Synod," as one historian claimed.[14] Pobedonostsev had limited authority; he could only coax, not coerce, bishops to do his bidding. As he wrote to a close associate: "Juridically, I do not have any kind of power to give orders in the church and its domain. It is necessary to bring everything before the Synod."[15] Nor could he issue directives to diocesan

13 See Pobedonostsev's account of a foiled attempt in June 1905, in K. P. Pobedonostsev, "Mat' moiu, rodimuiu Rossiiu, uroduiut. Pis'ma K. P. Pobedonostseva S. D. Sheremetevu," *Istochnik*, 1996, no. 6: 8–9.

14 A. G. Galkin, "Sudebnaia reforma 1864 g. v kontekste obshchestvenno-politicheskoi zhizni poreformennoi Rossii (1864–1904 gg.)" (dokt. diss., Moskovskii gosudarstvennyi pedagogicheskii universitet, 2011), 148.

15 S. I. Alekseeva, *Sviateishii Sinod v sisteme vysshikh i tsentral'nykh gosudarstvennykh uchrezhdenii poreformennoi Rossii 1856–1904 g.* (St. Petersburg: "Nauka," 2006), 30.

bishops; time and again he turned aside requests to intervene in diocesan affairs, with the candid explanation that the bishops were a difficult, independent lot, and jealously defended their prerogatives and power. Initially the chief procurator had some rapport with ranking prelates, but those relations steadily deteriorated. Even when the two sides agreed that something must be done, the Synod and diocesan bishops resisted Pobedonostsev's proposals.

More striking still, from the mid-1880s Pobedonostsev made few initiatives and concentrated on implementing measures adopted earlier—expanding the network of parish churches, tightening discipline in seminaries and academies, and above all building a large network of new parish schools. Here he had notable success, especially in persuading the state to fund a tenfold increase in parish schools. But he also stepped on many toes and, despite his conservatism and piety, turned many prelates into bitter adversaries. In 1905, the presiding metropolitan in the Synod, Antonii (Vadkovskii), colluded with ranking state officials to recommend radical structural reform in the church, including reestablishment of the patriarchate (to neutralize the chief procurator's role) and convocation of a church council (*pomestnyi sobor*) to address the many issues that had accumulated in the church. Pobedonostsev managed to persuade Nicholas II to delay the council as inexpedient amid the current revolutionary upheaval, but he could only defer, not deflect, the mounting demands for fundamental reform in the church.

Religious views and practices

Pobedonostsev's personal piety was indeed authentic and intense: he filled his diary with religious asides and affirmations, preferred to spend high holidays at a favorite monastery,[16] confessed that his love "for church services borders on a passion,"[17] and read widely in religious literature. Indeed, he not only read but wrote devotional tracts. His very first work, begun in 1856, described personal experiences on twenty-three church holidays. Later published as *The Lord's Holidays*, it was reprinted multiple times before the Revolution of 1917 and again in post-Soviet Russia.[18] Although devoted to Orthodoxy, Pobedonostsev not only read but also translated non-Orthodox texts; his first, appearing in 1869, was Thomas à Kempis's *The Imitation of Christ.* His preface to the translation explicitly prioritized faith over dogma:

> The book, *The Imitation of Christ,* undoubtedly does not have the authority of the church if one looks at it from a dogmatic point of view; however, there

16 Pobedonostsev to E. F. Tiutcheva, March 31,1877, in O. Maiorova, "Pishu ia tol'ko dlia vas. Pis'ma K. P. Pobedonostseva k sestram Tiutchevym," *Novyi mir,* 1994, no. 3: letter 9.

17 Pobedonostsev to E. F. Tiutcheva, June 12, 1878 (Nauchno-issledovatel'skii otdel rukopisei Rossiiskoi gosudarstvennoi biblioteki [NIOR RGB], f. 230, k. 4408, d. 13, l. 21 ob.).

18 Pobedonostsev, *Prazdniki Gospodni* (St. Petersburg: Tipografiia A. Benke, 1893).

> are many books that lack dogmatic authority, but nonetheless constitute the favorite reading of simple and pious people.[19]

He later claimed that Alexander II kept this translation at his bedside and prized it greatly.[20]

After the late 1880s Pobedonostsev turned his attention primarily to religious texts. Although he still published historical and legal texts, these actually represented work he did much earlier and often bore a brief preface confirming that they consisted of old research and notes. His new writings, from the 1890s and later, were mainly religious tracts of one kind or another, with the explicit goal of inspiring and edifying the *prostoi narod* (simple people). In his mind, at least, the believers—not institutions, clergy, or dogma—constitute the real church. In that sense, he was what the distinguished theologian G. V. Florovskii called a *narodnik* (populist)—not, of course, the revolutionary variety, but one who identified with the mass of peasant believers.[21] It was to them that he now devoted his writing talents. Scripture, not dogma, was most important, an idea that inspired him to provide a fresh translation of the New Testament—a central preoccupation of the last fifteen years of his life. His goal was to produce a translation closer to Church Slavonic than the official Synodal Bible published in 1876.[22] In his view, the Synodal text was gratuitously vernacular, needlessly replacing familiar Church Slavonic expressions with modern Russian, thereby increasing the gap between the traditional liturgical texts one heard in church and what one read in the Synodal text. His aim was to serve the needs of simple believers who had traditionally based their faith on church services, and who were only now becoming literate.

Despite opposition from ranking prelates, who regarded the Synodal text as the obligatory standard, in 1892 Pobedonostsev solicited commentaries from New Testament specialists at the ecclesiastical academies,[23] and three years later

19 Foma Kempiiskii, *O podrazhanii Khristu*, 6th ed. (St. Petersburg: Sinodal'naia tipografiia, 1896), v.

20 Pobedonostsev to Alexander III, *K. P. Pobedonostsev i ego korrespondenty,* 2 vols. (Minsk: Kharvest, 2003), 2:532 (February 7, 1893).

21 G. V. Florovskii, *Puti russkogo bogosloviia*, 2nd ed. (Paris: YMCA Press, 1981), 410. Florovskii's brief analysis, which treats Pobedonostsev's popular Orthodoxy negatively, receives a fuller exposition in Thomas C. Sorenson, "The Thought and Policies of Konstantin P. Pobedonostsev" (PhD diss., University of Washington, 1977).

22 On the contested history of Russian Bible translations, see Stephen K. Batalden, *Russian Bible Wars* (Cambridge: Cambridge University Press, 2013). Criticism of the Synodal Bible has not disappeared; the need to correct, if not replace, the Synodal Bible is currently under official consideration by the Moscow Patriarchate. For an overview in 2013 by a ranking patriarchal official and chairman of the Synodal Biblical and Theological Commission, see Metropolitan Ilarion (Alfeev), "Perevod Biblii: istoriia i sovremennost'," www.patriarchia.ru/db/text/3394042.html.

23 "Ob ispravlenii russkogo perevoda knig Sviashchennogo Pisaniia," *Tserkovnye vedomosti,* Pribavleniia, 1892, no. 33: 1129.

he published a manuscript translation by the poet V. A. Zhukovskii (1783–1852) with this explanation:

> In this work the late Zhukovskii embraced the idea that one should not translate the expressions of Church Slavonic into Russian without special need—so as not to vernacularize the text hallowed by church use because of its power and expressiveness.[24]

Significantly, Pobedonostsev was forced to publish the Zhukovskii translation in Berlin. As a professor at the St. Petersburg Academy explained, "the Synod did not permit him to publish Zhukovskii's translation of the New Testament."[25] Pobedonostsev continued working on his own translation and initially published individual books of the New Testament,[26] with this caveat: "Published at the order of the chief procurator of the Holy Synod (in a small number of copies and not for public circulation)." The full text of his translation appeared in 1906 and has recently begun to attract scholarly attention and earn praise for its originality.[27]

Diversion from church administration to religious writing reflected Pobedonostsev's admiration of the "simple people" as the bearers of true, traditional piety. To that faith he contrasted the indifference of the educated: "Everywhere the people are still pious, and all the worshippers cannot fit into the church here. But the so-called intelligentsia is mired in the search for pleasure and in perverse thoughts."[28] Indeed, Pobedonostsev conflated popular Orthodoxy with the church, as in an article he first published in 1873:

> From time immemorial, our church has had and today preserves its significance as a popular (*vsenarodnaia*) church and the spirit of love and

24 V. A. Zhukovskii, *Novyi zavet Gospoda Nashego Iisusa Khrista* (Berlin: Tip. P. Stankevicha, 1895), i.

25 Letter from 1905, included in the commentary to a reprint of the Zhukovskii text: V. A. Zhukovskii, *Polnoe sobranie sochinenii i pisem*, 20 vols. (Moscow: Izdatel'skii dom IASK, 2016), 11/2:514.

26 *Deianiia sviatykh apostolov i sobornye poslaniia v novom russkom perevode* (St. Petersburg: Sinodal'naia tipografiia, 1905), ii.

27 K. P. Pobedonostsev, *Novyi Zavet Gospoda Nashego Iisusa Khrista v novom russkom perevode. Opyt k usovershestvovaniiu perevoda na russkii iazyk sviashchennykh knig Novogo Zaveta* (St. Petersburg: Sinodal'naia tipografiia, 1906). E. E. Remorova, "Lingvostilisticheskie osobennosti perevoda Chetveroevangeliia, vypolnennogo K. P. Pobedonostsevym" (kand. diss., Novosibirskii gosudarstvennyi universitet, 2017). The subtext about "originality" is the oft-repeated charge of plagiarism and intellectual dishonesty; see, for example, Byrnes, *Pobedonostsev*, 284–90. Strikingly, two recent biographies barely mention Pobedonostsev's New Testament translation or ignore it altogether: S. L. Firsov, *Konstantin Pobedonostsev, Intellektual vo vlasti* (St. Petersburg: Vita Nova, 2016), 414, 498; Polunov, *K. P. Pobedonostsev*, 217.

28 "38 pisem byvshego ober-prokurora Sv. Sinoda K.P. Pobedonostseva k vysokopreosviashchennomu Makariiu Tomskomu," in K. P. Pobedonostsev, *Gosudarstvo i tserkov'*, 2 vols. (Moscow: Institut russkoi tsivilizatsii, 2011), 1:601.

> undifferentiated community. Our people survive through faith to this time—despite all the hardships and calamities; if something can sustain it, can strengthen and renew it in the future, then it is its faith, and only this church faith.[29]

Toward the end of his life, he quoted, approvingly, a friend's statement: "I believe only in the parish church"—a remarkable revision of the Nicene Creed ("I believe in the one, holy, catholic, and apostolic church").[30] As chief procurator, he disparaged erudite theological tracts that failed to appreciate the liturgy so dear to believers. As he complained in 1884, "Learned, superficial priests—who have lost touch with the beauty of the church and its services—have caused us much woe."[31] He later wounded the pride of a learned bishop who had just published a ponderous theological tome and exulted over positive reviews abroad by declaring that "the church does not need such erudite books" because "the people will not understand anything in such a book."[32] However much he himself might read and even translate European texts, he castigated the tendency of church academies to offer courses incorporating "German university elements alien to an Orthodox ecclesiastical school."[33]

Not that he was unaware of the shortcomings in popular Orthodoxy. Indeed, he was candid about the folk's religious ignorance:

> What a mystery is the religious life of a people such as ours, uncultivated and left to itself! ... To the illiterate the scriptures are unknown; there are church services and a few prayers, which, transmitted from parents to children, serve as the only link between the church and its flock. It is known that in some remote districts the congregation understands nothing of the words of the service, or even of the Lord's Prayer, which is repeated often with omissions and additions that deprive it of all meaning.[34]

In Pobedonostsev's view, however, the fault rested not with the believers but with priests and bishops: "Our clergy teach little, and seldom; they celebrate the

29 Pobedonostsev, "Vestminsterskoe abbatstvo," in Pobedonostsev, *Gosudarstvo i tserkov'*, 1:449.

30 See "Dva pis'ma Andreia Nikolaevicha Murav'eva k K. P. Pobedonostsevu," *Russkii arkhiv*, 1905, no. 7: 415–16. For Pobedonostsev's reference in 1905 to the Murav'ev letter, which he had arranged to have published only the previous month, see Pobedonostsev, "Mat' moiu, rodimuiu Rossiiu, uroduiut," 10.

31 Pobedonostsev to Nikanor, March 16, 1884, "Perepiska Pobedonostseva s preosv. Nikanorom," *Russkii arkhiv*, 1915, no. 7–8: 347.

32 Serafim to Flavian [undated, 1900–01] (RGIA, f. 796, op. 205, d. 744, ll. 47–48).

33 Comments during a visit to the Kiev Academy in the fall of 1880, cited in N. Iu. Sukhova, *Vysshaia dukhovnaia shkola: problemy i reformy* (Moscow: Pravoslavnyi Sviato-Tikhonovskii Gumanitarnyi Universitet, 2006), 348.

34 K. P. Pobedonostsev, *Moskovskii Sbornik,* 5th ed. (Moscow: Sinodal'naia tipografiia, 1901), 165.

service in the churches and direct the administration of the parishes."[35] The chief procurator therefore assigned the highest priority to religious education, a view that led to his unrelenting commitment to building a thick network of parish schools.

Reservations about the pious folk, however, also generated skepticism toward demands that the laity be given greater authority in the church, especially at the parish level. Despite his growing and overt disdain for prelates and priests, Pobedonostsev looked askance at proposals for parish reform that would give the laity control over parish funds and the appointment of local clergy. In part, no doubt, his reaction reflected a visceral disbelief in institutional panaceas that flowed from the pens of bureaucratic reformers ensconced in their Petersburg chancelleries. But the procurator was no less critical of proposals for parish reform that emanated from his Slavophile associates and friends.[36] At work here, no doubt, was his pragmatic inclination: if given full authority, most parishioners would cease to pay the diocesan levies that sustained local administration and seminaries. While the seminaries, in his view, certainly were in need of reform and tighter control from above, the chief procurator had no illusions about finding alternative funding and, instead, sought to focus any state allocations on parish schools and subsidies for parish clergy.[37]

As the procurator encountered growing resistance from ranking clergy, from the mid-1880s he became ever more engaged in broader social and political issues. To be sure, his primary interest remained "simple believers," but he saw their defense to lie far beyond the realm of the church itself. While this view was partly due to the deterioration in his relations with the episcopate, it also reflected his belief in the intertwining of the spiritual and secular, the state and church. Despite all his philosophical conservatism, he subscribed to the activist "this-worldly" perspective that had gained acceptance since midcentury, with its insistence that the church must engage with social and political questions. As he argued in *Moskovskii Sbornik*, "The church cannot renounce its influence on civil and public life; the more active it becomes, the more it senses its internal and vital force, then the less can it be indifferent to the state."[38] That was a critical impulse to his tireless effort to address a full gamut of secular issues that lay well outside the ecclesiastical domain for which he was responsible. In his mind, the church and state were so inextricably intertwined that he was duty bound to ensure that the church's view was expressed.

35 Ibid.

36 For a Slavophile complaint about the sorry state of the parish, see the diary comments by a Pobedonostsev confidant: *Dnevnik A. A. Kireeva, 1905–1910*, ed. K. A. Solov'ev (Moscow: ROSSPEN, 2010), 39, 69, 78, 195.

37 See Gregory L. Freeze, "Konstantin Pobedonostsev: Chief Procurator as Chief Parishioner," *Canadian Slavonic Papers* 61, no. 3 (2019): 261–87, DOI:10.1080/00085006.2019.1636631.

38 Pobedonostsev, *Moskovskii Sbornik*, 22.

Jurisprudential ideas and legal practice

Central to Pobedonostsev's thinking was historicism, the idea that each nation must follow its own path of development, its unique *Sonderweg*.[39] Historicism was widespread among his colleagues at Moscow University, including the famed historian Sergei M. Soloviev, but Pobedonostsev drew principally on German legal scholarship, especially the work of Friedrich Carl von Savigny, whom Pobedonostsev greatly admired and recommended to his students in the early 1860s.[40] Historicism inspired Pobedonostsev's extensive research in Russian legal history that led to several historical studies and source collections,[41] and this knowledge of Muscovite and imperial history reinforced his belief that Russia had developed differently from Western Europe.[42] Although his legal research ended in the mid-1860s, he continued to publish what he had amassed early in his career. It was not just authorial hubris that inspired these later publications, but a belief that Russia was sorely deficient in jurists prepared to navigate the complexities of the country's legal history. In 1872, for example, he published a judicial guide with a collection of rules, statutes, and examples from civil procedure; his express goal was to help officials and lawyers contend with the new legal system.[43] Later he published documents and materials collected during his earlier research, including his notes from the Russian legal code—which he found to be poorly indexed and poorly understood.[44]

His research and university lectures provided the basis for a major legal work, the three-volume *Course of Civil Law*. The first volume appeared in 1868, followed later by volumes 2 and 3, with the entire set published in 1896. It earned praise from contemporaries and has even been reprinted in post-Soviet Russia. It covers patrimonial property (volume 1), family, inheritance, and testaments (volume 2), and contracts (volume 3). Each section begins with a summary of

39 K. A. Salekhov, "Konservatizm kak konstruktivnyi printsip podkhoda K.P. Pobedonostseva k izucheniiu politiko-pravovykh iavlenii," *Iurist-Pravoved,* 2015, no. 1 (68): 110–13.

40 Savigny emphasized that a lawgiver must incorporate both theoretical and practical elements: *System des heutigen Römischen Rechts,* 8 vols. (Berlin: Veit und Comp., 1840–49), 1:xix–xx. See A. E. Nol'de, "Obzor nauchnoi iuridicheskoi deiatel'nosti K. P. Pobedonostseva (nekrolog)," *Zhurnal Ministerstva narodnogo prosveshcheniia,* 1907, Novaia seriia, ch. 10, August: 83–116; and E. V. Timoshina, "Politiko-pravovye vzgliady K. P. Pobedonostseva" (kand. diss., Sankt-Peterburgskii gosudarstvennyi universitet, 1998), 3–48.

41 K. P. Pobedonostsev, *Istoricheskie issledovaniia i stat'i* (St. Petersburg: Tipografiia Ministerstva putei soobshcheniia, 1876). See Iu. G. Stepanov, "K. P. Pobedonostsev kak istorik krepostnogo prava," in *Konstantin Petrovich Pobedonostsev*, ed. Vedernikov, 18–28.

42 Polunov, *K. P. Pobedonostsev*, 62.

43 K. P. Pobedonostsev, *Sudebnoe rukovodstvo. Sbornik pravil, polozhenii i primerov, izvlechennykh iz teorii i praktiki grazhdanskogo sudoproizvodstva* (St. Petersburg: Tipografiia I. P. Anisimova, 1872).

44 K. P. Pobedonostsev, *Istoriko-iuridicheskie akty perekhodnoi epokhi XVII i XVIII vekov* (Moscow, 1887); Pobedonostsev, *Materialy dlia istorii prikaznogo sudoproizvodstva* (Moscow: Universitetskaia tipografiia, 1890); Pobedonostsev, *Vypiski iz Polnogo sobraniia zakonov* (St. Petersburg: n.p., 1895).

Roman, French, and German law, followed by the main text on the historical development of Russian law.[45] In 1896 he published an index, expanded bibliography, and glossary of terms for his *Course*.[46] Although arid and prone to archaic language,[47] the *Course* does engage contemporary issues, such as proposals to allow civil marriage (shifting control from religious organizations to the state) and to liberalize divorce.[48] About divorce, he digresses to write:

> In recent years, in the liberal organs of our press one often hears voices for a secularization of ecclesiastical justice in matters of marriage and associated questions. These opinions obviously did not arise from a popular source but have come from without. They are based only on abstract principles of theory and are usually accompanied by polemics against a so-called clerical tendency. But, it seems, ancient historical experience has already made it very clear how dangerous is any reform emanating from abstract principles and not corresponding to the practical conditions of the country and the matter itself.[49]

With his relocation to St. Petersburg in 1865, Pobedonostsev ceased to teach and conduct research and instead began to apply what he had learned to contemporary politics. For the next four decades, he expounded and applied six main principles, summarized below.

1. Unlimited autocracy

Pobedonostsev was a categorical supporter of unlimited autocracy, which he saw as critical to Russia's survival. As he explained to Nicholas II in 1895, "The autocratic power of the sovereign is not only *necessary* for Russia, it is not only the guarantee for internal stability, but it is the essential condition for national unity and the political might of our state."[50] The emperor, he argued, must exercise

45 Although critics complain that Pobedonostsev simply juxtaposed Western and Russian law without direct comparisons and conclusions, in some cases the juxtaposition did not require elaborate comment. In the case of divorce, for example, volume 2 provides a long summary of the grounds for annulment and divorce in Western law, followed by a review of acceptable grounds in Russia. See K. P. Pobedonostsev, *Kurs grazhdanskogo prava*, 3 vols. (St. Petersburg: Sinodal'naia tipografiia, 1896), 2:83–96, 97–116.

46 *Ukazateli i prilozheniia k Kursu grazhdanskogo prava* (St. Petersburg: Sinodal'naia tipografiia, 1896).

47 The first volume is titled *Votchinnye prava*, invoking the medieval term for "property" (*votchina*). This penchant for archaic language reflects Pobedonostsev's historicism, but also his aversion to neologisms from European jurisprudence, despite his long comparative sections and close knowledge. Nol'de, "Obzor," 110.

48 Pobedonostsev, *Kurs grazhdanskogo prava*, 2:72, 110–11.

49 Ibid., 2:110.

50 Iu. B. Solov'ev, "Nachalo tsarstvovaniia Nikolaia II i rol' Pobedonostseva v opredelenii politicheskogo kursa samoderzhaviia," *Arkheograficheskii ezhegodnik*, 1972, 316–17.

that vast power and satisfy the expectations of the people, who believed that "the tsar can do everything and that his word can transform the face of the Russian land."[51] It was therefore unthinkable that the tsar accede to demands for a constitution, which could only divert Russia from its natural path and alienate the people. As he wrote during the political crisis of the late 1870s, the entire population believed that "it is better to have a revolution than a constitution. It is still possible to overturn the form and establish order; the latter [a constitution] is a poison for the organism."[52] His antipathy toward "liberal bureaucrats" intensified when the leading officials sought to impose limits on autocracy. In response, he offered this colorful description of Petersburg elites during the crisis of autocracy:

> I see a lot of people of every rank and station. From all the local officials and learned people my heart is aching, as if I were in the company of half-crazed people or perverted apes. Everywhere I hear the one memorized, false, and accursed word: constitution.[53]

Only autocracy, he argued, could govern the empire—with its vast expanse, backwardness in economic and cultural development, and complex ethnic and religious composition.

2. *Good officials, not ideal laws and institutions, are needed*

Pobedonostsev expounded a premise more appropriate for a religious thinker than a legal scholar: what really mattered was personnel, not institutions and laws. In good measure, that conviction grew out of his historical research and administrative experience: no matter what the formal law might say, it was the individual administrator and his moral backbone that was important, not the Digest of Laws or the Complete Collection of Laws of the Russian Empire. In his words, "I have more faith in an improvement of people than institutions."[54] Indeed, the exponential profusion of laws during the Great Reforms only made matters worse. As he wrote in 1873, "one wants to believe in new people, not new laws: the latter have already piled up such that one cannot cope with them."[55] The flood of confusing laws merely antagonized the folk, who "understand only too well that there is no sense, but just a burden, from the proliferation of decrees and directives, which are either unimplemented or only result in the imposition of new burdens."[56] But Pobedonostsev was especially hostile toward the "enlightened

51 K. P. Pobedonostsev, *Pis'ma k Aleksandru III,* 2 vols. (Moscow: Izdatel'stvo "Direkt-Media," 2014), 2:142 (November 25, 1887).

52 Ibid., 1:247 (December 14, 1879).

53 Ibid.

54 Pobedonostsev to S. A. Rachinskii, in A. Iu. Polunov, "K. P. Pobedonostsev, Sviateishii Sinod i arkhierei v 1881–1894 gg.," *Vestnik Moskovskogo universiteta,* Seriia 8, 1994, no. 4: 22.

55 Pobedonostsev, *Pis'ma k Aleksandru III,* 1:21 (November 5, 1873).

56 Pobedonostsev, *Pis'ma k Aleksandru III,* 1:265 (January 31, 1880).

bureaucrats" who engineered the Great Reforms, and he denounced their penchant for fashionable doctrinairism and ignorance of Russian realities outside the capitals. Indeed, the dearth of qualified officials was one reason why Russia needed autocracy and centralization: "We have not had, and do not have, an estate [*soslovie*] of jurists. Strong, experienced professionals are very few; everywhere one is forced to appoint inexperienced, sometimes incompetent youths."[57]

3. *Incrementalism*

Although he disparaged modern doctrines and doctrinaires, Pobedonostsev did not propose to return to some glorious lost past. In contrast to the Slavophiles, he had conducted too much historical research to idealize Muscovite Russia. That was evident, for example, in 1882, when he adamantly opposed an attempt to resurrect the medieval *zemskii sobor* (assembly of the land). Nor was he disposed to favor reestablishment of the patriarchate; rather, he defended the Petrine church reforms that replaced the patriarchate by the Holy Synod, notwithstanding his own conflict with the Synod. Despite the widespread stereotype, Pobedonostsev did not oppose all change but only insisted that it be incremental, and that it commence with what is, not what might have existed in some remote or imaginary past. Thus, in 1884 he opposed plans for a radical revision of the university statutes, with this explanation: "Change some articles [in the university statute], limit the democratic principle, enhance the authority of the administrators, but do not smash the very core of this entire organization!"[58]

4. *Restricted freedom of conscience*

Demands for freedom of conscience became more insistent in late nineteenth-century Russia, not only among the liberal educated public but also among high-ranking state officials, who were disposed more toward *raison d'état* than defending church interests. Pobedonostsev, however, opposed concessions to religious minorities and especially any concessions that would allow proselytizing by the non-Orthodox. Although personally respectful of other Christian confessions[59] and circumspect about conversion to Orthodoxy,[60] Pobedonostsev

57 *K. P. Pobedonostsev i ego korrespondenty,* 1:62 (undated).

58 Pobedonostsev, *Pis'ma k Aleksandru III,* 2:168 (January 1888).

59 A. Iu. Polunov, "Protestantizm i katolichestvo v otsenkakh 'Russkogo Torkvemady': K voprosu o religioznykh vozzreniiakh K. P. Pobedonostseva," *Vestnik PSTGU,* Seriia 1, 2016, vyp. 5 (67): 24–32. On Pobedonostsev's response to the Jewish question, see S. L. Firsov, "K. P. Pobedonostsev i 'evreiskii vopros' v Rossii," *Studia culturae* 1(23) (2015): 110–32. See, for example, the fascinating account about the American ambassador, Andrew White, who had extensive conversations with Pobedonostsev: V. N. Pleshkov, "Endriu Dikson Uait o vstrechakh s K. P. Pobedonostsevym," in *Konstantin Petrovich Pobedonostsev,* ed. Vedernikov, 81–86.

60 When the bishop of Riga reported a movement of Estonians and Latvians to convert to Orthodoxy, Pobedonostsev urged caution: "I advised him to act with extreme caution in this

adamantly rejected proposals to legalize proselytizing by the non-Orthodox as a mortal threat to simple believers. He framed the religious struggle in global terms, as in the case of Catholics in the western provinces: "It is obvious that a systematic campaign against Russia and its cause has been undertaken in the West, and it is guided by the Catholic Church in close alliance with the Austrian government and the Polish national party."[61] But he also warned about internal religious threats—from Old Believers and sectarians in the Russian interior. That fear inspired his opposition to the publication of a Baptist catechism in Russian: "In my opinion, one should absolutely not permit the publication of a Russian translation of a catechism for Baptists. The publication of this catechism is obviously undertaken for the sake of propaganda among Russians."[62] Faced with growing resistance from state officials to support such repression, whether from personal conviction or bureaucratic convenience, Pobedonostsev realized that the Orthodox Church itself must assume primary responsibility in combatting the spiritual threats.[63]

Pobedonostsev hardly bore sole responsibility for religious repression; other authorities, central and local, also played a role.[64] But his prominence as chief procurator made him the target of criticism, especially from religious groups abroad.[65] That was particularly evident in the case of the prosecution of Baltic Lutheran pastors for violating the empire's laws on reconversion. In a letter to the president of the Swiss Evangelical Lutheran Committee, the chief procurator even argued that Russia had unparalleled religious tolerance: "Nowhere in Europe do other Christian and even non-Christian confessions exercise such broad freedom as among the Russian people. Alas, Europe does not want to recognize this truth."[66] But Pobedonostsev was losing the argument not only abroad but at home: in the postreform era the government gradually adopted concessions that would culminate in the decree of April 17, 1905, "On the Strengthening of the

important matter (which, I dare think, is unclear and ambiguous). It is difficult to believe that the sudden movement [to convert] was absolutely sincere and disinterested." Pobedonostsev to D. A. Tolstoi, July 14, 1883 (NIOR RGB, f. 230, k. 10802, d. 6, ll. 18–19).

61 *Pis'ma k Aleksandru III,* 1:350–51 (November 11, 1881). He made a similar complaint about the transnational Jewish campaign against Russia, *K. P. Pobedonostsev i ego korrespondenty*, 2:501–5.

62 Pobedonostsev to N. P. Ignat'ev, in R. M. Kantor, ed., "Pis'ma K.P. Pobedonostseva k gr. N. P. Ignat'evu," *Byloe,* 27–28 (1925): 66 (December 7, 1881).

63 In an 1893 letter about sectarians, Pobedonostsev declared that "this evil is spreading and intensifying." Although state authorities had prosecuted and deported members, such "measures are only auxiliary," for the church must be the main agency to repulse this threat—"through services and singing in church and instruction in the schools." See his letter in "Pis'ma K. P. Pobedonostseva Preosviashchennomu Ilarionu, arkhiepiskopu Poltavskomu," *Russkii arkhiv,* 1916, no. 1–3: 153.

64 "K. P. Pobedonostsev," *Otechestvennaia istoriia,* 2013, no. 1: 102.

65 Hermann Dalton, *Offenes Sendschreiben an den Oberprokureur des russischen Synods, den Wirklichen Geheimrat Konstantin Pobedonoszeff* (Leipzig: Duncker & Humblot, 1889).

66 Pobedonostsev, "Pis'mo Ober-prokurora Sv. Sinoda k Eduardu Navilliu," in Pobedonostsev, *Gosudarstvo i tserkov',* 1:477.

Principles of Religious Toleration." Predictably, Pobedonostsev castigated the decree as conferring "equality of confessions," giving Catholic clergy the freedom to entice vast numbers of Orthodox, and he warned that opening the door to Muslim propaganda was "something terrible."[67]

5. *Judicial counterreforms*

Of the various counterreforms (first proposed in the mid-1870s, but proliferating under Alexander III), Pobedonostsev was particularly determined to revise the Judicial Reform of 1864 that he had helped to write. His earlier role, even if more limited than once thought, was nonetheless undeniable, and he was not wont to invoke memories of his participation. By the 1870s, he had become increasingly critical and later claimed that discontent with the new courts was universal: "All across Russia, from the people there arises a wail of grumbling at the judicial institution."[68] Rhetoric turned into formal deliberations on counterreform under Alexander III, and in early 1885 Pobedonostsev submitted a memorandum on what needed to be done. The memorandum was quintessential Pobedonostsev: "As experience has proven" (a typical emphasis on practice, not theory), the judicial order created in 1864 was incompatible "with the needs of the people and the conditions of its way of life" (an allusion to the country's backwardness and expanse) as well as "with the general structure of state institutions in Russia" (that is, autocracy). Characteristically, however much Pobedonostsev disliked the current judicial order, he insisted that it be changed "gradually," not in one fell swoop.

His memorandum itemized various failings beginning with the irremovability of judges, but now argued that the reforms had failed to work because of the lack of a "judicial estate" and the appointment of untrained and even unethical judges. A second target of criticism was the "publicity of all court sessions," which had led to a "demoralization" of society as the public became avid spectators to horrendous crimes. His memorandum also castigated the new liberal profession of lawyers, created in 1864 in an attempt to replicate the "advocate estate" in European countries. Arguing that this attempt to replicate the European model had badly failed, Pobedonostsev declared that "it is necessary to take decisive measures to curb and limit the arbitrariness of lawyers." Pobedonostsev was also critical of the jury system established in 1864. Citing multiple shortcomings, such as the practical impossibility of mandatory court presence in a far-flung country, the appointment of unqualified justices of the peace, and the massive backlog in judicial cases, he declared the jury system unworkable:

> The establishment of a jury in the criminal court system has proved to be totally wrong for Russia. It is totally incompatible with the conditions of our

67 Iz chernovykh bumag K. P. Pobedonostseva," *Krasnyi arkhiv* 5 (18) (1926): 204.

68 Pobedonostsev to A. N. Shakhov, *K. P. Pobedonostsev i ego korrespondenty*, 2:46 (March 10, 1884).

> way of life and with the structure of our courts; it is false in its essence and under conditions here has served to bring about a fatal demoralization of public conscience and the perversion of the essential goals of justice.[69]

In the ensuing years, the government did reconstruct the judicial system, but incrementally, as Pobedonostsev insisted—through a series of adjustments, not a single radical measure.

Pobedonostsev's criticism of the 1864 system was hardly unique; his was not "a voice crying in the wilderness," to use one of his favorite expressions. On the contrary, by the mid-1870s the initial enthusiasm for the Judicial Reform had dissolved into a fierce debate. The new system had some defenders but also many critics.[70] Regarding the jury system, for example, opponents complained of leniency (a high rate of acquittals)[71] and various problems—some practical (juror truancy), some cultural (jurors' tendency to privilege their own notion of justice over statutory law), some political (the infamous acquittal of the terrorist Vera Zasulich).[72] Nor did the new system of advocates work as smoothly as once hoped; the number, quality, and performance of the "estate of advocates" left much to be desired. Indeed, some blamed the judicial system for an apparent upsurge in crime. Although contemporary statistics leave much to be desired, they reinforced the perception that a poor judicial system had actually led to a sharp increase in crime. Although Western historians generally support the view of prerevolutionary liberal lawyers, some take a more critical view—closer to that of Pobedonostsev than of his adversaries.[73] Recent Russian scholarship, with a mass of empirical case studies, also inclines toward the more critical view.

69 *K. P. Pobedonostsev i ego korrespondenty,* 2:65–72 (zapiska, 1885).

70 For an overview of the debate about the jury system, see A. A. Sorokin, "Vopros o reforme mestnogo suda Rossiiskoi imperii: vlast' i obshchestvo (1889–1912 gg.)" (kand. diss., Natsional'nyi issledovatel'skii Nizhegorodskii gosudarstvennyi universitet, 2017).

71 See: Girish Narayan Bhat, "Trial by Jury in the Reign of Alexander II: A Study in the Legal Culture of Late Imperial Russia, 1864–1881" (PhD diss., University of California, Berkeley, 1995); N. V. Cherkashina, "Sudebnaia reforma 1864 g. v Rossii (po materialam Vladimirskoi gubernii)" (kand. diss., Nizhegorodskaia pravovaia akademiia, 2006); O. A. Puzanova, "Sud prisiazhnykh vo Vladimirskoi gubernii" (kand. diss., Vladimirskii iuridicheskii institut, 2005); A. A. Demichev, "Sravnitel'no-pravovoe issledovanie suda prisiazhnykh v Rossii (istoriia i sovremennost')" (dokt. diss., Nizhegorodskaia akademiia MVD, 2003); O. E. Gromikova, "Sud prisiazhnykh v Rossii vo vtoroi polovine XIX–nachale XX veka" (kand. diss., Penzenskii gosudarstvennyi universitet, 2012).

72 On the Zasulich case, see Chapter 7 of this volume.

73 The conventional historiography, influenced by articulate liberal lawyers, has tended to idealize prerevolutionary lawyers with such comments as "legal professionals appeared with an unprecedented ethical commitment to the law and a knowledge of law and legal practice" (Richard Wortman, "Russian Monarchy and the Rule of Law: New Considerations of the Court Reform of 1864," *Kritika: Explorations in Russian and Eurasian History* 6 [2005]: 159). Revisionists have been less generous. See, notably, Jörg Baberowski, *Autokratie und Justiz: Zum Verhältnis von Rechtsstaatlichkeit und Rückständigkeit im ausgehenden Zarenreich 1864–1914* (Frankfurt am Main: Vittorio Klostermann, 1996), 481–614. See also

6. *Social conservatism*

Pobedonostsev also applied his conservative outlook to the social sphere. Whereas the Great Reforms had begun to dismantle the estate (*soslovie*) boundaries erected earlier to thwart excessive social mobility (deemed responsible for upheavals and revolution in Western Europe), the postreform government sought to bolster such boundaries—a policy that Pobedonostsev enthusiastically supported. That informed his opposition to the creation of an inclusive "all-estate township" (*vsesoslovnaia volost'*) as the basic unit of local administration in order to overcome the boundaries separating the peasantry from other estates. Pobedonostsev, who feared exposing the simple folk to pernicious elite influence, castigated the draft proposal as a "nightmare," adding: "In recent years I have read a lot of crazy, incoherent, illiterate, and worthless proposals, but nothing the likes of this. It is just as if some boys were playing a game of making state laws."[74]

Such social conservatism likewise informed Pobedonostsev's views on the family and women. One of his earliest translations was Heinrich Thiersch's book on the Christian foundations of the family,[75] and the family remained a constant theme thereafter, the leitmotif being that "the true foundation and guide for a good citizen must be sought in the *home* and in the *family*."[76] In the legal sphere, this view inspired his strict opposition to civil marriage, on the grounds that each confessional group must regulate the family as its faith dictates, thereby making secularization and state control unthinkable. He was particularly opposed to the growing demand for divorce reform and, while willing to make ad hoc exceptions,[77] defended laws that made divorce difficult and punitive for the

---

Jane Burbank, "Discipline and Punish in the Moscow Bar Association," *Russian Review* 54 (1995): 44–64. On the shortcomings (and shortages) of the prerevolutionary legal profession, see William E. Pomeranz, "The Emergence and Development of the Russian *Advokatura:* 1864–1905" (DPhil diss., University of London, 1990); E. D. Blagodeteleva, "Moskovskaia korporatsiia prisiazhnykh poverennykh: formirovanie professional'noi gruppy (1866–1914)" (kand. diss., Moskovskii pedagogicheskii gosudarstvennyi universitet, 2012).

74 Pobedonostsev to D. A. Tolstoi, *K. P. Pobedonostsev i ego korrespondenty*, 1:323 (September 11, 1883).

75 Heinrich Thiersch, *Über christliches Familienleben* (Frankfurt am Main, 1854), which Pobedonostsev later published as *Khristianskie nachala semeinoi zhizni* (St. Petersburg: Sinodal'naia tipografiia, 1899).

76 [Pobedonostsev], "Nravstvennyi kharakter grazhdanina v khristianskom obshchestve," *Tserkovnye vedomosti,* 1902, no. 12 (March 23): 415.

77 Pobedonostsev was willing to make exceptions so long as that did not mean changes in the fundamental laws on divorce. He made that clear in a letter to Alexander III on May 23, 1883, suggesting how one noblewoman, denied divorce and permission to remarry, might circumvent existing law by arranging an illegal marriage and then appealing to the emperor to order that an investigation be terminated. See Pobedonostsev, *Pis'ma k Aleksandru III,* 2:33–35. The following year, in a conversation with General A. A. Kireev, the chief procurator sought to rebut complaints from conservatives about the steady rise in divorces by offering this explanation: "It is necessary to leave a 'little window,' for if we are too rigorous in applying all the laws, then you may well lead things to the point of provoking a whole

"guilty" party. The reason, he explained to Alexander III, was a moral decline that threatened the very stability of the family:

> Especially under the present ease of marriage and separation of spouses, such an imperial order could serve to intensify debauchery. Now people who have thoughtlessly married, soon, at the smallest disagreement, think about divorce and arrange it such that one of the sides assumes the guilt of adultery in the hope that it will then be possible to ask that the ban on remarriage will be lifted.[78]

Pobedonostsev also opposed giving a broader social role—and higher education—to women because of the threat it posed to the traditional family order.[79] He argued that the "women's question" itself was an import from the West:

> Along with many ideas that have penetrated our society from Western Europe since the 1860s, there has come the idea of women's emancipation, and it has begun to affect people's thinking and to spread. Fanatics have appeared who favor the equality of women and men in all public rights, the establishment of women's courses [for higher education], and the admission of women to the university.[80]

Assessment of legacy

Pobedonostsev, long the target of ridicule and vituperation, has enjoyed an astonishing rehabilitation in post-Soviet Russia, with a flood of reprints and anthologies, and numerous scholarly works, including several biographies, more than a dozen dissertations, and a plethora of scholarly collections and articles devoted specifically to him. These works do not spring from a cult of personality but from a nationalist conservatism that has steadily gained momentum since the fall of the Soviet Union. The key precipitant was the disastrous "katastroika" of the early 1990s, when the new regime of Boris Yeltsin eagerly adopted the nostrum of the "Washington consensus," promising that a neoliberal Russia could magically transform the Soviet system into a prosperous free-market economy. Nothing of the sort transpired; on the contrary, the Russian gross domestic product plummeted on a scale greater than during the Great Depression, inflation ravaged private savings and income, and by the late 1990s the country was effectively bankrupt. Disenchantment derived too from the country's decline in political and military power accompanied by Western aggressiveness—from the expansion of

revolution against the church." Entry in Kireev's diary from February 1884 (NIOR RGB, f. 126, k. 3, d. 9, l. 305).

78 Pobedonostsev, *Pis'ma k Aleksandru III,* 2:34 (May 23, 1883).

79 Pobedonostsev to Alexander III, *K. P. Pobedonostsev i ego korrespondenty,* 2:509–10 (May 22, 1891).

80 Pobedonostsev, *Pis'ma k Aleksandru III,* 2:233–37 (May 1891).

NATO (previously disavowed) to the marginalization of Russia as a global power. The influx of missionaries, religious and secular, only reinforced anti-Western sentiment and suspicions.

Pobedonostsev, along with other prerevolutionary conservatives, has benefited from the new awareness that Russia *is* different and need not succumb to "imperialism," whatever form it might take—economic, political, or cultural. If anyone from the Russian past might seem to have been a difficult case for rehabilitation, it was certainly Pobedonostsev. Yet within two years of the dismemberment of the Soviet Union, conservative nationalists had begun to praise his views and reprint his works. Although the Russian Orthodox Church has been remarkably reticent, conservative nationalists have been unabashedly enthusiastic about promoting his legacy and ideas. That is apparent in the online site Russkaia Liniia (www.rusk.ru) as well as in the publications of the Institute of Russian Civilization. Many, in Russia and abroad, take exception to the excesses of such nationalists, but the nationalists have made Pobedonostsev's work available, not only as reprints, but as well-edited collections based on materials available only in major research libraries. Certainly, some of Pobedonostsev's ideas, such as his tirades against women's emancipation, are anathema to the modern reader, but others resonate not only with Russian nationalists eager to stress their country's special path but in the West, where the simple-minded universalism of "globalization" has long since given way to "glocalization" that valorizes the uniqueness of individual countries and their cultures. Although Pobedonostsev's illiberal populism is no panacea, his popularity shows that scholars and politicians must respect national traditions, national culture, and national values, even as they rightly promote universalizing principles.

6 Boris Chicherin

Christian modernist

Gary M. Hamburg

Boris Chicherin (1828–1904) was the Russian Empire's most important liberal intellectual. He was a tireless advocate of the Great Reforms of the 1860s, a lifelong defender of religious toleration and freedom of conscience, and a trenchant critic of political extremism from the left and right. From the mid-1860s to the turn of the century, he was a delegate in the Kirsanov zemstvo (land council) in Tambov province, and, for eighteen months in the early 1880s, he served as the mayor in Moscow's city council. During his term in those offices, he became one of Russia's best-informed and energetic proponents of elected local self-government. In the 1860s, he was skeptical about Russia's readiness for national representative government, but later he decided constitutional monarchy was the best hope for redressing the many problems assailing Russia. He is remembered today for his political activism in what turned out to be the losing cause of rule-of-law liberalism as the empire careened toward revolution.

For our purposes, the two most interesting aspects of Chicherin's legacy are his modernist religious views and his philosophy of law. As we shall see, he broke sharply from those contemporaries who saw Orthodox Christianity as the necessary underpinning of positive Russian law, and he bitterly rejected Vladimir Soloviev's doctrine of free theocracy.

Intellectual biography

Chicherin was the eldest of eight children born into a prosperous noble family in Tambov province. Like his siblings, he was initially educated at home in ancient and modern languages, history, and literature. He attended Moscow University as an undergraduate from 1845 to 1849, and took a master's degree there in the history of Russian law in 1856. In the course of his studies, he developed wide interests—in European and Russian history and in law, politics, and philosophy. From the late 1840s on, he styled himself a disciple of Georg Wilhelm Friedrich Hegel; in the 1880s, he was still a stout defender of Hegel's philosophical assumptions, but by then he also embraced Immanuel Kant's ideas concerning the centrality of human personhood in society. Chicherin therefore played an instrumental role in the revival of idealism in Russia in the two decades before 1905.

DOI: 10.4324/9781003017097-6

In 1861, Chicherin took an appointment at his alma mater's faculty of law. During his tenure there, he served as tutor in political theory to Grand Duke Nikolai Aleksandrovich, the oldest son of Tsar Aleksandr II. The grand duke's tragic death in 1865 altered the succession to the throne and changed Chicherin's life by removing his principal royal patron. Chicherin remained a university teacher until Dmitrii Andreevich Tolstoi, the minister of education, engineered his resignation in 1868.

After leaving Moscow University, Chicherin returned to his father's estate in provincial Tambov, where he lived out his days, except for brief residency in Moscow and Yalta. Chicherin married late—in 1871, at the age of forty-three. His young, wealthy, and well-educated wife, Aleksandra Alekseevna (née Kapnist, 1845–1920), proved herself an able manager of the family's estates and a worthy intellectual companion to Chicherin. In the evenings at their estate, they read aloud poetry, novels, plays, memoirs, and political tracts in various languages. Together they curated one of the best private collections of European art in Russia. After Chicherin's death in 1904, Aleksandra Alekseevna organized his papers, keeping them safe during World War I and the revolutions of 1917. She died in 1920, poverty-stricken and virtually alone.

In his published works before 1861, Chicherin made the case for understanding Russian historical development in the wider context of European history. On his reading of the historical evidence, the Russian past was peculiar in certain respects (the centuries-long dominance of private law and of special regulations, the late appearance of modern legal codes and of a rationally organized centralized bureaucracy), yet, he maintained, the country had nevertheless developed in the same general direction as its European counterparts, especially France. Chicherin categorically rejected the Slavophiles' notions of Russian uniqueness and religious exceptionalism. In various articles published abroad in the 1850s, he described what he saw as the next logical steps for Russia if it were to continue to advance on the Western European pattern. They included the abolition of serfdom and the establishment of freedom of conscience, freedom of speech, freedom of the press, academic freedom, transparency of governmental operations, and public access to legal proceedings. His political program helped generate momentum for the abolition of serfdom and the Great Reforms, which the government promulgated between 1861 and 1874.

From 1861 on, Chicherin wrote a series of books aiming to win adherents to his *Rechtsstaat* (rule-of-law state) liberalism. *Several Contemporary Questions* (1862) made the case for support of the government's emancipation of the peasantry, for conceiving the state as "the nation's living bond," and for regarding an educated citizenry as the "crown of humanity." *On Representative Government* (1866) argued that successful constitutional governments require a degree of political maturity, social cohesion, and respect for law that Chicherin thought Russia still lacked. He maintained that the establishment of civil rights (freedom from arbitrary arrest and unreasonable search and seizure, the right to own property, freedom of press and academic freedom, freedom of assembly, the right to trial before an independent court) must historically precede the granting of political rights (the right to vote and the right of society to govern itself through elected representatives). He called on the government and society to collaborate in support of civil rights as prerequisites of a future representative government. In *Property and the State* (1882–83), Chicherin tried to show that the free individual and a free economy are necessary foundations for the modern political order. His *Philosophy of Law* (1899–1900) argued that the government should commit itself to the protection and advancement of liberty. Finally, Chicherin's *Russia on the Eve of the Twentieth Century* (1900) claimed that the time had come at last to inaugurate a constitutional regime in Russia.

Chicherin's liberalism was an attempt to stake out the contested middle ground between revolutionaries and social conservatives, between autocracy's extreme critics and its hardline defenders. Predictably, he fell under attack from both camps. The socialist Aleksandr Herzen accused Chicherin of revering "the idol of the state with the tsar at the top and the hangman at the bottom."[1] Meanwhile, in the mid-1860s, the government distanced itself from Chicherin, whom it increasingly viewed as an unreliable ally and dangerous critic.[2] Thus, Chicherin constantly had to defend himself against the Left's accusations that he was a blind statist and against the Right's charge that he sought to overthrow legitimate authority. The precariousness of his position was largely the consequence of three strong cultural currents in imperial Russia: the tradition of the "censure of law," Orthodox hostility to "Europeanism," and the radicalization of educated society. The failure of Chicherin's liberal program was also rooted in the relative weakness of Russia's middle classes. His liberalism therefore lacked the constituency it might have enjoyed in other circumstances.

Institutional contexts

Chicherin wrote his books in one formal conventional context and in several less formal ones. For more than ten years Chicherin studied at Moscow University, and then served seven years as a professor. It is scarcely surprising that he elaborated his basic legal and historical views while at the university, or that many of his later projects testified to the intellectual agenda he had worked out there. In this respect, he followed the pattern established in the Catherinian era by Ivan Andreevich Tret'iakov and Semen Efimovich Desnitskii, the university's pioneers of legal study. Chicherin's training and early career were not very different from those of his teachers Konstantin Dmitrievich Kavelin, Nikita Ivanovich Krylov, and Petr Grigor'evich Redkin. Nor did his trajectory differ much from that of his coeval Konstantin Pobedonostsev, although Pobedonostsev entered government

1 Aleksandr Ivanovich Gertsen, *Byloe i dumy,* in: *Sobranie sochinenii v tridtsati tomakh* (Moscow: Izdatel'stvo Akademii nauk SSSR, 1954–64), 9:252–53.

2 For the history of Chicherin's demonstrative resignation from the university faculty and the official pressure to which he responded, see G. M. Hamburg, *Boris Chicherin and Early Russian Liberalism* (Stanford, CA: Stanford University Press, 1992), 311–30.

service while Chicherin stayed out of it.[3] Study of jurisprudence followed by teaching and research in that discipline was also an established pattern in Germany, where Friedrich Carl von Savigny, Rudolf von Gneist, and Eduard Gans wrote monumental studies of Roman law. In England, incidentally, the connection between high-level scholarship and the university track in jurisprudence was less firm: William Stubbs, the author of *The Constitutional History of England in Its Origin and Development* (1873–78), took degrees in classics and mathematics; Frederic William Maitland studied the moral sciences before embarking on his *Constitutional History of England* (1908). Stubbs earned his living mainly from the pulpit, Maitland from a law practice, before both returned to the university to teach law. In France, the best work on jurisprudence, Montesquieu's *On the Spirit of the Laws* (1748), was done outside the university altogether.

Yet if Chicherin could boast of roots in Moscow University, he also moved in less formal contexts. In the late 1840s, he partook of Moscow salon discussions, which introduced him to the Westernizer-Slavophile debate. In the late 1850s, he joined the philosophical circle of the Hegelian Aleksandr Vasil'evich Stankevich, who became his closest friend and later his most reliable sounding board. In the Stankevich circle, Chicherin met Leo Tolstoy, whom he tried to convert to Hegelianism, and with whom he struck up a durable acquaintance. Also in the late 1850s, Chicherin involved himself with Konstantin Kavelin and others in the writing of "manuscript literature"—that is, nineteenth-century *samizdat* works that circulated from hand to hand in the Russian capitals before being published abroad. Before 1865, as noted above, Chicherin tutored the heir to the throne. In the early 1860s, he also cultivated the government's leading young statesmen, such as Nikolai and Dmitrii Alekseevich Miliutin. In the early 1870s, Chicherin developed ties with zemstvo activists and spoke at a clandestine zemstvo congress, where he inveigled members to support a constitution. In 1885, he joined the Moscow Psychological Society, a circle devoted to promoting idealist philosophy. After his marriage in 1871, Chicherin mostly lived in rural Tambov, where his estate, Karaul, was like an island of European culture. From there he plied friends and family with countless letters in which he solicited new books and journals, tried out his political ideas, and reacted to ideological currents of the day.

In other words, Chicherin operated in the conventional university space but also outside of it—in licit settings (his country estate, the government and royal family, the Moscow Psychological Society), in semilicit settings (critical salon discussions), and in illicit ones (the manuscript literature campaign of the late 1850s, the zemstvo congress of 1871). The variety of venues in which he was active contributed to his knowledge of Russian educated society and thus to his often penetrating judgments concerning the country's legal consciousness and political maturity. The combination of conventional and unconventional venues

3 For sketches of Russian legal thinkers, with much biographical information on their formations and careers, see V. A. Tomsinov, *Rossiiskie pravovedy XVIII–XX vekov: ocherki zhizni i tvorchestva*, 2nd rev. ed., 3 vols. (Moscow: Zertsalo–M, 2015).

lent a liminal quality to his liberalism: it was a way of thinking that, in Russia, occupied the border between positive law and moral imperative.

Religious convictions

Chicherin grew up as an Orthodox Christian, but in the mid-1840s he became an atheist. In this regard, he shared the path of many young intellectuals who found their way to religious doubt and unbelief.[4] Two factors seem to have precipitated his skepticism: a required theology class at Moscow University which was so badly taught that it left his childhood convictions in ruins, and the reading of David Strauss's *Das Leben Jesu* (1835–36), which analyzed Jesus as a historical figure principally by stripping away the "Oriental myths" informing the gospels.

Chicherin did not begin to return to belief in God until 1865, when he nearly died of miliary fever; even then, he rejected the reality of an afterlife. Over the next decade, he underwent a "long conversion to Christianity" in which key moments were his marriage, the deaths in infancy of his first two children (in 1874 and 1875), and careful study of the rational component of Christian belief. We can reconstruct the conversion process partially, on the basis of letters to his wife and to Stankevich, but uncertainty about his inner world makes understanding his spiritual transformation a matter of speculation. At first, all Chicherin could do was to posit God's existence: he felt indifference to the afterlife. Later, he accepted the reality of an afterlife but could say nothing about its nature and therefore derived little satisfaction from its prospect. The passing of his children impelled him to confront the apparent injustice of early death, so he began to see why there must be justice in the next world. In other words, the main obstacles to religious belief were probably emotional, although, as we shall now see, his writings approached faith primarily from an intellectual perspective.

In March 1876, Chicherin planned a book on "knowledge and faith" (in correspondence with a friend, he referred to the title as *La science et la foi*).[5] He started writing in the winter of 1877–78 and finished the book's first draft just before Easter 1878. The book finally appeared as *Science and Religion* (*Nauka i religiia*, 1879; 2nd ed., 1901). Its aim was to find a convincing resolution of the tensions between reason and faith.[6] The book consisted of three parts: an analysis of the reason-faith question from a rational philosophical perspective; an analysis of faith "as a manifestation of the human spirit, of the striving toward living communion with the Absolute" (212); and an analysis of human history from the dual perspectives of reason and faith.

4 Victoria Frede, *Doubt, Atheism, and the Nineteenth-Century Russian Intelligentsia* (Madison: University of Wisconsin Press, 2011).

5 See his letter to Baroness Edita Fedorovna Rahden on March 23, 1876, in Gosudarstvennyi Arkhiv Rossiiskoi Federatsii (GARF), f. 1154, ed. khr. 63, l. 127 ob.

6 Boris Nikolaevich Chicherin, *Nauka i religiia* (Moscow: Tipografiia Martynova i Kompaniia, 1879). Parenthetical page citations in the text are to this edition.

Book one of *Science and Religion*—"Reason" or "Knowledge" (*nauka*)—acknowledged the importance of empirical science, of knowledge drawn from experience and observation, in framing human perceptions of the world. However, it also insisted that our minds operate on the basis of innate rules that give us the capacity to order our sense impressions. According to Chicherin, these rules constitute the essence of reason, which possesses its own logic, its own principles and laws. He argued that analysis of these principles and laws can lead us from the particular to the general, from the finite to the infinite, from bounded matter to Absolute Spirit. He accepted elements of the ontological, cosmological, and teleological proofs of God's existence. He asserted that reason can lead us to an appreciation of God's Trinitarian nature: God's first person being "Might" or "Power," God's second person being "Reason" or "Word," and God's third person being life-giving "Spirit" (113–14).

Recognition of God as living being came with the assumption of God's freedom to intervene in human history. It also led to the corollary that, if human beings are modeled on God, then we, too, must possess freedom of choice. In Chicherin's words, "the human soul is the arena of freedom [*poprishche svobody*]" (120).

Chicherin posited that, being free, we human beings can recognize and may follow our abstract duty to uphold the universal good. At the same time, we may also yield to selfish desires or vicious impulses. In other words, every day we must distinguish right from wrong and choose between them. Chicherin maintained that choosing the good entails identification with the moral law and with the community of rational beings, whereas choosing evil involves "putting oneself in contradiction to the common moral law" and to the rational community. Of course, it followed that because human beings perpetually face moral choices and because we may, at any time, be drawn toward evil, "there is no person immune to evil [*net cheloveka, iz"iatago ot zla*]" (142). It also followed that, absent the freedom to choose, we cannot be held morally responsible for our acts. As Chicherin put it, "we [may properly] regard only those acts as moral that are done freely, not those accomplished under coercion." To dismiss freedom of the will, as Arthur Schopenhauer and other nineteenth-century thinkers had done, was "to annihilate individual responsibility" (143). Chicherin asserted that the only fully persuasive philosophical position is idealism—that is, recognition of the free Absolute Being, of human beings' innate moral sense, and of the fact that "freedom originates in the metaphysical essence of the individual, an essence inaccessible to empirical analysis" (146).

Turning to the problem of the individual and society, Chicherin defined society as "the union of rational beings." He insisted that, because members of the community are subject to moral law, "there is no human community without religion." He also maintained that individual members of the community "are defined by right, which is closely connected with morality, and which, like the latter, depends on recognition of the absolute principles of human life." Chicherin followed Kant in asserting that the dignity of the individual derives from the status of human beings as bearers of the Absolute. According to Chicherin,

> an individual can demand respect only by virtue of being a bearer of the Absolute. Otherwise, there is no justification for not placing him or her in the sort of subordination in which one places the other animals to whom no one attributes rights.... Only by virtue of this metaphysical essence is a human being recognized as free.... And from this [freedom, right, and dignity] flows the legal equality of human beings.

Chicherin maintained: "Those who speak about liberty, about equality, about human rights, while simultaneously rejecting metaphysics and deriving their understanding of anthropology from empirical data, do not know of what they speak" (149).

Having come close to equating morality (*nravstvennost'*) with right (*pravo*), Chicherin now made a crucial distinction. Like morality, right may be grounded in freedom, but whereas morality is "inner liberty," right is "external liberty." Because the external liberty of one individual may conflict with the external liberty of another person, the right of one is necessarily limited by the external freedom of others. By definition, therefore, right (*pravo*) entails mutual limitation of freedom under law (148). To enforce liberty's mutual limitation, positive law penalizes those who violate it—that is to say, statutory law is necessarily coercive. In Chicherin's opinion, however, morality may be understood as prescriptive in the sense that our sense of duty may make us feel bound in conscience to behave in conformity to the moral law, whereas "positive law [*zakon*] prescribes nothing; rather, it permits everything compatible with the liberty of others. And [under positive law] moral principles have no force: an immoral act may be legally permissible" (148–49).

Here, *in nuce*, was Chicherin's distinction between morality and positive law. The former is the arena of metaphysical choice between right and wrong, and therefore the arena of liberty. The latter is, paradoxically, both inherently coercive and nonprescriptive. On this distinction Chicherin built his conception of human history. On one hand, because human beings are by nature metaphysically free, they will strive to embody that liberty in their social arrangements, which over time will reflect that underlying liberty to an ever greater degree. On the other hand, because individual freedom must always be constrained to a lesser or greater extent by the freedom of others, hence by positive law, social arrangements can never escape some element of coercion. Thus, it may be true both that the arc of history bends toward liberty and that the kingdom of God is not of this world.

Before leaving his analysis of rational knowledge, Chicherin elaborated his views of the soul and the afterlife. Admitting that "of the soul's immortality we cannot know from experience" (161), he imagined the soul as an intermediary between body and reason or mind, as a meeting place of the material world and Supreme Reason (187). At death, when the body disintegrates, the soul can no longer occupy the intermediary position between the physical and the Absolute, so it "fuses itself with the universal spiritual substance that has been poured into the world and that constitutes the essence of humanity" (190). If the individual soul loses its particular identity, mind or reason does not. The individual's capacity to reason constitutes a share of universal reason, but of that portion of the universal reason to which an individual adds over a lifetime his or her distinctive consciousness: it is this consciousness, more or less virtuous, that survives death. Thus, in Chicherin's opinion, there are two sorts of immortality: the impersonal merging of the soul with the universal spiritual substance and personal immortality inhering in rational consciousness.

Chicherin believed that, after death, virtue will be rewarded and vice punished. A rational person adheres to the moral law in part because that person knows that virtuous conduct before death will lead to felicity after death. Were this not so, we should all ask with the German poet Heinrich Heine: "Why does the just man walk, bloody and unhappy, under the cross/ while the evil man rides, happy, as victor, on horseback [*Warum schleppt sich blutend, elend / Unter Kreuzlast der Gerechte, / Während glücklich, als ein Sieger, / Trabt auf hohem Ross der Schlechte?*]" (195). In Chicherin's view, the assurance of justice in the afterlife finally redeems history. Even as human societies advance toward greater perfection, that perfection can only be relative. Generation after generation must engage in manual labor to subdue nature, while a tiny minority enjoys prosperity. If the goal of history is personal material satisfaction, then the human past is a mockery of the simple laborers who have sacrificed their lives without tasting happiness:

> Even if we should imagine that humanity has finally attained complete prosperity equally distributed to each member of society, then the most recent generations would still be privileged in comparison with earlier ones. To them [recent generations] would befall the ultimate happiness, the complete realization of human significance, but what will have come of their predecessors who prepared the way? What can redeem their sufferings and tears? Did they endure oppression and poverty only so that future generations might live better than they did? Even if we assume that, at the end of historical time, individuals will be able to attain their full potential, that fact will not change the lots of the many millions who have perished on the way. Shall we claim that they were instruments of humanity's highest aspirations and that their purpose consisted in playing the role of tools? The moral law forbids us to view the individual merely as a means: while serving higher purposes, the individual is also an end, for he or she is the bearer of an absolute principle, and [only] if this personal [moral] end is not attained, can one say the individual's significance will not have been fulfilled. Therefore, it will not do to appeal to the future perfection of the human species: the demand that full human potential be achieved must apply equally to past and present generations, for human nature is the same in all.
>
> (200–01)

The second book of *Science and Religion* focused not on rational proofs of God's existence but on religion per se, which Chicherin defined as "the human striving toward living communion with the Absolute" (211). In Chicherin's opinion, the aspiration to reach God is rooted in our emotional identification with a being or principle greater than we are. This aspiration is not irrational, for it is the nature of sentient creatures to seek perfect reason. In fact, Chicherin argued, religion "is by its very nature emotion shot through by reason." This observation was the premise for his historical account of religious differences over time: "Religion is subject to development," he wrote, "not because [religious] emotion develops, but because reason does" (216).

Nineteenth-century critics of religion often pointed to what they saw as the "primitive" content of theological systems. For Chicherin, however, a given theology constitutes only a certain stage in reason's grasp of the divine. Similarly, critics ridiculed religious rituals as strange, arbitrary, indeed irrational rites. Chicherin conceded that certain rituals may reflect a low level of doctrinal sophistication, but he insisted that Christian rituals often convey profound truths in an artistic fashion. That is why he thought the Christian sacraments so helpful in facilitating believers' communion with God (223–24).

At bottom, Chicherin thought, every religion manifests the "religious instinct," an innate longing for God. Whereas primitive faith traditions tended to seek God in nature, as a spirit either embodied in matter or manifested in natural phenomena, more sophisticated faiths imagined God apart from nature and therefore as transcendent. Whereas many ancient religions had a purely national or "tribal" character, Buddhism, Christianity, and Islam assumed a universal character (275). Chicherin followed Augustine and the German comparative religionist Max Müller, who ascribed to every faith tradition some truth. Yet Chicherin argued that Christianity, with its postulate of a transcendent God and its universalism, is superior to competing faiths because it harbors a larger component of truth than they do.

Among Christian confessions, Chicherin maintained, there is a shared common belief system, but there are also key differences in governance. Roman Catholicism had tended to demand blind obedience from its adherents, whereas Protestant denominations had emphasized individual freedom to interpret the scriptures. Catholicism had too often degenerated into spiritually destructive authoritarianism, especially where the church had cultivated alliances with secular powers (278); Protestantism had undercut legitimate church authority over doctrine and had elevated rationalism over divinity itself (270–71). What Chicherin sought was a middle way that would protect the individual believer's freedom of conscience while also acknowledging the church's legitimate role in preserving doctrinal integrity. This middle way entailed the rejection of any kind of theocracy but also of any church monopoly over worship in a given state. Chicherin therefore attacked nineteenth-century Christian denominations that aligned themselves with conservative governments against revolutionary ideas, for any such alliance was bound to prove counterproductive for both church and state.[7] He wanted church and

7 See the discussion of the church's role in religion, especially the comments on church-state relations, in Chicherin, *Nauka i religiia,* 262–81.

state to be separate entities, with the church acting as a voluntary association of believers and the state as the entity responsible for protecting believers' freedom of conscience and for protecting the church's status as a free organization.

Chicherin therefore emphasized reason's role in the development of faith traditions, though not to the exclusion of the religious instinct itself. He stressed the centrality of freedom of conscience in the political realm, though not to the detriment of the church's role in maintaining doctrinal adherence. His idea of religion therefore combined progress in two senses: progress in humans' insight into God's purposes, and progress in reconciling freedom of conscience with proper religious authority. His sense of ever-developing theology and his tolerance of religious pluralism marked him as a religious modernist.

As one would anticipate, Chicherin was cautious in his comments about Russian Orthodoxy. His criticisms of those Christian denominations that had aligned themselves with secular authority nevertheless amounted to an implicit indictment of Russian Orthodoxy under the Petrine settlement. He hoped the Russian state would, in the future, protect Orthodoxy without discriminating against other faith traditions. He upheld an "ideal" form of church administration in which a monarchical chief priest (*pervosviashchennik*) presided over the "aristocratic" clergy and the "democratic" laity, with monastics serving as a link between the latter. Adopting Chicherin's model church government would have required the Orthodox Church to jettison the Holy Synod in favor of returning to a patriarch as the church's chief official. Chicherin's program of restoring the patriarchate can be read both as reversion to the medieval ecclesiastical model and as a liberal reformist attempt to remake Russian church governance on the mixed model of government that Chicherin defended in the secular realm.

Book three of *Science and Religion* spelled out the links between faith and historical progress alluded to above. The earliest religions imagined the world and every feature of human life as manifestations of God's will; in other words, these faith systems worshipped the "God of Might." Because early peoples did not distinguish sacred from secular authority, the earliest polities were theocracies. In medieval Europe, educated Christians generally understood God in moral terms; they took Christ as the incarnation of moral perfection—as "God of the Word." In Western medieval Christendom, the tension between sacred and secular authorities usually ruled out theocratic government, even if it did not prevent church officials from trying to institute theocracy. According to Chicherin, the medieval religious synthesis dissolved under pressure from Protestantism and the Enlightenment. Chicherin now expected nineteenth-century secularism to yield to a new religious development, an age of "God of the Spirit," an age of "the Good." He predicted that this new epoch would witness the overcoming of materialism through a rational metaphysics that would enable human beings to arrive at a new level of communion with God.

From the beginning, Chicherin's method had been to combine empirical knowledge (derived from experience) and deductive reasoning. He now supposed that the dialectical union of experience and reason, of matter and spirit, would bring about an "epoch of universalism" dominated by rational faith and communion in the Divine (511). In his view, recognition of reason's proper place in religion would be consistent with *Rechtsstaat* liberalism in the secular realm. For him, rational faith and rational politics went hand in hand.

Chicherin's *Science and Religion* came uncomfortably close to a theodicy, for the book posited a theory of human progress based on the logical revelation of God's Triune nature. Although Chicherin had defended freedom of conscience as imperative and had treated tolerantist liberalism as the secular culmination of history, he sensed that the logically determined culmination of history by divine ordination seemed to mock this liberty. Chicherin answered this objection in two ways. First, he noted that, from a human perspective, individuals have always been free to understand and to observe the moral law, so historical progress can be measured by charting the degrees of that free understanding and free adherence. Second, he maintained that, from a divine perspective, history is the story of humans' return to God. Because God is the beginning, middle, and end of history, the human movement from worship of the God of Might to worship of the God of the Word and, then, the God of the Spirit represents stages in humanity's return from the Good to the Good (519).

Law in theory and practice

Chicherin's metaphysical grounding of moral freedom was a key element of his religious teaching, but he had buried the distinction between morality and law *in medias res* among more important points such as God's existence, the soul's nature, and the afterlife. He returned to the morality/law distinction three years later in his grand meditation on the "social question," *Property and the State* (*Sobstvennost' i gosudarstvo*, 1882–83; 2nd ed., 2005). This polemical work consisted of three parts: a book on legal philosophy, titled "Law" or "Right" (*pravo*); a second book devoted to "Economy" or "Industry" (*promyshlennost'*); and a third book on "The State" (*gosudarstvo*). Chicherin designed the volume to show that philosophy of law is the foundation for understanding liberal economics, and that these two elements—the free individual and a free economy—must undergird the political order and, in turn, be protected by it. Therefore, the distinction between morality and law was foundational to *Property and the State* in a way it could not be in *Science and Religion*. Because of the centrality of the distinction to the argument of *Property and the State*, Chicherin explained it more clearly and added nuances missing in the earlier volume.[8]

8 He returned to the distinction in *Philosophy of Law* (*Filosofiia prava*, 1900), the work that is generally regarded as his masterpiece. I focus here on *Property and the State* because it is Chicherin's original formulation of his mature legal philosophy and because it more clearly shows the development of his views in relation to *Science and Religion*. An exposition of *Philosophy of Law* can be found in G. M. Hamburg, "Boris Chicherin and Human Dignity in History," in *A History of Russian Philosophy, 1830–1930: Faith, Reason, and the Defense of Human Dignity*, ed. G. M. Hamburg and Randall A. Poole (Cambridge: Cambridge University Press, 2010), 111–30.

Chicherin used the first chapter of book one to spell out his basic orientation. He argued that human beings are social animals, and that we are distinguished from other animals by a moral consciousness (*soznanie*) that enables us to choose how to behave and tells us how to define positive laws.[9] In his opinion, the capacity for moral choice, springing from the innermost recesses of human nature, makes human beings metaphysically free. He contended that this freedom may manifest itself externally, in actions affecting others, or internally, through self-mastery. He conceded that human societies often restrict the external liberty of their members and sometimes even enslave them. He argued that early in human history slave ownership had advanced the development of civilization by giving slave owners the wherewithal to act as citizens. In modern Europe before the French Revolution, he noted, society had advanced under the aegis of political absolutism that violently suppressed oppositional movements (65–66). Chicherin maintained, however, that even though unfreedom had manifested itself in the past, human progress is the story of liberty's gradual realization in society.

The advance of external liberty has a number of causes, Chicherin thought, but the main one is human nature itself. Because human beings are morally free, they naturally seek liberty, for they sense that their dignity as human creatures rests on the assertion of freedom. Over time, he claimed, as human beings have come to understand the need to express their inner liberty ever more fully, they have insisted on statutory laws to protect their persons from external interference. Therefore, in modern times, between inner and external liberty there had appeared a mutually reinforcing relationship: "Without inner liberty, external liberty lacks support and meaning.... [Meanwhile] inner liberty without external liberty lacks actuality" (62).

As he sketched the relationship between inner and external liberty, Chicherin made his crucial distinction: inner liberty is the *moral freedom* to choose between right and wrong, and, because inner liberty is rooted in the moral impulses of individuals, it is a metaphysical phenomenon beyond the reach of statutory law. He maintained that external liberty, which by definition operates in the interpersonal sphere, is subject to legal writ and therefore to state coercion. On these postulates Chicherin argued that statutory law must never trammel inner liberty, for interference in metaphysical freedom is the very essence of tyranny. A government should make only laws affecting external relations among people, and it should ground those laws only on protection of individuals against others' unwarranted interference in their lives or on the welfare of society as the sum of individuals.

Chicherin treated moral imperatives and statutory provisions as theoretically independent of one another, whether they coincided or contradicted one another in practice. To illustrate this independence, let us take two simple examples—prohibitions against killing and provisions to render assistance to others. The

9 B. N. Chicherin, *Sobstvennost' i gosudarstvo*, ed. I. I. Evlampiev (St. Petersburg: Izdatel'stvo RKhGA, 2005), 49–50. Parenthetical page citations in the text are to this edition.

moral law against killing one's neighbor coincides with statutory rules against murder. In Chicherin's opinion, however, our moral sensibility serves only to identify right actions and to censure wrong ones, leaving the individual free to choose between good and evil. In Chicherin's abstract view, no agency on earth can rightly compel the individual to choose the good, because inner liberty is the arena in which conscience operates autonomously from external coercion. Statutory rules, on the other hand, spring from the need of society to protect citizens from harm, and laws always entail coercion. Therefore, out of self-protection, a political community prohibits murder and enforces that prohibition by jailing violators. To the naive eye, it may seem that the penal code punishes immoral conduct (killing), but in Chicherin's opinion the penal code actually punishes *antisocial* conduct (murder). This may seem a distinction without a difference, but in Chicherin's theory, protecting the autonomy of the moral realm was paramount.

The distinction between moral and statutory authority comes clearer if we focus on provisions for assisting others. Because the moral law demands that one love others, a good person may feel conscience-bound to give alms to a needy neighbor. In Chicherin's view, however, if the state requires citizens to render aid to others on pain of arrest or loss of property, it infringes on the almsgiver's moral freedom by making charity a compulsory rather than a voluntary act.

In the second chapter of *Property and the State*, Chicherin discussed the problem of right in relation to liberty. He distinguished right viewed from the perspective of the individual—so-called subjective right—from right understood as a binding legal condition—objective right. He asked whether liberty should be interpreted as originating from objective law (*zakon*) or whether objective law is merely the means to define and preserve already existing freedom. This question, he noted, is a philosophical issue that had been debated since antiquity.

According to Chicherin, Roman jurists had tended to see subjective right (the justice deserved by individual citizens) as fundamental and objective right (statutory law) as derivative from it (76–77). Most modern political thinkers since Grotius had made the cardinal error of effacing the distinction between moral imperatives and statutory law, thus making ethical principles legally binding (77–79). In eighteenth-century England and France, there developed a new school of legal thought positing individual rights as the basis of positive law. By century's end, this way of thinking had led to the Declaration of the Rights of Man and of the Citizen. Chicherin criticized eighteenth-century thinkers of the individualist school for failing to justify their assumption that liberty is an inherent fact of personhood:

> If we ask on what basis this theory [of individual rights] rests, we will find no answer among eighteenth-century philosophers. Their theory is the pure result of an analysis dividing human society into its constituent parts and of imputing rights to each [member of society] as inherent and inalienable. But on what basis are such rights attributed to these individuals?
>
> (79–80)

Chicherin considered the individualist theory of jurisprudence not only as philosophically shallow but also as dangerous. Instead of constituting ideal norms toward which human beings should strive, thinkers of the individualist school regarded rights as imperatives against which no one could legitimately object. Moreover, under individualist assumptions, rights were not balanced by duties, except those freely accepted by individuals. The result, Chicherin thought, would be a society based solely on principles of individual right, a society that would tend to disintegrate over time (79–80).

Over the moral and individualist schools of jurisprudence, Chicherin preferred the idealist approach. He accepted Kant's assumption that inner liberty is an inherent property of personhood that each individual should express without impediment in the moral sphere and that deserves protection under statutory law. Chicherin also agreed with Kant that, in the external sphere, freedom should be regarded as an important desideratum, as a worthy human aspiration, but not as an absolute. In Chicherin's opinion, Kant's theory of law had been broadly accepted in early nineteenth-century Europe alongside Hegel's theory of law as the product of free will (81–82). As Chicherin contended, "Philosophers and jurists, liberals and conservatives, partisans of philosophical deduction and defenders of empirical experience—all had come to see right as a manifestation of external individual freedom guaranteed by statutory law" (83).

At the end of Chapter 2 of *Property and the State*, Chicherin returned to his distinction between inner and external liberty, but he now introduced certain complications relevant to his philosophy of law. As before, he defined inner liberty as a moral phenomenon preceding the law, whereas he saw external liberty, by its nature, as subject to juridical regulation. But he now admitted that when human beings "transgress [moral] boundaries and violate the law, it becomes necessary to define their guilt, and that cannot be done without entering the sphere of inner liberty." Criminal law therefore concerns itself with a defendant's state of mind, with the degree of "corruption" of the defendant's will, and with the defendant's intentions or "inner justification [for acting]" (119). Chicherin now defined civil law as the arena in which the individual "acts as a free, autonomous person" with respect to others; thus, civil law is "a sphere in which individualism predominates." He defined public law as "the realm of social liberty," wherein the individual appears not as an autonomous entity but rather as "a member of the community in which he or she has entered as a free but subordinate person" (120).

These new distinctions between moral norms and criminal law, and between civil and public law, enabled Chicherin to argue that there is, after all, a concrete link between moral liberty and civil liberty, and thus that civil liberty is an inherent right of the individual flowing from moral liberty, something that should be protected by the government against arbitrary interference. Meanwhile, he acknowledged that public law may be adjusted as society's needs change, and therefore that the rights assigned to individuals in the public sphere "may be granted or withdrawn according to society's needs" (121–22).

In laying out his morality/law distinction, Chicherin marked out the basis of his differences with the novelist Fyodor Dostoevsky and the philosopher Vladimir

Soloviev. Like Dostoevsky, Chicherin defended metaphysical freedom as central to human identity. To infringe upon the freedom to choose between right and wrong is an assault on human personhood, a monstrous act worthy of the Grand Inquisitor. Like Dostoevsky, Chicherin distinguished between moral and statutory law. Because Dostoevsky regarded moral rules as the linchpin of human society, he thought of moral law as the foundation of rightful statutory authority. However, he considered many provisions of existing public law to be either superfluous (having nothing to do with the moral code on which human behavior should be based) or harmful (contradictory to the moral code). Dostoevsky's utopia—the state's transformation into the church—would eliminate the superfluous and harmful provisions of public law by aligning statutes with the moral code while at the same time striking down the state's penal authority. In his ideal society, there would be no need for government to resort to coercion to enforce the law because individuals would conform to moral law out of fear that the church and their fellow Christians would disapprove of unrighteous conduct. In Dostoevsky's best case, good Christians in an ideal community would obey the moral law habitually out of love for one another. As noted above, Chicherin's distinction between moral and statutory law operated differently.

Judging by Soloviev's *The Critique of Abstract Principles* (1880), the young religious philosopher shared a number of premises with Chicherin, among them the metaphysical value of the individual and the conviction that individuals, as bearers of right, should never be treated merely as means but always as ends in themselves. Indeed, Soloviev concluded, "Recognition that each human being contains something of higher value than *any* material interest is the basic precondition for moral activity and for a normal society."[10] Soloviev went on to prepare his readers for his main conclusion: the achievement of the good in human society can occur only under the aegis of religious faith. Here he was careful to distinguish false conceptions of religion from true. He attacked those religions—Islam and Catholicism—that present God as a being external to nature and humanity, for he felt that such religions, if they are self-consistent, must logically make war on outsiders, on reason, on freedom of conscience, and on human sexual expression. In the West, he averred, clerical power failed to defeat its secular opponents, so it struck a cynical deal with the secularists by separating church and state according to the formula "a free church in a free state." But Soloviev was convinced that absolute separation of church and state was bound to be a disaster in ethical terms. Government can interest itself only in formal justice, whereas the church's interest must be the promotion of active love and eternal justice. Often, the two goals are flatly contradictory. How, Soloviev wondered, does a Christian judge in a murder trial simultaneously love the defendant and sentence the defendant to be hanged? Soloviev's solution for this contradiction

10 V. S. Solov'ev, *Kritika otvlechennykh nachal*, in *Sobranie sochinenii Vladimira Sergeevicha Solov'eva*, ed. S. M. Solov'ev and E. L. Radlov, 2nd ed., 10 vols. (St. Petersburg: Knigoizdatel'skoe Tovarishchestvo "Prosveshchenie," 1911–14), 2:v–397, here at 140.

was an all-encompassing church to which secular authority freely submits itself. He called this solution "free theocracy."

It was on this point, in an essay titled *Mysticism in Scholarship*, that Chicherin parted ways with Soloviev. Chicherin observed that Soloviev demanded a unitary social order in which all particularity was to be subordinated to a single mastering principle—the moral law. In Chicherin's opinion, the moral law is a behavioral code ethically binding on every individual, but, given human nature, impossible to enforce in practice. Any attempt to do so, he thought, "would be the most terrible tyranny imaginable."[11] Soloviev's system of free theocracy would, in reality, lend to society an enormous authority over the individual, would corrupt individual conscience by insinuating social imperatives into it, and would thereby destroy the basis of subjective ethical judgments. "As soon as the inner voice of conscience is transformed into an organ of social consciousness or social imperatives," Chicherin wrote, "the individual will cease to be a free and consequently a moral person." Soloviev's *Critique* could lead "only to the complete negation of freedom."[12]

Late in his life, Chicherin regarded the most pressing practical legal questions confronting Russia to involve the protection of religious practice. In *Russia on the Eve of the Twentieth Century* (*Rossiia nakanune dvadtsatogo stoletiia*, 1901) and *The Polish and the Jewish Questions* (*Pol'skii i evreiskii voprosy*, 1901), he criticized religious discrimination and religious persecution in the Russian Empire. These books rehearsed the turbulent history of Russian-Polish relations since the three partitions in Catherine II's reign. Chicherin accused Catherine of "extraordinary acts of violence" (*samye vopiiushchie nasiliia*) against Polish Catholics and of forcing the Poles "to sign their country's death sentence."[13] When the Poles rose to restore their independence in 1830– 31 and 1863–64, the Russian government responded with punitive measures intended to diminish the influence of the Polish language and the Catholic Church. The government's desire to prevent the spread of Catholic religious influence led it to approve the forced conversion of Polish Uniates.[14] Chicherin repudiated these policies and criticized Russian Polonophobes who sought to control the preaching of Polish priests. He reminded his readers that the state

> has no right to interfere in matters of conscience.... When any earthly authority, driven by political interests, intrudes into this reality, it crosses the ethical limits of its right and becomes an oppressor. This is the cornerstone of the individual's inner freedom, on which depends human dignity in its entirety.[15]

11 Boris Nikolaevich Chicherin, *Mistitsizm v nauke* (Moscow: Tipografiia Martynova i Ko., 1880), 59–60.

12 Ibid., 62–63.

13 Boris Chicherin, *Pol'skii i evreiskii voprosy. Otvet na otkrytye pis'ma N. K. Rennenkampfa*, 2nd ed. (Berlin: Izdanie Gugo Shteinits, 1901), 11–12, 17. Parenthetical page citations in the text are to this edition.

14 B. N. Chicherin, *Rossiia nakanune dvadtsatogo stoletiia*, 4th ed. (Berlin: Izdanie Gugo Shteinits, 1901), 64–66.

15 Chicherin, *Pol'skii i evreiskii voprosy*, 33–34.

He also attacked Russians' general condescension toward Poles because such condescension "breeds the kind of arbitrariness and persecutions that … twist people's souls." He called on Russian statesmen to liberate Poland, an act that "would raise Russia to that height that it had once achieved in the Napoleonic wars, when it became the liberator of Europe."[16]

In *Russia on the Eve of the Twentieth Century,* Chicherin attacked Konstantin Pobedonostsev, the chief procurator (*ober-prokuror*) of the Holy Synod, for initiating restrictions on Russian Baptists (*Shtundisty*) and Doukhobors (*Dukhobortsy,* "Fighters of the Spirit"). Chicherin lauded Leo Tolstoy for raising money to support the Doukhobors. In contrast to Tolstoy's philanthropy, Pobedonostsev's immoral policy had caused an "international scandal."[17]

According to Chicherin, perhaps the most lamentable policies pursued by the Russian government were the "severe restrictions" on Russia's Jews that had led in 1891–92 to the expulsion of Jewish artisans from Moscow.[18] In his book on the Polish and Jewish questions, he tried to explain the various factors contributing to anti-Semitism in Russia: the mistaken notion that Russian Jews had nothing in common with the biblical people of Israel[19]; the prejudice that the Jews are "enemies of Christ" (49–50); the confusion about Christianity held by some Christians who supposed that "one might be a hater and oppressor of Jews and still think of oneself as a genuine Christian" (51); the conceit that oppression of the Jews should be abolished only gradually (52–54); the fear of Jews based on their energy, industriousness, and high level of culture (55–57); and, finally, the mistaken assertion that, by virtue of their kahals, Jews constitute "a state within the state" (59–61). In the end, such views were nothing but old prejudices of the sort convenient to "short-sighted bureaucrats," officials accustomed to considering "the development of liberty as *dangerous*" (62). In Chicherin's view, genuine statecraft "must not consist of petty oppressions. [Officials] should instead take a wider view and should look at the individual's rights, rights which spring from the very nature of human beings and without which there can be no prosperous civic life, no fruitful social development" (62–63).

Assessment

Russian philosophers and non-Marxist political thinkers have given Chicherin a mixed reception. His closest disciple in the Silver Age was probably Pavel Novgorodtsev, who credited Chicherin for profound exploration of the worlds of religion and philosophy and for his philosophical defense of human dignity.[20] Novogorodtsev's best book, *On the Social Ideal* (*Ob obshchestvennom ideale,*

16 Ibid., 41–42.

17 Chicherin, *Rossiia nakanune dvadtsatogo stoletiia*, 59–60.

18 Ibid., 60–64.

19 Chicherin, *Pol'skii i evreiskii voprosy*, 46–48.

20 Pavel Ivanovich Novgorodtsev, *Boris Nikolaevich Chicherin* (Moscow: Universitetskaia tipografiia, 1904).

1917) was an antiutopian treatise built on Chicherin's conception of a strong *Rechtsstaat*.[21] Writing in *A History of Russian Philosophy*, the religious philosopher Vasilii Vasil'evich Zen'kovskii described Chicherin as a "transcendental rationalist," a passionate believer in human dignity, whose ideal of the free personality saved the individual from being swallowed up by society. However, Zen'kovskii worried that Chicherin imagined human beings as being of one substance rather than a vehicle for heterogeneous sensations and therefore susceptible to irrationalism.[22] Nikolai Onufrievich Losskii's *History of Russian Philosophy* (1951) faulted Chicherin for exaggerated individualism.[23] The wisest and most penetrating account of Chicherin's political theory in any language belongs to the Polish historian of philosophy Andrzej Walicki, who underscored Chicherin's attempt to vindicate the rule of law in an intellectual environment hostile to it, and to salvage individual freedom in the face of overwhelming pressure from that "new Moloch," society.[24] We might add to Walicki's assessment that Chicherin's bold defense of freedom depended fundamentally on his religious beliefs. After his long conversion, he understood, as had some of his predecessors in the Russian Enlightenment, that faith and reason, moral imperatives and statutory law, should be interpreted as supplementing rather than as contradicting one another.

In the last half century, jurists and historians inside Russia have shown keen receptiveness to Chicherin's thought. Valerii Dmitrievich Zor'kin's 1975 revisionist book on Chicherin's liberalism underlined the value of his commitment to a rule-of-law state.[25] This book proved a landmark in Russian jurisprudence, not only because of Zor'kin's academic status as the leading Soviet expert on legal philosophy, but also because, after the disintegration of the Soviet Union, he became chair of the Constitutional Court of the Russian Federation. His position in the legal community helped legitimate studies of Chicherin in the post-Soviet period. Since 1991, two biographies of Chicherin have appeared,[26] both treating his political and legal philosophy. Probably the most energetic Russian proponent of Chicherin's philosophy of law since 1991 has been Igor'

21 For a discussion of Novgorodtsev's legal thinking and of his debt to Chicherin, see Andrzej Walicki, *Legal Philosophies of Russian Liberalism* (Oxford: Clarendon Press, 1987), Chapter 5. See also Chapter 11 of this volume.

22 Vasilii Vasil'evich Zen'kovskii, *Istoriia russkoi filosofii v dvukh tomakh* (Paris: YMCA-Press, 1948–50), 2: chap. 6; English edition, V. V. Zenkovsky, *A History of Russian Philosophy*, trans. George L. Kline, 2 vols. (New York: Columbia University Press, 1953), 2:606–20.

23 N. O. Lossky, *History of Russian Philosophy* (New York: International Universities Press, 1951), chap. 9.

24 See Walicki, *Legal Philosophies of Russian Liberalism*, 105–64.

25 Valerii Dmitrievich Zor'kin, *Iz istorii burzhuazno-liberal'noi politicheskoi mysli Rossii vtoroi poloviny XIX–nachala XX v. (B. N. Chicherin)* (Moscow: Izdatel'stvo Moskovskogo universiteta, 1975); see also Zor'kin., *Chicherin* (Moscow: Iuridicheskaia literatura, 1984).

26 Aleksandr Stepanovich Kokorev, *Sotsial'no-politicheskoe nasledie Rossii: kontsa XIX–nachala XX veka (B. N. Chicherin)* (Tambov: Izdatel'stvo TGU, 2001); Boris Vladimirovich Emel'ianov, *Boris Chicherin* (St. Petersburg: "Nauka," 2016).

Ivanovich Evlampiev, who republished Chicherin's *Property and the State*,[27] with an introduction pointing, among other things, to Chicherin's ideas of religion and law. Evlampiev's recent book on Chicherin's political philosophy stressed the centrality of religion and law in Chicherin's thinking, this time in the context of his *History of Political Ideas* (*Istoriia politicheskikh uchenii*, 5 vols, 1869–1902). In his conclusion, Evlampiev offered the hope that Chicherin's work would make Russians mindful of the balance between liberty and responsibility, but also that it would push their society in the direction "of ever greater liberty."[28] More than a century after his death, Chicherin's admirers can ask for no better legacy.

27 See note 9.
28 I. I. Evlampiev, *Politicheskaia filosofiia B. N. Chicherina* (St. Petersburg: Izdatel'skii dom Sankt-Peterburgskogo gosudarstvennogo universiteta, 2013), especially 7–33, here at 223.

7 The civic religion of Anatolii Koni

Tatiana Borisova

Anatolii Fedorovich Koni (1844–1927) was a brilliant and unusual figure in the history of Russian law. His name acquired notoriety in connection with the sensational trial of Vera Zasulich in 1878, where Koni was the presiding judge. The acquittal of the terrorist was perceived by many as Koni's doing—as an unforgivable and brazen escapade of the rising star of the capital's jurisprudence.

While in fact a splendid jurist, Koni was by nature more of an artist than an official. The art world surrounded him from childhood. Koni's father was a theater critic and man of letters. Koni's mother was a well-known actor and an activist in the emerging women's movement in Russia. Koni called himself "a child of the footlights."[1] His godfather was the well-known writer Ivan Lazhechnikov, author of *The House of Ice*. As a youth, Koni already had a passion for reading, and as his personal archive attests, he wrote poetry throughout his life. However, Koni chose jurisprudence, not literature or art, as his life's work. In jurisprudence he occupied a special place, becoming a civic preacher. His eloquence was known far beyond St. Petersburg and Moscow. Representatives of all social strata turned to him for help, writing him letters from all over Russia. Koni's eloquence is attested by his innumerable civic homilies, delivered as public lectures or published in newspapers and journals.

Many studies of Koni have been written.[2] They convey the style of the author, who stands out first of all as a fighter. Sometimes Koni's fighting spirit so enthuses historians that they neglect his own statements. For example, in the Zasulich case, Koni underscored the central role of the jury and even indicated that he was not

1 This chapter is the product of a research project implemented as part of the Basic Research Program at the National Research University Higher School of Economics, Russian Federation.

R. M. Khin, "Pamiati starogo druga," in *Pamiati A. F. Koni* (Leningrad: Trudy Pushkinskogo doma, 1929), 55–79, here at 63.

2 Carla Cordin, *Anatolij F. Koni (1844–1927) zwischen Herrscher und Volk: ein liberaler Jurist und seine autobiografische Praxis in Zarenreich und Sowjetunion* (Cologne: Böhlau Verlag, 2019); V. N. Sashonko, *A. F. Koni v Peterburge-Petrograde-Leningrade* (Leningrad: Lenizdat, 1991); V. I. Smoliarchuk, *Anatolii Fedorovich Koni* (Moscow: Izdatel'stvo "Nauka," 1981); Sergei Vysotskii, *Koni.* Zhizn' zamechatel'nykh liudei (Moscow: Molodaia gvardiia, 1988).

DOI: 10.4324/9781003017097-7

in agreement with their decision, but the historiography still ascribes the authorship of the acquittal specifically to him.[3]

Despite the abundance of publications on A. F. Koni's distinguished service to jurisprudence during the era of the Great Reforms, the question of his motivation has still not been thoroughly researched. The existing historiography is devoted mainly to the professional and political fronts of his struggle. His personal life has not been studied. He thought of himself as a sickly man. Unmarried, he often lamented that he had no family to give him emotional support. However, he was always surrounded by influential women who supported him, enhanced his moral authority in the upper ranks of society, and helped him in his professional work.[4] In this chapter, we are concerned with the moral component of Koni's vocation and its religious underpinning.

Koni's moral authority is confirmed by the fact that he was one of the few prerevolutionary jurists to whom the Soviet regime gave due recognition, perhaps because he never openly criticized the Soviet regime. Moreover, from his starting point in jurisprudence, he worked on a topic of great interest to the Soviets—the ethics of communal living. Indirect evidence of Koni's special relationship to the Soviet state was the permission, after his death in 1927, for his burial in a cemetery of outstanding figures of Russian culture at the Alexander Nevsky Monastery in Leningrad. In 1929, at the height of the Soviet attack on religion, a massive wooden cross was erected on Koni's grave. After World War II, in 1946, Koni's friend E. A. Sadova called the attention of the authorities to the fact that the cross, "erected with such difficulty," was badly tilted, which amounted to "black ingratitude" toward Koni, who, as Sadova reminded them, was "a remarkable man, a deep thinker and writer, the 'leading judge' of Russia, the friend of many outstanding people of our Homeland, a helper and teacher of his contemporaries."[5]

This testimony raises the central question of this chapter: what understanding of the Christian religion did Koni, a baptized Orthodox Christian, profess in his social and professional activism?

Answers to this question can be found in Koni's numerous publications and memoirs, in official documents and correspondence, and in unpublished sources from Koni's personal archive. Relying on these sources, I will speak first about the prehistory of the "Koni phenomenon." Then I will turn to the personages who figure in his notes and homilies. Here I will pay attention to Koni's use of religious language and other elements of his civic preaching. From Koni's preaching, I will turn to his legal cases, examining those in which his civic religion and

3 See discussion in Cordin, *Anatolij F. Koni*, 206–11; and A. M. Larin, "Anatolii Fedorovich Koni," in A. F. Koni, *Izbrannye trudy i rechi* (Tula: Avtograf, 2000), 15–45, here at 32–33.

4 S. A. Domanova, "Perepiska Koni kak istoricheskii istochnik" (kand. diss., Rossiiskii gosudarstvennyi gumanitarnyi universitet, Moscow, 1999), 136–37, 141, 153.

5 Elena Aleksandrovna Sadova, Pis'mo v Litfond soiuza pisatelei (Otdel rukopisei, Rossiiskaia natsional'naia biblioteka [OR RNB], f. 666, op. 2, d. 219, l. 1 ob.).

his relationship to the state's ecclesiastical policies appear most clearly. In the concluding section, I will speak about the final years of Koni's life and the thick file in his archive—a file to which no attention has been paid—where his religious searchings are reflected.[6] The file contains prayers written in Koni's hand (ll. 16, 25–27). For example:

> Lord, your name is love: do not reject me, a man astray
> Your name is strength: strengthen me, for I am fainting and falling
> Your name is light: illuminate my soul, which worldly passions have darkened
> Your name is peace: calm my rebellious soul
> Your name is mercy: do not cease to have mercy on me[7]
>
> (l. 25 ob.)

The file also contains two particularly poignant pages responding to the question, "Is life worth living?" (ll. 43–44). Koni posed the question of suicide to himself in 1918, when the Russian Empire was collapsing before his eyes.[8] Responding to his own question, he described schematically the conditions of life in Russia that induced him to wish for death. Religion was one of the rubrics of these sad reflections. Written in large letters, clearly and legibly, this document was a verdict upon imperial Russia, including the empire's religious policies. Yet, as the documents show, despite his disappointment in the Orthodox Church, Koni's personal faith led him to choose life. What sort of faith was it?

Koni's moral tuning fork

In his essay on "Pushkin's Moral Temper," Koni wrote that, already as a young man, Pushkin became aware of the calling that made him the genius of Russian literature. Koni formulated this calling as "the search for truth in sincerity and justice." The outcome of Pushkin's search was "mercy for the fallen," when one "celebrates forgiveness as victory over the enemy."[9] Pushkin's example became Koni's moral "tuning fork."

6 A. F. Koni, Materialy o religii, 1890–1920 (Institut russkoi literatury [IRLI: Pushkinskii dom], f. 134, op. 1, d. 136).

7 "Mercy" is underlined in the document.

8 A letter from a friend of his later years, Mikhail Teodorovich, who arranged the posthumous publication of Koni's memoirs on the Zasulich case, provides indirect evidence of Koni's contemplation of suicide. See Pis'mo M. Teodorovicha k Koni 1920g. (IRLI, f. 134, op. 3, d. 1692, l. 5 ob.): "The same thoughts you shared with me sometimes occur to me too, but like you, I try to drive them away." See also the essay on suicide Koni published in 1923: "Samoubiistvo v zakone i zhizni," in A. F. Koni, *Sobranie sochinenii v vos'mi tomakh*, ed. V. G. Bazanov et al. (Moscow: Izdatel'stvo "Iuridicheskaia literatura," 1966–69), 4:454–81.

9 A. F. Koni, "Nravstvennyi oblik Pushkina," in A. F. Koni, *Ocherki i vospominaniia: publichnye chteniia, rechi, stat'i i zametki* (St. Petersburg: Tipografiia A. S. Suvorina, 1906), 1–35, here at 24–25. The quoted phrases are drawn, respectively, from Pushkin's "Ia pamiatnik sebe

I use this metaphor following Andrei Zorin, who has shown how the modernist agenda of a new type of personhood appeared in Russia in the late eighteenth and early nineteenth centuries.[10] This agenda took the form of a specific cultural code of moral conduct. Reading and literary creativity were distinctive means of relating a personal moral tuning fork to the ideals, feelings, and mentality of the people of one's own circle. Such practices of affirming personhood were part of the repertoire of the Enlightenment, and, as Zorin shows, the Russian public quickly grasped this particular genre of epistolary self-affirmation and construction of a circle of kindred persons in letters, diaries, and memoirs.

In Russia, as in Western Europe, the modernist personality went through a definite evolution. At first it manifested itself through ethical and aesthetic experience in the private sphere: love, friendship, family relationships. The ethics of the new person were based on the daily choice of truth and justice in the face of conflict with the conventions of existing hierarchies. Beginning in the 1840s, modernist rhetoric of the new personhood became a mode for the development of the public sphere. Clear evidence of this was the appearance of the first literary weekly, *Literaturnaia gazeta* (Literary gazette), in 1840. The editor was Koni's father, Fedor Alekseevich Koni. As stated by the critic V. G. Belinskii, the famous promoter of the modernist agenda in Russian literature, the materials of this newspaper were expected first of all to answer to the criterion of "modernity," that is, "to have lively, contemporary interest."[11] Readers were not simply to receive information or moral instruction, but to be actively involved in the ethical evaluation of a fast-changing world.

Anatolii Koni was born when *Literaturnaia gazeta* was just four years old. The modernity of his father's views was solidified through conflicts with the censors. F. A. Koni was the writer who first made the *feuilleton* an indispensable rubric in a Russian newspaper.[12] His biting *feuilletons*, satirizing the stagnant moral norms of Russian life, eventually led to his departure from the newspaper.

The authorities' vengeance on F. A. Koni's boldness endangered the material situation of the Koni family. In the 1850s, F. A. Koni published the literary-theatrical journal *Panteon* (Pantheon), in which he printed sarcastic stanzas rumored to have elicited the anger of Nicholas I. During the Crimean War, *Panteon* was not permitted to reprint telegrams from the official military newspaper, *Russkii invalid* (The Russian invalid), something A. F. Koni subsequently viewed as an act of reprisal by the emperor. *Panteon* collapsed. One day, returning home from

---

vozdvig nerukotvornyi" ("I erected a monument for myself not made by human hands") and "Pir Petra pervogo" ("The Feast of Peter the First").

10 A. L. Zorin, *Poiavlenie geroia. Iz istorii russkoi emotsional'noi kul'tury kontsa XVIII– nachala XIX veka* (Moscow: Novoe literaturnoe obozrenie, 2016). On major trajectories of narratives of personhood in Russia, see D. Ia. Kalugin, *Proza zhizni: russkie biografii v XVIII–XIX vekakh* (St. Petersburg: Izdatel'stvo Evropeiskogo universiteta v Sankt-Peterburge, 2015).

11 V. G. Belinskii, *Polnoe sobranie sochinenii v trinadtsati tomakh* (Moscow: Izdatel'stvo AN SSSR, 1953–59), 3:380.

12 G. P. Talashov, *Literaturnaia gazeta 1840–1845 godov* (St. Petersburg: Roza mira, 2005).

school, young Koni discovered that his family's furniture had been sealed up to settle accounts with his father's creditors. He had to do his homework on the windowsill.[13]

Thus, Koni discovered early both the joy of acting in accordance with high principles and the burden of humiliating retribution for this joy. The vulnerability of his parents' vocation as artists influenced his choice of jurisprudence as his calling. In 1865, he finished his studies in the law faculty of Moscow University. Despite his great literary gifts and deep interest in literature, he came forward as a writer only after he had established himself professionally as a jurist. He was eventually elected to the Russian Academy of Sciences in two fields: law (1896) and literary criticism (1900).

Koni chose to pursue the legal profession in state service rather than private practice. He understood very early that the state was the most influential player in social and professional life. He believed that it was possible to put the state's resources to work in the service of justice and to attract others to this service. The Judicial Reform of 1864 and the liberationist agenda of the reforms of Emperor Alexander II opened all sorts of possibilities for this. As the first historians of the Judicial Reform wrote, new principles for the "liberation of persons" were built into its foundation.[14] For Koni, the new judicial statutes were a landmark of liberation from social bondage and hierarchy. They created a foundation for *service* to the principles of justice.

Fathers and children of the Judicial Reform

Koni began his service in the field of jurisprudence the day after the opening of the St. Petersburg Judicial Chamber. On April 18, 1866, he was named assistant to the secretary of the chamber. His talents were recognized, and in late 1866 he began working in the procuracy of the Moscow Judicial Chamber. He quickly ascended the career ladder. Working in Moscow, Kharkov, and Samara, Koni got to know the people in his circle, those for whom the Judicial Reform provided an opportunity to "serve justice." I will show below how Koni took this rhetoric from the "fathers" of the Judicial Reform and reworked it in a new genre—the genre of civic preaching.

In the Koni archive one can find journal and newspaper clippings castigating the old court system. One can assume that it was with special love that Koni saved an article from the pen of one of the fathers of the Judicial Reform, Sergei Ivanovich Zarudnyi: "Letter of an experienced official of the 1840s to a young colleague entering state service."[15] The editor claimed in a note that the letter had

13 Khin, "Pamiati starogo druga," in *Pamiati A. F. Koni*, 64.

14 P. I. Liublinskii, "Sud i prava lichnosti," in *Sudebnaia reforma*, ed. N. V. Davydov and N. N. Polianskii, 2 vols. (Moscow: "Ob"edinenie," 1915), 1–41, here at 3.

15 Sergei Ivanovich Zarudnyi, "Pis'mo opytnogo chinovnika sorokovykh godov mladshemu sobratu, postupaiushchemu na sluzhbu" (1850) (IRLI, f. 134, op. 5, d. 181). The clipping

been "passed along" to him by Zarudnyi. We will return to the fiction of indirect authorship later.

In his "Letter," the "experienced official" advised the novice to avoid resolving even a single case, but to respond to all cases in purely formal terms. He went on to note that any ethical or moral conflict had to be suppressed:

> Handling cases in this way, you will smother your inborn sense of justice, and compassion for the unfortunate will be unknown to you. Hence:
> — never try to uphold the side of truth when falsehood armed against it is stronger and is sheltered by legal forms; by upholding the truth, you will only bring suspicion upon yourself; no: in such instances, always refuse, uphold the side of the strong, and you will enjoy the reputation of being a scrupulous official.
> — never pay as much attention to the substance of a case as to the people involved.
> — never do what ought to be done; do what the superior authority wishes.[16]

I have cited this satirical passage to demonstrate the existence of a new cultural code of *service* in a government job, a code which both the fathers and the children of the Judicial Reform shared. It was based on a sharp break with hypocrisy. Richard Wortman called this code "legal consciousness."[17] Legal consciousness implied that the recognition of human dignity, of the value of human life, and of the natural rights of human beings should be foundational. This consciousness was an important condition for the implementation of the Great Reforms of Alexander II in the 1860s and 1870s. Koni described the break between the old and the new with great clarity in the collection of essays he organized for the fiftieth anniversary of the judicial statutes, *Fathers and Children of the Judicial Reform*.[18]

The demand that one's own and others' actions should be moral, that they should correspond to "truth," became an important paradigm in the demolition of the traditionalist model of hierarchical power. Zarudnyi satirized those who slavishly served their superiors rather than freely serving their principles. People of the new type should decide independently what should be done according to principles and notwithstanding the tastes of their superiors, and then they should be held accountable for their actions.

However, Zarudnyi's "Letter" was written in a typically schematic way, without concrete details. The safely anonymous tone was typical of compositions of

---

is from *Russkaia starina*, 1899, vol. 100, no. 12: 543–46. See also "Sergei Ivanovich Zarudnyi," in Koni, *Ocherki i vospominaniia*, 625–45.

16 *Russkaia starina*, 1899, vol. 100, no. 12: 545–46.

17 Richard S. Wortman, *The Development of a Russian Legal Consciousness* (Chicago: The University of Chicago Press, 1976, 2010).

18 A. F. Koni, *Ottsy i deti sudebnoi reformy (K piatidesiatiletiiu Sudebnykh Ustavov). 1864–20 noiabria–1914* (Moscow: Izdanie Tovarishchestva I. D. Sytina, 1914).

this type published before the Great Reforms. Critical details often pointed to a personal acquaintance whom the author was castigating, but neither the author's name nor concrete hints as to the identity of the persons or place of the affair were indicated in such publications. Such a style was a safe means for state servants to criticize the work of other officials.[19]

Koni broke decisively with anonymous and indirect authorship, where the critic was an unnamed accomplice in the events he censured. As a "son" of the Judicial Reform, Koni wrote in a completely different way. In his many speeches, he provided numerous details of a personal kind when he celebrated his heroes, that is, those who implemented desired changes. He praised those who, on their professional path, performed acts of "civic heroism" (*grazhdanskii podvig*) in the service of humanity and homeland. If, in the earlier period, we find anonymous publications for one's own circle, now we have colorful speeches crammed with details of a personal sort and delivered in public venues such as an academic auditorium, an open lecture, or the meeting of a professional or civic society.

"Civic hagiography": F. N. Plevako

Koni applied the term "civic heroism" to the activity of a far from simple figure among Russian lawyers, Fedor Nikiforovich Plevako. I will take a detailed look at Koni's portrait of him because the religious component of Koni's civic preaching appears there with great clarity. I call Koni's presentation "civic hagiography" (*grazhdanskoe zhitie*), a composition where the saintliness of the hero is disclosed through the courageous mastering of a thorny professional path.

Koni chose an interesting format for his account of Plevako by comparing and contrasting him with another son of the Judicial Reform, the well-known Moscow lawyer Prince A. I. Urusov. Koni compared the two in "Two Judicial Orators" (1910), a lecture he presented to the Society of Lovers of Oratory not long after Plevako's death.[20]

Koni began by stating that both his heroes rejected the assumption that "new people will not be found for the new cause." Both Urusov and Plevako were new people, sons of the Judicial Reform, but they were very different sons. Urusov,

19 See Tatiana Borisova, "Legislation as a Source of Law in Late Imperial Russia," in *From the Judge's Arbitrium to the Legality Principle: Legislation as a Source of Law in Criminal Trials*, ed. George Martyn, Anthony Musson, and Heikki Pihlajamäki (Berlin: Duncker & Humblot, 2013), 295–315, here at 304–08. Also available as Chapter 3 of Tatiana Borisova, "The Emergence of the Legality Tradition in Russia, 1800–1918 (PhD diss., University of Turku, 2017) at www.utupub.fi/bitstream/handle/10024/129875/Borisova_DISS_2016.pdf.

20 A slightly revised version appears as "Kniaz' A. I. Urusov (um. 1900) i F. N. Plevako (um. 1908)," in Koni, *Sobranie sochinenii*, 5:123–37. An offprint of the original lecture is archived: A. F., "Dva sudebnykh oratora" (OR RNB, f. 423, d. 1020). On Plevako, see V. I. Smoliarchuk, *Advokat Fedor Plevako: ocherk o zhizni i deiatel'nosti advokata F. N. Plevako* (Cheliabinsk: Iuzhno-Ural'skoe knizhnoe izdatel'stvo, 1989). On Urusov, see A.V. Stepanova, "A. I. Urusov—iurist i sudebnyi orator" (kand. diss., Saratovskii gosudarstvennyi universitet, 2005).

the scion of an old Moscow family, symbolized the continuity of an earlier, traditional lineage of elite power. Plevako, born almost a thousand miles east of Moscow in Orenburg Province, was the illegitimate son of a Pole and a Kirghiz woman. As Koni saw it, the radically different backgrounds of these two men played a defining role in their differing conceptions of law and the judicial process. Koni used the comparison with Urusov to underscore all the more emphatically the novelty of Plevako, a "tribune" of the people in the Russian judicial system.[21]

Urusov and Plevako represented different cultures. Urusov bore the "stamp of the hereditary gentry and a centuries-old culture"; "in his movements and gestures, the refined upbringing of a man educated in the European manner shone through" (5:123). Plevako came from an indigenous Russian culture:

> In contrast to the aristocratic Urusov, Plevako had the manner of a democratic plebeian, a person who knew native life in all strata of Russian society—someone who, without losing his dignity, could ascend to the top or descend to the "bottom"—someone who, on both levels, understood everything and was understood by all, always responsive and unaffected.
>
> (5:124)

In Koni's view, in the activity of the plebeian Plevako, "the element of service to society predominated" (5:133). This became apparent in the different ways in which Plevako and Urusov viewed the Judicial Reform of 1864:

> For Urusov, a European to the bottom of his soul, the new statutes were a fragment and a manifestation of Western political life, a life he treasured in his dreams but which we had not yet experienced [in Russia].... In his speeches to juries, one could discern the broad education of a man … who popularized his view of the case at hand in order to influence those who chanced to sit before him, people to whose low and various levels of development he artfully calibrated the exposition of his train of thought.
>
> (5:129–30)

As Koni saw it, Urusov continued the old tradition of a Russian elite positioned above the people, whereas the "democrat" Plevako actually embodied the people. For Plevako, the new judicial laws "were the sacred gates through which newly awakened Russian thought and the legal consciousness of the people entered into the life of society." For him, jury trial was "a venue for the spirit of the people, a spirit called to show itself in questions of conscience and in defense of the people's worldview on fundamental principles of social structure" (5:129).

21 "Kniaz' A. I. Urusov (um. 1900) i F. N. Plevako (um. 1908)," in Koni, *Sobranie sochinenii*, 5:123–24.

Koni thought it especially important to emphasize how differently Urusov and Plevako related to jurors. Plevako's relationship was "heartfelt":

> For him, they were the chosen bearers of the people's wisdom and sense of justice. He refrained from trying to teach them or manage them. Without separating himself from them, he entered into their milieu with his powerful discourse and immersed himself along with them in the feelings he aroused and, at times, in their age-old worldview.
>
> (5:130)

Koni used Plevako to underscore how the Judicial Reform signified a new direction in Russian social life. The reform produced heroes who opened the doors of the court not to educate the people, but to listen to them and to heed "the people's justice" (*narodnaia pravda*). For Plevako, the judicial statutes were not a copy of Western models as they were for Urusov, but a means of hearing his own people.

The civic hagiography devoted to Plevako is full of Christian rhetoric, including direct references to holy scripture, which Koni himself marked as quotations:

> He [Plevako] often turned the weapons of his own powerful discourse to the defense of the "humiliated and abused," to representing the cause of poor, weak, and primitive people who broke the law as a result of confusion or because others, while treating them lawfully perhaps, did not treat them "in God's way."
>
> (5:133–34)

Koni emphasized that the law in the codes was essentially an incarnation of Christian law. Thus, when a defendant, Abbess Mitrofaniia, tried to justify her fraudulent acts by saying that "as a woman" she did not know she was breaking the law, Plevako implacably reminded her, "From the summit of smoking Sinai it was stated, 'Thou shalt not steal.' … You could not have been ignorant of this, so what are you up to?" (5:126–27).[22]

Such a sense of justice was a help to Plevako when he was poorly prepared for a trial. Koni observed that, unlike the meticulous Urusov, Plevako did not always study the details of the case before him. But for Koni, such carelessness was not a critical factor: Plevako had a sense of justice and the ability to communicate it to others. To describe Plevako's talent in this regard, Koni again alluded to religious or mystical experience:

> For the most part, his speeches were marked by unfeigned inspiration. It took possession of him, at times probably without his expecting it. At these

22 Abbess Mitrofaniia (Baroness Praskov'ia Grigor'evna Rozen) was convicted in 1874 of forging promissory notes to fund projects of the convent she supervised.

> moments, he was like Russian sectarians, members of mystical denominations who, during their rituals, suddenly enter a state of ecstasy and explain it by saying that "the spirit descended upon them." So, too, did it descend upon Plevako.
>
> (5:127)

Koni went on to give an example of how Plevako experienced and communicated to others the transcendental experience of communion with a source of gracious truth that revealed itself to him when, in Koni's words, "the spirit descended upon him." On one occasion, in a closed session in the Senate, Plevako was defending the presiding judge of a major court who was accused of allowing his subordinates to embezzle funds designated for repair of the court. The prosecutor in the case recalled the words of holy scripture: "to whom much is given, much will be required" (Luke 12:48). Koni continues:

> The factual side of Plevako's speech [for the defense] was weak—he confused the witnesses and kept losing his train of thought. But, remembering the prosecutor's words, Plevako pulled himself together and said in a voice that carried from one soul to another: "the prosecution tells you that [the defendant] once stood high but has now fallen low, and on these grounds strict punishment is being solicited because 'much should be required' of this man. But, gentlemen, here he is before you, the one who stood so high! Look at him, and think about his broken life. Has much not been required of him already? Just think of what he has had to suffer while awaiting his inevitable appearance on the court bench and even now while sitting on it. He stood high … he has fallen low … but note, this refers only to the beginning and the end of his story. What about everything he has experienced in between? Gentlemen, be merciful and just, and being mindful of his high position as well as of how low he has fallen, ponder the arc of his fall." Pushkin said that "as soon as the divine word touches his heedful ear, the soul of the poet is roused like an awakening eagle."[23] But the divine word speaks to the heart of a heedful person not only in words about beauty and love: it awakens in him also the feeling of forgiveness and mercy. Such a voice obviously sounded for Plevako, forcing him to wake up and rouse himself. One had to hear him at these moments, to see his gestures, to understand from the expression on his transfigured face—transfigured by an inner rapture—that "the spirit had descended upon him."
>
> (5:128–29)

As we have seen, the new court in which "tribunes" like Plevako could present themselves was for Koni a place where, alongside the letter of the law with which the legalist Urusov complied, the spirit of the people's justice could thrive. The

23 Koni quotes from Pushkin's poem "Poet" ("The Poet").

spirit of truth "descended" through this man of the people. For him as for the jurors, bearers of "the people's justice," the essence of the laws was revealed as resting upon the Christian principles of forgiveness and mercy. The experience of such divine revelation in court was possible precisely because of the innovations in legal procedures springing from the Judicial Reform of 1864, which Koni never ceased to defend with ferocity.

The struggle for justice against the Pharisees: the acquittal of Zasulich

The authorities soon noticed the brilliant procurator Koni and transferred him to the capital, where, beginning in 1875, he headed up the work of the Department of the Ministry of Justice. In this position, he coordinated all cases under the command of the justice minister, Count K. I. Pahlen. At the beginning of 1878, Koni was named presiding judge of the St. Petersburg District Court. Here the greatest professional ordeal of his life awaited him: the trial of Vera Zasulich, a terrorist who had attempted to assassinate the governor of St. Petersburg in January of that year. From personal materials in the Koni archive and from his own memoirs, we know that he thought much about the meaning of life, religion, and his own faith during the severe personal crisis connected with the acquittal of Zasulich.

After the scandalous acquittal of the terrorist, Koni's professional standing was shaken. The proposal of the minister of justice that Koni retire caused him great moral suffering and, as he himself wrote, "emotional pain." The minister's proposal, Koni lamented, "was directed at an irremovable judge because he [the judge] acted as a servant of the law under conditions outlined by the Judicial Statutes [of 1864], not as an obliging accomplice in the implementation of decisions made in advance."[24]

Koni became ill from the strain. Only two individuals among his fellow officials did not shrink from showing him friendly concern. These were the minister of internal affairs, Dmitrii Miliutin, in whose chancellery Koni worked shortly after graduation from the university, and Konstantin Pobedonostsev, a former professor who remembered Koni as one of his talented students.[25] Koni kept up a correspondence with Pobedonostsev throughout his life, despite the political friction between them. It is known that Pobedonostsev severely censured Koni for the Zasulich verdict and warned Emperor Alexander III that he should not trust Koni with the responsible post of chief procurator of the Senate.[26] Yet Pobedonostsev's

24 "V doroge," in A. F. Koni, *Na zhiznennom puti*, 2 vols. (Moscow: Tipografiia I. D. Sytina, 1916), 2:340. Koni served four more years as president of the District Court, but, tired of the constant criticism, he was pleased at his transfer to the Civil Department of the Judicial Chamber, whence, in 1885, he was transferred to the Senate.

25 "V doroge," in Koni, *Na zhiznennom puti*, 2:340.

26 *Pis'ma Pobedonostseva k Aleksandru III*, 2 vols. (Moscow: "Novaia Moskva," 1925), 1:119.

letters to Koni always contained a Christian component. Their contents allow us to suppose that relations of spiritual closeness existed between them.[27]

For Koni, the Zasulich affair was the moment when his professional and personal ethics crystallized, as did his faith in justice and human beings. It was precisely after the acquittal and the disgrace that resulted from it that Koni began his civic preaching. It is interesting that he started writing detailed memoirs about the Zasulich case in 1904, but he was not able to finish them before the end of his life.[28] The fact that Koni continued working on the memoirs during the 1920s and was still not ready to publish them testifies to the great significance the Zasulich case had for him.[29]

The story of the Zasulich trial began with the sharpening of the conflict between old and new principles in Russian jurisprudence. The minister of justice asked Koni, the presiding judge, to use his good offices to incline the jurors to convict Zasulich. Koni replied that such an understanding of the role of the presiding judge was not admissible:

> The president of the court is a judge, not one of the parties, and in conducting a criminal trial, he holds a veritable chalice containing the sacred gifts. He does not dare to tip it to one side or the other—otherwise, the gifts will be spilt.[30]

Koni insisted that a court does not render services to anyone. In accordance with the ordinances of the fathers of the Judicial Reform, a court must serve justice, not individuals. The liturgical metaphor of the chalice with the holy gifts underscores the exalted institutional significance of the court as an institution in which high justice is accomplished, the same thing we saw in Koni's "hagiography" of Plevako.

So Pahlen tried to influence Koni in a different way. To remind him of his professional duty and the fact that the emperor was the supreme lawgiver in the Russian Empire, Pahlen organized an audience with Alexander II two weeks before the trial, on the occasion of Koni's inauguration as presiding judge of the St. Petersburg District Court. Such an audience was not stipulated by protocol. Koni understood that it had been organized because of the approaching trial, and, in agitation, he pondered how to share his feelings about the case with the Tsar-Liberator. At the reception following the Sunday liturgy, deep disappointment

27 In a letter of April 6, 1882, Pobedonostsev wrote Koni: "Christ is risen. Rejoice, and remember me" (IRLI, f. 134, op. 3, d. 1320, l. 1).

28 Vospominaniia A. F. Koni o dele Very Zasulich. August 15, 1904 (Gosudarstvennyi arkhiv Russkoi Federatsii [GARF], f. 564, op. 1, d. 200, 201), unfinished manuscript. The memoirs were published posthumously by Koni's friend and collaborator M. F. Teodorovich: A. F. Koni, *Vospominaniia o dele Very Zasulich*, ed. M. F. Teodorovich (Moscow and Leningrad: Academia, 1933).

29 See L. Utevskii, "Poslednii etap zhiznennogo puti," *Pamiati A. F. Koni*, 79–101, here at 96.

30 *Vospominaniia o dele Very Zasulich*, in Koni, *Sobranie sochinenii*, 2:85–86.

awaited Koni. The emperor, a very weary man unacquainted with the details of the Zasulich case, shook his hand and inquired briefly about his previous government service.[31]

Thus, Koni had to decide for himself how to act in the case, and he chose the path that seemed to him the most congruent with seeing justice done. To this end, he made the principled decision for which he was subsequently censured. At the trial, he allowed the defense to rehearse the circumstances which provoked Zasulich to commit her crime. Zasulich testified that she was not personally acquainted with the student Bogoliubov but had read a newspaper account of the harsh suppression of disorders in a preliminary detention facility, disorders resulting from the shameful flogging of Bogoliubov for supposedly failing to remove his hat in the presence of D. F. Trepov, the governor-general of St. Petersburg. The humiliation of a man already deprived of his rights and the defenselessness of his fellow prisoners compelled Zasulich to take her desperate step. By her attempt on Trepov's life, she wanted to turn society's attention to this unconscionable state of affairs.

Koni's decision to allow the reading of the aforementioned newspaper article in open court and to permit the interrogation of eyewitnesses fundamentally altered the significance of the trial. Pahlen intended to present the trial as the adjudication of a criminal case in which the basic motive was Zasulich's desire for vengeance against Trepov for the humiliation of Bogoliubov, with whom it was rumored she was having an affair.[32] Under Koni's presidency, the trial went from being a private case to being a social case: Zasulich's act was interpreted as an all but necessary step of self-defense by society against arbitrary state power.[33] This was the interpretation the trial received in a number of St. Petersburg newspapers. In the detailed reporting on the case in *Novoe vremia* (New times), for example, the reader is struck by the fact that most of the space was devoted to the defense's argument, while the prosecution's side was presented very laconically.[34]

In the end, the case against Zasulich became a case against the unlawful exercise of power. In point of fact, Trepov's order to have Bogoliubov flogged exceeded the limits of the law. Punishment of this type could be applied to a convict only when he was serving his sentence, whereas the events in question took place in a preliminary detention facility.

In his memoirs, Koni paid attention to an interesting detail that bears on the role of religion in this story. He wrote that not long before the Bogoliubov affair,

31 Koni emphasized, however, that it was considered an honor to merit a question from the emperor.

32 Letters intercepted by the secret police testify to the existence of these rumors in St. Petersburg. See GARF, f. 93, op. 1, d. 5.

33 See Tatiana Borisova, "Public Meaning of the Zasulich Trial 1878: Law, Politics and Gender," *Russian History* 43, no. 3–4 (2016): 221–44; and T. Iu. Borisova, "Neobkhodimaia oborona obshchestva: iazyk suda nad Zasulich," in *Kembridzhskaia shkola: teoriia i praktika intellektual'noi istorii*, ed. T. Atnashev and M. Velizhev (Moscow: Novoe literaturnoe obozrenie, 2018), 232–57.

34 *Novoe vremia*, 1878, no. 755.

in social circles and state institutions, people had begun talking about the need to reinstitute flogging as a patriarchal method of reasserting control over young people. Trepov's order to have Bogoliubov flogged was issued in this context. It was a response to the demand to "restore" peace and quiet by force.

Koni also highlighted the fact that Trepov once came to see him and, "crossing himself before the icon," tried to convince him that he did not know that his action violated the law. Trepov also kept insisting that, after the flogging, he had sent tea and sugar to Bogoliubov as a token of reconciliation. Amused by this supposedly Christian act on Trepov's part, Koni said he doubted that Bogoliubov drank Trepov's tea. As for Zasulich, Koni wrote that, already before her trial, Trepov went around saying he forgave Zasulich and did not wish her ill, although he did not appear in person at her trial. For Koni, Trepov's declarations amounted to nothing but Pharisaism, something he was well acquainted with in his milieu, and which he more than once denounced in his memoirs on the Zasulich case.

Public opinion eventually inclined to the view that Koni did not violate judicial procedure in the Zasulich trial.[35] The fact that the jury acquitted Zasulich indicated the presence of a moral conflict in society between "fathers" and "children." The fact that the defense of Trepov's right to life lost the argument in court indicated the victory of "mercy" for the children. As Koni saw it, this outcome was an important victory for the new court system as a social institution which might facilitate the reconciliation of the two sides.

The Multan case

The Multan case, like the Zasulich case, had great social resonance. Koni, who from 1885 was the chief procurator of the Criminal Cassation Department of the Senate, took a principled position in the case.

This case, which has not escaped the attention of researchers, is especially interesting to examine in contrast with the Zasulich case.[36] In both instances, a crime was committed against the right to life. In both instances, a jury examined the case. Newspapers showed great interest in the trials. As the archival materials demonstrate, Koni's participation was central in both instances.[37] Here, however, the similarities end. The greatest difference between the trials sprang from the contrast between the "civilized" urban center where jurors were able

35 Koni's colleague and former professor Boris Chicherin, who attended the trial, wrote a short but very influential note in which he authoritatively confirmed the legality of the entire judicial procedure in the Zasulich trial. See B. N. Chicherin, "O dele Zasulich," in Koni, *Vospominaniia o dele Very Zasulich*, ed. Teodorovich, 376–84.

36 See the review of the historiography in I. V. Loginova, "Otnoshenie rossiiskoi obshchestvennosti i vlasti multanskomu delu v kontse XIX veka" (kand. diss., Nizhegorodskii gosudarstvennyi pedagogicheskii universitet, 2002).

37 Ugolovnogo kassatsionnogo Departmenta Pravitel'stvuiushchego Senata delo o multanskom zhertvoprinoshenii (Rossiiskii gosudarstvennyi istoricheskii arkhiv [RGIA], f. 1363, op. 2, d. 452).

to understand and forgive Zasulich and the "backward" province where peasant-jurors twice convicted the innocent Votyaks.

In 1894, in the village of Staryi Multan, far from the capital, a peasant named Kanon Matunin was murdered. The murder took place in a ritual scenario, which immediately led investigators to seek suspects among the local Votyaks—an ethnic group Christianized early in the nineteenth century but still maintaining some of their traditional rituals. (In today's Russia, the Votyak ethnos is called by its indigenous name: Udmurt.) At the first trial, the jurors convicted the Votyaks. Thanks to the vigilance of the defense, however, it was revealed that the criminal investigation suffered from serious breaches of procedure, including the flogging of the accused and of witnesses. A second trial ensued, but a fresh panel of jurors once again convicted the Votyaks.

The writer V. G. Korolenko, invited by the defense to attend the trial, became an important participant in the event. Thanks to his journalism, the public in the capitals came to learn of the sorry consequences to which the patriotic rhetoric of the defense of Christian values could lead.[38] The basis of the prosecution's case was the assertion that the Votyaks were primitive, which was automatically taken to imply that they had engaged in human sacrifice. The Votyaks' supposedly primitive state was established with the help of various experts. Besides ethnographers who confirmed "scientifically" the existence of rituals of human sacrifice among the Votyaks, Orthodox clergy played a role.[39]

The first indictment was based on two witnesses for the prosecution—a ninety-five-year-old man, Iustin Danilov Ivantsev, whose nephew the Votyaks supposedly intended to offer as a sacrifice, and the priest Mikhail Yakimov, who claimed to have knowledge of two instances of human sacrifice by the Votyaks.[40] The counsel for the defense, Mikhail Deriagin, correctly protested that the charge was based on hearsay.[41]

As in the Zasulich case, newspapers played an important role.[42] The Senate, upon receiving Deriagin's appeal, demanded an explanation from the Kazan district procurator. Moreover, a clipping from *Russkie vedomosti* [Russian news] containing Korolenko's reporting on the trial was dispatched to the procurator, whose response the Senate wished to receive.[43] The procurator was asked to respond to two serious charges by Deriagin and Korolenko concerning the

38 Korolenko wrote ten articles on the case. See V. G. Korolenko, *Polnoe sobranie sochinenii*, 9 vols. (St. Petersburg: Izdanie Tovarishchestva A. F. Marks, 1914), 4:303–464.

39 On the role of ethnographic expertise in the Multan case, see Robert Geraci, "Ethnic Minorities, Anthropology, and Russian National Identity on Trial: The Multan Case, 1892-96," *The Russian Review* 59, no. 4 (2000): 530-54.

40 Ugolovnogo kassatsionnogo Departmenta Pravitel'stvuiushchego Senata delo o multanskom zhertvoprinoshenii (RGIA, f. 1363, op. 2, d. 452, l. 93).

41 Ugolovnogo kassatsionnogo Departmenta Pravitel'stvuiushchego Senata delo o multanskom zhertvoprinoshenii (RGIA, f. 1363, op. 96, d. 452, l. 3).

42 See Loginova, "Otnoshenie rossiiskoi obshchestvennosti i vlasti multanskomu delu."

43 Clipping from *Russkie vedomosti*, October 18, 1895 (RGIA, f. 1363, op. 96, d. 452, ll. 95, 95 ob., 96).

quality of the judicial procedure: the intimidation and beating of Votyak witnesses, and the fact that the court bailiff, Shmelev, administered the oath to the witnesses not on a Bible (as should have been done because the Votyaks were baptized) but on a bearskin.

On October 20, 1895, the procurator of the Kazan Judicial Chamber, N. D. Chaplin, presented a detailed report to the minister of justice. "Aside from a certain tendentiousness and mode of exposition betraying the participation of the defense counsel in their compilation," he wrote, "I personally find that the factual material in these documents is laid out truthfully enough and accords with the factual material submitted to the ministry by me and the procurator of the Court of Sarapul" (ll. 99–99 ob.). Following this personal introduction, in which he tried to show that he was a modern man and did not object in principle to newspaper reports on judicial proceedings, the procurator went on the attack. As I will show below, he allied himself with the authority of local knowledge, the local administration, and the local church.

Rejecting reports of an oath "on a bearskin" and the beating of witnesses as "not at all plausible," the procurator stated his assurance that:

> as he had learned from a fellow procurator who supervised the investigation, these reports were dreamt up by the witnesses Mikhail Tikhonov and Konstantin Moiseev with the aim of justifying their denial of the original depositions establishing the guilt of their relatives. The procurator suggested that the district police chief should quietly correct these details.
>
> (l. 101)

Thus, while rejecting the plausibility of reports of beatings and a pagan oath, the procurator nevertheless ordered the removal of these details from the minutes of the session where they were recorded as a complaint on the part of the defense counsel.

What made the procurator so sure that he was right? First, he cited:

> the impression made by the anxious, overwrought, and one-sided personal opinion of Mr. Korolenko and his colleagues, who are scarcely competent to judge an episode from the daily life of an ethnic group whose morals and customs are in many respects still hidden from the view of specialist ethnographers and, if you will allow me to say so, are better known to the population of the Vyatka region who have contact with the life of the Votyaks than to the specialists.
>
> (l. 102)

Appealing to local knowledge, knowledge presumably inaccessible to visiting journalists, the procurator insisted that even among Votyaks "who have been enlightened by the Orthodox religion," pagan rituals continued to exist, a fact about which "there is no doubt, either in the general population or among the clergy or among the state authorities or among researchers" (l. 102 ob.).

Next came the procurator's weightiest argument:

> The pagan rituals of the Cheremiss and the Votyaks, even those who have converted to Orthodoxy, long ago attracted the attention of the government and precipitated measures designed to uproot them. By order of Emperor Nicholas I, missionaries for this purpose were designated for Vyatka Province beginning in 1827; in some degree, the illustrious Metropolitan [of Moscow] Filaret supervised the missionary work. However, the successes recorded during the first period of the mission did not in the end produce favorable results and, as stated above, pagan rituals are still practiced, and not only among the Votyaks of Vyatka Province, but among other indigenous groups in neighboring provinces.
>
> (l. 102 ob.)

As chief procurator of the Department of Criminal Cassation of the Senate, Koni did not find the explanation of the Kazan procurator convincing. He was indignant at how quickly representatives of the judiciary and the police, along with local priests, were prepared to present the Votyak peasants as savages and to exclude them from the operation of laws that provided for the defense of the rights of individuals under investigation. To vindicate justice, Koni used formal criteria. The decision of the Department of Cassation of the Senate, which he prepared, abounded with references to specific articles of criminal law that had been violated in the Multan case. Koni's position appeared on the pages of *Novoe vremia* (New times) and was incorporated into the collection of his speeches published in 1896.[44]

Koni wrote that he explained to the minister of justice, N. V. Murav'ev, who had hinted at the emperor's displeasure, that if the accused Votyaks were going to be convicted of human sacrifice to pagan gods, this should be done formally:

> by observing with complete accuracy all the forms and rituals of the legal system, because, through such a decision, not only would the existence of a frightful and bloody custom be confirmed by the authoritative word of a court, but the question would also inevitably arise as to whether Russia, which has governed the Vyatka region for several centuries, has taken sufficiently effective measures to fulfill its mission of Christian and cultural enlightenment.[45]

In this way, Koni sought to reverse the argument about the allegedly primitive Votyaks. He tried to show that a verdict based on their primitive state cast doubt

44 "Po delu o Multanskom zhertvoprinoshenii," in A. F. Koni, *Za poslednie gody: Sudebnye rechi. Vospominaniia i soobshcheniia. Iuridicheskie zametki* (St. Petersburg: Tipografiia A. S. Suvorina, 1896), 243–59.

45 "V. G. Korolenko i sud," in A. F. Koni, *Izbrannoe* (Moscow: "Sovetskaia Rossiia," 1989), 217–22, here at 221.

on how civilized the government's mission of enlightenment actually was. A fair review of an unlawful investigation and flawed trial, along with the correction of all breaches of due process, could restore "civilization" to the government's own administrative procedures.

Summing up

Koni's position on the Multan case was a continuation of his position at the Zasulich trial. He spoke out unambiguously against the tendency to militant conservatism in the political discourse of the Russian Empire at the time. Koni understood that the discourse of war, punishment, and intransigent confrontation with external and internal enemies would lead to the diminishment of the rights of persons. He saw the task of the judicial system to lie in mercy, reconciliation, and the restoration of peace. As the eminent lawyer N. P. Karabchevskii wrote, Koni believed "in human beings."[46]

Religious discourse played an important role in the moral confrontation between conservatives and innovators like Koni. Sergei Uvarov's triad—Orthodoxy, Autocracy, Nationality[47]—inspired the patriotic rhetoric that lavished praise on M. N. Murav'ev, the pacifier and "hangman" of Poland, who put down the Polish rebellion of 1863. Newspapers called Murav'ev a "saint of the state" (*gosudarstvennyi podvizhnik*). After Karakozov's attempt on the life of Emperor Alexander II in 1866, Murav'ev's harsh but "just" policy was transferred from the rebellious western borderland to the heart of the empire: he was appointed to chair the Extraordinary Criminal Commission investigating the attempt. In his petitions to the emperor, Murav'ev never ceased to insist that the press was infecting the youth of the empire with the Polish "contagion," that is, harmful "social ideas" emanating from the West.[48] The infected individuals should be subjected to the harshest punishments and quarantined. This call for "hygiene" and discipline through punishment, censorship, and prosecution appeared very clearly during the 1860s.

Against such state-sponsored "saintliness," which sowed fear, dissension, and suspicion, stood Koni's "civic heroism" in the service of mercy, reconciliation, and justice. Koni preached forgiveness for the weak but retribution for persons in positions of authority who abused their power. New people like Plevako and Koni himself used judicial institutions to defend the humiliated and oppressed and to oppose injustice. As his copious correspondence and the memoirs of

46 N. P. Karabchevskii, Piatidesiatiletie sudebnoi i obshchestvennoi deiatel'nosti A. F. Koni (September 30, 1915) (OR RNB, f. 423, d. 1057, l. 3). Karabchevskii mentions that when he was a young man, Koni extricated him from a group of defendants on trial for revolutionary activity.

47 Sergei Semenovich Uvarov (1786–1855) was a scholar and statesman who served as education minister (1833–49) under Nicholas I.

48 GARF, f. 95, op. 1, d. 439.1, d. 439.2. See Claudia Verhoeven, *The Odd Man Karakozov: Imperial Russia, Modernity, and the Birth of Terrorism* (Ithaca: Cornell University Press, 2009).

contemporaries prove, Koni used his position to do everything he could to help countless petitioners who sought him out to defend them against injustice.[49]

In Koni's view, the new courts, along with the provision for jury trial, made it possible to realize the people's hopes for justice. Here Koni continued an established tradition in Russian philosophy of law, namely, an emphasis on the normative significance of law. It was this principled meaning of "justice" (*pravda*) in Russian law that Ivan Kireevskii underscored in his article "In Response to A. S. Khomiakov" (1839).[50] Kireevskii held that the procedural approach to law dominant in the West reduced law to a lifeless formula, whereas in Russia law ascended directly to justice and truth that could not be given or taken away. He developed this thought in his philosophical "Fragments": "Justice, morality, the spirit of the people, human dignity, and the sanctity of lawfulness [*sviatost' zakonnosti*] can all be felt only with an awareness of the eternal religious relations of humanity."[51] In Koni's view, too, an unjust law could not be applied in court without negative consequences for civil peace.

However, as in the cases of Zasulich and the Votyaks, Koni was convinced that judicial procedures, namely *due process* in the Western sense, made it possible to contest the unjust actions of the police. The court became the arena for restoring justice in the conflict between justice and order. The order imposed by Trepov and the Vyatka investigators, based as it was on using force against people whose rights were already sorely impaired, could be contested on two grounds: its unlawfulness and its injustice. The court could expose and censure the unlawfulness of the flagrant violation of rights through procedural breaches of administrative rules, thereby giving voice to people who held those breaches to be not only unlawful but unjust.

In this sense, one can agree with Jörg Baberowski that the Judicial Reform of 1864 had constitutional significance for Russia.[52] As a distant echo of the unwritten English constitution with its Act of Habeas Corpus, the Judicial Reform made the guarantee of the procedural rights of human beings an important criterion of legality. Koni's civic advocacy played a huge role in spreading precisely this understanding of the possibility and necessity of justice in Russian law during the reform period. The distinctiveness of Koni's view lay in how he linked guarantees of due process with popular ideas of justice. Rejecting the notion that judicial

49 A. F. Koni, Pis'mo N. S. Tagantsevu (December 5, 1878) (OR RNB, f. 760, no. 236, l. 2). "Perepiska s L. N. Tolstym," in Koni, *Sobranie sochinenii*, 8:103–05. See also Smoliarchuk, *Anatolii Fedorovich Koni.*

50 I. V. Kireevskii, "B otvet A. S. Khomiakovu" at http://az.lib.ru/k/kireewskij_i_w/text_0080.shtml.

51 Ivan Kireevsky, "Fragments," in *On Spiritual Unity: A Slavophile Reader*, ed. and trans. Boris Jakim and Robert Bird (Hudson, N.Y.: Lindisfarne Books, 1998), 275–91, here at 291.

52 Jörg Baberowski, "Law, the Judicial System and the Legal Profession," in *The Cambridge History of Russia*, vol. 2, *Imperial Russia, 1689–1917*, ed. Dominic Lieven (Cambridge: Cambridge University Press, 2006), 344–68.

procedures borrowed from the West ran ahead of the natural course of events and were not appropriate for the primitive population of the Russian Empire, Koni insisted that the people knew when justice was violated and were prepared to fight for justice in court.

As we know, Koni rejected Stolypin's invitation to become minister of justice after the Revolution of 1905.[53] He continued to work in the Senate. Disappointed in the capacity of state institutions to oppose the forces of conservatism, he retired from the judiciary but continued to take part in legislative activity and redoubled his preaching of faith "in human beings." Adding to his many portraits of saintly activists in Russia, he wrote a separately published biographical sketch of the famous saintly doctor F. P. Gaaz.[54] At Koni's request, the minister of justice, N. A. Manasein, gave a copy of this work to Emperor Alexander III on February 28, 1898, and the emperor expressed his gratitude to Koni.[55] Koni gave copies of his writings to all three of the last Romanov emperors with the aim of letting them, too, hear his preaching of mercy and forgiveness.

In 1903, promoting his idea of the need for civic reconciliation, Koni tried to realize the project of creating a special hospital for political prisoners on the Valaam Islands, where, with the help of the Orthodox monks of Valaam, prisoners could prepare themselves to reenter society. In this way, Christian love and mercy would overcome the injustice of the existing social order. It is clear from the documentation that Koni traveled to Valaam and attempted to implement his plan.[56] Notebooks preserved in his personal archive with extracts from the Gospels are clearly devoted to one overarching theme—mercy, Christian love, forgiveness (ll. 6–11 ob., 46–49).

Koni experienced the tragedy of 1917 in a deeply personal way. Giving serious thought to the question of suicide ("Is life worth living?"), he made a depressing reckoning of the fall of the Russian Empire, which he presented schematically under the following rubrics: "my personal situation, the spiritual aspect, the people, the intelligentsia, the homeland, the Russian person, general conclusion." He defined the spiritual aspect categorically in terms of two things he fought against throughout his life: "the profanation of ideals and principles" and "the subversion of public service by time-servers" (l. 44).

In the section on "homeland," there is separate subdivision for religion where Koni briefly summarized his verdict on the ever-submissive Orthodox Church:

> Vague concepts of God and sin. In place [of God], obscure dogma. Relics. Distortion of the meaning of icons. Replacement of dogma by ritual. Elimination of the mystical character of ritual. Prayers for the tsar, the Holy

53 Petr Arkad'evich Stolypin was prime minister of Russia from 1906 until his assassination in 1911.

54 A. F. Koni, *Fedor Petrovich Gaaz: Biograficheskii ocherk* (St. Petersburg: Tipofgrafiia A. S. Suvorina, 1897). Also in Koni, *Sobranie sochinenii*, 5:288–422.

55 Koni, Materialy o religii (IRLI, f. 134, op. 4, d. 18, l. 8).

56 Koni, Materialy o religii (IRLI, f. 134, op. 1, d. 136, ll. 84–86 ob.).

> Synod, for "Our Lord-Bishop-So-and-So," for the Christ-loving army. Loss of respect for the church. The latrine, cigarettes.
>
> (l. 85)

His point was that the Orthodox Church, subordinate to the state and put to the task of serving the police functions of the throne, had lost the confidence of the people, who were quick to make a "latrine" of it as soon as the political regime that protected it fell. But the need for justice and mercy did not vanish with the collapse of the empire. During the Civil War, Koni courageously chose life in response to the greatest challenge facing his fellow citizens at the time, namely, the reduction of life to mere survival, to the maxim: "Don't survive in order to live, just live in order to survive" (l. 44).

In 1918, while Vera Zasulich was dying in hungry Petrograd in a small apartment crammed with baskets of rotting produce, Koni was giving lectures on ethics.[57] His contemporaries often mentioned that teaching—that is, systematic civic preaching—was a necessity for him. As an old acquaintance, the psychiatrist S. M. Lukianov, attested, even though Koni had no need for additional income, from 1876 to 1883 he taught the theory and practice of criminal procedure in the Imperial School of Jurisprudence.[58]

Following the Russian Revolution, Koni was in great material need. Deeply ashamed that he was forced to live and work in such conditions, Mikhail Teodorovich asked Koni to accept the financial assistance that Teodorovich was able to give—two thousand rubles.[59] Lecturing became Koni's chief means of support. In 1918–22, he devised a course on "The Ethics of Communal Living," which he delivered in the Institute of Cooperators and the Institute of the Living Word at Petrograd University.

Continuing his civic preaching, Koni lectured on the contribution of the heroes of Russian literature (Tolstoy, Dostoevsky, Turgenev) to the understanding of human nature. Like Pushkin, he sought "to foster benevolent feelings," even at the height of the Civil War.[60] Koni had already developed a keen interest in psychiatry, and now, besides his lectures on the ethics of communal living before wide audiences in the young Soviet republic, he lectured with increasing frequency to doctors on the subject of medical ethics.[61] Perhaps he hoped in this way to make his own contribution to the understanding of human nature and its potential for improvement.

The last works of Koni's life clearly illustrate how he understood the essence of jurisprudence. For him, serving society meant serving people's needs, especially

57 Antonina Fedorovna Peshekhonova, Byloe: Vospominaniia 1905–1919 (1949–1952), Tetrad' 2 (OR RNB, f. 581, d. 70, ll. 138–39).

58 S. M. Luk'ianov, "Pamiati A. F. Koni," *Zhurnal dlia usovershenstvovaniia vrachei*, 1927, no. 10: 733–38, here at 737.

59 Pis'mo M. F. Teodorovicha A. F. Koni 1919 (IRLI, f. 134, op. 3, no. 1692, l. 1).

60 The quotation is from Pushkin's "Ia pamiatnik sebe vozdvig nerukotvornyi."

61 Luk'ianov, "Pamiati A. F. Koni," 738.

the needs of the oppressed: the more people stood in need of the restoration of justice, the more selflessly Koni devoted himself to their affairs. In the courts, in the procuracy, in the judicial institutions of the Russian Empire, and in his lectures to the hungry population of Petrograd during the revolutionary period, Koni promoted the view of the sociopolitical process that Karamzin had articulated almost a century earlier: "It's not forms that matter, but people."[62]

62 N. M. Karamzin, *Zapiska o drevnei i novoi Rossii v ee politicheskom i grazhdanskom otnosheniiakh* (Moscow: "Nauka," 1991), 98.

8 Leonid Kamarovskii

Christian values and international law

Vladimir A. Tomsinov

Kamarovskii and the modern science of international law

Leonid Alekseevich Kamarovskii (or Komarovskii, 1846–1912) was a scholar of encyclopedic knowledge who left a huge body of work—more than two hundred books, articles, and essays. A number of his works were dedicated to various aspects of the internal political life of Russia in his day, including constitutional law, parliamentarism, governmental power, and political parties. He also wrote on Russian foreign policy, particularly Russia's relationship with the Balkan states, and published articles on university education. However, works on international law and international relations are the most significant part of his scholarly legacy, in both scope and intellectual content.[1] In the words of Sergei Kotliarevskii, international law "was not just the object of Count L. A.'s professional *work*, but the object of his profound faith and devotion."[2]

As a scholar, Kamarovskii addressed nearly every principal problem of international law: the nature, objective conditions, and concrete forms of international law; the rights of sovereign states to security, development, and equality; the means and methods of resolving international disputes; the idea of an international court; and problems of international organization. But the principal theme of all his work on international law was the idea of peace. As he put it:

> No critical, dispassionate mind can fail to see that the higher the moral and intellectual level of humanity rises, and the more perfect the organization of states becomes in terms of freedom and stability, the more completely war contradicts these developments. In our day, when society has reached such a high level of culture and even aspires to call itself Christian, war is a scandalously discordant element.[3]

1 The most complete bibliography of Kamarovskii's published works is in A. S. Iashchenko, "Graf L. A. Kamarovskii: Zhizn' i nauchnaia rabota," *Izvestiia Ministerstva inostrannykh del*, 1913, kn. 1: 117–34, here at 129–34.

2 S. Kotliarevskii, "Neskol'ko slov pamiati gr. L. A. Kamarovskogo (1846–1912)," *Iuridicheskii vestnik*, 1913, kn. 4: 222–23, here at 222.

3 L. Kamarovskii, *Voina ili mir?* (Odessa: Tipografiia Isakovicha, 1895), 8–9.

DOI: 10.4324/9781003017097-8

Kamarovskii believed that the establishment of "the most equitable and stable peace possible among states by means of a special international organization" should be the main goal of international law. He qualified this view by declaring that peace should be taken to mean

> not the utopia of eternal, i.e., universal and uninterrupted peace on earth, but peace understood only as a juridical principle.... This principle is much more concrete, definite, and limited, and it is quite realizable. The establishment of *such* a peace is a straightforward and noble task. Will a broader and more lasting peace thereby arise on our planet? Only future ages—in all likelihood, far removed from us—can answer this question.[4]

Kamarovskii did not just investigate specific problems of international law. He also attempted to establish what can be called *the ideology of modern international law*. He saw that it is impossible to establish a stable order of international law when, in the global arena, the actions of individual states are governed solely by self-interest. Accordingly, he expressed the view that

> the exclusively political interests of individual states—interests which lead to universal hostility and anarchy, or to temporary and artificial compromises—should be replaced by international legal principles which, while respecting the independence and autonomy of nations, bind them together as members of humankind into a higher, living whole.

Kamarovskii felt that the best way to shed light on these principles was "to eschew the opinions of diplomats and listen instead to public opinion" when it is expressed with total candor.[5]

At the same time, he saw the Christian religion as the prototype of universally accepted, hence universally binding, principles of international law capable of putting an end to incessant hostility between states. Inherently cosmopolitan and universal, Christianity is

> diametrically opposed to the pagan religions, all of which were national in character. Although Christianity was not the immediate source of international law, it was the factor which more than any other cleared the way for it because of the profound inner kinship that exists between the ideas and commandments of Christianity on one hand and the principles of international law on the other.[6]

4 L. A. Kamarovskii, *Ob osnovnoi zadache mezhdunarodnogo prava*, Rech', proiznesennaia v torzhestvennom sobranii Imperatorskogo Moskovskogo Universiteta, 12-go ianvaria 1898 goda (Moscow: Universitetskaia tipografiia, 1898), 3.

5 Kamarovskii, *Voina ili mir?*, 22.

6 L. Komarovskii, *Mezhdunarodnoe pravo* (Moscow: Tipografiia Obshchestva rasprostraneniia poleznykh knig, 1900), 8.

A. S. Iashchenko, Kamarovskii's pupil, wrote a biographical portrait in which he sought to define his teacher's place in the history of the science of international law. Iashchenko called Kamarovskii "a representative of the religious-philosophical tendency" in international law.[7] However, this is not a completely accurate assessment of Kamarovskii's approach to the subject. While paying attention to the inner kinship between the principles of the Christian religion and the ideas of international law, Kamarovskii qualified this point by saying that

> international law as a juridical system *is not to be identified with either religion or morality but rests upon independent principles of law*. International law will gradually be extended to all the nations in the world as they come to understand its nature and purpose [italics added].[8]

Kamarovskii viewed international law not from the religious or moral standpoint but from the juridical standpoint. Thus, he predicted that international law would eventually include nations professing religious beliefs quite different from Christianity. He believed that the significance of Christianity for international law lay not in its particular religious content but in its general worldview. Kamarovskii emphasized repeatedly that Christianity did not create international law, but played the enormous role of forming the cultural and spiritual community among nations which is the necessary objective condition of the existence of international law. As he put it, "In its basic idea and commandments, Christianity has expressed what international law aspires to convey in juridical language" (22).

According to Kamarovskii, three Christian ideas facilitated the emergence of the spiritual community from which international law sprang up. The first was *the idea of the unity of all humankind*. The second was *the idea of the brotherhood of all human beings*. According to Christian teaching, "all human beings, as sons of God, are brothers, regardless of nationality, class, or social standing." The third idea, derived from the other two, is *peace*. Kamarovskii firmly believed that "Christianity is the most sublime teaching of peace the world has ever known" (22). In *The Idea of Peace and the Church*, Kamarovskii supported his view with specific references to canonical Christian texts. "According to the Gospels," he observed,

> the commandment of peace is one of the fundamental commandments for all Christians. This is attested not only by the whole spirit of the Gospels, but also by many other texts, the plain meaning of which cannot be obscured by certain passages and [historical] facts which appear to contradict this spirit.... [A]postles constantly and insistently repeat the commandment of peace. In their epistles, they use this word to greet the faithful, they view God as the

7 Iashchenko, "Graf L. A. Kamarovskii," 123.

8 L. Kamarovskii, *Osnovnye voprosy nauki mezhdunarodnogo prava*, *Uchenye zapiski Imperatorskogo Moskovskogo universiteta*, Otdel iuridicheskii, vyp. 10 (Moscow: Universitetskaia tipografiia, 1895), 1–201, here at 57.

> foundation of true peace, and they even call their whole teaching *the ministry of reconciliation.*[9]

While remaining separate from the norms and principles of international law, the spiritual values of Christianity helped to strengthen the order of international law by their moral effect on it. "There is no doubt that a lasting improvement of international relations cannot be achieved unless the moral level of both rulers and peoples is raised," Kamarovskii averred, adding that "morality, in turn, finds its deepest and most lasting basis in religion."[10]

On March 12, 1903, Kamarovskii delivered a public lecture at Moscow Diocesan House on the importance of Christian morality for normal international relations. He remarked:

> No matter how perfect our laws and state institutions might be (and they are very far from perfect), they will always need the support of morality. There are two reasons for this. First, in both life and consciousness, morality precedes law and makes up for its gaps and deficiencies. Second, morality deepens the meaning of the ideas expressed in law, provides these ideas with practical application, and opens the way for their improvement in the future. The life of a community in all its forms—from families to international alliances—does not rest on compulsion but on the animating effect of a moral principle. Moreover, when we speak of this principle, we do not mean autonomous morality based on the idea of humans as rational beings belonging to this world alone. We mean Christian morality, which draws its principles from divine revelation. Of all systems of morality proposed so far, Christian morality is the most profound intellectually and the most applicable to everyday life.[11]

"A most idealistic and deeply religious man"

Kamarovskii's Christian worldview enabled him to appreciate the qualities that make international law one of the grandest phenomena in the life of human society. But Kamarovskii was not only a scholar with a pronounced Christian style of thought, he was also a Christian by education, temperament, and mode of life. A. S. Iashchenko, who knew Kamarovskii well, noted:

> Count Kamarovskii was unusually truthful, guileless, and honest. In all his relationships, this guilelessness lent him an endearingly old-fashioned

9 L. Komarovskii, *Ideia mira i Tserkov'* (Moscow: Tipografiia G. Lissnera i A. Geshelia, 1899), 4, 6. Kamarovskii is referring to 2 Cor. 5:18: "All this is from God, who through Christ reconciled us to himself and gave us the ministry of reconciliation" (Revised Standard Version).

10 Kamarovskii, *Osnovnye voprosy nauki mezhdunarodnogo prava*, 55–56.

11 L. A. Kamarovskii, "Khristianskaia nravstvennost' i mezhdunarodnye snosheniia," *Vera i Tserkov'*, 1903, kn. 5: 810–27, here at 810–11. Moscow Diocesan House was an Orthodox educational center in central Moscow which opened in 1902. It now houses St. Tikhon's Orthodox University of Humanities.

quality—aristocratic, simple, and a bit naïve amid the political and social chicanery of our complicated age. He was a very religious person, a believing Christian, and completely devoted to the precepts of the Orthodox Church. He would begin every important undertaking with a prayer, and prior to every decisive step in his life he would pray before the icon of the Iberian Mother of God. He was close friends with many hierarchs of the Russian Orthodox Church, including Anastasii, vicar bishop of Serpukhov, and especially Arsenii, archbishop of Novgorod, doctor of theology, former rector of Moscow Theological Academy, and a member of the State Council.[12]

In 1900, Arsenii was bishop of Volokolamsk. In that year, he wrote in his diary of a visit with the "most estimable and kind" Kamarovskii family: "I spent a very pleasant two hours with them. A family like this one is very rare. They exude such purity and sincerity, such a welcoming spirit, that you seem to be raised to a higher plane."[13] In the same diary entry, Arsenii called Kamarovskii "a most idealistic and deeply religious man." This characterization agrees completely with the opinion of Iashchenko, who wrote:

> [Kamarovskii's] modest, almost ascetic mode of life, his profound religiosity and abiding simplicity of heart, the kind yet stern, ascetic features of his slender, immobile face—all this conveyed the impression of something close to holiness and made one think of the ancient Russian saints.[14]

Leonid Alekseevich Kamarovskii was born into a noble family on March 15, 1846, in Kazan. His father, Aleksei Evgrafovich Kamarovskii, was a landowner. His mother, Adelaida Albertovna, was the daughter of Baron Albert Karlovich Pirch, a Kazan landowner of German descent. Initially, Leonid was educated at home by teachers who administered the standard gymnasium curriculum. Religion was also part of Kamarovskii's early training. As Iashchenko remarked, "with respect to religion, his education was closely supervised by his mother, who was deeply devoted to the precepts of the Orthodox Church and imparted her religiosity to her son."[15] In 1864, as a nonmatriculant, Kamarovskii passed the entire course of study in the First Kazan Gymnasium and enrolled in the law faculty of Moscow University.

As a student, Kamarovskii had a wide range of interests. Both Russian state law and ancient Roman history attracted him, and the latter was actually the subject of his first thesis.[16] But international law eventually became the chief focus of his

12 Iashchenko, "Graf L. A. Kamarovskii," 121.

13 Arsenii (Stadnitskii), mitropolit, *Dnevnik*, vol. 1: 1880–1901 (Moscow: Izdatel'stvo Pravoslavnogo Sviato-Tikhonovskogo universiteta, 2006), 360.

14 Iashchenko, "Graf L. A. Kamarovskii," 121.

15 Ibid., 117.

16 Kamarovskii's candidate's thesis, "Studies on Roman Finance and Economics," came out as a monograph: *Ocherki Rima v finansovom i ekonomicheskom otnosheniiakh* (1869; Moscow: LENAND, 2018).

attention. From his student years to the day of his death, he treated this discipline as if it were his religion.

After completing his undergraduate studies in 1868, Kamarovskii stayed on in the department of international law to write a master's thesis. In 1871–72, he studied international law at Heidelberg University under Johann Kaspar Bluntschli.[17] Professor Bluntschli showed great cordiality toward the young Russian scholar and was happy to offer him advice and guidance. Kamarovskii treated Bluntschli with great respect, although he did not accept all of his views on international law. In the foreword to his master's thesis, *The Principle of Nonintervention*, Kamarovskii wrote:

> I am particularly grateful to Professor Bluntschli of Heidelberg University, who was always ready to guide me with advice and supply me with books from his library during my stay of nearly a year and a half in picturesque Heidelberg. The days I spent with this worthy servant of science are among the most radiant memories of my life.[18]

Kamarovskii shared Bluntschli's view that Christianity played a prominent role in the development of international law. Kamarovskii called the following passage from Bluntschli on this point "superb":

> Many Christian ideas paved the way for international law. Christianity regards God as the father of human beings and human beings as children of God. This view recognizes in principle the unity of humankind and the brotherhood of all nations. The Christian religion restrains the pride and conceit of the ancient world and demands humility; it cuts off egoism at the root and teaches self-denial. It places self-sacrifice on behalf of one's neighbors above domination. In this way, it removes the obstacles that hindered the emergence of international law in antiquity. It elevates and liberates human beings, purifying them and reconciling them with God. Its message is peace. It would therefore be quite natural to translate these ideas and commandments into the principles of a humane international law that recognizes all nations as members of one great family of humankind, protects

17 Johann Kaspar (also Caspar) Bluntschli (1808–81) was a jurist of Swiss origin, the author of *Moderne Kriegsrecht der civilisierten Staten, als Rechtsbuch dargestellt* [The modern law of war of civilized states, expounded as a code] (Nördlingen: C. H. Beck'sche Buchhandlung, 1866) and *Das moderne Völkerrecht der civilisirten Staaten, als Rechtsbuch dargestellt* [The modern international law of civilized states, expounded as a code] (Nördlingen: C. H. Beck'sche Buchhandlung, 1868). Kamarosvkii edited the Russian translation of the latter: I. Bliunchli, *Sovremennoe mezhdunarodnoe pravo tsivilizovannykh narodov, izlozhennoe v vide kodeksa*, trans. V. Ul'ianitskii and A. Lodyzhenskii, ed. L. Kamarovskii (Moscow: V tipografii Indrikh, 1877).

18 L. Kamarovskii, *Nachalo nevmeshatel'stva* (Moscow: V Universitetskoi tipografii [Katkov i Ko.], 1874), iv.

> peace everywhere, and even in times of war demands respect for universal human rights.[19]

On October 14, 1874, Kamarovskii delivered his introductory lecture as a privatdocent in the law faculty of Moscow University. The title was "Comments on the Relation of International Law to Other Branches of Jurisprudence."[20] Such was the beginning of a teaching career of thirty-eight years at Moscow University.

On December 5, 1874, Kamarovskii successfully defended his master's thesis, *The Principle of Nonintervention.* At the defense, he called his thesis the first result of his study of international law and politics. As for the topic, he went on to say:

> Anyone who devotes himself to the study of a specific discipline will naturally direct his attention to the general and fundamental problems of the field he has chosen. In the field of international law, *the principle of nonintervention* is indisputably this kind of problem. On the one hand, a scientific understanding of the subject becomes clearer to us as we learn more about the life of states and the laws that govern it; on the other hand, actual practice at every turn brings us face to face with the interference of one state in the affairs of another.[21]

Kamarovskii fully recognized the strangeness of trying to apply some sort of legal norms to intervention, that is, to the display of force and selfish calculations by intervening states. Obviously, such excesses occur when "by force or clever intrigues states can benefit from the troubles and discord of their neighbors." He went on to explain, however, that "to renounce the desire to grasp and define the various forms of intervention is tantamount to relegating all relations between states to brute force alone—a conclusion that contradicts the fundamental idea of international law" (99).

Seeking to understand the principle of nonintervention, Kamarovskii began by examining theories expounded in the foreign literature. Next, he examined diplomatic documents related to defensive intervention: in connection with the French Revolution at the end of the eighteenth century, and in connection with the activity of the Holy Alliance (Russia, Austria, and Prussia) during the 1820s. The design of Kamarovskii's work had an obvious shortcoming in that he discussed

19 Quoted in Kamarovskii, *Osnovnye voprosy nauki mezhdunarodnogo prava*, 23. The quotation is from Bluntschli, *Das moderne Völkerrecht der civilisirten Staaten*, 12. See also Bliunchli, *Sovremennoe mezhdunarodnoe pravo tsivilizovannykh narodov*, 15.

20 "Zamechaniia ob otnosheniiakh mezhdunarodnogo prava k drugim otrasliam pravovedeniia." The lecture was published in the newspaper *Moskovskie vedomosti* in October, 1874. The following year it was published in French translation: L. A. Kamarowsky, "Quelques réflexions sur les relations entre le droit international et les différentes branches de la jurisprudence," *Revue de droit international et de legislation comparée* 7 (1875): 5–21.

21 *Sbornik gosudarstvennykh znanii*, ed. V. P. Bezobrazov, vol. 2 (St. Petersburg: V tipografii V. Bezobrazova i Ko., 1875), Otdel kritiki i bibliografii, 98–103, here at 98–99.

theories of nonintervention and the practice of international relations separately, which made it impossible to assess the theories properly. Grouping theories of nonintervention by the nationality of their authors was also a flaw.[22] Another shortcoming was Kamarovskii's failure to analyze the Monroe Doctrine (1823), which vowed noninterference by the United States of America in the internal affairs of the European states and demanded the noninterference of the European states in the political affairs of the Americas.

The greatest shortcoming of Kamarovskii's thesis was a contradiction in its basic concepts. While insisting on the need to distinguish intervention from mediation and war,[23] and while demonstrating the extreme danger of interventionism, Kamarovskii nevertheless recognized the legitimacy of intervention on the basis of "the higher demands of altruism" for the purpose of protecting certain common human interests. Kamarovskii did not reckon with the fact that such a vague argument could be used in practice to justify virtually any interference in the internal affairs of another state. Numerous instances of intervention by the United States of America in our own day are justified as a means of defending "common human interests," whereas in fact we see the egotistical interests of national or global elites at work.

F. F. Martens, an authoritative Russian scholar of international law, declared that "all exceptions to the principle of nonintervention" are "dangerous." Nevertheless, he allowed that intervention in the internal affairs of states is permissible in certain cases, such as:

1) where intervention is based on a treaty, e.g., where one state has promised to guarantee the system of another. It goes without saying that a guarantee to preserve the existing order of another state is atypical, but if it is based on a treaty, it cannot be negated.
2) where a coup d'état violates the positive legal rights of other powers;
3) where intervention is prompted by the intervention of another state (counterintervention).[24]

In contrast to Kamarovskii, Martens found the legal basis for intervention in the violation of laws, not of interests.

22 Most of Kamarovskii's book is devoted to summarizing the views of his European and American contemporaries: Karl von Rotteck, Heinrich von Rotteck, Carl Friedrich Heiberg, August Wilhelm Heffter, Johann Kaspar Bluntschli, Henry Wheaton, William Beach Lawrence, Carlos Calvo, Richard Wildman, Robert Phillimore, Augustus Granville Stapleton, Paul Pradier-Fodéré, Pellegrino Rossi, Terenzio Mamiani, Pasquale Fiore, Ercole Vidari, Augusto Pierantoni, and Giuseppe Amari. The book also takes into account an essay by the Russian legal scholar M. N. Kapustin, "Pravo nevmeshatel'stva, ogranichivaiushchee nezavisimost' gosudarstv," in Kapustin, *Obozrenie predmetov mezhdunarodnogo prava*, vyp. 2, otd. 2–6 (Moscow: Universitetskaia tipografiia, 1856), otd. 6.

23 Kamarovskii, *Nachalo nevmeshatel'stva*, 103.

24 F. F. Martens, *Sovremennoe mezhdunarodnoe pravo tsivilizovannykh narodov*, 2 vols. (St. Petersburg: Tipografiia Ministerstva Putei Soobshcheniia [A. Benke], 1882–83), 1:297.

Subsequently, Kamarovskii himself was highly critical of his first scholarly work on international law. He admitted that, owing to his youth and to the incompleteness of his research, the results of his first study of the principle of nonintervention were "obviously quite deficient."[25]

In his master's thesis, Kamarovskii expressed not only his scientific ideas but also his political convictions. In this connection, he presented a critique of the views that Friedrich Brockhaus expounded in *The Principle of Legitimacy*.[26] Brockhaus attempted to show that the legitimacy of a ruler is based on the mere fact that the ruler is in possession of supreme power. "I must confess," Kamarovskii wrote,

> that I cannot agree with Brockhaus's conclusion. Supreme power cannot be regarded as belonging exclusively to the one who is the most audacious. It also acquires its sanction juridically: through inheritance of the throne in absolute monarchies, through religious ideas in theocracies, or through the respect and love of the people in enlightened countries. *The nation, as a living political person, is not a thing that can be treated irresponsibly* [italics added].[27]

In 1874, another significant event occurred in Kamarovskii's life: he got married. His bride was Ekaterina Aleksandrovna Shirinskaia-Shikhmatova. They had three children: Sergei (b. 1876), Ekaterina (b. 1878), and Mariia (b. 1883).

L.A. Kamarovskii's doctoral dissertation: *On an International Court*

Kamarovskii spent 1878–79 in France doing research for his doctoral dissertation. He chose to write on the question of an international court. Kamarovskii deduced the idea of such an institution from the nature of the modern state. The modern state cannot exist without interacting with other states. However, it is not possible to create a global central government to regulate relations among states, since in that case the states would cease to be states and would become the provinces of some kind of world state. Since sovereignty is an essential feature of the modern state, it follows that an international union to regulate relations among states can only be *juridical*, not political, in character. Kamarovskii was fully aware that international life is not a replication of the internal life of states on a larger scale. It transcends the latter and, as a special sphere of human existence, requires a special form—an international juridical organization. He believed that such an organization is not the product of abstract theoretical conceptions but must grow out of the actual practice of interstate relations. The primary

25 Kamarovskii, *Nachalo nevmeshatel'stva*, 100.

26 Friedrich Brockhaus, *Das Legitimitätsprincip: Eine staatsrechtliche Abhandlung* (Leipzig: F. A. Brockhaus, 1868). The author was the grandson of the eminent publisher Friedrich Arnold Brockhaus (1772–1823).

27 Kamarovskii, *Nachalo nevmeshatel'stva*, iv.

nucleus around which the international juridical order, or positive international law, will crystallize, is an *international court*, the expression and embodiment of the juridical principle of community.

Investigating the question of an international court, Kamarovskii did not confine himself to the search for the sources of his idea or to the analysis of the development of the idea in scholarly works. He also constructed an actual model: the theoretical foundation of the institution and the practical principles of its organization, internal structure, and operation. The pages of his doctoral dissertation on which this model is described are the most valuable part of the work.[28]

In 1881, Kamarovskii successfully defended his dissertation before the council of the law faculty of Moscow University, and the work was published the same year. In 1887, it came out in French translation.[29] As W. E. Butler has observed,

> Kamarovskii's contemporaries were amazed by the logic and pragmatism of his model of the international court, and many elements of his model were subsequently incorporated in the Permanent Court of Arbitration (est. 1899) and the Permanent Court of International Justice (est. 1920) in The Hague. Kamarovskii's book richly deserves its reputation as the first and most fundamental work on this subject.[30]

Kamarovskii maintained that the international court would become the highest organ of human justice on earth and would be the nucleus and chief basis of an international organization comprising the states of Europe and America without those states having to sacrifice their independence and nationality. "Only a reform of this sort," he averred, "can make international law fully positive."[31] At the same time, Kamarovskii tried to convince his readers that an international court, in and of itself, did not represent anything especially new or unusual. It arose from the same conditions and considerations that often led states to prefer the practice of arbitration to the wiles of diplomacy and the devastation of war. However, an international court "transforms an impermanent court of arbitration into a permanent institution governed by juridical principles and providing its members with all desirable guarantees" (524).

Kamarovskii formulated the organization and activity of the international court on the basis of the principles governing the formation of a judiciary in any developed state. The first principle he posited was independence: "In the international domain, the court must be independent of the parties whose case it

28 L. Kamarovskii, *O mezhdunarodnom sude* (Moscow: Tipografiia T. Malinskogo, 1881), 519–38.

29 L. Kamarowsky, *Le tribunal international*, trans. Serge de Westman, intro. Jules Lacointa (Paris: A. Durand et Pedone-Lauriel / G. Pedone-Lauriel, 1887).

30 U. E. Batler, "Graf L. A. Kamarovskii i sozdanie mezhdunarodnogo suda," in L. A. Kamarovskii, *O mezhdunarodnom sude*, ed. L. N. Shestakov (Moscow: Zertsalo, 2007), xxxv–xliii, here at xlii–xliii.

31 Kamarovskii, *O mezhdunarodnom sude* (1881), 459.

is considering and of all political tendencies and opinions." Second, the international court must be based on the principle of *collegiality*, as is the case with the organization of the judiciary everywhere. Other principles Kamarovskii singled out included "oral, adversarial proceedings," "public access" to judicial proceedings, and "the principle of two instances," that is, the right of appeal (519–20).

It is interesting to note that Kamarovskii assigned a legislative function to the international court. As he conceived it, the court

> should seek to identify the juridical elements in the claims of the contending parties, to invest those claims to the extent possible with the forms of a regular judicial proceeding in keeping with concrete juridical principles, with the aim of establishing a new relationship between the contending parties. Thus, the court first applies existing law, but when it finds omissions and contradictions in the latter, it heeds the directives and demands of life and undertakes to ***draft new international laws.*** These it develops methodically with the participation, if necessary, of competent and enlightened statesmen and jurists and forwards them, with an accompanying rationale, for consideration and approval by the respective governments.
>
> (529–30)

On October 30, 1881, Kamarovskii was awarded a doctorate in international law by the council of Moscow University and was appointed ordinary professor in the Department of International Law.[32]

Kamarovskii's doctrine of the nature and content of international law

The 1880s and 1890s were a time of intense scholarly activity in Kamarovskii's life. He presented more than thirty papers at meetings of the Moscow Juridical Society. He published dozens of articles in scholarly journals on a wide range of topics: "The Institute of International Law in the Last Five Years, 1876–1881,"[33] "On the Idea of Peace Among Nations," "The Laws of Land War," "Toward a Theory of Treaties," "On the Admission and Expulsion of Foreigners," "On the Organs of Modern International Unions," "The Attempt to Codify Private International Law—The Hague Conference of 1893," "On the Meaning of War for Modern Society," "International Law as a Subject of Self-education," "The Question of the Reduction of Modern Armaments," and many others.[34] He also

32 Tsentral'nyi istoricheskii arkhiv goroda Moskvy (TsIAM), f. 418, op. 50, d. 223.

33 The Institute of International Law was founded in 1873 in Ghent, Belgium. Kamarovskii became a corresponding member in 1875 and a full member in 1891.

34 "Institut mezhdunarodnogo prava za poslednee piatiletie, 1876–1881," *Iuridicheskii vestnik*, 1882, vol. 10, no. 6: 171–200; no. 7: 367–81. "Ob idee mira mezhdu narodami," *Russkaia mysl'*, 1884, no. 7, pt. 1: 120–35. "Zakony sukhoputnoi voiny," *Iuridicheskii vestnik*, 1885, vol. 19, no. 8: 703–28. "K ucheniiu o traktatakh," *Iuridicheskii vestnik*, 1887,

published a number of books and pamphlets: *On the Political Causes of War in Modern Europe*, *On International Measures in the Battle against Epidemics*, *The Eastern Question*, *On the Fundamental Problem of International Law*, and *Some Successes of the Idea of Peace*, among others.[35]

Kamarovskii's most significant works during this period were *Fundamental Questions of the Science of International Law* (1895) and a textbook, *International Law* (1900).[36] In these works, Kamarovskii expounded his views on the origin and nature of international law as well as its contents, objective foundations, and connection with other branches of law. He also explored the application of international law and the scientific and practical significance of studying it. In Kamarovskii's opinion, international law did not exist in antiquity or the Middle Ages. Its origin can be traced to the seventeenth century, the early modern period, when all the objective conditions necessary for its inception were in place: 1) the existence of numerous states; 2) the existence of independent, sovereign states; and 3) the existence of states connected by a common culture. Kamarovskii thought that this last condition was particularly important in the formation of international law because international law could arise only where states were conscious of "their solidarity in the accomplishment of shared cultural tasks."[37] Thanks to this solidarity, and despite political differences generating disharmony, nations

> began to converge because of common ideas and common interests into a kind of union, which, over the centuries, was transformed from a simple *de facto* order into an increasingly well-defined, genuine *juridical union*. The idea of such a union, like that of any association or union, assumes that its members recognize the principle of mutual equality and the necessity of self-limitation in the service of the common interest. In this way, the egoism

vol. 25, no. 5: 114–23. "O dopushchenii i izgnanii inostrantsev," *Iuridicheskii vestnik*, 1889, vol. 3, no. 12: 519–33. "Ob organakh sovremennykh mezhdunarodnykh unii," *Russkaia mysl'*, 1892, no. 12, pt. 2: 161–82. "Opyt kodifikatsii chastnogo mezhdunarodnogo prava—konferentsiia v Gaage 1893 g.," *Zhurnal iuridicheskogo obshchestva*, 1894, no. 6: 1–18. "O znachenii voiny dlia sovremennogo obshchestva," *Severnyi vestnik*, 1895, no. 2, pt. 1: 127–41. "Mezhdunarodnoe pravo kak predmet samoobrazovaniia," *Sibirskii vestnik*, 1895, no. 12: 46–68. "Vopros o sokrashchenii sovremennykh vooruzhenii," *Russkaia mysl'*, 1898, no. 10: 118–21.

35 *O politicheskikh prichinakh voiny v sovremennoi Evrope* (Moscow: Universitetskaia tipografiia, 1888). *O mezhdunarodnykh merakh bor'by s epidemiami.* Rech', proiznesennaia v torzhestvennom sobranii Imperatorskogo Moskovskogo Universiteta, 12-go ianvaria 1893 goda (Moscow: Universitetskaia tipografiia, 1893). *Vostochnyi vopros* (Moscow: Izdanie knizhnogo magazina Grosman i Knebel' [I. Knebel'], 1896). *Ob osnovnoi zadache mezhdunarodnogo prava* (1898; see note 4). *Uspekhi idei mira* (Moscow: Izdanie knizh. magaz. Grosman i Knebel' [I. Knebel'], 1898).

36 *Osnovye voprosy nauki mezhdunarodnogo prava* (see note 8). *Mezhdunarodnoe pravo* (see note 6).

37 Kamarovskii, *Mezhdunarodnoe pravo*, 9.

> and brute force typical of the *de facto* order give way to principles of commonality and solidarity leading to relations that are regular and enduring, i.e., organized.
>
> (9)

Kamarovskii's starting point was an understanding of international law as a juridical phenomenon. "International law," he wrote,

> should be understood as a set of norms which are binding on states and their subjects in their relations to each other and, in general, to other people who are currently members of the International Union, but also, speaking more broadly, [members] of humankind as a whole.[38]

Here, Kamarovskii understood the term "binding" to mean "juridical." "International law" he explained,

> is composed of *binding* norms. This means that its norms are not just moral principles or political rules, but essentially juridical norms, i.e., norms that are protected by law and, in extreme cases, *by force*. The association of these norms with law is determined by their nature and purpose: the object of law is to protect human beings' life together in society.[39]

In the structure of international law, Kamarovskii distinguished three parts that tend to evolve into separate disciplines. The first, *public international law*, comprises norms protecting the interests of the state as a whole. It includes: 1) the study "of states as international persons," their emergence, rights, and termination; 2) the study of the territorial principle and of international agreements; and 3) the study of conflicts between states and various methods of resolution.

The second part comprises norms protecting the interests of individuals living in foreign lands. Kamarovskii believed that such norms should be distinguished from public law and assigned to the field of *private international law*. The third branch comprises norms protecting the practical social concerns embodied in international networks such as the postal service, the telegraph, railroads, industry, literature, and the like. Kamarovskii called the juridical norms associated

38 Kamarovskii, *Osnovnye voprosy nauki mezhdunarodnogo prava*, 6. It is interesting that, while Kamarovskii looked at international law as "a set of norms which are binding on states and their subjects in their relations to each other and, in general, to other people," his teacher, Bluntschli, represented international law as a world order—a political rather than a normative phenomenon. "International law," wrote Bluntschli, "is a recognized world order linking different states into one universal-human juridical association and guaranteeing to all subjects of these states equal defense of their particular and generically human rights" (I. Bliunchli, *Sovremennoe mezhdunarodnoe pravo tsivilizovannykh narodov*, 65).

39 Kamarovskii, *Osnovnye voprosy nauki mezhdunarodnogo prava*, 6.

with these concerns "*social international law,* a discipline which falls somewhere between public and private international law" (9).

When Kamarovskii spoke of the objective foundations of international law, he meant conditions that are independent of acts of will, be it the will of individuals or of powerful states. These conditions include "the distinctive physical characteristics of Europe," "the ethnic kinship of the European peoples," "their spiritual kinship," and "the parallelism of their historical growth and development" (17). Kamarovskii regarded Russia as a "special world," a country that "differs more from Europe than the individual European nations differ from one another." Russia's difference consists not just in the great size of the country and its geographical location between the European and Asian worlds, but in other facts of Russian history, such as the adoption of Christianity from Byzantium rather than Rome, the long struggle against plunderers from Asia, the long separation from Europe, and so on. "But Russians, like the Slavs in general," Kamarovskii believed,

> are members of the great European family of nations, first of all, because they are Christian, and second because, like the Romans and Germanic peoples, they are Aryans and possess the talents common to the latter. Thus, while international law has its roots in the soil of Western Europe, it is not foreign or hostile to Russia and the other Slavic peoples; rather, while respecting and recognizing their particular characteristics, international law unites all Christian peoples into one great, living family.
>
> (30)

Kamarovskii believed that the science of international law is "a logical deduction from the principles of all other disciplines of law and [also] their natural and profound culmination." In a striking analogy, he opined,

> international law occupies the same place in the system of jurisprudence that philosophy occupies with respect to the branches of human knowledge in general: it unifies and completes them. However, there is also an important difference. Whereas philosophy plays a purely theoretical, abstract, and logical role, international law is *living*, hence *versatile* and *real.*
>
> (84)

Thus, in the scholarly study of jurisprudence, Kamarovskii regarded international law as *the science of sciences.* He believed that a basic knowledge of international law was obligatory not only for jurists but also for statesmen, politicians, journalists writing on international themes, and so on:

> A broader knowledge of the principles of international law among the educated classes is highly desirable. This will enlighten the minds of the populace, moderate its passions, and augment peace. Political opportunists and

hack journalists will have fewer opportunities to toy with the destinies of nations to accomplish their dark personal goals.

(91)

Kamarovskii in early twentieth-century Russia: political views

December 19, 1897, was the twenty-fifth anniversary of Kamarovskii's teaching career at Moscow University. According to the university charter, professors who had served this length of time had to be elected by the departmental council to another five-year term. A two thirds vote was required. On February 26, 1897, Kamarovskii was confirmed for another five years.[40] On December 19, 1899, he was awarded the title of distinguished ordinary professor.

The last decade of Kamarovskii's life was filled, as before, with intense scholarly activity. His publications in this period include: "Russia's Proposal on Arms Reductions," *International Law in the Nineteenth Century*, "The United States of Europe (On the Question of the International Organization of Europe)," *On the Question of the International Organization of Europe, Fundamental Principles of the Law of War, The Law of War*, and others.[41] V. E. Grabar wrote of Kamarovskii:

> Love of work made him the most productive of Russian internationalists, and not just Russian. All his works are permeated by one thought and one spirit: heartfelt devotion to the idea of international community, international organization, pacifism. In this respect, he was a very unusual and original person.[42]

January 12, 1905, was the 150th anniversary of Moscow University. Russian scholars planned to celebrate the day with a series of festivities. There were to be celebratory orations as well as speeches making specific proposals for the improvement of university education in Russia. A banquet was to be held in St. Petersburg, at which the organizers planned to read "A Memorandum on the Needs of Education," a document addressed to the Russian government and signed by some of Russia's most authoritative scholars. The events in St.

40 TsIAM, f. 418, op. 463, ed. khr. 28, ll. 162–67.

41 "Predlozhenie Rossii ob ogranichenii vooruzhenii," *Russkaia mysl'*, 1900, no. 5, pt. 2: 69–99. *Mezhdunarodnoe pravo v XIX veke* (Moscow: Tipografiia Tovarishchestva I. N. Kushnerev i Ko., 1901). "Soedinennye shtaty Evropy (po voprosu o mezhdunarodnoi organizatsii Evropy)," *Russkaia mysl'*, 1902, no. 9, pt. 2: 1–31. *Po voprosu o mezhdunarodnoi organizatsii Evropy* (Moscow: Tipo-litografiia Tovarishchestva I. N. Kushnerev i Ko., 1902). *Osnovnye nachala prava voiny* (Moscow: Tipo-litografiia Iu. Verner, 1904). *Pravo voiny* (Moscow: Tipo-litografiia G. I. Prostakova, 1905).

42 V. E. Grabar', *Materialy k istorii literatury mezhdunarodnogo prava v Rossii (1647–1917)*, ed. U. E. Batler and V. A. Tomsinov (Moscow: Zertsalo, 2005), 391.

Petersburg on January 9, 1905 ("Bloody Sunday"), forced cancellation of the celebration. Instead, the "Memorandum" was published with the signatures of 342 persons, including sixteen full members of the Imperial Academy of Sciences, 125 professors, and 201 privatdocents of Russian higher educational institutions. Kamarovskii was among the signatories.

The "Memorandum" was a true political manifesto. It made a direct connection between the improvement of the educational system and the full and fundamental transformation of the Russian state on the basis of legality, political freedom, representative government, and control over the administrative actions of the government. The scholars knew how perilous it was to sign this document. All were government servants whose position brought them considerable material benefits and the opportunity to do creative work in their chosen fields. "Everyone can understand the position of a person who suddenly loses his livelihood, can understand the sufferings to which he and his family are condemned," wrote K. A. Timiriazev, "but not everyone can appreciate what a scholar deprives himself of—a scholar not in status only, but by vocation—when he deprives himself of the environment without which his work is unthinkable."[43] Indeed, the authorities were preparing to punish the signatories of the "Memorandum." There was talk in the Ministry of Education of terminating them or withholding their salaries. In a circular letter, the president of the Academy of Sciences, Grand Duke Konstantin Romanov, accused the signatories of interjecting politics into science and recommended that they refuse to accept their salaries from "the government they were censuring." But the scholars were fearless. Academician Aleksei Liapunov sent the Grand Duke the following answer:

> We feel that it is our clear responsibility to indicate what we consider to be the way out of the present dire situation. This is our moral duty—to the fatherland to which we owe our high positions, and to the people from whose resources our state salaries are paid.[44]

The further course of events in Russia in 1905 forced the government to forget about the scholars' oppositional sally. The political crisis, especially in St. Petersburg and Moscow, became so acute that many political activists began to speak of revolution. In these conditions, the autocracy began to make concessions. On October 17, 1905, the government issued the "Proclamation on the Improvement of the State Order" ("October Manifesto") promising "to grant the people civil liberties based on the inalienable rights of the individual, including freedom of conscience, speech, assembly, and association." Immediately after

43 K. A. Timiriazev, *Nauka i demokratiia: sbornik statei, 1904–1919 gg.* (Moscow: Izdatel'stvo sotsial'no-ekonomicheskoi literatury, 1963), 60.

44 Quoted in G. D. Komkov, B. V. Levshin, V. K. Semenov, *Akademiia nauk SSSR: Kratkii istoricheskii ocherk*, 2nd ed., 2 vols. (Moscow: Izdatel'stvo "Nauka," 1977), 1:315.

this proclamation, political parties appeared. The Constitutional Democratic Party was the first. Its founding assembly took place on October 12–18, 1905. Many jurists joined this party.

Kamarovskii did not stand apart from the party movement unfolding in Russia. He decided to link his political fate to the Union of 17 October, a party that began to organize itself in late October 1905 and held its first assembly in February 1906. The Octobrists' political program called for "a hereditary constitutional monarchy in which the emperor, as the bearer of supreme power, would be limited by Fundamental Laws [that is, a constitution]." Kamarovskii fully embraced this ideal.

The Third All-Russian Assembly of the Octobrists was held on October 4–8, 1908, in Moscow, in the hall of the Polytechnical Society. Kamarovskii delivered the opening address and also made a presentation on religious policy on behalf of the party's central committee. Kamarovskii himself wrote the presentation, which reflected his views on the relation between state and church:

> Freedom of religion means the officially recognized right of every person to profess his faith without interference and to express it in rituals together with other persons of the same religion. But this freedom cannot be unconditional. It is not equivalent to the separation of church and state. Our state, as a Christian state, must give special protection to Christianity owing to the fact that the principle of the Christian religion is the chief support of human law and the foundation of the civil order. In the Russian state, Eastern Orthodoxy must be granted preeminent and official status owing to the fact that the Orthodox faith is historically linked to the destiny of the Russian state and undergirds the worldview of the overwhelming majority of the Russian people.

However, Kamarovskii underscored that "the privileges of the established Orthodox Church must not involve the persecution of other religions."[45]

Kamarovskii was highly critical of the organization of the Russian Orthodox Church. Among the chief deficiencies, he identified the following:

> 1) weakening of the vital connection between the members of the church, 2) absence of initiative in the internal life of the church community, 3) extreme formalism and bureaucratism in all areas of church life, and 4) the excessive influence of the state, which deprives the church of the freedom and independence it deserves.
>
> (100)

45 *Partiia "Soiuz 17 oktiabria,"* vol. 2: *Protokoly III s"ezda, konferentsii i zasedanii TsK, 1907–1915 gg.* (Moscow: ROSSPEN, 2000), 100–01.

In 1909–10, a number of events confirmed that Russian society recognized Kamarovskii's scholarly achievements in the field of international law. In 1909, Nicholas II appointed him as the Russian delegate to the Permanent Court of Arbitration in The Hague. On December 4, 1910, Kamarovskii was elected corresponding member of the St. Petersburg Academy of Sciences in the section of history and philology. The Academy of Sciences did not have a section for jurisprudence.

In 1909, Kamarovskii was elected dean of the law faculty of Moscow University. Insufficient compensation forced him to lecture not only at his alma mater but also at the A. L. Shaniavskii People's University and the Advanced Law Courses for Women. On April 22, 1911, a new university rector was to be elected by the council of Moscow University. Since February 1, 1911, Kamarovskii had filled in as temporary rector after the retirement of A. A. Manuilov, and it is certain that he would have been elected if fate had not been cruel to him. An absurd and tragic incident prevented him from becoming rector. Kamarovskii's daughter, Ekaterina Leonidovna, described the incident in her memoirs:

> He was on his way to participate in the election [at the university], but because he was practically deaf in one ear, he did not hear an approaching tram and was struck by it. I vividly remember every detail of this incident and everything I experienced at the time. I have preserved numerous clippings from newspapers where this accident is described in detail. The election was postponed, and papa subsequently withdrew his candidacy on account of illness.[46]

Kamarovskii never recovered from the tragic accident of April 22, 1911. Weakness caused by the trauma aggravated his chronic tuberculosis. On December 8, 1912, at the age of sixty-six, he passed away.

International law, Christian ethics, and the destiny of humanity

More than a hundred years have passed since Kamarovskii's death, but his thoughts on international law remain relevant. He understood that the future of humankind depends largely on its ability to establish a stable international legal order that will curb the egoistic ambitions of world powers, counteract the parasitism of states that exist by pitilessly exploiting other states, and support international peace. He believed that such a legal order could be established if international relations were grounded not only in the norms of international law but also in accord with the principles of Christian ethics. For Kamarovskii, "two fundamental duties incumbent upon nations in their relations with each

46 Grafinia Kamarovskaia, *Vospominaniia*, in E. L. Kamarovskaia and E. F. Komarovskii, *Vospominaniia* (Moscow: Zakharov, 2003), 149.

other follow from Christian ethics: mutual respect and mutual assistance."[47] He explained that "the duty of mutual respect is deeper and broader than what internationalists usually mean when they speak of the right to honor and respect," inasmuch as this duty, being a moral principle, "does not depend on contractual agreements, and second, imparts greater force and meaning to them [contractual agreements]." He went on to develop this idea:

> Nations, as collective persons, live in states, and the latter, by virtue of the aforementioned duty, must refrain not only from all acts infringing on the honor, rights, and interests of other states, both their official organs and their citizens, but from all acts which, although frequent in practice and not punished by formal law (still highly imperfect), are nevertheless *grave moral crimes, because they nullify the foundations of society.*
>
> (816)

Kamarovskii had the following acts in mind:

1) Oppression of weaker nations or even whole nationalities by conquest, by disrespecting their just claims, or by treating them as a tool to achieve one's own ends, ends which are alien to them.
2) The desire, through envy or ill will, to impede the internal development of other states [by bribing foreign officials,]… by intrigues involving party leaders,… by encouraging the populace to rebel [against legitimate authority,]… by employing secret agents and instigators on foreign soil, [and so on].
3) Obstructing the development of peaceful relations among nations because of a false conception of one's own independence, or because of laziness or confused thinking.
4) Starting a war without having recourse to all peaceful methods [of resolving a dispute], especially adjudication of the case before a court of arbitration in order to resolve misunderstandings that have arisen between states.

Listing war as one of these crimes, Kamarovskii nevertheless made the following important qualification:

> Given the imperfect conditions we live in, war is permissible as an extreme defense of the right of nations to independence and freedom. But from the point of view of pure Christianity and absolute morality, it goes without saying that war, especially between civilized nations, should never take place.
>
> (817)

Kamarovskii's reflections here and elsewhere can be viewed as idealistic and even utopian, for human society is set up in such a way that all that is humane and

47 Kamarovskii, "Khristianskaia nravstvennost' i mezhdunarodnye snosheniia," 816.

good seems idealistic and utopian, whereas evil and cruelty seem to be objectively real. Evaluating Kamarovskii's contribution to the science of international law, Sergei Kotliarevskii wrote:

> He introduced a humanitarian and idealistic tendency into the study of international law. He believed that destructive conflict and unbridled egoism cannot be the ultimate law of human society. Hence his firm belief in the gradual evolution of world peace. He bore no resemblance to the type of international law professor common in Germany, a type that ardently glorified war. At times, his idealism could seem almost strange in the context of an international reality where the last word still belongs to force. When he collided with this reality, he became indignant and sorrowful, but he did not lose his faith.[48]

Kamarovskii's ideas, while they appeared idealistic and utopian, were in fact the reflection of a genuine reality, albeit not the reality manifested in international crimes, military aggression, the hostile acts of one state against another, predations, and the use of state power to physically, economically, or culturally annihilate whole peoples. Kamarovskii's idealistic humanism was based on a deep understanding of the true nature of human society. This understanding led him to conclude that hostility between nations, devastating and destructive wars, the parasitic existence of some states at the expense of others—all these things serve to undermine the foundations of human society and lead humanity to ruin. Compared with these negative outcomes, Kamarovskii's ideas of universal peace and the construction of a world order based on legal and moral principles conform fully with the foundations of human civilization. These principles signify the real conditions under which human society exists—conditions that assure its progress and further development.

48 Kotliarevskii, "Neskol'ko slov pamiati gr. L. A. Kamarovskogo (1846–1912)," 222–23.

9 Vladimir Soloviev

Faith, philosophy, and law

Paul Valliere

Vladimir Sergeevich Soloviev (1853–1900) was not a jurist, but he has a place in the history of Russian Christian legal thought as the first Russian thinker to forge a comprehensive synthesis of Christian faith, philosophical idealism, and juridical values. His achievement contributed to the rise of a distinctive neo-idealist philosophy of law in Russia at the turn of the twentieth century. The last four jurists surveyed in this volume—Pavel Nogorodtsev, Sergei Kotliarevskii, Nikolai Alekseev, and Ivan Ilyin—all belonged to this "Moscow school of jurisprudence."

Boris Chicherin (1828–1904), the most accomplished liberal political thinker in Russia when Soloviev launched his career, also played a crucial role in the genesis of the Moscow school. In strictly professional terms, Chicherin's contribution was weightier than Soloviev's, whose role pertained to the wider cultural context. Rising to prominence as a young Slavophile, Soloviev was expected to censure legalism as something alien to Russia.[1] The fact that he did the opposite caused his audience to stop and think, to consider juridical values in a new light. Moreover, Soloviev's religiosity had an immediacy about it that Chicherin's lacked. As Gary Hamburg shows in Chapter 6 of this volume, Chicherin took religious questions seriously, but faith did not come easily to him. Soloviev, by contrast, was a "God-intoxicated man."[2] He discerned the divine on every level and in every aspect of reality, and he had the intellectual tools to articulate his religious vision with rigor.

A young Slavophile

Vladimir Soloviev was born in Moscow to a prominent academic family.[3] His father, Sergei Mikhailovich (1820–79), descendant of a long line of Orthodox

1 Portions of this chapter were originally published in *The Teachings of Modern Orthodox Christianity on Law, Politics, and Human Nature*, ed. John Witte Jr. and Frank S. Alexander. Copyright © 2007 Columbia University Press. Reprinted with permission of Columbia University Press.
See Andrzej Walicki, *Legal Philosophies of Russian Liberalism* (Oxford: Clarendon Press, 1987), Chapter 1: "The Tradition of the Censure of Law."

2 Novalis's characterization of Spinoza applies equally well, if not better, to Soloviev.

3 The classic Russian portraits of Soloviev's life and thought are Evgenii Trubetskoi, *Mirosozertsanie Vl. S. Solov'eva*, 2 vols. (Moscow: Put', 1913); K. Mochul'skii, *Vladimir Solov'ev:*

DOI: 10.4324/9781003017097-9

clergy, was a professor at Moscow University and the most eminent Russian historian of his generation. Vladimir's mother, Poliksena Vladimirovna (d. 1909), came from a military family of Polish and Ukrainian extraction. Soloviev entered Moscow University in 1869 after receiving an excellent classical education. He chose to study the natural sciences, although he completed his degree in history and philology. After graduation in 1873, he spent a postgraduate year at Moscow Theological Academy. This was an unusual step for a man from Soloviev's elite academic milieu and attests to his unconventional personality as well as to his religious interests. In 1874, Soloviev returned to Moscow University to defend his master's thesis, *The Crisis of Western Philosophy (Against the Positivists)*.[4] The following year, he began teaching at his alma mater but soon departed for a year's study in London. There he did research on mysticism in the British Museum and mixed with the local spiritualist community. In the museum, he had a vision of Divine Wisdom ("Sophia," appearing as a beautiful woman). She directed him to travel to Egypt, promising to reveal herself again—which she did, although not

---

zhizn' i uchenie, 2nd ed. (Paris: YMCA-Press, 1951); S. M. Solov'ev, *Zhizn' i tvorcheskaia evoliutsiia Vladimira Solov'eva* (Brussels: Izdatel'stvo Zhizn' s Bogom, Foyer Oriental Chrétien, 1977), republished as *Vladimir Solov'ev: zhizn' i tvorcheskaia evoliutsiia* (Moscow: Respublika, 1997); and A. [F.] Losev, *Vladimir Solov'ev i ego vremia* (Moscow: "Progress," 1990), republished with supplements, Moscow: Molodaia gvardiia, 2000. The work by S. M. Soloviev (Vladimir's nephew) is available in English: Sergey M. Solovyov, *Vladimir Solovyov: His Life and Creative Evolution*, trans. Aleksey Gibson, 2 vols. (Fairfax, VA: Eastern Christian Publications, Inc., 2000). See also Thomas Nemeth, *The Early Solov'ëv and His Quest for Metaphysics* (Cham, Switz.: Springer, 2014) and *The Later Solov'ëv: Philosophy in Imperial Russia* (Cham, Switz.: Springer, 2019). A collection of Soloviev's letters is available in English: *The Karamazov Correspondence: Letters of Vladimir S. Soloviev*, ed. and trans. Vladimir Wozniuk (Boston: Academic Studies Press, 2019). (The title of this publication is misleading. Except for a brief note from Soloviev to Dostoevsky, the collection contains no correspondence between the two, nor does Soloviev discuss *The Brothers Karamazov* in any detail in these letters.)

The Russian, European, and North American literature on Soloviev has grown exponentially since the end of the Soviet period and is too vast to be summarized here. For an overview of Soloviev's religious thought with bibliography and suggestions for further reading, see Catherine Evtuhov, "Vladimir Soloviev as a Religious Thinker," in *The Oxford Handbook of Russian Religious Thought*, ed. Caryl Emerson, George Pattison, and Randall A. Poole (Oxford: Oxford University Press, 2020), 205–19. For contemporary Russian scholarship, a good place to begin is *Solov'evskie issledovaniia*, a journal of Solovievian studies published since 2001at Ivanovo State University of Energetics: http://ispu.ru/node/6623. The first decade in particular contains numerous articles on Soloviev's philosophy of law.

In the twentieth century, the standard edition of Soloviev's writings was *Sobranie sochinenii Vladimira Sergeevicha Solov'eva*, ed. S. M. Solov'ev and E. L. Radlov, 2nd ed., 10 vols. (St. Petersburg, 1911–14; reprint, Brussels: Foyer Oriental Chrétien, 1966; supplementary vols. 11–12, Brussels: Izdatel'stvo Zhizn' s Bogom, Foyer Oriental Chrétien, 1969–70). The Institute of Philosophy of the Russian Academy of Sciences is currently bringing out a critical edition of Soloviev's complete works: V. S. Solov'ev, *Polnoe sobranie sochinenii i pisem*, 20 vols. (Moscow: "Nauka," 2000–).

4 Vladimir Solovyov, *The Crisis of Western Philosophy (Against the Positivists)*, ed. and trans. Boris Jakim (Hudson, NY: Lindisfarne Press, 1996).

until Soloviev nearly lost his life at the hands of hostile Bedouin on a walk in the desert near the pyramids.

In 1876, Soloviev resumed teaching at Moscow University, but before the end of the academic year he moved to St. Petersburg, where he accepted a sinecure in the ministry of education and began lecturing at the university and in the Higher Women's Courses. It was becoming obvious that Vladimir Sergeevich disliked trodden paths. Restless, visionary, impulsive, he would have made a fine bohemian were it not for his work ethic. He wrote his second monograph, *The Philosophical Principles of Integral Knowledge*, in 1877, composed and delivered his celebrated *Lectures on Divine Humanity* in 1878, and defended his doctoral dissertation, *The Critique of Abstract Principles*, in 1880. The author of four books in six years was twenty-seven years old.[5]

Soloviev never married, although he had several significant relationships with women. Sophia Tolstaia, widow of the poet Aleksei Tolstoy, was an important mentor and patron. Soloviev fell passionately in love with Tolstaia's married niece, Sophia Khitrovo, who remained close to him for the rest of his life. In 1891, he formed an attachment to another married woman, Sophia Martynova, a relationship that inspired him to write "The Meaning of Love" (1892–94).[6] The recurrence of the name Sophia in Soloviev's erotic relationships was connected with his devotion to heavenly Sophia, the muse of his private-speculative religiosity as well as of his public vocation (philosophy).[7] Soloviev's unmarried state facilitated his detachment from a settled existence. Never establishing a permanent home or institutional base, he lived the peripatetic life of an ancient philosopher. The lifestyle brought him material discomforts, but his capacity for love and friendship and his closeness to parents and siblings ensured that there were always people on hand to help him.

In St. Petersburg, Soloviev lectured in both academic and popular venues, promoting the Slavophile notion that Russia had a message the rest of the world needed to hear. The message was the advent of a new cultural synthesis combining the values of the European Enlightenment with the truths of Christianity. In *The Crisis of Western Philosophy (Against the Positivists)*, Soloviev argued that all Western philosophical systems suffered from the spell of abstractions resulting in one-sided approaches to the world. In *The Philosophical Principles of Integral Knowledge*, he outlined the case for a new philosophical synthesis in positive but

5 Vladimir Solovyov, *The Philosophical Principles of Integral Knowledge*, trans. Valeria Z. Nollan (Grand Rapids, MI: William B. Eerdmans Publishing Company, 2008); Vladimir Solovyov, *Lectures on Divine Humanity*, ed. and rev. trans. Boris Jakim (Hudson, NY: Lindisfarne Press, 1995). *The Critique of Abstract Principles* is not available in English.

6 "The Meaning of Love," in V. S. Soloviev, *The Heart of Reality: Essays on Beauty, Love, and Ethics*, ed. and trans. Vladimir Wozniuk (Notre Dame, IN: University of Notre Dame Press, 2003), 83–133.

7 The indispensable study of "Sophia" in Soloviev's life and work is Judith Deutsch Kornblatt, *Divine Sophia: The Wisdom Writings of Vladimir Solovyov* (Ithaca, NY: Cornell University Press, 2009).

fragmentary terms. In *The Critique of Abstract Principles*, the masterpiece of his early career, he rewrote and expanded both his critique of Western philosophy and his case for a new synthesis.

In *Lectures on Divine Humanity*, Soloviev focused on the theological substance of his vision, what he called *Bogochelovechestvo*. The term is an abstract noun derived from *Bogochelovek* (Godman, Christ). Translated into English as Godmanhood, divine humanity, or humanity of God, *Bogochelovechestvo* thematizes the Orthodox Christian doctrine of the Incarnation. In Orthodox theology, God's becoming-human accomplishes not just the moral salvation of humanity (Christ "for" us) but an ontological transformation (Christ "in" us). Soloviev gave this conception a historical and prophetic application: the divine-human union accomplished in the Incarnation points the way to the cultural synthesis of the future by offering the world a better moral and spiritual goal than the "godless human individual" of modern Western civilization or the "inhuman God" of Islam. Orthodox Russia, poised between West and East, has the providential mission of proclaiming and instantiating the good news of "divine humanity."[8]

Fyodor Dostoevsky, whom Soloviev had met in 1873 through family connections, attended the young philosopher's lectures on divine humanity. Following the death of Dostoevsky's three-year-old son, Alyosha, in 1878, the philosopher and the novelist made a pilgrimage together to Optina Hermitage, a center of the nineteenth-century monastic revival in Russia. The excursion occupies a special place in Russian literary history because Optina Hermitage was the model for Dostoevsky's portrait of Russian monasticism in the novel he was conceiving at the time, *The Brothers Karamazov* (1878–80).[9] Not surprisingly, scholars have looked for Soloviev's portrait in *The Brothers Karamazov*, although none of the three brothers corresponds exactly to the real-life Vladimir Sergeevich. On the level of ideas, however, there is definitely a connection. Early in the novel, during his family's visit to a monastery, Ivan Karamazov becomes involved in a conversation about the jurisdiction of ecclesiastical courts.[10] Ivan's thesis is that the modern state, because it has severed its connection with the church, cannot deal with crime and punishment in moral and spiritual terms but can only administer justice in a utilitarian way. Incapable of fostering repentance and regeneration, the state can do no more than repress and confine criminals. Criminals respond

8 The terms "godless human individual" (*bezbozhnyi chelovek*) and "inhuman God" (*bezchelovechnyi bog*) are taken from Soloviev's lecture "Three Forces" ("Tri sily," 1877), but the same conceptual scheme informs *Lectures on Divine Humanity*. The three forces are the humanistic but godless West, the religious but despotic Islamic East, and the higher synthesis of humanism and religion in Orthodoxy/Slavdom. See "Three Forces," in *Enemies from the East? V. S. Soloviev on Paganism, Asian Civilization, and Islam*, ed. and trans. Vladimir Wozniuk (Evanston, IL: Northwestern University Press, 2007), 24–33.

9 On the friendship between Dostoevsky and Soloviev, see Marina Kostalevsky, *Dostoevsky and Soloviev: The Art of Integral Vision* (New Haven: Yale University Press, 1997), 49–80. See also Soloviev's memorial lectures of 1881–83, "Three Addresses in Memory of Dostoevsky," in Soloviev, *The Heart of Reality*, 1–28.

10 *The Brothers Karamazov*, pt. 1, bk. 2, chap. 5.

by construing their relationship to the state in equally utilitarian terms, regarding their crimes as justifiable acts of rebellion against an oppressive social order. If Russia is to avoid such an outcome, Ivan argues, the state must reaffirm and expand the ministry of the church, especially in relation to crime and punishment. In *The Critique of Abstract Principles*, Soloviev advocates a social and political order similar to Ivan's, envisioning a theocracy of love inspired and guided by the Orthodox Church.[11]

Law and the theocracy of love

Soloviev's first elaboration of a philosophy of law appears in *The Critique of Abstract Principles*.[12] The social and political ideal Soloviev advances in this work is a symphonic community in which "all constitute the end of each, and each the end of all" (3:117). As soon as the project of realizing this kingdom of ends begins, however, one-sidedness undermines the task. Even when human beings embrace the all-inclusive ideal, they find it difficult to do justice to "each" and "all" at the same time. Those who lean to "each" generate individualism; those who lean to "all" generate some form of collectivism; and so the project of building the good society is undermined. Instead of addressing living human beings in the actual world, ethicists and political philosophers ponder the "individual" and "society." But these are abstractions.

Soloviev's critique targeted two influential social and political visions of his day: socialism and legalism. Soloviev affirmed socialism in its demand for an economic order embodying ethical norms. The error of socialism lies in the assumption that a material or economic order per se generates ethical norms,

> that an unexampled economic set-up (some kind of fusion of capital and labor, the organization of industry by unions, etc.) is obligatory in and for itself, unconditionally normative and moral, that is, that this economic set-up as such already contains a moral principle and is the sole condition of social morality.

This assumption is a classic example of one-sidedness: "the moral principle, the principle of the obligatory and the normative, is determined exclusively by one of the elements of the totality of human life—the economic element" (3:128). Other elements, however, also need to be accommodated in a social and political ethic.

One of these elements appears already in the rhetoric of socialism. Socialists typically cloak their preferred economic arrangements in discourse about a "just"

11 In the first of his memorial lectures on Dostoevsky, Soloviev wrote: "The Church as a positive social ideal was to appear as the central idea of a new novel or a new series of novels, of which only the first was written—*Brothers Karamazov*" (Soloviev, *The Heart of Reality*, 12).

12 *Kritika otvlechennykh nachal*, in V. S. Solov'ev, *Polnoe sobranie sochinenii i pisem*, vol. 3 (2001), 7–364. Page references in parentheses are to this edition.

economy and the "rights" of workers. But the concepts of justice and right cannot be derived from a material-economic process. Interests can be derived from it, but not rights. Rights pertain to *persons*, beings capable of freedom and rationality. Personhood transcends "every material interest"; it is a "res sacra" (3:133–35). Far from springing from the material-economic order, it reveals a higher order: the juridical order.

The juridical order, however, is no more immune than the economic order to the spell of abstract principles. Here the warring abstractions are the "abstract-historical concept of law" and the social contract theory, which Soloviev calls the "abstract-utilitarian concept of law" (3:137–41). The historicist concept was connected with Romantic conservatism; contract theory, with liberalism and revolution. Both theories are right in what they affirm, but wrong in what they deny. Historicists are right to insist that law develops organically through the historical process, but they are wrong to suppose that the essence of law is satisfactorily accounted for by its genesis. Contract theory, on the other hand, is too mechanical and utilitarian. It conceives of human beings as generic individuals who, lacking an inner spiritual connection with each other, contract to provide a framework in which they can pursue their private ends. The historicist account of law focuses on all to the detriment of each; contract theory, on each to the detriment of all.

What is needed is a higher synthesis. The juridical order provides such a synthesis, Soloviev believes, but only formally or negatively. "Law is freedom, conditioned by equality." This definition signifies a higher synthesis because freedom and equality, taken separately, are competing, not complementary principles, yet law necessarily brings them together. If a system of law fails to serve freedom, it depersonalizes its subjects and becomes an instrument of force, while a legal system that treats its subjects preferentially rather than equally becomes a vehicle of injustice (3:145–46). What makes the juridical synthesis formal or negative is that it does not prescribe the end or goal to which its subjects should direct their freedom.

> Law provides a normative definition of the means or *mode* of action, but not the ends or objects of action. For [law] there is no *normative* end, no normative will or intention. Heroic self-sacrifice and selfish calculation make no difference to law; it does not demand the former and does not forbid the latter.... [The juridical order] cannot require that all *should assist* each, and each all; it demands only that no one *should do harm* to anyone else.
>
> (3:147)

If the juridical order does not prescribe an ultimate end, where should one look for it? The material-economic order is not an option, because looking in that direction would mean regression: trading the personhood revealed in the juridical order for something less. More, not less, is needed. "Unconditional form [personhood] demands unconditional content. Beyond the legal order, the order of negative means, there must be a positive order defined by an absolute end" (3:148–49). The absolute end is the focal point of the "mystical attractions" of human beings, the aspiration "to be one with the whole of things" (*byt' vseedinym*). This is the substance of the "religious principle." The contrast with the juridical principle is clear: law demarcates, distinguishes, divides; religion connects, embraces, unites. Religion is about love—the loving union realized in "a mystical or religious community, that is to say, *the church*" (3:149–51).

The religious principle complicates social and political life because of the tension between love and law. The tension might not be a problem if the two orders could be confined in separate spheres, but this is not possible. Law and religion pertain to "one and the same sphere, namely the sphere of practical, moral, or social life." Soloviev rejected the attempt to reconcile the two through compartmentalization. For example, he denied "that I could *actually* show Christian love to a neighbor whom, in my capacity as a judge, I send to the gallows" (3:152–54). Love and law demand acknowledgment from the same person at the same time in the same society. An "inner, harmonious relation or synthesis" of the two is needed. Soloviev called this harmonious synthesis a "free theocracy" (3:155).

By calling his social and political ideal a theocracy, Soloviev guaranteed controversy. Boris Chicherin excoriated him for introducing "mysticism" into "scholarship."[13] Others were baffled by the apparent oxymoron: how can a theocracy be free? Yet Soloviev's terminology is clear enough when one examines it in context. Free theocracy forms a triad with two other "theo" terms in *The Critique of Abstract Principles*: free theosophy and free theurgy. Taken together, the three terms represent Soloviev's adaptation of the familiar Kantian-idealist triad: pure reason, practical reason, and creative reason, all of which Soloviev originally intended to critique in his book. He overreached: *The Critique of Abstract Principles* lacks the theurgy. But it contains the theocracy (critique of ethics, politics, law, and church; Chapters 3–26) and the theosophy (critique of epistemology, science, and theology; Chapters 27–46). *The Critique* is theological throughout because the whole point of the work is to expose the divine dimension in every act of knowing, doing, and creating, the relatedness of all knowing, doing, and creating to the divinely grounded whole of things (*vseedinstvo*, "all-unity").

As for "free," the tag signifies that Soloviev was a post-Kantian critical thinker. He had no interest in calling people back to their dogmatic slumbers. Science, morality, politics, creative activity—all of these pursuits have to be free (in the sense appropriate to each), and all were to be pursued in the context of the global civilization of the nineteenth century. Soloviev's "theo" projects were modern, not primitivist or medievalist.[14] He distinguished his social and political vision from "false theocracy" and "abstract clericalism," projects based on the

13 B. Chicherin, *Mistitsizm v nauke* (Moscow: Tipografiia Martynova i Ko., 1880). See the discussion of Chicherin's criticisms in Chapter 6 of this volume and in Nemeth, *The Early Solov'ëv*, 200–09.

14 For an example of Soloviev's unromantic view of ancient and medieval Christianity, see his 1891 essay, "On the Decline of the Medieval Worldview," in *Freedom, Faith, and Dogma: Essays by V. S. Soloviev on Christianity and Judaism*, ed. and trans. Vladimir Wozniuk (Albany: State University of New York Press, 2008), 159–70.

absolutization of the religious principle. The religious order of love transcends the juridical order, but it must not violate the juridical order. A theocracy that does so vitiates not just law but religion. False theocracy reduces God "to the thunder and lightning which extinguish completely the still small voice of reason and conscience" (3:151–52). Reason, conscience, the material world, too—all of these are God-given and divinely grounded. A free theocracy must incorporate them without violating their integrity.

By positing an order of love transcending the juridical order, Soloviev broke with the Hegelian mainstream of idealist political thought and its derivatives. He did not regard "the state as the highest and final form of human society and the universal kingdom of law as the apogee of human history" (3:149). Human beings need more than law and the state to order their affairs and fulfill their humanity. They need the church, the community of love, and they need hope for the restoration of all things in the kingdom of God.

By underscoring the centrality of the kingdom of God in the Christian message, Soloviev was ahead of his time. The majority of liberal and modernist Christian ethicists in the nineteenth century were tone-deaf to the theocratic dimension of the gospel. For them, Jesus preached an inner, spiritual kingdom that was to be distinguished from the supposedly crude nationalist theocracy of the Jews. Soloviev rejected this one-sided spiritualizing of the gospel, anticipating Albert Schweitzer and other Protestant biblical scholars who rediscovered the Jewish apocalyptic roots of Christianity around the turn of the twentieth century. Soloviev also anticipated twentieth-century Christian ethicists who recovered the political seriousness of the gospel, such as Jacques Maritain, Reinhold Niebuhr, Martin Luther King Jr., and John Howard Yoder.[15]

Soloviev's activism

Soloviev's views underwent a change in the 1880s. The decade began with a national tragedy. On March 1, 1881, Emperor Alexander II was assassinated by revolutionaries. As Russians reeled in horror, Soloviev publicly called on the new tsar, Alexander III, to deal with his father's murderers in the spirit of Christian love by refusing to impose the death penalty—an interpretation of Christian monarchy the tsar and his government rejected with indignation.[16] The political fallout from this episode, uncertain prospects for a university professorship, and

15 Continuing in this tradition, Timothy P. Jackson has proposed that liberal democracy will find its future and its fulfillment in "political *agape*," a proposal much like Soloviev's free theocracy. See his *Political* Agape*: Christian Love and Liberal Democracy* (Grand Rapids, MI: William B. Eerdmans Publishing Company, 2015), and further discussion of the theme in *Agape, Justice, and Law: How Might Christian Love Shape Law?*, ed. Robert F. Cochran Jr. and Zachary R. Calo (Cambridge: Cambridge University Press, 2017).

16 See Manon de Courten, "The Prophet Intervenes: Solov'ëv's Lectures after the Murder of Tsar Alexander II," in *Vladimir Solov'ëv: Reconciler and Polemicist*, ed. Wil van den Bercken, Manon de Courten, and Evert van der Zweerde (Leuven: Peeters, 2000), 297–312.

his own persistent restlessness led Soloviev to leave St. Petersburg in 1882. He also began to reassess his concept of theocracy. While not abandoning the theocratic ideal, he reconsidered some of the forms in which he had been preaching it, especially the eliding of Christian faith with Russian institutions. He also began saying positive things about the West, including the Roman Catholic Church. His Slavophile friends soon closed their journals to him.

Soloviev pursued the case for a more comprehensive understanding of theocracy by taking a critical look at how the Russian Orthodox community related to its non-Russian and non-Orthodox neighbors, inside and outside the Russian Empire. In *The National Question in Russia*, a collection of essays begun in 1883, Soloviev criticized the Russian state's denial of the human rights of its ethnic and religious minorities. In "The Development of Dogma and the Question of Church Union" (1886), he examined Orthodoxy's relations with the Roman Catholic Church and promoted what would eventually be called ecumenism, that is, the rapprochement or even reunion of the divided churches of Christendom.[17] In 1886, he visited Croatia for discussions with two Roman Catholic prophets of ecumenism, Bishop Josip Juraj Strossmayer and Canon Franjo Rački. In 1888, Soloviev spent most of the year in France, where he arranged for the publication of another ecumenist monograph, *Russia and the Universal Church* (1889). In the introduction, after explaining that censorship barred publication of the work in Russia, he declared, "I firmly hope to see the day when my country will possess the good it needs first of all—religious liberty."[18]

A new relationship between Christians and Jews was another component of Soloviev's theocratic project.[19] To Soloviev, the Jews were exactly who they claimed to be: the chosen people, the theocratic people par excellence. He regarded the Hebrew Bible, with its detailed account of the collaboration of prophets, priests, and kings in the history of Israel, as the original constitution of theocracy. When he designed *The History and Future of Theocracy*, which was to be a three-volume study of the theocratic idea in human history, he devoted the first volume to ancient Israel.[20] To enhance his expertise, he studied Hebrew with the help of Faivel B. Gets, a Russian Jewish intellectual who became one of his closest friends.

Soloviev reflected on Judaism in several essays. In "Jewry and the Christian Question" (1884), he argued that the so-called Jewish question actually pertains

17 "Dogmaticheskoe razvitie tserkvi v sviazi s voprosom o soedinenii tserkvei," in *Sobranie sochinenii Vladimira Sergeevicha Solov'eva*, 11:1–67.

18 Vladimir Soloviev, *La Russie et L'Eglise universelle*, 4th ed. (Paris: Librairie Stock, 1922), lxi.

19 The most comprehensive source in English on Soloviev and Judaism is Vladimir Solovyov, *The Burning Bush: Writings on Jews and Judaism*, ed. and trans. Gregory Yuri Glazov (Notre Dame, IN: University of Notre Dame Press, 2016).

20 The first volume was the only one Soloviev completed as planned. He composed the work in 1885–87 but could not publish it in Russia because of censorship. For the text, see *Sobranie sochinenii Vladimira Sergeevicha Solov'eva*, 4:241–639. *Russia and the Universal Church* is a version of what was to have been the third volume.

to Christians, not Jews.[21] In their mistreatment of Jews, Christians violate the ethic of love, the moral core of their religion. Since it is Christians, not Jews, who stand in need of repentance and amendment of life, the Jewish question turns out to be a Christian question. In "The Talmud and Recent Polemical Literature about It in Austria and Germany" (1886), Soloviev promoted a positive attitude toward Jewish law. He pointed out that, while Christians tend to make a sharp distinction between their religion and Judaism, most Christians have never read, much less studied, Jewish law. If they did, they would discover that Jewish and Christian ethical values are much the same. What Christianity has to offer is not a new ethic but the redemptive humanity of God in Christ. This is a gift that Jews, too, need to receive, but they should not be expected to receive it until Christians do a better job of showing how their proclamation actually transforms life. The enduring paganism of nominally Christian societies and the sectarian divisions within Christianity itself present a sorry spectacle. Soloviev imagines Jews saying to Christians:

> In our view, truth cannot be abstract, and cannot be separated from practical life. We are a people of the Law, and for us truth itself is not so much an intellectual idea as a *law of life*.... Your religious ideal is the expression of supreme sanctity, but the law of your life is and remains the law of sin and of injustice.[22]

The remaking of a Romantic-idealist Christian as a liberal universalist was by no means unknown in nineteenth-century spiritual culture (consider Victor Hugo), but such a conversion usually involved the abandonment of dogmatic and theocratic beliefs for a more secularized faith. Soloviev, by contrast, was able to hold the entire value spectrum together in a highly original synthesis, a union of opposites grounded in divine humanity. As he saw it, people do not have to choose between Orthodoxy and modernity, tradition and freedom, religion and science, Christian faith and religious universalism, gospel and law, God and the world. How is such wholeness of life possible? It is possible because "the Word was made flesh and dwelt among us" (John 1:14). In Christ—the humanity of God—all things in heaven and on earth are reconciled and destined for incorporation in the kingdom of God.

The Justification of the Good

In the 1890s, Soloviev pulled back from the activism of the 1880s and returned to writing projects in philosophy. His shift is often interpreted as evidence of his loss of faith in religious activism, but it is preferable to see it as a response

21 "Jewry and the Christian Question," in *The Burning Bush*, 277–329.

22 "The Talmud and Recent Polemical Literature about It in Austria and Germany," in *The Burning Bush*, 346–76, here at 374–75.

to new opportunities to pursue his original vocation. In 1889, Nikolai Grot founded Russia's first professional philosophical journal, *Voprosy filosofii i psikhologii* (Questions of philosophy and psychology). Soloviev was one of the collaborators. In 1891, Soloviev was appointed philosophy editor of the multivolume Brockhaus-Efron *Encyclopedic Dictionary*, a position that provided him with some income as well as intellectual stimulation. During this last decade of his life, he published many philosophical essays, including his magnum opus, *The Justification of the Good* (*Opravdanie dobra*, 1897; 2nd ed., 1899), which, to this day, remains the most comprehensive work of moral philosophy in the Russian tradition. With his brother Mikhail Sergeevich and close friend Sergei Nikolaevich Trubetskoi, Soloviev also embarked on the ambitious project of translating the complete works of Plato into Russian.[23]

Soloviev's mature philosophy of law is found in *The Justification of the Good* and a shorter, overlapping work, *Law and Morality* (1897).[24] In these compositions, Soloviev presents a more dynamic and nuanced view of the relationship between law and morality than in *The Critique of Abstract Principles.* There, as we have seen, Soloviev drew a sharp distinction between the formal or negative character of law and the substantive or positive ends of morality. He had little to say about how law and morality should interact, even though his theocratic ideal demanded interaction. In *The Justification of the Good*, Soloviev construes law not just as a formal structure but in positive terms as the "*compulsory demand for the realization of a definite minimum of good, or for a social order which excludes certain manifestations of evil*" (Jakim 320, Nemeth 331, *OD* 17.6). This definition obviously rules out the contention in *The Critique of Abstract Principles* that law can accommodate any end.[25]

23 Soloviev completed only one volume before he died: *Tvoreniia Platona*, trans. Vladimir Solov'ev, vol. 1 (Moscow: Izdanie K. T. Soldatenkova, 1899). The volume contains seven dialogues: *Theages, Alcibiades 1* and *2*, *Ion, Laches, Charmides*, and *Lysis.* On Soloviev's Plato scholarship, see Frances Nethercott, "Between Christian Platonism and the 'Father of Idealism': Solov'ëv as a Translator and Interpreter of Plato," in *Vladimir Solov'ëv: Reconciler and Polemicist*, 251–66; and Iu. B. Tikheev, "Vladimir Solov'ev—Izdatel' 'Tvorenii Platona,'" *Solov'evskie issledovaniia*, 2015, no. 1 (45): 6–15.

24 There are two English translations of *The Justification of the Good*: Vladimir Solovyov, *The Justification of the Good: An Essay on Moral Philosophy*, trans. Nathalie A. Duddington, ed. Boris Jakim (Grand Rapids, MI: William B. Eerdmans Publishing Company, 2005), and *Vladimir Solov'ëv's Justification of the Moral Good: Moral Philosophy*, ed. and trans. Thomas Nemeth (Cham, Switz.: Springer, 2015). In references to *The Justification*, I cite both editions. Quotations are from the Duddington-Jakim translation, which I have altered to Americanize spelling and secure gender-neutral language. To facilitate location of passages in Russian editions, I supply Soloviev's chapter and section numbers of *Opravdanie dobra* (abbreviated *OD*). An English translation of *Law and Morality: Essays in Applied Ethics* is found in *Politics, Law, and Morality: Essays by V. S. Soloviev*, ed. and trans. Vladimir Wozniuk (New Haven: Yale University Press, 2000), 131–212.

25 For his notion of law as the requirement of a "minimum of good," Soloviev was indebted to Georg Jellinek (1851–1911), whose concept of law as an "ethical minimum" gained wide

Soloviev still recognized that law and morality should not be elided. The differences between them endure in the notion of a minimum of good and in the idea that law eliminates "[only] certain manifestations" of evil. These limitations cannot apply to morality. Moral demands are unlimited, never finished, and effected voluntarily. "Be perfect, therefore, as your heavenly Father is perfect" (Matthew 5:48) is the standard of morality. Legal demands, on the other hand, are limited, realizable, and compulsory. Nevertheless, Soloviev construed the evangelical call to perfection in such a way as to affirm relative goods, not just the absolute Good:

> The *absolute* moral principle, the *demand*, namely, or the *commandment* to be perfect as our Father in heaven is perfect, or to realize in ourselves the image and likeness of God, already contains in its very nature the recognition of the *relative* element in morality. For it is clear that the demand for perfection can be addressed only to a being who is imperfect; urging him to *become* like the higher being, the commandment presupposes the lower stages and the relative degrees of advance.
>
> (Jakim 312, Nemeth 323, *OD* 17.1)

Law is a relative good because it pertains to imperfect beings, yet imperfect beings are advancing, heeding an upward call, experiencing a process of transformation extending from here to eternity. This understanding of progress makes it possible to define law in terms of a necessary ethical minimum without severing law's connection with the moral and spiritual maximum.

Soloviev saw the need for legal prescriptions of an ethical minimum in response to three manifestations of collective evil: the immoral relations between nations, between society and criminals, and between social classes. The first evil appears in nationalism; the second, in vindictive judicial practices, such as capital punishment; the third, in systemic poverty.

On the national question, Soloviev tried to steer a middle course between nationalism and cosmopolitanism. The evangelical commandment to love one's neighbor as oneself relativizes national boundaries and rules out national egoism. Yet actual neighbors are not abstract beings, but always members of a particular tribe, people, nation, or other group. Hence, the evangelical commandment must be taken to mean: "*we must love all nations* [tribes, peoples, etc.] *as we love our own*" (Jakim 257, Nemeth 265, *OD* 14.5). A Christian is not called to be "the abstract *human being in general* [*obshchechelovek*] of the philosophers and jurists," but is indeed called to be a "concrete *universal* human being" (*vsechelovek*) (Jakim 246, Nemeth 254, *OD* 14.3).[26]

currency. See E. A. Pribytkova, "Pravo kak 'eticheskii minimum' v filosofsko-pravovykh kontseptsiiakh G. Ellineka i Vl. Solov'eva," *Solov'evskie issledovaniia*, 2008, no. 2 (17): 266–85.

26 Dostoevsky featured the notion of a *vsechelovek* (lit. "pan–human being") in his famed Pushkin Speech of 1880. See Kostalevsky, *Dostoevsky and Soloviev*, 71–77.

Soloviev does not discuss international law in *The Justification of the Good*, but he does include a chapter on "The Meaning of War" (Chapter 18). He offered further discussion of the subject in his last book, *Three Conversations on War, Progress, and the End of World History, Including a Short Story of the Anti-Christ* (1899–1900). Rejecting Tolstoyan pacifism, Soloviev argued that Christian love requires one to protect the defenseless, by force if necessary, if it is in one's power to do so. Or more colorfully: after the murder of Abel by Cain, "justly fearing lest the same thing should happen to Seth and other peaceful people, the guardian angels of humanity mixed the clay with copper and iron and created the soldier and the policeman" (Jakim 348–49, Nemeth 361, *OD* 18.6). In *Three Conversations*, Soloviev pressed his case by invoking the contemporary example of the ethnic cleansing of Armenia by Turkish and Kurdish forces during the Russo-Turkish War of 1877–78, atrocities that recurred in the Armenian massacres of the 1890s.[27] As a nineteenth-century progressive, Soloviev believed in "the approaching end of wars"; but he also believed "it would be irrational … to think and to act as though that approaching end had already come" (Jakim 343, Nemeth 355, *OD* 18.4).

In his treatment of penal law, Soloviev rejected the traditional conception of criminal justice as retribution as well as the Tolstoyan view of criminal law as state violence. Both ideas fail to discern the essential hallmark of justice, which is neither force nor retribution but "right." A system of criminal justice must reckon with three rights: the right of the injured party to defense and compensation, the right of society to security, and the right of the criminal "to correction and reformation" (Jakim 278, Nemeth 287, *OD* 15.6). The first two rights are generally accepted. The third is controversial, because it challenges popular judicial practices that violate the humanity of the criminal. These include not just bloody and cruel acts of vengeance but any type of punishment that treats the offender simply as a means to an end. This is why Soloviev rejected capital punishment, a practice that violates not just the humanity of the criminal but the very notion of the "common good":

> Common good is *common* just because in a certain sense it contains the good of *all* individual persons *without exception*; if it did not, it would be the good of the majority.… But the conception of the *common* good implies with logical necessity that in *restricting* particular interests and activities within common bounds it cannot *do away with* a single bearer of such interests and activities by depriving him of life or of all possibility of free action. The common good must, in one way or another, be the good of *this individual also.*
>
> (Jakim 327, Nemeth 338, *OD* 17.9)

27 Discussion of political violence in the Ottoman Empire and elsewhere appears throughout this work of literary and philosophical genius. See Vladimir Solovyov, *War, Progress, and the End of History: Three Conversations, Including a Short Story of the Anti-Christ*, trans. Alexander Bakshy, rev. Thomas R. Byer Jr., intro. Czeslaw Milosz (Hudson, NY: Lindisfarne Press, 1990). Soloviev did not live to witness the Armenian genocide of the twentieth century.

The penal system should instruct and correct offenders, not destroy them. Since correction implies the possibility of repentance and amendment of life, Soloviev also rejected mandatory life imprisonment.

In *Law and Morality*, Soloviev offered a biblical argument against capital punishment. In biblical history, he identified three critical moments relevant to capital punishment: the punishment of Cain, reserved to God alone (Genesis 4:15); the institution of retributive justice after the Flood, an accommodation accepted into the Mosaic law; and a "return to the norm" in the Hebrew prophets and Christian gospel, both of which proclaim that God alone will repay sinners, and will repay them according to the principle, "I desire mercy, and not sacrifice" (Matthew 9:13 and 12:7; cf. Hosea 6:6).[28] Soloviev was convinced that a person who considers the biblical revelation as a whole rather than seizing on bits and pieces of it will conclude that capital punishment violates the divine norm:

> The Bible is a complex spiritual organism which developed over a thousand years. It is completely free of external monotony and unilinearity but amazing in its internal unity and in the harmony of the whole. To snatch out arbitrarily from this whole only intermediate parts without a beginning and an end is an insincere and frivolous business; and to rely on *the Bible in general* in favor of the death penalty—attests either to a hopeless incomprehension or a boundless insolence. Those who, like Joseph de Maistre, draw together the concept of the death penalty with the concept of a sin offering, forget that a sin offering has already been brought for all by Christ, that it has abolished all other blood sacrifices, and itself continues only in the bloodless Eucharist—an amazing lapse in consciousness on the part of persons who confess the Christian faith. Indeed, to permit any kind of sin offerings still—means to deny that which was accomplished by Christ, which means—to betray Christianity.[29]

Soloviev devotes a chapter of *The Justification of the Good* to economic justice. He argues that, even if the plutocrats of his day could demonstrate that the prosperity of the many was the sure outcome of the suffering of the few, unregulated capitalism would still be wrong because it reduces some human beings to the status of a means only. Here, too, the common good must be "the good of all and each and not of the majority only" (Jakim 294, Nemeth 305, *OD* 16.5). This principle led Soloviev to formulate the most celebrated concept in *The Justification of the Good*: the right of all human beings to a "dignified" or "worthy" (*dostoinyi*) existence. Human beings should live decently. An economy that produces or

28 Soloviev, *Law and Morality*, 175–76.

29 Ibid., 176. The depth of Soloviev's engagement with the Bible has not been sufficiently appreciated. For a corrective, see E. B. Rashkovskii, "Sovremennoe i bibleiskoe v nasledii Vl. Solov'eva, ili o dukhovnykh predposylkakh solov'evskogo 'liberalizma,'" *Solov'evskie issledovaniia*, 2008, no. 1 (16): 17–38.

tolerates degradation is immoral, and collective action should be taken to change it. "The duty of society is to recognize and to secure to all of its members and their families the *right* to enjoy unmolested *worthy* human existence" (Jakim 294, Nemeth 305, *OD* 16.5). "To recognize and *to secure*": Soloviev's emphasis on guaranteeing decent economic circumstances for all people made plain the need for economic legislation, law being an arrangement that actually effects a certain outcome as opposed to merely recommending it. Soloviev was an early advocate of the modern welfare state.

While there is much in his criticism of capitalism that approximates socialism, Soloviev never accepted the economic determinism of socialism. He also rejected its radical egalitarianism.

> It is one thing to strive for an impossible and unnecessary equalization of property, and another, while preserving the advantages of larger property to those who have it, to recognize the right of everyone to the necessary means of worthy human existence.
>
> (Jakim 298, Nemeth 308, *OD* 16.5)

Not equality but dignity should be the aim of economic legislation.

Soloviev's conception of the right to a dignified existence resulted from the synthesis of his idea of law with the Orthodox Christian view of human nature as capable of deification (theosis):

> The absolute value of human beings is based, as we know, upon the *possibility* inherent in their reason and their will of infinitely approaching perfection or, according to the patristic expression, the possibility of becoming divine (*theosis*). This possibility does not pass into actuality completely and immediately, for if it did human beings would be already equal to God—which is not the case. The inner potentiality *becomes* more and more actual, and can only do so under definite real conditions.
>
> (Jakim 296, Nemeth 306–7, *OD* 16.5)

To appreciate this passage, one must keep two points in mind. First, before the nineteenth-century Russian monastic revival and the labors of twentieth-century patristics scholars, the concept of theosis was in deep eclipse, even in Orthodox theology. Soloviev was one of the first modern thinkers to recognize the vast implications of the idea. Second, it was unprecedented to find the concept of theosis in an essay on economic justice. The passage just quoted comes from a page of *The Justification of the Good* where Soloviev adduces social statistics establishing a correlation between income level and life expectancy in modern urban society. By interjecting the concept of theosis into this discussion, Soloviev manages to connect the *summum bonum* of contemplative monks with the travails of the working class in places like Paris and St. Petersburg. A passage like this helps us appreciate why it was Soloviev, more than anyone else, who inspired the Russian religious-philosophical renaissance of the early twentieth century. Soloviev had a genius for reconciling opposites: gospel and law, church and world, contemplation and social action, Orthodoxy and humanism, God and human beings. Soloviev loved the Good—the whole of it.

Soloviev believed that the Christian church had an indispensable role to play in the "moral organization of humanity as a whole," as the last chapter of *The Justification of the Good* is titled (Chapter 19). Without the church and the kingdom of God to which it bears witness, the end of life would be opaque; history would lack direction. In these matters, the state must look to the church. As always, however, Soloviev's theocracy is free, not authoritarian. Church and state, while connected, must respect each other's integrity:

> *The state recognizes the supreme spiritual authority of the universal Church, which indicates the general direction of the goodwill of humankind and the final purpose of its historical activity. The Church leaves to the state full power to bring lawful worldly interests into conformity with this supreme will and to harmonize political relations and actions with the requirements of this supreme purpose. The Church must have no power of compulsion, and the power of compulsion exercised by the state must have nothing to do with the domain of religion* [Soloviev's italics].
>
> (Jakim 394, Nemeth 407–8, *OD* 19.17)

Soloviev's longstanding advocacy of religious freedom in the Russian Empire also informed his position here.

Many interpreters of Soloviev have underscored the contrast between his earlier works and *The Justification of the Good*, construing the former as vehicles of theocratic utopianism, the latter as evidence of the "dissolution of theocratic views."[30] The issue is what Soloviev meant in practical terms when he wrote that "the state recognizes the supreme spiritual authority of the universal Church." Walicki claims that, for the later Soloviev, "'free theocracy' was, so to speak, stripped of its millenarian features and reduced to something like a Kantian 'regulative idea' in ethics."[31] But this seems to understate the case. In the table of contents of *The Justification of the Good*, Soloviev still promised a description of Christianity "as an absolute *event*, an absolute *promise*, and an absolute *task*" (Jakim xxv, Nemeth xxiv, *OD*: Oglavlenie 11.8). In the last chapter, he still wrote of a "Christian state" whose "progressive activity" is "to prepare humanity and the whole earth for the Kingdom of God" (Jakim 391–92, Nemeth 405, *OD* 19.16). He still entrusted the moral organization of humanity to a "harmonious cooperation" of prophet, priest, and king (Jakim 401–03, Nemeth 415–17, *OD* 19.20). Is this language merely ornamentation for an essentially secular ideal? In a perverse way, Boris Chicherin was closer to the truth when, in his review of *The Justification of the Good*, he accused Soloviev of taking positions "which

30 Trubetskoi, *Mirosozertsanie Vl. S. Solov'eva*, 2:190–94.
31 Walicki, *Legal Philosophies of Russian Liberalism*, 191.

Torquemada could adopt."[32] It was an unfair comparison, of course. Soloviev never preached clericalism, not to speak of an inquisition. Still, Chicherin sensed something in Soloviev that many of the latter's cultured admirers tended (and tend) to minimize or to miss: for all his modernism and moderation, the author of *The Justification of the Good* remained a mystic, a prophet, and a theocrat.

An arresting example of the impact of Soloviev's Christian faith on his view of law is found in his observations on Plato's *Laws* in a late essay.[33] Both Plato's *Laws* and *The Justification of the Good* are essays of applied ethics in which a mature philosopher attempts "to reconcile an ideal with practical reality by combining minimalism in terms of the ideal with maximalism in practice."[34] Soloviev gave a sobering account of the path that led Plato, in the *Laws*, to absolutize the juridical order. Smitten as a young man by the goodness, truth, and beauty revealed in Socrates, Plato became increasingly frustrated by his inability to realize those values in the world of flesh and blood. This led him, in the *Republic*, to harness such atrocious means of social order as slavery, war, and tyranny to the service of his ideal. Finally, in the *Laws*,

> a direct, principled renunciation of Socrates and philosophy is expressed by Plato in those laws, by virtue of which any man who rejects or upsets the authority of the ancestral laws, both relative to the gods and relative to the public order, is subject to the death penalty.
>
> Thus the greatest disciple of Socrates, who had been called to independent philosophical creativity by his indignation at the *legal* murder of his teacher, toward the end totally rests on the point of view of Anytos and Melitos, who had obtained the death sentence for Socrates precisely because of his liberal attitude to the established religious-civil order.[35]

32 Chicherin's review of *The Justification of the Good* appeared as B. N. Chicherin, "O nachalakh etiki," *Voprosy filosofii i psikhologii* 8, no. 4, kn. 39, pt. 1 (1897): 586–701 ("Torquemada" at 644). Soloviev's reply appeared as "Mnimaia kritika. (Otvet B. N. Chicherinu)," ibid., pt. 2: 645–94. Further discussion appeared in the next issue: B. N. Chicherin, "Neskol'ko slov po povodu otveta g. Solov'eva," *Voprosy filosofii i psikhologii* 8, no. 5, kn. 40, pt. 2 (1897): 772–79; and Vl. S. Solov'ev, "Neobkhodimye zamechaniia na 'Neskol'ko slov' B. N. Chicherina," ibid., 779–83. Another eminent jurist who reviewed Soloviev's opus was G. F. Shershenevich: "Po povodu knigi Vl. S. Solov'eva 'Opravdanie dobra,'" *Voprosy filosofii i psikhologii* 8, no. 3, kn. 38, pt. 2 (1897): 456–74, followed by Soloviev's response: "Zamechaniia na stat'iu prof. G. F. Shershenevicha," ibid., 475–84. As a legal positivist, Shershenevich held a different view of the nature of law than Soloviev's. For a summary of these and other exchanges on *The Justification of the Good*, see Nemeth, *The Later Solov'ëv*, 232–48.

33 "Plato's Life-Drama," in *Politics, Law, and Morality*, ed. Wozniuk, 213–54.

34 Viach. Ivanov, "O znachenii Vl. Solov'eva v sud'bakh nashego religioznogo soznaniia," in *Vl. Solov'ev: pro et contra. Lichnost' i tvorchestvo Vladimira Solov'eva v otsenke russkikh myslitelei i issledovatelei, Antologiia*, 2 vols. (St. Petersburg: Izdatel'stvo Russkogo Khristianskogo gumanitarnogo instituta, 2000–02), 2:771–82, here at 774.

35 "Plato's Life-Drama," 252–53.

How could this have happened to Plato? It happened, Soloviev believed, because Plato attempted "the *reform* of societal relations" without believing in "the *regeneration* of human nature" (250). He did not believe in the regeneration of human nature because he did not know "the One who has the power of resurrection to eternal life." Plato knew Socrates, but not Christ, the "authentic, substantive *God-Man*" (254).

Soloviev's legacy

Soloviev died on July 31, 1900, following a brief illness. His influence, far from contracting, expanded in the two decades thereafter. The Russian Silver Age, as this period is called, was a time of extraordinary creativity in all fields of cultural endeavor: social, political, and legal thought, religion, literature, music, dance, painting, and more. Soloviev's ideas had an impact in several of these areas. All the young religious philosophers who sprang up at this time—Nikolai Berdiaev, Sergei Bulgakov, Semyon Frank, Lev Karsavin, Pavel Florenskii, and others—took Soloviev as their starting point, and much of their work may be seen as attempts to advance his agenda in one way or another, albeit with significant revisions.[36] The makers of the Symbolist movement in Russian literature—Aleksandr Blok, Andrei Belyi, Viacheslav Ivanov, and others—were profoundly indebted to Soloviev's mysticism and theurgic aesthetics. The composer Alexander Scriabin was an admirer. *Vekhi* (*Landmarks*, 1909), the most important work of self-criticism on the part of the Russian intelligentsia in the late imperial period, struck Solovievian chords.[37]

Soloviev also influenced the philosophy of law in Russia, but it is important to recognize the kind of influence it was. Pavel Novgorodtsev addressed this question in the issue of *Voprosy filosofii i psikhologii* dedicated to Soloviev's memory.[38] He argued that Soloviev was not important because of contributions to the specialized literature in philosophy of law. Indeed, Soloviev's jurisprudential writings contain "many blunders and oversights" and "definitions that willy-nilly offend a jurist's ear" (126, 128). Soloviev's contribution was on another level: he masterfully defended "the idea of law," "the ideal essence of law," and "trust in the moral power of law" (112–14). Novgorodtsev's point was that the finest professional jurisprudence in the world will have little effect where people do not have faith in law to begin with, or regard the idea of law as inherently contingent and negotiable. Novgorodtsev also praised Soloviev's criticism of religiously motivated indifference and even hostility to juridical values on the part of the

36 For an introduction to this large subject, see P. P. Gaidenko, *Vladimir Solov'ev i filosofiia Serebrianogo veka* (Moscow: Progress-Traditsiia, 2001).

37 See Chapter 14 of this volume (312–13) for a brief discussion of *Vekhi* (*Landmarks*).

38 P. Novgorodtsev, "Ideia prava v filosofii Vl. S. Solov'eva," *Voprosy filosofii i psikhologii* 12, no. 1, kn. 56 (1901): 112–29. See also M. G. Galakhtin, "Vladimir Solov'ev i moskovskaia shkola iurisprudentsii," *Solov'evskie issledovaniia*, 2005, no. 1 (10): 109–22.

Slavophiles and Tolstoy. Soloviev offered a metaphysical and religious justification of law.

Most of the religious thinkers of the Silver Age shared Soloviev's commitment to juridical values. Several were graduates of law faculties, and all were involved in one way or another in the struggle for political rights and church reform. What Soloviev taught this generation of neophytes was that the struggle for human rights and lawful political institutions, far from being something religiously awakened persons are free to disregard, is a religious imperative. As Irina Borshch puts it, "The justification of law cannot be a matter of indifference to the Christian conscience because, in the last analysis, it is bound up with the justification of human beings."[39] Accordingly, the Solovievians of the Silver Age inaugurated a "dialogue" between jurisprudence and religious philosophy within which a "Russian Orthodox legal consciousness" began to take shape. The dialogue was fated to be short lived because of the upheavals of the Russian Revolution and the suppression of the tradition of Russian legal education in the Soviet period. The final chapter of the dialogue took place in the early 1920s, when Novgorodtsev, Bulgakov, and Nikolai Alekseev served together as members of the Russian Law Faculty in Prague.[40]

For most of the Soviet period, Soloviev was a nonperson. None of his works were republished. The existence of prerevolutionary editions, however, enabled a few highly motivated individuals to explore what was there. Father Aleksandr Men' (1935–90), the spiritual guide of a generation of Moscow intelligentsia in the 1960s and 1970s, began reading Soloviev in the late 1950s. His understanding of Christianity was strongly Solovievian.[41] Aleksei Losev (1893–1988), a philologist and philosopher who had experienced the Silver Age as a young man, survived repression and decades of obscurity to emerge as a mentor to the new generation at the same time. A harbinger of change appeared in 1970 with the publication of a high-quality encyclopedia article on Soloviev by a team of authors with ties to Losev and Men'.[42] Losev managed to publish a small book on Soloviev in 1983; an expanded, more accessible version came out in 1990.[43] Since then, there has been a steady stream of publications, conferences, and public discussion of Soloviev's life and work.

39 I. V. Borshch, *Russkaia nauka tserkovnogo prava v pervoi polovine XX veka: Poisk metodologii*, prefaces by A. Arzhakovskii and O. A. Sedakova (Moscow: URSS, 2008), 115.

40 Ibid., 44.

41 See E. B. Rashkovskii, "Vladimir Solov'ev i protoierei Aleksandr Men' v dinamike istorii rossiiskoi," *Solov'evskie issledovaniia*, 2011, no. 2 (30): 33–44; and Kateřina Kočandrle Bauer and Tim Noble, "Alexander Men and Russian Religious Thought in the Post-Soviet Situation," in *The Oxford Handbook of Russian Religious Thought*, 627–41.

42 V. Asmus, E. Rashkovskii, I. Rodnianskaia, and S. Khoruzhii, "Solov'ev," in *Filosofskaia entsiklopediia*, 5 vols. (Moscow: Sovetskaia entsiklopediia, 1960–70), 5:51–56.

43 On the drama surrounding the publication Losev's book, see A. A. Takho-Godi, "Iz istorii knigi o Vl. Solov'eve," in Losev, *Vladimir Solov'ev i ego vremia* (2000), 5–10.

Soloviev is now a classic. His place in the history of Russian thought needs no defense. The question concerning his legacy for Russian jurisprudence today is whether the prophetic edge of his thought—his passionate "justification" of human rights, his advocacy of love and mercy as virtues for public, not just private life, and his inclusive, universalist vision of the Christian faith—will play a role in shaping the mentality of the Russian state and the Russian Orthodox Church in the twenty-first century.

10 Between law and theology

Russia's modern Orthodox canonists

Vera Shevzov

The overhaul of Russia's universities by Emperor Alexander II (r. 1855–81) as part of his broader reformist endeavors was a landmark in the history of Orthodox thought on church/canon law in modern times. Though not without debate, under pressure from faculties of law, the 1863 University Regulations established departments of "church jurisprudence"—officially renamed "church law" in 1884—within university law faculties. These new departments joined a cohort of some twelve others across different fields of law, together comprising Russia's discipline of jurisprudence until the Bolshevik coup of 1917.[1]

Although the study of church/canon law in terms of "church justice" (*tserkovnoe pravosudie*) alongside "state justice" had been proposed for Russia's first institution of higher learning—Moscow's Slavo-Greco-Latin Academy—as early as 1668, that effort came to naught.[2] The study of church/canon law was

1 *Universitetskaia reforma 1863 goda v Rossii*, ed. V. A. Tomsinov (Moscow: Zertsalo, 2012), lxxxiv–cxvii. For debates regarding the establishment of departments of church law within faculties of law, see "Novye predlozheniia otnositel'no kafedr tserkovnoi istorii i tserkovnogo zakonovedeniia v nashikh universitetakh," *Pravoslavnoe obozrenie*, 1864, vol. 13, no. 1 (Jan.): 93–104; *Zamechaniia na proekt obshchogo ustava Imperatorskikh Rossiiskikh universitetov*, pts. 1–2 (St. Petersburg: Tip. Imperatorskoi Akademii Nauk, 1862); and A. S. Pavlov, *Sokrashchennyi kurs lektsii tserkovnogo prava* (Moscow, 1895–96), 42–43.

2 Sergei Smirnov, *Istoriia Moskovskoi Slaviano-Greko-Latinskoi Akademii* (Moscow: Tip. V. Got'e, 1855), 12. For examples of histories of canon law as an academic field in Russia's universities, see the numerous publications of A. A. Dorskaia, especially *Gosudarstvennoe i tserkovnoe pravo Rossiiskoi imperii: problemy vzaimodeistviia i vzaimovliianiia* (St. Petersburg: Izd. RGPU im. A. I. Gertsena, 2004) and *Vliianiia tserkovno-pravovykh norm na razvitie otraslei rossiiskogo prava* (St. Petersburg: Asterion, 2007). Also see, E. V. Beliakova, *Tserkovnyi sud i problemy tserkovnoi zhizni* (Moscow: "Dukhovnaia biblioteka," 2004); I. V. Borshch, *Russkaia nauka tserkovnogo prava v pervoi polovine XX veka: Poisk metodologii* (Moscow: URSS, 2008); N. I. Komarov, D. A. Pashentsev, S. V. Pashentseva, *Ocherki istorii prava Rossiiskoi imperii: vtoraia polovina XIX-nachalo XX v.* (Moscow: Statut, 2006). For brief overviews, see I. V. Botantsov, "Sootnoshenie istochnikov svetskogo i tserkovnogo prava v Rossiiskoi imperii 1832–1917," *Leningradskii iuridicheskii zhurnal*, 2016, no. 2 (44): 9–19; O. E. Rychagova, "Razvitie nauki tserkovnogo prava v XIX-nachale XX veka v Rossii," *Vestnik Omskogo Universiteta*, 2002, no. 2: 96–99; John D. Basil, *Church and State in Late Imperial Russia: Critics of the Synodal System of Church Government (1861–1914)*, Minnesota Mediterranean and East European Monographs, no. 13 (Minneapolis: Modern Greek Studies, University of Min-

DOI: 10.4324/9781003017097-10

officially introduced into Russia's theological academies in the eighteenth century, when higher education in Russia was divided into two parallel tracks.[3] This dual arrangement included an imperial state university system, structured on Western European models, and an academy system overseen by the church with a curriculum including the "theological sciences" alongside other areas of study.[4] In the academies, the subject of church/canon law was at first loosely grouped with the theological sciences, but with time it became a nomadic field, lacking a fixed disciplinary or departmental home, and the training of specialists lagged well into the mid-nineteenth century.[5]

The study of church law in Russia's universities was not unknown, however. Prior to 1863, universities taught church jurisprudence, but only among other courses on Orthodox theology. Overseen by a theological academy graduate—usually an ordained priest who concurrently served as the university chaplain—universities' single-member departments of theology were, by design, independent within the curriculum and thus marginalized from other faculties.[6] Although professors of theology may have taught a course on church jurisprudence specifically to law students as early as 1835, it was mandatory only for students belonging to the "Orthodox confession" (*Greko-rossiiskogo ispovedaniia*).[7]

The migration of church/canon law from the confessional canopy of university theology departments to secular faculties of law in 1863 was thus a momentous, though publicly little noticed, occasion in the history of Orthodox academic thought in Russia. On one hand, as newcomers to university faculties of law, canonists initially often found themselves in the role of Orthodox apologists, attempting to justify not only the necessity of knowing church/canon law as part of the history of law in Russia, but also the importance of the related subjects of basic theology and religion for the modern jurist. On the other hand,

nesota, 2005), 35–59; N. N. Glubokovskii, *Russkaia bogoslovskaia nauka v ee istoricheskom razvitii i noveishem sostoianii* (Warsaw, 1928), 94–100.

3 A. E. Ivanov, *Vysshaia shkola v Rossii v kontse XIX–nachale XX veka* (Moscow: Akademiia nauk SSSR, 1991); F. A. Petrov, *Formirovanie sistemy universitetskogo obrazovaniia v Rossii*, 4 vols. (Moscow: Izd-vo Moskovskogo Universiteta, 2002–03); A. Iu. Andreev, *Rossiiskie universitety XVIII–pervoi poloviny XIX veka v kontekste universitetskoi istorii Evropy* (Moscow: Znak, 2009). For the history of the teaching of the theological sciences in Russia's universities, see N. Iu. Sukhova, *Vertograd nauk dukhovnyi: sbornik statei po istorii vysshego dukhovnogo obrazovaniia v Rossii XIX–nachala XX veka* (Moscow: Pravoslavnyi Sviato-Tikhonovskii gumanitarnyi universitet, 2007), 326–44.

4 N. Iu. Sukhova, *Vysshaia dukhovnaia shkola: problemy i reformy* (Moscow: PSTGU, 2006).

5 N. K. Sokolov, *O vliianii tserkvi na istoricheskoe razvitie prava* (Moscow: Universitetskaia tip., 1870), 6–8; N. Iu. Sukhova, "Tserkovnoe pravo v pravoslavnykh dukhovnykh akademiiakh Rossii: problemy i traditsii," *Religii mira: Istoriia i sovremennost'* (Moscow and St. Petersburg: Nestor–Istoriia, 2012): 346–68.

6 *Materialy sobrannye otdelom vysochaishe uchrezhdennoi kommissii dlia peresmotra obshchego ustava Rossiiskikh universitetov pri poseshchenii ikh v sentiabre, oktiabre, i noiabre 1875 g.* (St. Petersburg: Tip. Balasheva, 1876), 251–53.

7 *Sravnitel'naia tablitsa ustavov universitetov 1884, 1863, 1835 i 1804 gg.* (St. Petersburg: Tip. St. P. Tiurmy, 1901), 87.

canonists were influenced by their new environment. Their reconsideration of church/canon law as a subject of study—its parameters and provisions, definition of terms, sources, history, and ultimate purpose—had as much impact on Orthodox thought as on jurisprudence in Russia.

Professional profiles

The formidable task of recasting church/canon law into the language of modern jurisprudence fell initially to a small but influential group of academic pioneers. Among the canonists who held the first positions of church jurisprudence were Moscow University's N. K. Sokolov (1835–74), St. Petersburg University's M. I. Gorchakov (1838–1910), and Kazan University's A. S. Pavlov (1832–98).

Over the decades, Russia's canonists taught thousands of law students, including, surprisingly, such figures as Vasily Kandinsky (1866–1944), Sergei Diaghilev (1872–1929), Georgii L'vov (1861–1925, head of Russia's Provisional Government in 1917), and Vladimir Ulyanov (Lenin, 1870–1924). Canonists were also vanguards of scholarship germane to modern Orthodox thought. The initially small cohort of university-based specialists expanded as some retired or passed away, new universities opened, and comparable departments emerged in other institutions of higher learning, such as the prestigious Imperial School of Jurisprudence in St. Petersburg and the Demidov Law Lycée in Yaroslavl. In addition, their ranks were matched by those of equal stature in Russia's four theological academies, which, in response to the demand for cadres to fill university positions, established parallel degree-granting departments of church law in 1884.[8] Thus, pioneers in Russia's university law faculties were soon joined by canonists such as I. S. Berdnikov (1839–1914), N. S. Suvorov (1848–1909), M. A. Ostroumov (1847– 1920), N. A. Zaozerskii (1851–1919), and N. D. Kuznetsov (1863–1936), among others.

Although operating in different methodological and disciplinary spheres, university and theological academy canonists became part of a broader network encompassing their distinct educational worlds. The nature of church/canon law as a subject encouraged such cross-pollination and collaboration. As Gorchakov maintained in the 1870s,

> for the sake of a rigorous academic … approach to their subject of study, and even for the soundness of their official position in the department, university canonists must possess such knowledge of theology so as to be in a position to explain the relationship between law and faith from a theological point of view, even to a theologian, and to find the means within this knowledge to defend juridical principles.[9]

8 Sukhova, "Tserkovnoe pravo," 358.

9 V. N. Beneshevich, "Pamiati Gorchakova," *Trudy iuridicheskogo obshchestva pri Imperatorskom S.-Peterburgskom universitete za 1911*, vol. 5 (1913): 201–17, here at 207.

At the same time, universities and theological academies enjoyed their distinct subcultures, often remaining mutually guarded. As late as 1906, some faculty at St. Petersburg Theological Academy viewed their colleague Vladimir Beneshevich—a brilliant Byzantinist and university-trained canonist who taught canon law at the academy—as an "outsider" (*chuzhak*). Theological academy professor Ilya Berdnikov encountered a similar sentiment during his tenure at Kazan University's faculty of law.[10]

A brief professional profile of university and theological academy canonists in the late nineteenth and early twentieth centuries illustrates the links—and distinctions—between the two scholarly worlds. Between 1877 and 1917, Russia's universities and theological academies granted a total of twenty-four master's degrees and fourteen doctorates in church law.[11] Not all graduates subsequently occupied university or theological academy positions in church law. Similarly, not all canonists holding university positions had formal juridical training.

The fourteen doctorates awarded during this period were split evenly between university and theological academy graduates.[12] All seven theological academy graduates were raised in clerical families, and most spent at least part of their careers teaching in secular universities.[13] Only two of the seven—Nikolai Zaozerskii and Timofei Barsov—taught exclusively in theological academies.

In contrast, only two of the seven doctoral graduates from university law faculties—Suvorov and V. K. Sokolov (1871–1921)—came from clerical backgrounds, and only Sokolov chose to attend a theological academy (Kazan) prior to embarking on university studies. Suvorov was among the few canonists who

10 D. A. Karpuk, "Nauchno-issledovatel'skaia i prepodavatel'skaia deiatel'nost' dotsenta Sankt-Peterburgskoi dukhovnoi akademii po kafedre tserkovnogo prava V. G. Solomina (1881–1918)," *Vestnik Istoricheskogo obshchestva Sankt-Peterburgskoi Dukhovnoi Akademii*, 2020, no.1 (4): 144–67, here at 146; Sukhova, "Tserkovnoe pravo," 356.

11 Nikolai Suvorov was granted Russia's first university graduate degree in church law in 1877 (master's degree, St. Petersburg University). In 1917, P. V. Verkhovskoi (1879–1943) and Nikolai (Iarushevich, 1891–1961), a future controversial metropolitan, earned the last graduate degrees in the field prior to the establishment of the Soviet regime. See A. N. Iakushev, "Organizatsionno-pravovoi analiz podgotovki nauchnykh kadrov i prisuzhdeniia uchennykh stepenei v universitetakh i akademiiakh Rossii, 1747–1918" (kand. diss., Sankt-Peterburgskaia Akademiia MVD Rossii, 1998), 262. Iakushev's list does not include Pavel Verkhovskoi's 1917 doctorate.

12 The information on dissertations specifically in canon law for master's and doctoral degrees is based on N. Iu. Sukhova, *Russkaia bogoslovskaia nauka (po doktorskim i magisterskim dissertatsiiam 1870–1918)* (Moscow: Izd. PSTGU, 2013), 183–85. Prior to 1884, students in theological academies who earned master's degrees and doctorates on topics in canon law were officially granted doctorates in theology. These canon law-based doctorates in theology are not included among the fourteen doctorates noted here.

13 N. A. Zaozerskii (Moscow Theological Academy), T. V. Barsov (1836–1904, St. Petersburg Theological Academy), M. A. Ostroumov (Kharkov University), P. A. Prokoshev (1868–1922, Tomsk Imperial University), A. I. Almazov (1859–1920), V. N. Myshtsyn (1866–1936), and V. A. Narbekov (1862–1932), who subsequently pursued an academic career in church archaeology.

held no theological academy degree, although he received a full seminary education in Kostroma.[14] Of the remaining five university doctoral graduates, two were from the nobility,[15] one was the son of a court bailiff,[16] and the social background of the remaining two is unknown.[17] Nevertheless, even the university-trained canonists Platon Sokolov and Pavel Verkhovskoi augmented their training with studies at St. Petersburg Theological Academy. Only one of the seven university doctoral graduates taught church/canon law at a theological academy (Vladimir Beneshevich, St. Petersburg Theological Academy, 1906–09).

With respect to master's degrees, only one student (in addition to the seven already mentioned who completed university doctorates) received a master's in church law from a university.[18] Theological academies were much more active on this front, granting master's degrees in church law to some six students between 1878 and 1917 (in addition to seven others who subsequently completed doctorates as well).[19] Among the theologically trained canonists at this level, only two were not raised in clerical families: Nikolai Kuznetsov, whose father oversaw the Imperial Moscow Foundling Home, and hiermonk Mikhail (Semenov), son of a Russian mother and a Jewish cantonist and convert to Orthodoxy. In addition, some of the earliest professors in university departments of church law—including Pavlov, whom the eminent historian Vasilii Kliuchevskii ranked among the "best experts in canon law in contemporary Europe"[20]—received no more than a master's degree in theology from a theological academy. Finally, neither the first specialist in church law at Moscow University (N. K. Sokolov, a graduate of Moscow Theological Academy) nor the last professor of canon law at St. Petersburg Theological Academy (V. G. Solomin, 1881–1918, a graduate of the same school) held any advanced degree.[21]

The vast majority of professors of church/canon law from the late 1860s to 1917 were laymen. Only four trained canonists during this period were clergy, and each was a unique case. Gorchakov, who taught at St. Petersburg University for more than forty years (1868–1910), was an ordained priest before he earned his two doctorates—from the faculty of law at St. Petersburg University and from St. Petersburg Theological Academy. Hiermonk Mikhail (Semenov), an extraordinarily popular and innovative teacher of canon law at St. Petersburg

14 A. A. Dorskaia, "Iuridicheskoe nasledie Nikolaia Semenovicha Suvorova," *Istoriia gosudarstva i prava*, 2009, no. 13: 17–20.

15 P. V. Gidul'ianov (1874–1937, Moscow University) and Pavel Verkhovskoi (Imperial University of Russia in Warsaw).

16 V. N. Beneshevich (1874–1938, St. Petersburg University, St. Petersburg Theological Academy).

17 M. E. Krasnozhen (1860–1934?, Moscow University, Yuriev University) and P. P. Sokolov (1863–1923, St. Petersburg University, Kiev Imperial University of St. Vladimir).

18 I. M. Gromoglasov (1869–1937), the son of a deacon.

19 Nikolai Kuznetsov, hiermonk Nikolai (Iarushevich), Ilya Gromoglasov, Nikolai Temnikovskii (1860–1934), hiermonk Mikhail (Semenov, 1873–1916), and S. V. Troitskii (1878–1972).

20 V. O. Kliuchevskii, *Pravoslavie v Rossii* (Moscow: Mysl', 2000), 327.

21 Karpuk, "Nauchno-issledovatel'skaia i prepodavatel'skaia deiatel'nost'," 144–67.

Theological Academy, was tonsured before embarking on his dissertation.[22] Two other canonists—Ilya Gromoglasov and Pavel Verkhovskoi—sought ordination following the Bolshevik coup of 1917, well after the establishment of their academic careers. The single exception to the predominance of lay canonists in secular departments of church law was at the Imperial School of Jurisprudence, which continued the former practice of appointing theologically trained priests to teach church jurisprudence and, simultaneously, to serve as the school's priest.[23]

University graduate students in church law regularly traveled abroad for study and research. For instance, Pavel Gidul'ianov, future professor of church law at Moscow University, spent two years studying in Berlin and Munich. Vladimir Beneshevich spent four years studying law, history, and philosophy at the universities of Heidelberg and Leipzig. Trips in search of sources also took him to Mount Athos, Sinai, Egypt, and Palestine. In 1903, V. K. Sokolov, a graduate of Kazan University's faculty of law, spent a year abroad familiarizing himself with scholarship on canon law in Germany. Mikhail Gorchakov studied at the universities of Tübingen and Heidelberg during his term as cantor in the Russian church in Stuttgart (1863–66). Hence, Russia's canonists were exceptionally well-versed in philosophical, theological, and jurisprudential trends among their European counterparts.

The primary sources detailing the canonists' thinking on the nature of law in general, and church/canon law in particular, are their lecture notes and publications. Given the novelty of their field and its new institutional university setting, a dearth of teaching resources meant university professors had to conceptualize and delineate their subject for themselves and for their students virtually *ex nihilo*. The result was the production of lectures in the form of lithographed student notes or formal textbooks. Leading university canonists whose notes or textbooks were published (sometimes posthumously) included Berdnikov, Gorchakov, Krasnozhen, Ostroumov, Pavlov, N. K. Sokolov, and Suvorov.[24]

That these textbooks differed widely in approach and content speaks less to a "lack of progress in the field," as one late nineteenth-century canonist argued, than to the complexity of the subject matter and the diversity of thought.[25] The

22 Semenov lasted only one year (1905–06) before being let go for his openly liberal, Christian socialist views. For a theological academy student's perspective on Semenov's views, see Viktor Vvedenskii, "Glavnye techeniia v nauke kanonicheskogo prava." Kursovoe sochinenie studenta IV kursa (Otdel rukopisei, Rossiiskaia natsional'naia biblioteka, f. 574, op. 2, d. 416).

23 Two of these professors published textbooks on church/canon law, both of which were more of a catechetical nature: Mikhail Bogoslovskii, *Kurs obshchego tserkovnogo prava* (Moscow: Univ. tip., 1885); V. G. Pevtsov, *Lektsii po tserkovnomu pravu* (St. Petersburg: Tip. St. P. Odinochnoi Tiurmy, 1914).

24 Other textbooks at the time included M. P. Al'bov, *Kratkii kurs lektsii po tserkovnomu pravu* (St. Petersburg: Tip. Balasheva, 1882); Bogoslovskii, *Kurs*; P. A. Lashkarev, *Pravo tserkovnoe v ego osnovakh, vidakh i istochnikakh. Iz chtenii po tserkovnomu pravu* (St. Petersburg: Izd. Ogloblina, 1889); Pevtsov, *Lektsii*.

25 M. A. Ostroumov, *Ocherk Pravoslavnogo tserkovnogo prava*, vol. 1 (Kharkov: Tip. Gubernskogo Pravleniia, 1893), 95.

textbooks provide invaluable insights into the varied and sometimes competing understandings of concepts at the heart of the field—church, law, canonicity, authority, and others. These books also testify to the sharpening of canonists' modern critical sensibilities in the setting of university-based teaching and research.

In scholarly productivity, no period in Russia's history before or since equals the achievements of both university- and theological academy-based canonists across virtually all realms of church/canon law. The canonists also located and published rare Byzantine, South Slavic, and old Russian canonical texts. These efforts were perhaps best epitomized in the work of Beneshevich, whose "fantastical plan," as he called it, was to publish a complete collection of all canon law (as he defined the term).[26]

In addition to primary sources, the canonists also published historically informed studies on issues of particular interest at the time: marriage and divorce; confession and penance; ecclesiastical courts; participation of women in church and liturgical church life (including the issue of deaconesses); internal church governance; and church-state relations in the history of Orthodoxy. Canonists also became increasingly interested in other autocephalous Orthodox churches and the ways in which they appropriated Byzantine church/canon law. Of no less interest was the history of the juridical/canonical foundations, justification, and impact of the jurisdiction of the Patriarchate of Constantinople over the Russian church (tenth to sixteenth centuries) with respect to the development of Russian legal consciousness. And, once discussion of church reforms in Russia began in earnest in the early years of the twentieth century, canonists contributed actively to the debates, especially around issues of laity and "church rights," freedom of conscience, and church-state relations. Indeed, the intellectual odyssey of the canonists proved critical for Russia's Orthodox Church following the significant shifts in its legal position in the Russian state in 1905.

The personal fates of Russia's canonists were as complex, and often as tragic, as those of the rest of the Russian population during the years that saw world war, revolutionary upheaval, the unraveling of the monarchy, the Bolshevik coup, and civil war. Some canonists did not live to see the atrocities of this period or of the Soviet regime that followed it.[27] Most, however, did. Demidov Law Lycée's Vasilii Myshtsyn (d. 1936), Kazan University's Vladimir Sokolov (d. 1921), Kharkov University's Mikhail Ostroumov (d. 1920) and Evgenii Temnikovskii (d. 1919), Kiev University's Platon Sokolov (d. 1923), and Novorossiisk University's Aleksandr Almazov (d. 1920) all died of health-related causes. Moscow Theological

26 Mitropolit Isidor (Tupikin), "Nauka kanonicheskogo prava v Sankt-Peterburgskoi dukhovnoi akademii i osnovnye ee predstaviteli," *Khristianskoe chtenie*, 2019, no. 2: 88–98, here at 92.

27 Canonists who died prior to 1917 included: Moscow University's Aleksei Pavlov (d. 1898), Kiev University's Petr Lashkarev (d. 1899), St. Petersburg Theological Academy's Timofei Barsov (d. 1904), Moscow University's Nikolai Suvorov (d. 1909), St. Petersburg University's Mikhail Gorchakov (d. 1910), and Kazan University's Ilya Berdnikov (d. 1915).

Academy's Nikolai Zaozerskii (d. 1919) and St. Petersburg Theological Academy's Viacheslav Solomin (d. 1918) also died of natural causes. Details surrounding the deaths of two other juridically trained canonists, Yuriev University's Mikhail Krasnozhen (d. 1934? 1941?) and Tomsk University's Pavel Prokoshev, are unknown. Five other canonists—Moscow University's Pavel Gidul'ianov (d. 1937) and Ilya Gromoglasov (d. 1937), St. Petersburg University's Vladimir Beneshevich (d. 1938), Warsaw University's Pavel Verkhovskoi (d. 1943), and the juridically and theologically trained canonist and practicing lawyer Nikolai Kuznetsov (d. 1936)—experienced arrests and imprisonments. Eventually, Beneshevich, Gromoglasov, and Gidul'ianov (despite Gidul'ianov's initial work as a consultant for the Soviet state's People's Commissariat of Justice, which oversaw early Bolshevik efforts to "liquidate" the Orthodox Church) were executed for counterrevolutionary activity.[28] Kuznetsov, who often represented the Orthodox Church legally before Soviet officials (1917–19), and Verkhovskoi faced several arrests, served time in notorious Soviet prisons or corrective labor camps, and eventually died in internal exile in remote regions. In the end, no university-based canonists or professors of church/canon law from Russia's theological academies were among the large wave of Russia's Orthodox émigrés through whom Orthodox thought eventually became known in the West.[29]

The canonists' challenge: Orthodoxy and church law in a modern age

As groundbreakers in the study of church/canon law—which, as Suvorov maintained in 1889, was among Russia's least developed academic fields—Russia's university-based canonists faced numerous challenges.[30] Among the most immediate was establishing the field's legitimacy, purpose, and relevance on two fronts. First, canonists faced students who tended to dismiss topics concerning the church, deeming them applicable only for clergy and—as taught in the past—epistemologically out of place in a largely secular educational milieu. Second, the canonists encountered an "onslaught" of criticism from church officials or academic faculty "who consider this field to be the monopoly of the spiritual

28 In his capacity as consultant for this commissariat, Gidul'ianov authored *Tserkov' i gosudarstvo po zakonodatel'stvu R.S.F.S.R. Sbornik uzakonenii i rasporiazhenii s raz"iasneniiami V otdela NKIu* (Moscow: Tip. GPU, 1923).

29 S. V. Troitskii received a master's degree in church/canon law in 1913 but did not become a professor of canon law until he assumed an academic position in the emigration in Yugoslavia. Nevertheless, he referred to himself as "the last of the Mohicans, the sole survivor among the canonists of the old Russian academic school." S. Troitskii, "O edinstve Tserkvi," *Vestnik Russkogo Zapadno-Evropeiskogo Patriarshego Ekzarkhata*, 1957, no. 26: 101–10, here at 110.

30 N. Suvorov, *Kurs tserkovnogo prava*, 2 vols. (Yaroslavl: Tip. G. Fal'k, 1889–90), 2: iii; N. Zaozerskii, "O zhelatel'noi postanovke prepodavaniia tserkovnogo prava v nashikh uchebnykh zavedeniiakh," *Chteniia v obshchestve liubitelei dukhovnogo prosveshcheniia*, 1910, no. 1 (Jan.): 26–35, here at 26.

domain."[31] Although united in the conviction that the study of church law was vital to church, state, and society, canonists varied widely in their understanding of, and approaches to, their subject.

Indeed, canonists grappled with the question "what is church law?" to clarify what one of them characterized as the "extremely garbled views on the nature of this 'thing' that is being studied."[32] Church/canon law by definition was interdisciplinary, including such wide-ranging matters as historical and contemporary reflection on church and authority in the context of ecclesial governance; the person (*lichnost'*) in relation to community and society; and the relationships among law (*zakon*), rule (*pravilo*), and *pravo*—a term historically linked in Russia with truth, integrity, authority, and freedom before it assumed the Western juridical meaning of "law" and "right" in the sixteenth and seventeenth centuries.[33] Also in need of clarification were the sources of church law and the roles of state and church in formulating and implementing both civic and church/canon law. Attempts to identify the provenance(s) of church/canon law resulted in canonists constructing often-competing historical narratives of Russia's interwoven Byzantine juridical heritage, Western Christian influences, and indigenous ecclesio-juridical traditions.

The study of church/canon law also involved methodological challenges. Russia's canonists were acutely aware of Orthodoxy's lack of an established system for the study of canon law comparable to that of their Western counterparts, although none would minimize the influence of church/canon law on the history of law in Russia more broadly.[34] As Suvorov explained, although Russia's Byzantine inheritance included collections of church rules, it did not include the *science* of church law: "the Byzantines could not bequeath that which they did not possess, and that in which they were not proficient."[35] To compensate for the lack of a well-defined Orthodox framework for studying church/canon law, and to present the subject in terms resonating with modern juridical discourse in Russia, most university-based Russian canonists turned to Western Christian counterparts, especially at German universities. The value of Western legal thought for Orthodox church/canon law, however, remained contested. A review of the thought of several prominent late nineteenth-century canonists offers insight into the diversity of views on the definition, nature, and significance of church/canon law on the eve of the Bolshevik Revolution of 1917.

The first canonist in St. Petersburg University's faculty of law, Mikhail Gorchakov, taught some eight thousand students during his lengthy career

31 Mikhail Gorchakov, quoted in Beneshevich, "Pamiati Gorchakova," 208.

32 Beneshevich, "Pamiati Gorchakova," 207.

33 V. V. Vinogradov, *Istoriia slov* (Moscow: Institut russkogo iazyka im. V. V. Vinogradova, 1999), 533–34.

34 David Wagschal, *Law and Legality in the Greek East: The Byzantine Canonical Tradition, 381–883* (New York: Oxford University Press, 2015), 80.

35 N. S. Suvorov, "Tserkovnoe pravo, kak iuridicheskaia nauka," *Iuridicheskii vestnik*, 1888, vol. 28, no. 8 (Aug.): 520–50, here at 522.

(1868–1910).[36] His full promise was cut short by the premature death of his wife, which left him to raise five children. Except for four monographs based on his dissertations in civil law and canon law, his publications included articles, published lectures, and reviews of doctoral dissertations. Nevertheless, the large library he willed to St. Petersburg University and incomplete drafts of book manuscripts testified to his academic aspirations. Referring to himself as "a liberal of the 1860s," Gorchakov retained his pro-reform sentiments to the end of his life. In 1905, at the age of sixty-seven, he was among the famous group of thirty-two St. Petersburg priests who signed the progressive memorandum "Thoughts on the Necessity of Changes in the Governance of the Russian Church." The document caused a public sensation and elicited criticism from some church officials.[37] Nonetheless, on the basis of his stature and erudition, in 1906 the Holy Synod ratified Gorchakov's participation in the newly formed State Council.

Unlike other textbook authors, Gorchakov linked his understanding of church law as a juridical discipline to his understanding of law and religion more broadly speaking. According to Gorchakov, law is a relational principle involving universal laws foreordained by the Creator and human-created laws designed to regulate social relations justly. In Gorchakov's estimation, humans do not have full knowledge of the universal laws—the laws of "absolute truth" (*absoliutnaia pravda*)—but, instead, are ever in the process of understanding them.[38]

Gorchakov identified both the individual person and communities as sources of human-created law.[39] The person is foundational. Self-aware of "possessing the potential, the ability, and the strength reasonably and freely" to realize themselves, persons strive to develop their individual natures according to their qualities. To achieve their goals, all persons also depend on others, for which reason communities are no less law-generating than individuals. Once one becomes a part of a community, however, the freedom to develop oneself risks limiting the freedom of others. Human-created law, then, involves managing freedom in a communal context. "No single person," Gorchakov argued, "can claim unconditional rights to fulfill their needs without any checks or interference from others."[40] Each member seeks to protect their rights to pursue their perceived "reason-

36 Biographical information is based on Beneshevich, "Pamiati Gorchakova"; "Gorchakov, Mikhail Ivanovich, prof. prot., Nekrolog," *Tserkovnye vedomosti*, 1910, no. 33 (Aug. 14): 1397–99; M. A. D'iakonov, *M. I. Gorchakov. Nekrolog* (St. Petersburg: Tip. Imperatorskoi Akademii Nauk, 1910); Nikolai Markov, "Gorchakov, Mikhail Ivanovich," *Pravoslavnyi bogoslovskii entsiklopedicheskii slovar'*, ed. A. P. Lopukhin (Petrograd: T-vo A. Lopukhina, 1900–11), 552–60; Aleksandr Bertash, "Gorchakov," *Pravoslavnaia entsiklopediia* (Moscow: Tserkovno-nauchnyi tsentr "Pravoslavnaia Entsiklopediia," 2000–), vol. 12: 156–58.

37 On the memo of the thirty-two priests, see Jennifer Hedda, *His Kingdom Come: Orthodox Pastorship and Social Activism in Revolutionary Russia* (DeKalb: Northern Illinois University Press, 2008), 154–58.

38 M. I. Gorchakov, *Tserkovnoe pravo: kratkii kurs lektsii* (St. Petersburg: Izd. Studenta A. Shiriaeva, 1909), 9–10.

39 The following summary is based on Gorchakov, *Tserkovnoe pravo*, 6–8.

40 Ibid., 8.

able needs" for the realization of their full human potential. Gorchakov thus identified law as "an expression of the understanding of justice" at a given time in a given society.[41] If humans collectively understood the foreordained universal laws and lived according to them, "absolute truth" would prevail. Having only vague knowledge of these universal laws, however, humans coexist with a variety of ever-changing and often seemingly competing understandings of justice.

Gorchakov's understanding of church law emerged from this conceptualization of law more broadly. He maintained that faith (or religion) was one of the reasonable needs that all humans possess by nature. Faith, Gorchakov argued, was "one of the most significant aspects of human life, be it in one's personal life, within society, or within the state."[42] Drawing on sociology, anthropology, phenomenology, psychology, and philosophy of religion, Gorchakov defined faith as a particular human disposition engaging "the totality of a person's powers and life capacities" and informing all relationships. As humans are social beings, people form relationships on the basis of shared faith-informed views.[43] These relationships, in turn, network into larger associations with their own rules, forms of governance, and relations with other religious associations. Gorchakov maintained that religion's intrinsic capacity to generate associations made it relevant to jurisprudence. A jurist's education remained incomplete without knowledge of such associations and their underpinnings.[44]

Gorchakov claimed that the laws governing these associations—including the Orthodox Church—should not be conflated with other branches of law, because their subject and object were a unique, sui generis community stemming from religion (or faith) in broad terms, not just Christianity or Orthodoxy in particular. Gorchakov directly linked the laws governing the Orthodox Church as a juridical discipline to the political and social sciences and, indirectly, to theology. The task of the academic study of church/canon law, then, was twofold. First, it aimed to "systematize in all of its totality the norms of the church's organization, its internal governance, its relationship to the state and to other social associations." Second, it aimed to clarify whether the "internal norms" of this law corresponded with the goals of the church as a community and institution, as well as with the general provisions of jurisprudence.[45]

Gorchakov advised law students to define religious communities on the communities' own terms rather than on the basis of abstract or politically motivated philosophical considerations. Since religious communities typically defined themselves on the basis of theological teachings, Gorchakov argued that these self-definitions were "givens": jurists must start with them. However, jurisprudence

41 Ibid., 10.

42 Ibid., 1.

43 Ibid., 8–9.

44 According to Gorchakov, jurists are "expected to know, understand, and explain the significance of any religious association that exists . . . within the bounds of the state" where they live. Gorchakov, Tserkovnoe pravo, 1.

45 Ibid., 23.

involves such theological givens only insofar as they apply to juridical issues. The specific content of theological views stands beyond the jurist's domain.[46]

Gorchakov's understanding of law and his emphasis on religion as a shared feature of the human condition eliminated any leanings in his work toward Christian or specifically Orthodox exceptionalism. They also underlay his interest in freedom of religion and conscience, topics to which he devoted considerable attention in his textbook. He maintained that Russia's legal designation of Orthodoxy as the "ruling" faith was based on Orthodoxy's majority status, not on confessional "superiority." Following the October Manifesto of 1905, Gorchakov was among the churchmen who advocated abolishing the term "ruling" (*gospodstvuiushchaia*) with respect to the Orthodox Church in Russian law.[47]

Aleksei Pavlov began his long career as a university canonist in Kazan, Russia's "window to the East." Born in the Siberian region of Tomsk to a church cantor, Pavlov graduated from seminary and enrolled at Kazan Theological Academy in 1854. The academy had recently acquired a rich collection of manuscripts related to canon law, and Pavlov's work with them sparked his lifelong interest in the subject.[48] The academy's dean at the time, Ioann (Sokolov, 1818–69)—future bishop of Smolensk and author of a textbook on church law—tapped Pavlov to mine the archive for sources Sokolov needed for his own work.[49] Following graduation from the academy, Pavlov taught for a semester at Kazan Seminary before returning to the academy to teach church law and liturgics. In 1864 Kazan University's faculty of law recruited Pavlov to fill the new position in church law.

Pavlov first studied abroad at the University of Heidelberg in 1867, working in particular with professor of Roman law Karl Adolph von Vangerow (1808–70) and Byzantinist Karl Zachariae von Lingenthal (1812–94). After returning to Russia, Pavlov accepted a position in church law at Novorossiisk University in Odessa. In 1875, he moved to Moscow University's faculty of law following the premature death of their young canonist, N. K. Sokolov. By all accounts, Pavlov accepted this offer because of the access to archives and libraries that residence in Moscow afforded him. He remained at Moscow University until his death, in 1898.

Like most other university canonists (except for Gorchakov), Pavlov introduced the study of church law in his works by highlighting the uniqueness of the Christian community. Christians from the very start distinguished themselves

46 Ibid., 14.

47 Ibid., 335; *Zhurnaly i protokoly zasedanii Vysochaishe uchrezhdennogo Predsobornogo Prisutstviia (1906 g.)*, 4 vols. (Moscow: Izdatel'stvo Novospasskogo monastyria, 2014), 2:539–40.

48 A. Dmitrievskii, "Nezabvennoi pamiati professorov A. S. Pavlova i N. F. Krasnosel'tseva," *Trudy Kievskoi Dukhovnoi Akademii*, 1899, no. 1: 59–104, here at 60–61.

49 Arkhimandrit Ioann, *Opyt kursa tserkovnogo zakonovedeniia*, 2 vols. (St. Petersburg: Tip. Fishera, 1851). This textbook is often cited as among the first systematic works on this topic in Russia. For Pavlov's assistance in Ioann's work, see P. Znamenskii, *Istoriia Kazanskoi Dukhovnoi Akademii za pervyi (doreformennyi) period ee sushchestvovaniia (1842–1870 gody)* (Kazan: Tip. Imperatorskogo Universiteta, 1891), 212.

through imperceptible sacred bonds uniting diverse peoples in a spiritually united transnational association sharing a vision of God and ultimate purpose eclipsing all other interests and identities.[50] According to Pavlov, the Christian church, as a sacred "organism," was autonomous and self-governing. Christians established the church's norms and rules (*prava*) according to what they considered divinely instituted principles facilitating the community's ultimate goals. Notably, in the context of nineteenth-century Russia and its Petrine system of church organization, Pavlov's narrative of church autonomy and Christian self-government carried potentially subversive political undertones.

In contrast to Roman law, where laws concerning religion fell under broader state-legislated domains of public or private law, Pavlov emphasized church law's particularity. He maintained that rules governing the church as a community could be formulated only by members of that community; the independence and autonomy of the church, in this respect, were absolute. To subsume church law under public law, as in Roman law and Justinian's *Corpus juris civilis*, would presume that the Christian religion was inherent to, and coincided with, the state. Pavlov was adamant that "Christianity … did not belong to anyone as a national religion, and the Church was not a state establishment."[51] Similarly, the church could not be considered a "state within a state," because the qualitatively different aims of church and state prevented the two from being equated, "even in circumstances when all peoples [within a given state] belonged to a single church … since the church was 'a kingdom not of this world.'"[52] At the same time, Pavlov emphasized that, as an association existing alongside others in a state, the church and its members were still subject to state laws.

Pavlov referred to the church's rules interchangeably as "canon" or "church" law. He attributed the distinction often made between these terms to the history of church/canon law in the West, a history not shared in his estimation by Christians in the Eastern Roman Empire.[53] Accordingly, he argued, Orthodox canonists could use these terms interchangeably.[54]

In contrast to Gorchakov, whose approach was influenced by sociology, anthropology, and the philosophy and phenomenology of religion, Pavlov adopted a historical-critical methodology. Maintaining that the study of church law focused on the "currently operative law of the church," Pavlov argued that appreciation of church law's "vital significance" necessarily involved a return to the sources that shaped this law. Church/canon law, in Pavlov's view, was genealogical in nature. Proper understanding and application involved tracing the origins of a given law, tracking its subsequent development, and "marking the local, national,

50 Pavlov, *Sokrashchennyi kurs*, 1–6.

51 A. S. Pavlov, *Kurs tserkovnogo prava* (Sviato-Troitskaia Sergieva Lavra, 1902), 11.

52 Ibid., 12.

53 According to Nikolai Sokolov, Pavlov's predecessor at Moscow University, the term "canon law" was not indigenous to Byzantine Orthodox Christianity, especially in Russia, since it grew out of the relationship between the Latin church and Roman law.

54 Pavlov, *Kurs*, 7–9.

and political influences" that produced its current form. By following any given rule's evolution or "genetic process," canonists demonstrated that church/canon law was a "living" law "with its own character."[55]

Pavlov's historical-critical approach, combined with his starting point as a person of faith, resulted in a theologically informed, ecclesio-juridical appreciation of canon law conveyed in the academic language of his time. While an academic canonist at a secular university, Pavlov maintained an ecclesiological purpose—to discern church/canon law's "link with the essential nature of the Church," whose primary goal, in turn, was transformation of the human person and his or her communion with God.[56] Echoing the imagery of "kernel" and "husk" used by Estonian-born Lutheran church historian Adolf von Harnack (1851–1930), Pavlov spoke about the hidden "essential core" of ecclesiastical institutions and rules in contrast to their visible, pliable, and historically conditioned "external wrapping" (*obolochka*), whose "look" could change over time.[57] Insights from detailed source analysis, he maintained, enabled the church to weigh the extent and kinds of reforms it could undertake without betraying its being and mission.[58]

Pavlov's contributions to Orthodox thought were far reaching. He maintained, for example, that the church as "an association for all peoples in all times" across cultures and historical-political circumstances resulted in the coexistence of diverse ecclesial rules considered normative by their respective communities. Pavlov also recognized the institutional mechanisms—councils in particular—through which Christian communities attempted to maintain unity in the face of variation and disagreements over competing practices. According to Pavlov, councils governed by "the principle of equality of spiritual authority of all hierarchs" were the highest administrative body of the church.[59] Yet in terms of reception, Pavlov maintained that not all Christian communities accepted the disciplinary rules and organizational norms which even imperially overseen ecumenical councils established: only the dogmatic decisions of these councils could claim that honor (and even then, only up to a point).[60]

Because the norms governing organizational and disciplinary matters of church life were formulated by particular persons in particular time periods, Pavlov maintained that church members had not only the obligation but the divinely given *right* to alter the outward shape of communal norms and governances to reflect changing historical circumstances—precisely to preserve the church's relevance.[61] More than a decade following his death, as debates about church reforms gained public attention in Russia, Pavlov's voice rang out in the

55 Ibid., 30–31.
56 Ibid., 5, 68.
57 Ibid., 9, 31.
58 Ibid., 30.
59 Ibid., 260.
60 Ibid., 52–53.
61 Ibid., 38–39.

writings of the next generation of canonists. Vasilii Myshtsyn, professor of canon law at Demidov Law Lycée, for instance, quoted Pavlov in 1910 to support his views that "church canons were not immutable or obligatory for all times," that canons can be changed or rescinded, and that reform cannot be equated with "restoration of all ancient canons."[62] In doing so, Myshtsyn corroborated earlier predictions that Pavlov's deep knowledge of the sources pertaining to church/canon law ensured that his works would have "classic, timeless significance" for future Orthodox thinking on canon law.[63]

In evaluating the evolving field of academic church law, Pavlov singled out two fellow canonists—Ilya Berdnikov and Nikolai Suvorov—as "extremes" in terms of methodological shortcomings.[64] According to Pavlov, Berdnikov was too theological in his approach, while Suvorov depended too heavily on Western legal jurisprudence.[65] While both canonists were lauded as "coryphaei" within the field, their disparate academic training and teaching environments contributed to stark diversity with respect to "ecclesiastical legal consciousness."[66] Highlighting the perceived differences, the juridically trained Suvorov referred to Berdnikov as a "spiritual writer," while the theologically trained Berdnikov noted Suvorov's self-regard as a "canonist of a special type."[67]

In 1888, Suvorov published an unfavorable review of Berdnikov's *Short Course on the Church Law of the Greco-Russian Orthodox Church*, the first textbook designed for both university law students and theological academy students. Berdnikov's response was eventually published in a 450-page monograph, *The Foundational Principles of Church Law in the Orthodox Church*.[68] The controversy centered on two primary factors: a) the relevance of Western canon law and jurisprudence more broadly for the study of Orthodox church/canon law, and b) the nature of the church and its governance, including church-state

62 V. N. Myshtsyn, *Naskol'ko obiazatelen avtoritet kanonov? O tserkovnykh kanonakh* (Moscow: Tip. Butaeva, 1910), 6, 9.

63 N. Zaozerskii, "Pamiati A. S. Pavlova," *Bogoslovskii vestnik*, 1898, vol. 3, no. 9: 348–55 (2nd pagination), here at 352.

64 Berdnikov, Pavlov's one-time student and a graduate of Kazan Theological Academy (1864), was professor of church law at the academy until his retirement in 1911, periodically also teaching at Kazan University. Suvorov bypassed a theological academy education and, after completing seminary, enrolled in St. Petersburg University. Upon completion of his master's dissertation under Gorchakov in 1877, Suvorov taught for two decades at the Demidov Law Lycée before replacing Pavlov at Moscow University in 1899, where he remained until his death, in 1909.

65 Pavlov, *Kurs,* 30.

66 *Pamiati professora Il'i Stepanovicha Berdnikova* (Kazan: Tsentral'naia Tip., 1915), 13.

67 Suvorov, *Kurs,* 1:31; I. Berdnikov, *Osnovnye nachala tserkovnogo prava pravoslavnoi tserkvi* (Kazan: Tip. Imperatorskogo Universiteta, 1902), 3.

68 I. Berdnikov, *Kratkii kurs tserkovnogo prava Pravoslavnoi Greko-Rossiiskoi Tserkvi* (Kazan: Tip. Imperatorskogo Universiteta, 1888). It should be noted that in his title, Berdnikov uses the adjective *rossiiskii* ("pertaining to the Orthodox Church in imperial Russia"), not *russkii* ("ethnic Russian"). For Suvorov's review, see note 35; for Berdnikov's *Foundational Principles*, see note 67.

relations, which at least some regarded as one of the least studied subjects among Russian jurists.[69]

Known for his deep admiration of Europe's historical accumulation of "juridical concepts, categories, and scientific classifications," Suvorov not only encouraged his students and fellow canonists to tap this "capital" but also insisted that its appropriation was necessary for organizing and understanding the "heap of materials" that presented itself as Orthodox church/canon law, especially in Russia.[70] A supporter of the Petrine church reforms, Suvorov spoke of church-state relations in Russia as a "mix of the Byzantine system and the Western system of state ecclesiality."[71] Contemporary church law could not, therefore, be conceptualized primarily in terms of Byzantine norms and laws established a thousand years earlier, as if those prescriptions were still "active."[72] European legal thought was essential to the academic study of Orthodox church law in Russia, a fact to which Berdnikov seemed indifferent.[73]

Suvorov also criticized Berdnikov's narrative of the history of the Orthodox Church's governance and juridical authority. In particular, Suvorov questioned the historical accuracy of Berdnikov's textbook depiction of the Orthodox Church—even after the conversion of the emperor Constantine—as an autonomous, internally self-governing association with its own rules and highest legislative authority vested in councils.[74] Furthermore, according to Suvorov, Berdnikov's identification of ordination and rank (*san*) as *the* criteria for church governance—including the assignment of legislative, administrative, and judicial roles—resulted in a faulty image of the church as comprising solely ordained clergy at administrative levels. It also reinforced the identification of the church as type of "state" in which no layperson—even emperors—could hold a position of governance without explicit hierarchal permission.[75] In Suvorov's estimation, this depiction of the Orthodox Church mirrored a "Roman Catholic construct."

Suvorov also criticized Berdnikov's conflation of "rule" (*kanon*) with "law" (*zakon*) and his use of "church law" to refer to both church canons and imperially issued church-related legislation. Berdnikov's textbook thus confused students regarding the church's "rule/law-creating" (*pravoobrazuiushchii*) authority.[76] For Suvorov, Berdnikov's use of terms suggested that the Orthodox Church was

69 N. Suvorov, "Kharakteristika katolitsizma i protestantizma v ikh otnosheniiakh k gosudarstvu," *Iuridicheskii vestnik*, 1887, vol. 26, no. 11 (Nov.): 492–503, here at 501.

70 Suvorov, *Kurs*, 2:iii; "Tserkovnoe pravo," 520–21.

71 Suvorov, *Kurs*, 2:492.

72 Suvorov, "Tserkovnoe pravo," 523–24; 533–34.

73 Ibid., 523, 524.

74 Ibid., 531, 533, 537. Suvorov cites Metropolitan Makarii Bulgakov's (1816–82) *Dogmatic Theology*, which was heavily influenced by Roman Catholic teachings, as a source of this teaching: Makarii, Mit. Moskovskii i Kolomenskii, *Pravoslavno-Dogmaticheskoe Bogoslovie*, 4th ed., 2 vols. (St. Petersburg, Tip. Golike, 1883).

75 Suvorov, "Tserkovnoe pravo," 533, 535.

76 Ibid., 527–31.

governed by its own authority and laws, to which emperors, as secondary, only formally assented.[77]

Even a cursory review of Orthodox church governance in the Byzantine past and Russian present, Suvorov maintained, offered a different picture. Suvorov maintained that with Constantine, the "norms of church law began to flow from two main sources: from church canons and from imperial legislation."[78] Initially, Constantine recognized church hierarchs as representing a spiritual authority distinct from imperial authority, identifying himself as "bishop [to those] outside the church." His task was to enforce "Christian law"—formulated by the church's hierarchy—as imperial law.[79] Nevertheless, Byzantine emperors often reverted to the Roman imperial identification of religion with state. Despite Justinian's well-known codification of two distinct, divinely given authorities in human society—the priesthood (*sviashchenstvo*) and the emperor—Suvorov maintained that this distinction in no way expressed imperial recognition of two *juridically governing* authorities.[80] A single legal governing authority—the emperor—oversaw both state and church. The emperor served as the juridically "highest church-governing authority" and "rule-generating" center of the institutional life of the Orthodox Church—both internally and externally.[81]

While refuting Western academic definitions of "Byzantinism" and "caesaropapism" to describe this phenomenon, Suvorov did not deny the phenomenon but reinterpreted it, focusing on the church hierarchy's response to the new imperial reality. The church hierarchs, Suvorov claimed, saw the emperor's role in their own terms. Like their Western Roman ecclesiastical counterparts, Byzantine hierarchs viewed the emperor's "earthly" power as secondary to, or lower than, their "spiritual" authority.[82] Byzantine hierarchs imagined the emperor as an administrative "organ" of the church to whom they had willingly *granted* ecclesiastical authority—along with symbolic liturgical functions—in exchange for the commitment to protect the faith and implement the church's "norms" as state law.[83] Thus, Byzantinism and caesaropapism, in Suvorov's estimation, did not represent the subjugation of church and clergy to state control (as Western scholars understood those terms) but constituted a unique form of "papism."[84] Byzantinism was an "expression of the church in the state and its imposition of law on the state."[85]

77 Ibid., 533–34.

78 Suvorov, *Kurs,* 1:223–24.

79 N. Suvorov, "Predislovie perevodchika," in Fridrikh Maassen, *Deviat' glav o svobodnoi tserkvi i svobode sovesti*, trans. and intro. by N. Suvorov, *Vremennik Demidovskogo Iuridicheskogo Litseia*, no. 29 (Yaroslavl: Tip. G. Fal'k, 1882), i–xxxvi, here at xxvi.

80 Ibid., xxvii.

81 Suvorov, "Tserkovnoe pravo," 531, 534, 539; *Kurs*, 2:63.

82 Suvorov, "Tserkovnoe pravo," 539; "Predislovie perevodchika," xviii.

83 Suvorov, "Predislovie perevodchika," xiv, xxi, xxviii.

84 Ibid., xv.

85 Ibid., xxi.

With respect to Russia specifically, Suvorov maintained that Peter the Great's reforms attempted to neutralize the church hierarchy's potential capacity to position themselves in society as an equal or higher authority, parallel to that of the emperor. The architect of the Petrine church reforms, the archbishop of Novgorod Feofan (Prokopovich, 1681–1736), attributed two distinct but coexisting "jurisdictions" or roles to Russia's ruler: a) "just a tsar," and b) a "Christian tsar."[86] According to Suvorov, Peter—in his role as just a tsar—attempted to abolish "the spiritual hierarchy's" realization of their imagined "higher authority" vis-à-vis the state by including the clergy as one among several state service ranks. In his second role, as a Christian tsar, Peter represented not a confrontation between two coexisting orders—state and church—but instead the efforts of an "energetic ... tsar-reformer" to overcome "ecclesiastical disorder" and clerical lethargy.[87]

Suvorov maintained that Berdnikov's description of Russia's church governance—a synod of bishops independently engaged in a "law/rule-creating culture" (*pravoobrazovatel'naia kul'tura*) with the emperor "on the sidelines"—implied a "dualism in governing authority" that overlooked the realities of the Petrine system and denied the legal role of the emperor with respect to the church as defined in Russia's law code.[88] By associating church governance, administrative functions, and church-legislative activity solely with the clergy and church hierarchy, Berdnikov once again revealed his inclinations toward Catholic teachings.[89] As a result, he virtually ignored the authority of the emperor, viewing it as "extraneous to the church," an institute of "secular," not church, law. As Suvorov saw it, Berdnikov's ecclesial understanding led to one of two conclusions: a) it implicitly rejected the reality that the emperor represented the law-generating center and highest office of church authority in the Orthodox Church; or b) it suggested that the emperor's legal role vis-à-vis the church was a form of "usurpation."[90]

Suvorov's focus on the emperor as the juridically unifying center of the institutional Orthodox Church had far-reaching consequences for his "canonical view" of Orthodox governance. In his estimation, neither bishops (including patriarchs), whose authority was territorially limited, nor ecumenical councils, which met only irregularly and under the emperor's aegis, could claim to represent a single administrative-juridical center within Orthodoxy.[91] The Byzantine church hierarchy attempted to counter this lack in various ways: with such notions as the pentarchy of patriarchs,[92] or with what Suvorov referred to as the Patriarchate of Constantinople's self-proclaimed "pretensions" to the position of the highest judicial authority among Orthodox churches (which Suvorov denied was ever

86 Suvorov, "Tserkovnoe pravo," 540.
87 Ibid., 541.
88 Ibid., 543.
89 Ibid., 544.
90 Suvorov, *Kurs*, 1:208n25.
91 Ibid., 1:62–63.
92 Ibid., 1:78–79.

ratified as a canon).[93] The same motive of providing an administrative-juridical center also led to the idea that ecumenical councils were the "highest linking church-administrative form," an idea which prevented local churches from being regarded as "self-sufficient organisms." Suvorov argued that autocephalous churches were in fact "separate juridical units," whose decision to participate in any council depended entirely on "the considerations of church authorities" in any given country.[94] He ascribed the efforts of "spiritual writers" to maintain otherwise as contributing to "ahistorical Orthodox self-understanding."[95]

While disagreeing with Berdnikov's view of the church as a fully autonomous, self-governing institution, Suvorov also disagreed with the widespread view that the Petrine system had resulted in the church's "fusion" with, or "absorption" by, the state.[96] Instead, based on his reading of recent European Protestant experience, Suvorov argued that the Petrine system required Russia's nineteenth-century canonists and jurists "to clarify the distinction between the emperor as head of state and the emperor as head of the church's administration," to demarcate the boundaries between the two and, thereby, the boundaries between state and church as well. In the end, Suvorov maintained, this was one of the most essential tasks facing modern jurisprudence in Russia.[97]

Berdnikov's response to Suvorov's review was no less direct. In response to Suvorov's depiction of his ecclesiastical views as essentially Roman Catholic, Berdnikov asserted that Suvorov's juridically secularist, Protestant-informed approach to Orthodox church/canon law resulted in an "original perspective" on church governance, authority, and rule-making that the Orthodox Church "never shared."[98] Berdnikov's rejoinder addressed three major areas of disagreement between the two canonists: their understanding of a) the nature of church legislation; b) church-state relations in Byzantium; and c) Russia's Petrine church reforms and the system of church governance in nineteenth-century Russia.

Suvorov's rejection of the working premise of Berdnikov's textbook—the view of the church as a historically independent association (*obshchestvennyi soiuz*) with its own "right of [internal] legislation"—steered Berdnikov's response. Reflecting on the dynamic nature and competing understandings of "law," Berdnikov contended that Suvorov's criticism of his interchangeable use of *zakon*, *pravo*, and *zakonodatel'stvo* (statute law, law/right, and legislation) for both church-issued rules (*pravila*, "canons") and state-enacted decrees was philosophically and politically driven. Pointing out that his own terminology corresponded to contemporary usage among canonists in Russia and Europe as well as church- and

93 Suvorov, "Tserkovnoe pravo," 540.
94 Suvorov, *Kurs*, 1:7.
95 Suvorov, "Predislovie perevodchika," xxii.
96 Suvorov, "Tserkovnoe pravo," 543.
97 Ibid., 543.
98 Berdnikov, *Osnovnye nachala*, 386–87. Initially Berdnikov published his response in a series of installments in the journal *Pravoslavnyi sobesednik* in 1889–91 and 1897. In 1902, they were published as *Osnovnye nachala* (see note 67).

state-related sources from late antiquity, Berdnikov argued that he had undermined Suvorov's working premise that "lawmaking" was an exclusive function of the emperor as the "highest source of justice [in society]" and the "supreme law-generating authority in all aspects of society's life."[99] Berdnikov's interchangeable use of these terms also pointedly undermined Suvorov's claim that, historically, Orthodox bishops had no "law-generating" authority. In Berdnikov's estimation, Suvorov's view that bishops did not "legislate" but merely "composed rules" (canons) that remained little more than "opinions" was historically untenable.[100]

From Berdnikov's perspective, Suvorov's understanding of law and authority implied that, prior to the fourth century, the church was not an autonomous "legal organism" (*pravovoi organizm*)—a view with which few historians would agree.[101] More importantly, Berdnikov disagreed with Suvorov's implication that, beginning with Constantine, the church as an institution had no internal, self-regulating life distinct from the state, and that imperial legislation "regulated all aspects of church discipline and even dogmas of faith."[102] Such a view led to a distorted understanding of Byzantine church-state relations and the "generative center" of church law.

In contrast, Berdnikov argued that episcopal councils not only retained their internal ecclesial "legislative" authority under Byzantine imperial rule but also overturned the traditional monopoly of the Roman state over religion-related legislation.[103] Byzantine emperors officially promulgated the church's rules/laws not as initiators of those laws or for purposes of "controlling" the church, but in order to confirm the Christian faith. In terms of sacrality, emperors generally viewed conciliar decisions on a par with scripture. Imperial appropriation of church-generated laws as imperial laws, Berdnikov argued, was a sign of the emperors' deference to the church as a means of ensuring divine favor.[104] In the end, in contrast to Suvorov's revisionist view of caesaropapism as applied to Byzantium, Berdnikov staunchly defended his position that the church remained a distinct "social organism" with its own law-generating functions, and that Byzantine emperors did not generally encroach on those functions without consulting the church hierarchy.[105]

Berdnikov was no less critical of Suvorov's reading of the fate of church/canon law in Russia's history. Suvorov appeared to believe that "lawmaking in the Orthodox Church belonged only to state authorities," and that without these authorities, Russia's Orthodox Church "had no established order."[106] Such views yielded statements that were, in Berdnikov's opinion, often contradictory and

99 Berdnikov, *Osnovnye nachala,* 24–28, 29, 35.
100 Ibid., 29, 95–96, 107.
101 Ibid., 32, 78, 102.
102 Ibid., 33, 103.
103 Ibid., 81.
104 Ibid., 103–05, 114.
105 Ibid., 107–08, 126.
106 Ibid., 373, 377.

incomplete. Suvorov claimed that ancient Rus' had exhibited little in terms of lawmaking before the sixteenth-century. While recognizing that the princes of Rus' had access to the translated body of laws they received from Byzantium, Suvorov minimized the influence of those texts, claiming that the princes were influenced more by indigenous common law and viewed Byzantine laws as ancillary.[107] Suvorov also saw little in terms of indigenous hierarchal initiative with respect to local church order and "rule-making" in Rus'. In response, Berdnikov asked what type of ecclesial rule-making or lawmaking there could be in Russia's church during a time when it remained officially under the jurisdiction of the Patriarchate of Constantinople. Until the fifteenth century, Russia's church officials were usually appointees from Constantinople and, therefore, mostly Greeks. Given the two canonists' competing reference points in their understanding of church administrative and legislative authority—the emperor for Suvorov, and the ecclesiastical hierarchy for Berdnikov—they also attributed the eventual surge in "indigenous" church governance and legislation to different causes. Suvorov tied this development to political centralization and the rise of Russia's autocrats, who inherited the notion of an inherent link between imperial and ecclesiastical authority from their Byzantine predecessors. Berdnikov, in contrast, attributed the surge to the church's newly established ecclesiastical independence after some four hundred years under Byzantine-Greek dominance, a change that gave the church the freedom to order its own affairs.[108]

In contrast to Suvorov, who praised Peter the Great's church reforms as introducing a period of "maximum energy in the generation of church law," Berdnikov remained reserved. He spoke more about a bygone era when councils were the main source of church lawmaking. While he did not find imperial ratification of synodal decisions problematic, he found the procedure by which ratification took place dubious. Committed to the notion of the church as an autonomous, self-governing institution, Berdnikov admitted that, in the nineteenth century, churchmen had no recourse but to seek ways to work "independently from the framework it has been [legally] assigned by the state."[109]

Among canonists with professional juridical training who spent their careers at a theological academy, Nikolai Zaozerskii was the best known.[110] The son of a rural priest, Zaozerskii enrolled in Moscow Theological Academy in 1872.

107 Ibid., 372, 373–75.

108 Ibid., 378.

109 Ibid., 382.

110 A. Bertash, "Zaozerskii," *Pravoslavnaia entsiklopediia*, vol. 19: 600–06; Sergei Golubtsov, *Moskovskaia dukhovnaia akademiia v nachale XX veka: professura i sotrudniki* (Moscow: Martis, 1999), 42–43; *Protokoly kommissii po tserkovnomu pravu pri Moskovskom iuridicheskom obshchestve za 1911–1912* (Moscow: Tip. G. Lissnera i D. Sovko, 1913). For the politics surrounding the appointment of Zaozerskii's replacement, see T. A. Bogdanova, "Iz akademicheskikh 'istorii': zameshchenie kafedry tserkovnogo prava v Moskovskoi Dukhovnoi akademii v 1910 godu," *Vestnik tserkovnoi istorii*, 2007, no. 1(5): 31–77. Eventually, the position went to Nikolai Kuznetsov.

Following graduation, he taught for two years in Kostroma Seminary before returning to his alma mater in 1878 to teach church law. Zaozerskii earned his master's and doctoral degrees from Moscow Theological Academy, writing dissertations on ecclesiastical courts in the early church and on authority in the church. Zaozerskii published on a variety of topics in church law, including Russia's ecclesiastical court system, relations between church and state, marriage and divorce, primacy, the parish, and the role of laity. From 1909 to 1912, he served as editor of one of Russia's premier theological journals, Moscow Theological Academy's *Bogoslovskii vestnik* (Theological herald). Retiring from teaching in 1911, Zaozerskii continued to publish, remaining an active member of the Moscow Juridical Society and, in 1912, standing as a candidate for the fourth State Duma. He died from health-related causes in 1919.

Unlike Gorchakov, Pavlov, Suvorov, and Berdnikov, neither Zaozerskii nor his students published a textbook based on his lectures. His views on church/canon law are thus found in other publications during his career.[111] His first work on the subject (1888) opened with his understanding of law broadly conceived, and only then proceeded to Orthodox church/canon law. His intended audience comprised those for whom Orthodox church/canon law seemed to have little to add to contemporary jurisprudence, as well as academic peers in the West who considered Russia's church law "unoriginal," "vague," and nothing but a "weak imitation" of its developmentally stunted, "long-fossilized Byzantine prototype."[112]

Defending the integrity of church/canon law as an independent field, Zaozerskii was unapologetically theological in his reasoning while remaining grounded in a historical-philological, analytical approach.[113] He defined the church as a moral and prophetic "social organism," whose ultimate goal was personal transformation through the spiritual gifts and divine enlightenment communally revealed and communicated by Christ to all people.[114] This social organism, Zaozerskii maintained, lived according to its own particular "genus" (*rod*) of law, which, given its divinely inspired nature, could not be conflated with other branches of jurisprudence. Hence, the church could not be considered "part" of any state.[115] The church enjoyed "the complete capacity and essential need to protect and develop its own law [*pravo*]."[116]

111 N. A. Zaozerskii, *Pravo pravoslavnoi grekovostochnoi russkoi tserkvi kak predmet spetsial'noi iuridicheskoi nauki* (Moscow: Tip. M. G. Volchaninova, 1888); *Istoricheskoe obozrenie istochnikov prava Pravoslavnoi tserkvi*, vyp. 1: *Kanonicheskie istochniki* (Moscow: Tip. M. G. Volchaninova, 1891); "O zhelatel'noi postanovke prepodavaniia tserkovnogo prava" (see note 30); *O sushchnosti tserkovnogo prava* (Sergiev Posad: M. S. Elov, 1911).

112 Zaozerskii, *Pravo pravoslavnoi grekovostochnoi russkoi tserkvi*, 1.

113 Zaozerskii identified his general approach as "church-historical" and "philosophy of law." Zaozerskii, *O sushchnosti*, 1.

114 Zaozerskii, *Pravo pravoslavnoi grekovostochnoi russkoi tserkvi*, 49–50, 54, 56.

115 Ibid., 53.

116 Ibid., 62.

Two German jurists—Rudolf von Jhering (1818–92) and Rudolf Sohm (1841–1917)—significantly influenced Zaozerskii's views on the nature of church/canon law. Drawing on Jhering's *The Spirit of Roman Law in the Various Stages of its Development*, Zaozerskii presented the task of the study of church/canon law as the "re-creation of the representations of the integral juridical image of the Church, which is given in the totality of its objective laws, as formulated in primary sources."[117] While the initial stages of this process included codification of church law, this alone was insufficient. Leveraging lengthy quotations from Jhering, Zaozerskii maintained that the academic canonist's goal was not to examine legal statutes for literal content, but to discern the underlying ecclesial principles informing them. This approach would then transform church/canon law from little more than a collection of seemingly outdated, disorganized, and arbitrary rules into a set of living principles which, in turn, could be tapped—individually or in various combinations—to generate new norms. Zaozerskii maintained that such an approach to church/canon law—an approach which included historical research, codification, logical systematization, and the final step of discerning the principles informing each rule—could provide the Orthodox Church in Russia with what Jhering called "simple reagents for limitlessly complex life situations."[118] The coordination of formulated norms with underlying principles reflecting the ultimate goals of church life would disclose that growth and development are as integral to church/canon law as they are to believers seeking communion with God.[119]

Zaozerskii's second lengthy reflection on the nature of church/canon law was prompted by a translation of Sohm's history of canon law.[120] In this polemical treatise against Roman Catholicism and revisionist challenge to late nineteenth-century Protestant views of the early church, Sohm argued that early Christian communities had no formal system of governance—no presbyters or bishops—but were organized by charisms of the Holy Spirit. As purely spiritual organizations, these communities "could not be grasped by any juridical understandings," which, in Sohm's estimation, were purely "worldly" constructs. For Sohm, the notions of church and law were antithetical.

Characterizing Sohm's view of the church as "an organization without rules," Zaozerskii argued that law was more than a worldly phenomenon based on force and coercion. Law was inherent to the human spirit, "deeply ingrained in the very nature of a rational moral being."[121] Zaozerskii defended law's spiritual foundation by appealing to psycho-philosophical studies (unnamed) tying the origins of law to the human striving for freedom and the sense of duty. Freedom

117 Ibid., 131.

118 Ibid., 140.

119 Ibid., 141.

120 Rudolph Sohm, *Kirchenrecht*, vol. 1: *Die geschichtlichen Grundlagen* (Leipzig, 1892), which appeared in Russian as *Tserkovnyi stroi v pervye veka khristianstva*, trans. A. Petrovskii and P. Florenskii (Moscow: D. P. Efimov, 1906).

121 Zaozerskii, *O sushchnosti*, 29.

and duty, in turn, were connected with an innate sense of justice. According to Zaozerskii, these basic human traits resulted in even small groups of persons binding together on the basis of mutually agreed-upon principles regulating their relations. These intrinsic principles, or laws, spiritually linked community members to one another. Thus, law related to the rights of others: "without this shared mutual sense of responsibility there were no rights/law (*prava*), and without rights/law there could be no freedom."[122]

Against Sohm, Zaozerskii maintained that church history did not involve a struggle against church law as inimical to the church's spiritual nature. Rather, church history reflected a "struggle with the *distortion* of the spirit and form of church law."[123] As a corrective, members of the church needed awareness of their mutual "responsibilities" and "duties" through "a sense of conscience and in the name of God," not through coercion.[124] In contrast to Sohm's charismatic communities, Zaozerskii focused on early Christian communities' disciplinary practices. These practices, according to Zaozerskii, embodied the "inner work" that the awareness of obligation and genuine freedom entail.[125]

With respect to Sohm's critique of hierarchy, Zaozerskii argued that "the hierarchical principle flows from the nature of the church; it is necessary to its organization as a religious community; [it] corresponds to Christ's principles and precepts, and at its root, it was his direct formation."[126] However, this claim involved a crucial caveat: "power" and "authority," as defined by "the imperium" and appropriated by the church following Constantine's conversion, were alien to hierarchy as understood in early Christian communities. The qualities defining the early church's orders—deacons, presbyters, and bishops—had nothing in common with the coercion and force Sohm associated with law; these offices were based on humility, integrity, duty, moral example, and spiritual guidance. Zaozerskii noted how early Christians appropriated a common civil legal practice used in the election of persons to public office—*cheirotonia*—as a communal recognition of a new pastor's authority. "The laying on of hands," he noted, indicated the community's spiritual unity.[127]

Among his contributions to the field of canon law, Zaozerskii is perhaps best remembered for his laity-minded ecclesial legal consciousness. Well before the revolutionary turmoil of the twentieth century, Zaozerskii promoted conciliarity as the foundational principle of Orthodox church governance, insisting also on conciliarity's "pan-ecclesial" quality (*vsetserkovnosti*). He considered the church's third-century councils memorable as "lawmakers" (*zakonodateli*). He compared these "church-constituent acts" to liturgical assemblies in which the entire

122 Ibid., 30.
123 Ibid., 20.
124 Ibid., 39.
125 Ibid., 45.
126 Ibid., 77.
127 Ibid., 71.

church participated.[128] Zaozerskii's promotion of lay participation in administrative church life resulted in Ilya Berdnikov critically dubbing him the "inspirer of the revivalists."[129]

This brief overview of some of Russia's "new canonist" pioneers illustrates their diversity of thought—not only concerning the sources, meaning, pliancy, permanence, and authority of the norms governing church life, but also with respect to decision-making in the church and church-state relations. Such diversity typified Orthodox Christian thinking on most topics at the time. In 1904, in a term paper on "The Main Trends in Russian Scholarship on Canon Law," a student at St. Petersburg Theological Academy, Viktor Vvedenskii, noted that canonists in Russia could not be grouped according to "schools" of thought. He doubted whether such schools would form until the field produced more generational "links" in the academic chain.[130] Changes in Russia's political landscape would soon challenge the very formation of such links in ways this young student could not have foreseen.

The canonists' council

In 1905–06, the legal relationship between state and church in Russia shifted dramatically—and permanently—as a result of what one juridically trained canonist called the "crumbling" of the existing state order.[131] With increasing civil unrest and a growing political liberation movement, Emperor Nicholas II (r. 1894–1917) established an elected assembly—the State Duma. Moving toward a constitutional monarchy, he decreed that "no law shall take effect without the State Duma's confirmation," a provision bolstered in the 1906 February Manifesto on the reorganization of the State Council.[132] Yet, at the same time, the accompanying 1906 revisions to Russia's Fundamental Laws contained no amendments regarding the juridical standing of the Orthodox Church. If, according to Russia's Petrine-inspired church law prior to 1905, "the emperor was the highest protector [*zashchitnik*] and preserver [*khranitel'*] of Orthodoxy in Russia," then, after 1905, that feature of imperial authority was essentially annulled. Consequently, the Orthodox Church remained juridically subject to an Orthodox emperor and now *also* subject to the Duma and State Council—elected parliamentary-type chambers with members representing an array of confessional affiliations or none at all. Given that these agencies held no historically based sacred authority comparable (at least in many believers' eyes) to the emperor's, this new legal arrange-

128 Zaozerskii, *Istoricheskoe obozrenie istochnikov*, 126–27.

129 I. Berdnikov, *Otkrytiia v oblasti tserkovnogo prava, sdelannye sovremennym tak nazyvaemym obnovlencheskim dvizheniem*, vyp. 1: *Smysl 13 Pravila Laodikiiskogo Sobora* (Kazan: Tsentral'naia tipografiia, 1908), 5.

130 Vvedenskii, "Glavnye techeniia," 9–10 (see note 22).

131 P. V. Verkhovskoi, *O neobkhodimosti izmenit' russkie osnovnye zakony v pol'zu zakonodatel'noi nezavisimosti Pravoslavnoi tserkvi* (Berlin, 1913), 9–10.

132 Ibid., 11.

ment threatened the perceived canonical integrity of the church in unprecedented ways.[133]

Regardless of how canonists greeted Nicholas II's reforms as a whole, in terms of the legal standing and interests of the Orthodox Church, they were left disoriented.[134] Nikolai Kuznetsov spoke for many Orthodox believers when he noted that the reforms of 1905–06 were formulated as if "no Orthodox Church exists in Russia, with which until this point the State had been closely tied."[135] According to Pavel Verkhovskoi, the new legislation only further shackled Orthodoxy to the state, reinforcing public perception of the Orthodox Church as nothing but a state church. The church's self-governance, Verkhovskoi insisted, depended on legal institutional autonomy, even if achieved via a "coup d'état."[136] Only then could the church embark on sweeping reforms enabling it to meet modernity's challenges, including what some canonists saw as the inevitable separation of the state from "religion" and the legal parity of all faiths.[137] Discourse among canonists and much of Russia's broader educated society shifted rapidly from "church law" to "canon law" or "canonicity" (*kanonichnost'*).[138] This shift did not signal Orthodoxy's institutional atrophy; rather, it testified to the awakening of an Orthodox legal consciousness and a growing awareness among Orthodox believers of the need for self-definition as a church independent from the state.

In response to public pressure, Nicholas II granted the Holy Synod permission to begin deliberations for a future All-Russia church council to oversee long-awaited reforms to ensure the vitality and integrity of Orthodoxy in the modern age.[139] Between March and December 1906, some forty-nine clergy and laymen (the latter constituting the majority) met as a Pre-Conciliar Commission (*Predsobornoe prisutstvie*) to draft a plan for the organization of a church council and various reform proposals. For success, reforms had to enjoy wide acceptance as canonical and, hence, authentically Orthodox. The commission, therefore, was by definition an ecclesial one; yet significantly, five of the eight participating canonists were university law professors who were now being asked to think in a theological environment, the conceptual working premises of which they often

133 Vladimir Rozhkov, *Tserkovnye voprosy v Gosudarstvennoi Dume* (Moscow: Krutitskoe podvor'e, 2004); *Zhurnaly i protokoly* (see note 47), 1:346.

134 For a review of the mixed motives behind various church officials' response to the Manifesto of 1905 and related decrees, see N. Zaozerskii, "O printsipe religioznoi svobody," *Bogoslovskii vestnik*, 1908, no. 3 (March): 506–16.

135 *Zhurnaly i protokoly*, 1:363–64.

136 Verkhovskoi, *O neobkhodimosti*, 14

137 *Zhurnaly i protokoly*, 1:347.

138 Following 1906, for instance, during discussions of parish reform, state officials sometimes resorted to the language of "canonicity" in their evaluation of proposals. See A. L. Beglov, "Pravoslavnyi prikhod Rossiiskoi imperii na rubezhe XIX–XX vv: sostoianie, diskussii, reformy" (dokt. diss., Rossiiskaia akademiia nauk, Moscow, 2019), 765–67.

139 See Chapter 1 of this volume for further discussion of the making of the council. The All-Russian Council of Moscow of 1917–18 opened on August 15, 1917.

worked to bracket in their professional capacities.[140] In addition, two practicing jurists—Nikolai Kuznetsov and Aleksandr Papkov—emerged as prolific, progressive canonists in their own right, whose contribution to the commission's deliberations were among the most influential and memorable.

To a large extent, the Pre-Conciliar Commission may be termed "the canonists' council." The commission merits the moniker not because the eight participating professional canonists contributed to quick confirmation of proposals (they did not), nor because the canonists spoke more than other members of the commission (they did), but because canons—their definition, interpretation, and authority—dominated the discussion of virtually every topic.[141] While the canonists were trained specialists on these topics, the commission's other vocal participants—theological academy professors of church history or patristics, parish priests, and active laymen—also spoke from their own authoritative, often experiential, perspectives.[142] Indeed, given the unprecedented nature of the commission's mandate and the rapidly evolving sociopolitical context, it is not surprising that virtually each participant considered himself a canonist to some extent. Arguably, then, the professional canonists' greatest contribution was to serve as catalysts for the articulation of the diversity—and divisions—brewing in modern Orthodox ecclesial legal consciousness.

A dissenting opinion ("Otdel'noe mnenie") produced by members of the Pre-Conciliar Commission on the composition of the anticipated church council highlighted the existing fault lines in Orthodox ecclesial legal consciousness. It also typified the criticism which some (though not all) canonists elicited from fellow believers with respect to the function and meaning of ancient canonical rules in contemporary church life. Noting the recently "awakened ecclesial self-consciousness" among Russia's believers, the dissenting opinion argued for an increased role for laity, criticizing the prevailing differentiation between the episcopate and the rest of the church's members as alien to the Orthodox understanding of the church as the body of Christ.[143]

140 The academic canonists present included Aleksandr Almazov, Timofei Barsov, Ilya Berdnikov, Mikhail Gorchakov, Mikhail Krasnozhen, Mikhail Ostroumov, Nikolai Suvorov, and Nikolai Zaozerskii. The practicing jurists included Nikolai Kuznetsov and A. A. Papkov (1853–1920), the latter a government official, one-time governor of Finland, and active Orthodox layman. Though a practicing attorney in 1906, in 1910 Kuznetsov replaced Zaozerskii as professor of church law at Moscow Theological Academy, a position he held until 1913.

141 It is noteworthy that canonists were the only lay academics invited from universities.

142 Among the non-juridically trained laymen who actively participated in the discussions, the most vocal was N. P. Aksakov (1848–1909), a Russian religious thinker and theologian who received his doctorate in philosophy from the University of Giessen in Germany in 1868. He subsequently published extensively on issues related to Orthodox canon law. See, for example, *Kanon i svoboda* (St. Petersburg: Tip. Merkusheva, 1905). For an overview of Aksakov's thought, see N. Antonov, *Nikolai Petrovich Aksakov i ego religiozno-obshchestvennoe mirosozertsanie* (St. Petersburg: Tip. M. Aleksandrova, 1912).

143 "Otdel'noe mnenie men'shinstva chlenov I otdela vysochaishe uchrezhdennogo pri Sviateishem Sinode Prisutstviia po voprosu o 'sostave Sobora'," *Zhurnaly i protokoly*, 1:641–51.

The authors of the dissenting opinion based their views on an ecclesial legal consciousness that identified the canonical foundation of church life in spiritual terms. From their perspective, canon law derived from a higher, unattainable living principle, an ideal inspired by the Holy Spirit which could never be fully realized; "it only sought out the best [already] existing forms for its expression."[144] Accordingly, while the living principles behind them remained eternal, the outward language and forms of the canons by definition were dynamic in light of the ever-evolving movement of human life.

Such a view of church/canon law was further informed by a vision of the church as a spiritual organism, the consciousness of which sparked to life on the day of Pentecost and became the "foundation of Church Tradition."[145] According to this view, the apostolic church, unified in heart and mind, drafted the earliest rules governing the Christian community. It did so through councils, not only under the perceived inspiration of the Holy Spirit but in an environment without juridically hierarchical regulation, with "neither superiors nor subordinates in the legal sense of this term."[146] As the authors of the dissenting opinion reasoned, because two centuries of the Petrine system had all but eliminated believers' conciliar sensibilities, the relationality presupposed by conciliarism (*sobornost'*) required restoration.[147] Given current realities, the authors maintained that bishops could no longer be presumed to represent the voice of the laity. Broad trust in the future council's decisions could be ensured only if those decisions were a "genuine expression of the voice of the entire Church." To this end, the council's participants would have to include believers across all ecclesial ranks and socioeconomic classes.[148]

Above all, the dissenting opinion's authors criticized some canonists' tendency to speak of the church primarily as a juridical institution rather than as a theologically defined living organism. Some canonists' proposals regarding the future council, the authors claimed, often resembled plans for "the convocation of a state parliament more than a gathering of believers in Christ."[149] The dissenting opinion, responding to existential challenges, articulated an understanding of the church primarily as a community (in contrast to an institution) and assigned ecclesial discernment a critical role in the divine-human synergism implied by the formation and interpretation of canons. Although no canonists were among the dissenting opinion's authors, the statement reflected views widely shared by canonists such as Nikolai Zaozerskii and, especially, Nikolai Kuznetsov and Aleksandr Papkov. Kuznetsov in particular penned numerous lengthy statements during the commission's proceedings in support of these views from his perspective as a canonist and practicing lawyer.

144 Ibid., 1:641.
145 Ibid., 1:642.
146 Ibid., 1:644.
147 Ibid., 1:643.
148 Ibid., 1:648.
149 Ibid., 1:645.

The identity of "some of the canonists" to whom the dissenting opinion refers remains unclear. Nevertheless, viewing the dissenting opinion primarily as a personal affront, Ilya Berdnikov replied formally in his own "Special Opinion," leveling three main criticisms.[150] First, he maintained that the dissenting opinion's definition of the "foundations of canon law" was based not on recognized Orthodox teachings but on something "completely subjective." The dissenting opinion's discussion of the church's canonical foundations was so vague that "even Solomon would not have been able to decipher them."[151] Second, maintaining that the dissenting opinion's overall ethos reflected the views of Rudolf Sohm, Berdnikov criticized the ease with which its authors dismissed existing canons on the basis of perceived historical relativism. Such an approach to existing canons overlooked the Orthodox Church's generally accepted teaching "obligat[ing] its members to follow canons issued by ecumenical and local councils."[152] Third, in contrast to the dissenting opinion's view of the laity as the source of episcopal juridical authority, Berdnikov located that source in the consecration to episcopal office (*chin*). The dissenting opinion's emphasis on the primacy of the laity was "a distortion of the Church's natural order."[153]

This exchange of opinions during the first weeks of the commission's sessions defined some of the competing principles characterizing Orthodox legal consciousness among professional canonists at this critical junction in the history of Russia's Orthodox Church. Several interrelated issues stood out for their tendency to elicit deep disagreement at a time when consensus seemed vital. First, canonists were not unanimous in their understanding of the nature of church/canon law, especially with regard to its permanence: were existing church laws and canons "a collection of [the] active laws in the church" or simply a "helpful archive" for consultation, a collection not exhaustive of all possible situations human life can pose (the latter view suggesting that, in new circumstances, new canons or ecclesial norms could arise)?[154]

Second, canonists disagreed over the guiding historical referent(s) of Orthodoxy's canonical tradition—apostolic times, Byzantium, or both. This disagreement was often linked with a third issue: the working approach to the church as a community or as an institution. Suvorov was reluctant to consider the internal organization of the early apostolic church a canonical norm.[155] Berdnikov did not regard the Apostolic Council (Acts 15) as "ecumenical" and maintained that the term "canonical," in common contemporary church usage, referred to

150 "Osoboe mnenie professora Kazanskoi dukhovnoi akademii Il'i Berdnikova po povodu otdel'nogo mneniia men'shinstva chlenov I otdela Vysochaishe uchrezhdennogo pri Sviateishem Sinode Prisutstviia po voprosu o sostave Sobora," *Zhurnaly i protokoly*, 1:142–51.

151 Ibid., 1:143.

152 Ibid., 1:143–46.

153 Ibid., 1:146.

154 *Zhurnaly i protokoly*, 1:168.

155 Ibid., 1:36, 223.

rules explicitly formulated during the imperial Byzantine period.[156] In contrast, Zaozerskii, who tended to conceptualize "church" in terms of community, disagreed, arguing that to bracket apostolic experiences when considering church/canon law would be "unecclesial," "unorthodox," and "unchristian."[157]

Finally, canonists disagreed over the ordering center of ecclesial life, hence over notions of authority. Most professional canonists, especially those in university faculties of law, were used to thinking about the church in institutional terms, focusing on relations between church and state, emperors, patriarchs, and church hierarchy. At this historical moment, the notion of popular sovereignty entered the fray, and the laity became a significant source of canonical preoccupation, especially in light of the traditional hierarchical ordering. Gorchakov reflected this internal conflict even within himself, mulling over whether laity should participate in the future council with only a "consultative voice" or with a "deciding voice" along with the hierarchy. On one hand, he adhered to the view of a "fixed" hierarchical ordering of the church, citing universal acceptance among all local Orthodox Churches and the oath every bishop takes upon consecration to uphold historic canons (not limited to those of the seven ecumenical councils).[158] On the other hand, he also maintained that the church was a community, and he advocated for the participation of parish priests and laity both in the future council (with a consultative voice) and on all levels of church administration, arguing that canons, unlike dogmas, pertain to the mundane level of church life shared by all.[159]

The Pre-Conciliar Commission's discussions of church reforms included periodic prescient observations by its members that they were witnessing the initial stages of a momentous "rupture" in the nine-hundred-year history of Russia: namely, the state's withdrawal from its relationship with Orthodoxy as the state religion, leaving the church "on a par" with other confessions.[160] Even if most commission members were critical of the Petrine system that shaped Orthodox church life as they had known it, and even though they were well-versed in European church-state relations and the history of canon law, the multidimensional challenges of reenvisioning, reforming, and reorganizing Russia's Orthodox Church in the face of early twentieth-century political, social, and cultural demands drew all Orthodox believers into canonically uncharted territory. This uncertain situation, complicated further by the Soviet experiment, continues to the present day.

156 Ibid., 1:36, 143.

157 Ibid., 1:33.

158 Ibid., 2:323.

159 Of the canonists present, only Gorchakov and Kuznetsov voted in support of a synod consisting of bishops, clergy, and laity, which in the newly reformed church would serve as the central governing body between meetings of the All-Russian Council. The four other canonists—Almazov, Berdnikov, Krasnozhen, and Ostroumov—voted for a synod consisting of hierarchs only. *Zhurnaly i protokoly*, 2:501.

160 Ibid., 1:347.

11 Pavel Novgorodtsev

Natural law and its religious justification

Konstantin M. Antonov

Pavel Ivanovich Novgorodtsev (1866–1924) was one of Russia's most systematic social, political, and legal thinkers, an outstanding representative of the trend in early twentieth-century Russian thought away from positivist and materialist principles to idealist and religious foundations. He was also a leading activist who participated in the shift from the revolutionary rejection of the "old world" to liberal reformism, reformism that also incorporated socialist ideas. A follower of the great nineteenth-century Russian idealists Boris Chicherin and Vladimir Soloviev, Novgorodtsev inspired a whole line of later thinkers, and in the last years of his life had a major intellectual role in the early Russian emigration.[1]

In the present chapter, I will examine (1) Novgorodtsev's biography; (2) the philosophical and social context of the formation and development of his ideas; (3) his views on the history of the philosophy of law, including questions of methodology; (4) his concepts of "natural law" and "the social ideal," and the critique of "utopias of earthly paradise" connected with them; and (5) his writings on political affairs. In conclusion, I will comment on the significance of Novgorodtsev's thought.

Biography: from Bakhmut to Prague

Pavel Ivanovich Novgorodtsev was born on February 28, 1866, into a well-to-do merchant family in the city of Bakhmut, Ekaterinoslav province (now Donetsk Oblast, Ukraine). In 1884, he graduated from the classical gymnasium

1 The first surveys of Novgorodtsev's life and work appeared shortly after his death. See I. A. Il'in, "Pamiati P. I. Novgorodtseva," in I. A. Il'in, *Sobranie sochinenii v desiati tomakh*, ed. Iu. T. Lisitsa, 10 vols. in 12 (Moscow: Russkaia kniga, 1993–99), 9–10:249–54 (first published in *Russkaia mysl'*, 1923–24, kn. 9–12); G .D. Gurvich, "Prof. P. I. Novgorodtsev kak filosof prava," *Sovremennye zapiski*, 1924, kn. 20: 389–93; and G. V. Florovskii, "Pamiati P. I. Novgorodtseva," *Rossiia i slavianstvo*, April 27, 1929. In English, the best survey of Novgorodtsev's work is Andrzej Walicki, *Legal Philosophies of Russian Liberalism* (Oxford: Clarendon Press, 1987), 291–341. Studies on Novgorodtsev, a chronology of his life, and a bibliography are published in *Filosofiia prava: P. I. Novgorodtsev, L. I. Petrazhitskii, B.A. Kistiakovskii*, ed. E. A. Pribytkova (Moscow: ROSSPEN, 2018). In contemporary Russia, Novgorodtsev is the subject of many dissertations and monographs.

DOI: 10.4324/9781003017097-11

in Ekaterinoslav with a gold medal and matriculated in the law faculty of Moscow University. Upon completing his studies in 1888, he stayed on in the department of the history of law to prepare for the professoriate. During the 1890s, he studied in European universities (Freiburg, Berlin, Paris), completing master's (1897) and doctoral dissertations (1902). He was appointed privatdocent at Moscow University in 1896, extraordinary professor in 1903, and ordinary professor in 1904.

In 1903, Novgorodtsev married Lidiia Antonovna Budilovich, the daughter of Professor A. S. Budilovich, a philologist of extreme Slavophile views. The couple had four children.

In 1911, with a number of other professors, Novgorodtsev resigned from Moscow University to protest measures taken by the minister of national education, L. A. Kasso, who had reduced the university's autonomy and imposed surveillance functions on the administration. Novgorodtsev was restored to his position in 1917. He also taught in the Higher Women's Courses and was a founder and the first director (1906–17) of the Moscow Commercial Institute, the leading academic institution for the study of economics in prerevolutionary Russia.[2] He also played an active role in the journal *Voprosy filosofii i psikhologii* (Questions of philosophy and psychology).

Novgorodtsev's political activism began in August 1903 with his participation in the "roving" founding congress of the Union of Liberation. He became a member of the council of the Union in 1904, joined the Constitutional Democratic Party (Kadets) in 1905, and was elected to the First State Duma in 1906. After the dissolution of the Duma in the same year, he signed the Vyborg Manifesto, which called on the Russian populace to protest the dispersal of the Duma by refusing military service and payment of taxes—that is, to engage in civil disobedience. For this, he was sentenced to three months' detention in prison and stripped of his voting rights. Thereafter, he abandoned political activism. During World War I, he participated in social organizations that assisted the government with the war effort but at the same time worked for political reforms in the country.

From the start, Novgorodtsev viewed the Revolution of 1917 with skepticism. This is the moment when we may begin to speak of a conservative turn in his political and philosophical thought. In March 1917, he joined the Central Committee of the Constitutional Democratic Party, where he argued against a coalition with the socialist parties. He participated in the League of Russian Culture, organized by P. B. Struve, and was elected to the All-Russian Constituent Assembly. He firmly opposed the October Revolution and collaborated actively in the anti-Bolshevik work of the Kadets. In May 1918, he went into hiding,[3] giving rise to a family drama: for the opportunity to leave Bolshevik Russia, Lidiia Antonovna

2 Now the G. V. Plekhanov Russian University of Economics.

3 Warned of an imminent search of his residence, Novgorodtsev went into hiding on May 18, 1918, but courageously took part in the dissertation defense of his student Ivan Ilyin the following day. See Il'in, "Pamiati P. I. Novgorodtseva," 253–54.

was forced to accept the ultimatum of the Soviet authorities that she divorce her husband. The reunification of the family took place only after Pavel Ivanovich's emigration in 1921.

In 1918, Novgorodtsev helped to prepare *Out of the Depths* (*Iz glubiny*), a collection of essays in which Russian religious thinkers subjected the revolutionary events in Russia to harsh criticism. During the Civil War, Novgorodtsev participated in the work of the Special Council (*Osoboe Soveshchanie*) under General A. I. Denikin and in the reforms carried out by the government of General P. N. Wrangel in Crimea in 1921.

Following evacuation from Crimea, Novgorodtsev settled in Czechoslovakia, where he became one of the intellectual leaders of the Russian emigration. He collaborated in the newspaper *Rul'* (The helm), published in Berlin by I. V. Gessen and V. D. Nabokov, former members of the Central Committee of the Kadets. In 1922, in the framework of the Czechoslovak government's support of Russians in exile, Novgorodtsev played the leading role in creating the Russian Law Faculty at Charles University in Prague. He took an active part in the activities of the Russian Academic Group and Russian National University in Prague, and in the organization of the Russian Student Christian Movement. Novgorodtsev died in Prague on April 23, 1924.

To this day, Novgorodtsev's personal religiosity has not been the subject of a special study. Scholars agree that he experienced a spiritual crisis during the final years of his life, as evidenced by the religious concerns that came to the fore in his last works. However, Novgorodtsev's thought manifested a religious dimension throughout his career. In Ivan Ilyin's words,

> This experience of mystery, this mystical principle, dwelt in him always. P. I. did not "become" a religious man in his last years, *he always was one*. And the deep wisdom of Russian Orthodoxy that he came to see in the years of upheaval and suffering constituted not the first, but a new and, as I believe, definitive form of his religiosity.[4]

Novgorodtsev's deep religious sensibility as he neared the end of his life made a powerful impression on those around him, including Father Sergii Bulgakov. In a diary entry from July 24, 1923 (July 11, Old Style), Bulgakov describes Novgorodtsev's participation in church life:

> A student conference has just taken place near Prague. I went there twice, served the liturgy, presented a lecture (on Peter and John), spoke. For its symptomatic character the conference was exceptionally significant: an Orthodox Christian intelligentsia, this is what I called the Russian intelligentsia to be all my life. There was a procession of the Cross from the [conference] building into an open field where, under a covered structure, an all-night vigil was

4 Il'in, "Pamiati P. I. Novgorodtseva," 251–52.

> held: I walked in the procession while P. I. N[ovgorodtsev], P. B. S[truve], V. V. Z[en'kovskii], G. F. Fl[orovskii] and the students carried the icons. A scene worthy of [the painter] Nesterov.[5]

Bulgakov commented on Novgorodtsev's death in a letter to Nikolai Berdiaev:

> the illness and passing of P. I. ... were drawn out and difficult, but also radiant and moving in the highest degree; it was 'a Christian end of life, blameless and peaceful.' Starting in March, I frequently administered confession to him, gave him the Eucharist, accepted his final wishes.... P. I.'s funeral, which took place on Good Friday, was splendid.
>
> (137)

Between positivist liberalism and historicist conservatism

The years of Novgorodtsev's formation fell during the reign of Alexander III, whose policy may be characterized as the conservative revision of the Great Reforms enacted by Alexander II. The new policy was endorsed by the Slavophile journalism of the time and enjoyed some support in the professoriate of the Moscow University law faculty while provoking protest and resistance from the radical and liberal intelligentsia, both in the zemstvos (local and provincial government assemblies) and in the universities. At the root of the opposition lay the contradiction between the idea of the worth of human persons that had taken shape in educated Russian society by this time and the repressive practices of the state designed to confirm autocratic government and bureaucratic methods of administration.

In the cultural-historical and philosophical situation of the 1880s and 1890s, Novgorodtsev emerged as a follower of Chicherin and Soloviev—in other words, as a representative of a liberal and religious Westernism seeking to ground the idea of the absolute worth of human persons in Christian universalism. He sought to vindicate this idea in opposition to several groups of thinkers. Many of the principal representatives of Russian legal science in Novgorodtsev's time, including most of his teachers in the university (A. S. Alekseev, N. P. Bogolepov), embraced the conservatism of the historical school of law. They regarded law as a manifestation of the moral life of the people, the result of organic historical development. The more liberal law professors (V. I. Sergeevich, G. E. Kolokolov, Iu. S. Gambarov, M. M. Kovalevskii, S. A. Muromtsev) were oriented to sociological positivism. A third group consisted of radical thinkers, populist or Marxist, who embraced positivism or materialism and held a nihilistic view of the value of law. A fourth group included the older Slavophiles and Leo Tolstoy. Their nihilism toward law was based on religion; they viewed the legal regulation of social life as a poor substitute for religious and moral principles. Finally, there was K. P.

5 S. Bulgakov, *Iz pamiati serdtsa* (Prague, 1923–24), 135–36.

Pobedonostsev, the chief ideologue of state-sponsored conservatism. In many respects, Pobedonostsev also relied on the ideas of the historical school, interpreted in such a way as to provide theoretical grounding for the Slavophile politics of the time. Hence, it was no accident that Novgorodtsev devoted intense critical attention to the "historical school of jurists" in his first published monograph.[6]

Problems of Idealism (1902), a collection of essays initiated by Novgorodtsev and Struve, was dedicated to the principled, frontal critique of positivism in both its variants, radical and liberal.[7] In both variants, as the authors saw it, the human person was swallowed up by one or another objectified principle, such as the state, the people, or class, in the name of which the ideologists of the corresponding tendencies elaborated their discourse. To these approaches Novgorodtsev and his colleagues, following Soloviev, sought to oppose a renovated conception of natural law, the most immediate basis of which was "ethical idealism." A religious perception of the world and of human beings was the deeper, ultimate foundation of natural law. This group of thinkers was affiliated with the right wing of the Constitutional Democratic Party, or party of "peaceful reform," and included E. N. Trubetskoi, P. B. Struve, S. A. Kotliarevskii, S. L. Frank, A. S. Izgoev, B. A. Kistiakovskii, N. A. Berdiaev, S. N. Bulgakov, and others. Novgorodtsev was a central figure in this movement.

Novgorodtsev's body of work is composed of several interlocking components. First, there are his studies of the history of the philosophy of law, including his master's and doctoral dissertations, lectures on the history of the philosophy of law in ancient and modern times, an essay on Vladimir Soloviev's philosophy of law, and other contributions. These works are not purely historical studies. The evolution of legal-philosophical ideas interested Novgorodtsev insofar as it opened the way for him to establish his own position and reveal the limitations of the positions held by his predecessors and opponents. The cycle of works titled *Introduction to the Philosophy of Law* occupies the central place in his oeuvre. He apportioned this overarching work into three parts.[8] The first, titled "The Rebirth of Natural Law," consists of two articles: "Ethical Idealism in the Philosophy of Law" (1902) and "The State and Law" (1904). Two important theoretical monographs form the second and third parts: *The Crisis of Modern Legal Consciousness* (1909) and *On the Social Ideal* (1919). While Novgorodtsev retains a historical perspective in these works, a purely theoretical objective occupies the foreground, namely, the validation of natural law as a kind of metajuridical court of appeal for the evaluation of juridical decrees, positive law, and legal institutions. Finally,

6 P. I. Novgorodtsev, *Istoricheskaia shkola iuristov, ee proiskhozhdenie i sud'ba. Opyt kharakteristiki osnov shkoly Savin'i v ikh posledovatel'nom razvitii* (Moscow: Universitetskaia tipografiia, 1896).

7 English edition: *Problems of Idealism: Essays in Russian Social Philosophy*, ed., trans., and intro. Randall A. Poole (New Haven: Yale University Press, 2003).

8 Novgorodtsev presents this three-part outline of his work in the preface to *The Crisis of Modern Legal Consciousness*; see P. I. Novgorodtsev, *Vvedenie v filosofiiu prava: Krizis sovremennogo pravosoznaniia* (Moscow: "Nauka," 1996), 8.

one can see the practical consequences of Novgorodtsev's theoretical position in his writings on political affairs. Here one should note the intellectual and political evolution that Novgorodtsev underwent. From his own distinctive interpretation of the Kadet political program he gradually moved to the right, a move that became particularly pronounced after the Revolution of 1917, especially following the October Revolution and his emigration. In this final stage, the religious elements of Novgorodtsev's worldview emerged into the foreground and began to influence his political and legal-philosophical ideas in an essential way. I will address each of the components of Novgorodtsev's work in turn.

History of the philosophy of law

Methodology: against historicism and sociologism

Novgorodtsev's reflection on the methodology of historical research in philosophy of law speaks already about his ambition to go beyond a purely historical approach and to demonstrate the more general significance of the concepts he analyzes. Novgorodtsev disputes the attempt of the historians of his day (in Russia: R. Iu. Vipper, D. M. Petrushevskii, I. M. Grevs, and others) to view the history of ideas, above all political ideas, as belonging to the domain of historical science alone. Against these thinkers, Novgorodtsev tries to construct a line of argument that allows him to preserve the history of philosophy of law and political thought as philosophical disciplines. In his view, beyond purely historical, psychological, or sociological explanations stand factors such as "the power of abstraction and the breadth of intellectual experience"—in other words, the inner logic of the work of thought and the abiding influence of intellectual traditions.[9]

These factors give rise to three purely philosophical tasks that complement historical study. The first is the systematic task of mapping the inner logic of a particular doctrine. The second is the critical task of discerning the value and shortcomings of a thinker's ideas and the place of those ideas in the history of thought. The third is the dogmatic task, the philosophical analysis and assessment of a doctrine apart from its historical preconditions or contemporary significance. Against historicism, Novgorodtsev postulates the unalterable logical basis of one or another political doctrine, its preconditions, and "the particular conclusions and demands that are logically connected with the fundamental principle under scrutiny" (23).

The dogmatic task of the study of ideas, the ambition to understand their significance "apart from their historical connections," comes more and more to the fore in Novgorodtsev's work with the passage of time, although, as we will see below, theory, historical analysis, and political application continually mediate each other in his work.

9 P. I. Novgorodtsev, *Kant i Gegel' v ikh ucheniiakh o gosudarstve i prave. Dva tipicheskikh postroeniia v oblasti filosofii prava* (Moscow: Universitetskaia tipografiia, 1901), 9.

The historical school and German idealism

In light of the above, Novgorodtsev's choice of a topic for his first dissertation was not accidental: "The Historical School of Jurists: Its Origin and Fate." Problematizing German historicism and positivism in law, Novgorodtsev indirectly criticized the corresponding elements in the ideas of the Germans' fellow travelers in Russia, in the liberal as well as the conservative camp. With this background in mind, one can see that Novgorodtsev set out to secure a foundation for natural law at the earliest stages of his scholarly career, and that this task had a political motivation from the beginning.

As Novgorodtsev shows, neither Friedrich Carl von Savigny (a conservative) nor Rudolf von Jhering (a progressive) nor the relativists Adolf Merkel and Karl Bergbohm succeeded in achieving a consistent historicism. Despite their criticisms, the significance of natural law as "the moral criterion for the evaluation of positive law" remained untouched.[10] In this way, Novgorodtsev's analysis of the development of the historical school opened the way to the rebirth of the doctrine of natural law.

In his second monograph, *Kant and Hegel's Doctrines of Law and the State*, Novgorodtsev addresses theoretical and political problems as well as the historical problem. Recognizing Kant's and Hegel's ethics and philosophy of law as classic examples of subjectivism and objectivism, respectively, Novgorodtsev sets out to clarify the "correct relationship" between the two approaches.[11]

Kant strictly distinguishes between theoretical and practical reason, hence between a scientific point of view relying on the principle of causality and the moral point of view relying on the idea of freedom. The individualism and formalism, or normativism, of Kant's ethics allows him to underscore the absolute value of human persons, to affirm their freedom. In this approach, however, the social-philosophical factor of objectivity, of how the absolute values of morality enter into the life of society, is overlooked (123).

This problem prompts the transition from Kant's individualistic normativism to Hegel's social-philosophical approach. In the latter, social life is seen "not as the restriction but as the incarnation of personhood," as "the necessary basis of rational existence" (216). This allows Hegel to include elements of objective morality, such as family, society, and the state, in the sphere that philosophy of law examines. However, despite his recognition of the principle of subjectivity and the powerful liberationist potential of his thought, Hegel runs the risk of subordinating subjectivity to moral unity.

Novgorodtsev views the relationship between these two German thinkers' philosophies of law as "more complementary than contradictory" (244). He concludes his monograph by asking how a more balanced and integral conception between these two positions might be imagined, a conception that would justify

10 Novgorodtsev, *Istoricheskaia shkola iuristov*, 213.
11 Novgorodtsev, *Kant i Gegel'*, 245.

the principle, "Persons do not exist for institutions, but institutions for persons" (222–23).

Soloviev's religious synthesis

Novgorodtsev considered the reconciliation of the aforementioned positions on the basis of Christianity to be the fundamental contribution of Vladimir Soloviev. In a memorial address dedicated to Soloviev's legal thought, Novgorodtsev was able to comment on the main tendencies of Russian social thought in his day by presenting Soloviev's ideas in the context of Russian debates, while at the same time comparing Soloviev's ideas with the legal-philosophical conceptions of European thinkers. In Novgorodtsev's view, Soloviev insisted on the importance of juridical ideals against positivism, Slavophilism, and Tolstoyanism, and kept pace with the main tendencies of philosophy in his time as he tried to synthesize Kant's normativism with Hegel's historicism in the context of "a living social Christianity."[12]

According to Novgorodtsev, the explicitly Christian thought of Soloviev, with its positive assessment of the important achievements of humanistic thought and practice in modern times, offered the most considered solution to the basic problems of philosophy of law, the closest approximation to achieving a balance between personal and social principles of morality and to understanding the moral factor in legal institutions and social organization.

The foregoing survey shows that the customary characterization of Novgorodtsev as a Neo-Kantian philosopher of law is oversimplified. While his conceptuality embraced the consistent distinction between "is" and "ought" typical of Neo-Kantianism, it also included aspects of their interaction typical of Hegelianism (a historicity not reducible to historical relativism) and the search for a Christian basis for this synthesis deriving from Soloviev and Chicherin. That search was the starting point for Novgorodtsev's development of his own legal-philosophical ideas, ideas connected first and foremost with the concept of natural law.

Natural law, the critique of utopias, and the social ideal

In his study of Kant and Hegel, Novgorodtsev singles out two basic dilemmas facing the philosopher of law: "the problem of the relationship of personhood to society" and "the relationship of law to morality."[13] Contrary to the main currents of nineteenth century thought, Novgorodtsev regarded the concept of natural law as the key to the analysis of these dilemmas and the most important instrument for their resolution. He admitted that historicist criticism had

12 "Ideia prava v filosofii Vl. S. Solov'eva," in P. I. Novgorodtsev, *Sochineniia*, ed. M. A. Kolerov and N. S. Plotnikov (Moscow: "Raritet," 1995), 285–99, here at 295.

13 Novgorodtsev, *Kant i Gegel'*, 111.

demolished transitory and antiquated elements of natural law theory such as: (1) the doctrine that law can be established by reason alone, without regard to concrete historical circumstances; (2) the idea of a single "system of norms which are suitable for all periods and all peoples"; and (3) "the attempt to attach immediate judicial significance to subjective legal ideals." Novgorodtsev found the true meaning of the concept of natural law in the recognition of "the whole corpus of ideal notions about law that have a purely moral character about them," whence two aspirations arise: (1) "the philosophical investigation of the basis of law," that is, the demonstration of the ultimate foundations and presuppositions of law; and (2) "the moral critique of positive law."[14]

Novgorodtsev's most important work, *Introduction to the Philosophy of Law*, is dedicated to realizing these aspirations. The author produced his trilogy over a period of almost twenty years (see above for the breakdown of its contents). Let us examine its basic ideas and inner logic.

The rebirth of natural law

Novgorodtsev thought about the problem of natural law in the context of the idealist movement of the early twentieth century in Russia. In the foreword to *Problems of Idealism*, he described this context: "The basic problem that is spurring the revival of idealist philosophy in our day is first of all a moral problem." He saw the heart of the problem as follows: "We seek absolute precepts and principles—for precisely here lies the essence of moral searching—yet we are told that everything in the world is relative and conditional."[15]

In *Problems of Idealism*, Novgorodtsev sought to provide a basis for ethical idealism in the philosophy of law. To this end, he tried to work out a basis for the autonomous philosophical investigation of law and a defense of absolute moral values against the totalistic pretentions of historical and sociological analysis. He combined this with the search for a new kind of historical thinking that raised the question of "the tasks and calling of the person, through whom the progress of history is accomplished."[16]

While he recognized the great methodological value of historicism and sociologism, Novgorodtsev criticized their claims to exclusivity and totality. The consistent implementation of these claims inevitably leads to the merging of "is" and

14 Novgorodtsev, *Istoricheskaia shkola iuristov*, 2–4.

15 Predislovie, *Problemy idealizma*, ed. M. A. Kolerov and N. S. Plotnikov (Moscow: Modest Kolerov and "Tri kvadrata," 2002), 233–36, here at 234; Novgorodtsev, *Problems of Idealism*, ed. Poole, 81–83, here at 82.

16 P. I. Novgorodtsev, "Nravstvennyi idealizm v filosofii prava (k voprosu o vozrozhdenii estestvennogo prava)," in *Problemy idealizma*, ed. Kolerov and Plotnikov, 505–74, here at 512; "Ethical Idealism in the Philosophy of Law (On the Question of the Revival of Natural Law)," in *Problems of Idealism*, ed. Poole, 274–324, here at 278. Parenthetical page references to this essay are first to the Russian edition, second to the English edition; translations are from the English edition.

"ought," violates the principle of objectivity and impartiality in historical analysis, and replaces "the question of the moral ideal" with "the question of a historically necessary result" (534/291). As Novgorodtsev believed, historicism and sociologism suffer from naive realism in that they take the categories of scientific analysis to be the actual relationships between phenomena. The consciousness of personal freedom inherent in human beings limits both approaches in principle. Historicism and sociologism ignore the consciousness of freedom for methodological reasons, yet this consciousness is a necessary factor in the historical process, in the life of society, and in legislative activity. Moreover, personhood relies on the consciousness of "ought," and this brings new factors into consideration. The psychological theory of law proposed by Leon Petrażycki is a step in the right direction, although it, too, fails to find its way from "the realm of the existent" into the sphere of "ought."[17]

To show this, Novgorodtsev analyzes the temporal component of legal consciousness. The concept of the imperfection of existing law raises the question of what law will be in the future. However, both the evaluation of the present and the construction of the future proceed "not from the point of view of causal historical succession, but from the point of view of moral 'oughtness' [*nravstvennoe dolzhestvovanie*]" (526/286). This very fact shows that a description of historical development does not exhaust the problematics of law. "Together with sociological inquiry, individual-psychological and normative-ethical inquiry must be recognized" (548/299).

Normative ethics is the most important element in Novgorodtsev's scheme. This means first of all a focus on individuals and their sense of absolute moral demands. However, because Novgorodtsev takes Hegel's and Soloviev's criticisms of Kantian subjectivism into account, "the principle of ethical individualism must be supplemented with the concept of social development," in accordance with which "ethics passes directly to pedagogy and public policy [*politika*]" (570/312). Nevertheless, Novgorodtsev still sees social progress as simply "a means to the development of persons" (570/312). The introduction of the social-historical factor into ethics forces the philosopher to postulate the formal, but not substantive, absoluteness of moral values, the highest value being personhood itself, understood as "a free and absolute center of independent decisions" (561/307). Such an approach leads the author to his own sort of personalist metaphysics (following Charles Renouvier and Chicherin against Émile Durkheim and Georg Simmel). Applied to law, this construction results in the "idea of natural law with changing content" (567/310), an idea which generated considerable potential for social and political criticism and even protest, which Novgorodtsev

17 The polemics with Petrażycki, often described as the collision of the Moscow and Petersburg schools of philosophy of law, were crucial in the formation of Novgorodtsev's position. See A. V. Poliakov, "P. I. Novgorodtsev i ideia 'vozrozhdennogo estestvennogo prava' kak kommunikativnaia problema," and A. Shliukhter-Rot, "Diskussiia Novgorodtseva i Petrazhitskogo: poniatie estestvennogo prava i zashchita prava," in *Filosofiia prava*, ed. Pribytkova, 51–77 and 428–45, respectively.

and his allies (Struve, Frank, Kotliarevskii, and others) directed not just against the Russian government of their day but also against the revolutionary parties.

Novgorodtsev sees the idea of natural law as having a three-tiered structure. On the lowest level, ethics makes common cause with the social sciences and carries out the construction of an ideal that correlates with the concrete conditions of social life. Towering above this level are "the abstract demands of the moral law," understood as "the highest principles" of natural law (571/312–13). Finally, the task of bringing together theory and practice, ethics and science, obligation and existence, "takes us beyond the limits of both positive science and moral philosophy" to metaphysics. Novgorodtsev's essay ends, in the spirit of Soloviev, with an essentially religious summons "to liberation from the illusory power of passing phenomena to the joyous recognition of absolute principles" (574/314–15).

In "The State and Law," Novgorodtsev seeks to make his conception concrete by taking the theory of the state as his example. The problem natural law theory is called to solve here lies in a basic tension. On one hand, the modern state views jurisprudence as the only legitimate, hence omnipotent, source of all law, yet on the other hand, the state is compelled to acknowledge the free human person as an indisputable limit on its supremacy."[18]

Novgorodtsev sees the source of this tension in a scientific jurisprudence that reifies the results of abstraction. In "the philosophy of positive law," a restrictive methodological device needed to give unity to a body of law morphs into the postulate of an entire worldview. In this view, law and the state are seen as consubstantial: "the law the state makes is at one with its source, which is the state." But this tautology is an abstraction that does not correspond to reality. In the actual historical process, there is "a permanent dualism, an endless succession of collisions between law [*pravo*] as it *ought* to be and state law [*zakon*]" (511). This manifest dualism is the point of departure for Novgorodtsev's theory of the state based on the concept of natural law. What does the theory of the state look like from this point of view?

First of all, the "natural-law theory of the state" radically alters the analytical perspective. "Instead of making law dependent on the state, this theory makes the state dependent on the ideal concept of law" (511). The theory does not occupy itself with explaining "the factual structure of relationships in the state," as historical and sociological analyses do, but propounds an ideal image of the state in which a moral idea provides the measure of positive law and evaluates it. "This is the basis of the idea of international obligations, the recognition of the inalienable rights of persons, [and] the force of constitutional guarantees"—in other words, the basic features of the modern state and modern law (513). Such an ideal construction of the modern state not only corroborated the theoretical relevance and vitality of the concept of natural law but also had a clear practical

18 P. I. Novgorodtsev, "Gosudarstvo i pravo," *Voprosy filosofii i psikhologii* 15, no. 4, kn. 74 (1904): 397–450; no. 5, kn. 75: 507–38; here at 397.

purpose. It was called to overcome the legal nihilism of the Russian liberationist movement by arming the movement with a powerful, ideally grounded juridical-political conceptuality capable of supporting a concrete program of political and judicial reforms.

The concept of natural law helped Novgorodtsev demonstrate the positive moral significance of the idea of the rule-of-law state. However, the existence of legal nihilism compelled him to approach the question of the limits of the rule-of-law state more responsibly. This led him to pose the problem of utopian consciousness.

Against "utopias of earthly paradise"

The idea of natural law, or more precisely, the natural-law construction of the idea of the modern state, was for Novgorodtsev the point of departure from which he attempted his own sort of "justification of law"—that is, the effort to meet the challenges facing the idea of law and the rule-of-law state as such. To this end, he painted a general picture of "the crisis of social and political ideas" from the eighteenth to the early twentieth centuries, a picture incorporating a critical analysis not just of future-oriented utopias such as liberalism ("the perfect rule-of-law state"), socialism, and anarchism, but of retrospective conservative utopias and Tolstoyan moralism as well. The common denominator of his critique was "the collapse of the idea of earthly paradise." Novgorodtsev believed that the collapse of utopianism showed that the way out of the modern sociopolitical crisis lay in "the replacement of the idea of ultimate perfection [*sovershenstva*] by the principle of infinite perfectibility [*sovershenstvovaniia*]."[19] Let us examine the basic elements of his critique.

For Novgorodtsev, the clearest manifestation of the crisis of the very idea of the rule-of-law state was to be found in the position of Leo Tolstoy, for whom "the refinement of the forms of law" was essentially "an illusion leading away from true progress." For Tolstoy, true progress was achieved only through "the religious and moral improvement of separate individuals."[20] This legal nihilism is correct to the extent that it underscores the significance of morality in opposition to the notion of the omnipotence of the rule-of-law state. However, against this extreme moralism, modern thought propounds a more realistic idea of morality, according to which "institutions grow together with people, and people improve together with institutions." In this account, the state does not possess absolute value but only practical value and can reach its goal only in conjunction with "moral factors" (253).

Analogously, the reactionary criticism of the rule-of-law state by such authors as Konstantin Pobedonostsev and Konstantin Leont'ev is correct to the extent that it exposes real problems, such as the deficiencies of the parliamentary system

19 P. I. Novgorodtsev, *Ob obshchestvennom ideale*, ed. A. V. Sobolev, et al., Iz istorii otechestvennoi filosofskoi mysli (Moscow: Izdatel'stvo "Pressa," 1991), 17.

20 Novgorodtsev, *Vvedenie v filosofiiu prava: Krizis sovremennogo pravosoznaniia*, 12.

and popular representation, and the contradiction between the principles of equality and freedom. Such criticisms are devastating for "simplistic and harmonious schemes ... for the solution of social contradictions" (256). However, reactionary criticism leads only to the idealization of the past and becomes a form of utopian consciousness in its own right. To be sure, the modern representative system reflects the popular will imperfectly, but its absence produces "the utter alienation" of the government from its people (139, cf. 113–15).

Novgorodtsev devotes the preponderance of his critical attention to "projective" utopias and their "faith in the possibility of paradise on earth," whether in the form of the political ideal of the eighteenth and first half of the nineteenth centuries (the idea of popular sovereignty) or in the form of the social ideal of the nineteenth and early twentieth centuries (socialism and anarchism). Despite their differences, the adherents of these schemes share a number of characteristics. They are convinced:

> (1) that humanity, or at least the chosen few, is approaching the final, blissful period of its existence; (2) that they know the final word, the saving truth, that will lead human beings to this higher and final summit of history.[21]

Following Alexander Herzen, Sergei Bulgakov, and others, Novgorodtsev was inclined to view utopias of this kind as quasi-religions. They all address "the problem of the salvation of human beings from the weakness and limitations of their personal capacities" and find the source of this salvation in "a perfect society," which is itself "the higher moral foundation that gives human beings both fullness of life and the meaning of their existence." In the end, "devotion to society replaces religious aspirations, the promise of paradise on earth takes the place of religious hopes" (42). Hence, the problem of the relationship of the individual to society becomes once again the central problem, a problem that is not only metajuridical or political but also religious. However, the principle of personhood explodes every utopian scheme.

For Novgorodtsev, the political utopia of the rule-of-law state was the crucial factor because the rule-of-law state is the foundational political principle of modern times, a principle which modernity cannot, and ought not, repudiate. Rousseau enunciated this principle with supreme clarity in *The Social Contract*. For this reason, the fate of Rousseau's ideas is the most important subject matter of Novgorodtsev's work on the crisis of legal consciousness. At the basis of this political utopia, which the French Revolution attempted to realize, lies Rousseau's principle of popular sovereignty and its realization in "the idea of a just state which harmoniously combines the freedom and equality of individuals with the supremacy and omnipotence of the general will."[22] Novgorodtsev traces the process of realizing this idea in the political theory and practice of the

21 Novgorodtsev, *Ob obshchestvennom ideale*, 23.

22 Novgorodtsev, *Vvedenie v filosofiiu prava: Krizis sovremennogo pravosoznaniia*, 40.

nineteenth century, when the separate elements of the idea underwent important changes and mutually limited each other. The crisis in the theory of popular sovereignty was the result of a crisis in the concept of personhood underlying the theory.

The idea of personhood typical of the eighteenth century, namely the "generic" notion of "the abstract human being who everywhere has one and the same nature and consequently the same needs and claims" (173), gives way in the nineteenth century to a new idea, an idea that emphasizes what is private, individual, and original in each human being, an idea that treats personality as "the original creative center of moral decisions" (205; cf. 180). This new idea of personhood explodes the political utopia of the rule-of-law state by denying the attainability of harmony "between personhood and the state" (204). As a result, the quasi-religious hopes for "a miracle of general moral renewal" (14) give way to the perception of the modern state as a necessary but insufficient condition of moral and cultural life.

However, the disharmony that came to light in this way was productive. A turn away from politics toward spiritual life and creativity ensued, and in the political sphere proper, there was "a transition from dreams to reality" (256), to the actualization of personal creativity in the sphere of social life. Paralleling this development, however, utopian conceptions of a new generation arose, namely socialism and anarchism, each proposing its own ultimate solution to the fundamental problem of social philosophy, the relationship between personhood and society. Anarchism absolutized the former; socialism, the latter. Novgorodtsev's best-known work, *On the Social Ideal*, is devoted to the critical analysis of these two outlooks.

Because Novgorodtsev did not complete his analysis of the anarchist utopia, which in any case follows the same methodology as his treatment of Marxism, we will concentrate our attention on his analysis and criticism of the latter. Marxism represents the most consistent attempt to realize the socialist, that is, collectivist, utopian project. Novgorodtsev offers a detailed, step-by-step description of the structure and inner logic of Marxism and its dialectical breakdown in subsequent social-philosophical thought.

Novgorodtsev considers the most characteristic feature of Marxism to be the way it combines its utopian and quasi-religious elements with its scientific, sociological, and rational-philosophical elements. This combination of elements explains the exceptional efficacy of Marxism, its capacity to influence the emotional-imaginative sphere as well as the intellect, and also its capacity to influence the masses as well as the intellectual elite. On the other hand, the tension between these elements explains Marxism's subsequent evolution and disintegration.

As a utopian vision, Marxism assigns absolute significance to all of its concepts. As a science, it sees all of them as necessary elements of the historical process. As a utopian ideal, Marxism possesses "faith in the possibility of the speedy attainment of the final, beneficent end of history" and "the final word by which it considers the attainment of this final goal to be guaranteed."[23] The future order is endowed with two supremely significant characteristics: "the unconditional rationalization of all social relationships and the unconditional control of nature by human beings" (224). "The cosmological problem of evil in the world" is swallowed up by "the sociological problem of social disorder" (224). The absolute means by which this absolute end is achieved is the proletariat, which accomplishes the social revolution, "making a leap from the realm of necessity into the realm of freedom." To the individual human being, Marxism promises "a new life where the bifurcation between persons and society will be eliminated, where full human emancipation will be achieved," in effect, a kind of salvation through "the merging of persons with the group, with society" (213–14).

In Novgorodtsev's view, it is the quasi-religious character of Marxism that produces, paradoxically, its inherent antireligiousness. Insofar as religion finds its source in "profound contradictions of personal consciousness which do not depend on the social structure" (219), the very existence of religion undermines Marxism's ambition to realize its ideal. Marxism has to narrow its anthropological horizon by regarding all transsocietal needs of persons—religious needs in particular—as illusory, as products of imperfect social interaction and practice. The principle of militant atheism is thus a necessary component of the Marxist program for realizing absolute socialism. Lowering the degree of its antireligious fervor, acknowledging religion as a personal matter, and allowing religious motivation to find a place in the socialist movement would be, in Novgorodtsev's opinion, indicators of Marxism's abandonment of absolutist utopian claims. These indicators mark the transition from an absolute to a relative socialism, a socialism that has turned into a program of social reform entirely consistent with the idea of the rule-of-law state.

Novgorodtsev has a similar view of the relationship of Marxism to law and the state. From the absolute political nihilism of the idea of the dictatorship of the proletariat and the dream of a stateless society, Marxism made a transition to constructive activity within the organs of power and to the patriotic sentiment of the early days of World War I.

The scientific elements in Marxism—its passionate scientism and economic, sociological, and historical objectivism—contributed to this transformation. While giving Marx's scientific discoveries their due, Novgorodtsev believed that the link connecting science with utopia in Marxist doctrine rested on its philosophy of history. This is where "ethical and metaphysical presuppositions imperceptibly encroach upon the positive theory of [social] evolution." Even Marx's purely economic views are infected; they manifest a kind of wishful thinking designed to confirm his essentially utopian outlook (235–37).

Novgorodtsev's analysis allowed him to expose the fundamental contradictions of Marxism: between the absolutism of a quasi-religion and the relativity of science, between deterministic fatalism and political pragmatism, between

23 Novgorodtsev, *Ob obshchestvennom ideale*, 228.

revolutionism and evolutionism. These contradictions on the level of theory became clear in the transition to practice and led to the disintegration of Marx's original conception among his epigones. Reformist socialism in Germany and revolutionary syndicalism in France were examples of this disintegration.

In the end, collectivist utopia cannot endure the test of personhood. The total subordination of persons to society turns out to be unrealizable both in theory and in social practice, while the truly vital content of socialism—"the idea of a dignified human existence to be secured for every person" (520)—is itself essentially personalist.

Novgorodtsev believed that the elevation of moral consciousness produced by Marxism—the recognition that overcoming poverty is a condition of human liberation and "fullness of life"— presented a challenge for the rule-of-law state. The state found itself obliged to carry out a series of complicated reforms that revealed the need to go beyond purely political means and enlist the moral forces of society.

Novgorodtsev's analysis of the utopian concepts of modern times allows him to outline the basic dynamics of utopian consciousness: the interrelationship between its emotional and rational elements, the internal contradictions of utopianism as it is put into practice, the link between utopian and real-world aspects of various social and political doctrines, and the interrelationship between their collectivist and individualist elements. Novgorodtsev's analysis also allows him to outline his own understanding of the social ideal, its structure, contents, and relation to real life.

Throughout his analysis, Novgorodtsev underscores the role of emotions and imagination in the genesis of utopian ideals. These ideals have a distinctly compensatory character because imagination is able to overcome the disharmony between the personal and the social, to overcome people's sense of their own imperfection. But the price of these victories is the erasure of the boundary between the relative and the absolute. The utopian project is a means of removing the psychological tension that appears along this boundary, but the means involve reversion to a less developed stage of consciousness. Utopias channel people's energy toward an illusory future while they destroy the real world around them. Novgorodtsev hoped that the rational critique of utopia would give this energy a more constructive purpose. As for religious consciousness, Novgorodtsev saw it as more mature and developed than the quasi-religious consciousness of utopianism, more sober and freer of illusions about the likelihood of achieving the ideal in the conditions of earthly life.

In the light of subsequent events, however, one must admit that Novgorodtsev's hope for rationally overcoming utopias through the gradual "education of the human race" proved to be utopian in its own right, albeit in a more restrained way.

The social ideal

Novgorodtsev's analysis of utopianism allowed him to outline his own understanding of the social ideal, its structure, contents, and relation to real life. In his view, neither religious eschatology nor empirical sociology can generate a satisfactory social ideal. Religion offers an otherworldly "ideal of absolute bliss" that rejects the relative values of history and culture. Empirical sociology can conceive of the social ideal "only as a temporary compromise" and rejects the absolute values of morality and religion. Only philosophy is capable of thinking through the problem of the absolute ideal—"the pursuit of which constitutes the truth and meaning of social life"—in such a way that the concepts of the absolute and the relative do not destroy each other but "come together freely in a concept of the historical process" (55, 71). As Novgorodtsev sees it, such a philosophical solution requires, on the formal side, an analysis of the interrelationship of the categories of absolute and relative and, on the substantive side, an analysis of the categories of personhood and society.

The formal task consists in defending "the value of relative goods" and "the idea of progressive development" (100). According to Novgorodtsev, such a defense is possible from the position of "ethical idealism," where the absolute ideal has a superhistorical essence that cannot be fully realized at any point in the historical process but can still be regarded as a moral demand addressed to each point along the way. Thus, the absolute ideal takes the form of an endless development in which "every epoch and every generation receives its justification not in relation to the future but in relation to the eternal" (65).

Novgorodtsev does not believe that the realization of the absolute ideal at each point in the historical process should be construed as the special action of "grace." Following Kant, he sees an element of eudaemonism in this view. Rather, realization of the ideal should be construed through the category of obligation as "the motivating force of human life." In relation to empirical reality, the ideal enters as "the demand of eternal progress toward perfection." Progress toward perfection is realized through moral activity, which involves striving for the ideal as an end and "the implementation of the moral law" in the concrete situation in which one exists (69). Ethical idealism in social philosophy demands the categorical rejection of eudaemonistic ethics (religious as well as atheist-utopian) and its replacement by pure deontology.

The substantive fulfillment of this imperative is clarified through analysis of the interrelationship between personhood and society. As in his criticism of utopianism, Novgorodtsev completely avoids any kind of concrete definition of the higher perfection, replacing it with categorical analysis (121). The social ideal emerges as a natural law formula that defines the vector of a lawful, ethically justifiable social movement.

This formula bears a distinctly personalist stamp. The basic moral norm "is the concept of personhood in its unconditional significance and infinite vocation" (103). Novgorodtsev thinks of personhood here as the unity of "a generic essence, uniformly replicated in separate individuals" with "an irreplaceable, unique individuality that cannot be replicated" (106–07). Such a concept of personhood complicates the idea of the moral law. The latter becomes not just the principle of personal duty, as it was for Kant, but "the moral norm of social interaction." The social reality that emerges on this basis constitutes "a new quality, a new concrete unity" resulting from the interaction of unique individuals. However, Novgorodtsev refuses to consider this social reality to be "a new independent substance" (108).

The relationship between unique individuals is better described as "a relationship of mutually interacting ends" than in terms of cause and effect. Personhood is the absolute end and value, but it is not self-sufficient, since a society consisting of other persons stands over against it. In turn, society serves as a means of developing personhood, but not only as a means, since it consists of persons who are ends in themselves. Society can be seen as an end only because "it consists of persons connected with each other by the unity of the moral ideal" (198). This relationship presupposes constant searching, mobility, disparity, and the impossibility of achieving complete harmony. Collectivism (Marx) and individualism (Nietzsche), moral objectivism (Hegel) and moral subjectivism (Kant, Tolstoy)—all of these propose more or less one-sided solutions, each expressing a certain aspect of the movement toward the ideal but failing to take the other important aspects into account, and failing to see that harmonization of the personal and the social is possible only on the basis of a higher, universal principle that embraces both.

The content of the social ideal may be expressed as "a free universalism," "a comprehensive union based on equality and freedom" (111). This formulation takes into account both the rights of persons (freedom and equality) and their duties (comprehensive union as panhuman solidarity and unity). In Novgorodtsev's conceptuality, this formulation conveys the categorical imperative of social life, "the idea of the right direction of social progress as an unconditional demand that applies always and everywhere" (110). This idea serves as the criterion of progress and as a universal principle of natural law enabling the moral evaluation of all forms of social organization, social transformation, legislation, laws, reforms, and the like.

In this connection, it is worth noting the important transformation of Novgorodtsev's point of departure. If, in the earlier parts of *Introduction to the Philosophy of Law*, the focus was on "natural law with changing content" as the standpoint from which to make a historically relative moral evaluation of positive law, here the focus has shifted to the universal content of the ideal, a content of transhistorical significance, where change means only the more or less clear and distinct disclosure of the components of the ideal—personhood, freedom, equality, solidarity, and the like, ideas which Novgorodtsev regards as implicit in "every *moral* effort of the human will" (114).

Obviously, the concept of "the absolute ideal," of which "the social ideal" is a partial concretization, involves not just metaphysical concepts but also religious concepts. It is no accident that Vladimir Soloviev is one of the authors Novgorodtsev now cites most frequently. The relationship between the absolute and the relative in which the absolute is not regarded as essentially separate from the relative and does not devalue it but rather gives it value and meaning by its abiding presence—this conceptuality fits nicely into the panentheistic conception of the relationship of the absolute and the relative in Solovievian metaphysics, although Novgorodtsev presents it here in the mode of practical philosophy with the help of Kantian categories. At the same time, again in a Solovievian key, the individualism of Kantian ethics is overcome, as moral personhood not only is released into society but turns toward the absolute.

The religious theme sounds most clearly in Novgorodtsev's late works, in which he dedicated himself to interpreting the Russian Revolution and its outcome. We will examine these works in the context of a survey of his writings on political affairs from 1905 to the end of his life.

Novgorodtsev's writings on political affairs

In his writings on the political affairs of his day, Novgorodtsev had three main concerns. Before 1917, he sought to apply the idea of natural law to the political program of the Constitutional Democratic Party. Following the February Revolution of 1917, he sought to work out the Kadet program for regulating the relationship between church and state. During and after the revolutionary upheaval of 1917, his thought took a conservative turn, which continued in his search for the meaning and intellectual unity of the Russian emigration.

Social liberalism

The clearest expression of Novgorodtsev's political and legal thought before 1917 was his idea of the right to a dignified human existence. He first proposed the idea in the context of the discussion of how Russia should develop following the Revolution of 1905, a discussion bearing on the relationship between liberalism and socialism, especially as it affected the program of the Constitutional Democratic Party. Novgorodtsev took the stage as a follower of Soloviev. In *The Justification of the Good* (1897), Soloviev became the first Russian writer to assert the right to a dignified existence as involving the right to "guaranteed means of existence," to physical rest, and to "leisure time for spiritual improvement." In this, he opposed Chicherin, who viewed "supporting the needy" as belonging to the sphere of ethics, not law.[24] Novgorodtsev offered a detailed defense of the right to a dignified human existence from the viewpoint of natural law theory. He deduced this right from the liberal understanding of law as "the protection of personal freedom" and from the fact that "the exercise of freedom can be completely paralyzed by a deficiency of means," whence the necessity of juridical recognition of "the need to provide the material means of freedom" as a condition of "the dignity of persons" (216–17). Policies answering to this view included the right to work (hence, the need for labor legislation and land reform), the right to organize unions, and "mandatory social and state care for the helpless and those incapable of working" (221). In contrast to some of his colleagues, such as S. L. Frank, Novgorodtsev believed it was necessary to include the right

24 P. I. Novgorodtsev, "Dva etiuda," *Poliarnaia Zvezda*, no. 3, Dec. 30, 1905, 216.

to a dignified human existence in a declaration of rights, seeing it not just as an important socialist element in the Kadet program but as the only possible basis of civil peace, "of the solidarity that saves us from both despotism and anarchy" (214).[25]

Church and state

In 1917, Novgorodtsev took part in the All-Russian Congress of Clergy and Laity (June) and in the work of the ninth congress of the Constitutional Democratic Party (July).[26] In both venues, he lectured on the Kadet party's program on the church question. His basic ideas were the liberation of the church from tutelage to the state—rejection of a state church but also of an immediate separation of church and state—and consistent application of the principle of freedom of conscience. Orthodox Christianity, as the religion of the majority, would continue to enjoy "a primacy of honor," which would be evident "in relevant aspects of state life."[27] Novgorodtsev's approach had a polemical edge in that it was directed against the programs of the socialist parties, where, as he believed, the demand for complete separation of church and state simply masked "hostility to things the human spirit holds sacred" (6). Novgorodtsev believed that respect for persons, freedom of conscience, and democracy mandated state protection of the church's "physical conditions of existence," its legal recognition, security, and material support (10). These rights would be extended to all religious organizations.

Already in this program, one senses the hopes Novgorodtsev placed on the Orthodox Church, as bearer of the Russian people's piety and ideals, in the work of national reconciliation.

The conservative turn

The problem of national reconciliation became much more acute following the October Revolution, the forced dispersal of the Constituent Assembly, and the beginning of the Civil War—events which forced Novgorodtsev to rethink many of his ideas and positions. He offered a diagnosis of the deepening crisis of the democratic idea in Russia, "the general crisis of consciousness in the Russian intelligentsia," and, closely connected with these crises, the destruction of the

25 Novgorodtsev and Frank agreed that a formal declaration of rights should be part of the arrangements for a constitutional monarchy in Russia. Frank drafted such a declaration: "Proekt deklaratsii prav," *Poliarnaia Zvezda*, no. 4, January 5, 1906, 243–54. There he notes his disagreement with Novgorodtsev about the place of "the right to a dignified human existence" in the declaration, but he does not go into detail.

26 On the Kadet congress and Novgorodtsev's role in it, see William G. Rosenberg, *Liberals in the Russian Revolution: The Constitutional Democratic Party, 1917–1921* (Princeton, NJ: Princeton University Press, 1974), 200–05.

27 P. I. Novgorodtsev, "Tserkovnyi vopros v programme partii 'Narodnoi svobody,'" vyp. 2 (Petrograd, 1918), 13.

Russian state and collapse of the Russian nation. He sought a way out of this situation through the actualization of the religious foundations of the nation's culture, through "the restoration of the holy." He also tried to formulate the particular features of the Russian tradition of philosophy of law, the sources of which he now found in the works of Dostoevsky.

It is fair to assume that the revolution provided the impetus for these new ideas. In a posthumous article, "The Restoration of the Holy," Novgorodtsev characterized the revolution as a "dissolution" involving the collapse of the political system, the economy, and everyday life. He characterized the administrative practices of the Provisional Government as "legalized anarchy," which led in turn to the despotism of the Bolshevik regime. He faulted "the sentimental and romantic populism" of the Russian intelligentsia for the upheaval.[28]

However, in Novgorodtsev's view, the Russian Revolution was just an exceptionally clear manifestation of a more general crisis. Democracy was "a system of freedom, a system of political relativism" (Hans Kelsen), but at the same time it was a system of political indeterminacy that exhausted people and provoked discontent.[29] As a result, "the whole world in our day is experiencing a grave crisis of legal consciousness."[30] Novgorodtsev characterized this crisis in harsh terms, unequivocally pointing to its religious causes. The way out lay in turning to religious foundations: justice must stand above democracy, a higher will above the popular will.[31]

It is essential to see that Novgorodtsev linked the turn to religious foundations with the turn to nation and state. The process of rebirth, the opposite of revolutionary dissolution, must rely on "the national principle." The restoration of the national culture and national state, however, must rely on the religious principle, "the holy." While Orthodox himself, Novgorodtsev refrained from identifying the holy with concrete and obligatory forms of faith, preferring to outline a kind of civil religion based on "guiding objective principles, before which individual consciousness bows, acknowledging them as something superior to itself."[32] Alignment with these principles does not impede the union of many different faiths (including unbelief), political views, and peoples in the framework of a common homeland.

Novgorodtsev linked his desired synthesis with overcoming the intelligentsia's apostasy and with the rebirth of the tradition of Russian thought connected with Chaadaev, the Slavophiles, Dostoevsky, Soloviev, and the authors of the essay

28 "Vosstanovlenie sviatyn'," in Novgorodtsev, *Sochineniia*, ed. Kolerov and Plotnikov, 424–43, here at 427, 431. The article was written in 1923 and published in 1926.

29 "Demokratiia na rasput'e," in Novgorodtsev, *Sochineniia*, ed. Kolerov and Plotnikov, 388–406, here at 393.

30 "Vosstanovlenie sviatyn'," 441.

31 Pavel Ivanovich Novgorodtsev, "On the Paths and Tasks of the Russian Intelligentsia," in *Out of the Depths (*De Profundis*): A Collection of Articles on the Russian Revolution*, ed. and trans. William F. Woehrlin (Irvine, CA: Charles Schlacks Jr., Publisher, 1986), 175–90.

32 Ibid., 186.

collection *Vekhi* (*Landmarks*, 1909).[33] To this heritage he also linked the Russian tradition of the understanding of law, a tradition he summarized in his article, "On the Distinctive Elements of the Russian Philosophy of Law" (1922–23). Here Novgorodtsev develops a philosophical and historical conceptuality where the distinctions between "discrete epochs" in the history of philosophy of law, and of philosophy itself, and the novel contributions of each epoch to the history of thought "lie in their changing relationship to religion."[34] Novgorodtsev links the coming of a new epoch of this sort with special features of Russian legal thought, among which "the law of Christ" as the basis of social solidarity and the grace of God as the determining factor come first. "Law and the state constitute only secondary stages of this development," the end of which can be reached only "in the church in its ideal sense." Religious catastrophism takes the place of the idea of the progressive rationalization of life. Law, state, and science are seen as secondary, auxiliary values.[35]

However, we should not exaggerate the extent of the transformation of Novgorodtsev's ideas. We are talking more about a redistribution of emphasis in the face of new circumstances and historical challenges, and a more detailed consideration of elements of his thought that remained in the shadows in a more peaceful time. A religious aspect was unquestionably present as the ultimate component even in the early version of his concept of natural law, but the religious foundation remained in the background compared with the analysis of its ethical component. Moreover, Novgorodtsev's late works retain the idea of natural law as the moral regulation of juridical relationships and the idea of the unity of morality and law. Nor is his prioritizing of the moral and metaphysical foundations of law over external forms and regulations something new. This was always his view. As for the critical state of democratic institutions, his discussion does not really go beyond his account of the crisis of legal consciousness written well before the Russian Revolution.

Novgorodtsev's awareness of the seriousness of the problems facing the democratic form of government did not lead him to reject democracy as "the system of freedom." His emphasis on the state and on civil religion and the corresponding nationalist rhetoric did not contradict "the ideal of free universalism" outlined in *On the Social Ideal*. In that work, too, he saw the nation-state as an intermediate stage in the development of a broader union. Moreover, the new emphases in Novgorodtsev's late works were prompted in many respects by the very specific crisis of the Russian state during the revolutionary period. As for the socially liberal components of Novgorodtsev's thought—personalism and the ideas of freedom, equality, and "the right to a dignified human existence"—these do not disappear. They remain necessary elements of a cultural synthesis grounded in

33 See Chapter 14 of this volume (312–13) for a brief discussion of *Vekhi* (*Landmarks*).

34 "O svoeobraznykh elementakh russkoi filosofii prava," in Novgorodtsev, *Sochineniia*, ed. Kolerov and Plotnikov, 367–87, here at 369–70.

35 Ibid., 373–75.

religion. Novgorodtsev's ideal was always "the combination of firm national-governmental and religious principles with the ideas of freedom and equality."[36]

Conclusion

In the course of his career, Novgorodtsev presented a critical interpretation of an enormous body of historical and philosophical material: the basic concepts of philosophy of law, of ancient social and political thought, and of modern European and Russian thought. This enabled him to create a multileveled theoretical conceptuality establishing the interconnection of religious values, moral principles, legal institutions, and political practice, and to defend the autonomy of their philosophical interpretation. His rehabilitation of natural law as a court of moral judgment on law and political practice was by no means outmoded. On the contrary, it anticipated (without coinciding with) analogous Western conceptions, in particular the ideas of Gustav Radbruch that provided the basis for the Nuremberg trials and Leo Strauss's rehabilitation of natural law. Novgorodtsev's concept also contains the potential for intelligent debate with Hans Kelsen's normativism.

Novgorodtsev's critical analysis of utopian consciousness, revealing the utopian element inherent in modern thought, also figured in twentieth-century discussions, from Ernst Bloch and Jürgen Habermas's apologetics for utopianism to the critical views of Karl Mannheim, Karl Popper, and Pierre Rosanvallon, especially in the discussion of the relationship of equality, freedom, and solidarity. Novgorodtsev also made a substantial contribution to understanding quasi-religions. After Nogorodtsev, the critique of utopianism became commonplace in Russian religious thought, appearing in Florovskii, Frank, Berdiaev, Vysheslavtsev, Ilyin, and elsewhere. One encounters it often in connection with the critique of irreligious humanism and in discussions of the crisis of Western culture as a whole.

In Russian thought, Novgorodtsev stands with Evgenii Trubetskoi as one of the founders of the legal-philosophical school based on moral idealism, personalism, and natural law. Nikolai Alekseev, Boris Vysheslavtsev, and Ivan Ilyin may be counted among his students. Struve and Berdiaev were also close to this group to one degree or another. Others who drew on Novgorodtsev's ideas include Father Sergii Bulgakov (on problems of canon law), S. L. Frank (on Christian ethics, social philosophy, and the moral foundations of politics), and Father Georgii Florovskii (on utopianism and personalism, which he carried into the theological sphere).

Through his philosophy of law, Novgorodtsev made a significant contribution to understanding the religious foundations of politics and social life as well as providing a conceptual structure to guide the active, constructive, and responsible participation of Christians in the life of contemporary society.

36 Novgorodtsev, "On the Paths and Tasks of the Russian Intelligentsia," 186.

12 Sergei Kotliarevskii

The rule of law in Russian liberal theory

Randall A. Poole

Friedrich Hayek, defining the idea of the rule of law, wrote that first of all "it constitutes a limitation on the powers of all government, including the powers of the legislature. It is a doctrine concerning what the law *ought to be.*" Because its source is not the state itself but rather the "moral tradition of the community," it is, he continues, "a meta-legal doctrine or a political ideal."[1] In Germany the rule of law was the guiding idea behind the *Rechtsstaat*, a concept that was inspired by Kant and achieved currency in the 1820s as the main goal of the liberal constitutional movement.[2] After the failure of the German Revolution of 1848, however, the meaning of *Rechtsstaat* was transformed from the rule of law to "rule by law," to adopt Harold Berman's distinction.[3] In this new positivist conception, the state itself was seen as the highest source of law, and the *Rechtsstaat* was reduced to a mere formal concept (*formelle Rechtsstaat*).[4]

German works on the *Rechtsstaat* began to be translated into Russian in the 1860s and 1870s, and by the 1880s the term *pravovoe gosudarstvo*, which I will translate as "lawful state," was being used for the German word.[5] Hiroshi Oda

1 This chapter appeared in an earlier version in *Dialogue and Universalism* 16, nos. 1–2 (2006): 81–104. The journal is published by the Institute of Philosophy, Warsaw University. I am grateful to the editors for permission to reprint the article.

F. A. Hayek, *The Constitution of Liberty* (Chicago: The University of Chicago Press, 1960), 205, 206, italics added.

2 Hayek, "The Origins of the Rule of Law," in Hayek, *The Constitution of Liberty*, 162–75; on the *Rechtsstaat*, see 196–204. On the development of the *Rechtsstaatsprinzip* in Germany, see also Hiroshi Oda, "The Emergence of *Pravovoe Gosudarstvo (Rechtsstaat)* in Russia," *Review of Central and East European Law* 25, no. 3 (1999): 373–434, at 375–81.

3 Harold J. Berman, "The Rule of Law and the Law-Based State with Special Reference to the Soviet Union," in *Toward the "Rule of Law" in Russia? Political and Legal Reform in the Transition Period*, ed. Donald D. Barry (Armonk, NY: M. E. Sharpe, 1992), 43–60, here at 47.

4 "Legal positivism from the very beginning could have no sympathy with and no use for those meta-legal principles which underlie the ideal of the rule of law or the *Rechtsstaat* in the original meaning of this concept, for those principles imply a limitation upon the power of legislature." Hayek, *The Constitution of Liberty*, 237.

5 *Pravovoe gosudarstvo* is typically translated "rule-of-law state," "lawful state," or "law-based state." "Lawful state" best fits Kotliarevskii's understanding of the concept, which encom-

DOI: 10.4324/9781003017097-12

argues that for Russian jurists, *pravovoe gosudarstvo* tended to reflect the pre-1848 meaning of *Rechtsstaat*, so that the Russian term *zakonnost'* (legality, in the sense of conformity with statutory laws) better corresponded to the post-1848 positivist meaning.[6] Article 47 of the Fundamental Laws of 1832 defined Russia as a lawful state in this latter sense: "The Russian Empire is governed on the firm basis of positive laws, establishments, and statutes, emanating from the autocratic power."[7] In other words, the tsar's will had to be obeyed because it was law—a debased sense of the concept.[8]

By the beginning of the twentieth century, the Russian constitutional movement was trying to change this state of affairs and adopted as its goal a *pravovoe gosudarstvo* in the sense of a state under the rule of law, the original meaning that *Rechtsstaat* had for German constitutionalists a century earlier.[9] More generally, *pravovoe gosudarstvo* could designate, even for positivist jurists, an evolution from rule by law (as in the *Polizeistaat* or "policing state") to the rule of law, or from the unlimited sovereignty of the state to the sovereignty of law.[10] One way or another, Russian liberal theorists developed the idea of the lawful state in the direction of the rule of law.[11] Those who were most concerned with justifying the sources of the supremacy of law were philosophical idealists such as Boris Chicherin, Vladimir Soloviev, and their successors.[12] The most systematic treatment of the specific topic of the lawful state is Sergei Kotliarevskii's work *Power and Law: The Problem of the Lawful State*.[13] It is a rich and rewarding study that merits careful exposition.

---

passes the entire history of the state's evolution (beginning with the biblical theocracies) toward ever more lawful forms. For Kotliarevskii, the rule of law is an ideal that no state ever perfectly realizes, so the term "rule-of-law state" risks conflating "what is" with "what ought to be." In his meaning, the *pravovoe gosudarstvo* is the state that is becoming ever more lawful, or the state that is developing toward and increasingly embodying the rule of law.

6 Oda, "The Emergence of *Pravovoe Gosudarstvo (Rechtsstaat)* in Russia," 373, 381–84.

7 Ibid., 385; see also Marc Szeftel, "The Form of Government of the Russian Empire Prior to the Constitutional Reforms of 1905–06," in *Essays in Russian and Soviet History*, ed. John Shelton Curtiss (New York: Columbia University Press, 1962), 105–06.

8 Oda, "The Emergence of *Pravovoe Gosudarstvo (Rechtsstaat)* in Russia," 385–86.

9 Ibid., 392–403.

10 Although positivism maintains that any legal limitation of state power is ultimately a self-limitation, some positivist approaches contend that law may become practically autonomous of its state origins and provide effective limits on arbitrary state power, so that rule by law evolves toward rule of law.

11 Gianmaria Ajani, "Russian Liberalism and the Rule of Law: Notes from Underground," in *Dimensions and Challenges of Russian Liberalism: Historical Drama and New Prospects*, ed. Ricardo Mario Cucciolla (Cham, Switz.: Springer, 2019), 15–26.

12 See Andrzej Walicki, *Legal Philosophies of Russian Liberalism* (Oxford: Clarendon Press, 1987), and Chapters 6, 9, 11, 13, and 14 of the present volume.

13 S. A. Kotliarevskii, *Vlast' i pravo: Problema pravovogo gosudarstva* (Moscow: Tipografiia "Mysl'," 1915). Walicki, *Legal Philosophies of Russian Liberalism*, succinctly identifies the thesis of Kotliarevskii's book (366). He refers to Kotliarevskii in the course of his analysis of Bogdan Kistiakovskii's theory of the lawful state (364–74), which makes clear that the two thinkers had similar ideas. Another important consideration of the lawful state is Pavel

Biographical and intellectual profile

Sergei Andreevich Kotliarevskii (1873–1939), a gentry landowner from Saratov province, was one of Russia's leading social philosophers and a public figure in the politics of Russian liberalism.[14] In 1898 he married Ekaterina Nikolaevna Orlova (a physician four years older than he); in 1906 they had a daughter, Pavla.[15] Kotliarevskii held the distinction of defending four dissertations at Moscow University, the first two on church history and the second two on constitutional law.[16] From 1899 he lectured in history as a privatdocent at Moscow University. With his second doctorate in 1910, he became a professor of state (constitutional) law. He also lectured at the Higher Women's Courses in Moscow (1908–17). In liberal politics, Kotliarevskii was a zemstvo constitutionalist (a district- and province-level deputy from Saratov), one of the organizers of the Russian Liberation Movement that culminated in the Revolution of 1905,[17] a founder and central committee member of the Constitutional-Democratic (Kadet) party, and a deputy to the First State Duma.[18] On July 8, 1906, the government dissolved the Duma. In response, the Kadets and their confrères issued an appeal from Vyborg, Finland (where they had convened), calling on the Russian citizenry to refuse to pay taxes or provide military recruits. Though he had misgivings, Kotliarevskii signed the Vyborg Manifesto, consequently losing the right to participate in Duma elections. He continued to work on the Kadet central committee, but gradually became disillusioned with the party and left it in 1912.[19] He collabo-

---

Novgorodtsev's *Krizis sovremennogo pravosoznaniia* (1909), which helped to shape Kotliarevskii's ideas. See Chapter 11 of this volume and Walicki, *Legal Philosophies of Russian Liberalism*, 318–28.

14 V. A. Tomsinov, "Sergei Andreevich Kotliarevskii (1873–1939)," in Tomsinov, *Rossiiskie pravovedy XVIII–XX vekov: ocherki zhizni i tvorchestva*, 2nd rev. ed., 3 vols. (Moscow: Zertsalo-M, 2015), 3:143–92.

15 Tomsinov, "Sergei Andreevich Kotliarevskii (1873–1939)," 144.

16 The first set was in the historical-philological faculty: *Frantsiskanskii orden i rimskaia kuriia v XIII i XIV vv.* (The Franciscan order and the Roman curia in the thirteenth and fourteenth centuries, 1901) for the master's degree, and *Lamenne i noveishii katolitsizm* (Lamennais and modern Catholicism, 1904) for the doctorate. The second set was in the law faculty: *Konstitutsionnoe gosudarstvo: Opyt politiko-morfologicheskogo obzora* (The constitutional state: An attempt at a political-morphological survey, 1907), and *Pravovoe gosudarstvo i vneshniaia politika* (The lawful state and foreign policy, 1909). All were published in the year indicated. For a recent edition of the third work, together with a work published in 1912, see S. A. Kotliarevskii, *Konstitutsionnoe gosudarstvo: Iuridicheskie predposylki russkikh osnovnykh zakonov*, ed. V. A. Tomsinov (Moscow: Zertsalo, 2004).

17 Kotliarevskii was a member of the first organized group of the Liberation Movement, the Beseda circle of the zemstvo opposition, formed in 1899, and contributed to one of its volumes: *Konstitutsionnoe gosudarstvo: Sbornik statei* (St. Petersburg: Izdanie I. V. Gessena i A. I. Kaminka pri uchastii redaktsii gazety *Pravo*, 1905). See Terence Emmons, "The Beseda Circle, 1899–1905," *Slavic Review* 32, no. 3 (1973): 461–90.

18 Tomsinov, "Sergei Andreevich Kotliarevskii (1873–1939)," 145, 147, 150–51. Tomsinov indicates that in 1905 and 1906, Kotliarevskii joined Masonic lodges in Paris and Moscow (148–49).

19 Ibid., 154–56, 170–73.

rated with Petr Struve on the liberal journals *Poliarnaia zvezda* (1905–06) and *Russkaia mysl'* (1907–18), and with E. N. and G. N. Trubetskoi on the liberal newspaper *Moskovskii ezhenedel'nik* (1906–10). During this period he was also part of the "Riabushinskii circle" of Moscow industrialists and national-liberal intellectuals.[20] In 1917 he helped Struve set up the League of Russian Culture, dedicated to the propagation of Russian national values.[21]

In the Provisional Government, Kotliarevskii worked on the law commission and on a commission to plan the Constituent Assembly.[22] On July 29, 1917, he was appointed deputy chief procurator of the Holy Synod. A week later, on August 5, the office of chief procurator was abolished, and a new Ministry of Denominations was established, with Kotliarevskii as associate minister. In that role, he participated in the All-Russian Council (*Sobor*) of the Russian Orthodox Church when it opened in Moscow on August 15.[23] In 1918 he contributed to *Iz glubiny* (*Out of the Depths*), a volume organized by Struve as a sequel to *Vekhi* (*Landmarks*, 1909), the famous collection of essays about the Russian intelligentsia. In his chapter, Kotliarevskii extolled religion as the antidote to the intelligentsia's delusional "subjective psychologism": "For if religion reveals itself to us in the secret depths of our spirit, then is not religious experience the very basis of the life of the individual, the guarantee that inherent in it is the very highest objectivity?"[24] At this time he became involved in the anti-Bolshevik All-Russian National Center and was arrested in late August 1919.[25] He was released but rearrested in February 1920 and given a five-year conditional sentence that permitted him to continue to teach at Moscow University.[26] Reconciling himself to Soviet power, he taught at Moscow University until the early 1930s, while also working for the Commissariat of Justice. In 1937 he wrote to Stalin—"Deeply respected Iosif Vissarionovich!"—supplicating him for academic work, appealing to Stalin's "exceptional concern for humanity," and reassuring him that he had "mastered

20 Kotliarevskii contributed an essay to the two-volume work produced by the group: "Russkaia vneshniaia politika i natsional'nye zadachi," in *Velikaia Rossiia: Sbornik statei po voennym i obshchestvennym voprosam*, ed. V. P. Riabushinskii, 2 vols. (Moscow, n.p. [1911–12]), 2:43–66.

21 On his work with Struve and the Riabushinskii circle, see Richard Pipes, *Struve: Liberal on the Right, 1905–1944* (Cambridge, MA: Harvard University Press, 1980), 21, 182, 236.

22 Tomsinov, "Sergei Andreevich Kotliarevskii (1873–1939)," 175.

23 Ibid., 178–79. See also *Time of Troubles: The Diary of Iurii Vladimirovich Got'e*, ed., trans., and intro. Terence Emmons (Princeton, NJ: Princeton University Press, 1988), 45–46. For Kotliarevskii's involvement in the church council, see James W. Cunningham, *The Gates of Hell: The Great Sobor of the Russian Orthodox Church, 1917–1918* (Minneapolis: Minnesota Mediterranean and East European Monographs, University of Minnesota, 2002); the index lists numerous page references for him.

24 S. A. Kotliarevskii, "Recovery," in *Out of the Depths* (De Profundis)*: A Collection of Articles on the Russian Revolution*, ed. and trans. William F. Woehrlin (Irvine, CA: Charles Schlacks Jr., Publisher, 1986), 145–55, here at 154.

25 Tomsinov, "Sergei Andreevich Kotliarevskii (1873–1939)," 183–86.

26 Ibid., 186–89. Got'e did not hide his contempt in writing that Kotliarevskii "wavered" and "compromised" himself. See *Time of Troubles: The Diary of Iurii Vladimirovich Got'e*, 378.

the methods of Marxism-Leninism" to such a degree that he could be helpful. His efforts seem to have yielded success, but only temporarily. He was arrested in April 1938 and executed a year later. He was rehabilitated in 1956.[27] How his reconciliation with Soviet power affected his religious-philosophical worldview must remain a matter of speculation.

Sergei Kotliarevskii was a religious idealist, metaphysical personalist, and liberal theorist whose ideas were closest to those of Sergei Trubetskoi (1862–1905), Evgenii Trubetskoi (1863–1920), and especially Pavel Novgorodtsev (1866–1924), his senior colleagues at Moscow University and in the Moscow Psychological Society. He combined philosophical idealism with a broad cultural and historical approach to liberalism. An astute student of religion and society, he became convinced that a liberal civic culture had its roots in a free and dynamic spiritual life. In his 1905 essay, "The Premises of Democracy," he described the type of religious consciousness that promotes the development and deepening of liberalism:

> Its binding force consists in the feelings of piety and worship that are inherent to a human being before the Unfathomable, the Divine. And these feelings are sufficiently powerful, sufficiently rich in creative force, to generate an infinite diversity of symbols and forms. The spiritualization of human life—here is the true premise of the principle of the "kingdom of freedom." It is impossible to imagine without religion, forging a link between the terrestrial and celestial.[28]

Not surprisingly, the author of these lines had a deep appreciation for the author of *The Varieties of Religious Experience*.[29] Through William James, Kotliarevskii became very interested in pragmatism, valuing it for its idea of the expansive possibilities of human experience, instead of the dogmatic constrictions and reductions of one or another monistic ideology. He believed that the pragmatist approach to the full range of human experience, including morality and religion, could promote the development of an integral, balanced, and liberal worldview.

Power, law, spirit

Pragmatism is the general philosophical framework within which Kotliarevskii conceives his project in *Power and Law: The Problem of the Lawful State*. The treatise opens with reflections on the nature of work—intellectual, moral,

27 Tomsinov, "Sergei Andreevich Kotliarevskii (1873–1939)," 190–92.

28 S. A. Kotliarevskii, "Predposylki demokratii," *Voprosy filosofii i psikhologii* 16, no. 2, kn. 77 (1905): 104–27, here at 126–27.

29 See Randall A. Poole, "William James in the Moscow Psychological Society: Pragmatism, Pluralism, Personalism," in *William James and Russian Culture*, ed. Joan Delaney Grossman and Ruth S. Rischin (Lanham, MD: Lexington Books/Rowman & Littlefield, 2003), 131–58. The second half of the essay is devoted to Kotliarevskii.

physical—and its value for personal, cultural, and even cosmic development. Work fashions both person and cosmos.[30] It is a creative and transforming process by which the initially given realities of the natural and human worlds are remade in a higher human and ultimately divine image.[31] Work is what brings the reality of "what is" closer to the ideal of "what ought to be." It is, in short, a spiritualizing process, the self-realization of a higher potential inherent not only in humanity but also in natural reality. Kotliarevskii relates these suggestions to the pragmatist approach to truth (1–2). His own conception was closest to the idea of the *plasticity* of reality, which the more speculative pragmatists, such as the British philosopher F. C. S. Schiller (1864–1937), used to convey the creative potential in our search for truth, a process in which reality to some extent realizes in itself our ideals.[32] As James put it, pragmatism was no mere epistemological matter. "*It concerns the structure of the universe itself.*"[33] This was precisely Kotliarevskii's idea of the cosmic-creative potential of work, including, of course, the work of discovering truth.

Kotliarevskii's pragmatist-inspired conception of work seems at first to have little to do with his main problem, power and law. In fact, however, this conception forms the underlying theme of his treatise: law is the ideal that is worked into the basic reality of the state—power—and progressively transforms it, in turn enabling higher levels of development. Law is part of the work that humanizes and spiritualizes reality, first of all the reality of unequal power in human relations. Kotliarevskii's approach was inspired not only by pragmatism but by a source closer to home: Vladimir Soloviev's concept of divine humanity (*Bogochelovechestvo*). For both Soloviev and Kotliarevski, law was integral to the work of spiritualization and ultimately of deification.

"Two Elements in the State" is the title of Kotliarevskii's first chapter. Despite the age-old striving to make the state more lawful, law is not the first, basic element of the state. Power is. It is primary and intrinsic to the state; law, as a matter of origins, is secondary and extrinsic. Power is the natural element; law is the ideal element, one that must be gradually realized in the state through work. Power, submission, and dependence are human psychological realities, and they are basic to the nature of the state. No abstract dialectical or formal juridical approaches are necessary to understand this, nor can they long deny it (5–6). Here Kotliarevskii followed the prominent Russian legal theorist N. M. Korkunov (1853–1904), who traced the source of power to the common human experience of dependence: it is the feeling of dependence in one person that

30 Kotliarevskii, *Vlast' i pravo: Problema pravovogo gosudarstva*, 1. Subsequent page references are cited parenthetically in the text.

31 Although pragmatism is the context here, Kotliarevskii could not have been unaware of Hegel's and Marx's ideas on the transforming power of work.

32 Kotliarevskii refers to the notion of the plasticity of reality in his essay, "Pragmatizm i problema terpimosti," *Voprosy filosofii i psikhologii* 21, no. 3, kn. 103 (1910): 368–79, here at 378.

33 William James, *Pragmatism* (New York: Dover Publications, 1995), 100. *Pragmatism* was first published in 1907.

gives power to another. Likewise with the state, which, according to Korkunov, derives its power not so much from coercion but from the consciousness, among its subjects, of dependence and subordination (6–8, 11).[34] Kotliarevskii thought this was paradoxical, as if to say that power is most present when it is least exercised, when people submit to it before its overt exercise. Overt or otherwise, it is basic to the state (14–17).

At this level (power), the state still has much in common with the brutish "state of nature" and is very much in need of ideal transformation and elevation to a higher level, which is the work of law. This is why Kotliarevskii insisted that power and law are two different elements of the state. The distinction is also relevant to his repeated efforts to resist political utopianism and its exaggerated claims for the role of the state in promoting human self-realization and perfectibility.[35] He wanted to stress that the possibilities of the state are limited by its own nature and means, which are relative ones inextricably tied to power relations. The rootedness of state power in flawed human nature is discounted by the rationalist faith in the realization of human perfectibility through political institutions and other external arrangements; similarly, by the anarchist faith in a natural human goodness that has been corrupted by politics but supposedly will reemerge with the state's destruction, as if power were an external matter. Both rationalism and anarchism share a "psychological utopianism" about human nature that is "one of the deepest roots of political and social utopianism" (18). In contrast to power and its reflection in the relative means of the state, law pertains to absolute ends and reaches beyond power relations to spiritual aspirations. Its possibilities, like the human spirit from which its demands come, are infinite, based on the realization that true transformation comes from within.[36]

Power is not unique to the state, of course, but pervades all types of human relationships and associations. "For a long time," Kotliarevskii writes, "dependence on kin, commune, and landlord was much more palpable and encompassed all moments in the life of the one under power and his whole field of consciousness, eclipsing the weak, dim power of the state." Gradually, however, the state triumphed over these groups, acquiring a monopoly over coercion. The general problem of power, in its relation to personal and social freedom, now tends to focus on the specific problem of state power. How, Kotliarevskii asks, are we to

34 On Korkunov's analysis of the phenomenon of power, see also Walicki, *Legal Philosophies of Russian Liberalism*, 214.

35 The philosophical critique of utopianism is a theme that runs through Kotliarevskii's works. See, for example, "Predposylki demokratii"; "Politika i kul'tura," *Voprosy filosofii i psikhologii* 17, no. 4, kn. 84 (1906): 353–67; and "Filosofiia kontsa," *Voprosy filosofii i psikhologii* 24, no. 4, kn. 119 (1913): 313–38.

36 Kotliarevskii's overall approach was much influenced by Pavel Novgorodtsev's *Krizis sovremennogo pravosoznaniia*, which argues that the specific institutions and mechanisms of the liberal democratic state are relative means that could never produce a perfect society or transform human nature, but that liberal democratic ideals, such as the rule of law, are indeed absolute ends, based ultimately on the idea of personhood.

resolve it? (17–18) With that question, he turns to the second element of the state: law.

The modern state, Kotliarevskii observes, reveals a profound change in the character of power. First, state power has generally come to be viewed as a means of fulfilling social functions and as an instrument of public policy. In terms of content, it is defined positively and invested with great social and national tasks (19–20). Second, state power has increasingly assumed a lawful form. There is, he explains, an undoubted link between the state's new social content and its legal form, which is that in both respects, state power has undergone a process of rationalization. But there is a certain antagonism as well. The antagonism between form and content arises precisely because the state's ever increasing activity in the social sphere requires that its legal character be defined negatively rather than positively.[37] Lawful form is, however, compatible with diverse and broad content; the issue is not what the state does but how it does it.

Defining the form and limits of state power negatively rather than positively, on the basis of prohibition rather than prescription, is Kotliarevskii's first criterion of the lawful state. "The concept of the lawful state," he writes, "at least initially meets the requirement of such a negative definition." The lawful state does not at all deny the principle of power, intrinsic as it is to human nature, but it does strive to balance this with other sides of human nature, first of all by preserving "a certain sphere of legal autonomy" (20). At the end of his study, he notes that the lawful state may have its origins in the "instinct" of limiting the feeling of personal dependence, the source of power and subordination, but his point is that the sphere of independence that law carves out is testimony to law's real, transforming force, for that sphere is the condition of all higher development (411).

The state is not the only organization where power and submission need to be limited by law. They also need to be limited in the family, the church, political parties, and "any union where there are people with their passions, with despotism and the temptation of subjection to another's will" (21).[38] But, Kotliarevskii continues, the main limitation on power in these groups is made by the state itself, which protects its members from being treated in ways contrary to their status as subjects and citizens. Since in the absence of a world government there is no organization higher than the state, it is essential that its power be lawfully limited so that it can serve as the model, institutional embodiment, and guarantor of the rule of law. "In contemporary circumstances," Kotliarevskii writes,

37 As Kotliarevskii puts it later in his study, "the expansion of state activity with positive tasks extraordinarily increases the government's force and, consequently, makes corresponding legal guarantees all the more necessary" (349n).

38 The importance that Russian liberals attached to dismantling the "interconnected structures of domestic patriarchy, *soslovie* society, and arbitrary autocratic and state power (*proizvol*)" has been masterfully demonstrated by William G. Wagner, *Marriage, Property, and Law in Late Imperial Russia* (Oxford: Oxford University Press, 1994) and Wagner, "Family Law, the Rule of Law, and Liberalism in Late Imperial Russia," *Jahrbücher für Geschichte Osteuropas* 43, no. 4 (1995): 519–35, here at 521.

"the lawful character imparted to state power is the necessary condition for the supremacy of law in all other social relations" (21).

This formulation—"the supremacy of law in all social relations"—nicely captures the main principle underlying Kotliarevskii's whole philosophy of law. The lawful state is the necessary condition for the rule of law elsewhere in society, and the rule of law is the necessary condition, in turn, for human self-realization and higher spiritual development. Law makes possible the fuller development of human potential by, in a sense, freeing people from the state of nature and reducing the element of power, force, and violence in human affairs. It makes people equal in a way that they are not in the state of nature or in unlawful societies, where the strong brutalize the weak—and brutalize themselves in the process. By equalizing human relations, law enables people to develop as persons. Law, in short, is an essential spiritualizing force. In this, Kotliarevskii's conception of law was classically liberal: law safeguards the scope of negative liberty necessary for self-realization by limiting arbitrary state power and the power of one person over another.

The striving for the supremacy of law over power is the defining, abiding feature of the lawful state. The institutions and practices of the lawful state, the various ways it seeks to realize the supremacy of law in practice, are all relative and subject to change, a matter of "political technics," but the ideal itself—"like the human spirit creating it"—is permanent (22). For this reason Kotliarevskii describes the concept of the lawful state as essentially "metajuridical";[39] its core principles are absolute ends that always transcend the specific juridical or political means used to approximate them in historical reality (22). In this connection, he specifies another basic premise of the lawful state: the relative mutual independence of law and the state (23). Clearly, this is a key formulation. We know that, for Kotliarevskii, the state's basic nature is power. Law by its nature and origins is different. It is extrinsic to the state but can be worked into it, limiting the arbitrary exercise of its power, making it lawful, and transforming its nature. To the question that inevitably arises—"What is the source of law?"—Kotliarevskii's answer is unambiguous, and he defends it throughout his treatise: the ultimate source of law is the striving of the human spirit, an autonomous ideal force capable of transforming external reality. This position is, of course, perfectly consistent with his overall philosophical idealism.

One of the basic claims of legal positivism is that the state is the source of law, a claim that Kotliarevskii is therefore obliged to refute. He focuses on the positivist approach to the problem of the legal self-limitation of state power. By "legal self-limitation," Kotliarevskii is not suggesting that state power is somehow self-limiting—although precisely this is the positivist position. He is interested more generally in why state officials, at a certain stage in the state's development, come to respect laws that also apply to the state's other subjects and that thus limit

39 Cf. Hayek's use of the term "meta-legal," quoted above.

their own power. Why, in other words, do state officials come to see themselves as under the rule of law and as equal to other subjects or citizens?[40] (32, 36–37)

The German legal theorist Rudolf von Jhering (1818–92) gave one answer to the problem: the state submits to its own laws because it is in its own best interests to do so.[41] Law is only an intelligent politics of state power, as Kotliarevskii puts it (34–35). He compares Jhering's theory to utilitarianism, which tries to explain morality as rational egoism. One of the dangers of Jhering's approach, he points out, is that the state is personified and depicted as a thinking and acting being. Kotliarevskii's main criticism, however, is that rational self-interest alone cannot explain the state's self-limitation. Jhering himself was eventually compelled to admit that moral factors are at work, without, however, recognizing that "this moral force is not contained within the bounds of even the most rational egoism; it rests on consciousness of responsibility and duty" (37). Kotliarevskii's overall conclusion is that Jhering's positivist approach prevents him from clearly appreciating that moral consciousness is the main factor in the legal self-limitation of state power; positivism must disguise this factor as "rational egoism."[42]

Kotliarevskii also considers the views of another prominent German legal theorist, Georg Jellinek (1851–1911),[43] who compares the state's legal self-limitation with the self-limitation of the human person submitting to the autonomous moral law. Although Kotliarevskii generally admired Jellinek, he rejects this comparison. First, Kotliarevskii is again wary of any psychological comparison of state and person. Second, as we know, he does not think it is correct to speak of law as an autonomous principle inherent in the state. A human being,

40 "The ideal of the rule of law requires that the state either enforce the law upon others—and that this be its only monopoly—or act under the same law and therefore be limited in the same manner as any private person. It is this fact that all rules apply equally to all, including those who govern, which makes it improbable that any oppressive rules will be adopted." Hayek, *The Constitution of Liberty*, 210.

41 For the Russian reception of Jhering's views, see Walicki, *Legal Philosophies of Russian Liberalism*, 143–44, 156, 185, 215, 227–30, 241, 261, 279, 302–04.

42 Kotliarevskii's treatment of Jhering is a good example of the "contraband" critique of positivism advanced by Russian neo-idealists. They believed that ethical, religious, and metaphysical suppositions were inevitable in human thought and needed to be acknowledged and justified. "Contraband" refers to the unconscious smuggling of these suppositions into areas of thought claimed by positivism as its own, and to the resulting intellectual distortion and muddling of concepts. The contraband critique of positivism was widely used in *Problems of Idealism*. See the editor's introduction to *Problems of Idealism: Essays in Russian Social Philosophy*, ed. and trans. Randall A. Poole (New Haven: Yale University Press, 2003), 1–78, esp. 35–42. Kotliarevskii helped to pioneer the contraband critique in his review of *Ocherki realisticheskogo mirovozzreniia* (1904), the leading positivist response to *Problems of Idealism*: see Kotliarevskii, "Ob istinnom i mnimom realizme," *Voprosy filosofii i psikhologii* 15, no. 5, kn. 75 (1904): 624–44. Walicki shows that Stanislaw Brzozowski, the Polish fin-de-siècle thinker, also used the contraband critique of positivism. See Walicki, *Stanislaw Brzozowski and the Polish Beginnings of 'Western Marxism'* (Oxford: Oxford University Press, 1989), 91.

43 For the Russian reception of Jellinek's views, see Walicki, *Legal Philosophies of Russian Liberalism*, 201, 314–15, 368–70.

in submitting to the moral law, follows the inner voice of conscience. The state, by contrast, takes law not from itself but from the "surrounding social sphere," in Kotliarevskii's phrase. "Law is a secondary element of state organization, and state recognition is not the primary source of its binding nature. For the original element of power, from which the state is created, law is heteronomous; it comes from outside." Power and law, he stresses, have different sources, and one or another combination of these elements determines the basic character of the state order (43–44). The lawful state cannot eliminate the element of power intrinsic to the state as such, but it can strive toward an ever fuller realization of the principle of law, "which is inseparable in the final account from religious-moral foundations" (45).

The religious roots of legal consciousness

One of the most important themes in *Power and Law* is that the very idea of the lawful state is not peculiar to modern constitutionalism but belongs to the "cultural inventory of humanity" (44). "It runs through the ages as the search for law, as the striving of the human spirit—silenced, rising again, never dying; only those political and social forms in which it has been embodied … die and are doomed to die" (233). In the third chapter of his study ("Historical Embodiments"), Kotliarevskii follows this perennial search for the ever more lawful state and its relative, historical approximations. His thesis is that the lawful state presupposes a certain legal consciousness. He is especially interested in how religious ideas and institutions have affected the development of this consciousness and its core moral conviction, that power ought to be limited by law.[44]

Kotliarevskii locates the ancient roots of the lawful state in the biblical theocracies. At first glance, this lineage might seem highly problematic; surely theocracy and the lawful state could be paired only as polar opposites. Kotliarevskii himself could not have been more critical of theocratic currents in modern social thought, beginning with Vladimir Soloviev's "free theocracy."[45] It is necessary, however, to distinguish among various senses of the term "theocracy" and to appreciate the historical context. What is retrograde in a more recent historical period might well have been progressive in an earlier one. Kotliarevskii argues that there is a

44 In addition to the religious roots of legal consciousness, Kotliarevskii also explores the "secular" Greek and Roman contributions to the idea of the lawful state (135–75).

45 Kotliarevskii and other Moscow Psychological Society philosophers, including Boris Chicherin, Evgenii Trubetskoi, and Pavel Novgorodtsev, were highly critical of Soloviev's theocratic utopianism, seeing in it the mirror-image of the subordination of church to state characteristic of modern Russian history. They argued that both systems were illiberal in the same way: they violated freedom of conscience and infringed the necessary autonomy of church and state. See Randall A. Poole, "Utopianism, Idealism, Liberalism: Russian Confrontations with Vladimir Solov'ev," *Modern Greek Studies Yearbook: Mediterranean, Slavic and Eastern Orthodox Studies* (University of Minnesota) 16/17 (2000/2001): 43–87 (on Kotliarevskii, see 66–67).

sense in which theocracy can refer to the limitation of secular power by the will of God and his earthly representatives. In this conception, religious sanction is given to secular power only conditionally and can be withdrawn, in which event it turns into a sanction for the overthrow of the offending government. "Here, under the defense of religious norms, the relative security of citizens can be preserved, as in other epochs and circumstances it is preserved under legal norms" (123–24).

The best example of this type of theocracy can be found among the ancient Hebrews. Kotliarevskii distinguishes between two types of theocratic ideals in the Hebrew tradition: priestly and prophetic. Both contributed to the development of legal consciousness, although Kotliarevskii believed that the prophetic-messianic tradition was the more significant, especially in its religious universalism, its fervent faith in a moral world-order, and its appeal to personal and social righteousness. The divinely inspired authoritative voice of the prophets acted as a restraining force against arbitrary power (127–28). The Israelite kings were not to rule despotically but according to God's will and law; "this is not so much monarchical power, as monarchical service" (132). Thus theocracy, as depicted in the Hebrew Bible, "itself provided a certain legal order, although by extra-legal norms: the will of the earthly ruler was concretely limited by a higher divine will" (131). Most important was the belief that divine dictates are not something external to human nature but are confirmed by conscience.

> Thus theocracy, limiting state power in its name, limits it by a norm flowing from human nature itself—from its natural law, it might be said. And it would be wrong to think that this nature was ascribed to only one selected nationality. The messianic ideal, transcending national exclusiveness, reveals a new world, where the wolf will graze with the lamb (Isaiah 65:25), where people from all nations and all ends of the earth will be saved (Isaiah 45:20, 22; Zechariah 2:11).
>
> (133–34)

Kotliarevskii attached great significance to the legal consciousness of ancient Israel as it developed alongside the Judaic monotheistic religious ideal. "Much of this spiritual wealth," he writes, "was inherited and reworked by future ages: much of it has left a clear mark on the history of the European state and its affirmation of legal principles" (134).[46]

Kotliarevskii contended that Christianity also made great and distinctive contributions to the idea of the lawful state. The first of these was religious freedom, a demand made by early Christian apologists against pagan Rome. They defended this demand as consistent with the legal principles recognized by Rome itself, principles that did not permit Christians to be denied their freedom without

46 Compare the view of one respected present-day historian: "It is not too much to say that, if the heart of political liberalism is the belief that power must be used within a moral framework independent of it, then its taproot is the teaching of the prophets." J. M. Roberts, *The Penguin History of the World* (New York, NY: Penguin Books, 1990), 110.

cause. The Christian apologists appealed to Rome to respect its own legal principles, and in doing so Kotliarevskii thinks they helped to deepen its legal consciousness. At the same time, the church itself became more authoritarian, hierarchical, and repressive—psychological traits "that did not remain without great influence on the relation of Christians to power and the state" (177–78). Externally, the church won an important victory in 313, when the Edict of Milan granted religious freedom to all Roman citizens. "But," Kotliarevskii adds cryptically, "another period soon begins," when the church will use its new power and privileges to suppress the religious freedom it had earlier championed. Here are the roots of medieval intolerance, yet the church's very power could also limit that of the state, as famously symbolized by Ambrose of Milan's excommunication of Emperor Theodosius in 390 (178).

The countervailing power of church and state produced the "medieval dualism" that, according to Kotliarevskii, so distinguished the Catholic West from the Orthodox East and excluded "state omnipotence" (179–80).[47] The church's power ran the risk, however, of compromising its spiritual vocation and distinctiveness as it assumed secular responsibilities in the highly decentralized feudal world.[48] The church recognized the dangers of internal secularization and tried to counteract them by several means: monasticism (especially with the Cluniac reform and founding of the mendicant orders); the reforms of Pope Gregory VII (1073–85), which asserted papal supremacy and condemned lay investiture, simony, and clerical marriage; and the systematization of cannon law. These far-reaching measures enabled the church to preserve its unity and independence (197–200).[49]

Through its monastic, clerical, and legal reforms, the medieval church tried to combine asceticism and theocracy. Following St. Augustine, it held that spiritual power over the world was justified only by ascetic rejection of the world.[50] Kotliarevskii believed this was a distinctive combination that had far-reaching implications for the later development of the lawful state. The church began to hold power as a function, not as property—***ministerium***, not ***dominium***, in Bernard of Clairvaux's expression (199). This sharply distinguished spiritual

47 "The very presence of the Catholic church," Kotliarevskii concludes, "limited state power" (207).

48 With regard to feudalism itself, Kotliarevskii argued that historians have exaggerated the extent and significance of its contributions to the rule of law (180–97).

49 Recall that the mendicant orders were the subject of Kotliarevskii's first master's thesis, *Frantsiskanskii orden i rimskaia kuriia v XIII i XIV vv.* (1901). On the Gregorian "Papal Revolution," see the Introduction to the present volume.

50 E. N. Trubetskoi's studies in the intellectual history of medieval theocracy develop this point at length. See Trubetskoi, *Religiozno-obshchestvennyi ideal zapadnogo khristianstva v V veke: Mirosozertsanie bl. Avgustina* (Moscow: Tipografiia E. Lissnera i Iu. Romana, 1892), 70–79, 257–70; and Trubetskoi, *Religiozno-obshchestvennyi ideal zapadnogo khristianstva v XI veke: Ideia bozheskogo tsarstva v tvoreniiakh Grigoriia VII-go i ego publitsistov–sovremennikov* (Kiev: Tipografiiia S. V. Kul'zhenko, 1897), 304, 318, 349–63. It is curious that Kotliarevskii cites neither of these works in this connection.

power from secular power, which was still "patrimonial," but which would later also come to be conceived as a function serving higher (state) purposes.[51]

Kotliarevskii further points to the late medieval conciliar movement which, although it ultimately failed within the church, became a crucial source of constitutional ideas in early modern political thought (200–01).[52] Other seminal Catholic contributions to the idea of the lawful state were natural law and contract theory (204).[53] Most important, the church preserved the autonomy of the religious sphere, both by its own spiritual/ascetic reforms and by its institutional power against the state. As a whole, the medieval West managed to avoid what Kotliarevskii calls "Byzantine caesaropapism" despite certain efforts in that direction by the Holy Roman Empire. He notes that historians have often recognized that the dualism of church and state was "highly favorable for European freedom," and he clearly agrees with them (205–06).[54] It is true that both church and state stood on theocratic ground, and that the state surpassed the church in persecution of heresy. But within the church's sphere there were limits to state power, and within this sanctuary Kotliarevskii sees the beginnings of freedom of conscience—with which, he says, all other freedoms are connected (206–07).

Problems of modern constitutionalism

From ancient and medieval "embodiments" of the idea of the lawful state, Kotliarevskii turns to the early modern and modern periods, to the progression from feudalism to absolutism and finally constitutionalism. A critical juncture in this progression was the transition from a patrimonial to a functional conception of power—the roots of which, as we have seen, he traced to medieval ascetic theocracy. Louis XIV's famous pronouncement, "L'état c'est moi," was made already at a time when "the power of the monarch was becoming separated from its patrimonial basis and turning into a state function demanded by the general

51 Cf. Ernst Kantorowicz's distinction between the immortal body politic and the mortal body of the king in Kantorowicz, *The King's Two Bodies: A Study in Medieval Political Theology* (Princeton, NJ: Princeton University Press, 1957).

52 Quentin Skinner's classic study, *The Foundations of Modern Political Thought*, vol. 2, *The Age of Reformation* (Cambridge: Cambridge University Press, 1978), emphasizes conciliarism and other Catholic sources of constitutionalism. More recently, see Francis Oakley, *The Conciliarist Tradition: Constitutionalism in the Catholic Church 1300–1870* (Oxford: Oxford University Press, 2003), and Paul Valliere, *Conciliarism: A History of Decision-Making in the Church* (Cambridge: Cambridge University Press, 2012).

53 Although Kotliarevskii does not cite him, E. N. Trubetskoi also refers to the church's use of ideas of popular sovereignty and contract theory against state absolutism. See Trubetskoi, *Religiozno–obshchestvennyi ideal zapadnogo khristianstva v XI veke*, 310–14.

54 He put it even more strongly in his 1907 book on constitutionalism: "The great service of Catholicism in the history of humanity . . . is that it defended a certain sphere of people's spiritual life from state intrusion." Kotliarevskii, *Konstitutsionnoe gosudarstvo: Opyt politiko-morfologicheskogo obzora* (St. Petersburg: Izdanie G. F. L'vovicha, 1907), 80–81.

good, and the monarch himself—into a state organ," his power no longer personal but derived from and thus (in theory) limited by the state (226).

This incisive formulation captures the distinctiveness of the modern lawful state and specifies a crucial threshold in its practical realization. Kotliarevskii's meaning is that the state turned from being (at least in part) the property or instrument of monarchical power into being the source itself of power, which would seem to transform the nature of state power and make it qualitatively more lawful than in previous embodiments of the lawful state. The state, once it is recognized as the only legitimate source of power in the public sphere, becomes the institutional embodiment of the rule of law, to which even (or especially) executive power is subordinate. As Kotliarevskii writes, "recognition of lawful supremacy presupposes only that the monarch be an organ of the state, and not stand above it" (244). The principle of the modern lawful state, he continues, excludes any patrimonial conception of power, for the monarch's (or any official's) power is not his own property but rather his competence; the "only subject" (or source) of power in the state is the state itself (246–47). In other words, there is no legitimate private (patrimonial) source of power in the modern lawful state; in the public sphere, all power is public and derives from the state. The modern form of the lawful state, so conceived, is the constitutional state, sustained by a relatively highly developed legal consciousness, which is also ultimately its very source.

In his consideration of the modern constitutional state,[55] Kotliarevskii emphasizes that it and the lawful state must not be equated. The lawful state is a meta-juridical concept that transcends any of its historical embodiments; in the modern era, its necessary form is indeed the constitutional state, but this is a historical form that may be superseded in the future (118, 234). Juridically, Kotliarevskii defines the constitutional state as one where only an act issued with the consent of popular representation can be recognized as a formal law (*zakon*) (234, 297). This definition indicates how the constitutional state provides for the supremacy of law over other acts of state power, and how law thus becomes the general norm for the state. The supremacy of law must also entail its universality, since this alone provides for equality before the law. The supremacy of law, so defined, is the main criterion of the constitutional state; other features, such as ministerial responsibility before parliament or whether the state is a monarchy or republic, are secondary (235–36).

By its very nature, the modern lawful state must give primary importance to the courts. They were, Kotliarevskii writes, the first branch of government to forcefully advance the principle of the legal self-limitation of the state. Long before the separation of the legislative and executive branches, the judiciary acquired its

55 This is the subject of his fourth chapter, "The Constitutional State as Embodiment of the Lawful State," most of which is devoted to contemporary constitutional politics and practices in Europe and elsewhere. The subject is also discussed at some length in his second chapter, a review of German, French, British, and Russian scholarship on the lawful state. He also devoted a separate book to the subject: Kotliarevskii, *Konstitutsionnoe gosudarstvo* (see note 54).

independence, a pivotal moment in the modern history of the rule of law. The Russian Judicial Reform of 1864, he observes, so successfully embodied the idea of an independent judiciary that the reformed courts were recognized (by friend and foe) as incompatible with autocracy. He opposed the retention of the *volost'* (township) courts because they operated according to unwritten customary law rather than ordinary civil law; therefore, he thought they impeded the final legal equality of the peasantry with other estates. In pointed references to Russia in his own day, he warned that any violation of established judicial procedure (such as trial by jury) was an infringement of the principle of law requiring not simple reference to state necessity but very weighty justification. This diminishment of law was even graver with any expansion of the jurisdiction of military courts, which had to be limited to absolute necessity (328–30).

Kotliarevskii was, of course, fully cognizant of the Russian context within which he was writing, and he no doubt hoped, as a civic-minded legal philosopher and historian, that his study of the development of the lawful state might reveal a "usable past" for Russia (albeit a largely foreign, Western one) as the country tried to build its own liberal future, one tied more closely to the West. He believed that the October Manifesto of 1905 signified Russia's transition to a constitutional order because it guaranteed that "no law can go into force without approval of the State Duma," which was his definition of the constitutional state (112–13, 236). In retrospect, this assessment was far too optimistic (and ironically for him, too juridical), but it gave greater practical relevance to recent Russian scholarship on the lawful state, including his own. In a succinct literature review, he highlights those Russian theorists who recognized that the legal limitation of state power was to be sought in the "normative consciousness" of citizens (N. I. Palienko) and that personhood was the ultimate metajuridical foundation of the lawful state (A. I. Elistratov) (113–18).[56]

The absolute worth of the human person was the basis, we know, for Kotliarevskii's negative definition of the modern lawful state. According to this definition, the state must recognize and guarantee the legal bounds surrounding individual persons and their various associations (119). "The necessity of a certain sphere of personal freedom" (including personal inviolability and freedom of conscience, expression, and association) has become "axiomatic" in modern legal consciousness and is today the "necessary premise" of any state under the rule of law (342).[57] But outside this sphere of negative liberty there

56 Kotliarevskii also considers the works of two other jurists, A. S. Alekseev and V. M. Gessen. Oda, "The Emergence of *Pravovoe Gosudarstvo (Rechtsstaat)* in Russia," refers to all these thinkers.

57 There is a succinct presentation of "The State and the Rights of the Citizen" in *Konstitutsionnoe gosudarstvo*, 80–101. David Wartenweiler, in his analysis of the idea of civil society in Russian liberal thought, highlights Kotliarevskii's contribution, quoting him from this source: "As Kotliarevskii remarked, the recognition and guarantee of individual rights 'proves to be fully effective only when the entire nation is imbued with consciousness of the importance of these individual rights, with consciousness of the great danger that comes

is broad scope for the positive activity of the state. In fact, what is distinctive to modern constitutionalism is its combination of negative legal form with positive social content and a broad commitment to welfare policies. Kotliarevskii strongly endorsed the social and cultural policies of the contemporary constitutional state, believing that they were not only compatible with but increasingly mandated by respect for the dignity of the human person. He wished to counter the view that the only tasks of the lawful state were to uphold law and order and to limit (to the extent possible) the state's interference in the life of citizens (119, 335–41). He even suggested that there is no necessary contradiction between socialism and the lawful state (339–41).[58] Like Vladimir Soloviev and Pavel Novgorodtsev, he championed a positive conception of the "right to a dignified existence" as the next step in the practical development of the constitutional state (346–50).

From personhood as the metajuridical foundation of the lawful state, Kotliarevskii drew other policy conclusions for modern constitutionalism. First, the idea of personhood utterly precluded capital punishment. This was a matter of great concern for him. "We can be sure," he wrote pleadingly, "that the growth of legal and moral feeling will lead to the state's complete renunciation of the death penalty, to the recognition of an impassable barrier, the absence of which in Christian Europe is one of the gravest indictments against contemporary civilization." Kant and Hegel's defense of the death penalty was, he added, a "sad aberration of great minds" (344).[59] The principle of personal dignity also prescribed equality of rights for every member of the state. Class or national inequality was thus a glaring violation of the rule of law. Here Kotliarevskii points to the egregious example of the legal position of Jews in Russia (344).[60] He

---

from their violation by state power, and with the readiness to defend them.'" David Wartenweiler, *Civil Society and Academic Debate in Russia, 1905–1914* (Oxford: Clarendon Press, 1999), 125, quoting Kotliarevskii, *Konstitutsionnoe gosudarstvo*, 99–100, translation slightly emended. Anastasiya Tumanova also quotes this passage, which makes clear, in her words, that "Kotliarevskii was a true exponent of the position of the 'revived natural law' school, which considered legal consciousness to be the source for the development of law and statehood." See Tumanova, "The Liberal Doctrine of Civil Rights in Late Imperial Russia: A History of the Struggle for the Rule of Law," *Cahiers du monde russe* 57, no. 4 (2016): 791–818, here at 808.

58 He refers here to Bogdan Kistiakovskii's essay, "Gosudarstvo pravovoe i sotsialisticheskoe," *Voprosy filosofii i psikhologii* 17, no. 5, kn. 85 (1906): 469–507, on which see Walicki, *Legal Philosophies of Russian Liberalism*, 369–74. Kotliarevskii's (like Kistiakovskii's) use of the term "socialist" is rather general; he affirmed the inviolability of property and condemned the 1905–06 agrarian programs of the extreme left-wing parties in Russia (340–41).

59 Kotliarevskii's opposition to the death penalty (which he repeats at 395 and 400) was another way in which he was a disciple of Vladimir Soloviev. For Soloviev's devastating critique of capital punishment, see *Politics, Law, and Morality: Essays by V. S. Soloviev*, ed. and trans. Vladimir Wozniuk (New Haven: Yale University Press, 2000), 111–23, 171–84.

60 But then he equivocates in his defense of this principle, writing, "This, however, does not entail national equality in the sense that individual national groups ought to have the same position in the state: to proclaim such equality among groups that are unequal in terms of population or culture would be a useless cause" (344).

also advocated for the rights of women, writing that the "humiliating and rightless position of women is not only a great moral evil, but also a cultural danger for any society that permits it. This is one of the main illnesses of the Muslim East, preventing its renaissance, and at the same time one of main advantages of Western civilization" (280).[61] The status of foreigners was another issue facing the constitutional state (346).[62] The resolution of all these problems would follow naturally from application of the basic principles of the lawful state: respect for human dignity, freedom, and equality. Kotliarevskii, ever the optimist, was hopeful about the future potential of the lawful state, even as it developed beyond its current constitutional embodiment. This was because "the lawful state relates to the world of ideas, but of ideas that are unfailingly realized and that transform facts"—the fact, first of all, of unequal power in human relations (350).

Justice, charity, and dignity

In his final chapter, "Metajuridical Foundations," Kotliarevskii presents his concluding philosophical justification of the lawful state. He introduces a new formulation of the position he has defended throughout his treatise. Behind the changing historical forms of the lawful state there remains a constant aspiration, which he now identifies as justice. "The state ought to be lawful," he writes, "because it ought to be just." The premise of justice is the dignity of the human person, the absolute value in the name of which state power ought to be limited and transformed (392, 394–95). Law, to the extent it does this, is just. Hence the idea of natural law, which Kotliarevskii simply defines as the juridical form of justice, writing that its "pragmatic task is to connect the legal order with its moral foundations" (396). At lower levels, justice is formal and deals with general norms (hence its affinity with law), but in limiting power and equalizing human relations, it makes possible progression to the higher morality of compassion, forgiveness, charity, and love (397–400).

In the Christian tradition, the most excellent virtue is charity (agape or love of God). In the *Summa theologica* (II-II, q. 23), St. Thomas Aquinas wrote that "charity is the friendship of man for God," an idea that suggests (and was certainly a source of) Soloviev's concept of divine humanity. According to Aquinas,

61 Since at least 1905, Kotliarevskii had supported women's suffrage in Russia. See K. F. Shatsillo, *Russkii liberalizm nakanune revoliutsii 1905–1907 gg.* (Moscow: "Nauka," 1985), 259–60.

62 Kotliarevskii cites V. M. Gessen, *Poddanstvo: Ego ustanovlenie i prekrashchenie*, vol. 1 (St. Petersburg: Pravo, 1909), which argued that growing recognition of the rights of foreigners was evidence of progress in international law. See Eric Lohr, "The Ideal Citizen and Real Subject in Late Imperial Russia," *Kritika: Explorations in Russian and Eurasian History* 7, no. 2 (2006): 173–94. Contrary to Gessen's and Kotliarevskii's optimism, violence against foreigners and "enemy" minorities (expropriations, looting, riots, purges, deportations) was a major dimension of Russia's wartime experience. See Eric Lohr, *Nationalizing the Russian Empire: The Campaign against Enemy Aliens during World War I* (Cambridge, MA: Harvard University Press, 2003).

no true virtue is possible without charity. Soloviev agreed. In *The Justification of the Good*, he wrote that if "justice demands charity and mercy … it clearly cannot be a virtue by itself, distinct from charity."[63] In the ordinary philanthropic sense of the term, charity begins privately, develops organizationally and institutionally in civil society (of which charitable associations are a major component), and may infuse the state itself with its spirit (401–03).[64] This last ideal, Kotliarevskii notes, was what Vladimir Soloviev meant when he called the state "collectively organized pity" and charged it with the duty of meeting every person's right to a dignified existence.[65] Kotliarevskii's ideas were deeply indebted to Soloviev:

> Power ought to be limited by law in the name of justice, and justice ought to be fulfilled by active charity, which in a certain sense is a higher justice, flowing from the dignity of the human person and from consciousness of cosmic and moral unity. The higher level gives true meaning to the lower, encompassing it. But it is impossible for society to ascend directly to the higher level, and here is the basic justification of the lawful state. Not only is there no contradiction between it and higher moral-cultural forms, but the path to them lies through it. The lawful state is, so to speak, a *threshold*. (403–04)

The lawful state is a step on the path toward the realization of divine humanity. Kotliarevskii's idea of the lawful state fitted perfectly into Soloviev's concept of the "justification of the good."

Kotliarevskii left no doubt that his philosophy of law required a theistic metaphysics. "The dignity of the human person," he wrote, "cannot be substantiated from a limited scientific-empirical worldview." Its source is transcendent and can be fully apprehended only in religious consciousness and experience (395, 411–12).[66] In this connection, he returned to the question of theocracy, recalling that it was the first form of the lawful limitation of power, at a stage when law was not clearly differentiated from morality and religion. But theocracy has long since outlived its historical justification and has become incompatible with modern legal consciousness in two main respects. First, "it imposes on the state tasks alien to its nature, tasks that it thus can realize only through constant extreme coercion, and moreover in spheres of the human spirit that most demand freedom and intimacy." Hence, the importance of separation of church and state

63 Vladimir Solovyov, *The Justification of the Good: An Essay on Moral Philosophy*, trans. Nathalie A. Duddington, ed. Boris Jakim (Grand Rapids, MI: William B. Eerdmans, 2005), 86. See also Walicki, *Legal Philosophies of Russian Liberalism*, 204.

64 See Adele Lindenmeyr, *Poverty Is Not a Vice: Charity, Society, and the State in Imperial Russia* (Princeton, NJ: Princeton University Press, 1996).

65 For the formulation of the state as collectively organized pity or compassion, see Solovyov, *The Justification of the Good*, 385.

66 Here he refers to the "great significance" of William James, especially his *Varieties of Religious Experience* (412n).

and freedom of conscience, without which the full development of religious consciousness and thus also the deepest type of respect for human dignity are impossible (412–13).[67] Second, theocracy debases the religious ideal by identifying it too closely with the temporal and relative. A proper balance must be sought between this type of conflation ("religious materialism"), on one hand, and absolute separation of the two worlds ("religious spiritualism"), on the other. "Above one-sided religious materialism and religious spiritualism, there rises faith in the drawing in of the world and humanity toward the divine" (414). This "drawing in" is nothing other than the process of divine humanity. For Kotliarevskii, the lawful state was an integral part (if only a part) of this process. "Its realization," he concludes, "is a necessary link in the creative work that raises humanity from captivity to its physical elements to spiritual freedom" (411).

67 Pointing to the central importance of the concept of human dignity in the American and French declarations of rights, Kotliarevskii notes that the revolutionary political philosophy behind them was closely tied to the religious movements of the seventeenth century, especially to the struggle for freedom of conscience (394n). He refers here to Georg Jellinek's classic work, *Die Erklärung der Menschen- und Bürgerrechte: Ein Beitrag zur modernen Verfassungsgeschichte* (Leipzig: Duncker and Humblot, 1895), which advanced the argument and was well known among Russian legal scholars. In *Konstitutsionnoe gosudarstvo*, Kotliarevskii writes, "Religious freedom was apparently the progenitor of all 'natural rights'—a fact that ought to be borne in mind by adepts of the exclusively economic interpretation of history" (81–82).

13 Nikolai Alekseev

Advocate of social justice and global peace

Martin Beisswenger

Nikolai Nikolaevich Alekseev (1879–1964) was not an entirely typical representative of the Russian religious renaissance of the early twentieth century. Like many other Russian religious thinkers of his generation, he underwent a transition from Marxism to idealism, and later to the Christian religion. He was unusual, however, in that besides his intellectual inquiries, he also spent considerable time and effort on practical issues directly related to his scholarly and philosophical ideas: as an organizer of student protests in imperial Russia, a patriotic activist during World War I, a pro-democracy agitator in the Russian Revolution and Civil War, a soldier of the White armies, a member of the Russian émigré Eurasianist movement, and an ecumenical Christian activist in the practice-oriented Life and Work movement (rather than its more theoretical counterpart, Faith and Order). Practical activity was essential to Alekseev's belief. As he declared in the late 1930s: "Faith proves itself through deed and wants to be realized; faith without deed is dead."[1] It is surprising that, despite his prominence both in Russia and abroad, Alekseev remains one of the least known and least studied representatives of the Russian religious renaissance.[2]

Alekseev's breadth of interest is astonishing. Trained as a legal scholar, he was interested in general questions of philosophical inquiry, epistemology, the intellectual history of legal, social, and philosophical concepts, international relations, Russian and European legal thought, Russian history, political and legal theory,

1 N. N. Alekseev, "Christentum, Recht und internationale Beziehungen," [Oekumenischer Rat für praktisches Christentum. Forschungsabteilung] [March 1937], 25, Bibliothèque de Genève, Alekseev papers (henceforth BdG AP), Ms. l.e. 284. Alekseev's statement echoes the view of faith and works in James 2:14-26. The Life and Work movement and the Faith and Order movement of the 1920s and 1930s were the two main streams of the Ecumenical Movement that combined to form the World Council of Churches in 1948.

2 Among the few studies devoted to Alekseev are several brief encyclopedia entries as well as a few comprehensive works: I. V. Borshch, *Nikolai Alekseev kak filosof prava* (Moscow: Iurlitinform, 2015) and B. V. Nazmutdinov, *Zakony iz-za granitsy: Politiko-pravovye aspekty klassicheskogo evraziistva* (Moscow: Norma, 2017). There are shorter biographical sketches of Alekseev's life and thought: V. A. Tomsinov, "Nikolai Nikolaevich Alekseev," in *Rossiiskie pravovedy XVIII–XX vekov: Ocherki zhizni i tvorchestva*, 2nd rev. ed., 3 vols. (Moscow: Zertsalo-M, 2015), 3:236–51.

DOI: 10.4324/9781003017097-13

human rights, and questions of war and peace. He commented on political and cultural issues of his time concerning not only Russia and the Soviet Union but also Europe, the United States, and beyond. Alekseev's life and work, and his intellectual journey from Marxism to idealism and, later, to Christianity, as well as his special focus on questions of religion, law, and the state, deserve detailed investigation.

From student radical to legal scholar

Alekseev was born in Moscow in 1879 into the family of a provincial noble from Ryazan Province. His father had studied law at Moscow University with Boris Chicherin and other famous Russian scholars and even envisaged a scholarly career. But after his marriage, Alekseev *père* had to abandon those plans and became a minor official in the Moscow Region Transportation Department.[3] Nikolai Alekseev's parents had a strong but rather contrasting influence on him. His father instilled in him a love for books, learning, and the desire to study some day at Moscow University. His mother, in her earlier years an emancipated "student radical," influenced his social and political outlook. Through her, Alekseev became familiar with the radical populism and nihilism of the 1860s and developed a passionate commitment to social justice. He came to despise government authority and, already as a schoolboy, having personally observed Emperor Aleksander III's visit to Moscow, concluded: "I am not with the tsar, I am with the 'populists.'"[4]

The 1896 Khodynka tragedy, where numerous people were killed in a panic during the celebration of Nicholas II's coronation, prompted Alekseev and his friends to embark on studying "serious" literature. They read the writings of radical thinkers, such as Dmitrii Pisarev and Nikolai Dobroliubov, as well as Aleksei Bakh's booklet *Tsar-Hunger*. During their summer holidays on the outskirts of Moscow, Alekseev and his peers were introduced through one of his friends into the milieu of "professional revolutionaries" and the incipient Social Democratic Party. By the end of the century, "the infantile-Bolshevik" period of Alekseev's life had taken full shape.[5] He was *au courant* with the radical revolutionary literature of the day, Russian and European, and studied and discussed Karl Marx's *Capital* together with his first girlfriend, as was the custom among the members of his circle.[6]

Alekseev's early radicalism gradually receded after he entered the law faculty of Moscow University in 1900. Eager to accomplish the scholarly career denied to his father, he enjoyed his new freedom for intellectual pursuits. His summer visit to Germany in 1901 gave him a more realistic view of the world.[7] But Alekseev's

3 N. N. Alekseev, "V burnye gody," pt. 1, chap. 1, "Roditeli," BdG AP, Ms. l.e. 282a.

4 Alekseev, "V burnye gody," pt. 1, chap. 3, "Pereezd v Moskvu i postuplenie v gimnaziiu," and chap. 4, "Kak my stali revoliutsionerami": ibid.

5 Alekseev, "V burnye gody," pt. 1, chap. 4: ibid.

6 Ibid.

7 N. N. Alekseev, "V burnye gody: Na pervykh stupeniakh nashei alma mater," *Novyi zhurnal*, no. 53 (1958): 172–88, here at 181 and 188.

deradicalization was due mostly to his acquaintance with Pavel Novgorodtsev, whose lectures on the history of political thought he attended in the 1901–02 academic year. Alekseev immediately fell under Novgorodtsev's personal and scholarly spell. Later he enthusiastically remembered how "the history of political thought became, in [Novgorodtsev's] presentation, a history of the philosophy of law, and even more, an introduction to social philosophy." Novgorodtsev also introduced Alekseev to the philosophy of Immanuel Kant, in particular the idea "that the human person is the highest value," that "one must not use the human being as a means," and that human beings are "ends in themselves."[8] Alekseev joined Novgorodtsev's "practical classes," which were attended by "the most intelligent and educated students of the entire Law Faculty."[9] Soon he became a member of Novgorodtsev's "school," which, according to Alekseev, included people with very different philosophical views, from materialists to Hegelians, the most prominent of whom were the emotional and passionate Boris Vysheslavtsev (later to become Alekseev's brother-in-law) and Ivan Ilyin, endowed with "pure intellect," the creator of "straightforward systems and lifeless schemas."[10]

Moscow University provided Alekseev with a stimulating intellectual environment. Still, his scholarly career nearly ended in 1902. Having moved away from radicalism, he nevertheless remained (as did Novgorodtsev) an advocate of democratic transformations in imperial Russia. During student protests in February 1902, he was among the nine hundred and twelve students of Moscow University who demanded student autonomy but also civil rights and the introduction of an eight-hour workday.[11] Together with the other protesters, he was arrested and sentenced to six months in prison. Although pardoned in July 1902, the students were banned from resuming their studies.[12] The ban was lifted the following year, but in the meantime, Alekseev found employment as tutor of the statesman and diplomat Count P. A. Shuvalov's grandson, with whom he spent the 1902–03 academic year in Dresden. This contact with imperial Russia's high society revealed to Alekseev the vast social and cultural gap separating the elite from ordinary people and fostered his pessimism about the empire's stability. At the same time, while in Dresden, Alekseev audited courses in physics and the history of philosophy at the Politechnikum and, at a meeting of Russian students, lectured on the landmark collection *Problems of Idealism* (1902) that had just caused a stir in Russia.[13]

8 N. N. Alekseev, "V burnye gody: Nash akademicheskii mir," *Novyi zhurnal*, no. 54 (1958): 148–63, here at 149.

9 Ibid., 148.

10 Ibid., 161.

11 N. N. Alekseev, "V burnye gody: Russkoe studenchestvo i revoliutsiia 1905 goda," *Grani*, no. 47 (1960): 102–15, here at 103–04.

12 Ibid., 105–10.

13 Alekseev, "V burnye gody," pt. 1, chap. 8, "Iz tiurmy v 'vysshii svet'," BdG AP, Ms. l.e. 282a. On *Problems of Idealism*, see Chapter 11 of this volume.

When Alekseev resumed his studies at Moscow University in the fall of 1903, he had wholly shed his infatuation with Marxism and had embraced idealism. In a report for Novgorodtsev's seminar that he soon turned into his first publication, Alekseev even declared the imminent decline of Marxism.[14] Still, he did not refrain from further civic and political engagement. In 1905, following the Bloody Sunday massacre in St. Petersburg, Alekseev again got involved in student unrest. He chaired a student meeting at Moscow University's law faculty and became a representative in the Central University Organ, a student assembly formed in 1905 at Moscow University to coordinate political activism.[15] This did not prevent him, however, from graduating from the university in the spring of 1906. Later that year he was awarded a scholarship to prepare for his master's examinations in public law in the department of the encyclopedia and philosophy of law, focusing on the history of political thought.[16]

After successfully passing his examinations in 1908, Alekseev received a generous research stipend that allowed him to spend two years abroad to prepare his master's thesis while studying with the most prominent philosophers of the time: in Berlin with Alois Riehl and Georg Simmel; in Heidelberg with Wilhelm Windelband and Georg Jellinek; and in Marburg with Hermann Cohen and Paul Natorp. Finally, he visited Paris, where he attended lectures by Henri Bergson and Joseph Barthélemy.[17] While Alekseev later claimed that he belonged to neither of the two German Neo-Kantian schools, he quite obviously "borrowed a lot" from German philosophers, developing his epistemological concepts on a solid Neo-Kantian basis.[18]

Alekseev's publications before World War I give evidence of a profound search for an original methodological approach to the human sciences, and to the philosophy and history of law in particular. He authored half a dozen book reviews and essays on such Russian thinkers as Boris Chicherin, Leon Petrażycki, and Sergei Bulgakov,[19] and on Western European scholars such as Rudolf Stammler and Georg Jellinek,[20] where he offered solidly Neo-Kantian investigations of the

14 [N. N.] Alekseev, "Razlozhenie marksizma," *Novyi put'*, 1904, no. 12: 86–115.

15 N. N. Alekseev, "V burnye gody: Russkoe studenchestvo i revoliutsiia 1905 goda," *Grani*, no. 47 (1960): 102–15, here at 114; no. 48 (1960): 136–49, here at 136, 139, 144n.

16 N. N. Alekseev, "Avtobiografiia," Zernov family papers, box 1, folder "N. N. Alekseev," Bakhmeteff Archive of Russian and East European Culture, Columbia University.

17 Alekseev, "Avtobiografiia."

18 Alekseev, "V burnye gody," pt. 1, chap. 11, "Dva goda za granitsei," BdG AP, Ms. l.e. 282a. On Alekseev's Neo-Kantianism, see Nina Dmitrieva, *Russkoe neokantianstvo: "Marburg" v Rossii. Istoriko-filosofskie ocherki* (Moscow: Rossiiskaia politicheskaia entsiklopediia, 2007), 197–201.

19 N. N. Alekseev, "Russkii gegel'ianets. Boris Chicherin," *Logos*, 1911, kn. 1: 193–220; "Osnovnye filosofskie predposylki psikhologicheskoi teorii prava L. I. Petrazhitskogo," *Iuridicheskii vestnik. Zhurnal Moskovskogo iuridicheskogo obshchestva* 4 (1913): 5–23; "Opyt postroeniia filosofskoi sistemy na poniatii khoziaistva [review of S. N. Bulgakov, *Filosofiia khoziaistva*]," *Voprosy filosofii i psikhologii* 23, no. 5, kn. 115 (1912): 704–35.

20 N. N. Alekseev, Review of Georg Ellinek [Jellinek], *Bor'ba starogo prava s novym* [Der Kampf des alten mit dem neuen Recht] (Moscow, 1908), *Kriticheskoe obozrenie*, no. 5 (10) (1908):

nature of scientific knowledge. He rejected both rigid naturalism and purely metaphysical skepticism and relativism and suggested a third way of inquiry. Alekseev's scholarly work of this time can be summarized by questions such as: What is the philosophy of law and legal thought? How is law possible? These questions also are at the heart of his master's thesis, "Social Sciences and Natural Sciences in the Mutual Interrelations of their Methods: Essays on the History and Methodology of the Social Sciences, Part One: Mechanical Theories of Society: Historical Materialism," which he defended at Moscow University in April 1911.[21] As the title suggests, Alekseev intended to complete his study with a second part, which would focus on organic theories of society. He envisioned this as his future doctoral dissertation. Because of the Revolution of 1917, he was unable to carry out this plan. Parts of his unfinished manuscript were later published in Moscow by his acquaintances.[22]

In 1911, Alekseev's adviser and mentor Novgorodtsev resigned from Moscow University to protest the de facto elimination of the university's autonomy. His new academic base was the Moscow Commercial Institute, whose director he had been since 1907. In 1912, Alekseev followed him and became extraordinary professor and secretary of the institute's academic council. Soon he was assigned the chair of international law. Alekseev was not much interested in international law, however, and published only one article in this field, on the legal status of prisoners of war.[23] Concurrently, he taught various law courses at Moscow University as a privatdocent before becoming extraordinary professor at the university in February 1917.[24]

Alekseev was working on his doctoral dissertation in Paris when World War I broke out. After a tiring journey back to Russia via Switzerland, Italy, and Constantinople, he felt compelled to join the patriotic effort.[25] Novgorodtsev was

62–65; "Sotsial'naia filosofiia Rudol'fa Shtammlera," *Voprosy filosofii i psikhologii* 20, no. 1, kn. 96 (1909): 1–26.

21 N. N. Alekseev, *Nauki obshchestvennye i estestvennye v istoricheskom vzaimootnoshenii ikh metodov: Ocherki po istorii i metodologii obshchestvennykh nauk*, Part 1: *Mekhanicheskaia teoriia obshchestva. Istoricheskii materializm* (Moscow: Tipografiia Imperatorskogo Moskovskogo Universiteta, 1912) (= *Uchenye zapiski Imperatorskogo Moskovskogo Universiteta. Otdel iuridicheskii*, vol. 38). See also Alekseev, "V burnye gody," chap. 12, "Moia akademicheskaia deiatel'nost i pervaia mirovaia voina," BdG AP, Ms. 1.e. 282a. The dissertation received several positive yet not uncritical reviews: P. I. Novgorodtsev, "Nauki obshchestvennye i estestvennye. (Neskol'ko zamechanii po povodu knigi N. N. Alekseeva)," *Voprosy filosofii i psikhologii* 24, no. 5, kn. 120 (1913): 716–22; V. I. Vernadskii, "Iz istorii idei," *Russkaia mysl'*, 1912, no. 10: 123–38.

22 N. N. Alekseev, *Ocherki po obshchei teorii gosudarstva: Osnovnye predposylki i gipotezy gosudarstvennoi nauki* (Moscow: Moskovskoe nauchnoe izdatel'stvo, 1919). See also Alekseev, "Avtobiografiia."

23 Alekseev, "Moia akademicheskaia deiatel'nost i pervaia mirovaia voina"; "Voennyi plen i mezhdunarodnoe pravo," *Iuridicheskii vestnik. Zhurnal Moskovskogo iuridicheskogo obshchestva*, 1915, no. 12: 17–33.

24 Alekseev, "Avtobiografiia."

25 Alekseev, "Moia akademicheskaia deiatel'nost i pervaia mirovaia voina."

then in charge of coordinating the fuel supply of Moscow. Alekseev, too, took up a logistical task. As representative of the Zemgor war aid organization, he left for the Turkish front, where he procured steamboats for the evacuation of wounded soldiers.[26] He was back in Moscow by February 1917 to witness another major watershed in Russia's history.

Revolution and emigration

Alekseev welcomed the February Revolution of 1917 "with that optimism with which it was welcomed by the majority of the Russian intelligentsia." He immediately plunged back into public activism. As a member of the Moscow Educational Commission, created "to prepare the population for the elections to the Constituent Assembly," he lectured soldiers on "the basic principles of the election law and the foundations of constitutional law." Very soon, however, he became disappointed with his mission and concluded that it was "very difficult to instill into the Russian popular masses the rightness of those political principles which, for the consciousness of the Russian liberal or radical intelligentsia, were axioms."[27]

Alekseev later claimed not to remember for which party he ultimately voted in the elections to the Constituent Assembly, but confessed that he had been torn between his social and political views: "Socioeconomically, I was closer to the leftists; politically, I thought that the forms of Western democracy do not suit us, that we need our own political forms." He was repelled equally by the demagogy of the political parties on the left and by "the tendencies toward restoration" on the right. Alekseev voiced his hopes and concerns about the fate of the Russian Revolution in four essays published between June and December 1917 on the pages of the Moscow journal *Narodopravstvo* (Popular rule), alongside articles by Nikolai Berdiaev, Georgii Chulkov, and others.

Alekseev did not welcome the October Revolution. Still, already in early December 1917 he came to the conclusion that the Bolshevik regime was there to stay for a long time.[28] This perspective filled him with anxiety: "The basic contradiction of my attitude then was that I sensed the inevitability of the Bolshevization of Russia ... and at the same time I was troubled by indignation about the violations of national values that accompanied Bolshevism at that time." In late summer of 1918, Alekseev left the country to avoid arrest by the Bolsheviks. He spent some time in Berlin and then joined the anti-Bolshevik White forces, a decision he later attributed to his hostility to the Bolsheviks' antinational agenda.[29]

26 N. N. Alekseev, "V burnye gody: Na turetskom fronte," *Novyi zhurnal*, no. 57 (1959): 191–205.

27 Alekseev, "Avtobiografiia."

28 N. N. Alekseev, "Sovremennyi krizis," *Narodopravstvo*, no.17 (December 7, 1917): 12–13.

29 Alekseev, "Avtobiografiia."

Alekseev's involvement in the Russian Civil War was complex. In the fall of 1918, he moved from Berlin to Kiev, then to Simferopol, where he briefly served as professor of constitutional law. In May 1919 he joined the anti-Bolshevik Crimean Cavalry Regiment, retreated to Kerch' with his unit, and participated in the armed struggle against the Bolsheviks. By early summer of 1919, he was working for the anti-Bolshevik newspaper *Velikaia Rossiia* (Great Russia) in Ekaterinodar. Later he collaborated with the White propaganda organization OSVAG (Information Agency). In March 1920, he was evacuated from Novorossiisk to Constantinople. After spending some time in Serbia, he returned to Crimea in a futile effort to support General Wrangel's last-ditch effort to resist the Bolsheviks. But in October 1920 he had to leave Russia for good and moved to Constantinople with the remnants of the White forces.[30] His life in emigration began.

Trying to find his place in a radically changed world, Alekseev lived for about a year in Constantinople, serving as an administrator in a Russian gymnasium. But soon he was able to resume his academic career. He was invited to Prague by the Czechoslovak government as professor and assistant to the dean in the recently founded Russian Law Faculty. The dean was none other than his mentor, Pavel Novgorodtsev.[31] Elected also as a professor at the Russian Scientific Institute in Berlin in 1924, Alekseev commuted regularly between Prague and Berlin until the early 1930s.[32]

In the interwar years, Prague and Berlin were prominent intellectual centers of the Russian emigration. The atmosphere of scholarly exchange stimulated Alekseev's further philosophical development and intellectual engagement. Although Alekseev began to discuss religious issues in print at this time, we know little about his private religious views and practices. In his memoirs, he mentioned observing religious holidays. But apart from that, his writings have a rather detached and sober attitude to questions of faith and religion. It was not until after World War II that Alekseev's engagement with the Orthodox Church grew stronger, when he played an active role in the life of a Russian parish in Belgrade.[33] It is obvious, though, that already by the early 1920s, Alekseev had developed a strong personal and intellectual interest in religion. Several circumstances may have contributed to this change: first, the experience of the revolution and Civil War, with their upheavals and unprecedented violence; second, his disenchantment with secular liberal democracies, a model which had not worked in Russia and was being increasingly challenged in Europe as well; finally, perhaps, the example of Novgorodtsev, who, after the revolution, wholeheartedly came to embrace religion as the foundation for his philosophy and his life.

30 N. N. Alekseev, "Iz vospominanii," *Arkhiv russkoi revoliutsii*, vol.17 (Berlin: Slowo, 1926): 170–255.

31 Alekseev, "Avtobiografiia."

32 Ibid.

33 V. Nekliudov, "Russkaia zhizn' v Belgrade (35-yi iubilei protoiereia I. Sokalia)," *Zhurnal Moskovskoi Patriarkhii*, 1948, no.1: 66–69, here at 66–68.

Alekseev's interest in religion may also have been stimulated by his engagement with the Eurasianist movement. The movement was founded in 1921 by Russian émigré intellectuals who famously claimed that Russia was neither a part of Europe nor a part of Asia, but a continent *sui generis*—"Eurasia." Recruited by the music critic Petr Suvchinskii and the religious philosopher Lev Karsavin, Alekseev joined the movement in 1926 and remained in regular correspondence with its members until the beginning of World War II.[34] Although he regularly published in the movement's periodicals, and in the 1930s organized its Paris-based section, conceptually Alekseev's Eurasianist affiliation was rather casual.[35] He shared the movement's view that the Russian Revolution was a popular reaction against the artificial Europeanization imposed by Peter the Great and that, over time, Soviet rule would be overcome from within, as soon as the Russian people, based on their Orthodox religion, became conscious of the country's Eurasian character. However, he rejected Eurasianism's fascination with the "East" and its positive evaluation of the Mongol and Muscovite periods in Russian history.[36] Ultimately, his ideas were not in any essential way shaped by Eurasianism. Neither did Alekseev contribute significantly to the movement's ideology.

A new chapter in Alekseev's life opened in the early 1930s. After the closing of the Russian Law Faculty in Prague in 1931 and of the Russian Scientific Institute in Berlin the following year, he moved to Paris, where he "was elected professor of the Russian Law Courses at the Sorbonne—courses that during this particular period eked out their existence in name only."[37] The same year also saw the publication of Alekseev's most comprehensive jurisprudential study, his *Teoriia gosudarstva* (The theory of the state), the latest in a series of publications that strongly resemble more traditional textbooks despite exhibiting some of the author's original ideas.[38] The Paris years also allow us a rare glimpse into Alekseev's private life. As his memoir and correspondence suggest, by the end of the 1930s he was married and was raising a twelve-year-old stepdaughter.[39] He

34 Gosudarstvennyi arkhiv Rossiskoi Federatsii [henceforth GARF], f. 5783, op. 1, d. 359, l. 172.

35 For a comprehensive analysis of Alekseev's role in Eurasianism, see Nazmutdinov, *Zakony iz-za granitsy*.

36 On the Eurasianist movement, see Sergey Glebov, *From Empire to Eurasia: Politics, Scholarship, and Ideology in Russian Eurasianism, 1920s–1930s* (DeKalb: Northern Illinois University Press, 2017).

37 Alekseev, "Avtobiografiia."

38 N. N. Alekseev, *Vvedenie v izuchenie prava* (Moscow: Izdanie Moskovskoi Prosvetitel'noi Komissii, 1918); *Obshchee uchenie o prave. Kurs lektsii, prochitannykh v Tavricheskom universitete v 1918/19 godu* (Simferopol, 1919); *Ocherki po obshchei teorii gosudarstva* (note 22); *Osnovy filosofii prava* (Prague: Plamia, 1924); *Obshchaia teoriia gosudarstva*, 2 vols. (Prague, 1925–26); *Teoriia gosudarstva. Teoreticheskoe gosudarstvovedenie. Gosudarstvennoe ustroistvo. Gosudarstvennyi ideal* (Paris: Izdanie evraziitsev, 1931).

39 N. N. Alekseev, "V burnye gody," pt. 3, chap. 1, "Vtoraia mirovaia voina i novoe pereselenie v Iugoslaviiu," BdG AP, Ms. l.e. 282b.

had been acquainted with his wife, Tat'iana Petrovna, also a Russian émigré, at least since the early 1930s.[40]

Beginning in the early 1930s, Alekseev's thought was increasingly shaped by the transformation of the Soviet Union and Nazi Germany into powerful totalitarian and antireligious states. He regarded these new political phenomena as an existential threat not only to the very nature of the state as such but also to the Christian churches, to religion generally, and, most alarmingly, to the human person. Whereas in the Soviet Union religion and the human person were destroyed in the name of class, in Nazi Germany this destruction occurred in the name of race.[41] Alekseev presciently predicted the inevitability of the two totalitarian regimes coming into violent conflict with each other, although he tried to assess ways in which this outcome could be avoided.[42] By 1935, Alekseev was convinced that humanity was threatened by its own technological and industrial achievements. Unless a new anthropology could be found, humankind was destined to end up in physical and moral degeneration.[43] In a series of articles, Alekseev attempted to provide a philosophical foundation for such a new anthropology and planned to turn these efforts into a book, tentatively titled *O poslednikh veshchakh* (On last things), which he never completed.[44]

At that time, Alekseev was concerned not just with philosophical considerations but also with more active strategies to counteract humankind's existential crisis. Already in the early 1930s he had been one of the editors of *Demain?*, an international journal devoted to questions of religious freedom and social justice. Published in Paris by the French-Irish Protestant aristocrat Hubert de Monbrison in collaboration with, among others, the Swiss nonconformist Denis de Rougemont, *Demain?* featured reports on the situation of believers in countries all over the world.[45]

Quite possibly as a consequence of his collaboration with *Demain?*, in 1935 Alekseev became involved in the ecumenical Life and Work movement based in Geneva. In preparation for the movement's Oxford Conference in 1937, he authored at least eight analytical essays on various current questions, such as the relations between church and state and the nature of the human person.

40 N. N Alekseev to P. N. Savitskii, October 16, 1930: GARF, f. 5783, op. 1, d. 425, l. 16–16 ob.

41 See, for instance, N. N. Alekseev, "L'Hitlérisme, le Racisme et la Religion," *Demain?*, no.14–15 (May-June 1933): 4–8.

42 N. N. Alekseev, "La Bataille de l'avenir: le communisme russe en face du national-socialisme," *La Revue hebdomadaire* 42, no. 23 (June 10, 1933): 139–50.

43 N. N. Alekseev, "Tot, kotorogo my ne znaem. Po povodu knigi D-ra Aleksisa Karrel' 'Chelovek, kotorogo my ne znaem,' Parizh, izd. Plon, 1935 [L'Homme, cet inconnu, Plon, 1935]," *Evraziiskaia khronika*, vyp. 12 (1937): 86–91.

44 See, for example, N. N. Alekseev, "Ob idee filosofii i ee obshchestvennoi missii," *Put'*, no. 44 (1934): 27–43.

45 The journal's full title was: *Demain? Bulletin Mensuel d'Information non-politique concernant: Les Mouvements Religieux. L'Athéisme International. L'Antireligion en U.R.S.S. "Les Forces Nouvelles."*

Some of these were published in the movement's collected volumes.[46] Alekseev's primary focus within the Life and Work movement soon became the role of religion and the churches in the solution of the international crisis and the prevention of another war. Alekseev participated in the Oxford Conference as a member of the Una Sancta and the World of Nations section, with a special focus on "The Christian Attitude to War."[47] In July 1939, Alekseev discussed the critical international situation in Geneva with more than thirty other ecumenical activists—a key event in the Ecumenical Movement's struggle for global peace and human rights.[48] From the mid-1930s, Alekseev's antiwar activities and Russian patriotism manifested themselves also in his active participation in the Defense Movement (*Oboroncheskoe dvizhenie*) that called Russian émigrés to the defense of the Soviet Union in case it was attacked by Japan or Nazi Germany.[49]

In late 1939, after the outbreak of World War II, Alekseev left Paris to become professor at the law faculty of the University of Belgrade, where he taught a course on the history of political thought until the spring of 1941, when, in the wake of the German invasion, all teaching was canceled.[50] In 1942 Alekseev was dismissed from the university altogether.[51] During the war he tried to stay clear of contacts with the German occupiers. Interestingly, in early 1944, in Belgrade, he met the German theologian and ecumenical activist Eugen Gerstenmeier, one of the conspirators against Hitler, who sought Alekseev's expertise for prospective separate peace talks with the Soviet government.[52] After the liberation of Belgrade by the Red Army, Alekseev was reinstated at Belgrade University and acquired Soviet citizenship. He continued to teach until the Stalin-Tito split in 1948 made his situation as a Soviet citizen in Yugoslavia unbearable. In 1950 he

46 N. N. Alekseev, "Das russische Volk und der Staat," in *Kirche, Staat und Mensch: Russisch-orthodoxe Studien* (Geneva: Forschungsabteilung des Oekumenischen Rates für Praktisches Christentum, 1937), 5–54; "Die marxistische Anthropologie," ibid, 152–74; "Gesellschaft, Staat und Kirche," in *Totaler Staat und christliche Freiheit* (Geneva: Forschungsabteilung des Oekumenischen Rates für Praktisches Christentum, 1937), 3–19; "The Marxist Anthropology and the Christian Conception of Man," in *The Christian Understanding of Man* (London: George Allen & Unwin, 1938), 83–137.

47 *The Churches Survey Their Task: The Report of the Conference at Oxford, July 1937, on Church, Community and State* (London: George Allen & Unwin, 1937), 306. See also Alekseev's report on the conference: "Vsemirnyi s"ezd prakticheskogo khristianstva v Oksforde," *Novyi grad*, vol. 13 (1938): 152–63.

48 John S. Nurser, "The 'Ecumenical Movement' Churches, 'Global Order,' and Human Rights: 1938–1948," *Human Rights Quarterly* 25 (2003): 851n40. Alekseev is the unnamed "Russian Orthodox" from Paris in Nurser's footnote.

49 See, for example, N. N. Alekseev, "Oboroncheskoe dvizhenie," *Novaia Rossiia*, no. 4 (1936): 10–12.

50 An abridged version of his Belgrade lecture courses on the history of political thought was published after the war: N. N. Alekseev, *Ideia gosudarstva: Ocherk po istorii politicheskoi mysli* (New York: Izdatel'stvo imeni Chekhova, 1955).

51 Alekseev, "Avtobiografiia."

52 Alekseev, "V burnye gody," pt. 3, chap. 4, "Germanskaia okkupatsiia v Iugoslavii," BdG AP, Ms. l.e. 282b.

resigned from his position and emigrated to Switzerland with the help of Henry-Louis Henriod, former general secretary of Life and Work in Geneva.[53] He lived in Geneva until his death in 1964. There Alekseev authored his memoirs and continued his philosophical meditations concerning the fate of humanity in an age of existential crisis and the threat of wholesale destruction.[54]

From Marxism to idealism and religion

Alekseev's thought mirrored his turbulent life and underwent transformations from radical revolutionary ideas to idealism and religion. What remained unchanged, however, was his quest for social justice, a goal to be attained in a lawful way and with the help of the state. The latter he understood as a rule-of-law state that protected the moral integrity and inviolability of the person. He rejected the unbridled individualism associated with the liberal idea of the state as a kind of night-watchman. He also refused anarchist concepts of society and, even more, the totalitarian state, in which the individual becomes a tool of state power.

Alekseev's first publication, "The Decay of Marxism," was a personal reckoning with his youthful radicalism. He characterized Marxism's epistemological method as "uncritical positivism" that was dogmatic and "based not on critical research, but on naive statements of ordinary human common sense."[55] At this time, when Russian thinkers became disenchanted with positivism, they turned toward an idealist, Kantian understanding of being. Idealism, Alekseev confidently argued, is not only based on a scientifically solid epistemology, it also "practically lifts up the significance of the human person and embodies the demands for its self-worth that are put forward by idealist philosophy."[56]

For Alekseev, rejecting Marxism as a philosophical guide was the easy part of the task. But what should replace it? In a series of critical essays on influential thinkers, both Russian and foreign, Alekseev sought to develop his own concept of how a society should be organized on idealist principles and how social justice should be achieved. In an examination of the German philosopher of law Rudolf Stammler, Alekseev sought to determine how social life could be philosophically understood and legally regulated. He acknowledged that Stammler had worked toward "a new spiritual- and cultural-historical worldview that would be opposed to the naturalism that dominates thus far in philosophy."[57] Yet, by focusing on "an external regulation or a social norm … that lies at the basis of the concept of people's social life," Stammler failed to provide a satisfactory

53 Alekseev, "V burnye gody," pt. 3, chap. 7, "Novaia sotsialisticheskaia Iugoslaviia i Belgradskii iuridicheskii fakul'tet," BdG AP, Ms. l.e. 282b.

54 See, for example, N. N. Alekseev, *Formy myshleniia i atomnaia revoliutsiia* (Geneva: n.p., 1959); *Mir i dusha. Filosofskie razmyshleniia o materii i dukhe na osnove dialekticheskogo realizma* (Frankfurt a. M.: Izdanie avtora, 1953) [pseudonym: N. Kolianskii].

55 Alekseev, "Razlozhenie marksizma," 92.

56 Ibid., 115.

57 Alekseev, "Sotsial'naia filosofiia Rudol'fa Shtammlera," 14–15.

answer. After all, Alekseev argued, social life could be organized according to different "social-philosophical principles" and, consequently, there could be different "social-philosophical types of society." Besides the "universalist" society championed by Stammler, there could be Stirner's "individualist" society or the "spiritual-organic" society developed by Aristotle, Hegel, or Vladimir Soloviev.[58]

Alekseev continued his argument against the absolutization of particular legal norms in a lecture on "Natural Law and Historicism," suggesting that natural law norms were by their very essence neither antihistorical nor valid "for all times and all peoples."[59] Instead, he claimed, it was possible to describe a historical approach to law "as having emerged and gradually developed from the very same natural law doctrine."[60] In Alekseev's view, there was no inevitable contradiction between natural law and history. Alekseev saw confirmation of this approach in the writings of Boris Chicherin, whose landmark *History of Political Ideas* influenced him significantly. Examining the famous polemics between Chicherin and Soloviev over the latter's *The Justification of the Good*, Alekseev sided with neither of them. He praised Soloviev for squarely posing the "problems of the social ideal," yet also agreed with Chicherin's strict methodological and historical critique. What was needed, Alekseev argued, was a synthesis of Chicherin's and Soloviev's ideas: this synthesis would have to "adapt [Chicherin's] theoretical premises, [and take] from Soloviev—the vivid content of the contemporary ideals of life."[61]

There is no doubt that, in the years before World War I, Alekseev himself attempted to produce such a synthesis. He wanted to return from the predominant naturalism of his day to the idealism and panlogism of Kant, Fichte, and Hegel, but without accepting these thinkers in their entirety. His ideal was "some kind of a middle line between Hegel's rationalism and panlogism and the empiricism and naturalism of the sociological and historical theories of the nineteenth century." According to Alekseev, the history of philosophy had already achieved some success in this respect. But the philosophy of law still needed to turn to history, to benefit from its insights, and to develop a new political and legal theory that could face the challenges of the current era.[62]

The Russian Revolution interrupted Alekseev's scholarly pursuits and forced him to turn his attention from abstract ideas to their political and social consequences. He mostly focused on the threat of anarchy, which he saw as a typical Russian phenomenon, a rebellion against all forms of law, order, and statehood. "Anarchists," he wrote, "are the greatest idealists," yet they have an "excessively naive faith in the potential of goodness." They tend to reject "all historical

58 Ibid., 23 and 25.

59 N. N. Alekseev, "Estestvennoe pravo i istorizm," *Voprosy prava*, 1911, no. 1, kn. 5: 5–29, here at 7.

60 Ibid., 28.

61 Alekseev, "Russkii gegel'ianets. Boris Chicherin," 212. On Chicherin and Soloviev see Chapters 6 and 9 of this volume.

62 Ibid., 220.

forms of social life, in particular the order of state and law."[63] The Bolshevik regime, Alekseev was convinced, satisfied the anarchistic and elemental forces of the Russian masses. It was an authentic voice of the Russian people, "a more *organic* phenomenon" than the Russian liberal intelligentsia was prone to think, and would therefore remain in power for years to come. Like earlier rebels, such as Sten'ka Razin and Emel'ian Pugachev, the Bolsheviks expressed the Russian people's yearning for the fusion of "objective truth" (*pravda-istina*) and "moral justice" (*pravda-spravedlivost'*) more convincingly than Russian intellectuals propagating the Western "political values" of a "constitutional regime, liberty, laws, guarantees, etc."[64]

Alekseev found another expression of Russian popular anarchism and antistatism in the postrevolutionary revival of Russian religious philosophy, including his mentor Novgorodtsev's turn toward Russian Orthodoxy and the "East." Russian religious culture, Alekseev admitted, had always prioritized "love of one's neighbor" over love of self, but at the same time, it was lacking in the principles of "order and law." Already, the Slavophiles, in particular Aleksei Khomiakov and Iurii Samarin, had understood the church as "the divine grace of mutual love," where there was no hierarchy, "no place for authority and respect," and where "all are equal, except God Himself." This understanding inspired "a free unity of people on earth, achieved by an inner law." Unfortunately, according to Alekseev, "the state and law cannot" be part of this unity; they "are simple historical outgrowths, epiphenomena."[65]

In Alekseev's view, it was "the tragedy of Russian history" that Russia had to build a state "that was not sanctified by the acceptance of supraindividual values" and that "laws had to be created without the acceptance of the moral force of laws." On the surface, the "ideology of Russian statehood" was an "ideology of theocratic absolutism that justified the divine foundation of the state's unlimited power." Yet "in its inner essence, this state absolutism demonstrates a certain ... *mechanical* character." Since Ivan IV (the Terrible, r. 1547–84), Alekseev argued, the Russian state "was not a reflection of the eternal order of the universe, not a likeness of the divine cosmos, [but] a defense against rebellion." Unlike Hobbes's "Leviathan," the Russian state was not created on the basis of a mutual political contract but was imposed upon its subjects from the outside by force.[66]

The preeminent task of the postrevolutionary philosophy of law, Alekseev concluded, was to change this attitude. It had to revise the fateful contradictions between religion, law, and the state in Russia. "Oddly enough, among the contemporary Russian religious strivings, sometimes views emerge that tend to destroy both law and the state. They declare law to be the equivalent of force,

63 N. N. Alekseev, "Anarkhizm," *Narodopravstvo*, no.2 (1917): 2–3.

64 Alekseev, "Sovremennyi krizis," *Narodopravstvo*, no.17 (December 7, 1917): 13.

65 N. N. Alekseev, "O kharaktere i osobennostiakh russkoi filosofii prava," *Novaia Russkaia Kniga*, 1923, no.2: 5–8, here at 5–6.

66 Ibid., 6–7.

and the state—the vessel of the devil. Russian religious philosophy must nurture [*vynosit'*] and bless the idea of law and of the state."[67] With this powerful statement Alekseev set the postrevolutionary research agenda that would occupy him for at least the next two decades and lead to a systematic examination of religious justifications of law and state—something more than the epistemological justifications that had satisfied him before the Russian Revolution.

Toward an Orthodox rule-of-law state

In three essays published in the second half of the 1920s, Alekseev examined the historical relation between the Christian religion, law, and the state, in effect producing a sweeping history of political thought. The Old Testament, Alekseev argued, depicted ancient Israel as a theocracy with a negative attitude to the earthly kingdom. The latter was seen as a punishment for the fall from divine grace. The state was portrayed "as the refuge of the impious, as the kingdom of the spirit of darkness."[68]

The New Testament presented a more ambiguous view of the state. Preaching loyalty to the secular powers, Christianity also welcomed the deposition of unjust rulers and could, under certain circumstances, reject worldly power and the state as creations of the Antichrist. Medieval Catholic authors later created the formula of the "just earthly state" (*pravednoe zemnoe gosudarstvo*) and developed "the basic dogmas of the democratic theory of the state: the teaching of the contractual origin of state power, of popular sovereignty, of resistance against unjust rule, etc." Thus, in one way or another, Christian authors agreed that "in a Christian state, the power of the state must be based on a contract as it was in the Bible."[69]

Christianity, Alekseev summarized, ascribes value only to earthly power that is "just," or, using Leon Petrażycki's terminology, "to power that is not the power of the master, but the power of service to society [*vlast' sotsialnogo sluzheniia*]." Here Alekseev advanced a concept of service that would later become central for his social theory. Already the church fathers "considered the legal interpretation of monarchy—the view of the king as the highest office, constrained by law—to be the only theory of kingly power in accord with Christianity." In other words, "they considered the view of the kingdom as *a rule-of-law state* to be compatible with the teaching of Christ."[70] Still, Alekseev observed, from the most ancient times there existed also a pagan tradition in which religion and monarchy were tightly

67 N. N. Alekseev, "P. I. Novgorodtsev i russkaia filosofiia prava," *Rul'*, no. 1038 (May 4, 1924): 7.

68 N. N. Alekseev, "Ideia 'Zemnogo grada' v khristianskom verouchenii," in *Russkii narod i gosudarstvo*, ed. A. Dugin and D. Taratorin (Moscow: Agraf, 2003), 21–47, here at 30 [originally in *Put'*, 1926, no. 5].

69 Ibid., 33, 38, 43.

70 N. N. Alekseev, "Khristianstvo i ideia monarkhii," in *Russkii narod i gosudarstvo*, 48–67, here at 55–57 [originally in *Put'*, 1927, no. 6].

intertwined with the idea of sacred kingship (*tsarebozhestvo*), so that ruler and god were one and the same. In this view, power can only be absolute. Emerging first in the Assyrian, Babylonian, and Persian empires, this model was later transferred to the Greco-Roman world and entered Christianity, manifesting itself in the "the divinization of emperors." Remnants of these pagan traditions were particularly evident in the Muscovite tsardom, both in the ideology of Iosif Volotskii and in the rule of Ivan IV, when "Orthodox monarchism was the Russian version of an ancient pagan idea somewhat softened by Christian influences."[71]

The repressive character of the Russian state was conditioned by the permanent threat from Asian nomads. This explains the character of the Russian state as a "military society, built like a large army and based on the principle of harsh service [*tiaglo*]." Still, alternatives to the "official" ideology of Muscovy were deeply embedded in the popular masses: the idea of a secular military dictatorship advocated by Ivan Peresvetov in the sixteenth century; the populist, democratic, but "politically amorphous" and "semianarchical" concept of Cossack freedom (*vol'nitsa*); and sectarian-utopian concepts of the state, such as those of the conservative Old Believers.[72]

In 1917, Alekseev argued, elements of all three concepts were fused with the Muscovite principle of dictatorship and realized under the guise of communism. The communist regime was destined to be a transitory phenomenon. "The ideas of democracy, dictatorship, and social justice," on the other hand, would remain essential for Russia's future. However, these ideas "need to be cleansed of materialism and transformed in a religious sense." The result would be an "*Orthodox rule-of-law state* able to combine firm authority (the principle of dictatorship) with popular rule [*narodopravstvo*] (the principle of *vol'nitsa*) and the service of social justice." This concept, too, had a precedent in Russian history in the "Orthodox rule-of-law monarchy," advocated already in the fifteenth century by Nil Sorskii and the Trans-Volga Elders, whose ideas were further developed by Vassian Patrikeev and Maksim Grek.[73]

In 1930, Alekseev complemented his historical argument for an Orthodox rule-of-law state with a philosophical argument. He now declared secular Western legal concepts, in particular those established by German idealism, insufficient. He criticized the Kantian categorical imperative as "empty," as ultimately leading merely to the establishment of an "order of [earthly] life." Due to this lack of content, the "ethics of idealism ... came close to the ethics of hedonism, utilitarianism, and materialism, which also denied the absoluteness of moral principles."

71 Ibid., 49, 51–52, 59, 64.

72 N. N. Alekseev, "Russkii narod i gosudarstvo," in *Russkii narod i gosudarstvo*, 68–119, here at 73, 83, 107 [originally in *Put'*, 1927, no. 8].

73 Ibid., 114–16, 84. Nil Sorskii (d. 1508) and the Trans-Volga Elders were contemplative monks who criticized the wealth of Russian monasteries. They also opposed reliance on state power and the use of violence to combat heresy. Vassian Patrikeev (d. after 1532) and Maksim Grek (Maximus the Greek, d. 1556) were monastic intellectuals whose editing of ecclesiastical books and discussion of other reforms earned them years of imprisonment.

Yet all moral values, Alekseev insisted, ultimately "receive their only genuine manifestation and expression in religion." The same is true for law, historically "equally connected with both religion and morality." In the process of secularization, however, the number of religiously mandated regulations decreased from a "moral maximum" to a "moral minimum," and "the laws of the state were torn away from religion and morality."[74]

Alekseev called for reconnecting the state and its laws with religion and morality, without, however, falling back into Ivan the Terrible's Orthodox dictatorship. For this purpose, Alekseev introduced the concept of "entitlement" (*pravomochie*), which ultimately allowed him, as he thought, to avoid the strict separation between laws that establish rights (*prava*) and laws that establish duties (*obiazannosti*). On one hand, there can be no duties without a certain freedom of choice. On the other hand, rights do not give unlimited freedom, but impose certain limits, although without directly establishing any duties. In Alekseev's view, entitlements could play a vital role in the organization of social life, replacing an abstract concept of law that all too often simply means "a coercive rule that established something as obligatory." Entitlements could provide a middle ground between social regulations that are solely "directed by the consciousness of duties," as in communism, and the other extreme, namely "personal responsibility and freedom," as in the pure form of liberalism.[75]

The conceptual basis for this new balance of rights and duties Alekseev found in the New Testament, in "the principle of service [*sluzhenie*]." This principle, rather than "the right to power," or "imperium," was "the characteristic of the genuine king, the Son of God." Here, "the external law acquires a purely relative meaning"; "personal conscience" and "spiritual consciousness" play a more important role. During the Protestant Reformation, Alekseev argued, demands for the respect of the human person became central, yet in their revolutionary zeal, the Reformers went too far, developing a "spirit of extreme and abstract individualism." This one-sidedness needs to be corrected: "The idea of personal rights must be confirmed in full force as a purely Christian idea, but right must not be torn off from duty; duty must be the ground of *entitlement* and merge in its legal relations into one organic unity." In Alekseev's view, Orthodoxy could play an essential role in this process: "The formation of such an organic teaching on the rights of the person is the basic task of the Orthodox philosophy of right and of Orthodox politics."[76]

But how exactly would this Christian concept of human rights look in reality in a "Christian state?" In Alekseev's view, several aspects were essential. First, there needs to be formal legality (*zakonnost'*): "the protection and defense of the autonomous person's rights must be the basic task of a Christian state." Yet the state must not merely refrain from interfering in people's lives (negative

74 N. N. Alekseev, *Religiia, pravo i nravstvennost'* (Paris: YMCA Press, 1930), 16, 19, 22–23, 30–31.

75 Ibid., 49, 55, 63.

76 Ibid., 91–93, 96–97.

freedom). On the contrary, "only a policy that vests the state with a positive mission complies with love and the service of society." The duty of the Christian state is to "improve the material conditions" of its people, to foster their "creative activities and to involve [them] in social construction." In other words, the state must provide people with positive freedoms; it must help them satisfy "their cultural and spiritual interests" on a broad scale.[77] Alekseev later systematized these principles into what he called the "guarantor-state" (*garantiinoe gosudarstvo*), a state with "a positive mission," called "to assist in the realization of certain positive social principles, of a certain permanent sociopolitical program." Far from being a totalitarian ideology, this program would be accepted "by people of a wide variety of philosophical, scientific, or religious convictions." At the same time, Alekseev's guarantor-state was an alternative to the liberal capitalist states of Western Europe and the United States, which he perceived as "night-watchmen states," "relativistic," lacking any positive mission, and prone to the accidental changes of parliamentary majorities.[78] What Alekseev had in mind came close to what we would now call the modern welfare state.

Christian churches in defense of the human person and global peace

Alekseev's concept of an Orthodox rule-of-law state also informed his contributions to the Life and Work movement in the 1930s. More explicitly than in his other writings, he emphasized here the key role of Christianity and the churches in preserving both the human person's spiritual freedom within states and the states' peaceful global coexistence. In Life and Work's discussions, the Russian Orthodox position Alekseev represented was close to that of the British delegates, who called for an active social and economic role for church and state and insisted on the need for state and society to conform to Christian values. His position contrasted with that of the German representatives, who conceived of the state as ultimately autonomous and superior to the church.[79]

Alekseev believed that states will exist as long as human beings exist. Their purpose is "not only to facilitate [the human being's] existence on earth, but also to enable him to enter the Kingdom of God." In order to pursue these goals and ensure that human beings are regarded in the political and economic spheres not as means but as ends in themselves,

> the state uses "positive morality," a value that in the West is usually called natural law. In the Christian sense of the word, "positive morality" is nothing

77 Ibid., 101–02.

78 N. N. Alekseev, "O garantiinom gosudarstve," in *Russkii narod i gosudarstvo*, 372–85, here at 372–73 (originally in *Evraziiskaia khronika*, vyp. 12 [1937]).

79 On these discussions, see Kenneth C. Barnes, *Nazism, Liberalism, and Christianity: Protestant Social Thought in Germany and Great Britain, 1925–1937* (Lexington: The University Press of Kentucky, 1991).

> but the secular emanation of Christian love, vested with a very specific normative form, the form of law or a legal norm.

The Christian state plays an essential and beneficial role: "as organizer of chaotic natural forces [the state] contained something of the divine Cosmos; it further developed these cosmic forces of nature, [and thereby] it prepares and creates the ground for the growth of spiritual energies."[80]

It is clear, then, that in Alekseev's opinion openly "anti-Christian states" are not governed by law and thus are incapable of improving human lives. Rather, they cause dehumanization, turning human beings into animals. But what exactly makes a state "legal" and, hence, from a Christian perspective, acceptable? In Alekseev's opinion, it was both necessary and sufficient that a state should accommodate both "centralized and decentralized social forces" and provide a certain degree of internal autonomy. At the same time, however, Alekseev saw no need for the church to advocate for the classical liberal state.[81]

By the mid-1930s, it had become clear that the human person as a free spiritual being was threatened not only by totalitarian states but also by a global war. Alekseev now stressed the positive role of the Christian churches for the pacification of international relations and the establishment of peace. In Alekseev's opinion, Christianity was uniquely suited for peacemaking because of its view that "all human beings are equal in God and in their effort to become like God." Christianity taught that all human beings live in a "mystical union with God and with all other human beings." In the Christian perspective, humanity became "a genuine universal 'communion,' a universal mystical community" that found its expression in the church. At every moment there was an "'all-unity' of all human souls in God." This new Christian concept of human equality, unknown to the pagan world, demanded "a revision of all pagan positive legal institutions" and the "creation of a more humane, more humanistic, and more universal legal system."

Unfortunately, at the time Alekseev was writing (March 1937), "Christian culture" was unable to complete this task, "being defeated in ordinary life by Roman law and the pagan state." Yet this defeat was not final: "the Christian ideal of love" retains its significance "for the further humanization of legal institutions and the institutions of the state."[82] War, Alekseev implied, was a predominantly pagan tradition, for in antiquity individual states considered themselves entirely sovereign. "Their highest law" in relations with other states "was the law of power," and "their last word was war." Yet slowly, among nations, "a consciousness of international solidarity" and an "international ethos" emerged that differed from the "exclusive ethos" of pagan states. Alekseev lamented the fact that the twentieth century witnessed "the rebirth of political and international

80 Alekseev, "Gesellschaft, Staat und Kirche," 12, 16.

81 Ibid., 14, 19.

82 Alekseev, "Christentum, Recht und internationale Beziehungen," 5.

ideologies that reestablish the old idea of the absolute self-importance of the state."[83]

According to Alekseev, only the idea and practice of "Christian peace" can avoid war. Several considerations were important. "Peace, first of all, needs to be a general peace," establishing peace in all spheres of social life. Under the social conditions of "envy, ambivalence, and widespread hostility," no "stable human organizations" can be established. Likewise, no peace can succeed without international organizations and treaties. Yet these organizations need to make clear that they do not shy away from coercion as "'the *ultima ratio*' of law," and that this coercion "will only be enacted if there is no other natural possibility to act otherwise." Ultimately, "the human being needs to justify every act of violence before God." Last but not least, one should not have exaggerated hopes for the Christian idea of peace: "[its] realization will not create the Kingdom of God on earth; it will merely build the conditions for an existence of human beings on earth that is worthy of God [*gottwürdig*]."[84]

Alekseev believed that Christianity had not only a special mission but also a unique ability to act in international relations. Christianity

> is not a theory of two worlds between which there is no transition. Deed serves as a bridge between faith and the real world. Faith proves itself through deed and wants to be realized.... On the other side, deed without leading principles, ideas, or ideals is blind.

Summing up his deliberations, Alekseev declared: "The church can and must lead spiritually." This leadership does not mean that the church "interferes in the struggle of contemporary ideologies but, on the contrary, that it unmasks this struggle and points to the properly Christian paths toward the reorganization of social life that is so urgently needed in our critical era."[85]

Post-Soviet legacy and reception

Alekseev's reception in post-Soviet Russia and elsewhere has thus far not served him very well. Although he is discussed in most recent Russian encyclopedias (with the notable exception of *Pravoslavnaia entsiklopediia*[86]), students of his life and thought have focused predominantly (and unjustifiably) on his affiliation with the Eurasianist movement.[87] One of the reasons for this imbalance

83 Ibid., 6, 9–10, 13–14.

84 Ibid., 23–24.

85 Ibid., 25.

86 *Pravoslavnaia entsiklopediia* (The Orthodox encyclopedia) is a publication of the Moscow Patriarchate. Since 2000, over forty volumes and numerous supplementary entries have appeared (www.pravenc.ru).

87 I. A. Isaev, "Nikolai Nikolaevich Alekseev," *Russkoe zarubezh'e. Zolotaia kniga emigratsii (pervaia tret' XX veka). Entsiklopedicheskii biograficheskii slovar'* (Moscow: ROSSPEN,

may be that the most readily available reedition of some of Alekseev's works was undertaken by the enterprising but controversial Neo-Eurasianist ideologist Aleksandr Dugin, who called Alekseev "the Russian [Carl] Schmitt."[88] Alekseev's Eurasianism also became the subject of less ideologically charged studies by Dmitrii Taratorin, another representative of Dugin's brand of Neo-Eurasianism, and by A. I. Ovchinnikov and S. P. Ovchinnikova.[89] A more serious study of Alekseev's Eurasianism was undertaken by Bulat Nazmutdinov, who failed, however, to fully contextualize Alekseev's Eurasianist activities in his more general views on philosophy, law, and religion.[90]

Alekseev's philosophy of law remains understudied, Irina Borshch's monograph being the exception that proves the rule.[91] Since the early 1990s, some of Alekseev's central monographs on the history and philosophy of law were reprinted, with informative but brief biographical sketches and summaries of his ideas.[92] More recently, Alekseev's post-World War II correspondence with his fellow Eurasianist Petr Savitskii has appeared in print.[93] It is much to be hoped that further editions and reeditions of Alekseev's works will follow and spark a new interest in this unique thinker, whose stormy life and unusually broad intellectual scope deserve to be known far more widely in Russia and abroad.

1997), 23–25; A. V. Sobolev, "Alekseev," in *Bol'shaia rossiiskaia entsiklopediia*, vol. 1 (Moscow: Bol'shaia rossiiskaia entsiklopediia, 2005): 461; Ia. A. Butakov, "Alekseev Nikolai Nikolaevich," in *Obshchestvennaia mysl' russkogo zarubezh'ia: Entsiklopediia* (Moscow: ROSSPEN, 2009), 173–77.

88 A. Dugin, "Teoriia evraziiskogo gosudarstva," in *Russkii narod i gosudarstvo*, 5–20, here at 9. This volume, initially published in 1998, was reissued twice (2000, 2003) with a total print run of several thousand copies. In addition to several of Alekseev's essays, it includes his monograph *Teoriia gosudarstva* (386–624), without, however, indicating its title. Many scholars have taken the title of Alekseev's introduction to the work ("Sovremennoe polozhenie nauki o gosudarstve i ee blizhaishie zadachi") for the title of the entire work. For the original edition (Paris, 1931), see note 38.

89 D. Taratorin, "Oderzhimyi Eidosom," *Elementy*, no. 9 (1998): 92–97; A. I. Ovchinnikov and S. P. Ovchinnikova, *Evraziiskoe pravovoe myshlenie N. N. Alekseeva* (Rostov-na-Donu: Izdatel'stvo SKNTs VSh MVD RF, 2002).

90 B. V. Nazmutdinov, *Zakony iz-za granitsy* (see note 2).

91 I. V. Borshch, *Nikolai Alekseev kak filosof prava* (see note 2).

92 N. N. Alekseev, *Osnovy filosofii prava* (1924; St. Petersburg: Iuridicheskii Institut, 1998); *Ideia gosudarstva: Ocherk po istorii politicheskoi mysli* (1955; St. Petersburg: Lan', 2001); *Ocherki po obshchei teorii gosudarstva: Osnovnye predposylki i gipotezy gosudarstvennoi nauki* (1919; Moscow: Zertsalo, 2008).

93 "'Dorogoi moi drug Petr Nikolaevich': Pis'ma N. N. Alekseeva k P. N. Savitskomu (1957–1961)," ed. B. V. Nazmutdinov and O. T. Ermishin, in *Ezhegodnik Doma Russkogo Zarubezh'ia imeni Aleksandra Solzhenitsyna,* 2017 (Moscow: Dom Russkogo Zarubezh'ia imeni Aleksandra Solzhenitsyna, 2017): 351–445.

14 Ivan Ilyin

Philosopher of law, force, and faith

Paul Valliere

Ivan Aleksandrovich Ilyin (1883–1954) was born in Moscow,[1] the son of Aleksandr Ivanovich Ilyin, an attorney. Ivan's mother, Ekaterina Iulievna Shveikert, was the daughter of a German Protestant physician who made his career in Russia. She converted to Orthodoxy when she married. The Ilyins were of noble rank and owned properties in Ryazan Province.

Ivan Aleksandrovich received a classical education in Moscow *gymnasia* and matriculated in the law faculty of Moscow University in 1901. Ilyin's student years were a time of intense political ferment in Russia, culminating in the Revolution of 1905. Ilyin was a political radical during his student days. His older brother Aleksei joined the Social Democratic Party in 1905 and took part in the armed uprising of Moscow workers in December of that year.[2] Ivan's radicalism, however, did not disrupt his academic work, and he graduated on schedule in the spring of 1906.

That summer, Ilyin married Nataliia Nikolaevna Vokach (1882–1963). Like Ilyin, Nataliia Nikolaevna came from a family connected with the legal profession. Her father was a Moscow attorney, while her uncle, Sergei Andreevich

1 The fundamental source for the study of Ilyin is the edition of his collected works prepared by Yurii Trofimovich Lisitsa. The first ten volumes appeared as a numbered series: I. A. Il'in, *Sobranie sochinenii v desiati tomakh*, ed. Iu. T. Lisitsa, 10 vols. in 12 (Moscow: Russkaia kniga, 1993–99). Volumes appearing since publication of the numbered volumes are identified by title. For Ilyin's biography, see Iu. Lisitsa, "Ivan Aleksandrovich Il'in: Istoriko-biograficheskii ocherk," in Il'in, *Sobranie sochinenii*, 1:5–36; V. A. Tomsinov, "Ivan Aleksandrovich Il'in (1883–1954)," in V. A. Tomsinov, *Rossiiskie pravovedy XVIII–XX vekov: ocherki zhizni i tvorchestva*, 2nd rev. ed., 3 vols. (Moscow: Zertsalo-M, 2015), 3:269–441; Aleksandr Sharipov, *Russkii myslitel' Ivan Aleksandrovich Il'in. Tvorcheskaia biografiia* (Moscow: Izdatel'stvo Glavarkhiva Moskvy/Izdatel'stvo "Delovoi ritm," 2008); and *Ivan Aleksandrovich Il'in*, ed. I. I. Evlampiev (Moscow: ROSSPEN, 2014). Biographical and bibliographical information can be found at www.nasledie-iljina.srcc.msu.ru. For a concise introduction to Ilyin by a leading American scholar, see Philip T. Grier, "The Complex Legacy of Ivan Il'in," in *Russian Thought After Communism: The Recovery of a Philosophical Heritage*, ed. James P. Scanlan (Armonk, N.Y.: M. E. Sharpe, 1994), 165–86. In the present chapter, Ilyin's name is transliterated Il'in in citations of Russian-language sources. The form of the name as it appears in translated works and secondary sources is preserved as published.

2 Tomsinov, *Rossiiskie pravovedy*, 3:287–88.

DOI: 10.4324/9781003017097-14

Muromtsev (1850–1910), was Russia's leading scholar of Roman law and an activist in the cause of constitutional government in Russia. In 1906, he served as chairman of the First Duma, Russia's first elected parliament. Nataliia Nikolaevna was an intellectual in her own right. Early in their marriage, she and her husband translated several works of European social and political thought, including Georg Simmel's *On Social Differentiation* and Paul Elzbacher's *Anarchism.*[3] Their marriage was a long and happy one. Ilyin dedicated most of his principal works to Nataliia Nikolaevna. The couple had no children.

Ilyin followed the conventional path of a young man headed for an academic career in one of Russia's top universities. With the support of his mentor, the Kantian jurist Pavel Novgorodtsev, Ilyin entered the master's program of the law faculty in 1906. He passed his examinations in 1909 and was elected in the same year to membership in the Moscow Psychological Society.[4] In 1910, his first scholarly article, "The Concepts of Law and Force," was published in the society's journal.[5] He also began teaching courses in Moscow academic institutions. Study abroad in Europe came next. The Ilyins traveled widely, although they spent more time in Germany than elsewhere. Ilyin's visit with Husserl in Göttingen, in the summer of 1911, may have been the most significant of his contacts for his philosophical development. Ilyin's intuitionism bears a resemblance to Husserl's.

One thing Ilyin failed to accomplish in Europe was completion of a master's thesis. A thesis on "the crisis of the rationalist philosophy of law in Germany in the nineteenth century" was one of the stated purposes of his sojourn abroad.[6] However, his growing interest in Hegel deflected him from his plan. Returning to Russia in 1912, Ilyin began work in earnest on what would become the most impressive scholarly product of his life, a two-volume exposition of Hegel's thought.[7] He defended the work as a master's thesis in May 1918, but his

3 See Il'in, *Sobranie sochinenii*, 1:363n35. Under her own name (Nataliia Vokach), Nataliia Nikolaevna published "Zigvart i problema logiki" [Sigwart and the problem of logic], *Voprosy filosofii i psikhologii* 22, no. 4, kn. 109 (1911): 449–71, and no. 5, kn. 110: 681–724; and "Bottichelli: Opyt po filosofii iskusstva" [Botticelli: an essay in the philosophy of art], *Russkaia mysl'*, 1915, no. 1: 95–123. The latter is reprinted in Il'in, *Sobranie sochinenii*, 6/1:415–44. Nataliia Nikolaevna contributed two articles on Pushkin to the journal her husband published in the emigration: I. A. Il'in, *Russkii Kolokol: Zhurnal volevoi idei*, ed. Iu. T. Lisitsa (Moscow: Pravoslavnyi Sviato-Tikhonovskii gumanitarnyi universitet, 2008), 225–30 and 757–63. She also published a historical monograph: Nataliia Il'ina, *Izgnanie normannov: ocherednaia zadacha russkoi istoricheskoi nauki* [The expulsion of the Normans: the next task of Russian historical science] (Paris: n. p., 1955).

4 Nataliia Nikolaevna was elected to membership in the Moscow Psychological Society in 1913.

5 "Poniatiia prava i sily," *Voprosy filosofii i psikhologii* 21, no. 2, kn. 101 (1910): 1–38. A version of the article appeared in German translation two years later: Iwan Iljin, "Die Begriffe von Recht und Macht: Versuch einer methodologischen Analyse," *Archiv für systematische Philosophie* 18, no. 1 (1912): 63–88; no. 2: 125–44.

6 Tomsinov, *Rossiiskie pravovedy*, 3:300–01.

7 I. A. Il'in, *Filosofiia Gegelia kak uchenie o konkretnosti Boga i cheloveka* (Moscow: Izd. G. A. Lemana i S. I. Sakharova, 1918), vol. 1: *Uchenie o Boge*, vol. 2: *Uchenie o cheloveke.* The work

examiners, Novgorodtsev and Evgenii Trubetskoi, were so impressed that they awarded him both the master's degree and a doctorate.

The Hegel book sheds light on how Ilyin positioned himself in the Russian religious-philosophical movement of his day. A protégé of Novgorodtsev, Ilyin had to decide whether he would be a keeper of the Kantian flame or do something new. He was a decade or more younger than Novgorodtsev and the other leaders of the Russian religious-philosophical renaissance. By the time he entered Moscow University, Russian idealism had emerged in both its Kantian and Schellingian-Solovievian versions. Ilyin showed character and originality when he decided to explore a less traveled path. In the study of Hegel, he found his *daimon*.

Because of the chaos of the Russian Revolution and Civil War, Ilyin's book on Hegel received little attention when it appeared, and the work was ignored in the Soviet Union. After World War II, however, Ilyin prepared an abridged German edition. Since then, the book has been much admired by Hegel scholars and others, including theologians, who have taken the time to study it.[8] *Pace* Feuerbach and Marx, Ilyin conveyed the theological seriousness of Hegel's thought. Hegel sought a grand synthesis of the Christian faith with scientific and humanistic culture. For Hegel, "the religious essence of the Christian religion, as the 'absolute' religion, is determined precisely by the good news of the realizability of the 'organic identity' of humanity and God."[9] What makes divine-human identity possible is what Hegel called *Geist* (spirit). *Geist* is both human and divine. Human beings fulfill their humanity through the clarification of *Geist* as freedom, while God fulfills God's divinity in and through the consciousness of human beings. The mutual actualization of human beings and God is what Hegel meant by spiritual life.

To what extent Ilyin shared Hegel's theological vision is a matter of debate. Igor Evlampiev, a contemporary philosopher who has written extensively on Ilyin, argues that the position Ilyin attributed to Hegel was his own, but that this fact has been obscured by "the myth of Ilyin as a strict Orthodox philosopher," a myth promoted by Ilyin himself after he moved to the right politically following the Russian Revolution.[10] Before 1918, Ilyin's occasional comments on Orthodox Christianity do not call up the image of a devoted churchman. He

---

appears under the same title in the edition of Iu. T. Lisitsa, 2 vols. (Moscow: Russkaia kniga, 2002). The work is available in English: I. A. Il'in, *The Philosophy of Hegel as a Doctrine of the Concreteness of God and Humanity*, ed. and trans. Philip T. Grier, 2 vols. (Evanston, IL: Northwestern University Press, 2010–11).

8 Iwan Iljin, *Die Philosophie Hegels als kontemplative Gotteslehre* (Bern: A. Francke AG. Verlag, 1946). Theologians and religious philosophers who have drawn on Ilyin's work include Emil L. Fackenheim, *The Religious Dimension of Hegel's Thought* (Bloomington: Indiana University Press, 1967); Hans Küng, *The Incarnation of God: An Introduction to Hegel's Theological Thought as Prolegomena to a Future Christology*, trans. J. R. Stephenson (New York: Crossroad, 1987); and Cyril O'Regan, *The Heterodox Hegel*, foreword by Louis Dupré (Albany: State University of New York Press, 1994).

9 Il'in, *The Philosophy of Hegel*, 1:258.

10 I. I. Evlampiev, "Ivan Il'in kak uchastnik sovremennykh diskussii," in *Ivan Aleksandrovich Il'in*, ed. Evlampiev, 8–28, here at 16.

complained about the "ecclesiastical rigmarole" (*naviazchivuiu tserkovnost'*) he had to go through to marry Nataliia Nikolaevna. He lamented the "hysterical prattling about Orthodoxy" (*istericheskie pravoslavnichaniia*) infecting Russian philosophy in his day.[11] When he talked about ultimate reality, he employed the Hegelian discourse of spirit. While the language of spirit may be heard by some as echoing the Orthodox mystical-ascetical tradition, Ilyin is generally talking about something else when he invokes spiritual life at this stage of his career (and even later). He is talking about cultural creativity in its several modes, such as literature, science, philosophy, and law. For Ilyin, as for Hegel, spiritual life was closely associated with the *universitas litterarum*.

Ilyin's debt to Hegel cannot be doubted, but neither should it be exaggerated. A humorous report preserved in Ilyin's memoirs is pertinent here. Ilyin was arrested and incarcerated by the young Bolshevik regime on several occasions between 1918 and 1922, but he escaped harsh punishment. He was told at the time that his apparent immunity was due to Lenin's esteem for his Hegel scholarship, Lenin valuing Hegel as a forerunner of Marx. As Ilyin reminisced,

> The "tame" Communists (and there were such) used to tell me that I had a good rating at the GPU [the secret police]: they saw me as a "*Hegelian.*" I usually answered that this was a confusion: that I was *never* a Hegelian and that Marx has nothing in common with Hegel. They replied: "Be quiet and make no objections! When we're no longer around, you can put it out that you're not a Hegelian; until then, that's your cover."[12]

During the Russian Civil War, Ilyin stayed in Moscow, lecturing and conducting seminars to the extent possible amid arrests and the upheaval of the time. Following the Civil War, Ilyin seemed to hope that he could resume his professional work under more normal circumstances. In the spring of 1922, he addressed a meeting of the Moscow Law Society, the first gathering of the association since 1917. His theme was "The Fundamental Tasks of Jurisprudence in Russia."[13] In September, however, he was expelled from the Soviet Union along with many other non-Marxist intellectuals. He and Nataliia Nikolaevna settled in Berlin, where, in the spring of 1923, Ilyin became one of the founding faculty members of the Russian Scientific Institute. The German capital would be his home until 1938.

Ilyin's legal thought

In his debut article, "The Concepts of Law and Force" (1910), Ilyin proposes a bold, categorical solution to the question of how we should understand the

11 Tomsinov, *Rossiiskie pravovedy*, 3:292, 322.
12 Tomsinov, *Rossiiskie pravovedy*, 3:353.
13 "Osnovnye zadachi pravovedeniia v Rossii," *Sobranie sochinenii*, 9–10:201–30.

titular concepts. Law and force, he argues, belong to entirely different "orders" of experience. The concept of force "lies always in the order of *the real.*"[14] It pertains to actual processes: physical, psychic, social, political, or metaphysical. Law is a normative concept. It pertains to the order of the obligatory "completely abstracted from any temporality and actuality whatever" (353). Law can be subjected to logical analysis, but this operation takes place within, not outside, the juridical order. The orders of law and force require different methodologies of those who would investigate them. Blurring this distinction vitiates the investigation from the start. Ilyin does not deny the possibility of studying law in terms of its engagement with "forces" of various kinds, as in the psychological, sociological, historical, or political investigation of law. However, he insists that "a juridical definition and examination of law is the logical prius" of all such enterprises (359). If the juridical moment proper (the norm and its logic) is eliminated or bracketed, the phenomenon under investigation will not be law at all but some sort of surrogate, or even its opposite. So, for example, a jurist will reject the definition of law as "defended interest" because an interest belongs to the psychological, not the juridical order, and "a 'defended' interest does not cease to be an interest." On the other hand, a division of labor is acceptable to Ilyin. In the example at hand, the jurist will study what it means to be "defended," while "the psychologist-legal theorist" will study interest "in the measure of [its] recognition through law" (371).

The normative and formalist idea of law that Ilyin elaborates in "The Concepts of Law and Force" stands in the Kantian tradition in which Ilyin was schooled, but the extremism with which he pursued the distinction between the normative and the "real" could not fail to invite criticism. Ilyin's most eminent critic was Bogdan Kistiakovskii, who incorporated criticism of Ilyin in his magnum opus, *The Social Sciences and Law* (1916).[15] Kistiakovskii was a Ukrainian idealist who distinguished his worldview, which he called "scientific-philosophical idealism," from the "metaphysical and mystical idealism" of Novgorodtsev and other religiously inclined philosophers (189–90). Kistiakovskii believed that the defense of absolute values against positivism could be, and should be, a secular and scientific enterprise.

Kistiakovskii criticized "The Concepts of Law and Force" on two grounds. First, he charged that Ilyin's position suffered from formalism. Ilyin "confuses

14 Philip Grier's translation of "The Concepts of Law and Power" is incorporated as an appendix in Ivan Alesksandrovich Il'in, *On the Essence of Legal Consciousness*, ed., trans., and intro. William E. Butler, Philip T. Grier, and Vladimir A. Tomsinov (London: Wildy, Simmonds and Hill, 2014), 341–73. The quoted phrase appears on p. 346. Grier's translation first appeared in *Journal of Comparative Law* 7 (2012): 63–87. In citations of Grier's translation, I have changed "power" (*sila*) to "force" following Andrzej Walicki, *Legal Philosophies of Russian Liberalism* (Oxford: Clarendon Press, 1987), 363. "Force" also exposes the common thread linking Ilyin's debut article to later works such as *On Resistance to Evil by Force* (discussed below).

15 B. A. Kistiakovskii, *Sotsial'nye nauki i pravo: ocherki po metodologii sotsial'nykh nauk i obshchei teorii prava* (Moscow: Izdanie M. i S. Sabashnikovykh, 1916), 301–17.

the concept of law with law itself"; he reduces norms to the logic of norms. For Kistiakovskii, the aim of law is always a norm *imagined as realized*, or at least *as capable of realization*, and this should be acknowledged even in a methodologically pure distillation of the concept. He agreed with Jhering's maxim that "law exists to be realized." By ignoring the intentionality of law, Ilyin steers legal thought in the direction of a "jurisprudence of concepts" and fails to provide criteria for distinguishing realizable juridical norms from fanciful products of the formalist imagination (313–17). By detaching concept from reality so categorically, Ilyin risks falling into a "scholastic Platonism" (308).

Kistiakovskii also criticized Ilyin for skating too lightly over the concreteness of law. Ilyin recognized that law "can be 'introduced' into the 'order' of the real and 'move' within it," but he failed to explain how this happens (312–13). This point was especially important to Kistiakovskii, who, besides being an eminent jurist, was a leading sociologist. He believed that the values of Neo-Kantian jurisprudence could be combined with the scientific method of sociology and other social sciences to advance the cause of the rule-of-law state in Russia.

Kistiakovskii's criticisms of "The Concepts of Law and Force" were for the most part fair. He could be faulted, however, for not underscoring the most important point of Ilyin's article, a point with which Kistiakovskii surely agreed: the *sui generis* character of law. Ilyin and Kistiakovskii wrote during a creative period of legal thought in Russia marked by the rise of new approaches emphasizing the "incarnate" aspect of law, as Kistiakovskii called it, that is, the embeddedness of law in social, psychological, political, and historical processes (317). Ilyin did not reject these approaches, but he was determined that law should not be swamped by the weight and complexity of the processes in which it is embedded. For Ilyin, no social science, however discerning, will ever arrive *unaided* at the idea of law. The idea of law must be there, and be recognized as there, from the beginning. It cannot be derived from something else. It certainly cannot be derived from force.

Ilyin took Kistiakovskii's criticisms to heart. In his most important jurisprudential work, *On the Essence of Legal Consciousness*, the titular concept presupposes the embeddedness of law in actual experience. The term "legal consciousness" does not occur in "The Concepts of Law and Force." By the time Ilyin began writing his new book, however, legal consciousness had become, and would remain, the focus of his legal thought. Ilyin wrote the first ten chapters of *On the Essence of Legal Consciousness* between 1916 and 1918. He completed the work after World War II. It was published posthumously in 1956 by the press of a Russian Orthodox monastery in Germany.[16]

The concept of legal consciousness (*Rechtsbewusstsein*) came into currency with Savigny and the historical school of jurisprudence in nineteenth-century Germany. However, Ilyin did not receive it from them, but from Novgorodtsev

16 I. A. Il'in, *O sushchnosti pravosoznaniia* (Munich: Tip. Obiteli prep. Iova Pochaevskogo, 1956). The work appears in Il'in, *Sobranie sochinenii*, 4:149–414. On the history of composition, see Grier's description in Il'in, *On the Essence of Legal Consciousness*, 6–7.

and Kistiakovskii. In 1909, Novgorodtsev brought out a survey of modern legal and political theories titled *Introduction to the Philosophy of Law: The Crisis of Modern Legal Consciousness.* In a lucid introduction, he identified the "crisis" as loss of faith in the transformative power of law. As Novgorodtsev saw it, faith in law reached its apogee in the French Revolution and the social and political philosophy of the German idealists. In that time,

> law appeared to be the crown and culmination of cultural development or, as Kant believed, the final end of world history. This was a kind of apotheosis of law issuing from faith in its divine destiny on earth. Hegel merely turned this faith into clear philosophical symbols when he called the state "an earthly god," "the incarnation of the ethical idea."[17]

The subsequent realisms, materialisms, positivisms, and failed revolutions of the nineteenth century undermined this faith. Novgorodtsev, however, did not accept the verdict of the nineteenth century as final. He sought to renew faith in law by making a case for natural law based on metaphysical idealism.

An essay by Kistiakovskii was also important in turning Ilyin's attention to legal consciousness. Kistiakovskii's "In the Defense of Law: The Intelligentsia and Legal Consciousness" appeared in *Landmarks: A Collection of Essays on the Russian Intelligentsia* (1909).[18] *Landmarks* (*Vekhi*) challenged the Russian intelligentsia to rethink their role in Russian society in light of the Revolution of 1905. Radical intellectuals, inspired by liberalism, populism, or Marxism, played a crucial role in making the revolution, but they failed to achieve their aims. Neither liberal democracy nor peasant socialism nor a workers' state resulted from the upheaval. What did result was the first constitutional limits on the power of the Russian monarchy along with the creation of Russia's first elected parliament. Most of the radical intelligentsia rejected this outcome. As they saw it, Russia needed a second, better revolution. The vocation of the intelligentsia was to bring it about. The *Landmarks* group dissented. What Russia needed most, they argued, was a season of peace, self-examination, and reconstruction. They acknowledged the deficiencies of the new institutions but believed it was possible to work within them for a better future. The group was not of one mind about how best to work for change. Some appealed to religious values, others favored cultural work. Kistiakovskii called for the cultivation of "legal consciousness."

As Kistiakovskii saw it, the low level of legal consciousness in Russia was "the result of a chronic evil—the lack of any kind of legal order in the daily life of the Russian people" (116). Instead of recognizing the absence of legality

17 P. I. Novgorodtsev, *Vvedenie v filosofiiu prava: Krizis sovremennogo pravosoznaniia* (Moscow: "Nauka," 1996), 15.

18 Bogdan Kistyakovsky, "In the Defense of Law: The Intelligentsia and Legal Consciousness," in *Landmarks: A Collection of Essays on the Russian Intelligentsia 1909*, ed. Boris Shragin and Albert Todd, trans. Marian Schwartz (New York: Karz Howard, 1977), 112–37.

as a problem, however, many Russian intellectuals preferred to celebrate it as a virtue. Conservative, religiously oriented thinkers regarded formal legality as morally flawed because it appeared to justify self-interest and individualism. Radicals viewed legality as a bourgeois stratagem for blocking the revolution. Even many Russian liberals were prone to minimize the importance of the legal order. Kistiakovskii cites the example of K. D. Kavelin, a mid-nineteenth-century Russian liberal who opposed the constitutionalist projects of his day because he believed they would be dominated by the nobility (and thereby vitiated). "While rejecting the constitutional state in the name of his own democratic aspirations, however, he ignored its legal significance" (119). Kistiakovskii faulted the liberals of his own day on the same grounds, namely, for putting political struggle (regime change, revolution) ahead of the struggle for legality, that is, for the cultivation of legal consciousness and the rule-of-law state.

In Ilyin's thought, the concept of legal consciousness functions as a means of linking the empirical and transcendental elements of law. His position may be summarized as follows. When one observes a legal system, one sees a set of concrete determinations designed to direct human conduct in a particular context. If one asks why these determinations command obedience, however, one confronts a problem: there is nothing in the determinations themselves to explain this. Even in a hard-wired positivist theory of law, human beings' recognition of law as law has to be explained, whether via quasi-biological concepts such as instinct or adaptation, or via the concept of self-preservation, or in terms of some other material factor. Empirically considered, law is not self-authenticating: it does not tell us why it is law. Terms such as right, justice, fairness, and the like are transcendental. They are nowhere to be found except in the mind, and it is an act of the mind, not something else, that links these unseen realities with the visible determinations of a legal system. This act of mind is the primordial act of legal consciousness. Legal consciousness is "*the living efficacy of law in the human soul.*"[19]

The idea of legal consciousness involves considerable optimism about human beings' ability to grasp standards of rightness. Ilyin embraced this optimism. He believed that "it is impossible for a human being not to possess legal consciousness."[20] Legal consciousness is "already given *in embryo* to each person" (121; cf. 334). This embryonic sense of rightness forms the basis of natural law. Natural law is the sum total of the transcendental values that stand above positive law and justify positive law as they take concrete form in it. The foundation of natural law is human beings' awareness of themselves as spiritual beings. For Ilyin, as for Hegel, spirit is the spark of the divine in the universe. Human beings possess an aboriginal "*will to spirit and to spirituality*" (186). Right springs from spirit. Hence, the most fundamental human right is "the right to lead a spiritually-dignified life" (156). From this right, Ilyin derived "the basic *axioms of legal consciousness*: a sense of one's own spiritual worth, the capacity for self-obligation

19 Il'in, *The Philosophy of Hegel*, 2:63.
20 Il'in, *On the Essence of Legal Consciousness*, 118.

and self-governance, and the mutual respect and trust of people in one another" (185).

If law is grounded in spirit, however, it is equally true that spirit needs law:

> Law in its original, "natural" sense is nothing other than a *necessary form of the spiritual being of a human.* It indicates that order of equal, *free self-sufficiency of each* in which alone spiritual life is possible on earth. From this it follows that law in this sense could be extinguished or become unnecessary only if the basic mode of human existence were to change, that is, if humanity ceased to be *a multiplicity of self-sufficient subjects*, united *by a shared basis of external life.*
>
> (158)

For this reason, Ilyin opposed visions of history or society that predicted the withering away of law, such as Marxism, anarchism, or Petrażycki's dream of an epoch when law will give way to love.[21] Freedom under law and law in support of freedom: this is the core of what may be termed Ilyin's liberalism.

The concept of legal consciousness has numerous practical applications in Iyin's jurisprudence. For example, it explains how legal systems change for the better. Laws improve as the people subject to them become more aware of the transcendental norms of law present in legal consciousness and find ways to concretize those norms more adequately. Improvement is always an option. Hence, a mature legal consciousness will affirm law *as such*, even in the face of unjust laws or poor administration of the law. Socrates's acceptance of the unjust verdict of an Athenian jury was the gold standard of legal consciousness for Ilyin.[22]

Ilyin also appeals to legal consciousness as a way of bearing the burdens involved in a system of positive law. Ilyin had a keen sense of these burdens:

> One who has lived under the burden of a totalitarian regime and terror; who has thought over the essence of material inequality and understood the regular connection between the sizes of the harvests in a country and the quantity of crimes against property; who is acquainted with the essence of the previous Russian suit for divorce; who has been in a convict prison and has heard the rattling of chains on human beings; who knows what corporal punishment is, and has had contact with a person condemned to capital punishment; who saw all that and understood that it is *also* carried out *in accordance with law*—such an individual possesses sufficient psychic motives to no longer trust in a single formulation of the problem of the spiritual justification of law.
>
> (148–49)

21 On the Polish-Russian jurist Leon Petrażycki (1867–1931) see Walicki, *Legal Philosophies of Russian Liberalism*, 213–90.

22 Il'in, *On the Essence of Legal Consciousness*, 165–66; cf. 183, 333.

Justifications of law based on pragmatic considerations such as self-preservation, security, and the like do not solve this problem. They might justify a legal system as a necessity, but they do not address the problem of moral degradation. "Only *a free recognition of law* is not degrading for a human being" (142). That recognition depends on legal consciousness; indeed, it *is* legal consciousness.

The proper exercise of judicial discretion also depends on legal consciousness. Only through an act of intuition, "an intuition of the whole," as Hegel called it, can a judge, "in the spirit of genuine right," bridge the gap between the rule or letter of the law and a singular case. Ilyin also followed Hegel in affirming trial by jury as the best way of engaging a defendant's legal consciousness in a judicial proceeding. Judgment by a jury of peers allows a defendant to see the court's verdict as if it came from his own soul.[23]

Force, fascism, and the future of Russia

"The Concepts of Law and Force" anticipated llyin's lasting concern with the problem of force. The events Ilyin and his generation were destined to endure—world war, revolution, civil war, exile, and a second world war—made this concern existential. The best known of Ilyin's writings on the subject is *On Resistance to Evil by Force* (1925), in which he advocated the use of violence in the struggle against Bolshevism. His rhetoric was at times extreme, as when he called for wielding "the Orthodox sword" against the Soviet regime.[24] The book sparked a storm of debate in the Russian emigration. Some of the leading lights of the religious-philosophical intelligentsia expressed shock at Ilyin's position, which they deemed unchristian. Nikolai Berdiaev branded Ilyin as a propagandist for "the evil good," comparing him to "inquisitors" such as Torquemada, Robespierre, and Dzerzhinsky (first head of the Cheka, the Bolshevik secret police). "The 'Cheka' in the name of God," Berdiaev averred, "is more repulsive than the 'Cheka' in the name of the devil."[25]

The polemics unleashed by *On Resistance to Evil by Force* can make it difficult to arrive at a fair assessment of its contents. It is worth noting, therefore, that Ilyin had covered much the same ground a decade earlier. In the opening months of World War I, he published an essay on "The Fundamental Moral Contradiction of the War," in which he explored the question, "Is it permitted to kill a human being?" Ilyin argued that the question of killing is perplexing because conscience responds to the question in contradictory ways. On one hand, conscience intuitively recognizes the guilt involved in taking a human life. In killing, human beings transgress God's sovereignty over life and death, they violate

23 Il'in, *The Philosophy of Hegel*, 2:64–65.

24 I. A. Il'in, *O soprotivlenii zlu siloiu*, *Sobranie sochinenii*, 5:31–220, here at 33.

25 N. Berdiaev, "Koshmar zlogo dobra (O knige I. Il'ina 'O soprotivlenii zlu siloiu')," in *I. A. Il'in: pro et contra. Lichnost' i tvorchestvo Ivana Il'ina v vospominaniiakh, dokumentakh i otsenkakh russkikh myslitelei i issledovatelei*, ed. I. I. Evlampiev et al. (St. Petersburg: Izdatel'stvo Russkogo Khristianskogo gumanitarnogo instituta, 2004), 658–73, here at 659, 665–66.

the social and spiritual love which knits the human race together, and they effect an outcome that cannot be rectified because it cannot be reversed. The burden of killing elicits responses like Tolstoy's: it is better to surrender one's earthly goods than to accept the defilement that comes from killing. Nevertheless, the same conscience that recoils from killing recognizes that there are also situations where yielding to aggression contradicts morality. For example, if someone tries to force another person to commit a despicable act or attacks a defenseless neighbor, conscience prompts resistance. In such cases, human dignity is at stake. Hence, the moral contradiction of war: conscience recognizes killing as a guilty act yet knows that there are times when one must vigorously combat evil. What is the way out of this dilemma? As Ilyin saw it, there is no way out. The human ethical situation is "*tragic*." The right path is the path of heroic endurance. One must "bravely accept *one's guilty mission*."[26]

Ilyin makes the same argument in *On Resistance to Evil by Force*. The main difference is that he adds Christian content to the argument. Christian faith does not figure in "The Fundamental Moral Contradiction of the War," not even in the pages on love. On love, Ilyin sounds like Hegel. Love is the "social-spiritual fabric of life ... the unbroken, continuous connection of all with all."[27] In *On Resistance to Evil by Force*, however, Ilyin loads his text with references to Jesus, the Gospels, and (to a lesser extent) the church. He also has more to say about love, which he now presents as grounded in God. In the effort to construe love in relation to the practice of force, Ilyin contends that the hero of conscience who raises the sword against an evildoer is actually performing an act of love—not positive love (subjective affection) but "negative" or objective love.

> A person who has smothered the image of God in himself, does not stand in need of a weak-willed, sympathetic "Yes," but of a severe, condemnatory "No," and this "No" that restrains him and brings him to his senses can and ought to have, as its genuine source, love for God in heaven and for the Divine in our fallen and spiritually extinguished soul.

Resistance to evil presents the "*negative face of love*."[28]

What made Ilyin's book controversial was not so much his core argument as his determination to Christianize it. To this end, he devised dubious interpretations of biblical passages, especially those concerning Jesus. With respect to Jesus's command to love one's enemies, for example, Ilyin argues that Jesus was speaking only about one's personal enemies, not "the enemies of God," whom, as Ilyin would have it, Jesus slated for punishment. He also argues that Jesus viewed capital punishment in a favorable light (5:141–43). At points such as these, one can appreciate Berdiaev's vexation: "It is monstrous to suppose that

26 I. A. Il'in, "Osnovnoe nravstvennoe protivorechie voiny," *Sobranie sochinenii*, 5:5–30, here at 29–30.

27 Ibid., 14.

28 Il'in, *O soprotivlenii zlu siloiu*, *Sobranie sochinenii*, 5:147.

the Son of God, the Savior and Redeemer of the world, concerned himself with questions of criminal justice and worked out a system of punishments." Berdiaev viewed the gospel according to Ilyin as "legalism devoid of grace."[29]

Despite the weaknesses of Ilyin's Christianization of the argument in *Resistance to Evil by Force*, his position was by no means the moral and religious travesty that his critics saw in it. Ilyin can certainly be exonerated of the charge that he proposed to induce virtue by force, like Torquemada or Robespierre. He explicitly rejected this idea.[30] He can also be exonerated of the charge of advocating holy war, although his position bears a resemblance to holy war in certain respects. The issue hangs on how one understands Ilyin's notion of "the guilty mission" that fighters for righteousness embrace. The Russian word translated as "mission" is *podvig*, a term redolent of the Orthodox Christian notion of holiness. Ilyin's point, however, lies not in the noun but the qualifier: "guilty." Far from being pure, Ilyin's hero recognizes that he is caught in a web of sin and guilt. For this reason, "the active, heroic struggle with evil *is not at all a direct and immediate path to personal holiness*" (5:187). On the contrary, "man is not righteous; and he does not conduct the struggle against evil as a righteous person or in the company of righteous persons" (5:179). The hero's situation is paradoxical: "he is not righteous, but *right*" (5:208). Ilyin's Christian soldier bears a resemblance to Luther's Christian person: *simul justus et peccator*, simultaneously righteous and a sinner.

Ilyin's exploration of this paradox suggests a wider context in which to set *Resistance to Evil by Force.* Ilyin was not the only modern thinker who wrestled with the challenge of reconciling Christian ethics with what Max Weber called an "ethic of responsibility."[31] In Russia, Vladimir Soloviev embraced the challenge a generation before Ilyin.[32] In the West, Reinhold Niebuhr and Paul Tillich embraced it in their effort to craft a Christian response to Nazism. Niebuhr's "Christian realist" attack on the pacifism of the interwar period turned on the same paradox as Ilyin's: Christians do not fight for the right as righteous persons but as sinners in need of forgiveness, even in their noblest actions.[33] Paul Tillich invoked Luther's idea of "the strange work of love." The strange work of love is the use of force "to destroy what is against love." This ethical formula involves the further discovery "that love's strange work, the compulsory element of power, is not only the strange but also the *tragic aspect* of love" (emphasis mine).[34] Tillich's position was the same as Ilyin's.

29 Berdiaev, "Koshmar zlogo dobra," 669–70.

30 Il'in, *O soprotivlenii zlu siloiu*, *Sobranie sochinenii*, 5:171.

31 Max Weber, "Politics as a Vocation," in *From Max Weber: Essays in Sociology*, ed. and trans. H. H. Gerth and C. Wright Mills (New York: Oxford University Press, 1958), 77–128, here at 119–21.

32 See Chapter 9 of this volume.

33 See "Why the Christian Church Is Not Pacifist" and other essays in Reinhold Niebuhr, *Christianity and Power Politics* (New York: Charles Scribner's Sons, 1940).

34 Paul Tillich, *Love, Power, and Justice: Ontological Analyses and Ethical Applications* (London: Oxford University Press, 1967), 49–51.

Ilyin differed from the Protestant realists in wanting to see a heroic element in Christian ethics. Niebuhr and Tillich would have agreed with Sergei Bulgakov's contention in *Landmarks* that Christian ethics involves a fundamentally different spiritual dynamic than the ethics of heroism: the Christian turns away from the voluntarism, egocentrism, and elitism of the heroic tradition to embrace humility and the theological virtues.[35] Ilyin, on the other hand, casts his Christian soldiers as heroes. They are knights in whom "the Orthodox chivalric tradition [still] lives."[36] They take the martial saints Michael and George as their models (5:141). They stand apart from the common crowd because, as Ilyin believed, the majority of human beings are rarely capable of heroism (5:138, 185). Appeals to heroism and moral aristocratism appear throughout Ilyin's writings. How well these Romantic, at times quixotic, appeals served him is questionable.

A darker fact must also be considered: Ilyin's relationship to fascism. Like Tillich and Niebuhr, Ilyin had to deal with fascism, but unlike them, he was sympathetic to it. His sympathy compounded the controversies surrounding his work, and these controversies have not ceased. Timothy Snyder, a distinguished contemporary historian of Eastern Europe, refers to our thinker as "the fascist philosopher Ivan Ilyin."[37]

Ilyin's contact with fascism began in 1924, when he visited Italy. The Mussolini regime was not yet two years old but had captured international attention. The following year, Petr Struve commissioned Ilyin to report on Italian fascism for his Paris-based Russian newspaper, *Vozrozhdenie* (Renaissance). The product of Ilyin's efforts was a series of impressions published in 1925–26.[38] Ilyin's portrait of Italian fascism was sympathetic but not uncritical. He commended the movement for steering Italy clear of the civil war that threatened it during the early postwar years. Here, as in many of Ilyin's writings on social and political topics in the emigration, the Russian Civil War loomed large as a point of comparison. Ilyin's chief caution regarding Italian fascism was that its patriotism, which he admired, could develop in the direction of an exclusivist nationalism, which he did not admire.

In 1927, Ilyin launched a journal of his own, *Russkii Kolokol* (The Russian bell).[39] Nine issues appeared between 1927 and 1930. In the one article where Ilyin discusses the possibility of a Russian version of fascism, he makes two distinctions that maintain distance between him and such a project. First, he explicitly distinguishes the émigré political association with which he himself was

35 See Sergii Bulgakov, "Heroism and the Spiritual Struggle," in *Sergii Bulgakov: Towards a Russian Political Theology*, ed. Rowan Williams (Edinburgh: T&T Clark, 1999), 55–112.

36 Il'in, *O soprotivlenii zlu siloiu*, *Sobranie sochinenii*, 5:33.

37 Timothy Snyder, *The Road to Unfreedom: Russia, Europe, America* (New York: Tim Duggan Books, 2018), 16.

38 Ilyin's "Pis'ma o fashizme" can be found in I. A. Il'in, *Stat'i, lektsii, vystupleniia, retsenzii (1906–1954)*, ed. Iu. T. Lisitsa (Moscow: Russkaia kniga, 2001), 223–61.

39 The complete journal is available in a single-volume edition. See note 3.

connected, the Russian General Military Union, from fascism. This organization stood on the right wing of Russian émigré politics, but it derived from the White Army of the Russian Civil War, not from contemporary fascist movements.[40] Second, Ilyin devotes most of his article to warning would-be Russian fascists against imitating existing fascist movements, since those movements were operating in contexts quite different from Russia.[41]

The high watermark of Ilyin's sympathy for fascism came in the spring of 1933, when he penned an article for *Vozrozhdenie* on Hitler's accession to power earlier that year.[42] Ilyin seems to have been as surprised as many other observers when Hitler took the helm of the German state in the wake of the Nazis' dramatic gains in the elections of 1932. Ilyin's first response, however, was positive. The point of his article was to combat what he viewed as the uncritical rejection of Hitler by liberals and leftists. He regarded Hitler and Mussolini as allies in the struggle against Bolshevism. He noted the Nazi government's assault on the civil rights of German Jews but did not regard those measures as a sufficient reason for calling the entire German fascist project into question. Ilyin's positive attitude toward the Nazi regime started unraveling soon enough, when he himself came under pressure as a foreign intellectual of independent views. In the summer of 1934, Ilyin was removed from his teaching position at the Russian Scientific Institute for refusing to promote anti-Semitic policies. He and Nataliia Nikolaevna abandoned Nazi Germany for Switzerland in 1938. They settled in Zollikon, outside Zurich, and resided there for the rest of their lives. Ivan Aleksandrovich died in 1954; Nataliia Nikolaevna, in 1963.

The question of Ilyin and fascism is best placed in the context of his political philosophy, the clearest exposition of which is found in the second half of *On the Essence of Legal Consciousness.* There Ilyin argues that the constitution of a state should be geared to the level of legal consciousness in the population the state is called to govern. A country where legal consciousness is rudimentary needs a different constitution than a country where legal consciousness is robust. Hence,

> the wise statesman, introducing political freedom, takes account of the cultural and spiritual level of the masses: he is firmly convinced that the spiritual

40 "O russkom fashizme," *Russkii Kolokol*, 258–68, here at 265–66. On the Russian General Military Union (ROVS), see Paul Robinson, *The White Russian Army in Exile 1920–1941* (Oxford: Clarendon Press, 2002).

41 Ilyin repeated the point in a lecture at a conference of Russian Christians in Geneva in 1937: "What is politically edifying in one country, for one people or at one period, may turn out to be destructive in different circumstances. Hence, Western Europe, which does not know Russia, has no basis whatsoever for imposing any sort of political forms on us—be they 'democratic' or 'fascist.' Russia will not be saved by any new versions of Westernism." I. A. Il'in, "Osnovy gosudarstvennogo ustroistva," *Sobranie sochinenii*, 7:488–509, here at 490.

42 "Natsional-sotsializm. I: Novyi dukh," in Il'in, *Stat'i, lektsii, vystupleniia, retsenzii (1906–1954)*, 316–24. First published, May 17, 1933.

> maturity of the population will inevitably take the form of political freedom; just as the premature seizure or the untimely bestowal of freedom can turn out to be a vain and fatal gift.[43]

"To find that historically best combination of 'solidary self-governance and ruling trusteeship' means to correctly solve the problem of the organization of state *power*."[44]

After World War II, Ilyin composed a series of journalistic pieces exploring what this optimal combination might look like in Russia following the demise of the Soviet regime.[45] His position was that post-Soviet Russia would not be ready for a maximalist liberal democratic constitution because "the art of freedom," that is, the proper balance between liberty and self-discipline, would be lacking in Russia. At least for a while, the country would require a top-down system administered by technically, intellectually, and spiritually qualified leaders. Ilyin described this regime as

> *a firm, national-patriotic, ideologically liberal dictatorship* [that would] *help the people prioritize their own best instincts and that would train the people in sobriety, in loyalty freely given, in self-government, and in organic participation in the building of the state.*[46]

Ilyin called his recipe "creative democracy," as distinct from "democracy at all costs." He believed that the introduction of "democracy at all costs" in post-Soviet Russia would land Russia in anarchy, as it did in 1917. Ilyin acknowledged that his recipe was "authoritarian." He denied that it was "totalitarian."[47]

One way to characterize Ilyin's political outlook is to apply the label that Ilyin's political mentor, Petr Struve, applied to himself: "liberal conservative."[48] One might object that Ilyin's call for an "ideologically liberal dictatorship" is a contradiction in terms, because any talk of dictatorship negates liberalism. On

43 Il'in, *On the Essence of Legal Consciousness*, 279.

44 Ibid., 231.

45 Ilyin's pieces took the form of bulletins to the members of the Russian General Military Union. The Union published a two-volume collection of the bulletins under the title *Nashi zadachi* (Our tasks) in Paris in 1956. The work appears in Il'in, *Sobranie sochinenii*, vols. 2(1) and 2(2). I cite a later edition: I. A. Il'in, *Nashi zadachi: Stat'i 1948–1954gg.*, ed. Iu. T. Lisitsa, 2 vols. (Moscow: Airis-press, 2008). By the time Ilyin wrote these bulletins, the Russian General Military Union had ceased to be a fighting force. It was a veterans' association.

46 "Demokratiia—nemedlenno i vo chto by to ni stalo," *Nashi zadachi*, 1:197–201 (No. 61, July 18, 1949), here at 199.

47 "Predposylki tvorcheskoi demokratii (1)," *Nashi zadachi*, 1:466–70 (No. 134, May 15, 1951), here at 469.

48 See Richard Pipes, *Struve: Liberal on the Right, 1905–1944* (Cambridge, MA: Harvard University Press, 1980), 374–76; and O. A. Zhukova, "Edinstvo kul'tury i politiki: liberal'no-konservativnyi proekt P. B. Struve v sozidanii Rossii," in *Petr Berngardovich Struve*, ed. O. A. Zhukova and V. K. Kantor (Moscow: ROSSPEN, 2012), 98–129.

the other hand, there is clearly a cluster of liberal values at the core of Ilyin's political thought. The entire second half of *On the Essence of Legal Consciousness* is devoted to the proposition that a political constitution must be founded on the irreducible freedom and dignity of the human person. Ilyin also emphasized the need for "*formal* legal guarantees" in contexts where "the best *substantive* guarantee—nobility of legal consciousness—is absent."[49] Comparison with Hegel is apt here. Victor Cousin wrote of Hegel that "he was profoundly liberal without being in the least republican."[50] Like Hegel, Ilyin was a statist and a monarchist, but to deny that liberal values occupied a central place in his political thought is a mistake.

For the same reason, it is a mistake to call Ilyin a "fascist philosopher."[51] Ilyin's thought never manifested such signal features of fascism as populism, totalitarianism, racism, anti-Semitism, thuggery, or the politics of hysteria. One may criticize Ilyin severely for not recognizing the catastrophic vices of fascism from the start. His expressions of sympathy enhanced the prestige of fascism in the Russian emigration and opened a wide door to harmful misuses of his thought. However, for a fairer assessment of Ilyin's lapses of judgment, we do better to cite a verdict Ilyin passed on someone else years earlier. As a graduate student, he wrote a paper for Novgorodtsev titled "Plato's Ideal State in Connection with His Philosophical Worldview." He concluded that "Plato's ideal state seeks to realize progressive principles by reactionary means."[52] The same reproach could be leveled at Ilyin forty years later.

Ilyin's Orthodoxy

Many of Ilyin's later works reflect his devotion to Orthodox Christianity. The best of these is *The Axioms of Religious Experience* (1953), which Ilyin conceived in 1919, although he wrote most of it much later.[53] In design and method, *Axioms* is a phenomenology of spirituality. Ilyin called it "a pneumatic actology," the "act" being the act of faith and its derivatives (1:11, 135–36). What lends *Axioms* an Orthodox Christian character is the extensive use Ilyin makes of source material from the mystical-ascetical tradition of the Christian East, that is, the Greek, Syrian, and Egyptian fathers of antiquity and the Middle Ages, along with studies of these sources by modern scholars. Yet Orthodox sources form only one stratum of the literature on which Ilyin draws in *Axioms*. Hindu, Buddhist, and

49 Il'in, *On the Essence of Legal Consciousness*, 234–35.

50 Ilyin cites Cousin's words in *The Philosophy of Hegel*, 2:275.

51 My conclusion on the question of Ilyin and fascism is basically the same as Paul Robinson's in *Russian Conservatism* (Ithaca: Cornell University Press/Northern Illinois University Press, 2019), 135–36. Robinson finds the "combination of authoritarianism and liberalism" (179) to be a fairly common phenomenon in Russian conservative thought.

52 Tomsinov, *Rossiiskie pravovedy*, 3:294–95.

53 I. A. Il'in, *Aksiomy religioznogo opyta: issledovanie*, ed. Iu. T. Lisitsa, 2 vols. (Moscow: Russkaia kniga, 2002–03).

other religious traditions figure prominently in the work, as do spiritual writers of the Western church and modern Western investigators of religious experience such as William James. Literary and philosophical references abound. Ilyin states that *Axioms* has an "Orthodox-apologetic purpose" (1:13), although he serves this end more by implication than directly. His handling of non-Orthodox and non-Christian spirituality is respectful. The apologetic force of the book lies in the author's assumption that Orthodox Christianity constitutes the fulfillment of human religious aspirations.

In the service of this vision, Ilyin posits a seamless continuity between Christian faith and what he takes to be universal human spirituality. Socrates is a "Christian who did not have to wait until Christ" (1:98). Plato keeps company with St. Basil the Great and St. Gregory the Theologian in "the aquiline soaring of the spiritual mind." To be "wounded by Perfection" (a Platonic trope) is to experience "the salvific wound of Grace." The "fervor" (*tapas*) of the Upanishads and "dry light" of Heraclitus are the same "immaterial, divine fire" that the ancient Christian ascetic Macarius the Great references in the *Philokalia* (1:225–27). Vasilii Zhukovskii, a Romantic poet, had it right when he wrote that "poetry is the earthly sister of the heavenly religion" (2:163). In a late essay on the kind of education he envisioned for the post-Soviet Russia of the future, Ilyin had no trouble imagining a perfect harmony between Aristotle and the Gospel: "For in actuality we all serve a higher Cause on earth—*God's Cause*—'the beautiful life,' as Aristotle called it, 'the Kingdom of God,' as the Gospel revealed it."[54]

Ilyin's elision of Christian piety with universal spirituality in *Axioms of Religious Experience* and elsewhere finds a parallel in the way he construes the role of the church in the constitution of the state in *On the Essence of Legal Consciousness*. "*Legal consciousness and the kingdom of God*," he opines, "live by one and the same psychic tissue, realize themselves in one and the same spiritual sphere. A mechanical separation of the 'Divine' from 'Caesar' will always remain a lifeless fiction, deprived of being and practical significance."[55] The "*spiritual solidarity*" of the body politic is "a living system of *brotherhood*, not only not contradicting Christianity, but corresponding to the spirit of the gospel doctrine" (220–21). In short, "in normal legal consciousness 'Caesar' and 'God' form a living unity" (226). Piety and patriotism also form a living unity for Ilyin, who, in a lecture in 1934, characterized "*the Native Land*" (*Rodina*) as "this living dwelling-place of the Spirit of God, this national treasure house of the Holy Spirit."[56] In formulations such as these, the church as an independent order of grace does not appear. The church forms part of a comprehensive synthesis, part of the "tissue" of state and society along with law, literature, science, and other departments of

54 "O vospitanii v griadushchei Rossii (2)," *Nashi zadachi*, 2:181–86 (No. 181, May 31, 1953), here at 181.

55 Il'in, *On the Essence of Legal Consciousness*, 320.

56 "Tvorcheskaia ideia nashego budushchego," *Sobranie sochinenii*, 7:453–88, here at 476.

the *universitas litterarum*. The integrative function belongs to the state. Ilyin was faithful to Hegel in this respect, but precisely for this reason one might say that he took the edge off the Gospel—the edge of grace, prophetic witness, radical transcendence, and eschatology. Ilyin rarely pondered the Gospel's judgment *upon* law. Nowhere in his writings, for example, does he discuss the jurisprudential implications of the judicial execution of Jesus—the execution of Socrates, yes, but not of Jesus. He passed over the more difficult case—more difficult, that is, for a jurist and philosopher of law.

Ilyin's legacy

Ilyin's way of construing the relationship between God and Caesar bears on his legacy in Russia today. Since the massive task of rebuilding the culture and polity of Russia got underway following the collapse of the Soviet Union in 1991, Ilyin's thought has appealed to those who seek to restore Orthodoxy as an essential element of Russian national identity and, to that end, promote a close relationship between the Orthodox Church and the Russian state. Given the arbitrariness and cruelty of the Soviet regime's repression of Orthodoxy, the restorationist movement is completely understandable. Nevertheless, it is fraught with tension. Post-Soviet Russia has a secular constitution, and although the Orthodox Church enjoys great visibility and patronage in Russian public life today, its position is not as secure as its quasi-established status might suggest. Collaboration between the church and Caesar in Russia today has an improvised quality about it because the constitution cannot sanction the integration of the two. How Orthodoxy should be accommodated in the legal and political order of Russia is a problem that neither Russian jurisprudence nor Russian Orthodox theology has solved. Ilyin's solution, which was the reestablishment of Orthodoxy as the state religion of Russia, is problematic in twenty-first century Russia, its appeal for some Orthodox traditionalists and Russian nationalists notwithstanding.[57]

The effort to reinstate Orthodoxy in Russian national identity also generates tension between Orthodoxy as a Russian patrimony and Orthodoxy as a global faith. Ilyin tended to elide the two, or at least to downplay the potential for friction between them. His Orthodoxy was very much a *Russian* Orthodoxy. The circumstances of his repatriation to Russia symbolize this feature of his faith. In October 2005, the mortal remains of Ivan Aleksandrovich Ilyin and Nataliia Nikolaevna Vokach-Ilyina were dispatched to Russia from Switzerland and interred in the cemetery of the Donskoi Monastery in Moscow. The patriarch of Moscow presided at the occasion, assisted by clergy from the Russian Orthodox Church Abroad, the émigré ecclesiastical jurisdiction to which the

57 In 1938, Ilyin drafted a constitution for a post-Soviet Russia. See "Proekt osnovnogo zakona rossiiskoi imperii," *Sobranie sochinenii*, 7:509–72.

Ilyins belonged.[58] This event anticipated by two years the formal reunion of the Moscow Patriarchate and the Russian Orthodox Church Abroad, one of the signal achievements of reconciliation in the Russian world during the post-Soviet era. Since that time, however, the Moscow Patriarchate's promotion of the reintegration of the Russian world has generated conflicts, not just with the worldwide Orthodox community but with some of its own affiliates, most notably in Ukraine. These are not conflicts that Ilyin's introverted Orthodoxy can settle. Only global Orthodoxy can resolve them.

In Russia's political culture today, Ilyin enjoys popularity among nationalists and authoritarians who admire his emphatic patriotism and his calls for strong state power in Russia.[59] Like many Russians before and after him, Ilyin believed that "*Either state power in Russia will be strong, or it will not exist at all.*"[60] But if this maxim has at times served to justify despotism in Russia, this was not Ilyin's purpose. He held a much more nuanced view:

> Strong state power is not ipso facto bureaucratic, or centralized, or military, or administered by a brutal police. To be sure, it is easier to create strong state power which is arbitrary, bureaucratic, centralized, military, and administered by a brutal police. But precisely these temptations, these easy paths, can and should be avoided.
>
> Russia needs state power which is strong, but differentiated. Strong, but consistently law-abiding. Strong, but not merely bureaucratic. Strong, but decentralized. Militarily defended, but only as a last resort. Protected by the police, but not inflating the competence of the police
>
> (7:498)

Ilyin repeated the same thought in a postwar series of essays on *sil'naia vlast'* (strong state power): "Strong state power in the Russia of the future should not be *extra*legal or *supra*legal; it should be ***drawn up by law*** and, ***in accord with law***

58 Sharipov, *Russkii myslitel' Ivan Aleksandrovich Il'in*, 298.

59 For a sample of Ilyin's popularity on the Russian Right, see the gift edition of some of his writings accompanied by illustrations on patriotic themes in the Russkaia imperatorskaia biblioteka series: I. A. Il'in, *Sil'naia vlast'. Russkaia ideia* (Moscow: Izdatel'stvo "E," 2017). The ultra-nationalist Institute of Russian Civilization has also brought out selections of Ilyin's works (and works by many other classical Russian thinkers) in anthologies designed to appeal to nationalist readers: Ivan Il'in, *Natsional'naia Rossiia: Nashi zadachi* (Moscow: Algoritm, 2007); *Mech pravdy Bozhiei: Iosif Volotskii, prp.; Il'in, I. A.* (Moscow: Institut russkoi tsivilizatsii, 2014); and Ivan Il'in, *Put' dukhovnogo obnovleniia* (Moscow: Institut russkoi tsivilizatsii, 2011). The editor of all three volumes was the head of the Institute of Russian Civilization, Oleg A. Platonov, who contributed prefaces incorporating his signature anti-Semitism, a theme which is not echoed at all in the works themselves.

60 "Osnovy gosudarstvennogo ustroistva," *Sobranie sochinenii*, 7:498.

and with the assistance of law, should serve *a nationwide legal order*."[61] Ilyin's nationalist and authoritarian admirers conveniently ignore his repeated emphasis on the rule of law as axiomatic for a just and stable political order in Russia.[62] Ilyin never preached state power as an end in itself. A rule-of-law state in Russia was always his goal.

61 "O sil'noi vlasti (3)," *Nashi zadachi*, 1:431–36 (No. 126, January 31, 1951), here at 433.

62 A good example is the Institute of Russian Civilization's anthology of Ilyin's writings, *Put' dukhovnogo obnovleniia* (note 59). The book is 1200 pages long, yet it contains no selections from *On the Essence of Legal Consciousness.* It is worth noting here that the handful of quotations from Ilyin's works that Vladimir Putin incorporated into speeches during his first three terms as president of Russia highlights the liberal rather than authoritarian aspect of Ilyin's thought. See Oksana Drozdova and Paul Robinson, "In Others' Words: Quotations and Recontextualization in Putin's Speeches," *Russian Politics* 2, no. 2 (2017): 227–53.

Afterword

William E. Butler

This book commenced with a tribute to Harold J. Berman for his pioneering work in exploring the interface between law and religion. It is only appropriate to close on the same note. Berman observed that there were at least four redeeming qualities of Russian life which "have given Russia greatness." The first was the reception of Christianity in Kievan Rus (ca. 988) with the development of a "special brand" of Christianity—Russian Orthodoxy. Coming to Russia from Byzantium, Orthodox Christianity differed from Western Catholicism and, of course, from the Protestant forms of Christianity that developed later on in the West. The choice of Christianity is said to have been a deliberate one: that Prince Vladimir of Kiev explored the possibilities of Islam and Judaism before preferring Byzantine Christianity.[1]

Before modern times, the Russian Orthodox Church produced few theologians or philosophers and, accordingly, little systematic theology or philosophy. However, the sermons and homilies that survive from medieval Russia figure in histories of Russian jurisprudence precisely because they address issues of right and wrong and have implications for the delineation of secular and ecclesiastical power and jurisdiction.[2] An impressive body of Russian legal theory developed in the nineteenth and early twentieth centuries, but the history of Russian legal theory was only beginning to be explored by the time of the revolutions of 1917. The eclipse of Russian legal traditions during the Soviet period delayed further work on the subject. This in itself gives occasion for the venture undertaken in this volume to examine distinguished Russian jurists, Christians all, for the role that their religious convictions may have played in their respective legal consciousness

1 Harold J. Berman, *Justice in the U.S.S.R.: An Interpretation of Soviet Law*, rev. ed. (Cambridge, MA: Harvard University Press, 1963), 220–21. The other three qualities were: universal compulsory service introduced by Mongol domination, mitigated by a sense of community supported by the Christian tradition; "inheritance of the Byzantine conception of the empire as sacred"; and the "energy of Westernization."

2 See W. E. Butler, *Russian Law and Legal Institutions*, 3d ed. (Clark, NJ: Talbot Publishing, 2021), 74–77.

and professional formation.[3] The individuals range from academic jurists to law reformers, legal practitioners, statesmen, judges, and philosophers, all of whom left a significant, even rich, legacy of published works and manuscripts.

Others might have been included. Baron Mikhail Aleksandrovich von Taube (1869–1961), for example, produced a major history of international law which placed Christianity at the center of its development.[4] In his view, different religious confessions contributed to competing trends of universalism and regionalism in international law. Among the regional traditions were Romano-Germanic, Byzantine-Slavic, and Asiatic. Differences among them originated partly in religious affiliations and views. Reflecting a comment often made about the development of Russian law, reference has been made to the "profound isolation" of the Orthodox world from Western Christendom in early modern times after the fall of Byzantium (1453).[5] Nevertheless, Orthodoxy is also "catholic" in the sense of universality, a concept that is nondenominational and does not belong to a localized nomenclature, but to the whole Church of Christ.[6]

There is another sense in which "universality" is sometimes understood with respect to the Russian legal profession and state system. It is sometimes said that in order for a foreign non-Orthodox individual to succeed in Russian state service, affiliation with Russian Orthodoxy was a practical, if not a strictly legal, requirement. Implied in that observation was an expectation of conformity to the Russian Church as a condition of employment, at least in the civil service. All of the individuals considered in the present volume were adherents of the Russian Orthodox faith, but not all Russian jurists in the eighteenth to twentieth centuries—the period considered here—were Orthodox. It had been widely believed, for example, that F. F. Martens (1845–1909), the leading Russian lawyer of his generation, orphaned as a child in Estonia, converted to the Russian Orthodox faith as he rose in the ranks to become one of the most celebrated international

3 For an analogous study emphasizing the rule of law, see Pavel Krasheninnikov, *The 12 Apostles of Russian Law: Lawyers Who Changed Law, State and Society*, trans. Christopher Culver (Moscow: Glagoslav Publications, 2019).

4 M. A. Taube, *Istoriia zarozhdeniia sovremennogo mezhdunarodnogo prava (Srednie veka)*, vol. 1, *Vvedenie i Chast' Obshchaia* (St. Petersburg: Tipo-Litografiia P. I. Shmidta, 1894); vol. 2, *Chast' Osobennaia: Printsipy mira i prava v mezhdunarodnykh stolknoveniiakh srednikh vekov* (Kharkov: Parovaia Tipografiia i Litografiia Zil'berberg, 1899); vol. 3, *Khristianstvo i organizatsiia mezhdunarodnogo mira* (St. Petersburg: Tipografiia V. Kirshbauma, 1902). Taube had wide-ranging religious interests. See, for example, M. A. Taube, *Agrafa: O nezapisannykh v Evangelii izrecheniiakh Iisusa Khrista*, published in Warsaw in 1936 by the Brotherhood of Orthodox Theologians in Poland. Taube also produced spiritual poetry. The United States Library of Congress holds a collection of seventy-five poems, one section of which is devoted to verses with Christian motifs, published in Paris in 1937. See W. E. Butler and V. S. Ivanenko, "Baron M. A. von Taube: Historian of International Law," *Jus Gentium: Journal of International Legal History* 4, no. 2 (2019): 495–525.

5 John Anthony McGuckin, *The Eastern Orthodox Church: A New History* (New Haven: Yale University Press, 2020), 6.

6 Ibid., 16.

lawyers in the empire and the world. From archival sources, we now know that Martens was born, raised, educated, married, and buried as a member of the Evangelical Lutheran church. The recent (2019) restoration of his grave in the Volkov Lutheran Cemetery, St. Petersburg, reinstalled a Lutheran cross.[7] There is every reason here to understand "Christian" in its broadest meaning.

Although the series in which this volume appears is devoted to great Christian jurists, it is no less appropriate to investigate great Jewish jurists or great Islamic jurists. In the case of Russia, this would draw attention to the multiethnic and multireligious composition of the Russian Empire and to the multiple legal systems operating simultaneously with Russian law and legislation generated or adopted by the central authorities and dominant nationality. Russian law has been multiethnic or multijurisdictional from the era of Kievan Rus, when each principality exercised jurisdiction over its own subjects.

The earliest documented Russian treaties and codes of law were limited in their territorial application, the true boundaries of which remain obscure. Legal historiography sublimates the realities of the reach of legal systems and rules in the interest of emphasizing the gradual formation, first, of the Muscovite state and later of the Russian Empire. But the development of centralized administration and expansion of frontiers were not the only factors at work in this history. One reason for the success of the Russian multinational empire was its ability and willingness to accommodate diverse legal traditions as the frontiers expanded. Whether this diversity took the form of Polish-Lithuanian (later Ukrainian Cossack), or Caucasian, or Baltic, or Eastern Polish, or Central Asian customary rules or bodies of legislation, these legal systems operated in tandem with the central authorities but were adapted to local circumstances. Their existence eventually led in the nineteenth century to the crystallization of private international law with the usual debate as to whether such law was confined to the conflict of laws or enjoyed a broader remit.

A key argument of those who drew attention to the importance of systematizing and codifying provincial or domestic regional legislation was precisely that such steps might form the foundation of a truly national body of imperial legislation, advanced in quality and benefitting from the advantages of harmonization and unification. In the end, there was a certain amount of systematization, commencing with individual regions (Baltic, Ukraine, and others), a tale discussed in some of the chapters of this volume. Fully fledged unification was, at best, pursued only episodically.

What did emerge, however, was an approach to the conflict of laws that eventually addressed domestic conflicts within the empire and foreign conflicts with

7 See W. E. Butler and V. S. Ivanenko, "F. F. Martens: Russian Scholar, Diplomat, and Arbitrator," *Jus Gentium: Journal of International Legal History* 4, no. 1 (2019): 145–78; and V. S. Ivanenko, *Sankt-Peterburgskaia shkola mezhdunarodnogo prava: Mesto i rol' Sankt-Peterburgskogo universiteta, ego uchenykh i vypusknikov v stanovlenii i razvitii nauki i praktiki mezhdunarodnogo prava*, pt. 1, *1720–1920-e gg.* (St. Petersburg: Izdatel'stvo "Iuridicheskii tsentr," 2019), 150–203.

jurisdictions beyond the boundaries of the empire. Some jurisdictional conflicts were purely territorial; others were founded upon religious differences and often simply left to each religious community to resolve or administer to their respective satisfaction. It would be an exaggeration to stress the legal rationality of the process. Passive recognition of diversity in certain contexts would be a more accurate description. Christianity in its Russian Orthodox embodiment dominated, to be sure, but the Russian state was usually clever enough to be at least minimally tolerant of alternative practices and approaches.

All of the individuals discussed in this volume appear to have treated Russian Orthodoxy as an important, if not integral, part of their personal and professional lives. They may have appeared on opposite sides of issues or may have related differently to trends or policies in legal developments, but they were serious about their faith, and that seriousness in turn affected their perceptions of right and wrong, good and evil, desirable and undesirable, or proper and improper. Each in his own way made a substantial contribution to the improvement of Russian law, legal doctrine, legal institutions, and legal education. They are, indeed, among the select who deserve the encomium of great Russian jurist.

Index

Taylor & Francis Group
an informa business

Taylor & Francis eBooks

www.taylorfrancis.com

A single destination for eBooks from Taylor & Francis with increased functionality and an improved user experience to meet the needs of our customers.

90,000+ eBooks of award-winning academic content in Humanities, Social Science, Science, Technology, Engineering, and Medical written by a global network of editors and authors.

TAYLOR & FRANCIS EBOOKS OFFERS:

- A streamlined experience for our library customers
- A single point of discovery for all of our eBook content
- Improved search and discovery of content at both book and chapter level

REQUEST A FREE TRIAL

support@taylorfrancis.com

Routledge Taylor & Francis Group
CRC Press Taylor & Francis Group

For Product Safety Concerns and Information please contact our EU
representative GPSR@taylorandfrancis.com
Taylor & Francis Verlag GmbH, Kaufingerstraße 24, 80331 München, Germany

www.ingramcontent.com/pod-product-compliance
Lightning Source LLC
LaVergne TN
LVHW011110300926
849160LV00008B/339